D1443937

Novels
for Students

Novels for Students

Presenting Analysis, Context, and Criticism on Commonly Studied Novels

Volume 9

Deborah A. Stanley
and Ira Mark Milne, Editors

Carol Jago, Santa Monica High School, Advisor
Kathleen Pasquantonio, Novi High School, Advisor

Foreword by Anne Devereaux Jordan, Teaching and Learning Literature

GALE GROUP

Detroit
New York
San Francisco
London
Boston
Woodbridge, CT

National Advisory Board

Novels for Students

Staff

Series Editors: Deborah A. Stanley and Ira Mark Milne.

Contributing Editors: Elizabeth Bellalouna, Elizabeth Bodenmiller, Sara L. Constantakis, Catherine L. Goldstein, Motoko Fujishiro Huthwaite, Arlene M. Johnson, Angela Y. Jones, Michael L. LaBlanc, Polly Rapp, Erin White.

Research: Victoria B. Cariappa, *Research Team Manager.* Cheryl Warnock, *Research Specialist.* Corrine A. Boland, Tamara Nott, Tracie A. Richardson, *Research Associates.* Timothy Lehnerer, Patricia Love, *Research Assistants.*

Permissions: Maria Franklin, *Permissions Manager.* Margaret A. Chamberlain, Edna Hedblad, *Permissions Specialists.* Erin Bealmear, *Permissions Associate.* Sandra K. Gore, *Permissions Assistant.*

Production: Mary Beth Trimper, *Production Director.* Evi Seoud, *Assistant Production Manager.* Stacy Melson, *Production Assistant.*

Imaging and Multimedia Content Team: Randy Bassett, *Image Database Supervisor.* Robert Duncan, *Imaging Specialist.* Michael Logusz, *Graphic Artist.* Pamela A. Reed, *Imaging Coordinator.* Dean Dauphinais, Robyn V. Young, *Senior Image Editors.* Kelly A. Quin, *Image Editor.*

Product Design Team: Cynthia Baldwin, *Product Design Manager.* Pamela A. E. Galbreath, *Senior Art Director.* Gary Leach, *Graphic Artist.*

Copyright Notice

Table of Contents

The Informed Dialogue: Interacting with Literature

When we pick up a book, we usually do so with the anticipation of pleasure. We hope that by entering the time and place of the novel and sharing the thoughts and actions of the characters, we will find enjoyment. Unfortunately, this is often not the case; we are disappointed. But we should ask, has the author failed us, or have we failed the author?

We establish a dialogue with the author, the book, and with ourselves when we read. Consciously and unconsciously, we ask questions: "Why did the author write this book?" "Why did the author choose that time, place, or character?" "How did the author achieve that effect?" "Why did the character act that way?" "Would I act in the same way?" The answers we receive depend upon how much information about literature in general and about that book specifically we ourselves bring to our reading.

Young children have limited life and literary experiences. Being young, children frequently do not know how to go about exploring a book, nor sometimes, even know the questions to ask of a book. The books they read help them answer questions, the author often coming right out and *telling* young readers the things they are learning or are expected to learn. The perennial classic, *The Little Engine That Could, tells* its readers that, among other things, it is good to help others and brings happiness:

"Hurray, hurray," cried the funny little clown and all the dolls and toys. "The good little boys and girls in the city will be happy because you helped us, kind, Little Blue Engine."

In picture books, messages are often blatant and simple, the dialogue between the author and reader one-sided. Young children are concerned with the end result of a book—the enjoyment gained, the lesson learned—rather than with how that result was obtained. As we grow older and read further, however, we question more. We come to expect that the world within the book will closely mirror the concerns of our world, and that the author will *show* these through the events, descriptions, and conversations within the story, rather than *telling* of them. We are now expected to do the interpreting, carry on our share of the dialogue with the book and author, and glean not only the author's message, but comprehend how that message and the overall affect of the book were achieved. Sometimes, however, we need help to do these things. *Novels for Students* provides that help.

A novel is made up of many parts interacting to create a coherent whole. In reading a novel, the more obvious features can be easily spotted—theme, characters, plot—but we may overlook the more subtle elements that greatly influence how the novel is perceived by the reader: viewpoint, mood and tone, symbolism, or the use of humor. By focusing on both the obvious and more subtle literary elements within a novel, *Novels for Students* aids readers in both analyzing for message and in determining how and why that message is communicated. In the discussion on Harper Lee's *To Kill a Mockingbird* (Vol. 2), for example, the mockingbird as a symbol of innocence is dealt with, among other things, as is the importance of Lee's use of humor which "enlivens a serious plot, adds depth to the characterization, and creates a sense of familiarity and universality." The reader comes to understand the internal elements of each novel discussed—as well as the external influences that help shape it.

"The desire to write greatly," Harold Bloom of Yale University says, "is the desire to be elsewhere, in a time and place of one's own, in an originality that must compound with inheritance, with an anxiety of influence." A writer seeks to create a unique world within a story, but although it is unique, it is not disconnected from our own world. It speaks to us *because* of what the writer brings to the writing from our world: how he or she was raised and educated; his or her likes and dislikes; the events occurring in the real world at the time of the writing, and while the author was growing up. When we know what an author has brought to his or her work, we gain a greater insight into both the "originality" (the world of the book), and the things that "compound" it. This insight enables us to question that created world and find answers more readily. By informing ourselves, we are able to establish a more effective dialogue with both book and author.

Novels for Students, in addition to providing a plot summary and descriptive list of characters—to remind readers of what they have read—also explores the external influences that shaped each book. Each entry includes a discussion of the author's background, and the historical context in which the novel was written. It is vital to know, for instance, that when Ray Bradbury was writing *Fahrenheit 451* (Vol. 1), the threat of Nazi domination had recently ended in Europe, and the Mc-Carthy hearings were taking place in Washington, D.C. This information goes far in answering the question, "Why did he write a story of oppressive government control and book burning?" Similarly, it is important to know that Harper Lee, author of *To Kill a Mockingbird,* was born and raised in Monroeville, Alabama, and that her father was a lawyer. Readers can now see why she chose the south as a setting for her novel—it is the place with which she was most familiar—and start to comprehend her characters and their actions.

Novels for Students helps readers find the answers they seek when they establish a dialogue with a particular novel. It also aids in the posing of questions by providing the opinions and interpretations of various critics and reviewers, broadening that dialogue. Some reviewers of *To Kill A Mockingbird,* for example, "faulted the novel's climax as melodramatic." This statement leads readers to ask, "Is it, indeed, melodramatic?" "If not, why did some reviewers see it as such?" "If it is, why did Lee choose to make it melodramatic?" "Is melodrama ever justified?" By being spurred to ask these questions, readers not only learn more about the book and its writer, but about the nature of writing itself.

The literature included for discussion in *Novels for Students* has been chosen because it has something vital to say to us. *Of Mice and Men, Catch-22, The Joy Luck Club, My Antonia, A Separate Peace* and the other novels here speak of life and modern sensibility. In addition to their individual, specific messages of prejudice, power, love or hate, living and dying, however, they and all great literature also share a common intent. They force us to *think*—about life, literature, and about others, not just about ourselves. They pry us from the narrow confines of our minds and thrust us outward to confront the world of books and the larger, real world we all share. *Novels for Students* helps us in this confrontation by providing the means of enriching our conversation with literature and the world, by creating an *informed* dialogue, one that brings true pleasure to the personal act of reading.

Sources

Harold Bloom, *The Western Canon, The Books and School of the Ages,* Riverhead Books, 1994.

Watty Piper, *The Little Engine That Could,* Platt & Munk, 1930.

Anne Devereaux Jordan, Senior Editor, TALL (*Teaching and Learning Literature*).

Introduction

Purpose of the Book

The purpose of *Novels for Students* (*NfS*) is to provide readers with a guide to understanding, enjoying, and studying novels by giving them easy access to information about the work. Part of Gale's "For Students" Literature line, *NfS* is specifically designed to meet the curricular needs of high school and undergraduate college students and their teachers, as well as the interests of general readers and researchers considering specific novels. While each volume contains entries on "classic" novels frequently studied in classrooms, there are also entries containing hard-to-find information on contemporary novels, including works by multicultural, international, and women novelists.

The information covered in each entry includes an introduction to the novel and the novel's author; a plot summary, to help readers unravel and understand the events in a novel; descriptions of important characters, including explanation of a given character's role in the novel as well as discussion about that character's relationship to other characters in the novel; analysis of important themes in the novel; and an explanation of important literary techniques and movements as they are demonstrated in the novel.

In addition to this material, which helps the readers analyze the novel itself, students are also provided with important information on the literary and historical background informing each work. This includes a historical context essay, a box comparing the time or place the novel was written to modern Western culture, a critical overview essay, and excerpts from critical essays on the novel. A unique feature of *NfS* is a specially commissioned overview essay on each novel by an academic expert, targeted toward the student reader.

To further aid the student in studying and enjoying each novel, information on media adaptations is provided, as well as reading suggestions for works of fiction and nonfiction on similar themes and topics. Classroom aids include ideas for research papers and lists of critical sources that provide additional material on the novel.

Selection Criteria

The titles for each volume of *NfS* were selected by surveying numerous sources on teaching literature and analyzing course curricula for various school districts. Some of the sources surveyed included: literature anthologies; *Reading Lists for College-Bound Students: The Books Most Recommended by America's Top Colleges;* textbooks on teaching the novel; a College Board survey of novels commonly studied in high schools; a National Council of Teachers of English (NCTE) survey of novels commonly studied in high schools; the NCTE's *Teaching Literature in High School: The Novel;* and the Young Adult Library Services Association (YALSA) list of best books for young adults of the past twenty-five years.

Input was also solicited from our expert advisory board, as well as educators from various areas. From these discussions, it was determined that each volume should have a mix of "classic" novels (those works commonly taught in literature classes) and contemporary novels for which information is often hard to find. Because of the interest in expanding the canon of literature, an emphasis was also placed on including works by international, multicultural, and women authors. Our advisory board members—current high school teachers—helped pare down the list for each volume. If a work was not selected for the present volume, it was often noted as a possibility for a future volume. As always, the editor welcomes suggestions for titles to be included in future volumes.

How Each Entry Is Organized

Each entry, or chapter, in *NfS* focuses on one novel. Each entry heading lists the full name of the novel, the author's name, and the date of the novel's publication. The following elements are contained in each entry:

• **Introduction:** a brief overview of the novel which provides information about its first appearance, its literary standing, any controversies surrounding the work, and major conflicts or themes within the work.

• **Author Biography:** this section includes basic facts about the author's life, and focuses on events and times in the author's life that inspired the novel in question.

• **Plot Summary:** a description of the major events in the novel, with interpretation of how these events help articulate the novel's themes. Lengthy summaries are broken down with subheads.

• **Characters:** an alphabetical listing of major characters in the novel. Each character name is followed by a brief to an extensive description of the character's role in the novel, as well as discussion of the character's actions, relationships, and possible motivation.

• Characters are listed alphabetically by last name. If a character is unnamed—for instance, the narrator in *Invisible Man*–the character is listed as "The Narrator" and alphabetized as "Narrator." If a character's first name is the only one given, the name will appear alphabetically by the name.

• Variant names are also included for each character. Thus, the full name "Jean Louise Finch" would head the listing for the narrator of *To Kill a Mockingbird,* but listed in a separate cross-reference would be the nickname "Scout Finch."

• **Themes:** a thorough overview of how the major topics, themes, and issues are addressed within the novel. Each theme discussed appears in a separate subhead, and is easily accessed through the boldface entries in the Subject/Theme Index.

• **Style:** this section addresses important style elements of the novel, such as setting, point of view, and narration; important literary devices used, such as imagery, foreshadowing, symbolism; and, if applicable, genres to which the work might have belonged, such as Gothicism or Romanticism. Literary terms are explained within the entry, but can also be found in the Glossary.

• **Historical and Cultural Context:** This section outlines the social, political, and cultural climate *in which the author lived and the novel was created.* This section may include descriptions of related historical events, pertinent aspects of daily life in the culture, and the artistic and literary sensibilities of the time in which the work was written. If the novel is a historical work, information regarding the time in which the novel is set is also included. Each section is broken down with helpful subheads.

• **Critical Overview:** this section provides background on the critical reputation of the novel, including bannings or any other public controversies surrounding the work. For older works, this section includes a history of how novel was first received and how perceptions of it may have changed over the years; for more recent novels, direct quotes from early reviews may also be included.

• **Sources:** an alphabetical list of critical material quoted in the entry, with full bibliographical information.

• **For Further Study:** an alphabetical list of other critical sources which may prove useful for the student. Includes full bibliographical information and a brief annotation.

• **Criticism:** an essay commissioned by *NfS* which specifically deals with the novel and is written specifically for the student audience, as well as excerpts from previously published criticism on the work.

In addition, each entry contains the following highlighted sections, set apart from the main text as sidebars:

• **Media Adaptations:** a list of important film and television adaptations of the novel, including source information. The list also includes stage adaptations, audio recordings, musical adaptations, etc.

• **Compare and Contrast Box:** an "at-a-glance" comparison of the cultural and historical differences between the author's time and culture and late twentieth-century Western culture. This box includes pertinent parallels between the major scientific, political, and cultural movements of the time or place the novel was written, the time or place the novel was set (if a historical work), and modern Western culture. Works written after the mid-1970s may not have this box.

• **What Do I Read Next?:** a list of works that might complement the featured novel or serve as a contrast to it. This includes works by the same author and others, works of fiction and nonfiction, and works from various genres, cultures, and eras.

• **Study Questions:** a list of potential study questions or research topics dealing with the novel. This section includes questions related to other disciplines the student may be studying, such as American history, world history, science, math, government, business, geography, economics, psychology, etc.

Other Features

NfS includes "The Informed Dialogue: Interacting with Literature," a foreword by Anne Devereaux Jordan, Senior Editor for *Teaching and Learning Literature (TALL)*, and a founder of the Children's Literature Association. This essay provides an enlightening look at how readers interact with literature and how *Novels for Students* can help teachers show students how to enrich their own reading experiences.

A Cumulative Author/Title Index lists the authors and titles covered in each volume of the *NfS* series.

A Cumulative Nationality/Ethnicity Index breaks down the authors and titles covered in each volume of the *NfS* series by nationality and ethnicity.

A Subject/Theme Index, specific to each volume, provides easy reference for users who may be studying a particular subject or theme rather than a single work. Significant subjects from events to broad themes are included, and the entries pointing to the specific theme discussions in each entry are indicated in boldface.

Each entry has several illustrations, including photos of the author, stills from film adaptations (when available), maps, and/or photos of key historical events.

Citing Novels for Students

When writing papers, students who quote directly from any volume of *Novels for Students* may use the following general forms. These examples are based on MLA style; teachers may request that students adhere to a different style, so the following examples may be adapted as needed.

When citing text from *NfS* that is not attributed to a particular author (i.e., the Themes, Style, Historical Context sections, etc.), the following format should be used in the bibliography section:

" Night." *Novels for Students.* Ed. Marie Rose Napierkowski. Vol. 4. Detroit: Gale, 1998. 34–5.

When quoting the specially commissioned essay from *NfS* (usually the first piece under the "Criticism" subhead), the following format should be used:

Miller, Tyrus. Essay on "Winesburg, Ohio." *Novels for Students.* Ed. Marie Rose Napierkowski. Vol. 4. Detroit: Gale, 1997. 218–9.

When quoting a journal or newspaper essay that is reprinted in a volume of *NfS,* the following form may be used:

Malak, Amin. "Margaret Atwood's The Handmaid's Tale' and the Dystopian Tradition," in *Canadian Literature* , No. 112, Spring, 1987, 9–16; excerpted and reprinted in *Novels for Students,* Vol. 4, ed. Marie Rose Napierkowski (Detroit: Gale, 1998), pp. 61–64.

When quoting material reprinted from a book that appears in a volume of *NfS*, the following form may be used:

Adams, Timothy Dow. "Richard Wright: Wearing the Mask," in *Telling Lies in Modern American Autobiography* (University of North Carolina Press, 1990), 69–83; excerpted and reprinted in *Novels for Students,* Vol. 5, eds. Sheryl Ciccarelli and Marie Napierkowski (Detroit: Gale, 1999), pp. 59–61.

We Welcome Your Suggestions

The editor of *Novels for Students* welcomes your comments and ideas. Readers who wish to suggest novels to appear in future volumes, or who have other suggestions, are cordially invited to contact the editor. You may contact the editor via e-mail at: mark.milne@galegroup.com. Or write to the editor at:

Editor, *Novels for Students*
The Gale Group
27500 Drake Rd.
Farmington Hills, MI 48331–3535

Literary Chronology

1469: Niccoló Machiavelli is born in Florence, Italy, on May 3.

1513: Niccoló Machiavelli's *The Prince*, dedicated to Lorenzo di Medici, is published.

1527: The Medici rule in Florence ends; the republic of Florence is restored; and Niccoló Machiavelli dies.

1660: Daniel Defoe is born in Cripplegate, just outside the walls of the City of London, to Dissenter parents, James and Alice Foe—Protestants who refused to accept the authority of the Anglican Church (also known as the Church of England).

1719: Daniel Defoe's *The Life and Strange Surprising Adventures of Robinson Crusoe* is published as a fictional memoir.

1731: Daniel Defoe, the author of *The Life and Strange Surprising Adventures of Robinson Crusoe*, dies.

1789: James Fenimore Cooper is born in New Jersey.

1819: Herman Melville is born in New York City.

1826: James Fenimore Cooper's *The Last of the Mohicans* is published.

1851: James Fenimore Cooper dies.

1885: Isak Dinesen is born (birthname Christence Dinesen) on April 17 in Rungsted, Denmark.

1891: Herman Melville dies in September.

1899: Vladimir Nabokov is born on April 23 in St. Petersburg, Russia.

1899: Nevil Shute (birthname Nevil Shute Norway) is born on January 17 in a suburb of London, England.

1900: Margaret Mitchell is born, and lives her entire life in Atlanta, Georgia, as had her parents and grandparents.

1914: Bernard Malamud is born in New York City.

1921: Alex Haley is born in Ithaca, New York.

1923: James Dickey is born in Buckhead, a suburb of Atlanta.

1924: Herman Melville's *Billy Budd* is published, when the work is discovered among Melville's papers, several years after Melville's death in 1891.

1929: Ursula K. Le Guin is born.

1936: Margaret Mitchell's *Gone with the Wind* is published, and becomes an immediate best-seller, bringing first-time novelist Margaret Mitchell an overwhelming amount of attention.

1937: Margaret Mitchell's *Gone with the Wind* wins the Pulitzer Prize.

1937: Isak Dinesen's *Out of Africa*, an autobiographical novel, is published, recounting the years Dinesen spent on a coffee plantation in East Africa.

1939: Margaret Mitchell's *Gone with the Wind* is adapted as a film—an achievement that wins ten Academy Awards.

1944: Rita Mae Brown is born in Pennsylvania.

1949: Margaret Mitchell dies after being hit by a car. She is mourned by millions of fans for whom *Gone with the Wind* had become an American classic.

1950: Julia Alvarez is born in New York City on March 27, the second of four daughters.

1950: S. E. Hinton is born, and lives her entire life in Tulsa, Oklahoma.

1955: Vladimir Nabokov's *Lolita* is published in Paris, and is soon banned for its controversial content.

1957: Nevil Shute's *On the Beach* is published.

1960: Nevil Shute, after suffering a major stroke in 1958 and another a year later, falls ill on January 12, while writing in his study, and dies later that evening.

1962: Isak Dinesen dies in Rungsted, Denmark, on September 7.

1966: Bernard Malamud's *The Fixer* is published while Malamud is at Vermont's Bennington College. This novel wins both the National Book Award and the Pulitzer Prize, and is made into a movie by John Frankenheimer in 1968.

1970: James Dickey's *Deliverance* is published with immediate critical and and popular success, followed by a similar reception for the movie that is adapted from the novel by Dickey and released two years later.

1973: Rita Mae Brown's *Rubyfruit Jungle* is published by a small feminist press and later reissued in 1977 by Bantam Books to sell over a million copies.

1976: Alex Haley's *Roots: The Saga of an American Family* is published, and becomes an immediate sensation. It is adapted into a popular miniseries and becomes one of the most-watched television programs in American history. Two sequels, *The Next Generation* and *The Gift,* quickly follow.

1977: Vladimir Nabokov dies on July 2 in Montreux, Switzerland.

1979: S. E. Hinton's young adult novel *Tex* is published.

1985: Ursula K. Le Guin's *Always Coming Home* is published, and wins the Kafka Award.

1985: Isak Dinesen's *Out of Africa* is adapted to film and wins an Oscar for best picture, prompting a resurgence of interest in the novel.

1986: Bernard Malamud dies in New York City.

1992: Alex Haley, on a lecture trip to Seattle, suffers a heart attack and dies at age seventy-one.

1994: Julia Alvarez's *In the Time of the Butterflies* is published, telling the story of Las Mariposas, or The Butterflies (code names of Minerva, María Teresa, and Patria Mirabal, three sisters who were key members in an underground movement to overthrow Rafael Trujillo, dictator of the Dominican Republic from 1930 to 1961).

1997: James Dickey, a professor of English at the University of South Carolina since 1968, dies.

Acknowledgments

The editors wish to thank the copyright holders of the excerpted criticism included in this volume and the permissions managers of many book and magazine publishing companies for assisting us in securing reproduction rights. We are also grateful to the staffs of the Detroit Public Library, the Library of Congress, the University of Detroit Mercy Library, Wayne State University Purdy/Kresge Library Complex, and the University of Michigan Libraries for making their resources available to us. Following is a list of the copyright holders who have granted us permission to reproduce material in this volume of *Novels for Students (NfS)*. Every effort has been made to trace copyright, but if omissions have been made, please let us know.

COPYRIGHTED MATERIALS IN *NfS*, VOLUME 9, WERE REPRODUCED FROM THE FOLLOWING PERIODICALS:

The American Scholar, v. 27, Autumn, 1958. Reproduced by permission.—*The Armchair Detective,* v. 27, May, 1994. Copyright (c) 1994 by The Armchair Detective. Reproduced by permission.—*Critical Quarterly,* v. 51, Summer, 1995. (c) Manchester University Press 1995. Reproduced by permission of Basil Blackwell Limited.—*The Dalhousie Review,* v. 56, Spring, 1976 for "The Creation of an Ordered World in 'Robinson Crusoe'" by Robert H. MacDonald. Reproduced by permission of the publisher and the author.—*English Journal,* v. 81, April, 1981 for a review of "New Writes of Passage," by Jean Duncan, Carol Dye, Joan Lazarus, Diane Schwartzmann, Jill A. Warner and Rita Hendin. Copyright (c) by the National Council of Teachers of English. Reprinted by permission of the publisher.—*Extrapolation,* v. 28, Winter, 1987. Copyright 1987 by The Kent State University Press. Reprinted by permission of the publisher.—*The Hudson Review,* v. XXII, Spring, 1969. Copyright (c) 1969 by The Hudson Review, Inc. Reprinted by permission of the publisher.—*Journal of Popular Culture,* v. 2, 1980. Copyright (c) 1980 by Phillip F. O'Connor. Reprinted by permission of the publisher.—*The New York Times Book Review,* May 6, 1938, September 20, 1985, June 6, 1988, December 18, 1994. Copyright (c) 1938, 1985, 1988, 1994 The New York Times Company. Reprinted by permission of the publisher.—*North Dakota Quarterly,* v. 54, Winter, 1986. Copyright 1986 by The University of North Dakota. Reproduced by permission.—*The Progressive,* v. 59, July, 1995. Copyright (c) 1995, The Progressive, Inc. Reprinted by permission from The Progressive, 409 East Main Street, Madison, WI 53703.—*Saturday Review,* September 10, 1966. (c) 1979, General Media International, Inc. Reproduced by permission of The Saturday Review.—*The South Atlantic Quarterly,* v. 72, Winter, 1973. Copyright (c) 1973 by Duke University Press, Durham, NC. Reprinted with permission of the publisher.—*Southern Humanities Review,* v. xxix, Summer, 1995. Copyright 1995 by Auburn University. Reprinted by permission of the author.—*The Southern Literary Journal,* v. XXVIII,

Spring, 1996. Copyright (c) 1996 by the Department of English, University of North Carolina at Chapel Hill. Reproduced by permission.—*Wilson Library Bulletin,* v. 66, June, 1992 for "On the Beach" by Gene LaFaille. Copyright (c) 1992 by the H. W. Wilson Company. Reproduced by permission of the author.—*The Yale Review,* v. LVI, March, 1967. Copyright 1967, by Yale University. Reproduced by permission of the editors.

COPYRIGHTED MATERIALS IN *NfS*, VOLUME 9, WERE REPRODUCED FROM THE FOLLOWING BOOKS:

Daly, Jay. From *Presenting S.E. Hinton.* Twayne Publishers, 1987. Copyright 1987 by Jay Daly.—Eisinger, Chester E. From "Lolita: Overview" in *Reference Guide to American Literature, 3rd edition.* Edited by Jim Kemp. St. James Press, 1994. Copyright (c) 1994 St. James Press. All rights reserved.—Levernier, James A. From "'The Last of the Mohicans': Overview" in *Reference Guide to American Literature, 3rd edition.* Edited by Jim Kemp. St. James Press, 1994. Copyright (c) 1994 St. James Press. All rights reserved.—Mansfield, Harvey C., Jr. From an overview of *The Prince* by Niccolo Machiavelli. Translated by Harvey C. Mansfield, Jr. University of Chicago Press, 1985. (c) 1985 by The University of Chicago. All rights reserved. Reproduced by permission.—Millichap, Joseph R. from *Twentieth-Century Young Adult Writers,1st edition,* edited by Laura Standley Berger, St. James Press 1994. Copyright (c) 1994 St. James Press.

PHOTOGRAPHS AND ILLUSTRATIONS APPEARING IN *NFS,* VOLUME 9, WERE RECEIVED FROM THE FOLLOWING SOURCES:

A scene from the film "Out of Africa", 1985, by Universal Studios, based on the novel by Isak Dinesen, photograph. Universal Studios. Courtesy of The Kobal Collection. Reproduced by permission.—"A Song to Liberty" (Mirabal sisters, mural on an obelisk), Santo Domingo, Dominican Republic, 1997, photograph John Riley. AP/Wide World Photos. Reproduced by permission.—Alvarez, Julia, photograph by Jerry Bauer. Reproduced by permission.—Atom bomb blast, Nagasaki, Japan, 1945, photograph by Scott Camazine. The National Audubon Society Collection/Photo Researchers, Inc. Reproduced by permission.—Bates, Alan (with Dirk Bogarde and other men, in film "The Fixer"), photograph. Kobal Collection. Reproduced by permission.—Brown, Rita Mae, photograph. AP/Wide World Photos. Re-

produced by permission.—Columbus, Christopher, drawing. Corbis. Reproduced by permission.—Cooper, James Fenimore, drawing by Cacilie Brandt. National Portrait Gallery, Smithsonian Institution. Reproduced by permission.—Dachau Concentration Camp, main entrance, 1949, Germany, photograph. AP/Wide World Photos. Reproduced by permission.—Day-Lewis, Daniel, in the movie "Last of the Mohicans," 1992, photograph. The Kobal Collection. Reproduced by permission.—Defoe, Daniel, photograph. Archive Photos, Inc. Reproduced by permission.—Dickey, James, photograph. AP/Wide World Photos. Reproduced by permission.—Dinesen, Isak, photograph. Archive Photos. Reproduced by permission.—Dominican refugees (resting on deck of cutter, with U.S. Coast Guard personnel), photograph. Corbis. Reproduced by permission.—Dragon sculpture at Taoist Temple, photograph. Corbis. Reproduced by permission.—English and Native Americans fighting the French, French and Indian War, painting. The Library of Congress.—Estevez, Emilio (with Matt Dillion and Meg Tilly, in film "Tex"), photograph. Kobal Collection. Reproduced by permission.—Fifteen views of British Man-of-war, photograph. Corbis. Reproduced by permission.—French and Indian War, 1689-1763, map by Molly Braun. From Atlas of the North American Indian, by Carl Waldman. Facts on File Publications, 1985. Copyright (c) 1985 by Carl Waldman. All rights reserved. Reproduced by permission.—Gable, Clark and Vivien Leigh, in the film "Gone with the Wind," 1939, photograph. AP/Wide World Photos. Reproduced by permission.—Group of Kenyan male warriors, from Kikuyu tribe, photograph. Corbis. Reproduced by permission.—Haley, Alex, photograph. Corbis. Reproduced by permission.—Hinton, S.E., photograph by Thomas Victor. Reproduced by permission of the Estate of Thomas Victor.—Hussey, Pat (with "Micky" Moorshead and Ann Grey), photograph. Corbis. Reproduced by permission.—Irons, Jeremy and Dominique Swain, in the movie "Lolita," 1998, photograph by Peter Sorel. The Kobal Collection. (c) Alphatex. Reproduced by permission.—Khrushchev, Nikita S., photograph. AP/Wide World Photos. Reproduced by permission.—Le Guin, Ursula, photograph by Lisa Kroeber. Reproduced by permission of Ursula Le Guin.—LeVar Burton, in a close-up scene from "Roots," photograph. AP/Wide World Photos. Reproduced by permission.—Lyon, Sue (in scene from "Lolita"), photograph. Corbis. Reproduced by permission.—Machiavelli, Niccolo, illustration.

Archive Photos, Inc. Reproduced by permission.—Malamud, Bernard, photograph by Jerry Bauer. Reproduced by permission.—Map showing Triangular Trade, sea trade routes between North America, England, and the Ivory Coast of Africa, illustration. The Gale Group.—Melville, Herman, painting. Archive Photos, Inc. Reproduced by permission.—Mitchell, Margaret, photograph. Corbis-Bettmann. Reproduced by permission.—Nabokov, Vladimir, photograph. AP/Wide World Photos. Reproduced by permission. "Napoleon on Horseback at the St. Bernard Pass," painting by Jacques-Louis David, 1801, oil on canvas. Corbis/Francis G. Mayer. Reproduced by permission.—Older Jewish man sitting in a synagogue, photograph. Bildarchiv Preussischer Kulturbestiz. Reproduced by permission.—Peachtree Street, building standing in ruins on corner, Atlanta, Georgia, 1864, photograph by George N. Barnard. National Archives and Records Administration.—Peck, Gregory (with Ava Gardner, in scene from "On the Beach"), photograph. Corbis. Reproduced by permission.—Quinn, Aidan, in the film "Crusoe," photograph. The Kobal Collection. Reproduced by permission.—Selling drugs (boy holding out handful of pills), photograph by Robert J. Huffman. Field Mark Publications. Reproduced by permission.—Shute, Nevil (with Moira Shearer), photograph. Corbis. Reproduced by permission.—Slaves planting sweet potatoes, James Hopkins plantation, Edisto, SC, 1862, photograph. Archive Photos. Reproduced by permission.—Stamp, Terence (as Billy Budd), photograph. Culver Pictures, Inc. Reproduced by permission.—Title page from The Life and Strange Surprising Adventures of Robinson Crusoe by Robinson Crusoe. The Granger Collection, New York. Reproduced by permission.—Typical slave family (men, women and children outside of cabin), photograph by T.H. O'Sullivan. The Library of Congress.—Villa Medici, drawing. Corbis. Reproduced by permission.—Voight, Jon, Burt Reynolds (drawing on bow), in the film "Deliverance," 1972, photograph. The Kobal Collection. Reproduced by permission.—Woman leading Gay Freedom Day Parade (holding sign reading "Lesbians are Beautiful"), photograph. Corbis. Reproduced by permission.

Contributors

Don Akers: Freelance writer, Harper Woods, MI. Original essay on *On the Beach*. Entry on *On the Beach*.

Betsy Currier Beacom: Freelance writer, North Haven, CT. Entry on *Billy Budd*.

Jane Elizabeth Dougherty: Freelance writer, Medford, MA. Original essays on *Roots* and *Tex*. Entry on *Roots*.

Logan Esdale: Doctoral candidate in the Poetics Program at SUNY-Buffalo. Original essay on *Billy Budd*.

Darren Felty: Visiting instructor, College of Charleston (SC); Ph.D. in Literature, University of Georgia. Original essay on *In the Time of the Butterflies*. Entry on *In the Time of the Butterflies*.

Jeremy Hubbell: Freelance writer; M.Litt., University of Aberdeen. Original essay on *Robinson Crusoe (The Life and Strange Surprising Adventures of Robinson Crusoe)*. Entries on *The Last of the Mohicans*, *Robinson Crusoe*, and *Tex*.

David J. Kelly: Professor of English, College of Lake County (IL). Original essays on *Deliverance*, *The Fixer*, and *The Prince*. Entries on *Deliverance*, *The Fixer*, and *The Prince*.

Tabitha McIntosh-Byrd: Freelance writer; M.Litt., University of Aberdeen. Original essays on *Gone with the Wind*, *The Last of the Mohicans*, and *Rubyfruit Jungle*. Entry on *Rubyfruit Jungle*.

Wendy Perkins: Assistant Professor of English, Prince George's Community College, Maryland; Ph.D. in English, University of Delaware. Original essays on *Lolita* and *Out of Africa*. Entries on *Lolita* and *Out of Africa*.

Michael Rex: Instructor at the University of Detroit Mercy. Original essay on *Always Coming Home*. Entry on *Always Coming Home*.

Rita Schweiss: Freelance writer, Roanoke, VA. Entry on *Gone with the Wind*.

Always Coming Home

Ursula K. Le Guin
1985

Always Coming Home, the Kafka Award-winning novel published in 1985, marks a departure for one of the world's foremost science fiction and fantasy authors. Often criticized for having too many male protagonists in her novels, Ursula K. Le Guin answers with two particularly strong women in this complex and difficult novel. Like many of her other novels, *Always Coming Home* deals with the duality of everything (life, sex, love, faith, fear), the individual's need to belong, and the interconnection of life with the universe. Le Guin uses the strong female characters Stone Telling and Pandora to explore a culture that is different, yet very familiar, to modern American society. The novel does not have one single story line, but is made of a collection of stories, poems, maps, dictionaries, charts, and songs held together by the three parts of Stone Telling's narrative and Pandora's footnotes and journal entries. Critics raved over the beauty of the poetry and the innovative narrative style, but did voice concern over the novel's difficulty.

Long heralded as America's J. R. R. Tolkien, Le Guin has produced *Always Coming Home,* which is most often compared to Tolkien's *Silmarillion*—a difficult, but brilliant anthropological exploration of Middle Earth. In her novel, Le Guin envisions a post-apocalyptic world, but one created by natural events and human evolution, not nuclear war. The Kesh live in a future time in what used to be Northern California. Their culture is technologically nonexistent, but socially and personally advanced far beyond twentieth-century American

Ursula K. Le Guin

culture. The Valley of the Kesh is a world in which Le Guin can argue for sexual equality, spiritual renewal, environmental awareness, and utopian ideology. By casting this novel as the work of an objective scientist, she can also explore the thin line between science fact and science fiction.

Author Biography

Born in 1929, Ursula K. Le Guin has always enjoyed reading, especially poetry and fiction dealing with other times and places. Her parents were both professionals, her father an anthropology professor and her mother a children's literature author, and they both encouraged her literary aspirations. She says that she was lucky to be born in 1929 instead of 1939 because of J. R. R. Tolkien's influence. In her introduction to her critical exploration of science fiction, *The Language of the Night: Essays on Fantasy and Science Fiction,* Le Guin muses, "what would have happened if I had ... first read Tolkien in my teens, instead of my twenties. That achievement might have overwhelmed me." Tolkien's influence is most evident in *Always Coming Home* in its portrayal of a future possibility as an already established fact and presenting all aspects of this future culture in a scientific, textbook

format. She began submitting stories for publication at age eleven and although she was not published that early, the real rejection slip from a real magazine only drove her desire for publication and fame.

Le Guin, in numerous interviews, never claims to be a science fiction/fantasy writer, but simply a novelist whose publishers market her work as science fiction/fantasy. When asked what kind of prize she would like to win, either a National Book Award or a Hugo, Le Guin said Nobel. She does not see a marked difference between writing fiction and writing science fiction. Both her academic training, including graduate work in French and Italian Medieval literature, and her desire to be a "name," have helped Le Guin carve out a unique position for herself in the second half of the twentieth century. She is one of the first women to reach national and academic acclaim in the genre of science fiction/fantasy. Beginning with her early "fairy tales in space suits" in the 1950s, Le Guin has produced over eighty novels and collections of short stories, storming the walls of both traditional science fiction readership and "serious" literary scholarship in an attempt to bring her version of feminist utopian ideology to a wider audience. Her success has inspired and encouraged the careers of other women science fiction writers like Amber Zimmer Bradley, Anne Macaffery, and Sheri Tepper.

Plot Summary

Always Coming Home marks a departure for Le Guin in its two female protagonists and its complex narrative structure. Although she routinely deals with issues of sexual equality, utopianism, and a hopeful outlook for the future, Le Guin's novel approaches these ideas through the use of sociology, anthropology, and folklore which forces her readers to explore and compare the cultures of the Kesh and Condors to their own.

Part I

After a two-page introduction on the idea of future archaeology, Le Guin launches into the single narrative thread of *Always Coming Home*—the life story of the Kesh woman known as Stone Telling. Her first name is North Owl and she begins by introducing the major influences in her life. These influences are her mother, Willow, her grandmother, Valiant, and her father, the Condor man, Kills. Stone Telling's story begins like most; she describes her home and how her family fits into the Keshian culture. Valiant is a weaver, yet the family has no sheep for wool, so Stone Telling's family is poor. She relates her earliest memories of her grandmother weaving and how cold the water is in the winter. The narrative continues in the same vein, discussing Stone Telling's childhood, which was normal for a Kesh child, yet did not make her feel a part of the community.

The main part of the first narrative concerns the family's trip to Kastoha-na. Valiant wanted to take the therapeutic waters there and visit relatives. While there, Stone Telling sees Condor men for the first time. The importance for both Stone Telling and her mother, Willow, is overwhelming. The Condor men are not part of the Kesh; they are, as Valiant says, of no House. Yet they hold an irresistible fascination for both Stone Telling and Willow. Willow regains some of her lost self-esteem as she talks to the men, mentioning the name of her husband. Stone Telling feels excitement because these men are the same as her father, a father she has never met. Her spirit quest does not quiet her fears about the Valley and she and her family return home more agitated and upset than before.

Kills (also known as Abhao) arrives during one of the Kesh's public religious ceremonies. His arrival is marked by disbelief and discord among the Kesh. War is not an honorable activity for the Kesh; they think it is a foolish, youthful pastime. Yet the Condor men are warriors, obviously on the war path. Many of Stone Telling's neighbors comment on the spiritual sickness of adults who insist on acting like children. Stone Telling, on the other hand, is fascinated and sickened by her father's return. She is torn between the two parts of herself: part of her wants to acknowledge the Condor blood in her veins, but a larger part finds it frightening and disgusting. It is only after she gets to know her father that Stone Telling comes to a greater understanding of her parents.

Abhao's arrival has a dramatic effect on the household. Willow becomes a full person again, happy and industrious. Valiant remains silent in her own home, but does not like Abhao's behavior, which she considers to be laziness. Abhao refuses to work for he feels that would be beneath him. He has returned to the Valley after nine years to see the girl he had seduced, believing that she would have gotten on with her life. He is pleased and surprised that Willow has waited for him and does not understand her anger at his impending departure a few months later. Willow insists that she will not

wait for him again; he must either choose to be with her or to be a warrior. He cannot be both.

Abhao chooses to obey his war orders, and Willow divorces him by putting his clothes outside the door. He storms about, and asks Stone Telling to wait for him. The first part of Stone Telling's narrative ends as her father marches away and her mother returns to her childhood name.

Part II

The second part of the narrative is filled with the grief of growing up and the heartbreak of lost love. Stone Telling is nine when her father left the Valley and she begins to search for a purpose in her life. At the same time, a new movement begins to grow in the Valley. The Warrior and Lamb Lodges gather members and train them in the ways of war. These lodges, spoken of as cults by most of the Kesh, differ from the rest of Keshian society in that they value killing and secrecy. The Kesh reject war and keep no secrets from each other.

Three people very close to Stone Telling become involved with the warriors. After her father leaves, her mother, now Towhee, joins the Lamb Lodge for warrior women, and Stone Telling's grandfather, part of the Warrior Lodge, moves back in. Valiant had never divorced him and now, feeling abandoned by her daughter, she has no choice but to take him back since she needs help around the house. The third is Stone Telling's first love, Spear. She has been very close to him and his sister, Cricket, for years and she "entered womanhood with that lion on" her mind. She feels she can never forgive the Warrior Lodge for taking Spear away from her and it is this feeling of abandonment that makes her decide to go with her father to the City of the Condor.

Five years after he left the Valley, Abhao returns. Stone Telling has fought with her grandmother and upon fleeing the house, she meets Abhao on the path outside their village. Their reunion is less than joyful since he does not recognize her, but she is determined to leave the Valley where she feels unwanted and unloved. Abhao agrees to take her with him and tries to teach her the ways of the Condor on their journey back to Sai. His language, terminology, and customs are foreign to Stone Telling, and she does not understand them. Her illiteracy is furthered by the fact that reading and writing are forbidden to Condor women. As their journey continues, Stone Telling finds a Condor feather and decides to keep her discovery a secret (she later learns that she could be put to death for

Le Guin's father, the anthropologist Alfred L. Kroeber, had a keen interest in Taoism, which led Le Guin to publish her version of Chinese poet Lao Tzu's Tao Te Ching, *one of the core texts of the ancient philosophy. The dragon pictured here adorns a Taoist temple in Cebu City in the Philippines.*

touching the feather). She also becomes disgusted and disturbed by her father's casual attitude toward death and killing. She silently says *heyas* for the animals that the men kill on the journey.

Once they arrive in Sai, the City of the Condor, life becomes even more unbearable. She is not allowed to ride her horse or even walk; she must travel in a wagon like an invalid. The attitude of the other Condor women reflect that of the men. Stone Telling is considered an animal because her mother was an outsider, or hontik. She is given a certain amount of rank when Abhao presents her to the Condor and he acknowledges her existence. However, Stone Telling is shrouded in a literal and metaphorical veil. She must remain covered and out of sight during the rest of her days as a Condor woman. She cannot even go above ground. This part of the novel ends as Stone Telling contemplates her current existence.

Part III

The third part of Stone Telling's narrative is the most horrifying for the reader. Here, she relates the illness that nearly kills her and the Condor remedy—marriage. Stone Telling's illness is more restlessness because she is not allowed outside, she cannot read, she cannot learn new arts, and, since she is a Condor's daughter, she cannot spin, weave, or create anything. The doctors recommend that she marry. Thus, Stone Telling becomes the "pretty" wife of an important Condor, Retforok Dayat. She is a sex object, nothing more. She gets pregnant twice, but aborts the first one because her husband raped her. The second pregnancy comes as a relief from the boredom of her life. Her daughter, Ekwekwe, not only brings meaning back to Stone Telling's life, but also convinces her to leave the Condors and return to the Valley. She finally is able to get her father to help her and she, her daughter, and servant, Esiryu, leave the City of the Condor.

Upon her return to the Valley, Stone Telling finds that much has changed. Her grandmother, Valiant, is dead and her mother has lost her mind. The Warrior and Lamb lodges have been disbanded and the unrepentant ones have been exiled from the Valley. Stone Telling becomes Woman Coming Home and learns to relish her life in the Valley. She also realizes that she does belong here with the Kesh and that she always did. Stone Telling does not marry again, but she does take in a gifted healer named Alder. She and Alder raise Ekwekwe, who becomes Shining, and enjoy happiness with their granddaughters. Thus, Stone Telling's narrative comes full circle: she is respected, accepted, and beloved.

Part IV: The Back of the Book

Interspersed between Stone Telling's narrative and the last 150 pages of the novel are what Le Guin calls the artifacts of the Kesh. These songs, jokes, short stories, glossaries, recipes, and editorial comments make up the bulk of the novel and yet do not directly tie into the narrative. They reinforce and explain elements of Stone Telling's narrative, allowing for a greater understanding of the story.

Characters

Abhao

Abhao is Stone Telling's father. He is a mighty Condor warrior, a general of great fame and ability. Unlike other Condor men, Abhao only marries Willow, not a Condor woman, and Stone Telling is his only child. This is a source of humiliation for him since his only child is not a son to carry on his family name or status. However, he seems to love his daughter and encourages her riding ability and intellect when they are both living in the Valley. He is happy when she promises to wait for him and delighted when she agrees to return to the Condor City with him.

Back with his own people, Abhao tries to turn his daughter into a Condor woman. This means she cannot go outside, ride horses, speak until spoken to, or control her life. He presents her to The Condor, who acknowledges her existence, which gives Stone Telling the status of being her father's daughter. Abhao puts all of his faith, trust, and obedience in The Condor even though he knows that The Condor's plans for conquest are unrealistic and fatal to his people. He sells his daughter into a loveless marriage and continues in his blind devotion and obedience to his leader. However, Abhao is redeemed when he defies all of his training, culture, and faith, allowing Stone Telling to escape Sai and return to the Kesh. Abhao never sees his daughter again.

Alder

Alder is Stone Telling's second husband—who is Keshian—although they never officially marry. They enjoy each other's company and he helps her realize that she does belong in the Valley with the Kesh. He also tells her that if she finds a man she likes better, he will go. However, she does not find a man she likes better than Alder. He becomes Stone Listening because he listens to his wife's visions, stories, and memories.

Ashes

See Willow

Media Adaptations

- The first edition of *Always Coming Home* was accompanied by an audio cassette entitled *Music and Poetry of the Kesh*. The music was composed by Todd Barton and set in a tone reminiscent of Native American songs and dances. Barton takes Le Guin's words and brings the Kesh to life. The cassette helps flesh out Pandora's textbook and makes the Kesh seem more real. It is an interesting departure for fantasy literature.

Ayatyu

See Stone Telling

The City of Mind

The City of Mind, known as The City, is the name given to the robotic computer system by the Kesh. The City is really a huge database, controlled by its own subroutines, which records everything about human existence on the planet. The database is open to anyone; in fact, there are terminals in all the major towns of the Valley and beyond. Some cultures, like the Condor People, restrict the information, but those decisions are made by the cultures themselves, not by The City. The City does not consider whether the information is good or bad, because all experience is knowledge. It also does not judge what people do with the provided information as good or bad, because that is not The City's function. The City only exists as a record of human events. The City encourages all people to contribute their life stories and events to its database, which will continue even after Earth's destruction—through its satellite network and backup systems scattered throughout the solar system. The City's network of terminals is also used for communication among different cultural groups involved in trade and commerce. Within the individual societies, the terminal network is used rarely and typically only for emergencies.

Condor People

The people of the Condor are a formerly nomadic, monotheistic, warrior society living outside the Valley of the Kesh, who call them the House-less Ones. They call themselves Dayao, the One-People. They believe that only they are truly people; everyone else is subhuman. They like to believe that they control the entire region, but the people living around them keep them contained. The society of the Condor people has three tiers. At the highest level are The Condor and his sons; the second tier is composed of the Condor's male relatives and their sons; and the third is composed of the Condor warriors and their sons. Women are not considered fully human by the Condor People, although daughters of Condor warriors are on a higher social level than other women.

Unlike the Kesh, people of the Condor live in one city, Sai, on a devastated plain of volcanic rock. They believe in the total domination of nature, the superiority of males, and the segregation and oppression of females. Information is strictly limited to the eyes and ears of the Condor, who rules arbitrarily and absolutely. Their religious beliefs are a mirror of their society. Their deity is the One God who is represented by the condor bird and demands absolute obedience and fear. In an age in which technology is useless, the Condor people waste vast amounts of food and fuel to create an armored tank and fighter-type balloon planes. Both these experiments with conventional weaponry fail just as the Condor city is failing due to starvation and disease. Le Guin uses the Condor people as a continual comparison to the Kesh, highlighting the vitality, openness, and success of the Keshian society with the dying, suffocating, and ultimately doomed culture of the Condor people.

Danaryu

See Ekwekwe

Dayao

See Condor People

Retforok Dayat

Retforok Dayat is Stone Telling's first husband. He is a Condor man of the second tier and highly involved in the political machinations surrounding the Condor. He took Stone Telling as his "pretty wife," or a wife whose only function was sex. Condor wives are expected to continually produce babies, especially boys, but "pretty wives" are not expected to have any children, but only to satisfy their husbands' sexual desires. Retforok Dayat ceases to be a problem for Stone Telling once she convinces her father to help her escape. Dayat does not go after Stone Telling since the only child she

bore him was a daughter and girls do not matter to the Condor men.

Editor

See Pandora

Ekwekwe

Ekwekwe, which means Watching Quail, is Stone Telling's daughter. Her Condor name, Danaryu, means One Given to Woman; in many ways she saved her mother's life. Ekwekwe is the child that Stone Telling wanted in order to relieve the boredom of her life as a Condor woman. However, as Ekwekwe grew, Stone Telling could not stand the idea of her daughter becoming just another Condor woman; this becomes the major reason Stone Telling attempts her escape. Ekwekwe is raised, loved, and accepted as a child of the Kesh and no one seems bothered by her mixed ancestry. Le Guin uses Ekwekwe to suggest that cultures are not necessarily bound together by common ethnic traits.

Esiryu

Esiryu is the hontik, or non-Condor, slave woman given to Stone Telling when she goes to live with her father in Sai. It is Esiryu who teaches Stone Telling the ways of the Condor culture, especially how women are supposed to behave. She also chooses to leave Sai with Stone Telling and Ekwekwe. When the women return to the Valley, Esiryu is so frightened of living a new way that she becomes Stone Telling's "shadow." Eventually this becomes her name as well. Even though she is frightened and repulsed by many of the Kesh's customs, she learns to enjoy and embrace life and eventually marries Stone Telling's cousin, Spear.

Houseless Ones

See Condor People

Kesh

Always Coming Home tells the story of the Kesh from an anthropological point of view. Their lives, customs, habits, literature, and culture make up most of Le Guin's novel. The Kesh are a society that works on lines of female descent with property, responsibilities, and more, passing from mother to daughter to her daughter and so on. Their religious beliefs include a female deity in the form of Coyote and the living interconnection of all things including animals, rocks, raindrops, and humans. For the Kesh, all living and nonliving things are people, just different kinds of people. The Kesh are divided into nine different "houses," which teach the trades or arts specific to individual houses. While the Kesh are willing to teach any trade to any single person, generally people learn the trades specific to their own houses.

Every Keshian town works the same way. There are five Houses of the Earth (Obsidian, Blue Clay, Serpentine, Yellow Adobe, and Red Adobe), which deal with physical or real things: farming, writing, carpentry, metal work, and tool making. The remaining four houses are Houses of the Sky (Rain, Cloud, Wind, and Air), which deal with spiritual or unnatural things: funeral ceremonies, windmills, and electricity. The Kesh have little use for technology, although they have access to the sum of human knowledge stored in "The City" and generally live their lives in harmony with nature. The Kesh do not believe in obtaining material possessions, whether it be food, goods, or services. Their concept of wealth is someone who gives unselfishly. Their culture seems, in many ways, at odds with late twentieth-century American culture and can be described as primitive, but the Kesh would consider a consumer culture to be the primitive one.

Sexual relations among the Kesh are considered a natural function and are not reserved for marriage, nor is homosexuality banned. Marriage does exist, called "going inland," but men become members of their wives' households with the children belonging to the women and their houses. Divorce is socially acceptable and when a couple divorces, the man returns to his mother's household. People of the Kesh generally have three names: a childhood "given" name usually coming from birds, an adult "self-chosen" name usually coming from some life experience, and the name of the "third" period, or old age, usually describes how the person lived out her or his life. When a Kesh dies, all three names are burned by her or his relatives at the Dancing of World following his or her death. The Kesh seem to have many cultural aspects in common with Native Americans, which becomes even more obvious when one listens to the recording of Keshian music and poetry that accompanies the novel.

Kills
See Abhao

North Owl
See Stone Telling

One Given to Woman
See Ekwekwe

One-People
See Condor People

Pandora

The only other major, consistent character in *Always Coming Home* is the Editor, who reveals her name as Pandora in journal entries scattered throughout the novel. She is a "future" archaeologist, who, through an undefined method of time travel, visits the world of the Kesh and describes their culture for her time period. The Editor expresses problems with understanding the Kesh, particularly in terms of their relationship to nature, their religion, and their social and sexual customs. Her inability to explain thoroughly these aspects of Keshian culture makes the novel difficult to read. She is constantly using footnotes and endnotes to explain how difficult the act of translation and cultural identification is without really adding to the narrative flow.

Pandora filters everything for the reader; she chooses what parts of the Kesh she relates and what she leaves unexplained. She is the most difficult character in the novel because she is walking a fine line between scientist and fiction writer. Pandora is not Le Guin, but is the character that Le Guin uses to explore the difficulty and the hypocrisy within the idea of scientific objectivity. Pandora is a product of her culture and so reads the Kesh and the Condor People through the lens of late twentieth-century technology, social relationships, and environmental relationships. Ultimately, she controls the image of the Kesh, so readers only see the Kesh as Pandora presents them.

Shadow
See Esiryu

Shining
See Ekwekwe

Stone Listening
See Alder

Stone Telling

Stone Telling is the only single character whose life becomes a major part of the narrative in *Always Coming Home.* She is the daughter of a Blue Clay woman and a Condor man and spent much of her early life feeling like a half-person since her father was not of the Kesh. Her story, told in three parts, holds the narrative of the Kesh together and gives a voice and a face to the "cold" scientific facts presented in the rest of the novel.

Home and family are not always comfortable places for Stone Telling and she dreams of a different kind of life. She feels unwanted and unaccepted in her community and tries to discover why by going on spiritual journeys, fasts, and physical pilgrimages. Stone Telling is overjoyed when her father returns to the Valley and stays with her family while training his troops for an attack on the Kesh's neighbors. Although Stone Telling does not say so, it seems that the Condor men do not bother the Kesh because her father is married to her mother. When her father leaves again, her mother tells him not to come back and puts his things on the porch, thus divorcing him. This scene ends the first part of Stone Telling's story.

Stone Telling's search for a place to belong leads her to leave the Valley, taking the name Ayatyu, and accompanying her father to the city of the Condor. There she comes face-to-face with the sexism and destructive nature of the Condor people. She is given status as the daughter of a Condor warrior, but her movements, her intellect, and her will are restricted. She lives the life of a Condor woman, including an arranged marriage. Only after the birth of her daughter does Stone Telling realize how awful her life has become and how much she misses and belongs in the Valley of the Kesh. She convinces her father to betray all of his beliefs and allow her and her daughter to escape. Stone Telling returns to the Kesh to find her grandmother physically dead and her mother spiritually dead. She spends the rest of her life coming to terms with what it means to "come home."

Towhee

See Willow

Valiant

Valiant is Stone Telling's grandmother and the matriarch of the family. She accepts Stone Telling as a whole person, even though Stone Telling does not believe that she does. Valiant tries to teach Stone Telling the ways of the Kesh, especially after her daughter Willow's divorce, but Stone Telling cannot make a connection with her grandmother. Valiant, who divorced her own husband, remarries her first husband because she feels abandoned by her family and needs someone to care for her in her old age. She dies while Stone Telling is living among the Condor people.

Watching Quail

See Ekwekwe

Willow

Willow is Stone Telling's mother. She defied her people and traditions by marrying a Condor *manconn*—a man of no House. Most of her neighbors do not believe that she and Stone Telling's father were actually married until he returns to the Valley when Stone Telling is eleven years old. She took the name, Willow, when he left her the first time, because, according to Keshian tradition, the willow tree weeps for a love lost. When Abhao returns, she is delighted and is able to sneer at her neighbors who said her child had no father. However, when he refuses to stay in the Valley with Willow, she "puts his clothes on the porch," which is a Keshian divorce, and returns to her childhood name, Towhee. She then joins the Lamb Society, a cult of women warriors that was disbanded by the Kesh in the face of an unrealized invasion threat by the Condor people. Stone Telling returns to the Valley as a young woman to find her mother a faded shadow of her former self. Willow has lost everything: her husband, her child, her social function, and her mother. She goes insane and Stone Telling renames her Ashes. Although Willow does not recognize either her daughter or the religious rituals of the Kesh, Stone Telling gives her a formal Keshian funeral and burns all three names at the Dance of the World following her mother's death.

Woman Coming Home

See Stone Telling

Themes

Sexual Equality

Gender equality has always been an important theme in Le Guin's fiction. She says, in *The Language of the Night: Essays on Fantasy and Science Fiction,* that she writes this kind of fiction because it allows her to explore how society would be without sexism and gender discrimination. The Kesh are essentially a nondiscriminatory people. A person's worth is not based on power or social relationships, but on how much he or she contributes to all major areas of society. The Condor society is diametrically opposite of the Kesh. Their society is based on male descent/relationship to the One Condor. This culture segregates women, keeping them ignorant and underground. Le Guin sets up these two societies, presenting the Kesh first, so that the shock and horror of the Condor society is more striking. The cultural criticism becomes more biting as Le Guin continually makes comparisons between the Condors and modern American society. The Kesh, with their open and equal attitudes toward sex and gender issues, are a thriving people. The Condors eventually destroy themselves, their sexist discriminatory culture collapsing under its own weight.

Spiritual Renewal

One of the major themes in *Always Coming Home* is that of renewal or regeneration, especially on the spiritual level. The world of the Kesh revolves around what they call "the hinge" of life. This is the point where the physical and the spiritual intersect, causing all people to examine who and what they are. The idea of spiritual growth and renewal is the common thread that holds not only Stone Telling's narrative together, but also the other narratives, short stories, poems, and songs of the Kesh.

Stone Telling's mother, Willow, and her grandmother, Valiant, both have so many problems finding meaning in their own lives that neither can spare any time to help Stone Telling with her life dilemmas. Willow's life falls apart because she cannot, as Lillian Heldreth suggests in *Mythlore,* accept or overcome the divide between what she wants (her warrior husband) and what her culture demands (that he give up being a warrior). She returns to her childhood name and eventually reverts to being a child. Willow cannot cope with losing everything that makes up her identity because she has no idea who she really is. Her husband, Abhao, is much the same. He cannot escape the bounds of his culture. When he takes Stone Telling with him to the Condor, he refuses to allow her to be free to become the person whom she would like to be. Abhao realizes that the Condor's desire for war and domination will destroy the Condors, but he cannot change the way things are. He tells Stone Telling that she made her choice to come to Sai and so she must remain until her death. However, because of his love for his daughter and granddaughter, Abhao does eventually help them escape the Condor, thus showing that he has grown beyond the rigid man he was at the beginning of the novel.

Environmental Awareness

One of the major differences between the Kesh and the Condors is their relationship with nature. All life is sacred for the Kesh and all living things are considered different kinds of "people." Le Guin goes to extremes to explain how the Kesh live as

Topics for Further Study

- Read Merlin Stone's *When God Was a Woman* and Anne Baring and Jules Cashford's *The Myth of the Goddess* and compare their arguments about the role of religion in the relationship of sexual equality to what Le Guin does with the Kesh and the Condor people. Investigate the idea of whether religion matters in the creation of culture.

- Investigate the role of technology in the development of modern culture, specifically the environmental movement of the 1980s and 1990s. How do these ideas about technology and the environment compare to the ideologies of the Kesh and the Condor people?

- Is Pandora, the editor, a "good" anthropologist? Compare Le Guin's ideas about future archaeology with current theories about how anthropology and archaeology work today.

- How do the political ideas of the societies in *Always Coming Home* compare to modern political ideas about communism, democracy, socialism, and totalitarian governments?

- Define, with examples, matriarchy and patriarchy. Do these systems satisfactorily define the Kesh and the Condor people?

- Research the dances, songs, and religions of various tribal societies. How do these cultures compare to the Kesh? How would you create a chant, choreograph a dance, or perform one of the pieces from *Always Coming Home?*

a part of the Creation; their religion and festivals are celebrations of Coyote's creation and participation in the life process. This attitude makes the Kesh profoundly aware of the environment. They have rejected the destructive technology that modern American society thrives on and work in harmony with nature. They kill only for necessity, asking forgiveness of the animals they kill and sing "*heyas,*" or hymns, as a part of the butchering ritual. Hunting is not an adult sport for the Kesh; it is something only children do, an activity put aside with maturity. Their agriculture, architecture, and even apparel are all focused on making as small an impact on the earth as possible. The Kesh believe that they are part of creation and must work within it, not against it.

The Condors, on the other hand, believe that they are directed by their god to dominate and use nature for their benefit. The One, the Condors' god, made creation, but is not part of it, and so does not care for it. Neither do the Condors; they see everyone and everything, save for Condor men, as animals or dirt (hontik). The lack of connection to the natural environment of the Condors is evident in the location of their city. Sai is built on an ancient lava plain where everything looks like death and nothing ever grows. This location is in perfect contrast to the Na Valley of the Kesh, which, even with toxic waste dumps and radiation poisoning, is green, alive, and inviting. The Condors do not care about scarring the land and are angered when the Kesh refuse to allow them to build a permanent bridge over the river. Nor do they give thanks or ask forgiveness from the animals they slaughter for food, horrifying a fifteen-year-old Stone Telling as she travels with her father. At Sai, the Condor sacrifices the health and well being of his city for the glory of polluting war machines that consume all the available food, causing the city to starve to death.

Utopian Ideology

Le Guin's use of utopian ideology differs from most of her contemporaries in the way she starts and sustains her utopia. Generally speaking, utopias grow out of some cataclysmic event, such as nuclear war, social collapse, or widespread religious persecution. Utopias are then sustained by the dedicated work of all citizens who are equally determined to see the utopia succeed. However, Le Guin does not create or sustain the utopian society of the Kesh in these ways. In their society, the people do not seem to care about their origins. They believe that they have always existed with no founders, first presidents, or list of creators of the Kesh culture. Revolting against both political and literary tradition, Le Guin insists that her utopia is the only rational evolutionary path if humanity is to survive. This view of utopia as an evolutionary end rather than a reaction to catastrophe makes *Always Coming Home* unique in modern science fiction.

The other part of Le Guin's unique approach to utopian ideology is the way she defines and sustains the utopia of the Kesh. There is no central government in the Na Valley; there is no local government in the individual cities either. The peace and stability of the culture are sustained by the desire of each individual to become the best she or he can be. This forms Le Guin's definition of anarchy, which J. R. Wytenbroek suggests she believes is the only form of government possible in a real utopia. He also says that Le Guin goes to great lengths to distinguish between armed chaos (terrorism) and the lack of an authority/government (anarchy). The idea of a perfect society without law, dogma, or technology puts *Always Coming Home* in a position to challenge the conventions of the very genre it claims to represent.

Scientific Objectivity

The structure of *Always Coming Home* lends itself more toward nonfiction than fiction. There is no real story line, action, or suspense, but rather a collection of artifacts presented to the reader as anthropological evidence. Le Guin is aware of and makes her readers equally aware of the problem of scientific objectivity. She introduces us to the Kesh first and so we see everyone else in the Na Valley and outside it through comparisons to the Kesh. We do not like the Condors because the Kesh do not like the Condors. Because each reader cannot meet the Kesh for him-or herself, Le Guin exposes the hypocrisy of scientific objectivity. No scientist, no matter how hard he or she tries, can ever break out of the bounds of his or her culture. Scientific objectivity cannot exist because every scientist must select the facts he or she is going to present. Reality, as Le Guin writes it, is always subject to interpretation.

Style

Point of View

Since *Always Coming Home* does not follow a traditional novel format, the point of view shifts continually. Both Pandora and Stone Telling's parts are told in first person, but these two sections make up less than half of the novel. Le Guin uses the framework of a scientific text to explore how a culture makes meaning, both for itself and for other cultures around it. Praised by some as lyrical and inventive, Le Guin's shifting between different "artifacts" makes following a single story, such as Stone Telling's narrative, difficult and, at times, frustrating. However, the intermixture of poems, songs, short narratives, religious ceremonies, and news bulletins help make sense of what Stone

Telling says and what she leaves out. The nonfiction aspects of this novel also help make it seem more plausible and real, lending a depth to otherwise shallow characters.

Names as Metaphor

The names in Le Guin's novel are descriptive because they not only name the characters, but they also describe the characters' personalities or circumstances in life. Pandora, for example, is the scientist who puts the entire collection of artifacts from the Kesh society together. However, Pandora was also the name of the first woman, according to Greek legend, who released all the evil in the world. The name, Pandora, also means "gift." Pandora, the editor in *Always Coming Home,* is keenly aware of the historical significance of her name. The names of both the Kesh and Condor characters are metaphoric as well. Pandora admits near the end of the novel that she has been using the English "meanings" of the Keshian and Condorian names rather than their real spellings. Le Guin does this for two reasons: one, she wants her readers to connect with her characters; and two, she wants her characters' names to reflect what her characters do.

If Pandora had used the Keshian and Condorian spellings for the names of the characters in this novel, the reader's level of identification would have been quite low, as would their attachment to the characters. Thus, Stone Telling is known as North Owl as a child or Woman Coming Home when she returns to the Valley. Willow becomes Ashes after her breakdown, and Stone Telling's warrior father is Kills. Readers can identify and pronounce these names, which lends to the credibility of these people. They do not have popular names, but they are recognizable and do reflect the characters' functions in the novel. For example, Abhao is called Kills because he is a warrior. Stone Telling becomes Woman Coming Home when she returns to the Kesh society, and Willow takes the name Ashes because she has become a burned-out remnant of who she used to be. Likewise, Stone Telling's friend becomes Shadow because she lives as if she were Stone Telling's shadow.

Symbolism

Symbolism plays a large part in *Always Coming Home.* Everything in the daily life of the Kesh is symbolic of the way they react toward their surroundings. From the way they build their homes to the way they farm, learn trades, and handle commerce reflects their belief in the interconnection of all living things. This allows Le Guin to express her ideas about progress, the future, and contemporary culture's fascination with technology and science. The Kesh have no leaders, no history that makes sense to Pandora, and no innovation. These qualities are not what science fiction usually attributes to an advanced culture. Le Guin makes very clear in her treatment of the Kesh and the technology-crazed Condors that this clash of progress with technology is the most serious problem facing human development and growth. By using every standard by which progress is measured in contemporary society as a symbol of decline, decay, and death, Le Guin attacks contemporary American culture on both practical and spiritual grounds.

Narrative Structure

The narrative structure of *Always Coming Home* is considered both interesting and difficult. The novel begins with two notes from the editor explaining that this work is different from anything else. She defines future archaeology and suggests that there is more than one way to read this, or any, novel. Often compared to J. R. R. Tolkien's *Silmarillion,* C. S. Lewis's *Lion of Judeah in Never Never Land,* and Gene Rodenberry's *Starfleet Academy,* Le Guin's novel uses a narrative structure that questions both her craft as a fiction writer and the craft of nonfiction writing. Stone Telling's coming-of-age narrative is broken into three sections, separated by collections of poems, shorter narratives, religious ceremonies, and news bulletins from the Exchange. All of these artifacts contribute to the fiction of "nonfiction" for the novel, but it makes for difficult reading and a sense of discontinuity. The second part of the novel, called "The Back of the Book," contains all the explanatory text necessary to thoroughly understand the first section. Le Guin is again playing with methods of reading because readers should read "The Back of the Book" (as she subtly suggests) before reading the front.

Historical Context

The Fiction of Scientific Progress

Always Coming Home allows Le Guin to question not only her craft, but contemporary notions of progress. Le Guin pits the Kesh, who do not use technology and are successful, against the Condors, who insist on using technology and ultimately fail. Le Guin maintains throughout this novel that technology without a connection to the universe is meaningless. The Condors fail to produce a massive killing machine because the technology-

Women participate in a civil defense exercise during the Cold War. At the time Le Guin wrote Always Coming Home, *the United States and the former Soviet Union were stockpiling weapons of mass destruction.*

saturated culture necessary for such a machine does not exist. The Kesh succeed because they have put technology in balance with nature, making real progress.

The Fiction of Scientific Objectivity

Le Guin's novel challenges the basic concept of scientific observation. She argues that a scientist cannot write outside of her culture and, therefore, must forget claims of objectivity. We see the Kesh and the Condors not as they are, but how Pandora sees them. This is the hypocrisy that Le Guin

challenges: the late twentieth century idea that science is not influenced by human behavior.

Fantasy Literature versus "Real" Literature

Science fiction and fantasy literature, along with other genres like mystery and detective fiction, is not considered "real" literature by many scholars and critics. This particularly irritates Le Guin, who always insists that she is writing fiction. In almost every interview or essay, Le Guin makes the comment that it is her publishers and marketers who label her a science fiction/fantasy writer. Le Guin is, however, one of the few science fiction writers to have breached the walls of scholarly opinion and her work is considered the best of the genre.

Critical Overview

When it was first published in 1985, *Always Coming Home* was heralded as a brilliant new work by one of America's favorite authors. There were the usual glowing reviews in *Newsweek* and *The New York Times Book Review* and the scholarly reviews in journals like *Mythlore* and *The Hudson Review.* All of the early reviews and articles said much the same thing: they praised the novel, but also commented on its strange narrative structure and length. Peter Prescott, writing in *Newsweek,* comments that the novel is too long and the situations cannot bear much examination but is well worth the reader's patience as an example of Le Guin's unique style. *New York Times Book Review* contributor Samuel Delany calls the book "a slow, rich read," advising the reader to savor Le Guin's prose since the storyline itself is weak and not action-filled. Dick Allen, who focuses, as most early reviewers did, on the utopian aspects of Stone Telling's narrative in *The Hudson Review,* waxes poetic about Le Guin's style and command of prose but worries that the narrative structure will intimidate readers unused to Le Guin's style and purpose.

The critical complaints over narrative technique and length soon gave over to genuine praise for a novel that is truly original in style and scope. Critics as diverse as Lillian Heldreth, Bernard Selinger, Lee Cullen Khanna, and Peter Fitting all have hailed *Always Coming Home* as a brilliant piece of work that has changed the genre of utopian literature forever. These critics have judged the novel as Le Guin's masterpiece in terms of its antiwar stance, its innovation in narrative technique, and its impact on utopian fiction.

The idea of war and technological progress being harmful to the human race is not new, but Le Guin reaches new heights according to Heldreth and J. R. Wytenbroek. In her essay, "To Defend or to Correct: Patterns of Culture in *Always Coming Home,*" Heldreth examines Le Guin's use of language as a map to understanding the miscommunications between people. These miscommunications often lead to war or violence in contemporary society, so Le Guin navigates these differences and shows how personal stubbornness and blindness lead to misery and pain. Le Guin's use of a people who reject war and yet still win, occupies the majority of Wytenbroek's essay *"Always Coming Home:* Pacifism and Anarchy in Le Guin's Latest Utopia." Here, Wytenbroek challenges contemporary readings of both Le Guin's pacifism and anarchy to suggest that she insists on both being present in a successful utopia. However, Le Guin plays with the idea of the Kesh being an utopian society by having both Pandora and one of her informants agree that the Kesh are not utopians. Yet everything used to describe the Na Valley is standard utopian fare. Le Guin creates a society that refuses to fight the Condors, but will do so if necessary. The warlike pacifism of the Kesh undercuts both the contemporary antiviolence campaigns in American culture and the wars that are standard science fiction narrative tools.

The narrative technique of *Always Coming Home* has also become one of the most lauded aspects of the novel. While most critics find themselves focusing on Stone Telling's narrative, all of them insist on mentioning the broken structure and interjected materials. Although one interesting fact of the novel is that it cannot be read like a normal novel, most of the critics that explore the use of narrative technique focus on the "normal" aspects of Stone Telling's narrative. Critics like Carol Franko and Bernard Selinger both commended Le Guin's novel as brilliant, complicated, and original in terms of technique, but both avoid the un-narrative parts of the novel. The poems, short stories, recipes, and glossary get very little attention in the critical literature, while Stone Telling's narrative becomes the focus. The original narrative technique gets lost in the search for the familiar.

By far the most important critical aspect of Le Guin's novel has been its impact on utopian fiction. According to both Lee Cullen Khanna and Peter Fitting, *Always Coming Home* marked a departure for both Le Guin and for feminist utopian fiction. During the 1970s and early 1980s, feminist utopian fiction became more and more depressing and defeatist. Novels like Margaret Atwood's *The Handmaid's Tale* (1985) and Suzette Haden Elgin's *Native Tongue* (1984) characterized this pessimistic view of the future. Khanna and Fitting both saw Le Guin's fiction as speaking to the times. America was mired in the arms race, the Cold War, and the introduction of the home computer. Video cassette recorders (VCRs), microwave ovens, and cordless phones were finding their way into the American marketplace. However, the threat of nuclear war was real, as then President Ronald Reagan called the U.S.S.R. the "evil empire" and asked Congress for the funds to outproduce them in weapons of mass destruction. In this world, where every other utopian author was writing works of failure and pessimism, Le Guin countered with *Always Coming Home,* what Fitting calls a turning point. Le Guin's novel describes a people who have rejected both war and technology and are thriving in a valley full of toxic waste and piles of radioactive garbage. Khanna and Fitting suggest, in their different essays, that Le Guin wanted to explore the possibilities of winning, of hope, of goodness within the human animal. She changed the face of utopian fiction and gave it life again.

Although it received a warm welcome when it was first published, many critics faulted the length and narrative technique of *Always Coming Home.* This criticism, however, did not hinder other critics from examining Le Guin's novel and ranking it among the best pieces of fiction produced in the 1980s.

Criticism

Michael Rex

Rex is an instructor at The University of Detroit Mercy. In the following essay, he explores how the issues of return and renewal in Always Coming Home *work to bring a narrative cohesion to disjointed text.*

It is an integral part of our culture. Home is where we feel secure, safe—where we belong. Home is also the place where we go if we are frightened, tired, or lonely because we know that there we will always find peace and love. Ursula Le Guin's novel *Always Coming Home* works on many levels, but the most interesting one is the theme of return or coming home. Le Guin could have named her book anything, but she chose *Always Coming Home.* The idea of the return to home is the central theme to all of the discordant parts of the novel. Many critics have commented on the odd narrative style, utopian aspects, and lack of character development, but few seem to deal with this issue. The return to "home" and spiritual renewal brings a narrative cohesion to the novel as all the various parts work together to explore humanity's need for home.

Pandora, or the Editor, plays a vital role in the novel. She is the scientist who presents the Kesh to the reader. She begins the novel by musing on the difficulty of doing "future archeology." But Pandora presents the reader with a double-edged problem. The Kesh are a people who might be going to live in Northern California several thousand years from now. All at once we become aware that the Kesh are fiction, but in order to make sense of the novel, we must accept that the Kesh are real and that Pandora has spent many months collecting the data which she presents as *Always Coming Home.* Even though she is a scientist exploring a new culture, Pandora is trapped in her own culture, viewing everything from her home. She originally has a problem locating the archaeological remains of the Kesh because she is thinking in terms of a modern American scholar. The contours of the map have to mean that a particular structure lies here, because that is how we would do it. So, a gate turns out to be a wall and Pandora initially sees the Kesh as a primitive, walled community too scared to leave home.

She realizes her mistake as she begins to explore the literature and culture of these primitive people. Pandora seems fascinated with the social structure and environmental ideology of the Kesh. The value they place on giving away to the community is particularly difficult for her to grasp. This idea, which is so alien to both the reader and the editor, forms the basis of Pandora's search for home. The Kesh believe that only when one gives away everything is one truly rich. Our society does not work that way, but neither does Pandora. She wants to know how the real people lived. She is a scientist unconcerned with the big, overall, simplified view of the Kesh. She wants the broken bowl, the little bits of daily life that will explain how the Kesh acted at home. Le Guin uses Pandora to expose the hypocrisy of scientific objectivity. Pandora cannot escape her own culture and so we see the Kesh and their neighbors, not as they really are, but as Pandora sees them. This becomes obvious when Pandora explains the Condor people and confronts her own scientific prejudices.

The Condor people are the enemy of the Kesh. They are the evil force threatening the utopia Le Guin has created. However, they hardly seem to be worth the fuss. Their society is on the brink of collapse and all they think about is war and domination. The way Le Guin presents the Condors is directly tied to what she wants to do with Pandora and scientific objectivity. The Condors are introduced only after we have met the Kesh. We do not

What Do I Read Next?

- Sheri Tepper's *Gate to Women's Country* (1988) deals with a world that has been divided into two: women and peaceful men living inside walled cities; and the warriors, banished to forts outside the city walls. It has been this way since an atomic war devastated the planet. These women must give up their sons, brothers, and lovers, yet something is just not quite right. Find out the secret that every Council in every Women's Country town knows and men must never find out.

- In a novel similar to Le Guin's *Always Coming Home,* Sheri Tepper envisions a world without technology and deeply withdrawn into the Jungian archetypes. *A Plague of Angels* (1993) follows the adventures of Abasio and Ellel as they attempt to prevent a family of power-hungry nobles from reaching the stockpile of nuclear weapons on the moon. Unlike Le Guin, Tepper refuses to give a happy or hopeful ending.

- Merlin Stone's *When God Was a Woman* (1974) explores the ancient Goddess worshipping cultures of the Middle East in order to explain how the relationships between women and men in terms of power, job opportunities, social status, and spiritual guilt changed with the introduction of male-dominated religion. Stone suggests that the current model of male-dominated culture is not natural, evolved, or normal. Her discussion of "Tales with a Point of View" is particularly useful in analyzing not only what Le Guin does in *Always Coming Home,* but other literature as well.

- The *Silmarillion* by J. R. R. Tolkien was not published until four years after his death in 1973, but it was written over twenty years earlier. Like Le Guin's novel, *Silmarillion* traces the anthropological aspects of Tolkien's Middle Earth. There is no real narrative, but the book is made up of songs, legends, maps, and short narratives that lay the ground work for his more familiar works, *The Hobbit* and *The Lord of the Rings.*

- Anne Baring and Jules Cashford's *The Myth of the Goddess* (1991) portrays the evolution of the female divinity. They explore how human culture in Europe and the Mediterranean celebrated and worshipped the Goddess from ancient times to the modern era and how her image became merged with the Virgin Mary. The development of this mythology and the idea of Coyote in *Always Coming Home* are remarkably similar.

- *The Left Hand of Darkness* by Ursula Le Guin astounded critics and readers alike when it was published in 1969. Here, Le Guin creates a race of people whose gender is not fixed and each individual can choose to change gender at will. The narrator of the novel is a human man who cannot handle or understand how to deal with this race. Le Guin says that her hero is a relatively stupid and shortsighted man because that describes most of her audience. *The Left Hand of Darkness* reinforced Le Guin's position as a major name in the world of science fiction and fantasy literature.

- Plato's *Timaeus* and *Critias,* both composed in the mid-fifth century BCE, describe the rise and destruction of Atlantis. As one of the first and most influential utopias, the story of Atlantis has held the imagination of readers and writers for centuries.

- *You Just Don't Understand: Men and Women in Conversation* (1990) launched Debrah Tannen's reputation as the pop culture expert on how men and women speak together and to each other. Her observations about conversation match Stone Telling's confusion about the Condor language and apply to Pandora's problems with translating the language of the Kesh.

- Sir Thomas More's *Utopia* (1516), like Plato's "Atlantis" dialogues and Le Guin's novel, sharply criticizes his contemporary society by creating a world in which he controls the truth. *Utopia* is presented as an eyewitness account of a "perfect" world. More's satire is more depressing and less hopeful than Le Guin's idealistic novel.

learn any stories, jokes, or customs of the Condors like we do the Kesh. So, of course we do not feel any connection to them. Although they are more like contemporary American culture, they lack a humanness that the Kesh possess. They dress like a buzzard bird that lives off the dead flesh of other animals. The Condors do not seem to notice the contradictions in their appearance and their attitude about themselves. Pandora, too, has problems being objective about the Condors. They are presented as a warrior society that is doomed to destruction under the weight of their hierarchical culture. But it is because we do not see them at home, being themselves, that they seem like monsters. Le Guin seems to be suggesting that our own desire for peace and prosperity masks a deeper ugliness, based on greed and the desire for destruction.

Pandora's scientific objectivity receives another blow when she tries to understand the Kesh and their lack of history. Unlike other societies, the Kesh have either always been or do not care where they came from. This attitude puzzles Pandora and she tries to unlock the idea of having no history, no beginning. She finds the Keshian creation stories unfulfilling and pushes the Archivist at Wakwah-na for clarity. The Archivist, a fellow scientist, whom Pandora greets as family, explains that most of the books are thrown away after a few years. The loss of information horrifies Pandora, who cannot see the practicalities of the Keshian system. She insists that data storage and retrieval systems could keep all of the valuable information that is now being lost. The Archivist counters that the City of the Mind already does that, and besides books are like people, mortal beings. She pushes Pandora further by questioning why Pandora insists on storing all information. What is the point? Does it create a system of power? A way to control others in the culture? Le Guin forces her readers to examine what we consider to be knowledge. Through her use of Pandora and her unfailing loyalty to her own culture, Le Guin suggests that we too use knowledge as a weapon to beat on each other. Pandora, even as she explores and explains the Kesh, is stuck in her own culture and cannot, or does not want to, see a way out. She is comfortable at home.

This comfort level with familiar things is a common human emotion. It is also the goal in most of the non-narrative text in *Always Coming Home*. The poems, short stories, dramas, and dances involve a journey away from home and celebrate the return. As Dick Allen says, the poetry is not profound, but it does speak to the peace and desire for

community. The first section deals with stories "told aloud." Their very title suggests a need for community, for home, for others. Each story tells of someone who felt outside the order. These characters did not belong in the situations they were in and the stories revolve around getting the individuals back home. This first sections deals with physical separations, followed by poems lamenting the nature of separation, and ending with a section on death customs among the Kesh. This structure follows the flow of Stone Telling's first narrative. She feels cutoff from her people, a part of them, but not fully whole. Her mother lives in a romantic fairy tale and dies, spiritually, when Abhao, her husband, leaves for the second time.

The next grouping of Keshian literature deals with romance, sacrifice for love, and "real" histories. The romances are not romantic as our culture would define romance. Instead they deal with the harsh realities of sexuality and taboo. The stories end unhappily because the characters want something they are not culturally allowed to have. This sense of loss and foreboding continues in the histories section. These histories show the Kesh at their ugliest. The Kesh are not happy-go-lucky, empty-minded Utopians. They are real people who love, hate, fear, and desire just like us. However, the Kesh seem more able than the societies around them to handle these pressures without imploding. But even here, the constant theme is one of community, belonging, fitting in. This again matches the narrative of Stone Telling.

In the second part of her story, Stone Telling dwells on her adolescence after her parents' divorce. She focuses on describing her actions, feelings, and fears as she grows into womanhood. She falls in love, not with a Condor like her mother did, but with a Kesh warrior, a young man named Spear. He is beautiful and soon becomes forbidden to her. He is a member of the Warrior Lodge, an outcast group within Keshian society, and he cannot associate with Stone Telling, since she is not a part of his world. Much like the lovers in the preceding romances, Stone Telling feels cut off from the object of her desire and lashes out at those who try to make her conform. She fights with her grandmother, who does not care for the warriors and leaves the house in tears. Here, Stone Telling is like every single teenager throughout time—confused, in between childhood and adulthood, but belonging to neither. She wants a community, a place to belong, and a place to call home. All of this confusion and desire push Stone Telling toward leaving the Valley. If she does not belong with her mother's people then she must belong with her father's kin.

In many ways, Stone Telling's leaving the Na Valley is both the best and the worst thing that could happen to her. She discovers that she is the product of opposites. Not only are her parents opposite genders, but their belief systems, ideologies, and life concepts are totally different. Abhao desires Willow as a Condor man wants any woman, as a possession or property. Willow wants Abhao to be a Kesh man and stay with her. Stone Telling is caught between these two systems. She is intelligent and keenly aware of her surroundings, but her father makes her feel stupid because she cannot learn his language and writing, as it is forbidden to her because she is a woman. We have to stop and wonder why Abhao takes Stone Telling with him to the Condor. She is female and half-animal (according to Condor theology) and will bring him nothing but shame. Yet Abhao wants to bring her to his home and make her part of his culture. He wants to show his culture that he is normal and can produce children. He wants to give his daughter a community, a place to belong, a home. Unfortunately, neither Stone Telling nor her father realize the dangers in trying to force square pegs into round holes.

The Keshian literature separating the second and final parts of Stone Telling's narrative illustrates these dangers. The dramas that immediately follow the second part of Stone Telling's story all deal with reality and deception. The first, "The Wedding Night at Chukulmas," tells the story of a long-dead groom who invades a real wedding looking for his long-lost bride. The live characters fear the bad luck that will come if the dead characters are not fulfilled. This fear continues in the other plays as characters who do not belong in the situations with which they are confronted react in increasing desperation and irrationality. The dances and the poems following the dramas add to the growing sense of dread. The excerpt from *Dangerous People* provides a foreshadowing of how Stone Telling's life will fall apart before she can find true happiness. We know that Stone Telling's life in the Condor City of Sai is not happy and the tales of loss, madness, and hysteria that proceed in the third section prepare the reader for the devastating reality of Condor life.

The third section of her narrative shows Stone Telling coming full circle. She experiences everything that we traditionally believe makes for happiness and belonging: family, marriage, and motherhood. However, Stone Telling's experiences with these factors only lead to her mental and physical collapse. It is only the birth of her daughter that forces her to take action. Stone Telling escapes from Sai and returns to the Valley. She has come home. She now knows where she belongs.

All of the elements, characters, and voices in this novel are always coming home. The journey is one full of danger and risk, but the rewards make up for them. Returning to a sense of community and belonging is the ultimate human goal. Le Guin suggests that this goal can only be achieved by first leaving, finding out who we are, and then finally coming home.

Source: Michael Rex, in an essay for *Novels for Students*, Gale, 2000.

J. R. Wytenbroek

In the essay below, Wytenbroek details the marked differences between the two societies portrayed in Always Coming Home *and notes how the work "adds a completely new dimension to Le Guin's study and presentation of war, as found in the rest of her science fiction."*

Ursula K. Le Guin is a pacifist, a fact she has made clear on numerous occasions, both in her writings and her political activities. Throughout her writings, she has dealt with war, or armed conflict, in various ways, examining it from a different angle in each work in which such conflict appeared. She examined the psychology of war to a large extent in *The Word for World is Forest* (1972), especially through the character of Captain Davidson. She looked at what happened to pacifists who could or would not fight back in *The Dispossessed* (1974), while she considered what happened to pacifists who did fight back in *The Eye of the Heron* (1978).

In her latest novel, *Always Coming Home,* Le Guin examines both the psychology and anatomy of war by examining an entire culture given over to war and conquering. She examines this culture from within the society itself, but through the eyes of an outsider who, initially willingly, becomes part of the society. The outsider, Stone Telling, daughter of a woman of the pacifistic Valley people and an important warrior of the constantly warring Condor people, is initially drawn to the power and excitement of her father's world. However, soon she discovers that the power of domination is not exciting when one is the dominated, and that a life based on power and violence is an extremely limited one, even for the powerful. These insights are gained by a free mind within an oppressed and oppressive society. Thus Stone Telling presents both societies, with their faults and strengths, with a clarity of vision that neither side, separated as they are physically and ideologically, is completely capable of achieving. Consequently, Le Guin is able to present a convincing portrait of the war machine and its necessary structure and operation through the eyes of an innocent, but objective observer. This novel, therefore, adds a completely new dimension to Le Guin's study and presentation of war, as found in the rest of her science fiction.

Unlike most of Le Guin's writings in which she examines the issue of war, there is no direct conflict between the two major groups being presented. However, through their contact with one another, there is a dialectical opposition set up between them. Both societies contrast with each other almost totally. This opposition is set up in every area except one (both societies are based on the extended family), and is an effective technique of analysis. Unlike most of Le Guin's works structured along dialectical principles, however, there is no synthesis of the two societies. Not only is their opposition extreme, but the total intractibility of the Condor mentality will allow for no possibilities but its own realities which the Valley people, flexible as they are, find repugnant and completely unacceptable. These feelings are evident in the people's dislike and eventual dissolution of the Warrior and Lamb lodges in the Valley, lodges concerned with the activities and attitudes of war, established during the influence of the Condor on the spiritually weak and the young. These lodges are allowed to exist for some time until the larger body of the people, aware of the danger of such an aggressive and unbalanced mentality amongst them, ask the Warrior and Lamb lodge members to either leave the community or to dissolve their lodges. A few choose the former, going off to the City to join the Condors. Most choose the latter. Thus a negative synthesis is refused by the Valley people, while a positive synthesis remains impossible.

The opposition is set up, then, between an essentially pacifist society and a militarist society. Not only is one side pacifistic, it is also anarchic according to Le Guin's definition of anarchy, as it appears in her introduction to the story "The Day Before the Revolution" in which she established the Odonian anarchy explored to such depth in *The Dispossessed*:

> Odonianism is anarchism. Not the bomb-in-the-pocket stuff, which is terrorism, whatever name it tries to dignify itself with; not the social-Darwinist

economic 'libertarianism' of the far right; but anarchism, as prefigured in early Taoist thought, and expounded by Shelley and Kropotkin, Goldman and Goodman. Anarchism's principal target is the authoritarian State (capitalist or socialist); its principal moral-practical theme is cooperation (solidarity, mutual aid). It is the most idealistic, and to me the most interesting, of all political theories. (*The Wind's Twelve Quarters*)

The Valley people, around whom *Home* is centered, inhabit the most fully realized anarchic state presented in Le Guin's writings to date. An anarchical society is community-based with no central government. All decisions are made by the members of the community who wish to participate in each decision-making meeting which, in the valley towns, seems to occur quite rarely. Life in the society is based on a system of freedom and mutual responsibility, each person walking his own path, yet aware of and concerned for his fellows as he does so. Thus the community is based on equality, each person being an equally important part of the whole. Each one is free to choose his own career, relationships, and the like, advice being offered when requested or when others feel it is necessary, but no control being enforced by any one person or group of people upon any other individual or group. This basic harmony and unity is maintained within the society, although the types of individual conflict which may arise whenever human beings live together is, naturally, present.

Thus the anarchical states in Le Guin's works generally create a natural, unified, free, and intrinsically peaceful way of life. The Valley people have an interesting set of ethical values, which are probably not foreign to the reader in type, but may be in application. For example, giving is central to the idea of mutual aid. Consequently, a wealthy family in the Valley is one which gives constantly into the town storehouses and to individuals. Each family gives what it can, whether it be in food stuffs grown, wool, woven cloth, pottery, or more technical skills. Lodges are established in which certain professions such as medicine are centralized, and where all learning regarding that profession takes place. Thus wealth is counted not only in goods given, but also in skills or learning used for the community. When Stone Telling returns to her hometown of Sinshan, after spending seven years in the City of the Condors, she decides it is time her family were wealthy. With the help of her daughter and a friend from the City, she builds up her sheep flock, begins a herd of goats, plants crops in the family garden plot and helps with the orchard harvesting. She also begins to weave. Within three years, she is able to give freely, and counts herself rich, but for her poverty of education in the history, poetry, and other intellectual pursuits of her people. She then begins to catch up, as much as she can, on these intellectual matters, eventually becoming the singer of one of the great poems of her people. Thus she becomes wealthy in all things, as she is able to give in every major area.

In a system where wealth is counted by how much one gives, and where personal possessions, position, and status mean nothing in themselves, there is little opportunity for a power structure to arise. A power structure, however, is absolutely essential for a primarily military society, as no true army can be run without a strict hierarchy of power and command. Thus the mighty Condors, the warrior-people of *Home,* live in a highly structured, hierachical society in which power, position, and possessions mean everything.

Power is, initially, appealing and exciting. Stone Telling is first drawn to power when her father, a commander of the Condor forces, lets her give instructions to his men who are building a bridge. Her own unhappy and disrupted home, her love for her father and her minor attraction to power, cause her to ask to go with him to the Condor City of Man. Once there, however, she begins to truly understand the power structure, because there she is amongst the lowest in the hierarchy: she is a woman. In the Valley, women are considered equal to the men in all things, and the family line is continued through the mother into whose house a man marries and children are born; in the City, women are considered utterly inferior to the men. They are kept within walls, usually a very negative symbol in Le Guin's works, living in women's quarters which are always on the lowest level of the underground houses. They rarely, if ever, go outside. They are not allowed to be educated in any way, and they are considered to have no souls. Their chief function is to bear children for the strength of their husbands' houses and for the glory of their god. However, Condor women, daughters of the powerful elite of the City, are not considered the lowest forms of life. Male farmers or workers (*tyon*) seem to be lower still, while *hontik* are at the bottom. *Hontik* seems to translate as animal or dirt, and includes all non-Condor women, all foreigners of either sex, and animals themselves. Thus the hierarchy is an extreme one, which recognizes nothing outside its ranks, and defines clearly what lies within those ranks.

Stone Telling makes it quite clear that the power-based society of the Condors is engaged in constant struggle and war. Even the lower orders, such as women, desire power because of their constant humiliation and dehumanization, and will exercise it whenever possible, while the powerful within the structure seek to maintain their power. Thus the strife is based on fear, envy, hatred, and suspicion, and yet the power structure breeds a desire for power. The internal, covert, mental, and emotional conflict of this society fuels the war machine and maintains the structure of the militarist society. A society based on such conflict must go to war to keep the structure from decaying or destroying itself. Hence, towards the end of the novel, when the Condors lose their grip on the people they have subjected, they turn within and begin to destroy their own people: buzzards tearing out and devouring their own entrails, as Stone Telling describes it.

Violence is, therefore, central to this society. When the Condors go to war, the killing is excessive and gratuitous—frequently all the men and children are killed, and the women kept for the pleasure of the soldiers. Within the society itself, life is uncertain. Everyone has a place in the hierarchy, but only for the lowest is that place permanent and secure. It is a society whose members' control over each other is both implicitly and, occasionally, explicitly violent. Stone Telling describes this violence with horror:

> It sounds strange when I say that disgrace could put a person in danger of his life; disgrace and shame are quite bad enough by themselves, among us in the Valley; but there, where every relationship was a battle, they were deadly. Punishment was violent. I have said that I was told that a hontik could be blinded for writing or reading, a woman killed for having sex; I did not see such things happen, but every day I did see or hear about violent punishments, striking children, beating slaves, locking up disobedient hontik or tyon; and later on, as I shall tell, it grew worse. It was frightening to live in this kind of continuous war. The Dayao [Condors] seemed never to decide things together, never discussing and arguing and yielding and agreeing to do something before they did it. Everything was done because there was a law to do it or not to do it. And if something went wrong it seemed never to be the orders, but the people who obeyed them, that got blamed; and blame was usually physical punishment. I learned caution daily. I learned, whether I wanted to or not, how to be a warrior. Where life has been made into a battle, one has to fight.

When rebellion breaks out amongst the slaves and *tyon,* Condor reprisals are immediate and harsh. The rebellion escalates, however, and, as the Condors' frustration grows, so does their desire to control and kill. Their society is a machine that, set going, cannot stop. Those who start the machine become part of the machine, until, finally, they become the machine and no longer control it. Thus, at some point in the development of the militaristic state, the war machine takes over, and human beings simply become its tolls. However, the war machine here is breaking down, collapsing under its own weight of greed and power. The society begins to destroy itself from within because of the potency of its own disease, which is overwhelming it. Le Guin is saying here that it is a society that not only promotes the most negative facets of the human personality, but that it is in a state of continuous suspicion and unrest in itself and therefore it feeds upon itself in its disease. Thus the society based on destructive traits and activities eventually destroys not only those in its immediate vicinity, but itself as well. The society that lives primarily in peace with others and within itself, like that of the Valley people, however, maintains itself and its values, and it grows and expands, within, as well as without.

Stone Telling, a daughter of the Valley people for fifteen years, with her people's ideas of freedom, responsibility, and equality, finds herself powerless in a highly stratified society, the daughter of a Condor and dirt. It is through her eyes that the reader sees the Condor people, and through her account of their society that the reader comes to see something of his own society from a fresh viewpoint, through new eyes. For Le Guin makes it quite clear in places that the Condor society is an analogy of our own militaristic western society. Indeed, at times the account almost seems an allegory. But there are many external differences between the two societies, even if the fundamental structures are rather similar, and thus Le Guin avoids the essentially didactic nature of the allegory.

Le Guin exposes and criticizes the militaristic society in *Home* through her direct comparison between it and the pacifistic, anarchical Valley community. Early in the novel, when the child North Owl (Stone Telling's "first" name) first sees the Condor soldiers of her father, she says:

> … I was not sure that the men there were human beings. They all dressed alike and looked alike, like a herd of some kind of animal, and they did not speak any word I knew. Whenever they came near my father they would slap their forehead, or sometimes kneel down in front of him as if they were looking at his toes. I thought they were crazy men, very stu-

pid, and that my father was the only real person among them.

The language used in this passage is important. Stone Telling's first impression of these men is that they are like animals. They dress alike and do not act or look like human beings in the Valley do. It is her first experience with the conformity necessary in a military hierarchy. Furthermore, the reference to animals has far-reaching reverberations, for it is six years later that she learns that Condors consider all non-elite Condors or farmers, "animals". Her perception in this passage is the reverse of that of the Condors; but whereas for her this observation remains *only* an observation, the Condors push their perception of non-Condors to a practical and frightening extreme. In their perception of others as only animals, they are freed of any human responsibility towards them and need not treat them as anything other than the lowliest of animals.

The term "animal", applied to humans, takes on further implications when Le Guin makes it clear that for the Valley people many animals, including the herd animals like sheep and goats to which Stone Telling compares the soldiers, are considered "people", and a distinction is made between human and other people when necessary. A Valley family is frequently numbered according to all its people, so that when Stone Telling returns from the City, she says her family includes her mother and five sheep. Thus, in the holistic Valley perception of life, all creatures are an integral part of the greater whole, which is life, or being. Humans are a part of this whole, but only one part, and must share the world with all others, in harmony with them, killing out of necessity, never pleasure. This attitude is completely alien, of course, to the hierarchical and exclusivist Condors, who believe that all the world exists only for their use and profit, life in general having no intrinsic value in itself. The Condors feel that they have no relationship to the rest of the world except that of their domination over it: "The Condor people seem to have been unusually self-isolated; their form of communication with other peoples was through aggression, domination, exploitation, and enforced acculturation". Consequently, the word "hontik" suggests both "animal" and "dirt", meaning that the *hontik* are as non-human and unimportant as animals or dirt to the elite. Of course, even dirt and rocks are part of the whole as perceived by the Valley people, and both are treated as sacredly as any other part of the people's teeming, living, holy world. These fundamentally spiritual perceptions of the world indicate the deep differences between the two peoples, their perceptions of each other and their relationships with the world about them.

The other word that is significant in the passage quoted earlier is "crazy". The Valley people view the Condors as "crazy" or "sick" or men "with their heads on backwards". In Valley society, only children play at games of war and hunting. Full-grown men who are hunters are considered adolescent, refusing to don the maturity of adulthood. Most of the meat-hunting for the towns is done by male adolescents, who usually take on some respectable trade when they become men. Thus the Valley people dismiss the Condors as children playing games, albeit dangerous ones, as they do the men who, under the Condor influence, form the short-lived Warrior Lodge. However, it is principally in terms of sickness or insanity that the Valley people view the Condor: "The people of the Condor, those men who have come here from that people, are sick. Their heads are turned backwards. We have let people with the plague come into our house". Le Guin herself, in a direct address to the reader, points out the difference between the Valley view of the power structure and its mate, war, and our own (which, she argues, is primarily the same as the Condors'): "To this I think the people of the Valley might have an answer, along the lines of 'Very sick people tend to die of their sickness,' or 'Destruction destroys itself.' This answer however, involves a reversal of our point of view. What we call strength it calls sickness; what we call success it calls death".

It is clear that the Valley people would have joined with other free peoples in their area to fight against the Condor if they had had to, to stop the spreading of the disease which breeds only more war and death. However, the overall desire was to cure or "quarantine", rather than to fight. The natural and non-violent method is always preferred. However, if there had been no choice, they were prepared to fight. Fortunately, the Condors destroy themselves before such a battle ever engages. Le Guin has worked through the results of an armed confrontation between pacifistic peoples and trained military groups elsewhere in her writings, and obviously, she is still not completely comfortable with a such a confrontation and its seemingly inevitable result. Consequently, in *Home,* she concentrates on revealing the differences between the two groups through simple juxtaposition, thus avoiding the necessity of an armed conflict.

However, fighting in general and a society based on conflict are considered essentially weak by the Valley people: "The weak follow weakness, and I was a child; I followed my father; ... ", Stone Telling says early in the story. Those who seek or exercise power are considered fundamentally weak because such external and imposed power is unbalanced, and does not draw from the power inherent in the harmonious participation in being, as Stone Telling says: "So I first felt the great energy of the power that originates in unbalance, ... ".

A power that does not proceed from balance cannot lead to wholeness of being, either for the individual or the society. This power, therefore, derives from "outside the world", as Stone Telling says repeatedly throughout the novel. Thus their pursuit of power places the Condor people as a group outside the world of being, wholeness, and harmony. Those who participate largely in being have their own kind of power, an internal power that seeks not to dominate but to be given in guidance, truth, or whatever is needed: " ... but Obsidian of Ounmalin stood forward to speak. She was the only person in the nine towns at that time called by the name of her House, the best-known of all dancers of the Moon and Blood, unmarried, single-sexed, a person of great power".

Because a power structure cannot admit of true freedom, one of the major differences between the two groups is that of freedom. A society based on power must move away from freedom, to stratification, intolerance, and inflexibility. Thus Terter Abhao, Stone Telling's father, refuses to help in the family garden plot when he stays in the village, because he is not a *tyon,* he is a Condor commander. He is unable to let go his position and status, even in a place where they are meaningless. He is not flexible within, nor is he flexible or free outside of himself. He leaves the Valley when he gets his orders. He has no choice. He must do what he is told, so unlike the Valley people, who come and go as they please, doing what they desire whenever they desire it, although these desires are schooled to consider, to some extent, the community and individuals around them. In the City, Stone Telling finds that the women are penned indoors like animals and have no real freedom of movement, being unable to go outside except with permission from the men. But the men, the elite, the Condors themselves, are in truth no freer. And they, like the women, servants, and slaves, live in fear and distrust, never knowing from day to day where blame or disfavor might fall, ending power, position, or even life.

Just as there is no freedom in the Condor society, there is also no participation in the decision-making process. All decisions are dictated by the One Condor, headman of the people. His advisors may suggest certain paths to take, but the ultimate decision rests with him. Furthermore, each advisor is in or out of favor with the One Condor according to the One Condor's feelings or desires at any time. Of course, no woman, *tyon,* or *hontik* ever has any input into what is decided. Le Guin sets up this situation in opposition to the Valley system, where all people have a right to participate in a meeting, and full agreement is always sought before any decision is carried through.

The idea of wealth is another part of the differences between the two groups. As mentioned earlier, wealth in the Valley is equated with the amount given. A family may feel shame if it must take more than it can give, although there seems to be no stigma attached to taking. There is, however, praise given for giving. In the Condor society, on the other hand, possessions indicate wealth. As Stone Telling traveled to the City with her father, she was amazed that the soldiers always took but never gave. Condor taking extended in every direction—they "increas[ed] their wealth and power by taking land, life, and service from other people". In the City, Stone Telling found that the same pattern continued. The wealthy were those who *had,* not those who *gave.* And amongst the many possessions a rich man might have, women, slaves, and children would be included. Thus a wife or a male child, like a servant or slave, *belonged* to the man. Le Guin seems to be suggesting here that possession is part of the military mentality, for it is in desiring to possess that one begins to take that which belongs to others. From an uncontrolled desire for wealth first arises theft and then, if condoned on a large scale, war.

One of the first things to be jealously possessed in a possessive society is knowledge. None but the True Condor men are allowed to learn to read. Women, *tyon,* or *hontik* caught reading are blinded or lose a hand. Consequently, knowledge and its distribution become tools of power in the hierarchy and help ensure the maintenance of that structure, for knowledge is an important part of power. If all have knowledge, all share, to some extent, in power. Hence, education and knowledge are highly valued amongst the Valley people, and those without an adequate education in culture, spiritual knowledge, and a trade are considered poor, as Stone Telling herself is when she first returns from the City. Thus, in the Valley, all share knowledge and all share

power. In the City, only a few hold power, and therefore only a few are allowed knowledge.

It is interesting that writing is considered sacred in both cultures. However, the definition of the word "sacred" varies. In the Valley society, where most natural beings and certain other things are considered sacred, and where all participate in and celebrate that sanctity, writing is learned by all. In the City culture, where only power and things of power are considered sacred, only a powerful few have access to writing. Le Guin states explicitly in the chapter "Pandora Converses with the Archivist of the Library of the Madrone Lodge at Wakwaha-Na", that there is a relationship between this withholding of information in the Condor society and that of our own world:

> ARC: Who controls the storage and the retrieval? To what extent is the material there for anyone who wants and needs it, and to what extent is it "there" only for those who have the information that it is there, the education to obtain that information, and the power to get that education? How many people in your society are literate? How many are computer-competent? How many of them have the competence to use libraries and electronic information storage systems? How much real information is available to ordinary, nongovernment, non-military, nonspecialist, nonrich people? What does "classified" mean? What do shredders shred? What does money buy? In a State, even a democracy, where power is hierarchic, how can you prevent the storage of information from becoming yet another source of power to the powerful—another piston in the great machine? … How do you keep information yet keep it from being the property of the powerful?

> PAN: Through not having censorship. Having free public libraries. Teaching people to read. And to use computers, to plug into the sources. Press, radio, television not fundamentally dependent on government or advertisers. I don't know. It keeps getting harder.

Through her juxtaposition of the two societies in *Always Coming Home,* Le Guin presents a powerful and timely anti-war statement. By her technique of examining the internal workings of the war machine through someone intelligent and thoughtful, yet largely innocent of any knowledge of power structures or war, Le Guin reveals the whole idea of the stratified power structure in a new way. For as the reader watches Stone Telling grow up, he becomes used to the Valley perception, strange though it may initially seem. Thus it may be something of a shock when the Condor are introduced and the reader recognizes many of the Condor views as ones with which he is culturally more conversant. So Le Guin acquaints us with the Valley people first, then presents the Condors through the eyes of the Valley people, which makes the Condors initially as alien to the reader as they are to Valley dwellers. Thus Le Guin can effectively present the evils of the militaristic and possessive society while the reader is still sharing Stone Telling's cultural disorientation. The emotional and intellectual effect of such a method is powerful and jolting, causing the very distance Le Guin desires the reader to have from a society all too like his own, so that he can dispassionately and objectively examine the principles and values upon which his own ideas of existence and social structures are based.

Le Guin occasionally sets up a specific correlation between the Condor society and our own, asking the reader to think about the direction of his own society, without setting up a constant one-to-one correlation that might antagonize the reader. And as always in her writings, Le Guin shows the reader what is wrong or unhealthy in his world only to suggest a way out—an alternative society, based on peace and freedom, and yet firmly grounded on possibility, requiring no fundamental changing of the human personality, only a shifting of perspective. *Always Coming Home* is a novel about challenges. It is a novel about possibilities. In a dark time, it is a novel about hope.

Source: J. R. Wytenbroek, "*Always Coming Home:* Pacifism and Anarchy in Le Guin's Latest Utopia," in *Extrapolation,* Winter, 1987, pp. 330-39.

Samuel R. Delany

Delany is an award-winning science-fiction writer and editor. In the following review, he praises Always Coming Home *as Le Guin's "most satisfying text among a set of texts that have provided much imaginative pleasure in her 23 years as an author."*

With high invention and deep intelligence, *Always Coming Home* presents, in alternating narratives, poems and expositions, Ursula K. Le Guin's most consistently lyric and luminous book in a career adorned with some of the most precise and passionate prose in the service of a major imaginative vision.

Mrs. Le Guin has created an entire ethnography of the far future in her book. It's called a novel. But even to glance at it is to suspect it's more than, or other than, that: the oversize trade paperback is boxed with a tape cassette of delicate songs, poems and haunting dance pieces, purportedly recorded on site. Liner notes are included. Are they by the composer, Todd Barton, or by Ursula Le Guin? It's not

indicated. I would like to know, since each entry, with its song or poem, is a small story in itself. Margaret Chodos's fine line drawings portray animals, birds, sacred implements and symbols, tools, mountains and houses (but no people); and we have charts, maps, alphabets and a glossary. The book contains a short novel, "Stone Telling," spaced out in three parts, narrated by a woman called Stone Telling; and "Chapter Two" from another novel, "Dangerous People", by Wordriver. Along with Marsh, Cowardly Dog and Mote, Wordriver is among the great novelists of the Kesh, the people of the Valley, the subjects of Mrs. Le Guin's pastoral vision. In addition there are poems, children's stories, adult folk tales, verse dramas, recipes, essays and a host of Kesh documents. Though the word "Indian" does not appear from one end of the book to the other, the reader is likely to feel after only a few pages that much Native American culture has become a part of this dark, wise, stocky people's way of life. Mrs. Le Guin has given us the imaginary companion volume of "Readings" that might accompany a formal anthropological study.

When did the Kesh live? They haven't, yet.

The Kesh have access to a daunting computer system. But they live 500 years or more in our future, on the northwestern coast of what's left of a United States gone low-tech and depopulated by toxic wastes and radioactive contamination. The Kesh are an attractive people. One noun serves them for both gift and wealth. To be rich and to give are, for them, one verb. They do not share the West's present passion for Origins and outcomes: their pivotal cultural concept is the hinge, the connecting principle that allows things both to hold together and to move in relation to each other. Their year is marked off by elaborate seasonal dances. Their lives and work are organized in a complicated system of Houses, Lodges, Arts, and Societies.

A minor tribal war occurs between some 30-odd young men of Sinshan, the Kesh village, and a few of the neighboring Pig People. There is a much larger and longer one between the Condor Men and the Valley people that occupies the periphery of "Stone Telling." In the end both wars are shown to share the same small-scale tribal form, for all their real deaths, real suffering, and real shame. But they are very different from the technological megawars of our century.

The emotional high point, for me, was the transcription of a Kesh play, "Chandi," a retelling of the biblical tale of Job. A society in which such a tale is important cannot be a simple utopian construct: a Job, (or a Chandi)—that most anti-utopian of myths—reminds us too strongly that as long as culture is fitted against nature, along whatever complex curve, the best of us may slip into the crack to be crushed by unhappy chance. The Chandi play is followed by a luminous meditation on a scrub-oak ridge by Mrs. Le Guin's ironic alter ego, Pandora—giver of all gifts, mother of all afflictions, guardian of hope—who, throughout the book, "worries about what she is doing," to the reader's delight and enlightenment.

Mrs. Le Guin has put some expository pieces in a 100-plus-page section called "The Back of the Book." These are among the most interesting, the most beautiful. I suggest going straight to them and reading "What They Wore," "What They Ate," and "The World Dance" before beginning the book proper. They will enhance Stone Telling's tale of her childhood considerably. (By the same token, don't read "The Train"—or you will spoil a pleasant narrative surprise earlier on.)

Grouped between the prose pieces, the 70-odd poems slow up a straight-through reading. Not particularly difficult or particularly bad. But a contemporary reader, for whom poetry is still a high art, and for whom the poet is at once on the margins of society while oriented toward the center of culture, simply finds it hard going through the Kesh's overwhelming poetic saturation. And while we understand the poems as simple surface utterances, at a deeper level, where we expect poems to be meaningful, they don't make much sense. I only wish Mrs. Le Guin had written more prose about the practice of poetry in the Valley with, say, the same energy and vividness she employed to write about the cosmogenic Dance of the World or the Saturnalian Dance of the Moon—two of the book's most spectacular set pieces.

Mrs. Le Guin is among the half-dozen most respected American writers who regularly set their narrative in the future to force a dialogue with the here and now, a dialogue generally called science fiction. She is also a much loved writer. And *Always Coming Home* is a slow, rich read, full of what one loves most in her work: a liberal utopian vision, rendered far more complex than the term "utopian" usually allows for by a sense of human suffering. This is her most satisfying text among a set of texts that have provided much imaginative pleasure in her 23 years as an author.

Source: Samuel R. Delany, "The Kesh in Song and Story," in *The New York Times Book Review,* September 29, 1985, pp. 31, 56.

Sources

Dick Allen, "Fire Burning in the Rain," *The Hudson Review,* Spring, 1986, pp. 135-40.

Samuel Delany, review in *The New York Times Book Review,* September, 1985, p. 31.

Peter Fitting, "The Turn from Utopia in Recent Feminist Fiction," in *Feminism, Utopia, and Narrative,* edited by Libby Falk Jones and Sarah Webster Goodwin, The University of Tennessee Press, 1990, pp. 141-58.

Carol Franko, "Self-Conscious Narration as the Complex Representation of Hope in Le Guin's *Always Coming Home,*" *Mythlore,* Spring, 1989, pp. 57-60.

Lillian M. Heldreth, "To Defend or to Correct: Patterns of Culture in *Always Coming Home,*" *Mythlore,* Autumn, 1989, pp. 58-63, 66.

Lee Cullen Khanna, "Women's Utopias: New Worlds, New Texts," in *Feminism, Utopia, and Narrative,* edited by Libby Falk Jones and Sarah Webster Goodwin, The University of Tennessee Press, 1990, pp. 130-40.

Ursula K. Le Guin, *The Language of the Night: Essays on Fantasy and Science Fiction,* edited by Susan Wood, G. P. Putnam's Sons, 1979, 239 pp.

Peter Prescott, review in *Newsweek,* November, 1985, p. 101.

Bernard Selinger, "*Always Coming Home:* The Art of Living," in his *Le Guin and Identity in Contemporary Fiction,* University of Michigan Press, 1988, pp. 127-47.

J. R. Wytenbroek, "*Always Coming Home:* Pacifism and Anarchy in Le Guin's Latest Utopia," *Extrapolation,* Vol. 28, No. 4, Winter, 1987, pp. 330-39.

For Further Study

James Bittner, *Approaches to the Fiction of Ursula K. Le Guin,* University of Michigan Research Press, 1984, 149 pp.
　　A holistic approach to the fiction of Le Guin that does not separate her science fiction from her fantasy. Explores all of her major fiction to date in broad terms of visions, praise, myth, and magic.

Robert Crossley, "Pure and Applied Fantasy, or From Faerie to Utopia," in *The Aesthetics of Fantasy Literature and Art,* edited by Roger Schlobin, University of Notre Dame Press, 1982, pp. 176-91.
　　Compares how fantasy has changed from absolute imagination like "Aladin's Magic Lamp" to more reality based utopias in the fiction of William Morris, Frank Balm, Charlotte Perkins Gilman, and Ursula Le Guin. Crossley suggests this is a development that shows a maturity in American literature.

Charles Crow, "Homecoming in the California Visionary Romance," *Western American Literature,* May, 1989, pp. 1-19.
　　Crow explores how descriptions of California differ in the works of John Griffith London, William Callenbach, and Ursula Le Guin. Suggests that the different utopias all see California as the ideal location.

Patricia Dooley, review in *Library Journal,* September, 1985, p. 93.

Unfavorable review of *Always Coming Home.* Says the novel is typical of Le Guin's style and manner, but too long and boring for most readers.

M. J. Hardman, "Linguistics and Science Fiction: A Language and Gender Short Bibliography," *Women and Language,* Spring, 1999, pp. 47-8.

A discussion of a selection of the novels used as texts in a course on language and science fiction taught by Hardman at the University of Florida. Novels included works by Nalo Hopkinson, Ursula Le Guin, and Elizabeth Moon. The relevance of each novel to the subject matter is included with its bibliographical citation.

Mary Catherine Harper, "Spiraling Around the Hinge: Working Solutions in *Always Coming Home,*" in *Old West-New West: Centennial Essays,* edited by Barbara Howard Meldrum, University of Idaho Press, 1993, pp. 241-57.

Discusses and explores Le Guin's ideas of dualism in terms of time, space, and characterization.

W. R. Irwin, "From Fancy to Fantasy: Coleridge and Beyond," in *The Aesthetics of Fantasy Literature and Art,* edited by Roger Schlobin, University of Notre Dame Press, 1982, pp. 36-55.

Discusses the change in imaginary writing from Coleridge to modern writers. Suggests that Coleridge changed the meaning of "imagination" and so opened the doors to fantasy literature.

Naomi Jacobs, "Beyond Stasis and Symmetry: Lessing, Le Guin, and the Remodeling of Utopia," *Extrapolation,* Spring, 1988, pp. 34-45.

Compares the narrative techniques and utopian ideologies in novels by Doris Lessing and Ursula Le Guin.

Patricia Linton, "The 'Person' in Postmodern Fiction: Gibson, Le Guin, and Vizenor," *Studies in American Indian Literatures,* Fall, 1993, pp. 3-11.

Explores how postmodern authors deal with issues of individuality, self-representation, and relationships with machinery and technology. Linton sees humanity losing a war against technology.

Richard Mathews, "Completing the Circle: Language, Power, and Vision," in *Fantasy: The Liberation of Imagination,* Simon & Schuster, 1997, pp. 135-151.

Examines Le Guin's trilogy (now four novels) *The Earthsea Series* in terms of language and power. Suggests that Le Guin sees the journey of the mind as important as the physical journey of reaching physical maturity.

Francis Molson, "Ethical Fantasy for Children," in *The Aesthetics of Fantasy Literature and Art,* edited by Roger Schlobin, University of Notre Dame Press, 1982, pp. 82-104.

Discusses the types of fantasy that contemporary culture finds acceptable for children. Suggests that children's fantasy literature must have clearly defined good and bad characters and situations, that good

must win, and that children must respect cultural limits put on them.

John Moore, "An Archaeology of the Future: Ursula Le Guin and Anarcho-Primitivism," *Foundation,* Spring, 1995, pp. 32-9.

Assesses Le Guin's theories of anarchy and utopia. Shows how her ideas compare to the theories of primitivism.

Patrick Murphy, "Voicing Another Nature," in *A Dialogue of Voices: Feminist Literary Theory and Bakhtin,* edited by Karen Hohne, University of Minnesota Press, 1994, pp. 59-82.

Explores how various twentieth-century women writers have used nature as a literary device. Murphy then compares these ideas to the literary theories of Mikhail M. Bakhtin.

Joseph Olander and Martin Greenberg, eds., *Ursula K. Le Guin,* Taplinger Publishing, 1979, 239 pp.

A collection of essays on Le Guin's early fiction. Various methodologies, literary theories, and critical approaches are used.

Richard Patteson, "Le Guin's Earthsea Trilogy: The Psychology of Fantasy," in *The Scope of the Fantastic—Culture, Biography, Themes, Children's Literature,* edited by Robert Collins and Howard Pearce, Greenwood Press, 1985, pp. 239-48.

Explores the psychological aspects of Le Guin's Earthsea Trilogy. Suggests that describing the interior working of the mind is Le Guin's strongest gift as a writer.

Oliver Scheiding, "An Archeology of the Future: Postmodern Strategies of Boundary Transitions in Ursula K. Le Guin's *Always Coming Home,*" *American Studies,* Vol. 41, No. 4, 1996, pp. 637-56.

Discusses *Always Coming Home* as a postmodern text and examines how Le Guin uses aspects of feminism, environmentalism, and technological progress to her own ends.

Jane Slaughter, "Ursula K. Le Guin," *The Progressive,* March, 1998, pp. 36-9.

Print publication of Slaughter's interview with Le Guin. Discusses her use of feminism, nature, and utopias in her work and where she plans to go in her future fiction.

Raymond Thompson, "Modern Fantasy and Medieval Romance: A Comparative Study," in *The Aesthetics of Fantasy Literature and Art,* edited by Roger Schlobin, University of Notre Dame Press, 1982, pp. 211-25.

Explores the relationship between romantic fiction of the Middle Ages to modern fantasy literature.

Sarah Jo Webb, "Culture as Spiritual Metaphor in Le Guin's *Always Coming Home,*" in *Functions of the Fantastic: Selected Essays from the Thirteenth International Conference on the Fantastic in the Arts,* edited by Joe Sanders, Greenwood, 1995, pp. 155-60.

Analyzes how Le Guin uses elements of the fantastic as metaphor.

Billy Budd, Sailor: An Inside Narrative

Herman Melville

1924

When Herman Melville began working on what was to be his final novel, *Billy Budd, Sailor: An Inside Narrative,* his years of renown as a celebrated American author were well behind him. He had worked in the New York Customhouse for nearly two decades, until 1885, when he retired from his job and returned to his writing. Sometime between 1885 and 1891, Melville wrote a poem, "Billy in the Darbies," about a young sailor who had been executed for his involvement in a mutinous plot. In 1888, Melville read an article called "The Mutiny on the Somers," which related the story of three sailors who in 1842 had been convicted of mutiny on board the U.S. brig *Somers.* Melville's older cousin had been one of the officers involved in the sailors' conviction, and his family knew details of the case that the public did not know. A split between what Melville biographer Leon Howard calls "the inside story and the historical record"—what really happened and what was reported—inspired Melville to expand his poem about Billy into a longer prose work with the subtitle "An Inside Narrative." However, Melville died in September 1891, six months after apparently finishing work on the book, and *Billy Budd* was left unpublished until 1924, when it was discovered among Melville's papers.

Raymond Weaver's 1921 publication of his Melville biography, *Herman Melville: Mariner and Mystic,* sparked a revival of interest in the works of the largely forgotten writer. In 1924, Weaver brought out *The Collected Works* of Melville, which includes the first edition of *Billy Budd,* and

critics greeted the short novel enthusiastically, admiring its perceptiveness and its moral and symbolic complexity. Treating such weighty themes as duty and conscience, good and evil, justice, and guilt and innocence, Melville's final novel is considered one of his masterpieces.

Author Biography

Herman Melville's reputation seesawed from popularity to obscurity and back again over much of his lifetime and beyond, but now his position is secure as one of America's greatest authors. Best known now for his masterpiece novel *Moby-Dick (1851)*, Melville first became popular as a writer in the 1840s for his novels of adventure in the South Seas: *Typee* (1846) and *Omoo* (1847). Born in New York City in 1819, Melville had been attracted to the sea and ships at a young age, and his first two novels, fictional romances inspired by his own seagoing adventures, were warmly received by readers.

After his early success with *Typee* and *Omoo,* Melville disappointed his audience with his third novel, *Mardi* (1849), which took a philosophical and metaphysical turn away from his previous narratives. More conventional sea novels *Redburn* (1849) and *White-Jacket* (1850)—his attempts to win his audience back—briefly appeased his readers, but then with the publication of *Moby-Dick* in 1851, followed by *Pierre* in 1852, Melville had lost his audience altogether. *Moby-Dick,* a novel ostensibly about whaling but actually about the human condition, had found a small but appreciative critical audience, but *Pierre,* a dark, somewhat autobiographical novel, was a critical as well as popular failure. The public who had loved his South Seas novels thought that Melville had gone mad.

After the dismal failure of *Pierre,* Melville decided to produce shorter prose pieces for publication in magazines. For a few years he honed his skill at writing these short works, producing such tales as "Benito Cereno" and "The Encantadas", before coming out with another full-length novel. *The Confidence-Man,* published in 1857, was the last prose piece that Melville would publish in his lifetime. This final novel, a satire which deals with confidence men on board a riverboat on April Fool's Day, was a failure.

Disappointed, Melville turned to writing poetry and eventually obtained a position as an inspector in the New York Customhouse, which he held for nearly 20 years. After his retirement, Melville continued to write poems, and sometime

Herman Melville

after 1888 he began work on a short novel—*Billy Budd, Sailor: An Inside Narrative*—which had grown out of his poem, "Billy in the Darbies". Melville's expansion upon the poem about the young sailor who had been implicated in a mutiny conspiracy was probably spurred by his having read an article about an 1842 mutiny plot on the U.S. brig *Somers*. Melville stopped work on *Billy Budd* in April, 1891, but then he died five months later, leaving the work unfinished and unpublished.

The manuscript of *Billy Budd* was not published until 1924, when it was discovered among Melville's papers. Modern, 1920s America was ready for Melville in a way that his own late nineteenth century had not been. With the 1921 publication of Raymond Weaver's biography *Herman Melville: Mariner and Mystic* and then the 1924 publication of *The Collected Works* of Melville, which contained the first published edition of *Billy Budd,* Melville's critical reputation soared, and the author who was virtually unknown at his death was essentially rediscovered and venerated.

Plot Summary

In *Billy Budd,* a navy sailor is accused of fomenting (or plotting) mutiny by an officer during wartime, at which point the sailor strikes the officer dead. To settle the issue quickly, the sailor is summarily tried and convicted by the captain for murder, and is hung at sunrise the following day. The novel presents different versions of the events themselves.

Arranged in thirty chapters, it is not until chapter 29 that the narrator quotes the official naval report on the murder. In no time at all, the events are summarized: "On the tenth of the last month a deplorable occurrence took place on board H.M.S. *Bellipotent.* John Claggart, the ship's master-at-arms, discovering that some sort of plot was incipient among an inferior section of ship's company, and that the ringleader was one William Budd; he, Claggart, in the act arraigning the man before the captain, was vindictively stabbed to the heart by the suddenly drawn sheath knife of Budd." In the end, this stands as one version of the novel's plot, but the other twenty-nine chapters tell a different story.

Chapters 1-8

In the first eight chapters, the narrator attempts to sketch the histories of these men—first Billy Budd, then Captain Vere, then John Claggart. Billy is "impressed" (forced) into the British navy, then (1797) at war with the French. A lieutenant boards the merchant ship, the *Rights-of-Man,* that Billy has worked on for some time, and selects only him to bolster the crew of the *Bellipotent,* without any consideration of Billy's or the merchant captain's desires. Apparently Billy was selected because he has the charismatic qualities of what the narrator calls the "Handsome Sailor," a leader both physically and morally. Billy appears to be exceedingly simple, an "upright barbarian," but factual knowledge of him is limited to his status as an orphan. Of his family history only speculation is possible. Captain Vere, on the other hand, traces his ancestors well back into the seventeenth century; he is well read, respected for his intelligence and open heart; he is a dedicated seaman and an efficient disciplinarian. About as much of Claggart's life before service on the *Bellipotent* is known "as an astronomer knows about a comet's travels prior to its first observable appearance in the sky."

Chapters 9-19

Chapters 9 through 17 develop the antagonism between Claggart and Budd—though "antagonism" must be used in a qualified manner since Budd holds no grudge against Claggart, and simply cannot understand why Claggart would dislike him. The reasons for this antagonism are unknown. The narrator suggests that perhaps the older man envied Billy's personal beauty, or saw in Billy the innocence he had lost. Because Claggart could "really form no conception of an unreciprocated malice," he contrives traps for Billy. Three incidents occur that test Billy's goodwill. Claggart has an underling disturb Billy's possessions so that he would fail inspection. Then Billy accidentally spills his soup in front of Claggart, who reads the mess as intentional. Finally, another stooge of Claggart's fails to tempt Billy into mutinous plots, even though Billy could justly resent having been impressed on board.

Since none of these incidents produce Billy's downfall, Claggart escalates his attack by taking advantage of a failed chase of a French warship, in chapter 18, to corner the captain and claim (falsely) that Billy had just revealed mutinous intentions. Vere is skeptical but arranges to question the two men privately in his cabin. In chapter 19, Claggart calmly accuses Billy, and instead of answering Claggart and clearing himself in front of the captain, Billy stutters and strikes Claggart directly on the forehead, killing him instantly.

Chapters 20-27

In chapters 20 and 21 Billy is tried before the captain and three officers. He says to the court, could "I have used my tongue I would not have struck [Claggart]." All four judges appear to believe in Billy's good intentions, but Vere ultimately convinces them all that their duty is to hang Billy. They must send a clear message to the sailors that even the taint of "mutiny" on your name will result in severe punishment. "For that law [the Mutiny Act] and the rigor of it," Vere says, "we are not responsible."

Chapters 22 to 27 describe the last few hours of Billy's short life. Vere tells Billy of his sentence, in such a way that added to the feeling he already had for the good captain, and Billy seems to respect Vere all the more. Billy has one more night and spends the time peacefully and alone. At sunrise, the "Handsome Sailor" is hung. There is some grumbling of discontent among the sailors at this seemingly unwarranted event, but naval discipline represses any actual signs of protest. The body is wrapped in what was once his hammock, and, like Claggart's body a few hours earlier, tossed into the ocean.

B i l l y   B u d d

After accidentally murdering the man who accused him of plotting a mutiny, Billy is sentenced to death by hanging in this 1962 film adaptation starring Terence Stamp as the eponymous hero.

Chapters 28-30

In the final three chapters, the narrator follows the fate of Captain Vere, includes the naval report on the incident, tells how the spar from which Billy was hung was "converted into a monument," and includes a poem by one of the sailors who knew Billy. Vere dies soon after in a fight with a French ship, and the men on board the *Bellipotent* who were present when Billy died all take a shard of the beam from which Billy was hung, since to "them a chip of it was as a piece of the Cross." With these shards, the men remember Billy. The poem "Billy in the Darbies," which speculates on how Billy might have spoken in his last hours, closes the novel: "I am sleepy, and the oozy weeds about me twist."

Characters

The Afterguardsman

The afterguardsman first appears as a mysterious whispering figure that awakens Billy as he sleeps on deck one warm night. He tries to draw Billy into a shady plot, which angers Billy. Billy sends the man away, raising a commotion, and when the others on board ask what is going on, Billy deliberates whether he should reveal what the afterguardsman has said to him. He decides not to be "a telltale" and keeps the incident to himself, although he is deeply puzzled by it. It is "the first time in his life that he had ever been personally approached in underhand intriguing fashion." When, during the next few days, the afterguardsman nods knowingly at Billy or speaks to him, Billy is "more at a loss than before." Billy's friend the Dansker connects the afterguardsman's act to Claggart's being "down on" Billy.

Beauty

See Billy Budd

"Board-Her-in-the-Smoke"

See The Dansker

Baby Budd

See Billy Budd

Billy Budd

In spite of the innocence and simplicity that characterize Billy Budd, he is a complex character in terms of what he represents. His name suggests an almost childlike youthfulness: Although he is an

V o l u m e   9

2 9

Media
Adaptations

- *Billy Budd* was adapted as a film in 1962 by Peter Ustinov, who directed, produced, and starred as Captain Vere in this version of Melville's novel. Terence Stamp, as Billy, won an Academy Award nomination for Best Supporting Actor. Other actors who starred in the film include Robert Ryan and David McCallum. The film is in black and white and is available on VHS.

- Benjamin Britten adapted *Billy Budd* as a four-act opera in 1951, with libretto by E. M. Forster and Eric Crozier. A production of the opera is available on video, released in 1988, starring Thomas Allen as Billy, and with the English National Opera Orchestra and Chorus conducted by David Atherton and directed by Tim Albery.

- *Billy Budd* is available on two audiocassettes, read by Simon Jones. The cassettes were released by Durkin Hayes Audio in 1987.

- Louis O. Coxe and Robert Chapman published *Billy Budd, A Play in Three Acts* in 1951 by Princeton University Press.

- A documentary on the historical incident that inspired *Billy Budd, The Curse of the Somers: Billy Budd's Ghost Ship* (1996) is an award-winning film narrated by Peter Coyote. The film looks at the controversial Somers Mutiny Affair, which Melville mentions in *Billy Budd*. This case resulted in the hanging of midshipman Philip Spencer and the court-martial of Captain Alexander Slidell Mackenzie. The film also includes underwater footage of an exploration of the Somers wreck. Information on the Somers Documentary Film Project can be found on the Web site: http://www.1somers.com/somers/film.htm.

---

adult, his name, William, is shortened into the child's nickname, Billy, and the Dansker refers to him as "Baby Budd" because he seems so young. His last name, Budd, suggests the immaturity of a flower that has not yet bloomed. And yet it is Billy's very immaturity that brings about his end.

Billy's innocence is the dominant aspect of his character. He is unable to distinguish between his friends and his enemies, or even to comprehend that he might have an enemy. Happy-go-lucky and popular with his fellow sailors, the handsome Billy is scrupulous about following orders and performing his duties correctly. Knowing nothing of his own heritage except that he was a foundling, Billy recalls "young Adam before the Fall": unburdened by a past, uncomplicated by civilization, meeting the world on his own terms, innocent of evil.

And yet this seemingly perfect human being is indeed flawed: Billy stutters when he becomes agitated. The narrator says that Billy's stutter is Satan's reminder that "I too have a hand here"; no one can escape his power. His innocence ironically comes to function as another flaw because he lacks "that intuitive knowledge of the bad which in natures not good or incompletely so foreruns experience." In Billy's encounter with the afterguardsman and his experience with Claggart—his first, puzzling brushes with corruption—"his innocence [is] his blinder," and he is unable to protect himself.

As he faces his execution, Billy exemplifies the Christlike nature which critics often note when discussing him. When Billy learns of Claggart's accusation, his face holds "an expression which was a crucifixion to behold." In spite of Captain Vere's decision to go through with Billy's execution, Billy's last words, illustrating his generous and forgiving nature, are "God bless Captain Vere!" At the moment of execution, the fleecy clouds in the eastern sky are "shot through with a soft glory as of the fleece of the Lamb of God seen in mystical vision." Then, recalling Christ's ascension into heaven following his resurrection, "Billy ascended; and, ascending, took the full rose of the dawn." The spar from which Billy is hanged takes on an almost religious significance for the sailors: "To them, a chip of it was as a piece of the Cross."

William Budd
See Billy Budd

The Chaplain
Meeting Billy as Billy prepares to die, the *Bellipotent*'s chaplain is amazed by Billy's peacefulness and realizes that he has little to give Billy. He finds Billy's ideas of death to be like those of a child; Billy is "wholly without irrational fear of [death]." And as the chaplain feels that "innocence [is] even a better thing than religion wherewith to go to Judgment," he does not impose himself on

Billy. The narrator cautions the reader not to expect the chaplain to speak out on Billy's behalf, having seen his essential innocence. Such an attempt to save Billy's life would be, the narrator points out, "an audacious transgression of the bounds of his function, one as exactly prescribed to him by military law as that of a boatswain or any other naval officer." The chaplain knows he must not step outside his realm of duties.

John Claggart

John Claggart, the master-at-arms on the *Bellipotent,* is a difficult character to grasp, even for the narrator: "His portrait I essay, but shall never hit it." Claggart's essential nature eludes not only the narrator and Billy Budd but also the perceptive Captain Vere; in fact, the only character who seems to understand Claggart and his motives is the wise yet taciturn Dansker. Claggart in turn is "perhaps the only man in the ship intellectually capable of adequately appreciating the moral phenomenon presented in Billy Budd," and ironically, Billy's goodness is what drives Claggart to destroy him.

Claggart is portrayed as being different from the other men on the *Bellipotent.* His physical description emphasizes his pallor, unusual among sailors and hinting of "something defective or abnormal." His background is mysterious, and he seems somehow foreign: "It might be that he was an Englishman; and yet there lurked a bit of accent in his speech suggesting that possibly he was not such by birth." He is not popular among the ship's crew, but "no man holding his office in a man-of-war can ever hope to be popular with the crew."

Having set Claggart up as an outsider on board the *Bellipotent,* the narrator goes on to establish Claggart's evil nature, which the narrator says is innate in him. Essentially envious of Billy's "significant personal beauty," Claggart is disdainful of Billy's simple innocence, and goaded by it: "to be nothing more than innocent!" Claggart's deep envy of Billy grows out of his sense that Claggart possesses "no power to annul the elemental evil in him[self], though readily enough he could hide it; apprehending the good but powerless to be it." The narrator refers to Claggart's "monomania," or obsession, which is "covered over by his self-contained and rational demeanor"; this controlled surface is what Billy sees and perceives to be friendliness towards him. Billy is incapable of comprehending how and why Claggart is against him, and when Claggart moves in for the kill, accusing Billy of mutiny, Billy is unable to defend himself, helpless in the face of Claggart's depravity.

The Dansker

Billy's confidant, the Dansker, is a man of few words, a navy veteran with a "wizened face" to whom Billy goes "for wise counsel." The Dansker, who dubs Billy "Baby Budd," tells Billy that Claggart is "down on" him. Billy cannot understand what the Dansker means; his innocence contrasts with his old friend's "pithy guarded cynicism." In spite of his wisdom, the Dansker chooses neither to interfere in Billy's business nor to give advice to the young sailor. The narrator attributes the Dansker's refusal to get involved to his experience with the world.

The Drumhead Court

Comprised of the *Bellipotent*'s first lieutenant, captain of marines, and sailing master, the reluctant drumhead court has no real choice but to convict Billy Budd and sentence him to death. In spite of their sympathy for Billy and their disbelief that he could be capable of mutinous plotting, as Claggart had insisted, the members of the court are obligated to support the King's law. Captain Vere senses the court's hesitancy to convict Billy and reminds them of their military obligation and corresponding lack of free will, and they decide Billy's fate accordingly.

The Foretopman
See Billy Budd

Captain Graveling

Commander of the merchant ship *Rights-of-Man,* Captain Graveling tells Lieutenant Ratcliffe about Billy's calming influence on the men on board his ship and laments, "you are going to take away the jewel of 'em, you are going to take away my peacemaker!" The captain is "a respectable man" who takes "to heart those serious responsibilities not so heavily borne by some shipmasters." He is disheartened to think of how his ship had been "a rat-pit of quarrels" before Billy came aboard, as he expects it to return to that state after Billy leaves.

The Handsome Sailor
See Billy Budd

Jemmy Legs
See John Claggart

The Master-at-Arms
See John Claggart

The Old Merlin

See The Dansker

The Purser

The purser confronts the surgeon several days after Billy's execution, asking the doctor why Billy had been so still during his hanging. The surgeon admits that "the absence of spasmodic movement" in Billy during the hanging "was phenomenal" in the sense that such spasms are normal and the absence of them in Billy is inexplicable. The purser wants the surgeon to concede that Billy was able, through his own will power, to remain still at the moment of hanging, but the surgeon refuses to agree. The conversation between the purser and the surgeon suggests that there was something super-human about Billy.

Lieutenant Ratcliffe

Ratcliffe is the "burly and bluff" lieutenant of the H.M.S. *Bellipotent,* the British warship whose crew Billy is compelled to join. Lieutenant Ratcliffe, looking for men to join his ship's crew, quickly chooses Billy when he sees him aboard the *Rights-of-Man* and then goes to help himself to Captain Graveling's spirit locker without an invitation from the captain. Ratcliffe is unsympathetic to Captain Graveling's dejection over losing Billy.

The Red Whiskers

When Billy is a newcomer on the *Rights-of-Man,* the fellow known as the Red Whiskers picks a fight with Billy, perhaps out of envy over Billy's popularity, and Billy gives "the burly fool a terrible drubbing." The incident serves as foreshadowing to Billy's later striking of Claggart.

The Surgeon

The surgeon is the *Bellipotent*'s doctor, "a self-poised character of that grave sense and experience that hardly anything could take him aback," and yet, when he examines Claggart and finds him dead, the surgeon is shocked. When Captain Vere immediately declares that Billy Budd must hang for killing Claggart, the surgeon thinks Vere is not in his right mind, and yet, he knows that to resist his captain "would be mutiny." So, out of duty, the surgeon carries out Captain Vere's orders.

Captain Vere

Noble, intellectual Captain Vere commands the *Bellipotent* and is an "austere devotee of military duty." He is, ultimately, responsible for Billy Budd's execution, as he instructs the drumhead court trying Billy's case in their responsibility to "adhere to ... and administer" the law, whether they agree with it or not. Respected by his crew, although seen by some as a martinet, Captain Vere is "an officer mindful of the welfare of his men, but never tolerating an infraction of discipline"; he believes that duty to the King comes before all else.

Captain Vere is an aristocrat, both by birth and in temperament, and his finely tuned "moral quality" enables him to be, "in earnest encounter with a fellow man, a veritable touchstone of that man's essential nature." The fact that Vere is puzzled by John Claggart and doubts his charges against Billy suggests that the events that follow Claggart's accusation will not be ordinary. Upon perceiving that Claggart is dead at Billy's hand, Captain Vere is transformed: "The father in him, manifested toward Billy thus far in the scene, was replaced by the military disciplinarian." The military relation overrides the emotional relation between Billy and Vere. When Vere speaks to the members of the drumhead court about the decision they must make regarding Billy's punishment, he tells them they are not "natural free agents" but officers of the King. Setting up the tension between emotion and intellect, Vere tells the officers, "let not warm hearts betray heads that should be cool"; in other words, they should not be swayed by emotion in Billy's case, hard as that may be. In spite of Captain Vere's words about military duty, his dying words, not long after Billy's execution, are "Billy Budd, Billy Budd," so it seems clear that Billy's fate has left its impression on the captain's heart.

Captain the Honorable Edward Fairfax Vere

See Captain Vere

Starry Vere

See Captain Vere

Themes

Duty and Conscience

Captain Vere's dilemma—whether to convict Billy and hang him in spite of his sense that the young sailor is innocent—arises from Vere's very nature. Captain Vere is characterized throughout *Billy Budd* as a man who heeds his duty. Even before Captain Vere appears, a description of the captain by minor character Captain Graveling of the *Rights-of-Man* anticipates the more central captain's problem: "His duty he always faithfully did; but duty is sometimes a dry obligation." The "dryness" of duty is in its disconnection from feeling or intuition: duty is intellectual rather than emotional. And Captain Vere is described as possessing "a marked leaning toward everything intellectual," and "never tolerating an infraction of discipline." He adheres to the law and expects his men to do so as well.

Captain Vere's nickname, "Starry Vere," comes from a poem by Andrew Marvell, in which allusion is made to the "discipline severe" of a figure called "starry Vere," actually an ancestor of the captain. These early references to Captain Vere's rigidness concerning law and duty create a character who later in the novel must face a moral dilemma and choose between his duty and his conscience. When Claggart comes to Vere with his accusation against Billy, Vere is wary of the strange officer's manner and doubts that Billy Budd could be involved in such a plot as Claggart implies. Yet Vere knows he must question Billy; this is the proper way to handle such an allegation. When Billy strikes Claggart, killing him, Vere reacts in "an excited manner [such as the surgeon] had never before observed in the *Bellipotent*'s captain." In this situation, Vere's duty is made unclear by his emotional response to "so strange and extraordinary a tragedy." Yet he immediately calls the drumhead court, leaving the surgeon to think that the captain has perhaps come "unhinged."

The members of the drumhead court, believing in Billy's innocence, are pulled by their conscience to vote to "convict and yet mitigate the penalty," but Captain Vere stands fast by his duty and reminds the court that they should not "Let warm hearts betray heads that should be cool." Billy's execution goes forward because of Captain Vere's intense focus on duty. As naval officers, he tells the court, "in receiving our commissions we in the most important regards ceased to be natural free agents." He goes on to ask them to "tell me whether or not, occupying the position we do, private conscience should not yield to that imperial one formulated in the code under which alone we officially proceed?" Essentially, the captain and his officers face a problem of whether to ignore their consciences, which speak strongly to them of Billy's innocence, or to follow their duty as officers in the King's navy and order Billy's death. The accusation of mutiny aside, the simple fact is that Billy, a foretopman, has struck and killed his superior, the master-at-arms. This fact, viewed objectively and according to the law, must result in

Topics for Further Study

- Research the Somers Mutiny Affair of 1842. Compare the events in that historical case to the events of *Billy Budd.* How did Melville depart from the events of the Somers case in his composition of *Billy Budd?* What events did he keep, and why?

- Watch the video of the 1962 film adaption of *Billy Budd.* What aspects of Melville's novel do the filmmakers emphasize? What do you think of the way the film was cast—are the characters portrayed as you would have expected? What do you think of the musical score's contribution to the film's mood?

- The narrator refers to Claggart's attitude towards Billy as "monomania." What does he mean by this term? Is there an equivalent in modern psychological parlance? Research how a modern psychologist might describe or explain Claggart's feelings towards Billy.

- Research the history of impressment into the British Royal Navy. Why do you think Melville made impressment into naval service a part of Billy's character? How might an actual sailor in Billy's time have felt about being impressed into service?

execution of the sailor, regardless of his innocent nature. Captain Vere, at his own death, appears still to be haunted by his decision in favor of duty: his last words are "Billy Budd, Billy Budd."

Innocence

Billy Budd's innocence—"his blinder," according to the narrator—is his tragic flaw. His innocence is what makes him the Handsome Sailor—it radiates from his laughing "welkin eyes" and makes him a peacemaker and a friend to all, drawing others to him. Yet aboard the *Bellipotent,* one of the men who is drawn to him is motivated by envy and malice: Claggart. Here, in his encounters with the scheming master-at-arms, is where Billy's innocence is his weakness. He cannot comprehend the evil in Claggart, nor can he grasp that it is directed at him.

A foundling with no knowledge of his parents, Billy is illiterate and has had little experience with the world, having spent much of his life on board ship. Billy is "little more than an upright barbarian, much such perhaps as Adam might have been ere the urbane Serpent wriggled himself into his company." Adamic innocence is the purest kind of innocence, and a comparison with Adam before the Fall implies a closeness to nature and an innocence that is untouched by even a suggestion of evil.

When Billy takes great care to keep his possessions in order and perform his duties correctly, he is puzzled when he finds "something amiss." When he consults the wise Dansker, Billy is even more perplexed when the latter implies that Claggart has had something to do with Billy's troubles. The Dansker's insistence that "Jemmy Legs is down on you" proves "incomprehensible to a novice, [and] disturbed Billy almost as much as the mystery for which he had sought explanation." Billy is fundamentally incapable of comprehending how or why someone could be out to get him. Not only is he young and inexperienced; Billy "had none of that intuitive knowledge of the bad," which others with less innocent natures may possess, enabling them to understand evil without having to experience it.

Law and Nature

Captain Vere defines the theme of law vs. nature when he admonishes the drumhead court to follow their duty to the King rather than listening to their hearts. He asks the members of the court how they can sentence to death "a fellow creature innocent before God, and whom we feel to be so?" When the court appears sympathetic to his question, he goes on, "I too feel that, the full force of that. It is Nature. But do these buttons that we wear attest that our allegiance is to Nature? No, to the King. Though the ocean, which is inviolate Nature primeval, though this be the element where we move and have our being as sailors, yet as the King's officers lies our duty in a sphere correspondingly natural? So little is that true, that in receiving our commissions we in the most important regards ceased to be natural free agents." Captain Vere's statement to the court highlights an opposition in the novel between human-made law and nature. Billy represents nature. The narrator calls him "a barbarian"; he "stands nearer to unadulterated Nature" than the other characters by virtue of his innocence. The manner in which Billy's case is handled represents the force of law upon nature: men who feel that Billy is innocent know that they must follow the King's laws against their better judgment. This problem is at the heart of the novel.

Evil

John Claggart personifies evil in *Billy Budd.* The narrator, who admits to his own tendencies toward innocence, claims not to be able to grasp Claggart's character in full: "His portrait I essay, but shall never hit it." Claggart is portrayed as mysterious and foreign. Little is known about him or his past. His complexion hints at "something defective or abnormal in the constitution or blood," and although he seems to have had an education, "Nothing is known of his former life." Claggart's characterization as dark and unknowable establishes a feeling of dread about him. Regarding the source of Claggart's evil, the narrator touches upon the question of whether one is born evil or learns to be so. In Claggart, he says, "the mania of an evil nature [was] not engendered by vicious training or corrupting books ... but born with him and innate, in short 'a depravity according to nature.'" Linked with such a nature is "an uncommon prudence ... for it has everything to hide." Claggart behaves courteously toward Billy, covering up his hatred and envy of the young sailor: his "monomania ... [was] covered over by his self-contained and rational demeanor." If Billy Budd is Adam before the Fall, Claggart represents the serpent who introduces the innocent man to pure evil.

Style

Point of View

The first-person narrator refers to himself as "I" and briefly talks about himself and his past experiences. He does not give his name and is not on board the *Bellipotent,* yet he speaks authoritatively about the events that take place there. The narrator has a limited omniscient point of view, which means that he is able to see nearly all of the novel's action, including some of the characters' thoughts. His admission of being unable to grasp Claggart's character—"His portrait I essay, but shall never hit it"—is one example of the narrator's limited omniscience, but it also contributes to the novel's overall depiction of Claggart's strangeness and foreignness.

The narrator tells of an experience he had as a young man, when "an honest scholar, my senior" spoke to him about a fine point of human nature, and the narrator says of himself, "At the time, my inexperience was such that I did not quite see the drift of all this. It may be that I see it now." He tells this story about himself to illustrate his similarity to and thus his empathy for Billy Budd. The narrator's empathy helps to shape the story, as it enables him to understand Billy's innocence: his tragic flaw.

Setting

The setting of *Billy Budd*—a British warship in the summer of 1797—is essential to the plot and meaning of the novel. The novel opens with the words, "In the time before steamships," immediately placing the action in a time relative to the development of naval technology: the reader envisions a ship with tall masts and huge sails, which is precisely where the novel's action is to occur. A few paragraphs later, the narrator introduces Billy Budd as a character and specifically identifies him as "a foretopman of the British fleet toward the close of the last decade of the eighteenth century."

The narrator's specificity about time and place sets the stage for what is to come. In chapter 3, the historic context for the novel's action is introduced: just prior to the novel's fictional events, which are set in "the summer of 1797," actual mutinies had taken place in the British navy in April and May of that same year. The mutinies at Spithead and the Nore still resonate on board the fictional *Bellipotent,* whose name means "strong in war." The *Bellipotent*'s sailors and officers continue to feel the tension from the two great mutinies: "Discontent foreran the Two Mutinies, and more or less it lurkingly survived them. Hence it was not unreasonable to apprehend some return of trouble." Melville uses this atmosphere of tension as background for his novel in order to create a sense of mutiny in the air, a weakening of trust between sailors and their commanders. He points out that "for a time [following the Two Mutinies], on more than one quarter-deck, anxiety did exist. At sea, precautionary vigilance was strained against relapse. At short notice an engagement might come on." An accusation against the innocent Billy Budd set at a different time, when the possibility of mutiny does not seem so palpable, might not end in tragedy. The narrator declares that "the unhappy event which has been narrated could not have happened at a worse juncture."

The shipboard setting, common among many of Melville's writings, presents a kind of microcosm of society, complete with hierarchies, laws

and a wide variety of personalities and backgrounds. Women are missing from this floating society, but in fact women would not have been part of the British navy at the time during which this novel is set. The narrator remarks that "the people of a great warship are ... like villagers, taking microscopic note of every outward movement or nonmovement going on." Such seemingly small incidents as Billy spilling his soup in the mess or the afterguardsman coming to speak to Billy at night take on a larger significance because everyone notices these moments and speculates about them, perhaps allowing them to mean more than they do.

Foreshadowing

Throughout *Billy Budd,* Melville makes use of foreshadowing—suggesting events that are to come—which gives the novel's events a kind of doomed, fated quality. Billy's initial description as "welkin-eyed"—his eyes are the color of the skies—identifies him with the heavens, suggesting his goodness but also suggesting that he will soon become a part of the celestial sphere. When, at the beginning of the novel, Captain Graveling relates the story of Billy striking the Red Whiskers out of anger, the incident sounds out of character for Billy. However, later on, when Billy strikes Claggart, killing him, the earlier incident reverberates. When Billy witnesses a fellow sailor being whipped as punishment for failing to do his duty, he is "horrified [and] resolved that never through remissness would he make himself liable to such a visitation or do or omit aught that might merit verbal reproof." Yet later, he himself is subjected to a punishment worse than whipping, and ironically his punishment comes about due to circumstances almost beyond his control. Melville's use of foreshadowing is effective in *Billy Budd* because it heightens the novel's irony and contributes to its tale of the ill-fated innocent.

Historical Context

The Royal Navy in the Late Eighteenth Century

Between 1794 and 1797, the number of seamen and marines serving in the British navy jumped from 85,000 to 120,000. England was at war with France at this time, and the navy's need for manpower was immense. Most of the men in the British naval service had not chosen to be there. While some men did join the navy, sailors could

Compare
&
Contrast

- **1790s:** Late eighteenth-century warships of the British navy are powered by sails. Seventy-four-gun ships—especially fast and easy to handle—are most common. Steam power is being explored as a means of ship propulsion.

- **1890s:** The United States begins building a "new navy" in the 1880s: ironclad steam-powered ships with a variety of weapons on board.

- **1924:** The Five-Power Naval Limitation Treaty, signed in 1922, restricts Allied countries from building new battleships until 1931 and orders that most battleships of outdated construction be destroyed. Naval aircraft technology is developed during this period.

- **Today:** Nearly half of the U.S. Navy's warships are propelled by nuclear reactors, which allow the ships to travel at high speeds without the need for fuel oil.

- **1790s:** During the American Revolution, capital punishment had come under fire in America as a deplorable institution from the reign of King George. By 1796, Melville's home state of New York has decreased the number of crimes punishable by death from thirteen to two—those being murder and treason.

- **1890s:** In 1890, the New York Assembly passes a bill abolishing capital punishment, but the State Senate votes the bill down. In August of 1890, William Kemmler becomes the first victim of execution by electrocution, hanging having been deemed too barbaric.

- **1924:** The infamous Leopold and Loeb murder case, in which teenagers Nathan Leopold and Richard Loeb are tried for brutally murdering fourteen-year-old Richard Franks, has many Americans demanding the death penalty for the defendants, who are found guilty of kidnapping and murder. The judge accepts renowned attorney Clarence Darrow's argument that Leopold and Loeb are insane and rejects the death penalty, instead sentencing them to life imprisonment at hard labor.

- **Today:** The U.S. Supreme Court abolished capital punishment in 1972 in *Furman v. Georgia,* but since that decision, rulings in other cases have chipped away at various aspects of the death penalty ruling, and executions continue to occur. In 1991, about 2,500 inmates were on death row. At the turn of the century, one debate over the death penalty focuses on whether lethal injection is more humane than the electric chair.

- **1790s:** In a nation of immigrants, white European settlers view Native Americans as "the other," and as impediments to their possession of the vast American land. In the South, African slaves are treated as property by their white slaveholders.

- **1890s:** American nativists grow uneasy about the enormous influx of immigrants into the country. In 1880, the U.S. Congress passed the Chinese Exclusion Act, prohibiting for ten years the entrance of Chinese laborers into the United States. In 1892, Congress renews the act for another decade.

- **1924:** Reflecting a national mood of anti-foreigner sentiment following World War I, the Immigration Act of 1924 establishes an annual quota for immigration into the United States.

- **Today:** "Multiculturalism," a movement aimed at engendering respect for other cultures, is taught in American schools and is a force in the popular culture.

also simply be taken off merchant ships by a warship's officer, as happens to Billy Budd. The sailors from merchant ships were valued for their sailing experience, and "topmen" such as Billy—those who could work up in the riggings—were especially useful.

Some men were "impressed" into naval service: these were the able-bodied men who could not be convinced to join the navy, so they had to be "pressed," or forced, to join, often through brutal means. Impressed men often resented their circumstances, but they had no choice but to stay aboard the warships, facing punishment if they shirked their imposed duty. When the afterguardsman comes to Billy to try to draw Billy into his mysterious plot, he first attempts to establish a bond with Billy regarding the way they were each brought onto the ship: "You were impressed, weren't you? ... Well, so was I ... We are not the only impressed ones, Billy. There's a gang of us." The context of this encounter is the tradition of impressment into the British navy and the resulting resentment, which has the potential to flower into mutiny.

Once on board the warships, sailors did not enjoy particularly healthful living conditions. A 74-gun ship, such as the *Bellipotent,* would have carried over 700 men, so quarters were crowded. Scurvy, a disease brought on by a lack of vitamin C, struck many sailors. In 1797, a British sailor could expect to eat salt beef and pork, oatmeal, cheese, bread, occasional fresh vegetables and assorted other foodstuffs. While a ship was at sea, the food often went bad: meat would decay, water would spoil, and the bread and flour would be invaded by mice, rats, weevils and other vermin. Officers and captains enjoyed a higher quality of food and food preparation than the sailors did, often supplementing their allotments of food with food they purchased themselves.

Mutinies at Spithead and the Nore

Chapter 3 of *Billy Budd* introduces the facts of the 1797 mutinies at Spithead and the Nore, two crucial events that occurred in the British navy during the Napoleonic wars. Spithead is a strait of the English Channel, located in the south of England between Portsmouth and the Isle of Wight; the Nore is a sandbank at the mouth of the Thames River in England, where the Thames enters the North Sea.

In 1797, Britain was at war with France, and the British navy had had to expand rapidly to fill the need for manpower on warships. However,

Melville's novel is set in 1797, during the early years of the long war England would wage against the French Revolutionary armies of Napoleon Bonaparte.

many of the men who entered the navy at this time did not do so voluntarily, and conditions on board the naval ships left much to be desired. The food was poor, the pay was paltry, medical treatment was substandard, and sailors were flogged for misconduct. Such circumstances contributed to a buildup of sailors' resentments. In April, when the commander of the Channel fleet's flagship, the *Queen Charlotte,* rejected the crew's demands to move the ship out to sea, the *Queen Charlotte*'s crew spurred other ships in the fleet to join them in protest. The mutineers presented a petition to the House of Commons, who in turn met some of the demands of the petitioners. The promises made to the mutineers included better pay, removal of some of the harshest officers in the fleet, and pardons for those involved in the mutiny. The mutineers had succeeded in securing some improvements in their lot.

The April mutiny at Spithead soon extended to include the North Sea fleet, which was anchored at the Nore. The mutineers at the Nore were not as readily satisfied as their counterparts at Spithead: when the government offered concessions to the protesters at the Nore, they were reluctant to accept. An ex-midshipman, Richard Parker, convinced his fellow mutineers that they should not accept the government's terms immediately but should hold out for more. The mutiny put Britain into danger for a time, as the Dutch—allies of France—nearly were able to invade England while the mutineers remained inactive.

In speaking to the members of the drumhead court, Captain Vere connects the mutinies at Spithead and the Nore to the events of *Billy Budd:* "You know what sailors are. Will they not revert to the recent outbreak at the Nore? They know the well-founded alarm—the panic it struck throughout England. Your clement sentence they would account pusillanimous. They would think that we flinch, that we are afraid of them." In this atmosphere of tension over the potential power struggle between captains and their crews, Captain Vere must decide how to handle Billy's impulsive killing of his superior.

Mutiny on Board the Somers, *1842*

Melville's narrator relates at the end of chapter 21 a connection between Billy's case and an incident aboard the U.S. brig *Somers* in 1842. This historic incident aboard the *Somers,* reports the narrator, culminated in "the execution at sea of a midshipman and two sailors as mutineers designing the seizure of the brig." The events on board the *Somers* and those on the *Bellipotent* are, he admits, "different from" each other, and yet "the urgency felt [by the officers deciding each case], well-warranted or otherwise, was much the same."

Melville's favorite older cousin when he was a child was Guert Gansevoort, who happened to be the first lieutenant of the *Somers.* When the three young sailors on board the *Somers* were suspected of planning a mutiny, Gansevoort had been among those officers called to advise the ship's captain, Alexander Slidell Mackenzie, as Mackenzie tried to decide the young men's fate. With no trial and no chance to defend themselves, the three sailors—one of whom, Philip Spencer, was the son of the U.S. secretary of war—were pronounced guilty and hanged from the ship's yardarm. Mackenzie was later tried for murder.

Critical Overview

Critical treatments of *Billy Budd* and of Melville abound, which is an irony given the origins of the novel. When Melville died in 1891, he

left behind the manuscript for *Billy Budd,* which would not be discovered among his papers for another thirty years. At the time of Melville's death, his reputation as a literary talent had faded, but a few obituary notices did take note of Melville's earlier success and fame. Some of what was written about Melville immediately following his death had a regretful tone, as if his slip into obscurity had constituted a loss for American letters. An obituary in the *New York Times,* alluding to Melville's past fame, remarked that "this speedy oblivion by which a once famous man so long survived his fame is almost unique, and it is not easily explicable." The obituary went on to wonder at "why [Melville's books] are read and talked about no longer. The total eclipse now of what was then a literary luminary seems like a wanton caprice of fame." However, in *North American Review* in 1892, W. Clark Russell wrote, somewhat prophetically, that "Famous he was; now he is neglected; yet his name and works will not die. He is a great figure in shadow; but the shadow is not that of oblivion."

Russell's words truly were prophetic, as around the centennial anniversary of Melville's birthday in 1919 a movement known as the "Melville revival" began to develop. In *The Gazette of the Grolier Club,* William S. Reese, a collector of Melville's works, attributed the emergence of the revival to both Melville's centenary and also to "the beginning of a more disillusioned, deterministic, post-war age," whose readers would be more receptive to Melville's works than his own contemporaries had been. Reese noted that "Melville's centenary in 1919 had brought numerous literary notices, and … In 1921 Raymond Weaver's biography, *Herman Melville, Mariner and Mystic,* came out, sparking further interest." *Billy Budd* was published for the first time in 1924 in a volume of Melville's work edited by Weaver, and thus, said Reese, "Melville was made generally accessible to readers."

In his 1921 biography of Melville, Weaver said that *Billy Budd* and other works in manuscript found after Melville's death were "not distinguished." Weaver added that *Billy Budd* "would seem to teach that though the wages of sin is death, that sinners and saints alike toil for a common hire." In the biography, Weaver also wrote that in *Billy Budd* Melville had lost "the brisk lucidity, the sparkle, the verve" of his earlier works and that "Only the disillusion abided with him to the last." Weaver seemed to contradict his 1921 statement in his introduction to 1928 *Shorter Novels of Herman*

Melville, where he said that *Billy Budd* is "unmatched among Melville's works in lucidity and inward peace."

Weaver referred in his introduction to *Shorter Novels of Herman Melville* to the "state of the *Billy Budd* manuscript," proclaiming that "there can never appear a reprint that will be adequate to every ideal." The difficulty of assembling a definitive text plagued Melville critics for decades. Weaver, the first critic to lay eyes on the manuscript, said that it is "in certain parts a miracle of crabbedness: misspellings in the grand manner; scraps of paragraphs cut out and pasted over disembowelled sentences; words ambiguously begun ... variant readings, with no choice indicated among them. More disheartening than this even, is one floating chapter ... with no numbering beyond the vague direction 'To be inserted.'" F. O. Matthiessen lauded Weaver's accomplishment in a footnote to his 1941 essay, "*Billy Budd, Foretopman*", because "The problem of editing Melville's one extant major manuscript was an exacting one" and thus critics should be "indebted to [Weaver's] enthusiastic and devoted pioneering for the first full-length study of Melville."

Another critic, Lewis Mumford, also found flaws in *Billy Budd;* he wrote in 1929 that what is missing in *Billy Budd* is "an independent and living creation." Mumford felt that while the story takes place on the sea, "the sea itself is missing, and even the principal characters are not primarily men: they are actors and symbols."

During the 1950s and 1960s, the body of Melville scholarship grew rapidly. Particularly after the 1962 publication of what was considered a definitive text of *Billy Budd*—edited by Harrison Hayford and Merton M. Sealts, Jr.—scholars approached Melville's final novel with renewed interest. Hayford and Sealts wrote in their preface to this definitive edition that in "the first quarter century of criticism (1921-46) [there] seemed to be virtually a consensus, that the work constituted Melville's 'testament of acceptance.'" The editors added that in the 1950s this earlier consensus had been "flatly contradicted ... by those reading the novel as an ironic reiteration of all his lifelong quarrels and denials."

Peter Shaw, looking back in 1993 at the development of *Billy Budd* scholarship, noticed that "resistance readings eventually began to take on the coloration of 1960s radicalism. Stimulated by the concept of innocent youth punished by paternal authority, critics in the 1960s imagined Melville to be finding fault with 'the system,' by which they sometimes meant the law and sometimes 'the tragic guilt' of society itself.... It followed that the story meant not only radically to champion 'the people,' but also amounted to 'a call for rebellion.'" Shaw maintained that the "resistance/ironist reading continued to hold sway in the 1970s." In the 1980s, Shaw said, critics began to "routinely [argue] that Vere's application of the law is arbitrary and unnecessary, that it springs from twisted psychological motives, and that it reflects the inherent cruelty of his privileged class."

Criticism

Logan Esdale

Esdale is a doctoral candidate in the Poetics Program at SUNY-Buffalo. In the following essay, he analyzes the self-conscious narration that exists in contrast to the apparent lack of self-consciousness in Billy Budd.

Herman Melville's *Billy Budd* has produced an astonishing diversity of equally plausible interpretations. Most critics consider finally whether they approve or condemn Captain Vere's decision to try and execute the sailor Billy Budd for the murder of the officer John Claggart. Invariably critics include in their analysis a statement made by the novel's narrator near the end that ostensibly apologizes for the meandering style and the unresolved questions: "Truth uncompromisingly told will always have its ragged edges." Following this proposition, the narrator concludes the history of Billy with three sequels—on the further adventures of the ship, the doomed captain, and the venerated spar from which Billy was hung—and a poem describing Billy's final moments in between life and death. The narrator includes as well a naval report that contradicts the version of events just given. This naval report is anything but ragged. It justifies the execution of Billy in the strongest terms, claiming that he "vindictively stabbed" the honorable John Claggart.

Judging by this report alone, there is no doubt that Billy's death answers for the life he took. For the good of the English nation Billy is hung. But there is no judging anything alone; everything has a context that, if explored, will lead to the digressions and ragged edges that the narrator understands both as a burden on the mind that desires order, and as a liberation from closure. With the

What Do I Read Next?

- "Young Goodman Brown," is a short story published in 1835 by Nathaniel Hawthorne. The character of Young Goodman Brown, an innocent, is tested by evil forces that are mysterious to him. He is nearly incapable of comprehending that the people he respects most might possess a capacity for evil. Melville was friends with Hawthorne and had the utmost respect and admiration for his work.

- Melville's *Moby-Dick* (1851), considered by most critics to be his masterpiece, is, like *Billy Budd,* a tale of good and evil set against the stark setting of the sea. Captain Ahab, who obsessively seeks the white whale, Moby-Dick, is identified as a "monomaniac"; Claggart in *Billy Budd* is described as possessing a "monomania."

- The Bounty Trilogy, a collection of three books by Charles Nordhoff and James Norman Hall, traces the historic mutiny aboard the H.M.S. *Bounty* and its aftermath as experienced by the captain and crew. The first book in the trilogy, *Mutiny on the Bounty* (1932), is an account of the 1788 voyage of H.M.S. *Bounty,* during which Fletcher Christian committed mutiny against Captain Bligh. In *Men Against the Sea* (1934), Captain Bligh, along with the nineteen men who chose to remain loyal to him during the mutiny, travel 3,600 miles in an open boat that they had been set out in by the mutineers. *Pitcairn's Island* (1934) tells of how Christian, his fellow mutineers, and a few Tahitians end up on a forsaken island in the Pacific following the mutiny.

- Melville's *Redburn* (1849) tells the story of an inexperienced yet proud young man who goes to sea and learns about the world through his difficulties with life at sea. While the innocent Redburn anticipates Billy Budd, the evil Jackson foretokens Claggart.

---

narrator, the reader will feel both disoriented and empowered—like the vertigo a person feels close to the edge of an abyss. Attention to all the facts puts the narrator in the impossible position of offering an endless series of contradictions, leaving readers uncertain about the intentions of the characters, and about the events themselves. Finally, the inclusion of other perspectives, like the naval report's, not only throws the truth of each account into doubt, but truth itself seems unreachable, a vanishing point on the horizon.

The novel—and language in general—structures itself through the use of binaries, such as child and adult, innocence and guilt, inner being and appearance, compassion and military or legal duty, the individual and the nation, sea and land. Looking carefully at all the facts tends to blur the difference between these "opposites." In a digression on the line between sanity and insanity, for instance, the narrator asks, "Who in the rainbow can draw the line where the violet tint ends and the orange tint begins? Distinctly we see the difference of colors, but where exactly does the one first blendingly enter into the other?" A question central to Melville's novel is where does the character "Billy Budd" end, and the character "John Claggart" begin? The two men appear to be utterly distinct, the one intent on doing good and the other intent on doing evil, but also, at times, the one seems to have merged with the other.

When does the past end, and the present begin? When does the future begin? These questions haunt the narrator, and the history of Billy Budd becomes itself a questioning of how history is written: the narration is self-conscious, which means that every general statement is qualified by a particular and contradictory statement, and that the lines among a character, the narrator, and the reader are blurred. The ragged edges of the story refer also to the rags or fragments of history the narrator finds and picks up as the story is written. An infinite number of sequels will still leave the story unfinished (as Melville left the manuscript unfinished at his death in 1891), and the narrator will consciously draw attention to this incompleteness. Critics have since 1924, when *Billy Budd* was first published, chosen either to write about the ragged edges, or write something like a naval report. Usually the critical imperative is to produce the latter; the chaos of events as they happen (in language) may be revealed, but everything will finally be put in order.

Is it possible to reach truth, or is truth only that which those with authority agree to call "truth"? The latter happens in the case of Billy Budd: the officers sentence him, not according to his innocence of fomenting mutiny and committing murder, which they believe, but according to military law. History records that Billy is "guilty." The narrator claims to be telling the truth about events that happened in 1797, decades earlier than "now" (for the narrator). In so doing, the narrator questions the truth of the naval report made at the time, and suggests that only at an objective distance from the events, something Captain Vere and the officers judging Billy lacked, can history be accurately written. In other words, the truth about the past can only be told once the past has ended. But is this possible? As readers (including the narrator) evaluate and judge the case, they realize that achieving objective distance is next to impossible. Perhaps the narrator tells us only what he wants to be true, slanting the facts to suit his purposes. And what is the reader's purpose?

This process of ordering chaos is habitual in us. Sailors live according to this habit. They need to trust in each other to survive. Any given ship was marked by diversity, "an assortment of tribes and complexions," so that the sailors, officers, and warship all appear together symbolically as a miniature nation. Some sailors chose to be on board, and some were forced (like Billy). Especially during war, when all differences among the enemy are ignored, any given nation glosses difference by transforming the characteristic habits of the people into instincts. "True" instinct, or that which defines the individual, are repressed. Common to all sailors was the "mechanism of discipline": "True martial discipline long continued," the narrator notes, "superinduces in average man a sort of impulse whose operation at the official word of command much resembles in its promptitude the effect of an instinct." In other words, what may appear natural or inherent in our behavior may be in fact merely habitual, in work on ship or on land. For writers this means that the discipline of writing creates the illusion of order; and critics are false witnesses (like Claggart) to readers and to them-

selves if they attempt to propose a single, totalizing account.

The lack of a stable ground upon which to build an orderly interpretation of events is an effect of the story's setting—the ocean. The ocean is "inviolate Nature primeval," or chaos, and resistant to mapping. The ocean and its effects on the story must have been implicit all along, but are not explicitly felt until well into the story, when Captain Vere meditates on the consequences of the two choices (between instinct and discipline) facing himself and the three officers of the drumhead court: Vere "to-and-fro paced the cabin athwart; in the returning ascent to windward climbing the slant deck in the ship's lee roll, without knowing it symbolizing thus in his action a mind resolute to surmount difficulties even if against primitive instincts strong as the wind and the sea."

Just as throughout the story the ship has been teetering back-and-forth, so too does the decision on Billy's fate move between innocent and guilty. This teetering might have continued indefinitely had Captain Vere not decided to prosecute Billy according to his deed (murder) and not his intention (defend himself). Vere eliminates ambiguity by executing Billy. Ultimately, the rights of the individual must be upheld in favor of the general "good." At the time, England was at war with France, and the navy had recently experienced two serious mutinies. "War looks but to the frontage, the appearance," Vere says, himself at war with indecision. Vere argues that the judgement must be made as if they were on (stable) land. He puts the ship back on even keel.

Naval battles are more explicitly described once we "sail away" from Billy's body on the surface of the ocean. Most striking in the sequels is the return to land—a return also to the beginning of the story, which opens on the border between land and ocean: "In the time before steamships, or then more frequently than now, a stroller along the docks of any considerable seaport would occasionally have his attention arrested by a group of bronzed mariners, man-of-war's men or merchant sailors in holiday attire, ashore on liberty." There are at least four liminal spaces—or, as in the story, those "deadly spaces between" two opposites—that affect the mood of indecisiveness, two of which are in this first sentence: the time or history that has passed between 1797 and "now"; and the dock or shore. The other two are the ocean surface, and the forehead of the human body.

Steamships are less determined by the arbitrary forces of nature than those powered by wind and sail, which implies that as time has proceeded, the forces (or instincts) themselves have not changed, but we have become further civilized or buffered from their strength and effects. Civilization, the narrator says, "folds itself in the mantle of respectability." Notice also that sailors ashore or along a dock are in the space between water and land, and are at "liberty." This particular reference to liberty or freedom suggests that on either side of a "dock space" people are subject to the "mechanisms of discipline." In a dock space or in the ocean, however, the diversity of forces is at play. An ocean surface can appear calm and serene, yet the struggle for life continues underneath between, simply enough, big and small fish.

Finally, in this short list of liminal spaces, the forehead marks the point between inside and outside, between body and mind. The forehead is the particular place Billy strikes on Claggart's body. Before this scene occurs, the narrator makes an odd comparison which helps explain the surprising effectiveness of the blow: "consciences are as unlike as foreheads." Why does Billy strike Claggart's forehead? Perhaps he did so because Claggart's "brow was of the sort phrenologically associated with more than average intellect." Phrenology claims that much about a person's character is revealed in the shape of the head. Billy was fooled by the humane aspect of Claggart's face (an ocean surface), never believing that Claggart harbored malicious intentions; but Billy seems also to know, unconsciously perhaps, that striking Claggart's (guilty) "conscience" would kill him. Billy strikes what was individual to Claggart. Had Billy struck elsewhere, Claggart probably would have lived. How did he locate Claggart's weak spot? What does Billy know about himself and Claggart?

Whether Billy lacks self-consciousness or comprehends the destructiveness in others and in himself is finally the question on which the novel turns. Billy Budd may well represent the complex tensions in American literature as a whole. Under pressure, Billy stutters: with "sudden provocation of strong heart-feeling his voice, otherwise singularly musical, as if expressive of the harmony within, was apt to develop an organic hesitancy, in fact more or less of a stutter or even worse"— silence. Poet and critic Susan Howe has said in *The Birth-mark: Unsettling the Wilderness in American Literary History,* that it is "the stutter in American literature that interests me. I hear the stutter as a sounding of uncertainty. What is silenced or not quite silenced. All the broken dreams."

Set in the Mediterranean Ocean on an English boat during a war with France, Billy is yet distinctly American. Given the chance to formulate dreams and ideals, America and "Billy Budd, the Handsome Sailor" (both are born in 1776) fail to realize them. Speculations on malice or difference "into which [Billy] was led were so disturbingly alien to him that he did his best to smother them," and so does America (consider in its history up to 1891 the silence on the slaughter of the natives as well as slavery, and that the majority of the population—including all women—do not have the right to vote, and are, in other words, unable to speak). Billy says at his trial, "Could I have used my tongue I would not have struck him" (consider the violence used in the making of history).

Melville stopped writing fiction for almost thirty years because his books received an almost uniformly hostile response. Out of this silence, *Billy Budd* surfaced and critiques an American reading public understood to be functionally illiterate. Billy is a big dumb kid, who certainly does not deserve to die, as the story is told, but who is—Claggart was right—dangerous. Claggart accuses Billy of harboring plots that would disrupt civil order. This accusation brings Billy's unconscious anger and fear to light and results in the deadly blow. The anxiousness on board about mutiny was caused by the sailor revolts just a few months earlier at British naval bases. But older captains in the British navy would have remembered the American Revolution, a mutiny on a national scale, in which the sailors (the colonies) overthrew the captain (the King). Melville wonders how an illiterate nation, one unable to speak for itself without using violence, is to survive.

There exists in Billy a refusal to be self-conscious, just as there exists in him an inability to speak during crisis moments, when ambiguity surfaces. Billy cannot and will not speak. The narrator attempts to repair this defect by writing a self-conscious history. *Billy Budd* represents the wildness of reading, and what is repressed during reading and interpreting. From the start, and at the end, both narrator and reader rock between writing an orderly report, or a self-conscious essay that tests the ragged edges, the gaps, or stutters in fiction and in history—a "sounding of uncertainty."

Source: Logan Esdale, in an essay for *Novels for Students,* Gale, 2000.

Tom Goldstein

In the following essay, Goldstein delves into the legal profession's view of Billy Budd.

It is a story of innocence and evil, of crime and punishment, of rationality and insanity, of motives tainted and pure. In short, material that lawyers thrive on, and since it was published posthumously in 1924, *Billy Budd, Sailor* has gripped the collective imagination of the bar.

Lately, a cottage industry has grown up in legal circles on the interpretation of Herman Melville's novella. It is taught in courses in jurisprudence, and books and law journal articles delve into whether Billy Budd, the protagonist, was unjustly executed and whether the man who sent him to his death, Captain Starry Vere, was a jurisprudential hero or villain.

Last fall a two-day colloquium on the law and Billy Budd was held at the Washington and Lee School of Law in Lexington, Va. And last week 150 lawyers listened to a prominent judge and professor debate the novel's meaning at the New York City Bar Association.

The novel, said one panelist, Prof. Richard Weisberg of the Benjamin Cardozo School of Law, causes lawyers "to reflect constantly upon our own values".

While some lawyers have long written fiction and some writers have long been fascinated by lawyers, only recently have law and literature become a fashionable and respectable area of legal scholarship. Courses are now offered at the best law schools, legal periodicals are filled with articles exploring [Fyodor] Dostoyevsky, [Franz] Kafka and [Herman] Melville, and at summer retreats, judges are as likely to discuss [William] Shakespeare as Tom Wolfe.

"Literature enriches our understanding of law", said David Saxe, an acting Supreme Court justice in New York City.

In the novel, Billy Budd, a popular sailor, has been impressed into service on a British warship. Soon afterward a petty officer, John Claggart, falsely accuses Billy of being a mutineer. When confronting his accuser, Billy cannot speak. The captain comforts him, saying there is no need to hurry. But Billy strikes Claggart dead with a single blow. The captain convenes a court-martial, whose members are inclined to leniency until the captain intercedes. Within 24 hours, Billy is hanged.

In the late eighteenth and early nineteenth centuries, men were often conscripted for the British Royal Navy because of the deplorable conditions and cruel mistreatment sailors suffered aboard such ships as the Man-of-War, *pictured here. Consequently, rebellious sailors, hungry for revenge, were likely to consider mutinious acts and turn on one another.*

Literary and legal critics have often viewed Captain Vere as an honorable man and able administrator who was forced to perform a distasteful task.

This view has been sharply challenged in lectures and articles by Professor Weisberg, who holds a doctorate in comparative literature as well as a law degree. He argued that the captain had acted improperly as witness, prosecutor, judge and executioner. In calling for summary execution, the captain, according to the professor, misread applicable statutes and committed procedural errors.

The professor presented a detailed review of court-martial procedures in effect in the 18th century, when the story took place, and concluded, "From the legal point of view, there was no justification of what Vere did".

His interpretation was disputed by Judge Richard Posner, a Federal appeals judge in Chicago who is a prodigious writer on the side; 13 books and 130 law review articles bear his name. The judge chided the professor for going beyond the text of the book for his evidence. Melville, he said, was "not writing the story for people expected to do legal research."

For Judge Posner, Vere was merely fulfilling his obligation. "We cannot bring a 1980's view of capital punishment to the story", Judge Posner said. "It was utterly routine in the 18th century".

Source: Tom Goldstein, "Once Again, *Billy Budd* Stands Trial," in *The New York Times,* June 10, 1988, p. 15, p. B9.

Charles A. Reich

In the essay below, Reich provides a detailed look at justice as portrayed in Billy Budd, *arguing that human law must address a man's actions as seen objectively within his situation.*

To read *Billy Budd* is to feel an intense and indelible sense of helplessness and agony. A youthful sailor, loved by his shipmates for his natural goodness, is put to death for the sake of seemingly formalistic, insensate law. In this final work of Melville's, law and society are portrayed in fundamental opposition to natural man.

The confrontation takes place in a stark and somber shipboard drama. Billy, the Handsome Sailor, is falsely and maliciously accused of mutiny by Claggart, the master-at-arms. Momentarily losing the power of speech while trying to answer, Billy strikes out at Claggart, and the blow kills. Captain Vere, who witnesses the act and must judge it, is caught in a "moral dilemma involving aught of the tragic." Knowing full well Billy's goodness, and that he did not intend to kill, Vere sees no choice but to apply the inflexible law of a military ship in time of war. Billy is hanged.

The problem of *Billy Budd* has produced much argument. Some critics have considered it Melville's "testament of acceptance," a peaceful, resigned coming-into-port after a stormy lifetime. Some have thought that Billy, though dead, triumphs because his sacrifice restores goodness to the world. Others have found the novel a bitter and ironic criticism of society. Most recently and persuasively, it has been called a Sophoclean tragedy, a contemplation of life's warring values. All of these views have merit. But there is still more to be seen in *Billy Budd*.

Melville's last book seems clearly to be different from his earlier works. It is true that Billy and Claggert are archetypal Melville figures. But in *Billy Budd* neither of these characters is developed or explained; each remains static. Instead, the focus is upon a new kind of character—the civilized, intellectual Captain Vere. He is the only character whose feelings we are permitted to see, and his is the only consciousness which seems to grow during the action. In addition, the book's focus is upon a new situation: not the old clash of good and evil, but an encounter of these natural forces, on the one hand, with society and law on the other. Significantly, Vere, and the dilemma of this encounter, were the last elements to be added when Melville was writing, as if he had started out to repeat an old drama but ended up with something new and unexpected. *Billy Budd* is also different in that the central theme is presented through the medium of a problem in law. And "law" is used not merely in the general sense of order as opposed to chaos. Instead we are given a carefully defined issue. This issue receives an extraordinarily full treatment which, together with its crucial position in the story, makes it the major focus of action and conflict.

In approaching *Billy Budd* almost all critics, whatever their ultimate conclusions, have started with the assumption that Billy is innocent, and that the issue is an encounter between innocence and formalistic society. But to say that Billy is innocent is a misleading start, for it invites a basic confusion and oversimplification. By what standard is he innocent? Is it by law deriving from nature, from God, or from man? And to what is the concept of innocence applied—to Billy's act or to Billy himself? Billy is innocent in that he lacks experience, like Adam before the Fall, but he is not necessarily innocent in that he is not guilty of a crime. The problem of justice in the book is a profoundly difficult one; its possibilities are far richer than is generally recognized. In turn, such recognition affects the reader's view of Vere and, ultimately, the understanding of the novel as a whole.

There are at least three basic issues in *Billy Budd*. First, how and by what standards should Billy, or Billy's act, be judged? …

In 1884, close to the time when Melville wrote *Billy Budd,* there came before the courts of England in a great and famous case a true-life sea tragedy, one which also presented a dilemma for the law. Three English seamen, Dudley, Stephens, and Brooks, and Richard Parker, an English boy of seventeen or eighteen, were cast away in an open boat 1600 miles from the Cape of Good Hope. For eighteen days they drifted, with no fresh water except occasional rain caught in their oilskin capes, and nothing to eat but two tins of turnips and a small turtle which they caught and which was entirely consumed by the twelfth day. On the eighteenth day, when they had been seven days without food and five without water, Dudley and Stephens, spoke of their having families, and resolved, if no help arrived by the next day, to kill the boy, who was lying helpless and near death in the bottom of the boat. On the twentieth day, no ship appearing, Dudley and Stephens, offering a prayer for God's forgiveness, told the boy his time was come, and put a knife into his throat, and the three men fed upon his body and blood. On the fourth day after the act they were rescued, in the lowest state of prostration. The three survivors were carried to Falmouth, and Dudley and Stephens were committed for trial on a charge of murder.

The decision of the case was rendered, for the Queen's Bench, by the Chief Justice of England, Lord Coleridge. It had been found that at the time of the killing there was no reasonable prospect of help, that had the men not fed upon the boy they would probably all have died before the rescue, and that the boy would probably have died first. In these circumstances, it was argued, the killing was not murder. In an elaborate and scholarly opinion which drew on the views of philosophers and legal authorities from the time of Henry III forward, Lord Coleridge rejected this defense. He found that no writer except one considered necessity a justification for killing, except in the case of self-defense, which differs because there it is the victim, and not some external element, who actively threatens the killer's life. The defense of necessity must be rejected, said the Lord Chief Justice, because law cannot follow nature's principle of self-preservation. "Though law and morality are not the same, and many things may be immoral which are not necessarily illegal, yet the absolute divorce of law from morality would be of fatal consequence...." Contrasting that morality with the law of nature, Lord Coleridge said:

> To preserve one's life is generally speaking a duty, but it may be the plainest and highest duty to sacrifice it. War is full of instances in which it is man's duty not to live, but to die. The duty, in case of a shipwreck, of a captain to his crew, of the crew to the passengers, of soldiers to women and children, as in the noble case of the *Birkenhead;* these duties impose on men the moral necessity, not of the preservation, but of the sacrifice of their lives for others, from which in no country, least of all, it is hoped, in England, will men ever shrink, as, indeed, they have not shrunk.... It is not needful to point out the awful danger of admitting the principle which has been con-

tended for. Who is to be the judge of this sort of necessity? By what measure is the comparative value of lives to be measured? It is to be strength, or intellect, or what? ... Such a principle once admitted might be made the legal cloak for unbridled passion and atrocious crime. There is no safe path for judges to tread but to ascertain the law to the best of their ability and to declare it according to their judgment; and if any case the law appears too severe on individuals, to leave it to the Sovereign to exercise that prerogative of mercy which the Constitution has intrusted to the hands fittest to dispense it.

> It must not be supposed that in refusing to admit temptation to be an excuse for crime it is forgotten how terrible the temptation was; how awful the suffering; how hard in such trials to keep the judgment straight and the conduct pure. We are often compelled to set up standards we cannot reach ourselves, and to lay down rules which we could not ourselves satisfy. But a man has no right to declare temptation to be an excuse, though he might himself have yielded to it, nor allow compassion for the criminal to change or weaken in any manner the legal definition of the crime.

Dudley and Stephens were sentenced to death. But the history does not end there. After an appeal for mercy, the Queen commuted their sentences to six months' imprisonment.

There are striking similarities between the history of Dudley and Stephens and the tale of *Billy Budd.* Billy, falsely accused before the Captain by Claggart, and unable to defend himself verbally because at the critical moment he cannot utter a word, responds to pure nature, and to the dictates of necessity. He is overwhelmed by circumstance, placed in the greatest extremity of his life. He stands "like one impaled and gagged," "straining forward in an agony ... to speak and defend himself" his face assumes "an expression which was as a crucifixion to behold." Suddenly he strikes a blow at the master-at-arms, and the blow kills. "I had to say something, and I could only say it with a blow, God help me!" Billy testifies later.

Captain Vere renders his judgement in much the same words as Lord Coleridge. He says "In natural justice is nothing but the prisoner's overt act to be considered?" Budd purposed neither mutiny nor homicide, Vere acknowledges. "And before a court less arbitrary and more merciful than a martial one that plea would largely extenuate. At the Last Assizes it shall acquit." But under the law, Billy's blow was a capital offense; the Mutiny Act made no exceptions for palliating circumstances. The officers' responsibility is to adhere to it and administer it. The exceptional in the matter moves the heart and the conscience, but it cannot move the upright judge.

In the discussion of the law that takes place aboard the *Bellipotent* among the members of the drumhead court, the first argument for Billy's innocence is based upon what is natural in the circumstances. Billy's act took place under the most extreme provocation. And it is described as almost automatic or instinctual, the unbearable tension of Billy's violent thwarted efforts at utterance suddenly finding outlet in a blow. If Billy is innocent for these reasons, it must be because of what Captain Vere calls "natural justice." Such justice, so Vere implies, looks to circumstances like self-defense, extreme provocation, or dire necessity. Natural justice exonerates, presumably, when the crime was forced upon the killer; when he did not kill by his own free choice. Billy was overcome by forces beyond his control. From the moment he was taken off the merchant ship *Rights-of-Man* and impressed into the King's service, until on the last night he lay prone in irons between two cannon upon the deck, Billy was "as nipped in the vice of fate." At the crucial moment when he was beset by Claggert's evil, society was not able to protect him; his separation from civilization is symbolized by the sea: in Vere's words, "the ocean, which is inviolate Nature primeval … the element where we move and have our being as sailors." The mood of the drama is all inevitability; against the impersonal movement of events Billy is but "Baby Budd." No wonder Vere whispers "Fated boy, what have you done!"

Billy, moreover, is presented less as a rational being than as a child of Nature. Illiterate, unselfconscious, "one to whom not yet has been proffered the questionable apple of knowledge," Billy was "little more than a sort of upright barbarian," one standing "nearer to unadulterate Nature." "Like the animals … he was … practically a fatalist." And although Claggart has the surface appearance of reason, he is as natural as Billy underneath. Like Heathcliff in *Wuthering Heights,* he personifies a nonhuman force. Although he has some very human qualities, the force that moves him is "Natural Depravity: a depravity according to nature," "born with him and innate." Like a storm or tidal wave, he represents "an unreciprocated malice." Billy's "mere aspect" calls up in Claggert "an antipathy spontaneous and profound." Thus their clash is as unavoidable as that of natural forces like fire and water.

The opinion of Lord Coleridge speaks to Billy's case as well as that of Dudley and Stephens. Like Billy, they found themselves in an extremity of circumstances, overwhelmed by forces beyond their control. Like Billy, they were called upon to act in the isolated universe of the sea and a boat, far removed from the protective influence of civilization. Like Billy, they acted as natural men.

Indeed, if Billy is innocent, why not Claggert? Is it just to blame Claggert for evil that was not his choice but was innate and inborn? His nature, "for which the Creator alone is responsible," must "act out to the end the part alloted to it." His antipathy was no more within his control than Billy's fist was under Billy's control. Billy's very existence and nearness was an excruciating, unbearable provocation to Claggart, as D. H. Lawrence's young soldier is to his superior in *The Prussion Officer.* In Lawrence's story, a striking parallel to the Claggart-Billy aspect of *Billy Budd,* a cold and haughty officer is assigned a youthful orderly, "an unhampered young animal" whose presence was "like a warm flame upon the older man's tense, rigid body." Something about the boy so disturbs and enrages the officer that he goads and torments the orderly until the boy, seized by a flaming, nearly suffocating instinct, breaks the officer's neck with his bare hands, then dazedly awaits his own death. In yielding to a similar provocation Claggart only shows the same inability to control his nature that Billy and, for that matter, Dudley and Stephens (who could not control the primal drive of hunger) have shown.

Nature contains both Billy's goodness and Claggert's evil. But in times of stress and extremity, the law of nature offers no support to goodness, and no check to evil. It interposes no objection when Dudley and Stephens kill the weak boy. And it allows Billy to kill a weaker man who was not immediately threatening his life. Human law must set a higher standard. To do so, it must look beyond the immediate theatre of action. Harsh though this may be, we must be judged by a universe wider than the one in which our actions are played out. The actions of Dudley and Stephens must be judged from England, and not from within the narrow universe of a lifeboat in the open sea. The act of Billy must be judged from outside his desperate "struggle against suffocation," and from beyond "the inner life of one particular ship."

In addition, man's law must posit a free will, an ability to choose. Not because free will always exists—or ever exists—but because law must rest on the assumption that man can control his own conduct, so that he may strive to raise himself above his natural state. Even psychiatry and psychoanalysis, the sciences which most strongly support a deterministic view of human nature, insist that an area of choice exists, and the patient can change his course. Even the psychotic makes some response to rules or law. Man must reject the concept of determinism if he is to live in and adapt to the society of others, whether that society is our complex twentieth-century world or the primitive grouping of four beings in an open boat. Not only Vere and Coleridge, but all men, wear the buttons of the King.

Natural justice, as the drumhead court sees it, has a second aspect; the guilt or innocence of the mind. Billy did not intend to kill. He testifies, "there was no malice between us … I am sorry that he is dead. I did not mean to kill him." Moreover, Billy's whole character shows an innocent mind. The sailors all loved him. His virtues were "pristine and unadulterate." He was the Handsome Sailor, blessed with strength and beauty, of a lineage "favored by Love and the Graces," with a moral nature not "out of keeping with the physical make," "happily endowed with the gaiety of high health, youth, and a free heart." Vere calls him "a fellow creature innocent before God." The chaplain recognizes "the young sailor's essential innocence." Even Claggart feels that Billy's nature "its simplicity never willed malice."

Of course Billy cannot escape all responsibility for the consequences of his blow. He intended to hit Claggart, although possibly not full on the forehead. Intending the blow, Billy took upon himself the responsibility for the possible consequences. But should not his responsibility be limited because this was an unintended killing? At first thought, we agree. The law does not punish children; it does not punish the insane. An accidental killing is not murder. The law recognizes the difference between premeditated killing and killing in hot blood, or by provocation, or in fear. Should not Billy's innocent mind be considered in extenuation? But although modern law is more flexible than the Mutiny Act, its basic approach is similar; primarily it judges the action and not the man or his state of mind. The law stands at a distance from the crime and the criminal, and judges "objectively." And while such an approach may not satisfy the demands of divine justice, it is the only possible basis for human law. Justice Holmes, in *The Common Law,* says:

When we are dealing with that part of the law which aims more directly than any other at establishing standards of conduct, we should expect there more than elsewhere to find that the tests of liability are external, and independent of the degree of evil in the particular person's motives or intentions. The conclusion follows directly from the nature of the standards to which conformity is required. These are not only external, as was shown above, but they are of general application. They do not merely require that every man should get as near as he can to the best conduct possible for him. They require him at his own peril to come up to a certain height. They take no account of incapacities, unless the weakness is so marked as to fall into well-known exceptions, such as infancy or madness. They assume that every man is as able as every other to behave as they command. If they fall on any one class harder than on another, it is on the weakest. For it is precisely to those who are most likely to err by temperament, ignorance or folly, that the threats of the law are the most dangerous.

The problem of subjectivity is shown by the case of Dudley and Stephens. They were, for aught that appears, the most upright and God-fearing of men, perhaps even the real-life equivalents of Billy. Possibly their motives were wholly altruistic. Maybe they would actually have preferred death to eating the flesh of the boy, but felt responsibility to wives and children. The necessity for their killing was far greater than the need which directed Billy's arm. Perhaps they, too, were men incapable of malice.

The divine law of the Last Assizes, a law that judges the totality of man, is beyond human ability to administer; more, it is beyond human ability to *imagine.* Such justice must ever remain unknowable to humans. When Claggart, the lying Ananias, is killed, Vere exclaims "Struck dead by an angel of God! Yet the angel must hang!" But this is no paradox. Men cannot enforce divine judgements.

Human law must accept the fact that the mind is largely unknowable; that motives can seldom be ascertained. How are we to judge a man who kills because he *thought* the other was threatening his life, or because he *thought* the other had killed his child, or because he *thought* God had commanded him to do the act? In such cases, the law ordinarily resorts to some objective test of the supposed state of mind. In a case of self-defense, we do not simply ask the killer what he thought at the time. We seek to determine on an objective basis whether the victim was actually approaching with a weapon in circumstances where the killer had no reasonable opportunity to escape. Provocation must likewise be determined not only by reference to the state of mind of the person provoked (he may be hypersensitive, or even paranoid) but by an objective look at the nature of the provocation. To some extent all law, and even more so the military law, "looks but to the frontage, the appearance." In sum, human law looks primarily to men's actions, the one objective reality that is presented. Human law says that men are *defined* by their acts they are the sum total of their actions, and no more.

In this light, the initial conflict in *Billy Budd* can be reassessed. Billy is not innocent in the sense in which that term is used in resolving issues of justice. Billy is innocent in what he is, not what he does. The opposite of his Miltonic type of innocence is not guilt, but experience. The conflict is not a "catastrophe of innocence;" it is a conflict between society and Nature that contains—even in Billy's case—both good and evil. It is "catastrophe of Nature." His inability to adapt to society is the inability of nature to be civilized. Billy is incapable of acquiring experience. And the failing that leads to his execution in his incapacity to use the civilized man's weapon of speech. In society, natural forces cannot fight out their battles; Billy cannot use his physical strength to strike back at Claggart. The novel, then is not an analysis of Billy or of Claggart. Instead, it asks the question *how did it fare* with Billy in the year of the Great Mutiny?

Source: Charles A. Reich, "The Tragedy of Justice in *Billy Budd,*" *Yale Review,* Vol. 56, 1967, pp. 368-89.

Sources

Harrison Hayford and Merton M. Sealts, Jr., eds., preface by Herman Melville, *Billy Budd, Sailor: An Inside Narrative,* University of Chicago, 1962, pp.v-vii.

Susan Howe, *The Birth-mark: Unsettling the Wilderness in American Literary History,* Wesleyan University Press, 1993.

F. O. Matthiessen, *"Billy Budd, Foretopman,"* in his *American Renaissance: Art and Experience in the Age of Emerson and Whitman,* Oxford University Press, 1941.

Herman Melville, *Billy Budd, Sailor,* edited by Harrison Hayford and Merton S. Sealts, Jr., University of Chicago, 1962.

Herman Melville's obituary, *New York Times,* October 2, 1891.

Lewis Mumford, "Melville's Final Affirmation," in his *Herman Melville,* Harcourt, Brace, 1929, pp. 353-54.

William S. Reese, "Collecting Herman Melville," *The Gazette of the Grolier Club,* http://www.reeseco.com/papers/melville.htm.

W. Clark Russell, "A Claim for American Literature," in *North American Review,* February, 1892.

Peter Shaw, "The Fate of A Story," *American Scholar,* Vol. 62, No. 4, p. 591.

Raymond M. Weaver, *Herman Melville: Mariner and Mystic,* George H. Doran, 1921.

Raymond Weaver, editor, *Shorter Novels of Herman Melville,* Horace Liveright, 1928.

For Further Study

Gail Coffler, "Classical Iconography in the Aesthetics of *Billy Budd, Sailor,*" in *Savage Eye: Melville and the Visual Arts,* edited by Christopher Sten, Kent State University Press, 1991, pp. 257-76.
    Coffler analyzes Melville's abiding interest in ancient Greek and Roman myth, law, and art. Billy Budd, the character, is a combination of Greek beauty and Roman strength.

Mervyn Cook and Philip Reed, editors, *Benjamin Britten: Billy Budd,* Cambridge Opera Handbooks, Cambridge University Press, 1993.
    A synopsis of Britten's opera, which is based on Melville's novel. In addition to the synopsis, the book includes an explanation of the opera's literary roots, a discussion of the librettist's and composer's work, and an interpretation of the music's tonal symbolism.

Clark Davis, *After the Whale: Melville in the Wake of Moby-Dick,* University of Alabama Press, 1995.
    A book-length assessment of Melville's lesser-known writings that came after the publication of *Moby-Dick.* This book won the 1993 Elizabeth Agee Prize in American Literature.

Kieran Dolin, "Power, Chance and the Rule of Law—*Billy Budd, Sailor,*" in *Fiction and the Law: Legal Discourse in Victorian and Modernist Literature,* Cambridge University Press, 1999, pp. 121-44.
    Discusses *Billy Budd* as one of the first explorations of the connection between law and literature. Dolin analyzes how "natural law," which involves ambiguities, was being increasingly replaced by "legal positivism," or a belief that law might be a precise science. Dolin argues that this shift in thinking is portrayed negatively in Melville's novel.

Lawrence Douglas, "Discursive Limits: Narrative and Judgement in Billy Budd," *Mosaic,* Vol. 27, No. 4, December, 1994, pp. 141-160.
    According to Douglas, Melville's novel is one of the earliest dialogues between law and literature, which is useful to students of both disciplines since it explores crisis in the act of and the art of judgement.

James Dugan, *The Great Mutiny,* Putnam's, 1965.
    This book discusses in detail the 1797 mutinies in the British Royal Navy at Spithead and the Nore, and the events leading up to these uprisings.

H. Bruce Franklin, "Billy Budd and Capital Punishment: A Tale of Three Centuries," *American Literature,* June, 1997, pp. 337-59.

Franklin examines the novel in the context of the contemporary (1880s) debate on capital punishment, a controversy particular to New York, where Melville lived at the time. The debate considered which offenses, if any, should carry the death penalty, and the exceptions that should occur during war.

Leonard F. Guttridge, *Mutiny: A History of Naval Insurrection,* United States Naval Institute, 1992.

Beginning with the infamous mutiny on the *Bounty* in 1787, this book traces the history of mutiny in the U.S. Navy as well as in other navies around the world. Guttridge dispels some of the myths of mutiny and shows how instances of mutiny have often grown out of individuals' reactions to specific historic circumstances.

Myra Jehlen, editor, *Herman Melville: A Collection of Critical Essays,* Prentice Hall, 1994.

This excellent critical anthology collects essays written in the 1970s, 1980s, and 1990s, on all of Melville's work.

Barbara Johnson, "Melville's Fist: The Execution of 'Billy Budd,'" *Studies in Romanticism,* Winter, 1979, pp. 567-99.

Perhaps the most comprehensive analysis both of the criticism prior to 1979 and the novel's ambiguities.

Charles Larson, "Melville's Marvell and Vere's Fairfax," *ESQ,* Vol. 38, No. 1, 1992, pp. 59-70.

Criticism of the novel has often considered the impact of the American and French Revolutions. Larson suggests that the English Civil War of the mid-seventeenth century should also be noted because of the novel's reference to Andrew Marvell's Civil War poem "Upon Appleton House," which was dedicated to a Puritan army commander, Lord Thomas Fairfax—an "ancestor" of Melville's Captain Vere.

Robert Milder, *Critical Essays on Melville's Billy Budd, Sailor,* G.K. Hall, 1989.

A selection of critical essays on Melville's works, ranging over the course of his career, with an introduction by editor Milder.

Susan Mizruchi, "Cataloging the Creatures of the Deep: 'Billy Budd, Sailor' and the Rise of Sociology," *Boundary 2,* Spring, 1990, pp. 272-304.

Mizruchi sees *Billy Budd* as a critique of the emerging discipline of sociology, which claims to be written by expert observers, and which homogenizes differences between people.

Kathy J. Phillips, "Billy Budd as Anti-Homophobic Text," *College English,* December, 1994, pp. 896-910.

Phillips discusses her experience teaching *Billy Budd* in the college classroom. With the impeded or prohibited speech of Billy in mind, the class thinks about homosexuality in the novel, and how, in general, vi-

olence instead of dialogue has typified America's relationship with "other" sexualities.

Laurie Robertson-Lorant, *Melville: A Biography,* University of Massachusetts Press, 1998.

A biography of Melville that draws upon research into Melville family letters, looks at the Melville-Hawthorne friendship, considers Melville's sexuality, and attends closely to Melville's writings as well as to the critical responses to his works.

Nancy Ruttenburg, "Melville's Anxiety of Innocence: The Handsome Sailor," in *Democratic Personality: Popular Voice and the Trial of American Authorship,* Stanford University Press, 1998, pp. 344-78.

In the context of American literature and history before 1891, *Billy Budd,* Ruttenburg argues, represents in its title character a paramount instance of the desire for an ideal figure, both innocent and beautiful. Emerson and Whitman had suggested and valorized this figure. Melville rejects it as an embodiment of an idealized American.

Eve Kosofsky Sedgwick, *"Billy Budd:* After the Homosexual," in *Epistemology of the Closet,* University of California Press, 1990, pp. 92-130.

This essay describes John Claggart as a homosexual, and considers the meaning of that man's death. Moreover, the entire cast of characters relate to one another according to male desire and intimacy. Like Johnson, Sedgwick undoes binary structure—this time between gay and straight. Sedgwick asks, Does male desire stabilize order, or disrupt it?

William T. Stafford, editor, *Melville's Billy Budd and the Critics,* second edition, Wadsworth, 1968.

This comprehensive collection of essays is helpfully arranged by themes and critical debates.

Christopher Sten, "Vere's Use of the 'Forms': Means and Ends in *Billy Budd,*" *American Literature,* March, 1975, pp. 37-51.

Sten compares Vere's authorship of Billy's trial and execution to Melville's authorship of Vere, and analyzes the motivations of each man.

Brook Thomas, "*Billy Budd* and the Judgement of Silence," *Bucknell Review,* Vol. 27, 1983, pp. 51-78.

Thomas examines Barbara Johnson's assessment of *Billy Budd,* and questions the political implications of her deconstruction of the text.

Howard P. Vincent, editor, *Twentieth Century Interpretations of Billy Budd,* Prentice-Hall, 1971.

Not as useful as Milder, Stafford, or Jehlen's compilations, Vincent's collection is divided into two sections, "Interpretations" and "View Points," indicating a loose gathering of responses to Melville and his final novel.

Deliverance

James Dickey
1970

When James Dickey's *Deliverance* was published in 1970, it was an immediate critical and popular hit. Critics and the general public also applauded the movie that was adapted from the novel by Dickey and released two years later. These two accomplishments were considered outstanding achievements for a writer who before *Deliverance* was known for his poetry. Like a poet, Dickey identified themes and images in his novel that resonate throughout the American psyche. His novel consists of adventure, suspicion, and murder in a natural setting.

In the book, four ordinary suburban men take a canoe trip through the wild hills of north Georgia, hoping to get away from their regulated, sterile lives for a weekend. Along the way they are accosted by uncivilized backwoods dwellers, and the travelers soon find themselves dealing with murder, a cover-up, and more murder and deceit. With sweeping descriptions and precise details, Dickey portrays the development of the novel's narrator, Ed Gentry, as he learns the ways of the forest and the river in his fight for his own survival. As he becomes more primitive, Ed finds himself grateful for this opportunity to live life to its fullest.

Author Biography

James Dickey's life was remarkable for the number of his vocations, any one of which could have kept another person busy for a lifetime. He was a soldier, a teacher, a hunter, a novelist, and

an advertising executive. Most of all, though, he was a poet, having produced a number of outstanding, award-winning volumes of poetry. Poetry was the main vocation that he claimed, and it was as a poet that he defined himself.

Dickey was born in 1923, in Buckhead, a suburb of Atlanta. His family was wealthy. In high school and college, he participated on the football team, but after his first year at Clemson, he enrolled in the Air Corps. During World War II, Dickey flew nearly a hundred missions in the Pacific. He claimed that it was while he was in the army that he started writing poetry, although he did not publish any until later. On returning from the war Dickey enrolled in Vanderbilt University, where he earned his bachelor's degree in English in 1949 and his master's in 1950. In 1956, teaching at the University of Florida, Dickey was in the middle of a controversy over a reading of his poem "The Father's Body," which some faculty members considered obscene. Angered by what he perceived as censorship, he went to work for a New York advertising agency, working his way up to an executive position before transferring to an Atlanta firm. While he was successful in advertising, he kept writing poetry. His first collection of poems, *Into the Stone, and Other Poems,* was published, and the following year, after winning a Guggenheim Fellowship, he quit advertising.

During the 1960s, Dickey was poet-in-residence at several colleges, and he published several more books, winning a National Book Award in 1966 for *Buckdancer's Choice.* In 1968 he became a professor of English at University of South Carolina, a position that he held until his death in 1997. *Deliverance,* his first novel, was published in 1970, and it became an immediate success. After the book's success and the success of the 1972 movie adaptation for which he wrote the script (and in which he appears briefly), Dickey became a popular speaker on college campuses, and he spent much of his time in the following years giving poetry readings. He wrote a poem for the inauguration of President Jimmy Carter in 1977, and published several volumes of poems for children. He published one more novel, *Alnilam,* in 1987, but it met with only modest critical success and lukewarm public attention.

James Dickey

take through the hills in the northern part of Georgia, where they encounter clannish, primitive people and hazardous natural conditions. Those who survive return to civilization feeling transformed by their experience. The novel starts out the day before the trip, with the four principal characters meeting in a bar to finalize their plans. Lewis Medford is the most dynamic of the group, the outdoorsman who has been to this river before, an avid hunter and fisherman. Bobby Trippe is a salesman of mutual funds, an amiable bachelor with a sarcastic sense of humor who enjoys comfort more than conquest. Drew Ballinger is a family man and a devoted employee of a huge soda pop company modeled on Coca-Cola. The narrator of the book is Ed Gentry: he is somewhat of an outdoorsman, in that he fires arrows for target practice with Lewis, but he is also a family man and a businessman, co-owner of an advertising firm. At the initial meeting all of the men agree to join Lewis, but each wants to bring one possession. Ed wants to bring his bow and arrows. Drew wants to bring his old Martin guitar. Bobby wants to bring liquor.

Ed goes back to his office, where he has to shoot photographs for a new ad layout. The ad, for a line of women's underwear, is to feature a young model wearing nothing but the underwear and holding a cat. While positioning her for the picture, Ed

Plot Summary

Before

James Dickey's novel *Deliverance* is about a canoeing trip that four men from suburban Atlanta notices a peculiarity in her eye, a golden glow. As soon as it strikes him, "she changed completely: she looked like someone who had come to womanhood in less than a minute."

September 14th

The first day of the trip starts with Ed waking in bed next to his wife, Martha. She questions whether it is her fault that he is going, if she is the reason he feels discontent with his ordinary life, and so they make love. Lewis comes soon after to pick him up, and they take off for the river. "Here we go," Lewis says as they take off, setting the tone for what's to come, "out of the sleep of mild people, into the wild rippling water." On the drive, they have a long discussion about their differing philosophies of life. For Lewis, life is a series of physical challenges, preparing himself for the day that society will break down and he and his family will have to survive on the canned goods and few other items that they have packed away in their fallout shelter. Ed explains his way of life as "sliding": living with the least friction, the most comfort.

In Oree, where they plan to take off, Bobby and Drew join them. They stop at a small country store to buy supplies and to hire someone to drive the cars down river so that they'll be there when the trip is done. At the store they meet a strange-looking albino boy, whose eyes look off in different directions. The boy plays a duet with Drew on his banjo, and gives the impression that he lacks intelligence, but he plays beautifully, providing a sign that something more artistic than intelligence is valued by the mountain people. At Griner Brothers' Garage, they are met with some hostility while trying to negotiate a price for having their cars delivered. Lewis is rough in offering less than what Griner is asking, but he also is confident in the honesty of these rural people and he fully expects the cars to be in the right place the next day. Both the old man at the grocery store and Griner express some skepticism as to why anyone would want to take a trip down the Cahulawasse River.

As the canoeists begin their journey, they glide through some peaceful scenery. They soon ride into a stretch of water filled with feathers and one decapitated chicken head as they pass a town with a chicken-processing plant. The water soon becomes calm and clean, and after a while they stop for the night. Their camp the first night is restful after hours of paddling. Drew plays the guitar, and they drink bourbon and eat steaks. During the night, an owl rests on top of Ed's tent, scratching through the nylon with its talons, like a mystical sign of nature seeking him out.

September 15th

Before the others are awake in the morning, Ed goes out into the fog-enshrouded forest, where he sees a deer. He fires two of his four arrows at the deer, but psychologically he is unable to kill it—his head jerks just before the arrow flies. Ed takes Bobby as his canoe partner because Bobby is complaining about the discomfort of his tent and the blandness of the camping food, and Ed is afraid Lewis will not put up with his complaining. The day trip is slow and leisurely.

At one point in the afternoon, when Ed and Bobby stop on the riverbank to rest, two men with a shotgun come out of the woods. The unknown men ask Bobby and Ed what they are doing there; Bobby insults them, and Ed inadvertently insults them even more by implying that they may be moonshiners. The men make Bobby and Ed march back into the woods. There, they tie Ed to a tree and make Bobby take off his pants and stretch across a log, and one of the men rapes him. The other man is just about to rape Ed when an arrow shot by Lewis, who has found his friends being attacked, goes through him from behind. The other attacker runs off into the woods.

There is a debate about what to do with the dead man's corpse. Drew supports taking it to the next town and telling the local authorities what happened. They all agree, however, that that would lead to a jury trial, and that the jurors in this part of the state would look on the four men as malevolent strangers. As Lewis puts it, "I'm goddamned if I want to come back up here for shooting this guy in the back, with a jury made up of his cousins and brothers, maybe his mother and father too, for all I know." They eventually decide to take the body into the woods, up a stream that branches off of the river, and to bury it in a lonely place. With that done, they leave that spot as quickly as they can.

They travel well for about an hour. As they approach turbulent water, Drew jerks upright and drops his paddle, turning the boat over and sending himself and Ed into the rough water. After struggling to survive the rapids, being dragged under water, and crashed against rocks, Ed surfaces downstream and finds Bobby and Lewis also thrown from their canoe. Lewis is suffering from a broken leg and, at this point, there is no sign of Drew. With one wounded and only one canoe, they are faced with the prospect that the partner of the man they killed is on a hill above the river waiting to shoot them all. Ed decides that someone has to climb up the rock cliff, up to where the man with the gun is, and kill him with a knife or an arrow. Since Bobby is too out of shape to climb a cliff, and he does not know how to shoot an arrow, it is up to Ed to do it. He starts his climb, torturously feeling out handholds, and at one point he stops with absolutely nothing onto which he can hold and keep from falling. Just as his strength is about to give out, he finds the slightest crack in the rock under one of his fingers, and, with renewed hope, pushes himself up into an open crevice.

September 16th

The last day of the trip begins with Ed in the crevice. After resting for a short while, he continues his ascent to the top and thinks about how he will kill the man. In thinking about him—who he is, what he wants, what assumptions he will make, and the way he will read the terrain—Ed realizes that he understands this man, that his mind knows exactly what he will do. At the top of the gorge, Ed looks for the place that the other man will think is the right place for shooting down at the river, and he climbs up a nearby tree and waits. A man with a shotgun comes along. Ed is not entirely certain that this is the man who was going to rape him, but when the man discovers him in the tree, he decides to move fast, and kills him with an arrow. The recoil of the shot makes him fall out of the tree, landing on the point of the other arrow, and he blacks out. When he awakens, he has to cut the arrow out of his side, and he tracks the trail of blood to find where the man has gone to die. After finding the body, he lowers it down from the top of the gorge with a rope and climbs down after it. He and Bobby tie rocks to the body and drop it out in the middle of the river.

After a while of proceeding down the river, they find Drew's body lolling against the shore. Neither Ed nor Bobby can tell if the wound on his head is a gunshot wound, or possibly a gash that he got rolling through the rapids. Lewis, near fainting from the pain of his broken leg, assures them that Drew's skull was grazed by a bullet. If it is a gunshot wound, the authorities will want to know who killed him and why, opening up an investigation into the other deaths. Thus, they tie rocks to Drew and drop his body in the river too. Further downriver, they decide on a place by a big yellow tree that they all will swear is where Drew fell out,

so that the authorities will not go looking for his body anywhere near where he really is.

At a point where a road passes over the river, they stop the canoe, and Ed walks up the road until he finds a gas station. The attendant calls for an ambulance, which comes for him and then has him take them to Lewis. The county sheriff's deputy asks a few questions, and Lewis is taken to the hospital. At the hospital, a doctor also sews up the arrow wound in Ed's side, and then drives him to the cars, which the Griner brothers brought down to Aintry, as planned. Ed and Bobby spend the night at a boardinghouse in town.

After

In the morning the sheriff's department raises some questions about their story: Bobby had told them that Drew had fallen out of the second canoe, but that canoe was found further upstream from where they said Drew had been lost. One of the sheriff's deputies is very hostile to them. It turns out that this deputy's sister had told him that her husband went hunting in the woods, in the area where the men were canoeing, and that he had never come home. The deputy is certain that they had something to do with his brother-in-law's disappearance, but the sheriff does not take him seriously. Ed argues back with the deputy, challenging him to find some evidence or to leave them alone. The sheriff permits them to leave.

Arriving home, Ed is reluctant to tell his wife what happened. She is very understanding, helping him redress his wound, and she goes with him to break the news about Drew's death to his wife. In the years that follow, Ed dreams about the river, now dammed up to form Lake Cahula. Bobby leaves town, but Ed and Lewis remain friends.

Characters

Drew Ballinger

Drew is a devoted family man who dies on the river. Before his death, he works for a large soft drink company and is loyal to them—he only shows anger when the company's good reputation is questioned. He is an excellent guitarist and brings his guitar along on the canoe trip, playing a duet with the banjo-playing albino boy at the grocery store where they stop for provisions. After the first death, it is Drew who argues for going to the authorities and explaining what has happened, but he is voted down by Lewis and the others. Further down the

Deliverance was made into a highly acclaimed film in 1972, starring Jon Voight (left) as Ed and Burt Reynolds (right) as Lewis.

river, Drew falls out of the canoe just as they approach some rapids. Ed, who was sitting behind him, is not sure that he was shot, but Lewis says that he was. When his body is found later it is not clear whether the gash on his head was caused by a bullet or by a rock that he hit. While burying his corpse in the river, Ed says, "You were the best of us, Drew … The only decent one; the only sane one." Drew is survived by a wife and a son, Pope, who has a deformity, a "hornlike blood blister" on his forehead, which the narrator describes as a reminder of "the true horrors of biology."

Sheriff Bullard

Sheriff Bullard is the sheriff of Helms County, where the canoe trip takes place. When Ed and Bobby return with their story that they lost Drew "on the river," Sheriff Bullard is skeptical of their story, but he is even more willing to believe that the missing brother-in-law of his deputy has disappeared for some reason that is unrelated to them. "And buddy, let me tell you one thing," he says to Ed as they are parting. "Don't ever do anything like this again. Don't come back up here." In part, his advice is meant for the canoeists' safety, an acknowledgment of the close call that they had on the river, but it is also a thinly veiled acknowledgment

that he knows there is probably something illegitimate about them that he just does not have the evidence to pursue.

Thad Emerson

Thad Emerson is Ed Gentry's business partner in Emerson-Gentry.

Dean Gentry

Dean Gentry is Ed's son.

Ed Gentry

The book's narrator, Ed Gentry is the vice president and art director for Emerson-Gentry, a small advertising agency. He is satisfied with his life before the trip, with his wife, Martha, and their son, Dean. He feels both that he is the master of his world and that he is enslaved by it. On the street after his lunch break, Ed looks around and finds himself surrounded by women, with no other men in sight. He develops an attraction for the Kitt'n Britches model who poses mostly nude for his camera, thinking of her periodically throughout the story. During the canoe trip, Ed is with Bobby when he is raped, and only escapes rape himself when Lewis intervenes. When Lewis is injured and Drew dies, it is up to Ed to take control of the situation, and from within himself he summons the mental and physical forces that allow him to scale a sheer cliff, kill a man, dispose of the body of a close friend, take control of the boat through raging rapids, and to boldly lie to the authorities about all that has happened.

Ed undergoes several changes while hunting the man that he thinks of as his enemy. At one point, he feels that his mind and the other man's have fused: "It was not that I felt myself turning evil, but that an enormous physical indifference, as vast as the whole abyss of light at my feet, came to me: an indifference not only to the other man's body scrambling and kicking on the ground with an arrow through it, but to mine." In shooting the other man he falls on his other arrow, which "opens him up," solidifying their spiritual union. After the trip, Ed fears when he hears a car outside that someone is coming for him, but he also feels a new source of strength for coping with the world. As he puts it, "The river underlies everything I do," including the art collages that he returns to making, years after having given up art, and the target archery that he still faithfully pursues.

Martha Gentry

Martha Gentry, an ex-nurse, is Ed's wife.

Griner

Griner is one of the proprietors of Griner Brothers' Garage. The men hire the two Griner brothers, plus a third man, to drive their cars down to the Aintry so that they will be there when the canoe trip is finished. Lewis bargains for a price with Griner, talking him down. He is confident that the backwoods people will be true to their words once the bargain is agreed upon. When the ambulance takes them back to Aintry after being treated in the hospital, both cars are there. Ed is certain to make sure that Griner gets the message that the rest of the money promised to him will be delivered.

George Holley

George Holley is a former employee of Ed's advertising agency who took his artistry seriously, which made Ed uneasy. He hung prints of paintings by French painter Maurice Utrillo in his cubicle and "was always talking about applying Braque's collage techniques to the layouts we were getting ready for fertilizer layouts and wood-pulp processing plants." Sometime after the river journey, Holley is rehired by the agency, where he becomes a fan of Ed's art collages and becomes Ed's best friend, next to Lewis.

Media Adaptations

- *Deliverance* was made into a major motion picture in 1972, with Burt Reynolds as Lewis, Jon Voigt as Ed, Ned Beatty as Bobby, and James Dickey himself in the minor role of Sheriff Buford. The script was written by Dickey and the film was directed by John Boorman.

- James Dickey is included on Caedmon's six-audio-cassette package, *Contemporary Authors Reading from Their Own Works,* along with Ernest Hemingway, William Faulkner, John Updike, and Tennessee Williams. Released in 1955, the cassettes were re-released in 1973.

- An interview of Dickey talking about *Deliverance* is available on a 1987 audio-cassette from New Letters.

Kitt'n Britches model

Early in the novel Ed has a photo shoot at his advertising agency for an ad for a line of women's underwear, Kitt'n Britches. He photographs a young woman wearing only her underpants, holding a cat. She has an irregularity in her eye, a "gold-glowing mote" that Ed thinks about several times during the canoe trip, comparing it to the moon's reflection on the water as a source of inspiration. After the trip, he mentions having taken her out for dinner a few times and having worked with her again on some occasions before losing interest.

Lonnie

Lonnie is the strange albino boy who plays a duet with Lewis on his banjo. Despite the fact that he is apparently retarded, his banjo-playing is impressive.

Shad Mackey

Lewis tells a story about a time when he was canoeing with Shad Mackey: Shad went off into the woods by himself and didn't return by nightfall. In the meantime, Lewis had made the acquaintance with one of the backwoods mountain men. The mountain man sent his son out into the darkness to find Shad, and eventually he brought him back with a broken leg. After he tells the story, Ed says that he never liked Shad very much, and Lewis agrees: "Not a good man. Drinks too much in an uncreative way. Talks too much. Doesn't deliver enough, either on the river or in business or, I'm fairly sure, in bed with his wife or anybody else, either."

Tom McCaskill

Tom McCaskill is a legendary wild man in the forest. Every few weeks, legend has it, McCaskill takes a jug of liquor out into the woods, lights a fire, gets drunk, and lets out loud, piercing screams.

Lewis Medlock

Lewis Medlock is the person who thinks up the canoe trip, the only one of the group to have any experience on the Cahulawassee River. He is a real estate man and a landlord. He is also an outdoorsman, bowhunter, and weightlifter, who is driven to mastering new challenges and excelling at physical tests. In regard to Lewis's devotion to physical activity, Ed says, "He had everything life could give, and he couldn't make it work. And he couldn't bear to give it up or see age take it away from him, either, because in the meantime he might be able to find what it was he wanted, the thing that must be there, and subject it to his will."

It is clear that Ed idolizes Lewis because he keeps seeking his approval, which he accepts like a blessing. To a limited extent, his idolization is justified. Lewis is cool under pressure, as when he appears out of nowhere, godlike, at the moment of Ed and Bobby's worst nightmare, to kill an armed man with his bow and arrow. When they go down the rapids, though, Lewis is incapacitated by a broken thighbone: while in an earlier chapter he had talked about walking three miles through the woods with a broken leg to safety, he spends the last half of this book in a pain-induced, feverish delirium. He speaks with complete confidence and lucidity when he declares the wound on Drew's skull to be from a gunshot grazing him, although Ed, possibly having lost some of his hero-worship, continues to have doubts about his assessment. At the end of the book, some time after the canoeing trip, Ed and Lewis own cabins on Lake Cahula, "on the other side of the state," and they shoot archery together. As a result of the trip, Lewis ends up with a mellower, more spiritual, personality: "he knows dying is better than immortality."

Deputy Sheriff Arthel Queen

Arthel Queen is the deputy sheriff of Helms County. Deputy Queen suspects right away that there is something false about the story that the men tell when they arrive back in civilization. He links them to the disappearance of his brother-in-law, saying that he has "a feeling" about their involvement, "And I ain't ever wrong about that." Ed is as forceful in his opposition to Deputy Queen as the deputy is about his insistence of their guilt. He calls Queen a "little bastard" and tells him, if he doubts that the river killed Drew, that he should "get [his] stupid ass on it and see for [him]self." The sheriff treats Deputy Queen as a fanatic who is blaming the men because they are "city fellows," implying Queen's deep country roots.

Benson Stovall

It is uncertain, but likely, that the man that Ed Gentry kills on top of the bluff is Benson Stovall. Deputy Queen's brother-in-law Benson is declared missing from the woods at the time that Ed kills the man; the man Ed kills has a card in his pocket saying that his name is Stovall and that he is a deputy sheriff of Helms County (although, as Lewis once pointed out, nearly everyone living in that region is a deputy sheriff); also, the man Ed shoots has dentures, which does not agree with his memory of the gruesome teeth on the man who assaulted them earlier. It is Sheriff Bullard's opinion that Benson, the deputy's brother-in-law, is not actually hurt. "Aw, he'll come in drunk," he tells Ed. "He's a mean bastard anyway. Old Queen's sister'd be better off without him. So would everybody else." Whether or not Benson and Stovall are the same person (a question Ed could easily clear up by asking the brother-in-law's last name), there is still a wide-open question about whether or not he was the one who participated in the molestation in the woods.

Bobby Trippe

Bobby Trippe is the weakest member of the group. He is overweight and out of shape, a bachelor with a perpetual good mood; a "born salesman." Bobby's one condition for this canoe trip is that he has to bring liquor along. After the first night on the river, he is the one who becomes exasperated—on the first morning he wants to give up and go home because of all of the discomforts. Ed takes Bobby in as his canoe partner because he is afraid that Lewis will become too impatient with Bobby's weakness. When they are accosted by two backwoodsmen, Bobby angers them with a facetious remark, and they end up sodomizing him. When Ed has to climb the cliffside to kill the man they think is stalking them, he orders Bobby to move out in the canoe in the first light. When he sees the canoe on the river later in the morning, he aims the gun he is holding at Bobby's chest. Back in civilization, Bobby proves quite adept at sticking to the lies that Ed has ordered him to follow. In the end, months after the incidents on the river, Ed says that "he had returned to the affable, faintly nasty manner he had always had, and I was as glad as not to leave him alone; he would always look like dead weight and like screaming, and that was no good to me." Ed hears from acquaintances that Bobby eventually moved to Hawaii.

Wilma

Wilma is the secretary of Ed's business partner, Thad. She is mentioned only twice, with references to her mouth. In the early scene at the advertising agency she is referred to as "mean-mouthed," and, when Ed is preparing to tie a rope to the body of the man he killed and lower it down the cliff, the dead face irritates him: "irritates me more than anything had in a long time; irritated me more than the set of Thad's secretary's— Wilma's—mouth and her tiresome, hectoring personality posing as duty."

Themes

Strength and Weakness

Lewis is, without a doubt, held up in this novel as an ideal of masculine strength. The narrator describes him as "one of the strongest men I had ever shaken hands with," and repeatedly points out the trials of physical endurance with which he challenges himself. Even more importantly, though, is that he is presented as having the psychological strength to overcome difficulty. His physical strength, as Lewis himself explains it, is just a tool to prepare him for a time he foresees in the near future when society will collapse, when people who rely on their social skills and positions will find themselves unable to survive. "Life is so fucked-up now, and so complicated, that I wouldn't mind if it came down, right quick, to the bare survival of who was ready to survive." One apocryphal story of Lewis's strength is when he broke his leg in the woods while fishing by himself and hopped three miles to his car. He then used a stick to push the gas pedal to drive it. On the canoe trip, though, the

Topics for Further Study

- Research the Depression-era Tennessee Valley Authority dam project, referred to in the novel as TVA. Report on how river damming affects rural life.

- In the end, Ed Gentry returns to his artistic interests, producing collages from newspaper pictures. Paste together a collage that you feel represents this novel, with pictures and headlines that capture the essence of particular moments.

- When he is taking aim at the mountain man, Ed explains that one must aim higher than seems necessary when one is shooting from above their target. Explain this fact.

- "I think machines are going to fail, the political systems are going to fail, and a few men are going to take to the hills and start over," Lewis tells Ed early in the story. Today, this view is even more prevalent in our society than it was when this novel was written. Research a separatist militia that Lewis might have joined, looking for points where their philosophy might disagree with his.

- Organize a class debate about whether hunting with a bow and arrow is morally superior to hunting with firearms.

- Hold a trial for Ed, Bobby, and Lewis for the murder of Deputy Queen's brother-in-law and/or for murdering Drew. Imagine what evidence, besides the actual bodies, an investigation might bring up. Try to convince jurors of possible motives for these crimes.

break in his leg is much more severe, up near the thigh: he does talk when spoken to, but for the most part the pain overcomes his strength, causing him to vomit and pass out.

Bobby, on the other hand, is the novel's example of weakness. He is fat and talkative: he "would not have been displeased if someone called him a born salesman." By the second morning of the trip, Bobby is complaining that he wants to go home, that the food is bad, and the tent is uncomfortable. As the story continues, Bobby and Ed are confronted by two rugged men who victimize them—one even rapes Bobby. Lewis, the strong character, comes to Bobby and Ed's rescue by sneaking up during the attack and killing Bobby's rapist.

Rites of Passage

The canoe trip represents a ritual that transforms Ed, the narrator, several times along the way. On the morning that he leaves home, while in Lewis's car, he contemplates the difference he sees in himself: "We were not—or at least I was not—what we were before." Later, when Ed relates the story of missing the deer with his arrow, he tells Lewis that he wishes Lewis had been there to take the shot, showing a confidence in Lewis's hunting skills. This confidence proves well-founded when Lewis is later able to kill a mountain man with one perfect shot through his back.

The rite of passage continues for Ed as he climbs up the rock cliff in an effort to stop the attacker. During this strenuous exertion, Ed recognizes that he is an element of nature, which helps him make a more difficult shot than Lewis did. The wound he incurs after killing the supposed attacker transforms Ed: "There had never been a freedom like it. The pain itself was freedom, and the blood." The arrow that he falls on, as he mentions several times, "opened" him up. For the rest of the trip Ed has increased awareness of the forces of nature, especially of the river. He has little patience for social amenities: he bullies and threatens Bobby and the Deputy Sheriff Queen. In the end, Ed reflects on how the river, which has been destroyed by the dam, still exists within his mind, and the friend and the enemy who were buried in the river are buried within his mind, too.

Identity

In this story, Ed goes through a process in which he finds himself identifying with different elements in the forest. The first night an owl lands on his tent, Ed reaches up and touches its talon. After that he imagines he can see what the owl sees when it flies up over the woods, hunting prey. When the men are carrying the body of the rapist upstream, Ed feels his identity meld with those of his three friends: "I bound myself with my brain and heart to the others; with them was the only way I would ever get out." When the canoe is turned over, he is thrown into the tumbling rapids and he

feels himself "fading out into the unbelievable violence and cruelty of the river, joining it." From that point on he is as violent and uncaring as nature, a killer. While hunting the man that he expects to find up on the bluff, Ed feels his mind "fuse" with the other man, so that he can anticipate his actions and predict where he will be and when. This fusion is so complete that after the man is dead Ed takes his gun and aims at Bobby, as the man would have. It is so complete that when he returns to the canoe, Ed talks like a backwoods man: "I killed him, and I'd kill him again, only better," he tells Bobby.

Natural Law

Trying to decide what to do once the first backwoodsman is dead, Lewis asks if anybody knows anything about the law. The best that the four men can come up with is that Drew was on a jury once. When Drew later points out that the murder of their first attacker is a matter for the law, Lewis responds, "You see any law around here? We're the law." The multiple killings in this book take place out in the wilderness, where the laws of courts and the judicial system do not apply, and these four men are left with the problem of determining justice themselves. The first killing is clearly justified—he had committed a heinous act, and was about to commit another. It becomes a little more complex regarding the man who may have shot Drew from the ridge—was it justified? A life for a life? By the time that Ed ascends the cliff and kills a man on top, the law of nature that commands self-preservation forces him to ignore the complication that this might not be the right man. When they return to civilization, they feel that the rights granted by the fight for survival still protect them, and they lie brazenly to the authorities who they feel have no right to question their actions.

Style

Setting

Dickey's fictional stretch of the Cahulawassee River between Oree and Aintry of Helms County, Georgia, is a thinly veiled version of the Coosawatee River between Ellijay and Carter's Quarters in Georgia's Rabun County. This setting is ideal for the story. The river has multiple levels of significance. It is a metaphor for the flow of life, for the lifeblood that flows through veins the way that water threads through a gorge. It represents the passage of time and becomes a character in the novel, with its own particular moments of anger and acts of kindness. It is a mirror of the narrator's subconscious, with bodies buried beneath its surface, and it can be interpreted as a culture on the verge of being sunk by the technology that dams its path. Dickey uses a setting that allows for the presence of scary, uncivilized characters; transportation that leaves the main characters vulnerable; and a body of water that moves the characters briskly from one situation to the next. Most importantly, the state of Georgia provides a stark contrast in setting in just a few hours of travel, from suburban Atlanta to the most primitive part of the Appalachians.

Narrator

Ed is the narrator, and is able to understand and explain the thoughts and actions of each character. Ed points out that Drew, the father of a deformed son, is the one who has the most invested in corporate life—he is offended if a competitor makes an false comment about his employers, and he shows his commitment to his company by keeping the company's official history on his coffee table at home. Although Ed prides himself on his company's nonassertiveness, he still is a vice president and co-owner, and by definition a corporate man. He is also a father, like Drew. Ed is less open about what he has in common with Bobby in his narration, possibly because there is so little admirable about him—he is a joker and a slick socializer, entirely inappropriate for the events of the weekend. Ed does note that Bobby "gave me the impression that he shared some kind of understanding with me that neither of us was to take Lewis too seriously." Though Ed's view of Lewis is critical at times, the bond between Ed and Lewis is strong, bordering on sexual. In his narrative, Ed is able to provide insight on Lewis and his intense love for the wilderness. It is thought that another narrator, such as Bobby, who also survives the trip, may not have represented the ideas of all of the men with as much understanding.

Doppelganger

A doppelganger is a character that represents the mirror image, or the dark, evil side, of another character's personality. Often in literature they are ghosts or other supernatural spirits used by authors to make protagonists come to grips with the aspects of themselves that they would like to ignore. In *Deliverance,* the mirror image to which Ed is bound is the man on the ridge. In order to hunt him, Ed finds that he has to *become* him, to some extent: he has to think just like him and read the signs just like the other man would. "I had thought so long and hard about him that to this day I still believe I felt, in the moonlight, our minds fuse," Ed tells the reader. After he has shot the man (and, incidentally, given himself an arrow wound at the same time, further indicating their bond), Ed tracks him down by crawling along the ground, feeling his blood, and even smelling it at times. Sometimes he finds what might be his own blood, and he has to assertively remind himself, "You haven't been here yet," uncertain of whether he is himself or the other man. Standing over the dead body of the other man, Ed considers eating him, as a primitive act of incorporating the man's spirit into his own.

Symbolism

It is difficult to separate many of the more poignant aspects of this adventure from their meaning. The banjo/guitar duet, for example, may be considered symbolic of the union of a civilized human with one who is inbred, but it could also be considered an actual, not a symbolic, relationship. One symbol that is mentioned consciously, and has no other purpose in the narrator's life except symbolism, is the half-moon mote that he sees in the eye of the Kitt'n Britches model. From the very first, this image is talked about as something that goes beyond its obvious significance: "it hit me with, I knew right away, strong powers," the narrator says. "It was not only recallable, but would come back of itself." This might be a symbol of beauty, longing, or the mysteries of the world. Or it may be a combination of all three. As he proceeds down the river, Ed sees this symbol in the moon on the water and, strangely, in the "yellow-tinged eyeballs" of the man who nearly rapes Ed. In the end, Ed says that the girl's "gold-halved eye had lost its fascination. Its place was in the night river, in the land of impossibility."

Historical Context

Aftermath of Civil Rights

In recent years, "militias" of white men in camouflage fatigues, gathering at camps in the woods to learn to protect themselves with weapons and survive on the land, resistant to government intrusion, have become common. Separatists who have attracted national attention include the Weaver family that had an armed confrontation with federal agents

Compare & Contrast

- **1970:** Americans are beginning to realize that the natural environment is in danger. The first Earth Day celebration is held on April 21. The Environmental Protection Agency is established and the Clean Air Act is passed.

  Today: Recycling is a way of life for most Americans, who realize that the water, earth, and sky are closed systems that cannot continually accept refuse.

- **1970:** The idea that drugs and music offered freedom from society's confining rules lost much of its credibility when Janis Joplin and Jimi Hendrix, both twenty-seven years old, die of drug overdoses.

  Today: High-profile celebrities still die of drug overdoses, but popular musicians are seen less as emblems of freedom and more as corporate products.

- **1970:** Several college campuses are closed in the spring because of riots protesting the Vietnam War. At Kent State, in Ohio, National Guardsmen open fire on protesters, killing four.

  Today: During the Gulf War and the military action against Bosnia in 1999, public opposition never rises to significant levels. Reasons for this include: both actions are over quickly; they are air wars, with Americans dropping bombs instead of dying in combat; and the government is more careful about limiting media access.

- **1970:** A special jury rules that a 1969 raid of the apartment of the Black Panthers, a revolutionary group, is justified, even though there is little evidence that anyone in the apartment fired back at the barrage of gunfire from the police.

  Today: The "underground" movement is more like what Lewis Medford imagines in *Deliverance:* people live in uncultivated areas of the country and train themselves in survival skills, waiting for the government to collapse.

- **1970:** The characters in the novel worry about the modern world becoming too complicated, encroaching on the individual's identity. Computers are run by integrated circuit boards, making them huge and slow, suited only for businesses. The first microchip, the Intel 4004, is introduced the following year.

  Today: Computers have made it possible to hold the information from shelves of books on a small disk. There is controversy about whether a wallet-sized card loaded with an individual's medical history would be helpful, in case of accidents, or subject to invasion of privacy abuse.

---

at Ruby Ridge in 1992; the Branch Davidian followers of charismatic religious leader David Koresh, whose standoff against Federal Bureau of Investigation (FBI) agents ended in the incineration of their bunker in 1993; and Timothy McVeigh, convicted of the bombing of a federal office building in 1995. Sociologists explain the behaviors of these and other groups like them as stemming from the sense of betrayal felt by white males after the civil rights advances made by women and minorities in the 1960s, which they feel diminished their social advantage.

At the start of the 1960s, positions of power in America were controlled, with few exceptions, by people who were white and male. The Civil Rights movement had made some gains for blacks in the 1950s, but these were mostly gains in the rights to participate in public discourse. The 1956 boycott in Montgomery, Alabama, changed the segregation rules, but that only allowed African Americans to ride buses. The landmark 1954 Supreme Court case *Brown v. the Board of Education* led to outlawing segregation in schools, but it did not guarantee blacks an equal place in society. The slow progress toward racial equality and the opposition of southern Congressional leaders to the 1964 Civil Rights Act that outlawed discrimination on the basis of color throughout the country led to frustration by blacks and the growing need to make their frustration noticed. In urban areas, race riots broke out throughout the latter 1960s, including the Watts section of Los Angeles in 1965; Chicago and Cleveland in 1966; and 127 U.S. cities in 1967. Black militants called for burning cities to the ground and killing police.

At the same time that blacks were becoming more vocal, the Women's Movement was on the rise. Much has been made of the fact that the widespread availability of the birth control pill in the 1960s gave women the freedom to explore sexuality without fear of unwanted pregnancy. It was a time of heightened consciousness about the rights of people who had previously been thought happy in subservient roles. The Women's Movement flourished in the 1960s. In 1966, the influential National Organization for Women (NOW) was formed, with activist Betty Friedan as its first president. The practice of burning bras to show freedom from shackles of confinement reached its peak in 1968. From 1964 to 1974, the divorce rate doubled, as married women from traditional homes realized that they could survive in the world without their husbands.

To white males, the advances toward liberation made by blacks and women seemed to be made at their expense. Civil rights protesters, as well as the young protesters on college campuses who opposed the war, targeted the people in power as the ones who had to be overthrown. White men were the faces of the enemy for an increasingly violent minority as they were the ones holding the political and economic power. For Lewis and Ed, who had grown up expecting to rule society with their white male friends, the civilized world had become hostile to them, causing them to become nostalgic for what they perceived to be an order closer to nature. In the natural world, they believed they could bond with others of their kind without being perceived as infringing on anyone's rights.

The Rural Poor

In the early 1960s, just after establishing the Peace Corps, President John Kennedy's administration had the idea to establish a National Service Corps to deal with similar problems on home soil. The idea was approved by the Senate, but the Congress objected and refused to provide funding. After Kennedy was assassinated, Lyndon Johnson came into office. One of Johnson's greatest concerns was his War on Poverty program. The premise of the program was that poverty in America could be eliminated. Johnson was more effective than Kennedy at getting domestic programs passed by Congress, and in 1964 the Economic Opportunity Act was passed.

The Economic Opportunity Act created several well-known programs, including Head Start and VISTA (Volunteers in Service to America). For a commitment of only one year and poverty-level wages, volunteers would be sent to poor areas of the country to teach, to help organize systems of self-help societies, and to work on community improvement. Among the projects that were aided by VISTA were credit unions, adult education programs, block watch clubs, and agricultural cooperatives.

Although the scope of the VISTA program included helping poor people in all fifty states, Americans came to associate the program with the rural poor. One reason was that VISTA advertisements often showed striking images from Georgia's Appalachian mountains or Kentucky's coal region, in order to impress viewers with the depth of poverty in this country (urban poverty, on the other hand, was explored nightly on the news). Also, there was a scandal with VISTA in Kentucky, where the governor charged members of the organization with sedition (the crime of inciting rebellion against the government). The VISTA program hit its high point in the early 1970s, but then dwindled. The Reagan Administration in the 1980s dismantled the budget for training and recruiting, but the program stayed alive, just barely. One of President Clinton's priorities when he took office was to revise the volunteerism that Kennedy had stressed, so he implemented the National and Community Service Trust Act of 1992, which incorporated VISTA and similar volunteer programs under the name AmeriCorps.

Critical Overview

Critics were very impressed with *Deliverance* when it was published in 1970. Geoffrey Wolff, reviewing the book for *Newsweek,* expressed appreciation for Dickey's craftsmanship, referring to his characterization of the four men in the story as "limned flawlessly by a few broad strokes," and the book as a whole as "rich with country lore and superb lyrical evocations of the wilderness, as we should expect from Dickey." *Time*'s reviewer praised Dickey for achieving "a small classic novel in which action and reflection are matched and a man's return to primitive produces some lasting fragment of interior knowledge." This review did find some fault with the way the novel slowed almost to a standstill, steeped in symbolism, during Ed's climb up the bluff to kill the stranger. "No single action is impossible to believe, but the accumulation—it eventually involves his singing a sort of victory song over the body and then lowering it from the cliff—is just a bit too much." This criticism is limited, however, because "the lapse is short."

Writing for *The New Yorker,* L. E. Sissman was completely swept up by what Dickey had achieved. He ended his review with glowing praise: "Having constructed his first novel, which brilliantly achieves what it sets out to do, and having given us a breathtaking adventure that is also an acute comment on America, Mr. Dickey has discharged his responsibilities as a first novelist with power, skill and grace."

Benjamin DeMott, in *The Saturday Review,* went beyond simply reviewing the book; he looked at it within several contexts: as it fit into Dickey's writings in general, as well as how it fit into the "More Life" school of literature. His essay, several pages long, only began evaluating the text near the end, where he identified the book's premise as a growing confrontation between Lewis's romantic self-importance and Ed's complacency with modern life. DeMott wrote: "Bringing off such a confrontation in a novel requires patience, humor, a speculative cast of mind and (most obviously) an interest in both normative and extreme experiences. Mr. Dickey doesn't bring the confrontation off." Instead of a conflict of values, DeMott noted an avoidance of conflict by having Lewis injured and having Ed instantly, almost magically, absorbing his worldview. "The result," DeMott wrote, "is that in place of a novel, where qualities of character and understanding are set in full view, compared and assessed, the reader is offered an emptily rhetorical horse-opera played in canoes."

Modern critics continue to struggle with the problem of balancing the book's mysterious implications with the desire to avoid over-intellectualizing. Keen Butterworth, writing in *The Southern Literary Journal* in 1996, established the characters as representatives of Freud's understanding of the psyche's id, ego, and superego, although he noted that "[i]n my own conversations with Dickey, however, he has denied that he was conscious of this division of the Freudian paradigm among the four characters of the novel. If this is so, an interesting

possibility is raised: Freudian metaphor has become so imbedded in modern thought that it often functions today at a subliminal level."

William G. Tapply, writing for a less intellectual audience in *The Armchair Detective* talked about having read the novel when it was first out and then rereading it recently, concluding that it is "a perfect book." Remembering the times that he was forbidden to teach *Deliverance* to his high school English classes because of its subject matter, Tapply took consolation from the fact that *Huckleberry Finn* has frequently been banned from schools and libraries too. He found no question that its quintessentially American themes make it an important part of the country's literature. If Dickey had been able to produce another novel of similar quality, his reputation as a novelist might have been secured, but as it stands *Deliverance* is usually discussed in literary circles as an outstanding achievement for a poet.

Criticism

David Kelly

Kelly is an instructor of creative writing at Oakton Community College and College of Lake County. In this essay, he suggests that, despite its grim subject matter, Deliverance *actually follows a common comic structure.*

Reading the last part of *Deliverance,* you get a funny feeling. Not "funny" as in odd, but the actual feeling that there is some sort of offensive dark comedy being played out with a perfectly straight face. James Dickey certainly isn't trying to amuse the audience—humor isn't this novel's reason for existing—but that does not mean that it can't stumble into some common comic strategy. There are all kinds of comic devices, such as wordplay and pratfalls and mistaken identities and an infinite variety more. One motif that comes up frequently in comedy is the humor that stems from watching a character ignore the perfectly obvious. In *Deliverance* Ed Gentry ignores the unignorable with a moral density that invites readers to laugh at him.

Usually in film and on stage this kind of humor from ignorance involves a character standing in the foreground, calm and collected, feeling he or she has life in control, while in the background the most incredible events take place. Often the background events involve danger to the oblivious

What Do I Read Next?

- Many of the situations in *Deliverance* are reminiscent of the struggle between man and water presented in *The Old Man and the Sea,* often considered Ernest Hemingway's best book. The 1953 Pulitzer Prize-winning novel tells the story of an old fisherman and his struggle to stay alive while battling against nature in his small, primitive boat.

- Contemporary poet Robert Bly has explored the theme of masculinity in his best-selling 1990 book *Iron John: A Book about Men,* where he mixes psychology, myth, anthropology, and literature to explain his theory of male sexual aggressiveness.

- Dickey's son, *Newsweek* Paris Bureau Chief Christopher Dickey, has published his memoir of life with his father. He especially focuses on the summer of 1971, when *Deliverance* was being made into a movie. He paints a portrait of a flawed, hard-working man in *Summer of Deliverance: A Memoir of Father and Son,* published in 1998 by Simon and Schuster.

- Many critics have compared the trip down the river that reveals the horrors of base instinct over intellect in this novel to the trip made by Joseph Conrad's Marlow in the short story "Heart of Darkness," from 1902.

- Dickey wrote the script for a television adaptation of Jack London's 1903 novel *Call of the Wild,* about a civilized man trying to survive in the Alaskan wilderness.

- Some of the themes in this novel were explored earlier by Dickey in his poem "On the Coosawattee," including a character named Lucas Gentry. The poem was included in his collection *Helmets* and can be found in *The Whole Motion: Collected Poems, 1945-1992.*

- Harry Crews is a Florida writer whose prose style and subject matter are reminiscent of Dickey, with the same tough fascination with maleness, but with a little more fanciful imagination. Several of his essays and a few full novels can be found collected in *Classic Crews: A Harry Crews Reader,* published in 1993 by Poseidon Press.

- In the late 1960s, cultural anthropologist Eliot Wigginton and his students went to the mountains in Georgia to study the folk ways of the natives. Their records of the folk customs were compiled in 1972 in *The Foxfire Book: Hog Dressing, Log Cabin Building, Mountain Crafts and Foods, Planting by the Signs, Snake Lore, Hunting Tales, Faith Healing, and Moonshining.*

party: a wrecking ball that swings over a man's head when he stoops to pick up a penny, or a tiger in the chandelier whose growl is never recognized for what it is. The last chapters of *Deliverance* operate on this same comic principle. Astute readers spend the end of the book with their jaws dropped, amazed at Gentry, wondering just when the seriousness of what he's done will register. The threat that Ed Gentry isn't perceiving is that he quite probably killed an innocent man, someone who showed up where he wanted a killer to be at the time he was expecting the killer to appear. Guilt may not sound like a threat to him—it's certainly not as

pressing as being picked off by a rifle shot to the head, which he fears when he kills the man—but for all of his moral posturing and claims of heightened awareness, he should be able to see that there is a difference between killing the right man and killing the wrong one. Failing to consider his probable guilt makes him a comic straight man, a stooge of his own obsessions.

Even without considering its ending, *Deliverance* already has a relationship to comedy. It holds a special place in American humor, strumming a chord of terror so deep that the only response is nervous laughter. It's that kind of laughter that bubbles up to protect us from fears we can't deal with rationally, a kind of whistle-past-the-graveyard defense that assures us that, though the crazed backwoods mountain men might have shotguns and anger, that their foolishness will always keep them down. To experience America's comic obsession with *Deliverance,* try mentioning the rural south or a long canoe trip in a crowded room: somebody is sure to whistle or sing out the opening notes for "Dueling Banjoes," the theme from the movie. For thirty years, those notes have been our national punchline for an unspoken joke about how the uncivilized resent the rest of us.

Critic Robert W. Hill put forth an argument in 1973 that Dickey was a comic poet, defining "comic" as "that which promises to go on: marriages are made, and fruitful continuance is implied." That works for this novel as well, as, at the end, Ed is presented as being back snugly in the comfort of his family, enjoying weekend water sports on the reservoir with Lewis, perhaps a better man of nature for having absorbed the Cahulawassee River into his memory. Hill cites some of the great critics of our time, Northrop Frye and Constance Rourke, on the subject of comedy: Frye talks of comedy stemming from a new society congealing around the comic hero's exploits, while Rourke, author of the comprehensive 1931 analysis *American Humor,* pegs comedy as the integration of several cultures into a single culture. These definitions certainly apply to the way *Deliverance* comes out, with the primitive and refined cultures combined in Gentry, his "new society" being a personal harmony of the both.

To find Gentry comically ignorant for being blind to a huge, obvious thing, there has to be something huge there, and it is obvious. Killing an innocent man is huge—in the realm of morality, it is just about the hugest thing there is. The novel seems not too impressed by killing; in fact, it seems to be an exercise in finding the circumstances under which it is right for a civilized man to kill. The killing instinct is high in Gentry. He watches another man sodomized right before his eyes. In the normal world this is horrifying enough, a breach of some our strongest taboos against rape and homosexuality. On this canoe trip, dominated by Lewis Medford's machismo, this crime of domination is even worse.

Nobody cares that the first rapist dies. Nobody is particularly interested in treating it like a crime that happened within the ordinary flow of ethics. The first rapist has canceled out any rights he may

have been born with, according to the men: Ed resists "drawing my family into the whole sickening, unresolvable mess, getting them all more and more deeply entangled in the life, death and identity of the repulsive, useless man at my feet." The man's death and identity are easy to forget because he was repulsive and useless, and for the threat he has posed to the families of the men. If ever there are going to be circumstances for killing and forgetting it, then rape, a threat to family, and the victim's repulsiveness come pretty close.

The second mountain man's crime is less certain, but Gentry sees a pretty clear case for why he must be killed. Granted, he isn't caught dripping with another man's blood, as the first man was, but from Gentry's point of view being hidden up on a cliff and shooting down anonymously makes him an even worse threat. On the other hand, the "self-defense" explanation that makes sense when someone is holding a gun to your neck stretches thin when you have to scale a rock cliff from sundown to sunup and then hide in a tree to get at him. It isn't so entirely clear that the second mountain man has to die, but Gentry's point in the novel is that the man presents so much potential danger that there can be no margin of error, that what he might do deserves a first strike. Legal scholars have disputed this, most famously in the case of Bernhard Goetz, who shot four men on a New York subway in 1986 because he thought they looked menacing as they approached: a grand jury indicted Goetz, and he was acquitted at trial. None of us knows what to do in extreme circumstances, and Gentry rests comfortably at the end of the book, feeling that he did the best with what he knew.

The obvious thing that he ignores is that the man on the bluff probably wasn't there to kill him. The evidence is just too slight, and the counterevidence too compelling. First, there is the question of whether anyone at all shot down on them. Lewis Medford had sworn that Drew was shot just before the canoes tumbled into the rapids, but the evidence of Gentry's own eyes never does support this claim. "He may have been shot," Gentry explains. "But I can't really say. I was looking right at him, but I can't say." Finding Drew's body later yields no definite evidence, just a gash that could be a bullet graze or could have come from scraping a rock.

The only person who would be shooting at them would be the man who tried to rape Gentry, whose friend was killed, but Gentry can't confirm whether the man he shoots is wearing the same clothes—they're similar, but most forest clothes are. The dead man has a dental plate: this proves that he is missing teeth, as the would-be rapist was, but more significantly it presents him as being much more civilized than the "repulsive, useless man" that Gentry has in mind. A deputy sheriff's brother-in-law has disappeared in those same woods, and the deputy has a gut instinct that he has been killed by these men—what a strange coincidence that would be, if his instinct were right about them killing somebody but wrong about who. The brother-in-law, Benson, is probably the man shot on the ridge. The sheriff says he was "a mean bastard," but that isn't very much evidence that he might be a murderer and rapist, that he would be the man who, as Gentry points out as he is tied to a tree, had probably done this before. There just isn't enough evidence that the man Gentry killed was guilty of anything more than walking by.

It is the author, James Dickey, who raises these questions about whether Drew was shot, whether the man's clothes were the same, whether he is the man named Benson. Dickey must have known that he was raising the prospect that his protagonist had killed an innocent man. Could he actually have been ignorant about how serious this is?

Unfortunately, it's actually quite easy to believe that he could have created this moral sinkhole and ignored its implications. After all, we are expected to ignore the synergy of anal imagery that keeps coming up throughout the novel—Dickey created *that,* too, but doesn't seem prepared to deal with it. Walking down the street, Gentry's mind is on the fact that "I kept looking for a decent ass"; the Kitt'n Britches ad centers on the model's behind, and in his tent at night Gentry has a fantasy about the cat clawing the girl's buttocks bloody; when he makes love to his wife, he takes her from behind; shimmying in the rock crevice is an erotic experience for him ("Then I would try to inch upward again, moving with the most intimate motions of my body, motions I had never dared use with Martha, or with any other human woman.").

Perhaps in another novel these images wouldn't add up to anything, and trying to make something of them would just be a case of snickering over a story about men among men. But the central action in *Deliverance* is, after all, sodomy: the failure to see the connection here falls either on the author or the narrator's psyche. As Charles Thomas Samuels asserts in a review for *The New Republic* that delves much further into Lewis and Ed's relationship, "perhaps the narrator doesn't discover latent homosexuality and symbolic transference be-

cause these are accidents of plotting and phrasing and are not essentials of the novel's purpose." In either case, though, the homoeroticism and the cold-blooded murder of an innocent man are there, and the characters look foolish if they don't see them.

Probably, Dickey raised questions about the identity about the man on the top of the ridge because he wanted to make a point about Ed Gentry's moral right to kill him, regardless of who he was. He makes a wrought-iron case for why the time is right for Gentry to kill somebody, a case that includes the mystical (he somehow knows that the next person he sees will be the man who molested him) and the childish (*Lewis* got to kill someone with an arrow) as well as the practical. The novel is less about the circumstances dragging a character into action than it is about them allowing him to act. Is there ever such a case, where a man's right to kill supersedes another's right to not be killed? No. In failing to take responsibility for whether or not he shot the right man, Ed Gentry looks as ridiculous as if he had failed to notice a tiger in the chandelier over his head. The more seriously he takes himself, the more readers have to laugh.

Source: David Kelly, in an essay for *Novels for Students,* Gale, 2000.

Sources

Keen Butterworth, "The Savage Mind: James Dickey's *Deliverance,*" in *The Southern Literary Journal,* Spring, 1996, pp. 69-78.

Benjamin DeMott, "The 'More Life' School and James Dickey," in *The New Republic,* March 28, 1970, pp. 25+.

Robert W. Hill, "James Dickey: Comic Poet," in *James Dickey: The Expansive Imagination,* edited by Richard J. Calhoun, Everett/Edwards, Inc., 1973, pp. 143-56.

"Journey into Self," in *Time,* April 20, 1970, pp. 92-3.

Charles Thomas Samuels, "What Hath Dickey Delivered?," in *The New Republic,* April 18, 1970.

L. E. Sissman, "Poet into Novelist," in *The New Yorker,* May 2, 1970, pp. 123-26.

William G. Tapply, "Because It's There: James Dickey and *Deliverance,*" in *The Armchair Detective,* May, 1994, pp. 342-35.

Geoffrey Wolff, "Hunting in Hell," in *Newsweek,* March 30, 1970, p. 75.

For Further Study

J. A. Bryant, Jr., *Twentieth-Century Southern Literature,*
The University Press of Kentucky, 1997.

    One of the country's leading literary critics examines
the background of Dickey's works. His poetry far
outshines his fiction in this review.

Richard J. Calhoun, editor, *James Dickey: The Expansive
Imagination,* Everett/Edwards, Inc., 1973.

    The essays collected by Calhoun in this book exam-
ine the poet and novelist as his style was still emerging and give insights into Dickey's reputation among
his peers at the time of *Deliverance.*

Richard J. Calhoun and Robert W. Hill, *James Dickey,*
Twayne Publishers, 1983.

    Calhoun and Hill, both professors of English at Clem-
son, take a personal as well as scholarly approach to
Dickey's career up to that point in time.

James Dickey, *Sorties: Journals and New Essays,* Double-
day and Company, 1971.

    This collection of miscellaneous pieces, published
around the same time as the novel, contains ample
information about Dickey's ideas, interests, and influences.

Susan Faludi, *Stiffed: The Betrayal of American Men,*
William Morrow and Co., 1999.

    A leading feminist critic explores the frustrations that
the changes in sexual roles in the last quarter century
have caused for men, who lack clear-cut heroes with
whom to identify.

Larry May, *Masculinity and Morality,* Cornell University
Press, 1998.

    This scholarly collection of essays by a philosophy
professor delves deeply and seriously into the ideas
that are hinted at in Dickey's novel.

The Fixer

Bernard Malamud
1966

Bernard Malamud based *The Fixer* on the case of Mendel Beilis, a Jewish bookkeeper for a brick factory who was accused of ritualistically murdering a Christian child. With very little evidence against him, the Russian government pushed for the conviction of Beilis in order to justify anti-Semitic policies that were being enacted at the time. The novel's protagonist, Yakov Bok, also works in a brick factory, and he is charged, for no particular reason except being Jewish, for a crime just like the one with which Beilis was charged. As in Malamud's fictionalized version, the actual case occurred between 1911 and 1913 in the Ukrainian capital, Kiev. The Beilis case is credited with being one of the main contributing factors in bringing about the Russian Revolution by raising the sense of distrust Russian citizens felt toward their government and the anger of people around the world. The political situation surrounding the case is hardly touched upon in *The Fixer*. Most of the book focuses on Yakov's life in solitary confinement, waiting for years in prison for the murder charge to be formally levied against him so that he can get on with the trial.

The Fixer was published in 1966, more than fifty years after the Beilis case had been settled in court, but Malamud could count on his audience to be familiar with the circumstances of what had happened because the case was and is an important event in the history of the Jewish struggle for peace and security. The book won the National Book Award and the Pulitzer Prize, and is considered one

Bernard Malamud

of the finest in the canon of books by one of America's finest authors.

Author Biography

Bernard Malamud was born in 1914 in New York City, in a neighborhood that had become famous as the settling place of Jewish immigrants throughout the first half of the twentieth century. His parents, Jews who had emigrated from Russia, worked sixteen hours a day in their grocery store. Malamud spent his childhood in Brooklyn, attending Erasmus Hall High School. It was in high school that he first began writing, starting with short stories about the life he knew best, urban Jewish life. He attended City College of New York— graduating with a Bachelor of Arts degree in 1936—and Columbia University, also in New York, where he earned a Master of Arts degree in 1942. While working toward his degree, he taught at high schools at night, and after graduation he continued to use his spare time writing and publishing short stories.

From 1949 to 1961, Malamud taught composition at Oregon State University in Corvallis. During this time, he wrote his first three novels: the

first one, *The Natural,* was published in 1952 and made into a popular movie over thirty years later. It was followed by *The Assistant* in 1957, and *A New Life* in 1961, the latter about a Jewish writer from New York who moves to Oregon to teach composition, as Malamud himself did. His first collection of short stories, *The Magic Barrel,* established Malamud as a contemporary master of the form, winning him the National Book Award as well as international respect. In 1961, he moved back to the East Coast to teach at Vermont's Bennington College. It was while at Bennington that he published *The Fixer* in 1966. This novel won both the National Book Award and the Pulitzer Prize, and was made into a movie by John Frankenheimer in 1968.

Malamud wrote three more novels in his lifetime: *The Tenants* (1971), *Dubin's Lives* (1979), and *God's Grace* (1982). *The Collected Stories of Bernard Malamud,* published in 1982, was considered a major event in the publishing world. Malamud died in 1986 in New York City. He is often categorized as a "Jewish writer" because many of the characters and themes in his books concerned Jewish history and especially the Jewish-American immigrant experience. However, he is also recognized as simply one of the best fiction writers of his generation, especially for his craftsmanship of the short story.

Plot Summary

Part I

The first section of *The Fixer* is divided into three chapters. The book's first chapter takes place at a point that is outside of the ordinary flow of time. While most of this book follows in chronological order, this chapter occurs after some of the plot events and before others. In the first chapter, Yakov Bok is already living at the brickyard when he hears the commotion of people running outside the factory gate because the body of a murdered boy, Zhenia Golov, was found stabbed to death. One of the drivers for the brickyard brings in leaflets from the Black Hundred, accusing the Jews of murdering the boy for his blood, which they would use for the making of Passover matzos. This chapter includes background information about other incidents of violence against the Jews. Within a year of Yakov's birth, his father had been killed by a pair of drunken soldiers out to shoot the first three Jews in their path, and Yakov himself had in his childhood survived one of the state-supported rampages against Jews, known as a pogrom. If this chapter were worked into the normal chronological order of the book, it would appear near the end of Part II, where the discovery of the boy's body, his funeral, and the public backlash against the Jews are recounted again.

The remaining two chapters of part I start with "five months ago, on a mild Friday in early November." Bok, whose wife has left him, is preparing to leave the Pale of Jews where he has been living to try to make a better life for himself in Kiev, possibly saving enough to go to Amsterdam and then to America. He has said good-bye to the few friends he had and traded the cow his wife kept for a horse her father used in his business, intending to take the horse and its carriage to the city, twenty miles away. Along the road, though, when he stops to pick up an old woman who turns out to be a Christian, the carriage wheel breaks, and he is left to ride on horseback as far as the bank of the Dnieper River. In order to get across the river, he trades the horse to an anti-Semitic ferryman. The first section ends with Yakov dropping his Jewish prayer things into the river.

Part II

The second section of the novel spans the five months between Yakov's arrival in Kiev and his arrest. On first entering the city, he lives in the Jewish quarter in the Podol district, working what few odd jobs he can find. One night, he finds a man drunk in the snow and helps him get home. The man, Lebedev, offers him a job fixing up an apartment upstairs in his house. Desperate for work, Yakov takes the job, even though as a Jew he is not supposed to. He gives a false, Russian name to hide his Jewish identity and answers questions carefully so that his identity will not be revealed. While he is working, Lebedev's daughter, a lonely cripple, seduces him. When the apartment is fixed up, Lebedev is so impressed that he offers Yakov another job, as overseer of a brick factory that he inherited from his brother. Yakov tries to turn the job down, but Lebedev keeps increasing his offer, with a free apartment at the factory and more and more money, until he accepts.

The workers at the factory resent him. They had been pilfering bricks and selling them on the side, and now must stop because Yakov has been put in charge of inventory. The foreman, Proshko, threatens Yakov carefully, alluding to his Jewish looks and asking about his work papers in order to convey the point that he knows Yakov could face

legal trouble. When Yakov finds an old Hasidic Jew wandering dazed in the snow, having been hit with stones thrown by some boys, he takes the man up to his apartment until the snow stops, but when Yakov falls asleep, he dreams of killing the man. The next day news arrives that a boy has been found dead in a nearby cave, and after several days of rising violence against Jews, the secret police show up at the brickyard and arrest Yakov.

Part III

The book's third section concerns Yakov's early days in confinement. When he is visited in his cell by the Investigating Magistrate, a man named Bibikov, he finds out how all of the events of his recent life have been twisted to make him seem guilty. Lebedev has testified that Yakov misled him in order to get the job at the brickyard; Zina testified that he tried to rape her; and Proshko testified about seeing the old Hasidic Jew, which is interpreted as evidence that the murder of Zhenia Golov was part of a Jewish conspiracy. Bibikov admits that the evidence is weak and gives Yakov hope that he might not be charged with murder and might only serve a month for being a Jew without the proper documents for working outside of the Jewish quarter. The Prosecuting Attorney, Grubeshov, pursues a conviction, and his political influence is stronger than Bibikov's. At the end of this section Yakov is thrown into a jail cell with other criminals: they all claim their innocence, but when they hear that Yakov is the Jew accused of killing the Christian boy, they gang up on him and beat him.

Part IV

In this section, more testimony emerges, as people spread lies that conflict with reality as Yakov knows it, but no one except Bibikov will believe his version of the facts. Yakov has to listen to Proshko's testimony that Yakov had cheated the brickyard and that he sneaked Jews into the brickyard. In his version of the night Yakov brought the battered old Hasid home, "they both tied horns on their heads and prayed to the Jewish God." He also testifies to having seen the old Jew burn down the stable while Yakov was in jail to destroy evidence. The dead boy's mother, who seems to babble like a crazy woman, says that her son told her he had been threatened with a knife by Yakov and also lured with candy to Yakov's apartment. Yakov is taken to the cave where Zhenia was found, and his body is dug up and returned to the scene of the crime. Father Anastsy, a local Catholic priest who has a reputation for being an expert on Jewish beliefs, spins a distorted history of folk tales and superstitions about Jews sacrificing Christian children at Easter time, drinking their blood and cutting their victims in the precise ways that the dead boy has been cut.

Part V

Yakov still holds hope that he might not be charged with a crime, that the weakness of the evidence will protect him from prosecution. Put into a cell with other prisoners, he fears another beating, but instead finds that one of them, Fetykov, dismisses the allegations against Yakov as fabrications. Unlike the superstitious people Yakov has been encountering, Fetykov has worked with a Jew and knows that the charge about blood rituals is ridiculous. Another prisoner, Gronfein, talks confidentially to him, offering to mail a letter for him, but fifteen minutes after Gronfein's release, the authorities have the letters Yakov wrote. Accusing him of conspiracy, they throw him into solitary confinement. When Bibikov visits him there one night, he goes over the details of the case that is being prepared against Yakov. Bibikov makes it very clear that he does not believe any of the charges against Yakov and that he thinks a jury probably will not either. At the end of this section, though, Yakov finds Bibikov in the cell next to his, having hung himself from the cell bars, beaten by the conspiracy.

Part VI

This part chronicles the slow deterioration of Yakov's mind in solitary confinement. He suffers freezing conditions, infections in his feet, and subtle poisoning of his food. Forbidden anything to read or anyone with whom to talk, he occupies his mind by recalling psalm verses that he learned in childhood. At one point he is transferred to the courthouse and is told that the indictment against him is finally ready. However, in his meeting with Grubeshov, the Prosecuting Attorney offers to have him driven to the border and released in exchange for a confession, a deal that Yakov does not believe and rejects. He is then refused the indictment for which he has been waiting, and he is sent back to the numbing boredom of his cell again.

Part VII

During his long wait, Yakov is allowed to read a New Testament that one of the guards has given him as well as parts of the Old Testament from a phylactery given to him in order to make him appear more Jewish to visitors. He also is allowed to read a long, rambling letter from Marfa Golov, the mother of the murdered boy, asking him to confess to the crime and stating her foolish prejudices about Jews. His father-in-law, Schmuel, arranges to sneak into the jail one night and visit him. Schmuel urges Yakov to rely on his religion to help him survive his ordeal, but Yakov rejects religion, still bitter about the unfair miseries that he has suffered.

Part VIII

The guard that Schmuel bribed to get into the prison has been found out immediately and transferred away. In his place is a new, meaner guard. At the same time, Kogin, the guard who never gave Yakov any help, talks to him, overcome with sadness about events in his own life: his son has been arrested for committing a murder during a robbery gone bad, and will probably be sent away. An indictment is issued, and Yakov is heartened to find that it is full of the same rumors and assumptions that Marfa Golov had in her letter, not at all the sort of thing a jury could take seriously. The next day, though, the indictment is taken back and called a mistake. To Yakov's surprise, his estranged wife, Raisl, is allowed to visit him. She tells him that she had a child after living with him and was abandoned by the man who is the child's father. She states that the people of the village treat her poorly because of this, and asks Yakov to write a letter saying that the child is his, although they both know it couldn't be. He agrees, and writes the letter on the back of an envelope containing another confession that the Prosecuting Attorney sent for him to sign. On the confession he writes, "Every word is a lie."

Part IX

In the novel's final section, Yakov listens to one more request from Grubeshov, the Prosecuting Attorney, to confess. Grubeshov proclaims that social violence that results from his trial will hurt the Jews. "You can take my word for it that in less than a week after your trial, there will be a quarter-million fewer Zhidy (Jews) in the Pale." After his refusal, Yakov is allowed finally to meet his lawyer, Julius Ostrovsky, who tells him about the recent history of anti-Semitism in Russia. He also reveals that the government wants Yakov convicted in order to convince the public that the crumbling of the economy is all part of a Jewish plot.

As he is finally being taken to trial, Yakov, who is ready to leave the jail behind him at whatever cost, is called back in by the Deputy Warden to suffer the indignity of a strip search once more.

When told to take off his last stitch of clothes, his undershirt, he throws it defiantly in the Deputy Warden's face. As punishment for insulting a prison official, the warden tries to shoot Yakov. However, his efforts are thwarted by Kogin the guard, and the warden shoots Kogin instead.

The carriage that finally takes Yakov to his trial is surrounded by mobs of Jews and anti-Semites. In the pandemonium that ensues, someone sets off a bomb that damages the carriage wheel, but it speeds off for the courthouse. As a result of the indignities suffered upon him, Yakov realizes that he must continue to fight for freedom, resolving to never give up. The book ends with him on his way to his trial, with no clear indication of the outcome.

Characters

Father Anastasy

Father Anastasy is the priest who offers moral support to Marfa Golov. He is a priest of the Orthodox Catholic Church, and is considered a specialist in Judaism. When the investigative party goes to the cave where the body was found, Father Anastasy gives a long, pseudo-scholarly history of ritualistic murders supposedly committed by Jews throughout history, giving twisted understanding of Jewish scripture as a basis of proof. "In the past," he says, "the Jew has had many uses for Christian blood. He has used it for sorcery and witches' rituals, and for love potions and well poisoning, fabricating a deadly venom that spread the plague from one country to another, a mixture of Christian blood from a murdered victim, their own Jewish urine, the heads of poisonous snakes, and even the stolen mutilated host—the bleeding body of Christ himself."

Berezhinsky

The guard who replaces Zhitnyak, Berezhinsky is an ex-soldier "with swollen knuckles and a broken nose." He taunts Yakov, pointing his gun at the prisoner and shouting "Bang!" to indicate how willing he is to shoot him. He is as cruel to Yakov as the Deputy Warden wants the guards to be, showing less mercy than Zhitnyak, but, in the end, when Yakov is leaving the jail to go to his trial, Berezhinsky tells him, "good luck and no hard feelings."

B. A. Bibikov

Investigating Magistrate for cases of extraordinary importance in Kiev, Bibikov is the person who questions Yakov after he is first arrested, and he turns out to be the only person of official capacity who is willing to believe that Yakov might be innocent. When he questions him in his cell, Bibikov is friendly, asking questions about philosophy, offering cigarettes, and even mentioning his own child's sickness. The next day, though, the interrogation in his office, in the presence of other Russians, is much more aggressive. Bibikov is divided between his suspicions that the case against Yakov is weak and the pressure from his superiors in the legal hierarchy, who want him to accept Yakov's guilt without question. Later, he visits Yakov in his cell to confide that there is little evidence against him, but that the authorities are set on having him found guilty. He promises to speak to a prominent lawyer about defending him. Soon after his visit, though, Yakov hears another prisoner being thrown into the cell next to him and tortured. Sneaking out of his cell, he is able to look into the other cell and see Bibikov hanging from his belt from the bars. Grubeshov later tells Yakov, "He was arrested for peculating from official hands. While awaiting trial, overwhelmed by his disgrace, he committed suicide."

Colonel Bodyansky

A military officer who is present when Yakov is interrogated by Grubeshov, Bodyansky threatens the suspect frequently with violence.

Yakov Shepsovitch Bok

Yakov is the "fixer" to whom the book's title refers. Thirty years old, he is despondent in the book's beginning because his wife has left him and run off with another man. Having nothing to live for in the "Step," the Jewish settlement in the countryside, he leaves for the city of Kiev, hoping to make enough money to someday immigrate to a country where Jews are treated more fairly. In Kiev, he first finds himself surprisingly lucky—a man he meets, Lebedev, gives him a job overseeing a brick factory. He is, however, a Jew in an area where Jews are not supposed to live or work. When a boy is found murdered nearby, others take advantage of Yakov's social disadvantage, and arrange to have him arrested. The workers under him want him out of the way so that they can continue the petty thievery they had practiced before he came, and the real killers, presumably the boy's mother and her boyfriend, use him as a scapegoat (the name "Bok" means "goat" in German).

At first, Yakov believes that his time in jail will go quickly, that the murder charge will be dropped

Yakov Bok, played by Alan Bates in the 1968 film adaptation of the novel, is unjustly arrested and incarcerated for murder.

and he will only be punished for living in the non-Jewish area, but as the novel progresses he finds out that the authorities intend to convict him for this crime. As time goes on, the evidence against him changes: witnesses claim to have seen him and other Jews holding ritualistic practices, to have seen him threaten the victim with a knife, and to have seen him with a body-shaped package on the night of the murder. For over two years, Yakov remains in jail, awaiting the formal indictment will start his trial. His health deteriorates, and he nearly goes crazy in solitary confinement. He is poisoned by the authorities and humiliated daily. Throughout this time, he learns that his religious faith, which he made light of before all of this trouble, is necessary in order for him to persevere. In the end, he accepts the fact that the government has made him a symbol of all Jews, and he vows to fight injustice at whatever cost, in the name of freedom.

Deputy Warden

The Deputy Warden is never called by name in this book, but he is Yakov's chief antagonist. His first words to Yakov are "Hello, blood-drinker, welcome to the Promised land … Here we'll feed you flour and blood until you shit matzos." He is the one who gives Yakov's guards their orders: when they feel some sympathy toward Yakov, they must take care that the Deputy Warden will not show up and prosecute them for disobeying. The Deputy Warden objects when Bibikov visits Yakov in jail, and soon after Bibikov is himself arrested and tortured. The Deputy Warden tries to make Yakov uncomfortable—holding out on firewood for his stove in the winter, keeping him chained to the bed, keeping him isolated, and strip-searching him several times a day. In the end, he pushes Yakov to the point of breaking, of openly rebelling, which would give the Deputy Warden a legal right to shoot him. One of his subordinates, Kogin, becomes tired of witnessing all of this cruelty and he intervenes, and the Deputy Warden kills him instead.

Yakov Ivanovich Dologushev

See Yakov Shepsovitch Bok

Fetyukov

Fetyukov is the murderer who shares Yakov's first jail cell. He is prepared to kill Yakov when he thinks the fixer is a stool-pigeon who has been put in the cell to spy on the prisoners there, but he believes Yakov when he says that he did not kill the child. Drawing from memories of a Jew for whom he had once worked, Fetyukov is too sophisticated to believe the gossip that the state presents as evidence for Jews' willingness to kill and drink blood.

Marfa Vladimirovna Golov

Marfa is the mother of the boy who was killed. She lives in a squalid little house near the brickyard. The story that she tells the prosecutors is inflated from the experiences relayed earlier in the book—for instance, she says that Yakov threatened her son with a knife, and that her son and another boy saw a jar of blood on Yakov's table (it was actually strawberry jam). Although the details of her life make her testimony suspicious—such as the fact that she blinded her lover, Stepan Bulkin, by throwing acid into his eyes but later reunited with him—the prosecutors still believe her over Yakov. As Yakov stares at her, wondering if she is insane, she shouts to the policemen to make him stop looking at her. Later, while Yakov is in jail, he receives a long, rambling letter from Marfa that alternates between begging him to confess to the crime and insulting him and all Jews. When the first indictment is handed down, Yakov suspects that the charges in it are based on the irrational claims in Marfa's letter.

Gregor Gronfein

A counterfeiter who is in jail with Yakov, Gronfein listens to Yakov sympathetically and gives him a pencil and paper with which to write letters to people who have not found out about his arrest. Gronfein offers to mail the letters, but instead he hands them over to the Warden, who is outraged. Yakov also finds out that Gronfein has claimed that Yakov spoke of being part of a well-connected conspiracy and that his friends would bribe Marfa Golov to change her testimony.

Grubeshov

Grubeshov is the Prosecuting Attorney in the case against Yakov and the Procurator of the Kiev Superior Court. While Bibikov is friendly toward Yakov and tries to assure him that the case against him is weak, Grubeshov is firm about seeking a conviction, threatening Yakov when he asks questions or gives answers that do not support the state's conspiracy theory.

Kogin

The less talkative of Yakov's two guards, he has worries on his mind—sometimes he mentions

Media Adaptations

- *The Fixer* was adapted as a film by John Frankenheimer in 1969, starring Alan Bates and Dirk Bogarde. The film was released by Metro-Goldwyn-Mayer/United Artists and is available from MGM Home Video.

- *The Short Stories of Bernard Malamud* is a six-cassette program released in 1988 from the Listening Library, Old Greenwich, Connecticut. The writings are read by Anne Jackson and Eli Wallach.

- Malamud's famous short story "The Magic Barrel" is included on the eighteen-hour collection *Jewish Stories from the Old World to the New*. The dozens of celebrity readers on this collection are as diverse as William Shatner, Joseph Gordon-Leavett, Julie Kavner, and Hector Elizondo. Available on eighteen compact discs, the collection was released by KCRW of Santa Monica, California.

his troubled son, who steals from him. It is Kogin who keeps a diary of Yakov's mutterings in his sleep, and although nothing from them is incriminating, his cries are nonetheless taken as signs of a guilty conscience. In the end, Kogin takes the one courageous act of anyone in the novel. Tired of watching the Deputy Warden abuse Yakov and distraught about his own son being in jail, he prevents the Deputy Warden from killing Yakov for insubordination by drawing his gun on the man. The Deputy Warden shoots Kogin dead.

Ivan Semyonovitch Kuzminsky

Kuzminsky is Bibikov's assistant. After being told that Bibikov is dead, Yakov asks to speak to Ivan Semyonovitch, hoping that he would have the notes that were compiled in the case, but he is told that the assistant was sentenced to a year in the Petropavelsky Fortress for failing to remove his hat when a band played "God Save the Tsar" at an Agricultural Fair.

Aaron Latke

Latke is a printer's assistant. When Yakov first moves to Kiev, he stays at Latke's flat while looking for work.

Nikolai Maximotitch Lebedev

Yakov helps Lebedev to his feet one night after finding him lying drunk in the street, despite the fact that he is wearing a double-headed eagle insignia on his coat—the sign of a society that hates and persecutes Jews. Lebedev does not realize that Yakov is Jewish, and as a gesture of appreciation hires him to paint an apartment in his building. Impressed with his work, Lebedev goes on to offer him a job as an overseer at the brick factory that he owns. Later, after his arrest, Lebedev testifies in his deposition that he had been suspicious of Yakov all along, but that he had been tricked and lied to.

Zinaida Nikolaevna Lebedev

The daughter of Yakov's employer in Kiev, Zinaida is a cripple, and lonely. She invites Yakov to have supper with her several times because her father, who drinks heavily, goes to sleep early. She then invites him to make love to her, but when he sees that she is menstruating, he cannot consummate their relationship, and so, apologizing, he leaves. After her arrest, she says in her deposition that he had tried to rape her that night in her room, despite the fact that a letter from her was found in his room asking him to come and see her again.

Tsar Nicholas II

Tsar Nicholas is the Monarch of Russia. Yakov imagines that the tsar visits him in his cell as he is awaiting trial. In the book's final, chaotic scene, Yakov imagines that Tsar Nicholas II is in the coach with him on the way to his trial. In this fantasy, he takes a gun and shoots the tsar through the heart.

Julius Ostrovsky

Ostrovsky is Yakov's lawyer, whom he is not allowed to meet until the final chapters of the book. In the course of explaining his chances for acquittal, Ostrovsky explains the social background, how Jews had been treated in Russia in recent decades and the significance that the government is putting on convicting Yakov.

Proshko

Proshko is the foreman at the brick factory. He resents Yakov from the start, because Yakov's presence makes it difficult for him to cheat his employer, Lebedev, by selling off some of the merchandise on the black market. Proshko suspects Yakov of being a Jew—"a man with a nose like that ought to be careful where he puts it," he says, as a veiled threat. He asks Yakov for his working permit, but Yakov lies and tells him that it has already been taken care of, fueling Proshko's suspicion further.

Shmuel

The father of Yakov's wife, Raisl Shmuel is ashamed of his daughter for having run away, but he is of a more forgiving and compassionate nature than Yakov, as evinced when he tries to borrow money from Yakov to give to a beggar. Before leaving the province for Kiev, Yakov trades his cow for Shmuel's horse and carriage. Shmuel visits Yakov in his cell one night, having bribed the guard and taking a chance with his life to do so. He continues to encourage Yakov to have faith in religion when all Yakov can feel is despair.

Zhitnyak

Zhitnyak is the guard who seems most compassionate to Yakov: he talks to him and shows interest in listening to Yakov recite the bible verses he has memorized. He shows some slight decency, trusting Yakov with a needle and thread to fix his raggedy clothes. It is Zhitnyak who, for a hefty bribe, allows Shmuel to visit Yakov in his cell, an infraction that is found out almost immediately by the Deputy Warden. Zhitnyak's fate following this event is unknown.

Zina

See Zinaida Nikolaevna Lebedev

Themes

Freedom

Yakov starts out very limited in his freedom and as the novel progresses finds he is losing more and more. From the beginning of the novel, he is limited in where he can live or travel or work since he is a Jew. Briefly, because he is willing to deny his Jewish heritage, he is free to go beyond his confines. However, this freedom does not last long and he is soon falsely accused of murder. While in jail, a period that makes up the bulk of the novel, Yakov becomes more and more confined. He loathes the first cell he is in because he is at the mercy of the other prisoners, but the solitary confinement he moves to is even worse. When he becomes accustomed to solitary confinement, his movement is limited further by being chained to the bed. And throughout it all the sadistic Deputy Warden conducts full body searches, looking in Yakov's mouth and anus while fully knowing that there is no way Yakov could have obtained a weapon: even the inside of his body is not free at this point. During his last days in jail he gives up on any hope of freedom, but on his ride to the courthouse, looking out of the carriage at all of his fellow Jews lining his route in defiance of the Tsar's government, he comes to believe in freedom. "Where there's no fight in it there's no freedom," he thinks. "Death to the anti-Semites! Long live revolution! Long live liberty!"

Religion

The political struggle between Christians and Jews depicted in this book has little to do with the actual beliefs of each group. More significant is the personal growth of Yakov as he goes from his initial disillusionment to embracing his identity as a Jew. In the beginning of the story he leaves the Pale of Jewish Settlement because he does not feel he belongs. "Torah I had little of and Talmud less," Yakov tells his father-in-law, Schmuel, "though I learned Hebrew because I've got an ear for language." With little work available, and his wife of six years having run away, he does not trust the consolations of his religious heritage. Instead, he has faith only in himself, as symbolized by his keeping his tool kit and dropping his prayer things into the Dnieper River.

Ironically, it is the authorities who try to force a Jewish identity on Yakov while he is in prison. They force him to grow his hair long, in the Jewish style. They give him phylacteries, small leather boxes containing parchments with Hebrew scripture quotations, which Orthodox Jews wear strapped to their heads and arms; he reads them eagerly to alleviate boredom. They give him a prayer shawl, which he clings to for warmth. Their purpose in giving him these things is to make him seem more likely to be part of an Orthodox Jewish conspiracy, but as he stays in jail Yakov learns to value his Jewish identity. This point becomes clear in the end, when he objects to having the Orthodox ringlets cut from his hair.

Class Conflict

In general, the classes represented in this book correspond to religious affiliations, with the Russian Christians comprising the dominant social order and the Jews kept in the lower class by government

Topics for Further Study

- Conduct a trial for Yakov Bok. Elect representatives from your class to play prosecutors, defendants, and witnesses.

- Some people have asserted that the 1994 murder trial of former football star O. J. Simpson was motivated by racism, making him a representative of blacks in the same way that Bok is made to represent all Jews in this novel. Research the facts of the Simpson trial and make a case for or against this theory.

- Interview some police officers or prison guards and see how they feel about prisoners who might be innocent. How much sympathy do they feel they are allowed to show the prisoners in their care?

- Compile a list of myths and superstitions that people have about others of different races, religions, and classes. What do these ideas tell you about the people who hold them?

- Make a chart comparing the rights that Jews had in Tsarist Russia, in Stalin's Soviet Union, and in Nazi Germany.

- Research a modern form of the pogroms that the Russians held against Jews, such as the "ethnic cleansing" campaigns in Rwanda, Serbia, or East Timor. Point out the similarities and the differences in the methods used to discredit the oppressed people.

- International awareness of the Nazi Holocaust made it possible and necessary for Jews to form their own country in 1948. Report on the Zionist movement, which had fought for a Jewish homeland since 1898, and how that led to the formation of Israel.

constraints. There are, however, significant cases in which religious differences are put aside and people relate as class peers. When Yakov first comes to Kiev, for example, Lebedev is impressed with him as a person and as a worker, and offers him the position as an overseer in the brickyard based on what he sees in him. He tells Yakov that he also worked up from poverty, establishing a bond based on recognition.

Later, when Yakov is in jail, he fears that his cellmates will blame him for the child's murder of which he is accused. However, the convict Fetyukov shows that, despite Yakov being from the lower class, he knows better than to believe superstitions about Jews. "When I was a boy I was apprenticed to a Jew blacksmith," he explains. "He wouldn't have done what they say you did. If he drank blood he would have vomited it up." A Christian Russian of a higher social class would not have had a similar contact with anyone Jewish, and would therefore have accepted rumors as truth. The most telling case of class affiliation overriding religious affiliation is Kogin's sacrifice at the end of the book. Because his own son is in jail, Kogin is able to empathize with Yakov more than with the Deputy Warden, even though he and the warden are in a sense coworkers. After treating Yakov indifferently through most of his confinement, Kogin, despite religious differences, ends up giving his life in order to save Yakov, feeling that if the system can treat one prisoner harshly it is just as likely to be unfair to his son.

Civil Rights

Modern American audiences often are outraged to read this story of a man held in prison for a crime he did not commit with no access to any help from outside. Because the U.S. Constitution specifically names the right to a speedy trial, and because organizations such as the American Civil Liberties Union diligently watch out for abuses of this right, Americans take for granted basic civil rights that simply are not recognized in repressive, totalitarian countries. Many countries offer no guarantee of the right to legal representation: in some, political prisoners are left to rot in jail while their families are not even told whether they are alive or not. Political prisoners are often killed in jail with the transparent excuse that "they were trying to escape," as Ostrovsky warns Yakov against in the book, while others are tortured and then left with the means to commit suicide, as is Bibikov. One sign of Tsarist society's recognition of the rights of prisoners is that in this novel nobody questions the fact that Yakov will have a trial once his indictment is handed down: a society without rules would not be bound by any such commitment.

Style

Point of View

Most of this novel is written in the third person limited point of view. This means that characters are referred to as "he" or "she." The narrator is not a character in the book and does not refer to him- or herself. The point of view is "limited" in that the narration is not free to describe anything that happens anywhere, but can only tell us about events and thoughts that are experienced by Yakov. Ideas in the minds of other characters, for instance, are beyond Yakov's knowledge, and so cannot be told to the audience. For instance, the book's narration cannot directly explain the political situation outside of the jail because Yakov would have no knowledge of what is happening. Since the narration is limited to what he knows, any background information is told to Yakov by Ostrovsky. The author uses this device to bring information into the novel that otherwise is beyond its range. Another element of the point of view is the tense: for the most part, this novel is told in the past tense describing the action as being in the past, as in "Yakov Bok *saw* people running," or "The fixer *remained* mute."

There are exceptions to the general point of view. The sixth chapter of section VI starts with Yakov himself functioning as the narrator, speaking in the first person ("I") present tense. The following chapter begins with one paragraph in the second person ("you") present tense. The first chapter of section VII starts with one sentence in the present tense form: "He waits." All of these have the effect of conveying Yakov's sense of reality unraveling as he sits in his cell, his mind deteriorating. Present and past, "me" and "you" and "him," all meld into one unclear frame of mind in his boredom.

Setting

Unlike some novels, which focus on the personal lives of their characters, the story of *The Fixer* places great emphasis on the time in which it takes place. Kiev, Russia, from 1911 to 1913, had just the right balance of political sophistication with peasant superstition; of dedication and corruption; of freedom and severe political consequences. Other settings have been dangerous for religious, political, and ethnic groups that were persecuted, but they have not ended in a few years with violent revolutions, and so they would have lacked the sense of hope that this story implies in the end.

Symbolism

Little is made of the fact that Yakov is a "fixer," other than the constant use of this word to refer to him. The term has literal significance in this story in that he is indeed a fixer, a handyman, as he proves with the work he does on Lebedev's spare apartment. As his troubles grow and freedom becomes less and less likely, he thinks of his tools more often. It is somewhat ironic that this novel is named *The Fixer* in spite of the fact that Yakov is trapped in his situation and for most of the book is unable to do anything to fix it. In the end, though, the purpose of the title becomes clear enough. In the last scene, he is hurtling along in a carriage with a broken, wobbling wheel that needs fixing (which echoes the wagon wheel that broke when he was first leaving for Kiev), trapped in a political system that also needs fixing. With his tools Yakov could fix the carriage, and by allowing himself to be a symbol of Jewish oppression he can further the growing revolution that might fix the corrupt government.

Folk Tale

Malamud has described this novel as a "folk tale." The key element of a folk tale is that, true or false, it is repeated frequently within a culture because, whether they know it or not, it helps people define who they are. Malamud mentioned that the story of Mendel Beilis, upon which this novel is based, is a story that his father told him when he was a little boy. A story like "Cinderella," for instance, has elements of tragedy (such as the death of the natural mother, the stepmother's cruelty, and the father's insensitivity), but it also ends in triumph, with the stepsisters defeated and the prince declaring his devotion.

The Fixer follows a folk tale pattern in that it starts with a man leaving his home and traveling to a place with which he is unfamiliar—a different world. In this case, he is moving from the Jewish Step to the Christian-dominated Kiev. By leaving out the trial and its outcome, though, the novel takes a turn toward abstraction that a folk tale would never take. There might be a good intellectual reason to leave the ending open, so that the reader will have to think about it and perhaps even look up the history of the case it is based on. However, folk tales, even when they are mysterious, seldom leave the reader with unanswered questions about what happened. Folk tales are repeated by listeners who have heard them and found them complete; they never leave readers unsatisfied.

Historical Context

Tsar Nicholas II

Nicholas II (1868–1918), who makes a brief appearance in Yakov's dream near the end of this novel, was the last tsar of Russia (the word is also translated as "czar"). He was driven from the throne and executed shortly after the events of *The Fixer* take place. To a large extent, it was Nicholas's arrogance and foolishness that brought about the Communist Revolution in Russia, although it is also likely that the country's weak economy would have crumbled under even the most competent monarch. Nicholas was a descendant of the Romanov dynasty, whose rule reached back to 1547, when the grand duke of Muscovy, Ivan IV (1530–1584), had himself crowned czar (the Russian word for "caesar"). His grand nephew, Ivan VI (1740–1764), was the first tsar with the Romanov name, a name that was passed down to Russian rulers until Nicholas was deposed. Nicholas himself became tsar in 1894, when his father became ill and died suddenly. Nicholas, then twenty-six, was unprepared for the throne, a fact that became clear almost immediately when thousands died attending his inauguration, trampled to death due to poor crowd control.

As the nineteenth century came to an end, while countries around the world were entering the Industrial Age, Russia struggled to end a feudal social order that locked peasant farmers into slave-like conditions. With the change in social order came massive poverty. From the 1870s on, revolution was in the air, with labor strikes and peasant revolts occurring frequently. Nicholas's answer to social unrest was to blame it on "outside agitators." In 1904, Russia went to war with Japan in a small dispute over land on the Korean Peninsula: one of the tsar's advisors had told him that "a victorious little war" would unite the population. Unfortunately and unexpectedly, Russia lost, further straining the economy. Strikes, demonstrations, and violence became common.

In 1905, hundreds of peasants, gathered outside the tsar's Winter Palace to present their grievances, were shot down by soldiers. To quell the public outrage that followed, Nicholas set up the Dumas, a Russian Parliament. He did not give the Dumas any political power, though, and the protests continued until later that year when he organized a second, functional Dumas. The public's distrust of the tsar and his family intensified in the following years as he came to rely on advice from

Jews were imprisoned and persecuted by Hitler's regime during World War II. At the first concentration camp, located in the Bavarian town of Dachau, more than thirty thousand people were murdered or died of starvation or disease.

Rasputin, a mystic known as the Mad Monk, who had won the Romanovs' trust by being able to treat their son Alexis's hemophilia. When Russia suffered heavy losses after World War I began in 1914, the fate of Nicholas II and his family was sealed. After the 1917 revolution led by Lenin, Trotsky, and others, the tsar abdicated his throne, and a Communist government was established in Russia. In 1918, Nicholas, his wife, and his children were executed, although unsubstantiated rumors persist to this day that one of his daughters, Anastasia, escaped.

Blood Libel

The myth that Jewish people murder Christian children to use their blood for mystical rituals is called a "blood libel," and has existed for hundreds of years. Similar accusations were levied against early Christians, who were a small, persecuted cult in the early centuries after the death of Jesus. The first record of a blood libel against the Jews dates back to the death of William of Norwich, who was found beaten to death in the woods on Holy Saturday (the day before Easter) in 1144. The proximity of the high Christian holiday certainly added to tensions between Jews and Christians, while the

specific details about the Easter cycle—the bloody death of Jesus, the offering of bread and wine as "body and blood"—are thought to have fueled imaginations about secret mystic rituals.

While blood libel stories existed for centuries, the first recorded one that had official church recognition was the "Cult of Anderl," which started in 1462. The cult celebrated the sainted Anderl von Rinn ("Anderl" is a Germanic form of "young Andrew"; Rinn is a city in the Tyrolean Alps). The death of Anderl, allegedly at the hands of Jews, became a part of the local folklore, handed down from generation to generation. In 1614, Dr. Hippolyt Guarinoni wrote a book, *Triumph, Crown, Martyrdom and Epitaph of the Holy Innocent Child*, recording the story of Anderl as he said it came to him in a dream. The cult of Anderl continues to this day. In 1985, in an attempt to end this anti-Semitic cult, the Bishop of Innisbrook had the boy's remains removed from the church and put into a grave, but followers still conduct annual processions to the boy's grave.

The blood libel has such deep roots in Christian folk tradition that the Brothers Grimm, German scholars who are famous for fairy tales like "Hansel and Gretel" and "Cinderella," wrote a version of it

Compare & Contrast

- **1913:** Tsar Nicholas II, political leader of Russia, follows a policy of persecuting and suppressing Jewish citizens in response to social unrest.

  1966: Leonid Brezhnev, premier of the Soviet Union, supports an official propaganda campaign to blame Russian Jews for the country's economic troubles.

  Today: With the economies of former Soviet countries unsettled, old questions of ethnic identity lead people to identify themselves with smaller groups and to also demonize other groups.

- **1913:** The American Cancer Society is formed at a time when 9 out of 10 patients diagnosed with cancer are destined to die.

  1966: The Surgeon General releases findings that smoking causes cancer, as well as numerous other health problems. Cigarette companies deny this claim.

  Today: Although the chances of surviving cancer has improved dramatically since 1913, the number of incidents of cancer has also increased, making it the second leading cause of death in America.

- **1913:** Distraught Russian citizens, upset with the country's backward economy and the government's inability to do something about it, riot frequently. The government fuels anti-Semitism in order to keep angry citizens distracted.

  1966: Race riots blaze across many major American cities, including Cleveland, Chicago, and Atlanta.

Today: Violent displays against social injustice have become rarer in the United States, having been replaced by more sophisticated forms of economic pressures.

- **1913:** The Russian government can hold a suspect in custody for as long as it wants without proceeding with a trial.

  1966: The U.S. Supreme Court rules in the case of *Miranda v. Arizona* that failure to allow suspects to have a lawyer present during questioning violates the Constitutional right against self-incrimination. At the same time, civil rights abuses are legendary in the secret workings of the Soviet Union's government.

  Today: The Soviet Union no longer exists, having given way to more democratic forms of government. Amnesty International is a respected worldwide organization that monitors abuse of political prisoners.

- **1913:** Before the First World War devastated their economies, the countries of Europe were the center of the world's finances.

  1966: In the middle of the Cold War, the world was defined by the competition between two Super Powers: the United States and the Soviet Union.

  Today: Since the Soviet Union voted to dissolve itself in 1991, the United States is recognized as the world's leading economic and military power.

---

in the 1400s. Their story "Der Judenstein" (The Jewry Stone) is about a father who sells his son to Jews, who kill the boy in a ritualistic fashion, tying the boy to a stone wheel and draining his blood. The blood libel has been authorized by Pope Sixtus V, who in 1588 gave official recognition to the martyrdom of Simon of Trent, allegedly tortured and murdered by Jews a hundred years earlier. To this day there are people who, like the Russian peasants in *The Fixer,* swear that Jewish people put

the blood of young Christian boys into the Passover matzos, citing the longevity of the blood libel as proof that it is true.

Mendel Beilis

The story of Yakov Bok is almost identical to the story of Mendel Beilis (also "Beiliss"), a bookkeeper in a brick factory in Kiev who was arrested in 1911 for suspicion of killing a Christian boy, Andrei Yushinsky. Beilis was held in jail for two years while the government tried to incite public anger against Jews. When Beilis finally did come to trial in October 1913, the jury unanimously declared him not guilty. Unlike Yakov, Beilis had a large family with whom he was reunited upon his release. The Russian government's attempt to distract citizens from the country's economic woes by stirring up religious conflict backfired, instead inciting international outrage against the government's anti-Semitic stance.

Critical Overview

The Fixer has always been considered Malamud's best work by literary critics. Specific arguments, however, have arisen regarding its strong ethnic cultural heritage and the disturbing imagery it presents. In 1965, the year before *The Fixer* was published, Sidney Richman wrote a book-length survey of Malamud's fiction up to that point, in which he examined the author's popularity and growing reputation. Richman experienced the uneasiness that critics often encounter when discussing works by authors with distinct social or religious backgrounds. On the one hand, Richman wanted to separate the literature from Malamud's heritage and discuss it in its own right, but he also acknowledged that doing that would be impossible, that Jewishness was part of the fabric of the author's works.

During the early 1960s, as Richman pointed out, works by Jewish authors were in vogue, with the best-seller lists being topped by works by Saul Bellow, Philip Roth, Harvey Swados, Herbert Gold, and others. He applauded the writers, including Malamud, for using Jewishness "to effect an imaginative entry into American literature." If, at the time, many more Jewish writers were making it to the best-seller lists than ever had before, then Richman was right to wonder whether Malamud's popularity was part of an overall trend or fad. However, Richman quickly dismissed this notion in his introduction and went on to offer a serious examination of the themes in each of Malamud's works. As Richman concluded prophetically, "Despite the evidence of his and our senses, he manages to affirm man, to find the vision through which the elusive and enigmatic sense of life's possibilities counters (all reality to the contrary) man's fall from grace."

Critics such as Dorothy Seimen Bilek have pointed out that *The Fixer* is an exception among Malamud's works. While many of his writings deal with characters that retain unassimilated Jewish values and who deal with the Nazi Holocaust of the 1930s and 1940s secondhand—through the window of history—*The Fixer* is rare in the immediacy of the horrors it recounts. Despite the difference in setting from Malamud's usual contemporary America, Sheldon J. Hershinow explained that there are many thematic issues that remained the same in *The Fixer*. "Bok is another of Malamud's poor Jews whose life seems to be an unending struggle to make ends meet," he explained. Hershinow went on to take note of a common criticism of the novel—that the characters, except for Yakov, are rather superficial and one dimensional, emphasizing the historical and symbolic over good writing. He agreed with this charge, pointing out as an example the character of Grubeshov, who is so fanatical in his anti-Semitism that he is willing to harm his career to persecute Yakov but at the same time is portrayed as a political opportunist. After recognizing this criticism, Hershinow countered by noting that providing more realistic opponents for Yakov would have made his experience less surreal and, therefore, less terrifying.

Other critics found the situations described in *The Fixer* to be less than compelling, in part because they are so cruel and difficult to experience, even from the distance of a reader's perspective. Whitney Balliet, writing for *The New Yorker* found the constant abuses of Yakov to be repetitive: "Human misery does not catalogue well," he observed wryly, to which critic Gerald Hoag responded in the *Western Humanities Review,* "If someone had long ago convinced Dostoevsky and some others of that principle, perhaps Malamud would not have found himself nose-to-nose with *The New Yorker* today." Hoag's point was that great writers always used human misery as subject matter, so it gives no reason to dismiss the quality of a work.

In fact, the disgusting details of Yakov's ordeal add to what critic Alan Warren Friedman, in *Bernard Malamud and the Critics,* referred to as the "Gothic" strain that could be found throughout Malamud's works. The unappealing nature of life is a fundamental part of the Jewish spirit that Malamud writes about, according to Friedman. In his essay "The Hero as Schnook," he summarized the relationship between the two: "The universe, the given, is impossibly antithetical to human dignity and worth, and its impoverished creatures struggle gamely to make a go of things."

Today, Malamud is remembered as much for his short stories as for his novels, possibly because his production of short stories stayed strong throughout his life, while his novel production became less frequent. *The Fixer* is still considered atypical for him because of its setting, but it is still among his most respected works, possibly because of the awards that it won. Most readers recognize Malamud's name as the author of *The Natural,* an early novel about baseball that was even more unusual than *The Fixer.* However, people are more aware of *The Natural* as it was successfully adapted into a blockbuster Hollywood movie starring Robert Redford and Glenn Close.

Criticism

David Kelly

Kelly is an instructor of creative writing and drama at Oakton Community College. In the following essay, he examines how the aspects of identity and responsibility inherent in parenthood are implied throughout The Fixer.

"Permit me to ask, Yakov Shepsovitch, are you a father?"

"With all my heart."

"Then you can imagine our anguish," sighed the sad-eyed Tsar.

This exchange, coming at the end of Bernard Malamud's most harrowing novel, *The Fixer,* represents a staple in the articles of faith followed by fiction writers: that the truth one feels is more significant than the sum total of what has gone on in life. Yakov Bok is charged with the mutilation of a twelve-year-old boy, a charge that the Tsar's government hopes will create social unrest between Christians and Jews and distract them all from the government's near collapse. In actuality, Bok has no children. Nor does he have any reason to lie and say that he has. This discussion takes place during a fantasy en route to the court date that will decide his fate, after two years of pointless abuse and humiliation. If we assume that he has no reason to answer other than truthfully in his fantasy, and that he is not mistaken about offspring (a subject that is so close to his heart throughout the book that he surely would remember), then we have to conclude that he is telling the truth; if not the literal truth, then a psychological truth.

There are other moments that shine throughout the final chapters of *The Fixer,* that leap out at the reader, that suggest themselves as the Key to What All of This Suffering Has Been For. There is

the sacrifice that Kogin the guard makes, for instance, putting his life on the line when he cannot witness any more torture, or Yakov defiantly throwing his filthy undershirt in the nameless Deputy Warden's face, or his exclamations in praise of liberty and revolution and "Death to the anti-Semites." These are all memorable dramatic moments, satisfying to readers who have spent several hundred pages waiting for something to happen. They all represent changes Yakov has gone through, and that the world had gone through because of him. All of the various dramatic moral twists come together in the question of fatherhood. In this novel, fatherhood represents both identity and responsibility, the two ways of knowledge that Yakov Bok has to accept if he is ever to escape his suffering. Responsibility is every parent's fate: it is in acting as a conduit, of conveying the identity of Judaism from previous generations into the future, that he fails and fails again until his sufferings have finally taught him better.

There is every reason for the thread of Jewish identity to die out with Yakov. Early in his life he learned the lesson that Judaism is trouble for its adherents. His father was killed for being a Jew, during an act of random violence that targeted him for nothing more than his religion. Yakov was raised in an orphanage, and, as if the story of his father's death hadn't been enough, experienced one of the periodical frenzies against Jews that swept over the Russian countryside in the late 1800s—a pogrom. Like a mythic hero, he had emerged from underground after three days, to take in the image of a Jew murdered and humiliated, his body being eaten by a pig. Of course nothing would be sacred for him. He had no religious training—"Torah I had little of and Talmud less," he explains of the orphanage he was raised in—but he was well trained in the social consequences of being a Jew.

One striking aspect of the early chapters of the novel, in Book I before Yakov leaves the shtetl, is the rapport that he has with his father-in-law, Shmuel. "A father-in-law's blood was thicker than water," he thinks regarding the uneven trade of his milking cow for the old man's decrepit horse. Still, it is not a blood relationship, but is founded on something that would seem even less substantial: their point of intersection is the wife who ran away from Yakov, and as a result one might expect his relationship to be even worse than an average in-law bond, not better. Yakov lets no opportunity pass to curse Raisl for leaving, and though it plainly hurts Shmuel he continually tries to soften his son-in-law, to make him a more forgiving man and consequently

What Do I Read Next?

- Austrian writer Franz Kafka's novel *The Trial*, first published in 1925, set the standard for novels about naive protagonists sucked into a complex, nightmarish legal system. Kafka's Joseph K. is so confused about of what he is supposed to be guilty that the term "Kafkaesque" has come to represent impersonal, irrational bureaucracy.

- Malamud has described *The Fixer* as a folk tale. Many of his shorter works fit this description. They have been collected in *The Stories of Bernard Malamud*, published by Farrar Straus Giroux in 1983.

- Isaac Bashevis Singer was a Polish-born Yiddish writer who won the Nobel Prize for Literature in 1982. Most of his stories take place in Jewish communities in rural Europe, and, like *The Fixer*, most of Singer's stories were written in a folktale style. Singer's first published novel, *Satan in Goray* (1935), deals with seventeenth-century pogroms in which Jews in Poland were brutally massacred by Cossacks.

- The case of Alfred Dreyfus, a Jewish army officer who was unjustly imprisoned for treason in France from 1894 to 1899, is mentioned in *The Fixer*. Of all that has been written about the case, which has come to be known as "The Dreyfus Affair," it is "J'Accuse," an 1898 letter about the case written by novelist Emile Zola, that has stood the test of time as a great work of literature.

- Bernard Malamud's friend Philip Roth is said to have patterned the character E. I. Lonoff, protagonist of his novel *The Ghost Writer*, on Malamud.

- Mendel Beilis, the man who was the model for Yakov Bok in this book, published an autobiography of his ordeal in 1926. Originally published as *The Story of My Sufferings*, it is currently available under the title *Scapegoat on Trial*.

- Another author, Sholom Aleichem, also wrote a novel based on the Mendel Beilis case, *The Bloody Hoax*, published by the University of Indiana press in 1991.

- Throughout *The Fixer*, the protagonist refers to his readings of the Dutch philosopher Baruch Spinoza. Spinoza's best-known work, his *Ethics*, is available in paperback from Everyman Press.

---

a better Jew. "What she did I won't defend—she hurt me as much as she did you," he tells Yakov. "Even more, when the rabbi says she's now dead my voice agrees, but not my heart … I've cursed her more than once but I ask God not to listen."

In no small way, Shmuel's relationship with Yakov mirrors the way Shmuel feels about his daughter: they both hurt him, but he absorbs it. It is not his religion that tells him how to accept misfortune, but instead he uses religion as a tool to put up with his lot. It is almost impossible to not see him as a father figure to Yakov, in the way that he frets, cajoles, bickers, pleads, and prays that the fixer will become a better man. When he visits Yakov in jail, though, his message is rejected. At

the height of his tribulation, the last thing Yakov wants to hear is that faith will make his misery worthwhile. "Ach, why do you make me talk fairy tales?," he asks, rejecting his people's faith while at the same time showing the speech pattern taught him by his culture. In the end, though, Yakov sees the full significance of his responsibility to Shmuel for what he has taught him about himself: "If I must suffer," he thinks, "let it be for Shmuel."

There are minor father figures among the Russians. When Bibikov first interrogates Yakov, he mentions as he is leaving, "I have to hurry now. My boy has a fever. My wife gets frantic." At the time, his domestic concerns might seem small to Yakov, faced with a fabricated murder charge, but in the greater scope of the novel Bibikov's intact family stands out as a healthy concern, especially when he is compared to the Russians who spend their time persecuting Jews. The fact that he mentions this small detail shows the closeness and confidentiality that he feels toward Yakov which, ultimately, is what gets him killed.

Lebedev's relationship with his daughter is inverted: he has become, through alcoholism, the child that has to be watched after, to be found in the streets when he doesn't come home, and tucked in when he does, and she in return is promiscuous. Marfa Golov's nightmarish relationship with her young delinquent son, Zhenia, whom she insists was a saint, proves abusive from her own oversweetened testimony, even without any proof that she was actually involved in his murder. It is the guard Kogin, though, who teaches Yakov the most about the suffering that must be borne in parenthood. Increasingly throughout the story, he expresses his worries about the trouble his son Trofim will get into, a fear that turns out justified when Trofim kills a man while robbing his house. "He came to an end I had predicted for him, all of a father's love gone for nothing," Kogin tells Yakov, and then he commits his most humane act toward his prisoner, offering him a cigarette. In the end, he takes responsibility for saving Yakov's life, the way he once took responsibility for his son, because he identifies with him: "I know his sorrows," he says while defending him.

While *The Fixer* moves upward, from the absent father figures introduced in the first chapter to fathers who accept their children and are willing to suffer for them, there is also a rise in the instances of child-images in Yakov's life. Chronologically, his story starts back even before the incidents that are described in the book. The chain of events is set into motion by his wife Raisl's abandonment of him, once it was determined that they could not conceive a child together. Early in the story, when her father asks him why he quit sleeping with her, he responds, "how long can a man sleep with a barren woman? I got tired of trying." His despair about being childless has led to Raisl leaving in frustration, which makes Yakov himself leave the shtetl. Departing from his religious surroundings gives him the illusion of freedom that makes him walk into the danger of working in an area where Jews are forbidden, which makes him a suspect. Much as he regrets not having children, he is not ready for fatherhood at the beginning of the novel. He is more prepared to be a drifter, lacking identity and lacking responsibilities. He is well suited to excel as a modern ur-

A Jewish man reads scripture in a synagogue.

ban man, with no family to tether his career, free to excel at his own pace. By going to Kiev instead of sitting around waiting for Raisl to come back or staying anchored within his religious community, he is making the most of his situation.

There are several ironies about his idea that Raisl is barren. First and most obvious is the fact that she is perfectly able to have children, proven by the fact that she becomes pregnant a few months after leaving Yakov. If the arc of events described in the novel springs from the idea that she could never conceive, it is sprung in error. Despair in itself is sad enough, but the despair that Yakov took for granted, the empty future he predicted, is a hoax in itself. Another twist of fate is that the family that would have held them together comes at a time when they can least use it: Yakov is in jail, and Raisl is struggling to make enough to feed herself and her father. Still, with no better reason than a growing sense of moral obligation, Yakov writes out a lie claiming responsibility for the child, an act that comes along with his refusal to lie about the truth of his guilt on a confession. Raisl's child, Chaiml, is Jewish, contrary to what Yakov has always suspected about the man with whom she ran away.

The one image of a child that shows readers that Yakov has come around to the mature sensibilities required by parenthood is the identification he has with the young Cossack soldier who is mutilated outside of his carriage during the chaotic final scene. Yakov notices him, riding on a gray mare, trying to keep the crowd in order, "[a]nd though he had no reason to, he smiled a little at the Cossack for his youth and good looks, and for being, as such things go, a free man, give or take a little." In the next minute, a bomb explodes, and as the smoke clears Yakov sees that the young man's foot has been blown off. As they carry him away Yakov feels empathy for this boy who is everything he is not—young, free, Catholic. He is able to understand the soldier's hurt and confusion, which mirrors his own suffering: "he looked in horror and anguish at Yakov as though to say, 'What has my foot got to do with it,'" showing a sense of absurdity with which Yakov could certainly identify.

From this experience, Yakov realizes that the fight is not between practitioners of different faiths or classes. He is as responsible for the young Cossack as he would be for his own son, and, when, in his fantasy, the Tsar tries to make himself a sympathetic figure by talking of his own son, Yakov realizes that he has a duty to all those who are suffering because of the privileged class. In his dream, he shoots the Tsar, so that in his reality he can make the world safe for the children of future generations.

Source: David Kelly, in an essay for *Novels for Students,* Gale, 2000.

Stephen Farber

In the following article, Farber evaluates the film version of The Fixer, *finding that it "inherits all of the weaknesses" of the "disastrous" novel that preceded it.*

The movies invariably "discover" a novelist just after he produces his poorest work. Bernard Malamud is a gifted writer, and *The Assistant* seems to me a remarkable achievement, subtly controlled, tartly observed, harrowing, yet a genuinely poetic and compassionate vision of human pain. In *The Fixer* Malamud abandoned a world he knew firsthand to grapple with the Jewish Problem and the indomitability of the human spirit: a fictionalization of the case of Mendel Beilis, a Jew accused of the ritual murder of a child in czarist Russia. The result was a pretty disastrous novel, but a natural for the best-seller list, with just enough pretension for the Pulitzer committee and plenty of lurid thrills for the hungry suburban sadomasochists. The prison scenes in the novel, savored in rancid detail,

are as sensational and as revolting as in any piece of porno-violence I can imagine, but since Malamud's reputation had already been secured, sophisticated readers were quite prepared to suffer along with Yakov Bok. Even the novel's tepid liberal sermon about injustice and conscience is a fraud. Ostensibly a protest against hate and prejudice, *The Fixer*'s cartoon-simple pageant of Russian sadists and bigots reveals exactly the kind of small-minded stereotyping that it pretends to deplore.

Now John Frankenheimer, one of the most talented American filmmakers working today, has fallen victim to the material. His film of *The Fixer,* though well photographed and well acted, inherits all of the weaknesses of the original. With a little less reverence for Malamud the film *might* have worked. The most interesting element in the novel was the characterization of Yakov Bok, particularly in the opening scenes. (These turn out to be the best scenes in the film too—Alan Bates perfectly captures Bok's timidity and self-deprecating sense of humor.) Malamud had done this character more fully before, and so had Saul Bellow, Philip Roth, Bruce Jay Friedman, and other Jewish writers. But to film audiences the character of the *schlemiel,* introverted, anxious, masochistic, may still be relatively fresh; only this past year, in Sidney Lumet's underrated *Bye Bye Braverman,* the first half of *I Love You, Alice B. Toklas,* moments of Barbara Streisand's performance in *Funny Girl,* have American movies begun to absorb some of the ethnic inflections of Jewish-American folklore.

But it was not the *schlemiel* hero of *The Fixer* that attracted Frankenheimer to the material. His films almost always deal with extreme forms of degradation, persecution, oppression, whether it is parental oppression in *The Young Stranger* and *All Fall Down,* political oppression in *The Manchurian Candidate* and *Seven Days in May,* or weird, inexplicable, almost preternatural oppression in the science fictional *Seconds.* And he has even done one other film about a man in solitary confinement, the excellent *Birdman of Alcatraz.* Frankenheimer is obsessively drawn to the figure of the victim, isolated, utterly defenseless, but struggling desperately to reassert his freedom against monstrous forms of tyranny. To say that there is something paranoid and masochistic in Frankenheimer's temperament is probably true, but those psychological labels do not help to understand his art. The pertinent point is that out of profound personal anxieties, he has created at least twice—in *The Manchurian Candidate* and *Seconds*—brilliant, original filmic nightmares of persecution. I felt that if anyone could salvage *The Fixer,* he could. I was not particularly looking forward to the film, but I thought it might turn out to be the definitive study of man in captivity. Instead, it remains a sluggish, morbid, pompous preachment.

The crucial question to be asked about the film, as about the novel: Why was it made? What is the purpose of *lingering* on the suffering of an abused Jew in pre-Revolutionary Russia? This may seem like a naive question; many people assume that the most awesome and uncompromising art concerns man's past barbarisms to his fellow man. I am not so convinced of the automatic relevance of watching the savagery of another era, and I should say that I am just as uneasy about most of the films that treat the Nazi experience: I resent the grim, gratuitous (though visually inventive) Czech film *The Fifth Horseman Is Fear* for essentially the same reasons that I resent *The Fixer.* It is supposed to be bracing to know of the atrocities that men have committed out of fear and hate and ignorance in this twentieth century. But we all do know by now. Does every reminder deserve our respect? Is it unreasonable to ask for some fresh insight, some illumination of our own society, or the human condition, or even the possible explanations for these atrocities? Just to *present* the atrocities is not illuminating.

Some of the best films ever made are historical fictions, but they do find a way of implicating us. Even simple horror films sometimes upset our complacency; *The Fixer,* gruesome as it is, only intensifies it. Audiences do penance for a couple of hours, devoutly acknowledging the wretchedness of the 1910 Russian Jew's existence, and then, cleansed of guilt, return to their newspapers and TV sets as stupefied as ever. The film doesn't connect with their own experience—it's too narrowly about a specific, remote time and place, and at the same time, paradoxically, too "universal", too general. It has no resonances, no aftertaste.

Of course it's easy enough to come up with some ringing statements about what *The Fixer* "really" means, but these probably don't have much to do with the experience of watching the film. For *The Fixer,* seizing at the prestigious laurels of High Art, in fact trades on the emotional responses of the very lowest. Who doesn't cringe at the closeup of a swollen, bloody foot or moan when a man is beaten to unconsciousness? Just as instinctively, the audience applauds when Yakov, ever humiliated, manages to score a minor point against his tormentors—identifying the Prosecuting Attorney's nose on a chart of "Jewish noses", or dressing up in prayer shawl and phylacteries to frighten off an idiot priest. The Torture Scene, The Triumph of the Underdog, even, for catharsis, The Martyr Thronged by Cheering Crowds—*The Fixer* is filled with familiar staples of pulp melodrama. These are the *easiest* responses a film can attempt, and the fact that *The Fixer* gets them should not be counted in its favor. The pity is that it so rarely tries for more subtle responses.

The screenplay was written by Dalton Trumbo, and it may not be farfetched to perceive an allusion to his own suffering under the notorious Hollywood blacklist of the McCarthy period: the scapegoat, innocent of all crimes, victim of a government's paranoid "international Jewish conspiracy" theory (the words are from the film), imprisoned and tormented because his ideas are alien. There are some leaden nuggets of political theory—people are united by hate, not love, and it serves the government's purpose if they hate the Jews rather than the czar—but it makes just as much sense to interpret the film's solemnity as Trumbo's self-pitying identification with the innocent man subjected to monumentally inhuman treatment. This interpretation does not, of course, make the film any more interesting.

Trumbo, always interested in themes of social significance, may have influenced the film in another, less obvious, but very important way. The express message of *The Fixer* is that Yakov Bok, through his suffering, develops for the first time a social and political conscience, a hitherto unfelt loyalty to the Jewish people, a sense of responsibility to his fellow man. As he tells the minister of justice "Something in me has changed. I fear less and hate more…. If the state acts in ways that are abhorrent to human nature, it's the lesser evil to destroy the state". His own degradation is supposed to have transformed him from a nonpolitical man into a quiet sort of political revolutionary. But at another point late in the film, Yakov's lawyer gushes, "It's a great honor to defend you", and Yakov replies determinedly, "It's just a dirty suffering. There's no honor in it". In fact, this is how the film looks to us—simply one dirty humiliation after another, without honor, without meaning. But then Yakov's passionate, defiant speech to the minister of justice seems incongruous. Is the imprisonment "just a dirty suffering" or is it a semi-heroic endurance that leads to a significant spiritual awakening? The film cannot really play for both cynicism and inspiration. It would be extremely difficult to dramatize an inner conversion, a growth of conscience and political involvement in any film. But it is *impossible* when another strain of the film—the desire to make the imprisonment look as dirty and gruesome as possible—is working directly against the conversion story. It is easy enough for Trumbo to write a few lines of dialogue in which Yakov *asserts* that a transformation has taken place, but film is a visual medium, and we believe what we see, not what we're told. A novel has an advantage in this respect because it *can* render the workings of consciousness. But the conversion motif was the book's biggest weakness too. Malamud tried to build the sense of Yakov's inner maturation through lengthy passages in which the fixer struggled with Spinoza, History, and Necessity or spoke sociology with a fantasized czar. These were the worst pieces of writing in the novel, because they did not belong to the consciousness of an ignorant handyman but were imposed from without, and written, besides, with all of the gassy awkwardness that usually overwhelms an artist when he wants to prove that he is also a philosopher. These monologues are luckily missing from the film, but nothing is there to replace them. Frankenheimer has been unable to find a way of visualizing an intellectual conversion, and so that conversion seems, as in the novel, merely a sop to the audience—a flimsy rationalization for all of the morbidity. Malamud and Trumbo and Frankenheimer piously raise their eyes to heaven at *The Fixer*'s finale; our eyes, unfortunately, are still on the shit on the prison floor.

What destroys the film is that Frankenheimer, fascinated by images of extreme suffering, cannot quite explore that obsession because he is burdened with Malamud's, and Trumbo's, and undoubtedly his own social pretensions. In a strange way I would have more respect for the film if it were a relentless, grotesque, hysterical study of confinement—in other words, more sadistic—because then the film would be truer to Frankenheimer's personal vision of oppression; and only this kind of intense personal document, even if shrill and overwrought, could unsettle us by touching on the unspoken terrors that we are share. But the film is too "tasteful", too "responsible" to abandon its flat message about political commitment for fullscale cinema of cruelty. That is *The Fixer* is not quite harrowing enough to involve us deeply, not quite cruel enough to be invigorating; it is just cruel enough, basted with unctuous moral fervor, to be unpleasant and offensive.

I have written about the film at this length partly because I dislike it, but also because I admire Frankenheimer and am concerned about his career. Even in *The Fixer* there are sequences that show unmistakable cinematic talent—the violently edited pogrom at the start of the film, a tense scene in which an old Hassid guiltily, embarrassedly eats a piece of matzo in Yakov's room, the startling cut from dark prison cell to the brightly lit palace of the minister of justice or, later, to the open air of Yakov's village as he escapes in a moment of fantasy. Frankenheimer does beautiful things with editing, and he can make just the sudden appearance of sunlight very moving. But like most American directors, Frankenheimer is at a tremendous disadvantage, in comparison with European directors, because he does not write his own scripts. He is at the mercy of other men's ideas. And he is all too susceptible to the Socially Significant theme, as he has already demonstrated in *The Young Savages* and *Seven Days in May.* The careers of our talented directors are likely to be crippled because they are rarely given complete freedom to explore themes that concern them; they rarely have an opportunity to experiment or to grow. They must buy best-sellers, and work from scripts by men whose concerns may be subtly different from their own. It is little wonder that so many American films are so messy. Of course some of the mess in *The Fixer* can be attributed to Frankenheimer's own uncertainties. It may be a personal desire to imagine the victim's triumph over tyranny that leads him to put so much false emphasis on Yakov Bok's internal transformation. *The Fixer* is not the first of his films to have an uplifting ending. (It may not be irrelevant that his two best films, *The Manchurian Candidate* and *Seconds,* are tragedies.) But the commercial system in which American films are made—the stress on properties from other media, the hostility between the Writers Guild and the Directors Guild, the pressure to make large statements that can make millions quiver—places an unnatural burden on the creative artist. Any artist may fail because of his *own* confusions; but the artist-in-Hollywood has to reckon with the confusions of too many other people. *The Fixer* represents a particularly sad example of what the outcome is likely to be.

Source: Stephen Farber, in a review in *Hudson Review,* Vol. XXII, 1969, pp. 134-38.

Granville Hicks

In the following essay, Hicks presents Malamud's The Fixer *as a work containing literary greatness, dealing with a man who suffered injustice and who learned both to endure and to resist.*

If I say, as I am prepared to do, that Bernard Malamud's *The Fixer* is one of the finest novels of the postwar period, I don't see how there can be much argument. If, however, I go on to agree with the publishers that it is a "great" novel, I may be in semantic difficulties. Recently I asserted that there is greatness in John Barth's *Giles Goat-boy*, which I believe to be true. Robert Scholes, on the other hand, writing in the *New York Times Book Review*, admitted of no qualification; he said flatly that it is "a great novel." He made a good case, too, but at the end he brought in an argument that I found disturbing. Barth's audience, he said, "must be that same audience whose capacities have been extended and prepared by [James] Joyce, [Marcel] Proust, [Thomas] Mann, and [William] Faulkner." He continued: "For some time we have been wondering what to do with the training given us by those giants of modern fiction, wondering whether we were really meant to expend our hard-earned responsiveness on such estimable but unexciting writers as C. P. Snow and Saul Bellow. The answer now seems clear. The difference between competence and genius can hardly be made clearer. And Barth is a comic genius of the highest order".

Who are the "we" who have been wondering? Mr. Scholes, I gather, and probably other academic critics. This calls to mind what Bellow said in his address to the recent International Congress of the P.E.N. Club. He complained that various critics in university posts had laid hold of the avant-garde heroes of an earlier generation, using their work to set a standard by which contemporary writers could be judged and condemned. In the version I read, in the *Times Book Review,* Bellow's argument wasn't completely clear, but I think I understand at least part of what he was saying. When Scholes calls Snow "estimable but unexciting," I can follow him, for Snow has deliberately adopted old-fashioned techniques, and the wonder is that he has managed to do as much with them as he has. But Bellow has constantly experimented with the form of the novel and has developed a powerful style that is peculiarly his. Bracketing Snow and Bellow tell us nothing about Barth—though something about Scholes.

What I am saying, of course, is what I have said before that there are more kinds than one of literary merit and even greatness. I think *Giles Goat-Boy* and *The Fixer* are both unusually good and unusually important novels, though they have little in common except their excellence. Malamud

has told a straightforward story in language of the greatest austerity. Although he began his literary career with a novel based on myth, *The Natural,* and has often introduced elements of fantasy in his short stories, *The Fixer* is realistic in the most precise sense of that term. But the story is told so purely and with such power that it has the large meanings—what some people call the "universal" meanings—of legend.

Malamud tells about a Jewish handyman who was arrested in Kiev in 1911, was charged with having committed a ritual murder, and suffered greatly for more than two years before being tried. To begin with, before I had read the book, I wondered why Malamud should expect his readers to be concerned about what happened to this one Jew half a century ago, in view of what had happened to six million Jews during the Second World War. It did not take me long to realize that Malamud had deliberately set himself this problem. Six million was a figure, but a man was a man. If he could tell this story well enough, he must have decided, this one unprepossessing man, this Yakov Bok, could represent not only the martyrs of Belsen and Auschwitz but all victims of man's inhumanity. We the readers could be made to feel for this one man what we could not possibly feel for the six million.

Malamud has written: "After my last novel I was sniffing for an idea in the direction of injustice on the American scene, partly for obvious reasons—this was a time of revolutionary advances in Negro rights—and partly because I became involved with this theme in a way that sets off my imagination in terms of art." He thought of civil rights workers in the South, of Sacco and Vanzetti, of Dreyfus, of Caryl Chessman, and then he remembered Mendel Beiliss, about whom his father had told him, and something happened. "In *The Fixer,*" he explains, "I use some of his [Mendel Beiliss's] experiences, though not, basically, the man, partly because his life came to less than he paid for by his suffering and endurance, and because I had to have room to invent. To his trials in prison I added something of Dreyfus's and Vanzetti's, shaping the whole to suggest the quality of the afflictions of the Jews under Hitler. These I dumped on the head of poor Yakov Bok…. So a novel that began as an idea concerned with injustice in America today has become one set in Russia fifty years ago, dealing with anti-Semitism there. Injustice is injustice."

Yakov Bok is nobody but Yakov Bok, and he is one of the most fully rendered characters in modern literature. An odd-job man, a Jack-of-all-trades, a fixer, he lives in a small Jewish community near Kiev. His wife, by whom he has had no children, has deserted him, and he finally makes a deal with her father and sets out for the city with the latter's horse and wagon. He is poor, proud, and bitter, with a fine sardonic wit. When his father-in-law tells him that, in going to the city, he is looking for trouble, he replies, "I've never had to look." When his wagon collapses, he asks, "Who invented my life?" Although he has had almost no formal education, he has read Spinoza and tried to understand him, and he calls himself a freethinker.

Even before he has reached Kiev, Yakov has encountered a violently anti-Semitic ferryman, and from the first he feels the hostility of the city. Bitter as he is, however, he has compassion for mankind, and when he sees a drunken Russian dying in the snow, he rescues him even though the man wears the badge of the Jew-hating Black Hundreds. Nikola Maximovitch, though he would exterminate the Jews, is capable of crying over the death of a dog, and he wants to reward his benefactor, whom he does not know to be Jewish. Thus Yakov is given a job, which he badly needs, in a brickyard. Because he is living in a district forbidden to most Jews, he is ill at ease, but he has to have money to live on.

When he is arrested, Yakov assumes that he is to be punished for some minor offense, and it takes him a while to grasp the horrible nature of the charge against him. Only when he is confronted with the witnesses for the prosecution, mostly men and women who are using anti-Semitic prejudice to conceal their own crimes, does he realize that he is the victim of a monstrous conspiracy. And he asks, as who wouldn't, why me?

Because the prosecution's case is so weak, Yakov's trial is postponed for two years, during which time his miseries multiply. Lodged in filth, never adequately fed, bowed down with disease, given little or nothing with which to occupy his mind, systematically tortured by the guards, finally chained to the wall of his cell, he endures such suffering as the reader is loath to contemplate. But Malamud, without sensationalism, without high-pitched emotionalism, makes us feel what we would prefer not to feel. Having himself fully entered into Yakov's ordeals in an extraordinary feat of empathy, he forces us to go at least some distance with him.

One of the ways in which Malamud compels realization of Yakov's suffering is to let him compare present with past. The life in the shtetl, which had once seemed to him poisonously narrow and dull, now takes on an idyllic aspect: "You can smell the grass and the flowers and look at the girls, if one or two happen to be passing by along the road. You can also do a day's work if there's work to do. Today there's a little carpentering job. You work up a sweat sawing wood apart and hammering it together. When it's time to eat you open up your food parcel—not bad. The thing about food is to have it when you want it. A hard-boiled egg with a pinch of salt is delicious. Also some sour cream with a cut-up potato. If you dip bread into fresh milk and suck before swallowing, it tastes like a feast…. After all, you're alive and free. Even if you're not so free, you think you are".

But later the miseries that made Yakov's pre-Kiev life appear a paradise come to seem a kind of happiness: "Yakov thought how it used to be before he was chained to the wall. He remembered sweeping the floor with the birch broom. He remembered reading Zhitnyak's gospels, and the Old Testament pages…. He thought of being able to urinate without having to call the guards; and of only two searches a day instead of a terrifying six. He thought of lying down on the straw mattress any time he wanted to; but now he could not even lie down on the wooden bed except when they released him to…. Yakov thought he would be glad if things went back to how they had once been. He wished he had enjoyed the bit of comfort, in a way of freedom, he had then".

Throughout the days and months and years of pain and despair, Yakov faces two temptations. What the anti-Semites in the government, from Czar Nicholas down, want to prove is that ritual murder is an essential part of the Jewish religion and that therefore all persecutions of the Jews are justified. More than once they promise Yakov that if he will testify that the boy was murdered by Jews for reasons of ritual, he himself will be treated leniently. Although he has never felt close to the Jewish community and has rejected the Jewish faith, he refuses to lend himself to so evil a conspiracy, even when his wife is sent to his cell with a confession for him to sign.

The other temptation is suicide. The idea inevitably occurs to him as soon as he understands the power of the forces drawn up against him. When the one Russian official who has shown a rudimentary sense of decency in his dealings with Yakov is framed because of that fact and sent to Yakov's prison, where he hangs himself, the poor persecuted Jew thinks of following his example. But he realizes that suicide would also be a betrayal of millions of people. "He's half a Jew himself, yet enough of one to protect them. After all, he knows the people; and he believes in their right to be Jews and to live in the world like men. He is against those who are against them. He will protect them to the extent that he can". "I'll live", he cries out in his cell, "I'll wait, I'll come to my trial".

All that he has endured has strengthened Yakov. Always a thinker in his uneducated way, he has recognized his historic role and, though he laments its being forced on him, he accepts it. "We're all in history", he thinks, "that's sure, but some are more than others, Jews more than some". As skeptical as ever about the existence of God, he believes that it is incumbent on men to stand for what they believe. Although in some ways more tolerant, for instance of his wife, he has not become saintly: "I'm not the same man I was. I fear less and hate more".

The climax of the novel comes in an imaginary dialogue between Yakov and the Czar. After describing his own misfortune, the latter says, "Surely it [suffering] has taught you the meaning of mercy"? Yakov replies, "Excuse me, Your Majesty, but what suffering has taught me is the uselessness of suffering, if you don't mind me saying so." He reminds the Czar of his failures as a ruler: "You had your chances and pissed them away. There's no argument against that. It's not easy to twist events by the tail but you might have done something for a better life for us all—for the future of Russia, one might say, but you didn't". While a carriage brings him closer to his trial, Yakov thinks: "As for history, there are ways to reverse it. What the Czar deserves is a bullet in the gut. Better him than us". "One thing I've learned, he thought, there's no such thing as an unpolitical man, especially a Jew. You can't be one without the other, that's clear enough. You can't sit still and see yourself destroyed". There the book ends, and, when one remembers what was in Malamud's mind when it was conceived, rightly ends. Yakov has learned not merely to endure, If I may use William Faulkner's favorite word, but also to resist.

Source: Granville Hicks, "One Man to Stand for Six Million," in *Saturday Review,* September 10, 1966, pp. 37-39.

Sources

Dorothy Seidman Bilek, "Malamud's Secular Saints and Comic Jobs," *Immigrant-Survivors: Post-Holocaust Consciousness in Recent Jewish American Fiction,* Wesleyian University Press, 1981, pp. 53-80.

Alan Warren Friedman, "The Hero as Schnook," *Bernard Malamud and the Critics,* edited with an introduction by Leslie A. Field and Joyce W. Field, New York University Press, 1970.

Sheldon J. Hershinow, *Bernard Malamud,* Frederick Ungar Publishing Co., 1980.

Gerald Hoag, "Malamud's Trial: *The Fixer* and the Critics," *Western Humanities Review,* Winter, 1970, pp. 1-12.

Sidney Richman, *Bernard Malamud,* Twayne Publishers, 1966.

For Further Study

Salo Wittemayer Baron, *The Russian Jew under Tsars and Soviets,* MacMillan, 1976.
This highly regarded book is out of print but still on the shelves of many school libraries.

Joel Carmichael, *The Satanizing of the Jews: Origin and Development of Mystical Anti-Semitism,* Fromm International, 1993.
This book examines the history behind the attitude that allowed the population of Kiev to be stirred up against Yakov and made them believe that, because of his religion, he would have perpetuated a ritualistic bloodletting.

Simon Dubnow, *History of the Jews,* 4th definitive revised edition, T. Yoseloff, 1973.
Dubnow is a greatly respected Jewish historian, and this work, originally published in Russian, contains the bulk of his life's work.

Robert Ducharme, *Art and Idea in the Novels of Bernard Malamud: Toward* The Fixer, Mouton Publisher, 1974.
One of the most thorough scholarly books written about *The Fixer,* examining it from all possible angles.

Charles Y. Glock and Rodney Stark, *Christian Beliefs and Anti-Semitism,* Harper and Row, 1966.
This book, published the same year as *The Fixer,* is part of a study that was being conducted by the Anti-Defamation League of B'Nai B'rith, a Jewish service organization.

A. S. Tager, *The Decay of Czarism: The Beilis Trial,* The Jewish Publication Society of America, 1935.
This early history of the Mendel Beilis affair was written when the Soviet Union was still young and old bitterness still seethed.

Gone with the Wind

Margaret Mitchell
1936

Published in 1936, *Gone with the Wind* became an immediate best-seller, bringing first-time novelist Margaret Mitchell an overwhelming amount of critical and popular attention. Awarded the 1937 Pulitzer Prize, the novel was adapted as a film in 1939—an achievement that won ten Academy Awards. A historical romance set in northern Georgia during the drama of the Civil War and Reconstruction years, *Gone with the Wind* traces the life of Scarlett O'Hara and her relationships with Rhett Butler, and Ashley and Melanie Wilkes. The novel addresses such themes as survival, romantic love, and the societal structuring of gender and class.

Early appraisals of the novel noted its memorable characters and historical accuracy as well as Mitchell's remarkable storytelling ability, though other reviews dismissed the novel as melodramatic and trite. Mitchell drew on her extensive knowledge of Civil War history in order to establish a believable setting for *Gone with the Wind,* but also spent considerable time fact-checking in the Atlanta Public Library. Biographers and critics have discovered striking similarities between real people in Mitchell's life and characters in the novel, though whether Mitchell intentionally modeled her characters after people she knew is unclear. What remains certain, however, is that her powerful, enduring story of love and survival set in the pre- and postwar South has made *Gone with the Wind* one of the most popular novels in American history.

Author Biography

Born in 1900, Margaret Mitchell lived her entire life in Atlanta, Georgia, as had her parents and grandparents. Mitchell grew up immersed in family history, listening to the stories of relatives who had survived the Civil War in northern Georgia. Both of her parents were well-versed in Georgian and southern history, and Mitchell's brother edited the *Atlantic Historical Bulletin.* This strong family interest in history helped Mitchell create a realistic backdrop for her novel *Gone with the Wind.*

Mitchell began writing as a young girl, often spending hours at a time composing stories and plays. She continued writing through her school years, and received encouragement from English teachers in high school and in college. Her English professor at Smith College considered her quite talented, but Mitchell distrusted her opinion.

In 1919, following the death of her mother, Mitchell dropped out of Smith and moved back to Atlanta to live with her father and brother. Three years later, she married Berrien Kinnard Upshaw, nicknamed "Red," but their stormy marriage ended quickly with an annulment. Mitchell's second marriage was to John Marsh, who had been the best man at her first wedding. At about this time she also started working at the *Atlanta Journal* as a feature writer. Linda Ludwig, writing in *American Women Writers,* states that Mitchell soon became known as a "talented and disciplined writer with an imaginative and witty style." After four successful years with the newspaper, Mitchell quit in 1926. She began writing *Gone with the Wind* that same year after an ankle injury forced her to remain in bed. Mitchell entertained herself during her convalescence by reading library books, but one day, Marsh, who had been bringing her the books, announced that she had exhausted the library's supply of interesting books. If she wanted something to read, he told her, she would simply have to write it herself. So Mitchell, accepting the challenge, sat down at her typewriter and commenced writing what would become the most popular novel in American history.

Mitchell wrote the last chapter of *Gone with the Wind* first, and thereafter proceeded somewhat chronologically, working steadily for several years. In 1935, a friend arranged for her to meet Harold Latham of Macmillan Publishing Company. Initially reluctant, Mitchell finally gave Latham her manuscript to read, and warned him of its deficiencies. Latham was captivated by the novel and

Margaret Mitchell

Macmillan published *Gone with the Wind* in 1936. It was an immediate best-seller, and Mitchell became an overnight celebrity, a role she did not entirely welcome. She was dumbfounded by the book's phenomenal success, maintaining that nothing about it warranted the attention it received. But the public obviously disagreed. *Gone with the Wind* won the 1937 Pulitzer Prize and was adapted as a film in 1939.

Mitchell never wrote another novel, but spent a considerable amount of time personally answering fan mail. When she died in 1949 after being hit by a car, she was mourned by millions of fans for whom *Gone with the Wind* had become an American classic.

Plot Summary

Twilight of the Old South

Scarlett O'Hara is the antiheroine of *Gone with the Wind,* a character who breaks the conventions of a romance novel from the first line of the book— "Scarlett O'Hara was not beautiful, but men seldom realized it." A spoiled, high-tempered, and strong-willed sixteen-year-old Southern belle, Scarlett is the eldest of three O'Hara daughters who live an idyllic life on a North Georgian plantation called Tara. In the opening scenes, the O'Haras prepare to entertain their neighbors with a barbecue, and Scarlett plots to capture the man she loves—Ashley Wilkes—from her friend, Melanie. However, Ashley rejects her, and Scarlett's nemesis, Rhett Butler, overhears her humiliation. Rhett, a wealthy outcast from high society who "looks like one of the Borgias," is both amused by and interested in Scarlett.

The Civil War

News of the war reaches Tara, and Scarlett's life and the lives of everyone around her are immediately and irrevocably altered. Frustrated by circumstances and rejected by Ashley, she marries Melanie's brother, Charles, stealing him away from India Wilkes. Charles goes to war and dies, like most of the young men who attended the O'Haras' party. Inglorious in Scarlett's eyes, Charles dies from measles, not fighting. The widowed Scarlett grows restless at her plantation home, and relocates to Atlanta, moving in with her sister-in-law Melanie and her Aunt Pitty. Melanie feels great love and respect for Scarlett, but Scarlett is jealous of her and hates her. Scarlett scandalizes Atlanta society with her defiant refusal to mourn her husband appropriately, and in a key scene dances at a charity ball despite the breach of etiquette such an action creates. Rhett is the winning bidder in the "auction" for her next dance, and though still in love with Ashley Wilkes, Scarlett soon comes to enjoy Rhett's company.

Rhett's "shady" activities now include blockade-running, and his outspoken views on both the war and Southern society make him even more of an outsider, albeit a gentlemanly one. Rhett and Scarlett argue incessantly, but he is the only person who really understands her. For the next few years, the condition of the Confederacy grows worse. Union troops begin to draw closer to Atlanta as Melanie is about to deliver a child, so Scarlett refuses to flee the city with the majority of its inhabitants. The city is set on fire and in a highly dramatic sequence, Scarlett is forced to deliver Melanie's baby. After Melanie gives birth, she, Scarlett, and the servants flee with the aid of Rhett.

Scarlett returns to Tara, and learns that the region has been nearly destroyed, along with her family. Her sisters have fallen ill, her father has had a mental collapse, and her mother is dead. The Union army has moved through the area, burning and looting the properties of her neighbors. Tara has been ransacked but left intact. There is no food to be had,

and Scarlett searches the grounds of the plantation and the surrounding countryside for something to eat. She does manual labor for the first time, and after her struggle, vows that she will "never go hungry again."

Reconstruction

When the war ends, the plantation recovers. Enormous taxes are levied on the property, and Scarlett decides to move to Atlanta to steal her sister's fiancé, Frank Kennedy, whose modest fortune will pay her debts. With the family home and finances secured, Scarlett now becomes an outstanding businesswoman, expanding Frank's sawmill business until it flourishes. On one outing she is harassed by a group of men, which includes some black men. This leads to a Ku Klux Klan response, which Rhett despises. During the attack, Frank is killed, and Scarlett becomes a widow once again.

Next, Scarlett marries Rhett. Their relationship is not a smooth one, but they have a child—Bonnie Blue—whom Rhett adores. Scarlett's ongoing obsession with Ashley begins to frustrate Rhett more and more, climaxing in a dramatic scene in which he forces her to have sex with him. In a deeply ambiguous sequence, this gives Scarlett the only true physical passion that she has ever had, underlining the themes of dependence, enslavement, force, and love that run throughout the novel. Scarlett becomes pregnant again, but loses the baby—another of the bitter disappointments that are growing between Rhett and his wife. Bonnie Blue—beautiful, headstrong, and high-spirited like her mother—is killed when she is thrown from a horse while making a jump that is far too high for her. Rhett is crazed with grief. Stunned, Scarlett retreats into coldness and, having already given birth to a son and a daughter by her two previous marriages, informs Rhett that she wants no more children. She insists that they maintain separate sleeping quarters and their relationship disintegrates.

Revelations

Melanie dies while giving birth, asking Scarlett to look after her bereft husband. Scarlett finally realizes that Ashley has always loved Melanie, and that she has never loved him—he's just a "child." Rhett is the "man"—the one she's loved all along. The knowledge comes too late. Tired at last of her feelings for Ashley, Rhett leaves her, no longer in love. She begs him to stay, asking him what she will do without him, and he replies with the book's most famous line, "My dear, I don't give a damn." Scarlett watches him go, and gradually gathers her strength. Vowing to go back to Tara and rebuild her life, she swears to get him back. As doubts assail her, she utters the novel's ambiguous closing words—"Tomorrow, I'll think of some way to get him back. After all, tomorrow is another day."

Characters

Archie

An ex-convict and former Confederate soldier who is taken in by Melanie.

Will Benteen

A former Confederate soldier, Will Benteen is on his way home from the war when his comrade leaves him at Tara because he's fallen ill with pneumonia. The O'Haras nurse him back to health and to show his gratitude he stays to help rebuild Tara. Although only a small "cracker" farmer, Will soon becomes instrumental in managing Tara. He eventually marries Suellen O'Hara.

Bonnie Butler

The spoiled, but adorable daughter of Scarlett and Rhett Butler. She dies tragically at the age of four when she is thrown from her pony.

Rhett Butler

Rhett Butler meets Scarlett for the first time at the Twelve Oaks plantation party and is immediately attracted to her high-spirited nature, eventually falling in love with her and convincing her to marry him. Tall, dark, and handsome with a hint of scandal about him, he succeeds in angering Scarlett when she discovers he eavesdropped on her impassioned conversation with Ashley at the party. Convinced he is no gentleman, Scarlett rebuffs him when he begins visiting her in Atlanta, but his charming manner and sense of fun usually wins her over. His cynicism and pragmatism concerning the Civil War lead him to become a blockade runner instead of a soldier, an occupation that makes him rich, and supremely attractive to Scarlett. His uncanny ability to read Scarlett completely is a source of constant irritation to her because she can never gain the upper hand with him as she does with other men.

After the death of Scarlett's second husband, she agrees to marry Rhett, though their marriage is not happy. Scarlett's persistent adoration of Ashley gradually wears Rhett down. After she and Ashley are caught embracing at the mill, Rhett, in a jealous, drunken rage, savagely seduces her by sweeping her off her feet and carrying her up to the bedroom—one of the most famous love scenes ever written. By the time Scarlett realizes her true passion is for Rhett and not Ashley, it's too late. Bonnie, the daughter Rhett doted on, is dead, and he has given up on Scarlett. With nothing left to tie him to Atlanta, he announces that he is leaving. Scarlett pleads with Rhett to stay, asking him forlornly what she will ever do without him. His famous, indifferent reply is, "My dear, I don't give a damn."

Cathy Calvert

One of Scarlett's old friends who is forced to marry the Calvert family overseer after her family loses everything.

Dilcey

An O'Hara slave, Dilcey married to Pork and mother of Prissy.

Hugh Elsing

Hugh is Mrs. Elsing's son and the unsuccessful manager of one of Scarlett's mills.

Mrs. Elsing

Friend to Aunt Pittypat, Mrs. Elsing is one of Atlanta society's most upstanding old ladies.

Grandma Fontaine

A shrewd old lady, part of the Fontaine clan, Grandma Fontaine gives Scarlett advice about surviving difficult times.

Johnnie Gallegher

Johnnie is one of Scarlett's mill managers who abuses the workers in order to generate high profits.

Charles Hamilton

Scarlett's first husband and Melanie's brother, Charles dies in the war.

Aunt Pittypat Hamilton

Aunt Pittypat is Charles and Melanie's spinster aunt with whom Scarlett and Melanie stay in Atlanta during the war. She leads a sheltered and pampered life and is incapable of making a decision without the help of her slave, Uncle Peter. Her love of gossip and silly, child-like demeanor make her a constant irritation to Scarlett.

The 1939 film of Mitchell's novel garnered ten Academy Awards. Vivien Leigh played the indomitable Scarlett and Clark Gable was the audacious Rhett.

Wade Hamilton

Scarlett and Charles Hamilton's shy son, Wade adores Melanie.

Ella Kennedy

Ella is Scarlett and Frank Kennedy's daughter, a silly girl who takes after Frank.

Frank Kennedy

Frank is initially Suellen's fiance whom Scarlett steals and marries because she needs his money to pay the taxes on Tara. Mild-mannered and old-fashioned, he is shocked by Scarlett's purchase and operation of a lumber mill, which ruins their reputation in Atlanta. He is killed during a Ku Klux Klan raid.

Mammy

Mammy is one of the O'Hara family house slaves, who initially belonged to Ellen. She helped raise the O'Hara girls, and her protective, mothering nature is sometimes overbearing. Scarlett often rebels against her strict standards for ladylike behavior. She remains loyal to the O'Hara family, staying with them after the war and looking down her nose at what she calls, "trashy free-issue niggers." She comes to Atlanta to live with Scarlett permanently after she marries Frank Kennedy.

Dr. Meade

Dr. Meade is husband to Mrs. Meade. Dr. Meade is unable to help Melanie with the delivery of her baby because he must tend to the soldiers wounded during the siege.

Mrs. Meade

An Atlanta lady who heads a hospital nursing committee for a war hospital, Mrs. Meade recruits Scarlett for her committee.

Mrs. Merriwether

Another upstanding matron of Atlanta and friend to Aunt Pittypat, Mrs. Merriwether goes into business selling homemade pies after the war.

Rene Picard

The colorful, Creole son-in-law of Mrs. Merriwether, Rene goes into business with her selling pies.

Careen O'Hara

Careen is Scarlett's meek, religious younger sister who is devastated by Brent Tarleton's death in the war. She eventually joins a convent.

Ellen O'Hara

Scarlett's mother, Ellen is a member of the well-known Robillard family of Charleston. Ellen is known throughout the county as a great lady, and Scarlett longs to be like her. She dies from typhoid fever, which she contracts while nursing the Slattery family through it.

Gerald O'Hara

Gerald is Scarlett's Irish-born father. A rough and wild-spirited man with a penchant for liquor, cards, and horseback riding, his brusque manner belies a gentler demeanor. His two greatest loves are his wife, Ellen, and his plantation, Tara. He relies almost completely on Ellen for the management of Tara. After Yankee soldiers destroy Tara almost totally and Ellen dies, he literally loses his mind. Because Gerald is incapable of rational thought, it is Scarlett that must take over the management of Tara after the war. He dies tragically in a riding accident after becoming upset over the Iron Clad Oath.

Scarlett O'Hara

Vain, flirtatious and utterly self-absorbed, Scarlett O'Hara makes an unlikely heroine. Other qualities, such as her courage and perseverance, ameliorate her bad points and make her an entertaining character. Although not particularly perceptive about people, she has a knack for seeing the reality of things, making decisions and following through on them no matter what she has to do. It is Scarlett on whom the whole family relies after the war. Her determination to save Tara becomes almost an obsession with her.

One of the most famous scenes of the novel is when Scarlett goes to Twelve Oaks plantation to look for food. Twelve Oaks has been burned to the ground, and the crops have been destroyed, but there is still food left in the slaves' garden. After digging for radishes, Scarlett makes a promise to herself, "As God is my witness, as God is my witness, the Yankees aren't going to lick me. I'm going to live through this, and when it's over, I'm never going to be hungry again. No, nor any of my folks. If I have to steal or kill—as God is my witness, I'm never going to be hungry again." This is a turning point for Scarlett, when she gives up all the trappings of the Southern belle and aggressively pursues financial security. Ironically, even though she longs to be a lady like her mother, everything she must do to save Tara makes her anything but a lady in the eyes of Southern society. Furthermore, she falls in love with Ashley because he's a beautiful gentleman and she wants to be his beautiful lady, not because she has anything in common with him. Scarlett goes after the superficial trappings of

Media Adaptations

- *Gone with the Wind* was adapted as a film in 1939, produced by David O. Selznick, and released by Metro-Goldwyn-Mayer Studios. The film stars Vivien Leigh, Clark Gable, Olivia de Havilland, and Leslie Howard.

ladyhood and love, never recognizing the true thing when she sees it, until it's much too late.

Suellen O'Hara

Scarlett's spoiled, older sister, Suellen proves virtually useless in restoring Tara after the war. Her shameless plan to get Gerald to sign the Iron Clad Oath leads to his death.

Uncle Peter

Uncle Peter is Aunt Pittypat's house slave.

Pork

Pork is Gerald's slave, whom he won in a poker game. Like Mammy, Pork remains loyal to the O'Hara family after the war, assisting with various tasks, such as hunting, around the plantation.

Prissy

Prissy is a slave girl who Scarlett takes with her to Atlanta the first time. She and Scarlett deliver Melanie's baby during the siege of Atlanta.

Big Sam

Former field hand at Tara, Big Sam is recruited to fight in the last days of the war. He saves Scarlett from being attacked by a gang of ex-slaves in Atlanta.

Emmie Slattery

A daughter of the poor Slattery family, Emmie marries the O'Hara's overseer, Jonas Wilkerson.

Beatrice Tarleton

Stuart and Brent's mother, Beatrice is known for her hot temper and expert horsemanship.

Brent Tarleton

Twin brothers Brent and Stuart are Scarlett's most ardent suitors. The novel opens with their visit to Scarlett in which they inform her of Ashley's engagement to Melanie. Stuart and Brent are killed in the war.

Stuart Tarleton

Brent's twin brother.

Belle Watling

Belle Watling is the madam of a whorehouse that Rhett Butler frequently visits. He befriends Belle, and subtle references are made to the fact that they had a son together. Together, she and Rhett help protect Ashley and other Ku Klux Klan members from being arrested for a raid on the ex-slaves that attacked Scarlett.

Mrs. Whiting

Another matron of Atlanta, Mrs. Whiting is part of Mrs. Elsing and Mrs. Merriwether's circle of friends.

Jonas Wilkerson

Overseer at Tara, Jonas is dismissed for impregnating Emmie Slattery. He and Emmie later try to buy Tara.

Ashley Wilkes

Ashley is the dreamy, golden-haired gentleman that captures Scarlett's heart. Educated and refined, he is the perfect picture of a Southern gentleman. But unlike Scarlett, he lacks the courage to succeed in the dramatically changed world in which they find themselves after the war. A member of the planter gentility, Ashley has been trained for nothing but the life of a gentleman plantation owner. He can't farm and he proves to be useless as Scarlett's mill manager. He symbolizes a bygone era, and is ruled entirely by his honor. His honor refuses to let him betray the Confederacy to save himself from going to jail during the war. It also prevents him from leaving Melanie for Scarlett, and keeps him from using the unscrupulous business practices that Scarlett employs to make money at her mill.

All of these honorable actions are incomprehensible to Scarlett, who is nothing if not pragmatic, selfish, and bold. Sadly, Ashley feels himself to be a coward. Rhett, who is supremely jealous of Scarlett's affections for him and scornful of his ideology, sums him up this way, "Ashley Wilkes—bah! His breed is of no use of value in an upside-down world like ours. Whenever the world upends, his kind is the first to perish. And why not? They don't deserve to survive because they won't fight—don't know how to fight."

Beau Wilkes

Beau is Melanie and Ashley Wilkes' son.

India Wilkes

Sister to Ashley, India intensely dislikes Scarlett. She catches Scarlett embracing Ashley at the mill along with Archie and Mrs. Elsing.

Melanie Hamilton Wilkes

Melanie becomes Scarlett's sister-in-law after Scarlett marries her brother. Somewhat plain and childlike in appearance, she is generous and kind to everyone, and is regarded as a lady of the first order. Her personality is almost the complete opposite of Scarlett's, although she adores Scarlett. Her inability to believe anything negative about the people she loves causes her to blindly defend Scarlett's scandalous behavior. Scarlett secretly hates her, resenting her marriage to Ashley. Only Scarlett's love for Ashley keeps her on good terms with Melanie, and forces her to stay with Melanie as she delivers her baby, Beau, during the burning of Atlanta.

Melanie's loving nature and humility in the face of her family's financial difficulties after the war make her popular among the upstanding Atlanta ladies who admire her attitude, and they immediately recruit her for their numerous charities and organizations. Her wise and nurturing personality make her the natural choice for people seeking refuge and understanding; she comforts people hurt or rejected by Scarlett, notably Rhett and Wade. Her sharp intelligence about people and her personal strength come into play when she must act quickly to save Ashley from being arrested for his participation in the Ku Klux Klan raid. Taking her cues from Rhett, Melanie ad-libs her way through a brilliant performance designed to elude the police, a performance that Scarlett would never be perceptive enough to carry off. Melanie's death at the end of the novel is a revelation for Scarlett, who realizes that Melanie is the only true friend she's ever had. It is also Melanie, in her final moments before death, who helps Scarlett to see how much Rhett loves her.

Themes

Gender and Social Class Structure

The world presented in *Gone with the Wind* is one defined by rigid gender and social codes of conduct. Clear rules govern the dress, actions, and speech of ladies and gentlemen, and the punishment for transgressions, especially those of a sexual nature, are severe. When Rhett first appears at the Twelve Oaks party, a scandalous rumor circulates about how he is not "received" in his home town of Charleston because he once stayed out all night with a woman and then refused to marry her, damaging both of their reputations permanently. Rhett is not considered a gentleman, a dangerous state, because, as Scarlett explains, "there was no telling what men would do when they weren't gentlemen. There was no standard to judge them by."

Although Scarlett tries to adhere to the social conventions of gender, she feels as constrained by them as Rhett does. When Rhett asks Scarlett to dance at a war fundraiser, she eagerly accepts, shocking Atlanta society by violating the mourning period required for the death of her husband. Later in the novel, after the war is over, Scarlett feels the training she received from her mother in being a lady is virtually useless to her in such changed and difficult circumstances. She succeeds financially in Atlanta by breaking all the rules, shocking society again when she buys and operates a lumber mill without the help of her husband, Frank Kennedy. Numerous references are made to the fact that this behavior "unsexes" her. Soon, like Rhett, she is not "received" by many families, save Melanie and Ashley's. Ironically, even the town whore, Belle Whatling, condemns Scarlett's "unladylike" behavior.

Mitchell illustrates the social class structure with various characters that represent different levels of society. At the very bottom of the white class structure are the Slatterys, the poor neighboring farmers of the O'Hara family, who own no slaves. Even Mammy looks down on them, calling them "white trash." Next up the ladder are the small farmers like Will Benteen, who own a few slaves and are moderately successful, but certainly not rich. At the top of society are the planter gentility with massive plantations and hundreds of slaves like the O'Hara family and their neighbors, the Fontaines, Calverts, Wilkeses, and Tarletons. The Civil War of course, obliterates these distinctions and everyone must make their own way, regardless of family name.

Financial ruin radically alters social class relations. Melanie and Scarlett are devastated when they learn of the engagement of their friend Cathy Calvert to the overseer of the Calvert's plantation, a man who is definitely "beneath" Cathy. Before the war, the O'Hara family never would have associated with Will Benteen, but Scarlett comes to depend on him to help rebuild Tara. Even among the slaves there is a certain hierarchy—house servants are superior to field hands. After the war, when the field slaves have run off and Scarlett asks Pork to go catch a sow that has escaped, he refuses at first saying, "Miss Scarlett, dat a fe'el han's bizness. Ah's allus been a house nigger."

Survival

Mitchell herself identified survival as the key theme of *Gone with the Wind,* claiming fascination with the topic of who survives during challenging times and why. In the Reconstruction era following the devastation of the Civil War, Rhett and Scarlett emerge as survivors while Ashley and Melanie flounder. The ability that Rhett and Scarlett both possess to assess circumstances realistically and adjust to the changing times greatly benefits them. One of Scarlett's biggest frustrations with everyone around her is that they persist in living in the past. Rhett is the one exception. A true opportunist, Rhett tells Scarlett early in the novel that there is money to be made both in the construction and destruction of a society. Instead of going off to war, Rhett profits from it by becoming a blockade runner, dealing in gold rather than Confederate currency, and keeping his money in stable European banks until the war is over. And Scarlett, seeing how necessary lumber will be for Atlanta's efforts at rebuilding, profits by buying a lumber mill.

At the opposite extreme are Melanie and Ashley. Ashley attempts to help out at Tara by farming, but proves a dismal failure. As Will Benteen tells Scarlett, "God knows he tries his best but he warn't cut out for farmin' and he knows it as well as I do … It ain't his fault. He just warn't bred for it." Later, as Scarlett's mill manager, his poor business sense and moral objections to using convicts and other unscrupulous business practices make him less financially successful than the manager of Scarlett's other mill. Groomed for life as the gentleman of a large plantation, Ashley is lost in the new South. His wife Melanie also remains faithful to the memory of the old days, loyal to old traditions. She becomes the leader of a group of Atlanta ladies who dedicate themselves to such organiza-

Topics for Further Study

- Research the New Deal programs implemented during the Depression era and compare them to programs initiated in the South during the Reconstruction period.

- Investigate the effect that Northern Carpetbaggers and Southern Scalawags had on Georgian politics and culture.

- Compare Mitchell's portrayal of slave life with slave narratives and other historical accounts of slavery. Which aspects of Mitchell's depiction of slave life on a plantation are realistic? Which are not?

- Trace the development and activities of the Ku Klux Klan from their formation to the present day.

- Imagine you could host a talk show with some of the characters from *Gone with the Wind*. One topic could be: Can Scarlett get Rhett back and can they salvage their relationship? Who would side with Scarlett? Rhett? Why? Think of two more topics and write three different episodes of the talk show.

tions as the Association for the Beautification of the Graves of Our Glorious Dead and the Sewing Circle for the Widows and Orphans of the Confederacy. These ladies spend most of their time complaining about Reconstruction and nostalgically looking back to antebellum days, activities that the forward-looking Scarlett cannot tolerate.

Romantic Love

The love triangle created between Scarlett, Ashley, and Rhett drives the narrative. For the majority of the novel, Scarlett believes herself to be in love with Ashley, never understanding how fundamentally different they are from each other. Furthermore, she fails to recognize the feelings she has for Rhett. And though Ashley finally admits to loving Scarlett, because of his honor he will not leave Melanie. Scarlett yearns for people to think of her

as a great lady; therefore, she never considers the ungentlemanly Rhett Butler as a serious suitor. More importantly, his annoying ability to expertly read her true intentions makes him the one man she can't easily manipulate.

Scarlett's first two husbands fall completely under the spell of her charms, never realizing she doesn't love them. She marries Charles simply to get back at Ashley for marrying Melanie, and steals Frank from her sister Suellen because of his money. When people admit their love for her, Scarlett takes shameful advantage of them. As Rhett says to Scarlett, "You're so brutal to those who love you, Scarlett. You take their love and hold it over their heads like a whip." Rhett falls in love with Scarlett almost immediately, recognizing a kindred spirit in her. But even though the twice-widowed Scarlett finally agrees to marry him, she lets him know that she does not love him. Over time, she becomes aware of the intoxicating effect he has on her, but by the time she realizes that she loves Rhett, he is worn out by her steadfast love for Ashley. At the end of the novel, Scarlett perceives that "had she ever understood Ashley, she would never have loved him; had she ever understood Rhett, she would never have lost him."

Style

Setting

Set in the tumultuous years between 1861 and 1873, *Gone with the Wind* shifts between two main locales: the O'Hara family plantation called Tara, located in the rolling foothills of northern Georgia; and the bustling, young city of Atlanta. The lush, fertile beauty of Tara and its importance to the O'Hara family is explained early in the novel by Scarlett's Irish-born father, Gerald, "Land is the only thing in the world that amounts to anything … for 'tis the only thing in this world that lasts, and don't you be forgetting it! 'Tis the only thing worth working for, worth fighting for—worth dying for." His words prove true as Southern sons march off to fight in the war a few chapters later to defend the land they love. Tara becomes a symbol of the old South and the lifestyle of the planter gentility, which is destroyed permanently as a result of the Civil War. Ransacked by Yankees at the war's end, Tara is left in ruins and Scarlett struggles to restore it to its former glory.

In sharp contrast to Tara stands the city of Atlanta, Georgia, a symbol of the new South. Mitchell describes Atlanta as a young, prosperous railroad town, more vital and exciting than the older Southern cities of Charleston and Savannah, which she likens to "aged grandmothers fanning themselves placidly in the sun." Although Sherman's troops set fire to the city in the final days of the war, the citizens of Atlanta waste no time rebuilding. Opportunities abound for new businesses as an interesting mix of Northern Carpetbaggers and Southern Scalawags begin to change the face of the town, and Scarlett aggressively pursues a lumber business of her own. Scarlett and Rhett flourish in the Reconstruction South, while characters such as Melanie and Ashley remain firmly tied to the life and customs of the old days.

Point of View

Although narrated in the third person, it is Scarlett whose thoughts and opinions are explored and revealed to the reader. The straightforward, linear narrative follows the course of Scarlett's life and is interrupted only to provide background information or delve into the personal histories of various characters such as the extended description of Scarlett's parents, Gerald and Ellen, in the opening chapters. Privy to Scarlett's true feelings, readers are made aware of her duplicity and manipulation of other characters. Mitchell's use of irony in several scenes throughout the novel depends upon the reader's ability to understand Scarlett's true motives. At the same time, a certain measure of sympathy for Scarlett can be more easily achieved by allowing the reader to enter her thoughts.

Use of Dialogue

Mitchell's characters come alive on the page through her skillful use of dialogue. The unique speech patterns Mitchell phonetically recreates, such as the slaves' black dialect, Will Benteen's "cracker" English and the Northern Carpetbaggers' accents add authenticity to their personalities. Set expressions such as Scarlett's "Fiddle-dee-dee!" or Gerald's "God's nightgown!" as well as Mammy's scoldings and Ashley and Rhett's propensity to quote are memorable aspects of their individual temperaments. And Rhett's cynical, mocking manner is convincingly developed through his irreverent comments. Most interesting, however, is Mitchell's use of dialogue to set and vary the mood of a scene, such as the final scene between Rhett and Scarlett. Rhett's resignation is conveyed almost entirely through his speech. As he tells Scarlett the reasons for his departure, a range of emotions surface: the tenderness of his past love for her, his grief over Bonnie's death, as well as his jealousy and anger over Scarlett's cruel treatment of him and her stubborn love for Ashley. However, all of these feelings are now tainted with bitter regret.

Use of Irony

Because of Scarlett's blindness to human nature, she lacks true understanding of those around her. This quality, combined with her vanity and selfishness, sets up several ironic situations in *Gone with the Wind*. The overarching irony of the novel, which propels the narrative, is that Scarlett's infatuation with Ashley prevents her from seeing that Rhett is her true soulmate until it's too late. Closely paralleling this is the fact that Ashley only recognizes the extent of his love for Melanie as she lies dying.

There are many other ironic situations in *Gone with the Wind*. For instance, the one person for whom Scarlett expends significant effort is Melanie, the same woman she desperately wishes were out of the picture. It's only because of her promise to Ashley that she doesn't abandon Melanie in the hospital to have her baby alone during the siege of Atlanta. And after Scarlett and Ashley are caught in a compromising situation, Melanie refuses to believe the rumors about them and is the one person who doesn't shun Scarlett. In fact, Melanie remains devoted to Scarlett throughout the novel, a fact that is supremely annoying to Scarlett.

The social upheaval created by the aftermath of the Civil War and the Reconstruction period provides another ironic twist in which Tara's former overseer, Jonas Wilkerson and his new wife Emmie Slattery, of the "poor white trash" Slattery family, try to buy Tara. Newly rich from Wilkerson's Scallawag job at the Freedmens' Bureau, they drive up to Tara in a fine carriage and beautiful clothes and offer to buy Tara from the now destitute O'Hara family. The O'Haras can't pay their taxes, but Scarlett throws them off the property, insulted that such low-class types would think they could live at Tara. The irony is heightened by the fact that the O'Haras and other wealthy plantation families tried for years to buy the Slattery property, but the Slatterys were too proud to sell.

Historical Context

The Great Depression and Reconstruction Eras

Although Mitchell's 1936 novel *Gone with the Wind* focuses on the Reconstruction years following the Civil War, many of Mitchell's initial read-

Wealthy plantation owners such as Scarlett's family, who used African-American slaves to work their land, had great influence on the economy and politics of the old South.

ers living through the Great Depression could iden-tify with the hardships endured by Scarlett and her family. When all the slaves of Tara run off, and Yankees loot the plantation by burning cotton and stealing valuables, the O'Hara family is left with very little. This experience was one shared by many plantation owners in the South, some of whom also lost their land because they were unable to pay the new taxes. Similarly, many people in the 1930s had lost their jobs, savings, and homes after the stock market crash of 1929.

Economic recovery during the 1930s was slow. Those who were lucky enough to keep their jobs often had to take salary cuts. Like Ashley, Melanie, and their son in *Gone with the Wind,* many people moved in with relatives, sharing resources to make ends meet. Others were much less fortunate. Many jobless, homeless people traveled across the coun-try in search of work. Some people who had lost their homes were forced to live in shacks, and lines at soup kitchens grew longer every day.

In order to save money, many Depression-era women began sewing their own clothes and pre-serving homegrown fruits and vegetables rather than buying them. Some enterprising families made extra money by taking in borders, selling home-baked goods, or doing laundry; these home-based

businesses were similar to those established by At-lanta families in *Gone with the Wind.*

The cloud of the Depression began to lift as a result of some of President Franklin D. Roosevelt's New Deal programs. The Civilian Conservation Corps, the Public Works Administration, and Works Progress Administration created jobs for people and helped stimulate the economy. The Fed-eral Emergency Relief Administration provided the states with money for the needy. Government poli-cies were passed at this time to ensure that such a widespread and devastating depression would not occur again.

Similar relief programs were instituted during the Reconstruction era. The Southern economy, based mostly on agriculture, had trouble recover-ing. Southerners financially devastated by the war had little money to invest in business or industry, so state officials worked to attract investment money from the North. State governments also of-fered financial assistance to various industries such as railroads and banks to spur economic growth and employment opportunities.

The Women's Movement

The time period in which *Gone with the Wind* takes place, 1861 to 1873, was a time in which

Compare & Contrast

- **1870s:** The only proper occupation for women is wife and mother. Only dire financial circumstances force women to work outside the home, and almost none own their own businesses.

  1930s: While it has become more acceptable for women to work, it is definitely not the norm; only 22 percent of women work outside the home and few women own businesses independent of their husbands.

  Today: Nearly 60 percent of women are now employed outside the home and 37 percent of all U.S. businesses are owned by women.

- **1870s:** Although the 14th Amendment guarantees the full citizenship of African Americans, including the right to vote, many Southern whites are appalled by this idea and begin terrorizing or murdering African Americans for exercising their right to vote.

  1930s: In the South, many African Americans are prevented from voting by educational tests they must pass or the poll taxes laws, which require them to pay a tax in order to vote.

  Today: The Civil Rights Movement of the 1960s abolished many discriminatory voting practices in the South, and now no legal barriers exist to prevent African Americans from voting.

- **1870s:** Many small farmers and plantation owners lose their land because they can't pay the new taxes; Reconstruction programs are implemented to stimulate the economy and create jobs by offering financial aid to various industries.

  1930s: Unemployment rates climb to 25 percent by the end of the decade; New Deal programs create employment for people to work on national projects such as highway construction and conservation.

  Today: Unemployment hovers around 5 percent, the United States enjoys a period of tremendous economic growth, and national and state governments push to drastically limit welfare programs.

- **1870s:** A large majority of the population makes its living by farming; in the South the entire economy is based on agriculture, but is beginning to undergo the transformation to a more industrialized economy.

  1930s Only 21 percent of the population works in agriculture; the Depression forces many to seek employment through Federal programs.

  Today: Now in the Information Age, less than 3 percent of the population makes its living by farming.

---

women had few rights and were not treated as the equals of men. They could not vote and were discouraged from pursuing an advanced education, mainly because they were considered intellectually inferior to men. Women who did attend college were thought by many to be unfeminine and even in danger of damaging their reproductive systems.

Particularly in the South, women were viewed as naturally weak and dependent and desperately in need of protection by men. A man's duty was to protect and provide for the women in his life and in exchange, women were expected to be obedient to men. A wife's role was to raise children and man-

age the home. Women who defied men or otherwise resisted their passive role in society were considered unfeminine and were ostracized. A perfect example of this is depicted in *Gone with the Wind* when Scarlett is labeled unladylike and is subsequently shunned by Atlanta society for disobeying her husband's wishes and buying and operating her own lumber mill. This contrasts greatly with the respectable and feminine home-based pie-baking business Mrs. Merriwether starts, especially since her father and son-in-law assist with the business. Similarly, Ellen O'Hara's skillful management of Tara is acceptable because it is an extension of home.

By 1936, when Mitchell wrote *Gone with the Wind,* the Women's Movement had improved some aspects of women's lives, but not all. Many colleges and universities opened their doors to women, though relatively few women enrolled, mainly because society still considered a man's education more important. Some women worked outside the home, but it was not the norm. A major achievement of the Women's Movement had been the Women's Suffrage Amendment. Introduced in 1878, it had finally passed in 1919, and by 1920 it was ratified into law as the 19th Amendment. However, by the 1930s the Women's Movement had fallen into a period of relative inactivity. With the vote granted, many women assumed the need for a Women's Movement had ceased to be important. Many inequalities still existed, but interest in women's rights would not rise again until the 1960s.

Critical Overview

Upon its publication in 1936, *Gone with the Wind* became an immediate best-seller. Before it even hit the bookstores, it was named as a Book of the Month main selection. In six months it sold a record-breaking one million copies and was well on its way to becoming the best-selling novel in history. To date it has outsold every other book except the Bible. The fervor it created extended to Mitchell herself, who quickly found that she could not leave home without fans begging her for autographs. Newspaper publishers and magazine editors offered her amazing sums for anything she would care to write for them. Hundreds of fan letters arrived at her home each day and her phone rang off the hook. *Gone with the Wind* was a national phenomenon.

Early reviews of the work spanned a wide range of opinions, but most were favorable. Many critics praised Mitchell for her attention to historical detail, her vivid characterization, and ear for dialogue. She was lauded as a gifted storyteller who held her readers spellbound. Edwin Granberry of the *New York Sun* compared her talent to that of the great Russian and English panoramic novelists, a comparison that other reviewers would draw as well. Herschell Brickell of the *New York Post* declared it the best novel written about the Civil War and its aftermath; furthermore, he predicted that *Gone with the Wind* would find a permanent place in American literature. In contrast, other critics dis-

missed the book as trite, overly sentimental, and full of cliches. Bernard DeVoto of the *Saturday Review of Literature* fell into this camp, deriding *Gone with the Wind* for its cheap sentiments, which he felt falsified true experience. In addition, there were reviewers who found aspects of the novel morally offensive. As Anne Edwards notes in her book, *Road to Tara: The Life of Margaret Mitchell,* some reviewers criticized *Gone with the Wind* for its "condescending portrait of blacks, the glorification of plantation life, and its lack of a political and social point of view."

In 1937, *Gone with the Wind* was honored twice: first with the Pulitzer Prize for fiction, and second with the annual prize for best fiction from the American Bookseller's Association. Following the release of the film in 1939, critical interest in the book virtually ended. Academics have since speculated that because *Gone with the Wind* was stylistically at odds with the modern literature published at the time and didn't fit easily into any school of literature, it was difficult for critics to assess. In addition, the novel's marketplace success and subsequent status as a pop culture icon has always been problematic, eclipsing everything else about the book for many critics. A resurgence of interest in the book occurred in the 1970s, but little consensus on its literary merit has been reached and criticism on it is still limited.

Mitchell herself admitted to being mystified by the book's mass appeal. Articles discussing the book's popularity appeared with some regularity in newspapers and magazines for a few years. Although several theories were debated, many reviewers attributed the book's success to the fact that Americans living through the Great Depression could readily identify with Scarlett's trials as she overcomes poverty and rebuilds her life in the Reconstruction South. But that seems only part of the book's allure, which continues to sell 250,000 paperback copies in the United States each year. As southern writer Pat Conroy expressed in his preface to the 60th anniversary edition of *Gone with the Wind:* "[The novel] works because it possesses the inexpressible magic where the art of pure storytelling rises above its ancient use and succeeds in explaining to a whole nation how it came to be this way. There has never been a reader or a writer who could figure out why this happens only to very few books … [*Gone with the Wind*] allows you to lose yourself in the glorious pleasure of reading itself, when all five senses ignite in the sheer happiness of narrative."

Criticism

Tabitha McIntosh-Byrd

McIntosh-Byrd is a doctoral candidate at the University of Pennsylvania. In the following essay, she analyzes Margaret Mitchell's Gone with the Wind *as an anti-Civil War novel at odds with its wider cultural interpretation.*

Gone with the Wind has sold an average of 500,000 copies each year since its publication in 1936. More Americans learn about the Civil War from Mitchell's novel than from any other single author, and even more Americans know the book through the movie that followed three years after its publication. David O. Selznick's 1939 film is still the most viewed movie in the history of cinema. *Gone with the Wind* holds an indelible place in U.S. culture as the great romanticization of the last days of the antebellum South.

Within this cultural enshrinement, Scarlett's character is collapsed into a broader understanding of Southern culture, becoming both metaphor and metonym of the South itself—the iconographic representation of Southern womanhood for every generation of girls born after 1939. Yet in striking ways, Mitchell's portrait interrogates both historical and contemporary mythologies of the war. Is Scarlett the ideal Southern Belle? Is the antebellum world the textual ideal? Are the Tarleton twins and Ashley the idealized and eulogized Southern Gentlemen whose passage is being mourned? The answers to these three questions are no—a suggestion made consistently and thoroughly throughout Mitchell's novel. In the final analysis, the glorious South of *Gone with the Wind* is as much and as little "authentic" as Vivien Leigh's Scarlett—a British actress of the 1930s portraying an American woman in the nineteenth century. Its status as a historical novel and its conscious reworking of history for contemporary ends elevates textual theatricality to its most opaque level. *Gone with the Wind* is acting a part, and in doing so it forces critical reevaluations of the script it is following.

From the first line, it is clear that *Gone with the Wind* is writing against expectations: its heroine is, "not beautiful, but men seldom realized it." Scarlett O'Hara is not an archetypal romance heroine or Southern belle, and the South that she represents is as paradoxically unattractive yet beguiling as she is. That Scarlett and the South are one and the same entity is an aspect of the novel that has been noted on many occasions. From the time

What Do I Read Next?

- *Lay My Burden Down,* edited by B. A. Botkin (1945), is a collection of interviews with former slaves, recorded and transcribed by the Federal Writers' Project. Men and women describe their experiences as slaves.

- *A Stillness at Appomatox* is Bruce Catton's 1953 history of the Civil War. The final book of his three-volume Army of the Potomac historical series, it won a Pulitzer Prize.

- *The Battle-Ground,* by Ellen Glasgow (1902), focuses on two aristocratic families who live on adjoining Virginia plantations during the Civil War era.

- James McPherson's *Ordeal by Fire: The Civil War and Reconstruction* (1982) traces Civil War events and also examines relevant pre- and post-war issues and activities.

- *Scarlett,* Alexandra Ripley's 1991 sequel to *Gone with the Wind,* continues the story of Scarlett and Rhett.

- Harriet Beecher Stowe's classic novel, *Uncle Tom's Cabin* (1852), chronicles the mistreatment of a slave named Uncle Tom at the hands of his cruel master, Simon Legree. Stowe wrote the novel, in part, to further the abolitionist cause.

of publication, reviewers and critics have characterized Scarlett as the personification of the acquisitive, mercantile zeitgeist of the New South, and she is clearly identified throughout the novel with Atlanta—that zeitgeist's representative city. At the same time, Scarlett embodies the culmination of the Old—the logical evolution, rather than transformation, of Antebellum into Reconstruction South. Scarlett passes from sanctioned performative gender play—a Judith Butler-esque negotiation of masquerading femininity and gender—to unmasqued businesswoman and schemer. This passage perfectly mirrors the transition of the grandiose antebellum South to the capitalist Reconstruction era: a parallel that reveals the fragile and paradoxical artifice of both Southern woman-hood and Southern gentility. Like Selznick's famous torching of the old Metro-Goldwyn-Mayer (MGM) sets to create the scene in which Atlanta burns, Scarlett's story tracks the conflagration of false fronts, and *tromp l'oeil.*

From the beginning of the text, Scarlett is both constrained by and in rebellion against the conventions of her society. As a child she can ride and climb as well as her male contemporaries; as a young woman she has become a "proper" young lady, trained to perform by her mother and her Mammy. Her performance is always just that—a self-consciously artificial masque embodying "outward signs" and betokening no "inner grace." Scarlett must "clothe" herself in femininity in the way that she literally clothes herself—a physical and mental distortion of natural form designed to create the illusion of an ideal. In doing so, her character calls into question not just the performative aspect of femininity, but also the performative aspects of a culture that demands such ritualistic self-presentation in order to function.

Scarlett's excellence at pretending to be feminine is the central paradox of the first section of *Gone with the Wind.* On the one hand, she is an ideal Southern young lady because she behaves exactly as the ideal is required to behave. On the other hand, it is her ability to scheme and "calculate"—both literally and metaphorically—that allows her to act this ideal. In other words, the very aspects of Scarlett's character that enable her to be "ideal" are precisely those attributes that are to be avoided. To "catch" her man she must be duplicitous; to "snare" a good marriage she must be "natural" and "unaffected." This series of irreconcilable paradoxes creates the sixteen-year-old heroine of the opening scenes, a girl who has learned to use the attributes of womanhood to further her "predatory" designs on men. Tellingly, mathematics is the only subject in which Scarlett has ever excelled—"calculating."

Scarlett's reaction to this endlessly self-generating cultural demand for calculated performance is not a positive one. It frustrates her, and over the course of the novel she becomes less and less willing to enact the required facades. Fundamentally, such facades are shown to be not only foolish, but also actively harmful. As her Mammy scolds her into remembering, in order to catch her man Scarlett must become completely "unnatural"—denying her actual hunger in the interests of seeming like a delicate young lady. In the complex exchange culture of Southern gender, Scarlett must deny her

physical reality in order to create a consciously false, quasi-Platonic Ideal of reality. The effort is exhausting and, more importantly, tends to the inevitable collapse of the Ideal. "Reality" cannot be denied. As Scarlett says, "I'm tired of everlastingly being unnatural and never doing anything I want to do." In an ironic foreshadowing of later events, this scene looks forward to the devastated Tara in which food is perilously scarce. Scarlett, like her culture, will experience a shift from feigned appetite to actual famine—from performance to reality—in one horribly ironic sequence. Reconstruction will depend on subduing all efforts to the goal of meeting the needs of bodies that had always been denied, ignored, and disguised. When Scarlett vows she'll "never go hungry again," the Southern lady disappears forever.

Scarlett's tendency to break the fourth wall of femininity shifts in meaning as the novel progresses. As the war forces a slow but total collapse of the old culture, so Scarlett's breaches of ritual become more and more essential to the survival of those around her. Melanie, the novel's true "ideal" lady, is able to easily shift her private self-sacrifice to a public self-sacrifice for the sacred Confederacy. While there is no real danger—and while the possibility of defeat is still safely in the North—the cultural goals that she embodies remain intact. Scarlett, who becomes a nurse simply because, "she didn't know how to get out of it," is the subject of outrage, preoccupied with her own aims and indifferent to the demands of Atlanta culture. The disintegration of the Confederacy and the arrival of war in Atlanta overturn the meaning of both the conventions she has ignored and the characteristics she refuses to hide. As Dr. Meade announces, "This is war time. We can't think of the proprieties now."

The currency has changed, and Melanie's "value" is debased entirely. Like the Confederate bonds in which the families have invested, old and privileged behaviors have no exchange value or functional meaning anymore. Significantly, Melanie is struggling in labor while Atlanta burns and Scarlett searches for help. Like her culture, she is unable to "reproduce" naturally—transmuting from a cherished ideal of weakness to a sickly liability during the course of the fire. The product of the cousin-marrying-cousin union of Ashley and Melanie, lady and gentleman par excellence, is unable to come into the world without the New South, Scarlett, who delivers the baby herself. From this point onwards, the traits that Ellen and Mammy have struggled to repress in Scarlett become the basis for her survival, and for the salvation of those who surround her. Melanie's world is too weak to survive into another generation without Scarlett, and reliance on Scarlett means accepting what Scarlett stands for, which in turn means accepting self-destruction. As Ashley says, it's the *Gotterdammurung*—the Twilight of the Gods—below the Mason-Dixon line.

The notion that Scarlett represents a critique of both Southern womanhood *and* manhood is suggested throughout *Gone with the Wind*. The gradual emergence of performative masculine gender behavior in Scarlett acts as a significant indicator of her character progression, from the little girl who was good at calculations, to the fully grown businesswoman who is better at calculating and dealing then the men who surround her. At the beginning of the novel, Scarlett is still engaged in the enactment of gender performance, and wishes she "was a man." While the Confederate cause was still glorious and while her culture remained ideal, Scarlett's yearning to psychically "cross-dress" is no more than appropriate cultural behavior—an extension of the ritualistic performance of femininity into which she is forced. By the end of the war she has begun to behave like a "real" man: now "her reactions were all masculine," and she "talked and acted like a man." Becoming almost a "garçon manqué," she wins a reputation for bravery among the ladies of Atlanta to the extent that Aunt Pitty and Melanie are willing to stay without a man if Scarlett is there. When Atlanta burns, Scarlett's role shifts between various masculine states, allowing her to become first a general in retreat, and then Tara's patriarch. The "real" patriarch is mad—both literally and metaphorically—and Scarlett becomes the family's provider and protector.

Scarlett's behavior throughout the Reconstruction period acts as a greater and greater critique of Southern gender assumptions than had her previous violations of convention. Having been the gallant savior of both Melanie and her surviving family, Scarlett now becomes a businesswoman. In the representation of this transformation lies a powerful reversal of entrenched masculine honor. First and foremost, Scarlett's "masculinity" shows itself to be based in acquisitiveness. She dedicates herself to amassing wealth at any human cost, orchestrating her marriages and trampling the affections of those around her to that end. Human relationships are reduced to financial transactions and calculations as Scarlett steals her sister's only beau, Frank Kennedy, for his money, offers her body to Rhett in exchange for money, and uses exploited convict labor to increase her profits. Lay-

ing bare the economic underpinnings of the old order, Scarlett justifies her actions with the comment: "You can't be a lady without money." Both the genteel femininity and protective masculinity of the antebellum South rested on assumptions of wealth and privilege. By laying these connections bare, Scarlett destroys their sum product. The New South that Scarlett represents is merely the Old South with its masque removed.

The idealized young gentlemen of the South— the Ashleys—have disappeared to battle, "gone with the wind" of "flamboyant patriotism" that made the war possible. By the novel's conclusion their glory has been debased and deflated, until they are, as Scarlett realizes, just "children." The benevolent white patriarchs are equally destroyed, reduced—like Gerald O'Hara—to madness and despair. Again, this is not a true transformation, but a breach of the facade—a revelation of reality. As the narrator says, the Old South was a "happy feminine conspiracy." Privilege rested with men, but power lay in the unspoken "conspiracy" of white Southern women. At Tara in the days before the war, "only one voice was obeyed on the plantation"—Ellen O'Hara's. The reality of gender and power remained hidden from Gerald, since "everyone from Ellen down to the stupidest field hand was in a tacit and kindly conspiracy to keep him believing his word was law." Gerald retains the performative aspects of masculine authority by tacitly accepting the condescension of his family and his slaves. Scarlett's masculinity and her naked ambition, calculation, and power shatter the illusion of the old patriarchy forever. Too "masculine" to be "feminine," and too "feminine" to be "masculine," Scarlett not only pulls down the structure of gender expectations and behavior, but also destroys the culture of which it was a product. The Scarlett who emerges from the war is the avatar of *de-* and *Re-* construction.

Source: Tabitha McIntosh-Byrd, in an essay for *Novels for Students,* Gale, 2000.

Joseph R. Millichap

In the essay below, Millichap provides a critical overview of Mitchell's novel and the circumstances around its writing and publication, taking special note of the elements that make the work especially appealing to young adults.

Although Margaret Mitchell did not consider herself a writer for young adults, her single masterpiece, *Gone with the Wind,* and its blockbuster film version have been perennial favorites of American

This photograph of Atlanta, Georgia, was taken in 1864. On November 15 of that year, General Sherman's troops burned and pillaged the city on their famous march to the sea, an event Mitchell vividly captured in her novel.

teenagers, to the point that both are often included in high school and college curriculums. The increased interest of recent years following the fiftieth anniversaries of both the novel (1986) and the film (1989), as well as the publication of an authorized sequel (1992) will surely extend the popularity of *Gone with the Wind* into the next century. This popular phenomenon proves most interesting as Mitchell's masterwork seems a nineteenth-century book in subject, theme, and style—a twentieth-century reincarnation of the Victorian "triple-decker" romance. Thus the book's remarkable popularity is a combination of tradition and change much like the narrative it relates. In critical terms, it is possible to read *Gone with the Wind* as a female development novel. At the novel's opening in 1861, Scarlett O'Hara is a sixteen-year-old coquette; when it concludes in 1873 she is a twenty-eight-year-old woman. In the twelve year span of the novel, she experiences Secession, Civil War, and Reconstruction, as well as romance, love, marriage, and motherhood. Scarlett lives through the adolescent trauma of American culture, which is matched by a traumatic personal history as much or more tumultuous. Energized by her own life, Mitchell created one of the most arresting tales of troubled adolescence in

American literature and in so doing created a novel which will continue to captivate teenagers and fascinate their teachers well into the next century.

For younger readers, Scarlett O'Hara's development from teenaged girl to mature woman proves as fascinating now as it did when the book was first published in 1936 or when the movie first appeared in 1939. The particular, indeed peculiar energy of the story proceeds from Mitchell's own girlhood, adolescence, and young adult life. During these years she heard the family legends of the Civil War era into which she projected her own development toward womanhood. The novel combines Mitchell's family and personal romances with historical facts to create powerful and popular fiction.

The popular image of Mitchell was as a Southern matron who turned to writing as her contemporaries might cultivate bridge, golf, or gardening. Although descended from old Georgia families and raised in comfortable circumstances, the future author was no simple Southern belle. Her mother's feminist leanings clashed with her father's conservatism, and a young Mitchell became a somewhat willful, rebellious tomboy, given to flights of imaginative fancy and a series of serious, debilitating accidents and illnesses. After the death of her first beloved on the Western Front and of her mother in the influenza epidemic, Mitchell became "a flapper," both living the wild times of the Jazz Age and writing about them in nonfiction. Her first marriage was a disaster, climaxed by spousal rape and scandalous divorce, while her second marriage mirrored her dependent, and sometimes stressful relationships with her father and brother. The writer's social, psychological, and sexual ambiguities found expression in her greatest creation, Scarlett O'Hara, while other people in her life provided models for other characters in *Gone with the Wind.*

The critical history of *Gone with the Wind* is contradictory, as might be expected from the writer's conflicted biography. The reaction of reviewers and of general readers was quite positive in 1936, for no one would deny that the novel was a great "read." Even the initial response of the literary community seemed laudatory. Comparisons were made with the great novelists and novels of the nineteenth century, such as [William Makepeace] Thackeray and *Vanity Fair,* [Leo] Tolstoy and *Anna Karenina,* and [Gustave] Flaubert and *Madame Bovary.* In terms of memorable characters, sweeping action, colorful settings, and grand themes the novel was a success. At the same time, qualifying statements about style, sentiment, racism, and melodrama raised legitimate questions about the book's literary status.

Unfortunately, the novel's existence as a cultural artifact subsumed its identity as a literary text and the immense power and popularity of the film version only complicated the situation. Book and film were conflated into a phenomenon of American and later international popular culture. Thus criticism was arrested at the levels of basic appreciation, often in the opposite poles of love and/or hate, and evaluation, again often in bipolar terms of praise and/or scorn. On the popular level the novel was lauded and in the literary world it was defamed.

This critical neglect continued well into the 1960s when reconsiderations of American culture and society elicited new readings of classic texts. Mitchell and her novel were seen as important symbols of American cultural forces. A serious biography in 1965 sparked reconsideration simply by the assumption of Mitchell's importance as a writer. Other reevaluations followed which asserted the literary quality of the work, notably in feminist terms. The critical neglect of the novel thus was explained in terms of the largely male critical establishment, and Mitchell became the subject of articles and dissertations in the 1970s. Finally, in the 1980s, the half-century anniversaries of both novel and film provided new perspectives for critical focus in a number of important critical works, including a definitive biography.

Source: Joseph R. Millichap, "Margaret Mitchell: Overview," in *Twentieth-Century Young Adult Writers,* 1st ed., edited by Laura Standley Berger, St. James Press, 1994.

Malcolm Cowley

Cowley has made several valuable contributions to contemporary letters with his editions of important American authors (Nathaniel Hawthorne, Walt Whitman, Ernest Hemingway, William Faulkner, F. Scott Fitzgerald), his writings as a literary critic for The New Republic, *and, above all, for his chronicles and criticism of modern American literature. Cowley's literary criticism does not attempt a systematic philosophical view of life and art, nor is it representative of a neatly defined school of critical thought, but rather focuses on works—particularly those of "lost generation" writers—that he feels his personal experience has qualified him to explicate and that he considers worthy of public appreciation. The critical approach Cowley follows is undogmatic and is characterized by a willingness to view a work from whatever perspective—social, historical, aesthetic—that the work itself seems to demand for its illumination.*

Gone with the Wind is an encyclopedia of the plantation legend. Other novelists by the hundreds have helped to shape this legend, but each of them has presented only part of it. Miss Mitchell repeats it as a whole, with all its episodes and all its characters and all its stage settings—the big white-columned house sleeping under its trees among the cotton fields; the band of faithful retainers, including two that quaintly resemble Aunt Jemima and Old Black Joe; the white-haired massa bathing in mint juleps; the heroine with her seventeen-inch waist and the high-spirited twins who came courting her in the magnolia-colored moonlight, with the darkies singing under the hill—then the War between the States, sir, and the twins riding off on their fiery chargers, and the lovely ladies staying behind to nurse the wounded, and Sherman's march (now the damyankees are looting the mansion and one of them threatens to violate its high-bred mistress, but she clutches the rusty trigger of an old horse pistol and it goes off bang in his ugly face)— then the black days of Reconstruction, the callousness of the Carpetbaggers, the scalawaggishness of the Scalawags, the knightliness of the Ku Klux Klansmen, who frighten Negroes away from the polls, thus making Georgia safe for democracy and virtuous womanhood and Our Gene Talmadge—it is all here, every last bale of cotton and bushel of moonlight, every last full measure of Southern female devotion working its lilywhite fingers uncomplainingly to the lilywhite bone.

But even though the legend is false in part and silly in part and vicious in its general effect on Southern life today, still it retains its appeal to fundamental emotions. Miss Mitchell lends new strength to the legend by telling it as if it had never been told before, and also by mixing a good share of realism with the romance. She writes with a splendid recklessness, blundering into big scenes that a more experienced novelist would hesitate to handle for fear of being compared unfavorably with Dickens or Dostoevsky. Miss Mitchell is afraid of no comparison and no emotion—she makes us weep at a deathbed (and really weep), exult at a sudden rescue and grit our teeth at the crimes of our relatives the damnyankees. I would never, never say that she has written a great novel, but in the midst of triteness and sentimentality her book has a simple-minded courage that suggests the great novelists of the past. No wonder it is going like the wind.

Source: Malcolm Cowley, "Going with the Wind," in *The New Republic,* Vol. LXXXVIII, No. 1137, September 16, 1936, pp. 161-62.

Sources

Pat Conroy, Preface of Margaret Mitchell's *Gone with the Wind,* Macmillan, 1996.

Anne Edwards, *Road to Tara: The Life of Margaret Mitchell,* Ticknor and Fields, 1983.

Linda Ludwig, "Margaret Mitchell," *American Women Writers,* Frederick Ungar Publishing Co., 1981.

For Further Study

Stephen Vincent Benet, "Georgia Marches Through," *Saturday Review,* July 4, 1936, p. 5.
    An early review praising the novel's realism and readability.

James Boatwright, "Totin' de Weery Load," *New Republic,* September 1, 1973, pp. 29-32.
    A review citing moral and political objections to *Gone with the Wind.*

Finis Farr, *Margaret Mitchell of Atlanta,* Morrow, 1965.
    The first definitive biography written on Margaret Mitchell.

Dawon Gaillard, "Gone with the Wind as 'Bildungsroman': or Why Did Rhett Butler Really Leave Scarlett O'Hara?," *Georgia Review,* Spring, 1974, pp. 9-28.
    Gaillard's essay discusses the relationship between gender and culture and argues that Mitchell is criticizing the Southern code of chivalry in *Gone with the Wind.*

Anne G. Jones, *"Tomorrow Is Another Day": The Woman Writer in the South, 1859-1936,* Louisiana State University Press, 1981.
    Jones's book places Mitchell in the context of a long line of Southern women writers who rebelled against Southern culture and a woman's place within it.

Richard Harwell, *Margaret Mitchell's "Gone with the Wind" Letters, 1936-1949,* Macmillan, 1976.
    A collection of the letters Mitchell wrote in response to the fan mail she received.

Darden Ashbury Pyron, *Recasting: Gone with the Wind in American Culture,* University Presses of Florida, 1983.
    A collection of critical essays, this book traces critical analysis of *Gone with the Wind* from its publication to the present.

———, *Southern Daughter: The Life of Margaret Mitchell,* Oxford University Press, 1991.
    An in-depth biography that also includes some critical analysis of *Gone with the Wind.*

In the Time of the Butterflies

Julia Alvarez
1994

When people think of the Dominican Republic in the twentieth century, two words most often come to mind: Rafael Trujillo. He ruled the island nation from 1930 to 1961. His dictatorship was defined by greed, a rigid control over the Dominican people, and unspeakable brutality. But many would also have people remember another history of the Dominican Republic, a history of brave resistance and immense sacrifice. Two different words come to mind when thinking of this history: Las Mariposas, or The Butterflies. These were the code names of Minerva, María Teresa, and Patria Mirabal, three sisters who were key members in an underground movement to overthrow Trujillo. On November 25, 1960, the dictator's men ambushed their car and the sisters were beaten to death. Since that time, they have become symbols of courage, dignity, and strength in their country.

In 1994, Julia Alvarez brought the Mirabals' story to an American audience through her novel *In the Time of the Butterflies*. Alvarez's connections to this story run deep, since her own parents were involved in the underground movement and fled to America before being arrested. She does not write a history or a biography, however. She fictionalizes the Mirabal sisters and depicts their lives through the voices she creates for them. She even includes Dedé Mirabal, the only sister to survive, as a voice of the present reflecting on the past. Through her characters, she stresses the need to remember the past, even times of great pain, while also striving for happiness in the present and the

Julia Alvarez

future. Perhaps more importantly, she stresses the need to see heroes not as superhuman, but as people who fight their own fears in order to fight injustice.

Author Biography

Alvarez was born in New York City on March 27, 1950, the second of four daughters. Shortly thereafter, the family moved to the Dominican Republic, where her parents were involved in an underground movement to overthrow Dominican dictator Rafael Trujillo. When the movement was discovered, the Alvarez family was forced to flee to escape imprisonment and possible death. They left the Dominican Republic on August 6, 1960, and moved to Queens, New York.

While living in New York, Alvarez had to perfect her English and adjust to life as an immigrant. She was alienated at school and subject to taunting from other students. As a result, she turned to reading for solace. These experiences proved important for her future writing. She writes in "A Brief Account of My Writing Life" for the Appalachian State University Summer Reading Program, "I came into English as a ten-year-old from the Do-

minican Republic, and I consider this radical uprooting from my culture, my native language, my country, the reason I began writing. 'Language is the only homeland,' Czeslow Milosz once observed, and indeed, English, not the United States, was where I landed and sunk deep roots."

Alvarez began attending a boarding school at age thirteen. By high school, she desired to become a writer. She was encouraged by teachers but not by her family. She explains to Jonathan Bing of *Publishers Weekly* part of her family's reasoning: "I grew up in that generation of women thinking I would keep house. Especially with my Latino background, I wasn't even expected to go to college.... I had never been raised to have a public voice." She pursued her writing interests at Connecticut College, however, where she won two prizes for her poetry in 1968 and 1969. She then attended Middlebury College in Vermont, where she won the Creative Writing Prize and graduated summa cum laude in 1971. She received an M.A. in creative writing from Syracuse University in 1975. While at Syracuse, she won the American Academy of Poetry Prize in 1974.

Between 1975 and 1977, she worked for the Kentucky Arts Commission, conducting poetry workshops throughout the state. In 1978, she worked in a National Endowment for the Arts bilingual program in Delaware and a program for senior citizens in North Carolina. From 1978 to 1988, she taught English and creative writing at a number of institutions. She began teaching at Middlebury College in 1988.

In 1984, she published *Homecoming,* a well-received collection of poetry. Her next major publication, *How the Garcia Girls Lost Their Accents,* appeared in 1991. This highly popular novel details the lives and struggles of four sisters who emigrated from the Dominican Republic to America. In 1994, she published *In the Time of the Butterflies,* which received much critical attention and praise. The following year, she published a second poetry collection entitled *The Other Side: El Otro Lado.* Her novel *!Yo!* appeared in 1997, and a collection of personal essays, *Something to Declare* was published in 1998.

Alvarez married Bill Eichner, an ophthalmologist, in 1989, and she continues to write and teach at Middlebury College.

Plot Summary

Set in the Dominican Republic, *In the Time of the Butterflies* depicts the lives of the Mirabal family between 1938 and 1994. The chapters are narrated by the four Mirabal sisters, Patria, Dedé, Minerva, and María Teresa, or Mate. Alvarez arranges events in roughly chronological order, though she excludes many years from the narrative and gives only brief treatment to the period between 1960 and 1994.

Section I: 1938 to 1946

The novel opens in 1994 with Dedé, the surviving Mirabal sister. She meets with an American woman who has come to interview her about her family. She recalls a time in 1943 when her father, Enrique, was predicting his daughters' futures. He tells Dedé that she will bury them all "in silk and pearls."

The second chapter is narrated by Minerva and depicts events in 1938, 1941, and 1944. Minerva and Patria go to boarding school at Inmaculada Concepción. Minerva befriends a withdrawn girl named Sinita Perozo. Sinita's male family members were murdered for opposing the Dominican dictator, Rafael Trujillo. Minerva is shocked to learn of Trujillo's cruelty, since all Dominican children are taught to revere him. In 1941, the married Trujillo seduces the most beautiful girl in Minerva's school, Lina Lovatón. After Lina becomes pregnant, Trujillo sends her to live in Miami. In 1944, Minerva, Sinita, and their friends Elsa and Lourdes perform a play for the country's Independence Day celebrations and win the opportunity to perform before Trujillo. During this performance, Sinita points a bow and arrow at Trujillo. Sinita is stopped by Trujillo's son, Ramfis, and Minerva intervenes by having everyone chant "*Viva Trujillo*," or "Long live Trujillo."

The third chapter consists of María Teresa's diary entries between 1945 and 1946. She describes her childhood pleasures, especially clothes. She also talks about Minerva's friendship with Hilda, a revolutionary fighting Trujillo. When Hilda is caught, María Teresa must bury her diary so the police will not find it.

Chapter four is narrated by Patria and begins in 1946. Patria wrestles with the question of whether she should become a nun. Soon, however, she falls in love with Pedrito González, a farmer, and they marry. They have a son and daughter, Nelson and Noris, but their third child is born dead.

Grief-stricken, Patria loses her religious faith. She regains her faith, though, when she hears the Virgin Mary speak to her through a church congregation gathered for worship.

Section II: 1948 to 1959

Chapter five opens in 1994 with Dedé telling the interviewer about Virgilio (Lío) Morales. Dedé privately recalls her own romantic interest in Lío when he was a young doctor and revolutionary. The narrative shifts to 1948, when the Mirabals met Lío. Dedé is beginning a romance with her cousin Jaimito, whom she soon marries. Minerva is attracted to Lío's Communist politics, though she never admits it to him. When Lío must flee the country, he asks Dedé to give Minerva a letter asking her to join him in exile. Dedé burns the letter.

Minerva narrates the sixth chapter, which begins in 1949. Three years after graduating Inmaculada, she is bored at home and wants to attend law school. She discovers that her father has four illegitimate daughters and that he has been hiding Lío's letters to her. The family goes to an outdoor party hosted by Trujillo, and Minerva slaps Trujillo when he becomes lewd while they are dancing. It begins to rain, and the Mirabals leave the party, even though it is against the law to do so. Minerva forgets her purse, which contains Lío's letters. Enrique Mirabal is soon arrested. After many weeks, Minerva and her mother secure his release by apologizing to Trujillo personally.

Chapter seven consists of entries from María Teresa's diary between 1953 and 1958. She discusses her father's death in 1953, her romantic dilemmas, Minerva's experiences in law school, and her own experiences at college. Minerva marries Manolo Tavárez, has a daughter, Minou, and earns her law degree, but Trujillo refuses her a license to practice. During the summer, María Teresa stays with Minerva's family. Minerva and Manolo have marital problems until they become involved in an underground movement against Trujillo. They explain the movement to María Teresa and reveal their code names. Minerva is Mariposa, or Butterfly. María Teresa joins them, largely because of her feelings for Leandro Guzmán, or Palomino, a man in the movement. She becomes Mariposa #2. She marries Leandro on February 14, 1958.

Patria narrates chapter eight, which covers 1959. She becomes pregnant and decides to name the child Raúl Ernesto after the Cuban revolutionaries Raúl Castro and Ernesto (Che) Guevara. The movement needs a place to meet, and Patria offers them her farm. Patria goes on a religious retreat. On the fourteenth of June, the retreat is bombed when Trujillo's forces attack rebels hiding in the mountains. Patria watches a boy die. She vows to help in the resistance, and she convinces Pedrito to do the same, though they will lose their farm if they are caught. The resistance names itself the Fourteenth of June Movement.

Section III: 1960

Dedé narrates chapter nine. She tells the interviewer that though she was sympathetic to the movement, she did not get involved in it because Jaimito would not. Dedé recalls that in 1960 she and Jaimito experience serious marital problems, but she stays with him. Minerva, María Teresa, and their husbands are arrested, along with Patria's husband and son, Nelson. Patria's family loses the farm.

Patria narrates chapter ten, which takes place between January and March, 1960. She lives at her mother's house, which is under constant surveillance. Captain Victor Alicinio Peña, one of Trujillo's top officials, begins to visit the house to keep tabs on the family. Margarita Mirabal, Patria's illegitimate half-sister, also visits with a prison message from María Teresa. Margarita's cousin is a guard in the prison, and the family sends the prisoners items through him. To gain favorable publicity, Trujillo allows Nelson to be released.

Chapter eleven consists of María Teresa's diary entries from March to August, 1960. She is in a cell with Minerva and twenty-two other women, most of whom are non-political criminals. She describes her prison experiences, including the women's routines, means of resistance, and the indignities they suffer. The worst incident María Teresa must endure is being electrically shocked before her husband. Seeing her pain, he agrees to cooperate with Trujillo's men. The Organization of American States sends inspectors to the prison. María Teresa secretly gives one inspector the story of her torture. Soon after, the female political prisoners are released.

Minerva narrates chapter twelve, which occurs between August and November 25, 1960. While under house arrest, she struggles to be her old, courageous self, but finds it hard to do so until faced with adversity. She discovers the hoped-for invasion of the island has been called off and most of the movement disbanded. Later, at a gathering, Trujillo declares that his only two remaining problems are the church and the Mirabal sisters. Manolo and

Leandro are transferred to Puerto Plata prison. The sisters must cross isolated mountain roads to get there for visitations. Minerva, María Teresa, Patria, and Rufino de la Cruz travel to the prison on November 25. On the way, they fear an ambush, but they arrive safely. They try calling home before heading back, but the line is busy.

Epilogue

In 1994, Dedé recalls the story of the sisters' and Rufino's deaths. On the road home, they were stopped by soldiers, who beat them to death then pushed them over a cliff in their car. Dedé recalls her slow process of healing and becoming the family spokesperson. She also recalls recently seeing Lío Morales at a reception and discussing the past and the current political situation with him. To Dedé, the Dominican Republic has become "the playground of the Caribbean" rather than its "killing fields." The materialistic young people have forgotten their past. Dedé asks herself, "Was it for this, the sacrifice of the butterflies?"

Characters

American Interviewer

An American woman of Dominican descent, the interviewer comes to speak with Dedé about the family history. She speaks poor Spanish. She strongly resembles Julia Alvarez herself.

Sor Asunción

As the head nun at Inmaculada Concepción, Sor Asunción tends to all of the Mirabal sisters. She prompts Patria to watch for God's call to become a nun.

Don Bernardo

When Chea Mirabal moves to town, Don Bernardo becomes her neighbor. Though his wife, Doña Belén, suffers from senility, he finds time to help the Mirabal family whenever they are in need.

Chea

See Mercedes Reyes de Mirabal

Rufino de la Cruz

Rufino is the Mirabal sisters' favorite chauffeur, and he is fiercely protective of them. He dies with Patria, Minerva, and María Teresa.

Manuel de Moya

De Moya is Trujillo's Secretary of State, but his actual job is to secure attractive young women for Trujillo. He arranges the meeting between Minerva and Trujillo at the Discovery Day Dance, where she slaps the dictator.

Enriquello

See Manolo Tavárez

Jaime Fernández

Jaimito is the Mirabals' cousin and Dedé's husband. He has little business sense, so he and Dedé suffer through financial hardship. He refuses to allow Dedé to become involved in her sisters' political activities because he fears reprisals. Because of his domineering ways, Dedé almost leaves him in 1960, but they stay married until they divorce in the 1980s. Though blustery, he often proves to have a good heart.

Nelson González

Patria's eldest child, Nelson, enthusiastically joins the underground when he is a young man. He is caught and imprisoned. Trujillo releases him for favorable publicity, and he goes to work for Jaimito on his farm.

Noris González

Noris is Patria's daughter. She goes with her mother to retrieve Nelson from prison.

Pedro González

A gentle, plainspoken farmer, Pedrito is Patria's husband. They meet when she washes his feet during a church ceremony. He loves his family and his land. He risks both, however, when Patria asks him to help in the underground movement. He is imprisoned and loses his farm when caught. After being released, he remarries and regains his land, but he is restless and does not resume farming.

Gringa Dominicana

See American Interviewer

Leandro Guzmán

Leandro, María Teresa's husband, is an engineer and revolutionary, code-named Palomino. He meets María Teresa while delivering guns to Manolo and Minerva's house. He is arrested in 1960. Like the other men, he is tortured. He agrees to help Trujillo's men after watching his wife being tortured by electric shocks. After his wife's death and his release, he follows Manolo for a time, then leaves politics. He becomes a successful

The painted obelisk "A Song to Liberty," erected in Santo Domingo in the Dominican Republic, commemorates the courage of the Mirabal sisters, the protagonists of Alvarez's book. Three of the women were murdered for their resistance to the ruthless dictatorship of president Rafael Trujillo.

builder in the capital, remarries, and has another family.

Hilda

A young revolutionary friend of Minerva's, Hilda must hide at Inmaculada Concepción to escape the police. She is arrested when seen leaving the school.

Jaimito

See Jaime Fernández

El Jefe (The Chief)

See General Rafael Trujillo

Lío

See Virgilio Morales

Lina Lovatón

The most beautiful girl at Inmaculada Concepción, Lina is seduced, impregnated, and then abandoned by Trujillo, whom she loves.

Media Adaptations

- The rights to a film version of *In the Time of the Butterflies* have been bought by Barnstorm Films and Phoenix Pictures.

Magdalena

Magdalena befriends and develops a romantic interest in María Teresa while they are in prison together.

Mamá

See Mercedes Reyes de Mirabal

Mariposa (Butterfly) #1

See Minerva Mirabal de Tavárez

Mariposa (Butterfly) #2

See María Teresa Mirabal de Guzmán

Mariposa (Butterfly) #3

See Patria Mercedes Mirabal de González

Mate

See María Teresa Mirabal de Guzmán

Enrique Mirabal

A successful farmer and store owner, Enrique Mirabal is the father of the Mirabal sisters and a man of means who accommodates the Trujillo regime rather than fighting it. Though he loves his children, he is disappointed that he has four daughters and no son. When María Teresa is still a young child, he begins a long-standing affair with another woman and has four daughters with her. He will not allow Minerva to attend law school, and he hides Lío Morales's letters to her. Minerva discovers his secret life, but they reach a truce and she accepts her half-sisters. After Minerva slaps Trujillo at the Discovery Day Dance, Enrique is arrested and kept in jail for weeks. He suffers a heart attack and nearly loses his mind before being released. He dies on December 14, 1953.

Margarita Mirabal

Margarita is the oldest of Enrique Mirabal's illegitimate daughters. She is a pharmacist and arranges for packages to be sent to Minerva and María Teresa in prison.

Dedé Mirabal de Fernández

Dedé is the second-oldest and last surviving Mirabal sister. In her late sixties in 1994, she is a successful life insurance agent. Since her youth, she has been very practical and good with math and business. In 1948, during her courtship with her cousin and eventual husband, Jaimito, she first meets Lío Morales, for whom she holds a secret attraction. She burns Lío's letter to Minerva asking her to go into exile with him. She and Jaimito have three sons, Enrique, Rafael, and David. Because she allows Jaimito to control their business ventures, the family is often in financial trouble. Jaimito forbids her from becoming involved in her sisters' political activities, and she gives in to his wishes because "She had always been the docile middle child, used to following the lead.... Miss Sonrisa, cheerful, compliant. Her life had gotten bound up with a domineering man, and so she shrank from the challenge her sisters were giving her." In 1960, she is unhappy in her marriage and almost leaves Jaimito, but they reconcile, though she still has serious doubts about their union. Once her sisters are arrested, she and Jaimito work hard to care for the family. She is devastated by her sisters' deaths, but she recovers and helps raise her sisters' children. She and Jaimito divorce in the 1980s, and she later survives breast cancer. Since 1960, she has helped keep the memory of her sisters alive.

Patria Mercedes Mirabal de González

Patria is the oldest and most religious of the Mirabal sisters. Her devotion to her religious pursuits catches the attention of the nuns at Inmaculada Concepción, and Sor Asunción tells Patria to watch for God's call to enter the sisterhood. Instead, Patria finds her call while washing Pedrito González's feet at a religious ceremony. She marries him when she is sixteen, and they quickly have two children, Nelson and Noris. Their third child is stillborn, which devastates them both. The child's death, coupled with her awareness of Trujillo's crimes, even causes Patria to lose her religious faith. She regains this faith, however, when on a pilgrimage. She hears the Virgin Mary speaking not through the Church but through the people themselves. Her religious belief is both transformed and strengthened by this experience.

When Nelson is in his teens, Patria worries about his desire to become involved with his aunts and uncles in the underground movement. Still, she and Pedrito allow the movement to meet on their land, but not in their house. She becomes pregnant again and decides to name the child Raúl Ernesto after the Cuban revolutionaries Raúl Castro and Ernesto (Che) Guevara. Patria becomes more intimately involved with the movement after attending a retreat in the mountains. The retreat is bombed when Trujillo's forces attack underground soldiers hiding in the mountains. Patria watches a teenaged boy be shot to death and feels a sharp kinship with him.

Upon her return home, she convinces Pedrito to hold the movement meetings in their home, which puts their farm at great risk. In 1960, Pedrito and Nelson are arrested and the government confiscates the farm. Patria moves in with her mother. She helps arrange secret contacts with her imprisoned sisters. Her contact is Margarita Mirabal, her illegitimate half-sister, and Patria sees her past rejection of Margarita as shameful. Patria is very adept at convincing Captain Peña to treat the family as well as possible, and she is overjoyed when he helps Nelson secure an early release from prison. Pedrito is not sent to Puerto Plata prison with Manolo and Leandro, but she accompanies her sisters on their final visit there. She is killed on their return trip.

María Teresa Mirabal de Guzmán

Born nine years after Minerva, María Teresa is the youngest of the Mirabal sisters. She is the most playful and, until her prison experiences, seemingly the most frivolous of the sisters. She attends Inmaculada Concepción during Minerva's last year at the school. She often covers for Minerva during this year to hide Minerva's subversive activities. María Teresa must eventually bury her first diary because she discusses the school's involvement with Minerva's revolutionary friend Hilda, who is arrested. After her father's death, María Teresa resents him because of his infidelities. She is having romantic difficulties with two of her cousins, who are competing for her affections. She eventually rejects them both, however.

After leaving Inmaculada, she goes to college with Minerva, and she lives with her sister and Manolo during one summer. She is appalled by their small house and witnesses their marital prob-

lems. She does not understand their reconciliation until Leandro Guzmán stores guns at their house and they tell her that they are involved in an underground movement. She immediately joins to be near Leandro. She continues her revolutionary activities while at college and marries Leandro in 1958. They have one daughter, Jacqueline. She is arrested in 1960 and shares a cell with Minerva and twenty-two other prisoners. She is miserable in prison, but she learns to adapt, forging a friendship with another prisoner named Magdalena. The prison guards torture her with electrical shocks in front of Leandro in order to secure his cooperation. She secretly writes of this experience to visiting officials of the Organization of American States, who come to investigate Trujillo's prisons. She lives in her mother's house after her release. Leandro is transferred to Puerto Plata prison, and she is killed with her sisters and their driver while returning from a prison visit.

Minerva Mirabal de Tavárez

Minerva is the third Mirabal daughter and the most committed to revolution. From an early age, she is sharp-tongued and self-confident. She wants to become a lawyer, though her father will not agree to this plan. He does, however, agree to let her attend Inmaculada Concepción with her older sisters. At Inmaculada, she quickly befriends a withdrawn girl named Sinita Perozo. Sinita tells Minerva about the deaths of her male family members. They were murdered for resisting Trujillo. This news shocks Minerva, and she begins the political questioning and fight for justice that will mark her future activities. Minerva, Sinita, and their friends Elsa and Lourdes perform a play before Trujillo, and Sinita aims an arrow at the dictator. Minerva diffuses the situation by chanting "*Viva Trujillo!*"

During her final year at Inmaculada, Minerva befriends a young woman named Hilda, who is a political insurgent. After Hilda is arrested, Minerva must destroy all evidence of their friendship. During her youth, she also meets and becomes interested in Lío Morales. She says she only feels a political kinship with him, but her feelings apparently run deeper than that. She spends three frustrating years at home after graduating. She then discovers that Lío has been writing her letters, which her father has hidden. She also discovers that her father has four other daughters by another woman. She reaches a truce with her father, but she is cold to him. She accepts her half-sisters and even arranges for their education. At a dance, she draws Trujillo's ire when she slaps the dictator for his sexual advances. She accidentally leaves her purse with Lío's letters behind at the dance. Her father is arrested, and she secures his release by apologizing to Trujillo.

Minerva then attends law school, where she meets Manolo Tavárez, whom she marries. They have two children, Minou and Manolito. She earns her law degree, but Trujillo denies her a license to practice. She and Manolo experience marital problems until they become involved in the anti-Trujillo underground movement. She is code-named Mariposa (Butterfly) and is a leader in the movement. After she is arrested in 1960, she retains her resolve in prison and organizes political classes for the women in her cell. She also turns down a pardon because the pardon would indicate that she did something wrong. When she is released, she lives with her mother and loses her political fervor for a time. She regains her resolve when she knows she must work to save her husband and to salvage the fractured underground. She is killed upon returning from her visit with her husband at Puerto Plata prison.

Virgilio Morales

A charismatic young doctor and a Communist revolutionary, Lío becomes close friends with Minerva. Dedé also has a silent infatuation with him. When he must flee the country, he sends Minerva a letter asking her to join him, but Dedé destroys the letter. He and Dedé meet in 1994 and discuss the past and the present state of the country.

Palomino

See Leandro Guzmán

Papá

See Enrique Mirabal

Pedrito

See Pedro Ganzález

Captain Victor Alcinio Peña

Peña is the head of the northern division of the SIM, Trujillo's security force. While the Mirabal sisters are in prison and under house arrest, he visits and keeps strict tabs on the family. He buys Patria's family's farm after the government confiscates it. He helps secure Patria's son Nelson's early release from prison in order to gain the support of the extended González family, who are laborers on the farm. Peña is alternately cruel and accommodating, depending on his purposes.

Sinita Perozo

Sinita attends Inmaculada Concepción after her male relatives are killed for opposing Trujillo. She teaches Minerva about Trujillo's crimes. While performing before the dictator, she points a bow and arrow at him but is stopped by Trujillo's son, Ramfis.

Mercedes Reyes de Mirabal

A very religious and strong woman, Chea Mirabal is the mother of the Mirabal sisters. She tries to protect her family from both outside harm and the harm they may bring on themselves. Her marriage is severely strained after she discovers her husband's long-standing infidelity. In 1960, when her daughters are arrested and Patria loses her farm, most of the family lives with her in her house in town. After the deaths of her daughters, she helps to raise their children. She dies in her sleep twenty years after her daughters' deaths.

Santicló

As a prison guard, Santicló (Santa Clause) receives his nickname by helping the women prisoners. He smuggles in items and delivers communications. He is Margarita Mirabal's cousin.

Manolo Tavárez

Manolo is Minerva's husband. Like her, he is a lawyer, but they are poor and Manolo is unfaithful early in their marriage. Their underground activities bring them closer together, and they both become leaders in the movement. After he is imprisoned, tortured, and loses his wife, he becomes famous in the country. He refuses to run for office, though, and takes to the mountains with a revolutionary force. He and his men are murdered after they surrender on December 21, 1963.

Minou Tavárez

Minou is Minerva's oldest child. She is close to her Mamá Dedé, who helped raise her. In 1994, she is a married woman with a child of her own, Camila.

General Rafael Trujillo

Trujillo is the Dominican dictator who ruled the nation from 1930 until his assassination in 1961. His greed, cruelty, and desire for total control over others inform the lives of all of the characters in the book. He tries to seduce Minerva, but she refuses him. He finally takes his revenge on the rebellious family by ordering the sisters killed.

Themes

Dominican Republic

As Alvarez indicates in her title, *In the Time of the Butterflies,* she is not just concerned with the Mirabal sisters themselves. She is concerned with an era and a way of life. To understand the impact of Trujillo's reign and the significance of the Mirabal sisters, readers must also understand the nation they inhabited. Therefore, Alvarez works to create a sense of the atmosphere of the country, its landscape, its institutions, and its people. The political environment, of course, is one of her chief topics. Trujillo's ruthless regime dominates this time period. By focusing on the country's tribulations over a long period of time, Alvarez communicates the disastrous consequences of Trujillo's rule on a nation and its citizens. She also reveals the changes the country undergoes after Trujillo is assassinated. The epilogue, in particular, stresses the traumas the country has suffered, the changes it has undergone, and the need to remember and learn from the "time of the butterflies."

Authoritarianism

Alvarez uses the Trujillo regime not only to depict the violent methods of this particular dictator but also to reveal the impact of authoritarian governments. Under Trujillo, anyone caught in "subversive" activity—even simply criticizing the government—is subject to imprisonment and, perhaps, torture and death. Dominicans, therefore, live in fear, however muted it may be. They censor what they say to one another, and many also censor their own thoughts. This atmosphere also makes people suspicious of one another, which hinders intimacies and ensures that people suffer in silence. Also, because Trujillo requires that his subjects display his portrait in their homes and that he always be characterized as the nation's hero, he thrusts himself into people's lives. He especially impacts the minds of children, who are taught to hold him on par with religious icons. These authoritarian methods allow dictators to enter and often control almost all spheres of people's lives. Alvarez stresses the consequences of this situation when she has Dedé hear a radio commentator say that dictatorships "are pantheistic. The dictator manages to plant a little piece of himself in every one of us." As Alvarez reveals, such a dictator also manages to satisfy his own monumental desires at the cost of the suffering of thousands.

Change and Transformation

In a novel in which the key word is "butterfly," readers might expect the theme of transformation to be a prominent one. Such is the case with this book. Alvarez focuses on the changes in the Mirabal sisters as they progress toward their revolutionary activities. In addition, she notes the subtle changes taking place in the country while Trujillo is alive. He comes under criticism from the Catholic Church, and more people join the resistance against him. These elements of the book stress both the dangerous and the liberating qualities of change, whether personally or politically. As Alvarez reveals in characters like Patria and in the country at large, people often must be forcefully thrust out of their patterns of existence, even when those patterns are detrimental. Though change can be painful, it frequently allows individuals or even a nation to discover stronger, richer, and more courageous versions of themselves.

Courage and Cowardice

Clearly, the Mirabal sisters are testaments to the power of courage. In Alvarez's rendering, the sisters also reveal fragility because they are not always courageous and self-assured. Their very fears make them all the more admirable, however, since they overcome them and find the strength to act. They draw strength from one another, as well, revealing that personal fortitude often requires a dependence on others. Bravery may come easier for some, but all of the central characters possess this quality. Minerva's courage is admired by all, but even she suffers from fear and doubt after her release from prison. Dedé, on the other hand, discusses her own lack of boldness when she refuses to join her sisters. She is afraid of losing her marriage, but she also is afraid for herself and for her sisters. Still, in moments of crisis, she also acts bravely to defend others. For instance, when stopped by Trujillo's men while with Minerva, she tells them that she is Minerva in an effort to protect her sister. She also has the courage to continue living after the loss of her sisters. Her nieces and nephews need her strength, and she gives it to them. In 1994, she has the fortitude to look honestly at herself and her country's past.

The courage of the Mirabal sisters is also contrasted with the essential cowardice of Trujillo's men and Trujillo himself, who struts, wears makeup and absurd medals, and constantly must hear about his own superiority. These men hold power and wield it unjustly and brutally. Even when Trujillo is obviously in the wrong, his men

Topics For Further Study

- Discuss whether writing a fictional account of real people is a valid or fair means of depicting them for an audience. Take into consideration Alvarez's comments in her postscript to *In the Time of the Butterflies.*

- Research the life of a woman who, like the Mirabals, fought for human rights or political change at great personal risk. The list of subjects is quite long, but some possible choices include Harriet Tubman of the Underground Railroad, Qui Jin of China, Ruth First of South Africa, Fannie Lou Hamer of the American Civil Rights Movement, Rigoberta Manchú of Guatemala, or Aung San Suu Kyi of Burma. You also may want to compare people's responses to these women to the Dominican people's responses to the Mirabal sisters.

- Compare the lives of Dominican women today to the lives of Dominican women before 1960. Explore their social positions, gender expectations, educational opportunities, familial roles, or their political impact.

- Compare contemporary political conditions in the Dominican Republic with conditions during the Trujillo regime.

- Research the relationship between the Trujillo government and the U.S. government. Choose a particular time frame or event that helps to clarify this relationship, and focus on one facet of their relationship, such as their economic ties, their political ties or disputes, or America's role in either maintaining or undermining Trujillo's dictatorship.

- Compare Trujillo's methods of gaining and maintaining power with the methods of another ruler, such as Francisco Franco of Spain, Joseph Stalin of Russia, Mao Tse-Tung of China, Fidel Castro of Cuba, François "Papa Doc" Duvalier of Haiti, or Saddam Hussein of Iraq.

- Construct a psychological profile of a dictator. Discuss his motivations, desires, needs, and possible fears. Address some of the root causes for the dictator's behavior.

- Research the 1937 massacre of Haitians in the Dominican Republic. Examine both its causes and its consequences. Then employ literary works, such as Edwidge Danticat's novel *The Farming of Bones* or Rita Dove's poem "Parsley," to explore how people have reacted to this terrible event.

---

carry out his orders to gain favor and prevent their own punishment. Their selfishness and cowardice further highlight the courage of the Mirabal family in resisting such greed and inhumanity.

Family Life

A depiction of family life is central to Alvarez's characterization of the Mirabals because she wants to portray them as Dominican women, not Dominican legends. The Mirabal sisters' families are core elements of their lives. They receive strength and support from their families because, despite their many conflicts, they aid each other even when in disagreement. Of course, their commitments to their families also make the Mirabals vulnerable to painful losses. For instance, Patria

grieves over her stillborn child and worries constantly over Nelson after his arrest. The sisters also suffer because of their father's infidelity, although they eventually come to accept their half-sisters. Dedé and Mamá Mirabal suffer acutely when Patria, Minerva, and María Teresa are killed. Alvarez also focuses heavily on the sisters' children. She effectively conveys the sisters' need for them and their willingness to sacrifice for their children's futures. By focusing on the children, Alvarez communicates the powerful loyalties that drive the sisters and cause them both guilt and pain. Without this familial emphasis, Alvarez would not as clearly communicate the sacrifices of the Mirabal family for a cause greater than themselves.

Gender Roles

Alvarez's focus on gender also stresses the achievements of the Mirabal sisters. They live in a country and era in which gender roles are clearly defined. Men hold positions of authority and women largely maintain domestic roles. Alvarez depicts these realities with Enrique Mirabal's attempts to force his daughters to abide by their gender limitations. For instance, he will not allow Minerva to attend law school despite her obvious ability. Alvarez also reveals the consequences of gender definitions through Dedé and Jaimito's marriage. Dedé is very intelligent with a strong business sense, but Jaimito keeps her from exercising these abilities because he wants to "wear the pants" in his family. He tries to maintain his view of masculinity, authority, and honor by running their business affairs, usually with disastrous consequences. Her business success after her divorce testifies to falseness of these gender distinctions.

Alvarez represents the complexity of women's lives by portraying women who challenge gender limitations, such as Minerva and her friends at school, many of whom go on to have successful professional careers. Even Patria, who enjoys the more traditional occupations of wife and mother, becomes involved in revolutionary politics. Alvarez also employs her female characters to depict changes in attitudes toward gender. The Mirabal sisters obviously step outside the boundaries of traditional feminine behavior in the country. Yet, Alvarez also presents the further defiance of the sisters' daughters and even their mother, who advises Minou, Minerva's daughter, to have a career before marrying, although she opposed this desire in Minerva years previously. Ultimately, Alvarez's focus on gender allows her to amplify the range of the Mirabal sisters' challenges and accomplishments in life.

Style

Setting

In the Time of the Butterflies is set in the Dominican Republic. The action takes place between 1938 and 1994, although many of these years are not depicted in the novel. This time period is characterized by Rafael Trujillo's authoritarian rule, which dominates both the country and, quite frequently, people's lives. The Dominican Republic is a largely Catholic country with a very influential Church. The country is also largely patriarchal, with the men holding positions of authority and women most often expected to forego individual careers, although this code is not as rigid as in the past. Trujillo's prisons also are featured prominently in the novel, and Alvarez effectively contrasts their harshness with the general lushness of the country's fertile regions.

Historical Fiction

By creating fictional characters and situations out of historical people and events, Alvarez raises questions about the role of the novel in understanding the past. Does representing actual people in a fictional context diminish their significance—or, worse, constitute unethical misrepresentation? Does changing facts from the era to suit a writer's purposes undermine the messages she is trying to convey? Alvarez addresses these and similar concerns in her postscript to the novel. She never claims historical accuracy in her work. Instead, she asserts that she wanted "to immerse ... readers in an epoch in the life of the Dominican Republic that I believe can only finally be understood by fiction, only finally redeemed by the imagination." Her apparent intent in the work is to convey the emotional and psychological reality of the situation, not strict facts. By fictionalizing, she provides readers with *her* sense of the Mirabal family, the political and social situations in which they lived, and the lessons we can draw from their lives and deaths. For Alvarez, such is the function of a novel, which she says is not "a historical document, but a way to travel through the human heart."

Multiple Points of View

Alvarez tells the Mirabal sisters' stories through their own eyes. Patria, Minerva, and María Teresa narrate three chapters each. Dedé narrates three chapters and the epilogue, which briefly discusses the years between 1960 and 1994. In her postscript to the novel, Alvarez says she began writing the Mirabals' story to understand what gave them their courage to oppose Trujillo's brutal regime. She asserts, though, that "the characters took over, beyond polemics and facts," and she began to invent them. Her use of multiple points of view allows Alvarez to create her fictional Mirabal sisters and to intimately explore the sisters' contrasting personalities. For instance, they each have different motivations for joining or not joining the underground movement against Trujillo, and their individual narratives reveal the development of their political beliefs. They also reveal the quality and depth of their love for others, as well as the difficulties they have maintaining their strength in the face of extreme adversity. This narrative technique helps Alvarez to avoid creating a "mythological" version of the Mirabals that she believes "dismiss[es] the challenge of their courage as impossible for us, ordinary men and women." Her use of individual perspectives, therefore, proves central to generating more human characters who she hopes are "true to the spirit of the real Mirabals."

Diary Entries

María Teresa's chapters consist of her diary entries from her girlhood, young womanhood, and her time in prison. These entries create a far more fragmented picture of events than do the chapters narrated by the other sisters. The diary entries of the younger María Teresa also offer a young girl's perspective on important events in the family's life, such as Patria's child being born dead, Minerva's friendship with the radical Hilda, and her father's death. All three journals contain drawings that reveal María Teresa's emotional and psychological progression. For instance, she draws shoes and a dress in her first journal; in the second, she draws a ring, Minerva's house, and a bomb; in the third, she draws the layout of her prison cell.

Flashbacks

Though the entire book is, in essence, a flashback to the lives of the Mirabals, Dedé's chapters employ this device most explicitly. Her chapters begin with her thoughts and conversations in 1994, then shift back in time when she immerses herself in her memories. This technique emphasizes the impact of the past on the present, as well as the great losses both Dedé and the country have suffered. The flashbacks also offer a contrast between Dedé's desire to keep the past alive and the desire of the country's youth to forget the past entirely.

Sense of Inevitability

By beginning the book with Dedé in 1994, Alvarez foregrounds the Mirabal sisters' deaths from the first chapter. This knowledge colors the reader's experience of the characters and their lives. Even in moments of happiness in the book, the inevitability of the sisters' murders generates a sense of impending doom and loss. It also shifts attention away from questions of plot because the reader does not wonder what will happen to the characters. Instead, the reader is invited to focus on questions of character, character relationships, the reasons behind the Mirabals' fate, and the consequences of their deaths.

Spanish Phrasing

Though she writes the novel in English, Alvarez consistently includes Spanish words or phrases, such as Sor (sister), Tía or Tío (aunt or uncle), por Dios (for Heaven's sake), and El Jefe (The Chief). In his review of the novel, "Sisters in Death" in *The New York Times Book Review*, Roberto González Echevarría contends that Alvarez has "marred" the book with these "Hispanisms" because "Once we accept the idea of English-speaking Mirabals, there is no reason for them to have accents." Isabel Zakrzewski Brown, however, disagrees with this assessment in her article "Historiographic Metafiction in *In the Time of the Butterflies*" in *South Atlantic Review*. She contends that Alvarez's method enables her to create "an artful means of approximating the English-speaking reader to the ambience within which the Mirabal sisters lived."

Historical Context

The Trujillo Regime

The time period of the novel, 1938 to 1994, is dominated by the political regime of dictator Rafael Leonidas Trujillo (1891–1961) and its aftermath. Trujillo ruled the Dominican Republic from 1930 until his assassination in 1961. Before 1930, he had been trained by the American military forces who had taken control of the nation in 1916 and left in 1924. In 1930, he used his position as head of the Dominican military to assume control of the country. To ensure his election as president, his men brutalized political opponents and terrorized voters. He further secured his power by creating a secret police force that violently suppressed opposition to his rule, maintaining networks of spies, and taking control of the press and national education. He took over industries in the country and accumulated an immense fortune. To further trade and strengthen his regime, he supported American business interests in the country and maintained a strong anti-Communist stance.

His reign was characterized by brutality and fear. He regularly employed torture and murder, and the Dominican population was largely terrified of his police forces. The most infamous episode of his dictatorship was the massacre of thousands of Haitian citizens in 1937. Haitian men, women, and children working as sugar-cane cutters or living in Dominican territory were murdered by Trujillo's

Dominican refugees are taken from a sailboat in the waters off the Florida Keys and boarded on a U.S. Coast Guard cutter before being interviewed by immigration officials. Many natives of the Dominican Republic left the island in reaction to the oppression of the government during and after Trujillo's reign.

soldiers. Estimates of the death toll range from 13,000 to 20,000 people.

Trujillo's methods also affected Dominicans' psychological and emotional lives. His presence dominated Dominican life. For instance, he changed the name of the capital city Santo Domingo to Cuidad Trujillo (Trujillo City) in 1936, and he put up signs that read "God and Trujillo." In school, Dominican children were taught to revere him. People were required to hang a picture of Trujillo in their homes. As Alvarez describes in her essay "Genetics of Justice," beneath the picture was the inscription "*In this house Trujillo is Chief.*" People learned to censor themselves and live in fear of reprisals. In the novel, Alvarez quotes a radio commentator who contends that in authoritarian countries, "The dictator manages to plant a little piece of himself in every one of us."

Political Resistance to Trujillo

Though Trujillo's methods of control were highly effective, he could not completely stop either criticism or secret challenges to his rule. He defeated an insurrection attempt in 1949, when ex-

iled Dominicans attempted to overthrow the government. In the 1950s, an underground movement developed. The movement was organized into small eight- to ten-member units or "cells." Many movement members had Communist leanings; others were simply dedicated to ending Trujillo's brutal reign. Exiles tried to invade the country on June 14, 1959, but they failed and were killed. These events spawned the Fourteenth of June Movement, which continued resistance efforts. Both the Mirabal sisters and Alvarez's parents were members of the movement, which planned to assassinate Trujillo in January of 1960. Their plans were uncovered, however, and the movement members either fled or were jailed, tortured, and often killed.

Late in his rule, Trujillo came under increasing international scrutiny. The Catholic Church began to openly criticize Trujillo in 1960. The United States feared his brutality would spawn a revolution directed by Communist rebels or those sympathetic to Fidel Castro, who overthrew Fulgencio Batista's government in Cuba and instituted a Communist regime. The Organization of American States was outraged by Trujillo's attempt to assassinate Venezuelan President Rómulo Betancourt in

Compare
&
Contrast

- **1960:** Trujillo rules the country. No opposition party exists. No genuine elections are held. Joaquín Balaguer is Trujillo's puppet president.

  1996: Balaguer steps down from the presidency. He held the office from 1966 to 1978 and from 1986 to 1996, winning in rigged elections. The new president, Leonel Fernandez Reyna, is elected with Balaguer's support. The election is judged non-corrupt. His vice-president is Jaime David Fernandez Mirabal, Dedé Mirabal's son. Patria Mirabal's son Nelson Gonzalez Mirabal is the vice-president's chief aid. Minerva Mirabal's daughter Minou Tavares Mirabal is deputy foreign minister.

- **1960:** A 137-foot obelisk stands in Cuidad Trujillo. The dictator erected it in his own honor.

  1999: The obelisk in the renamed Santo Domingo is adorned with a mural of the four Mirabal sisters. It is a monument to all who struggled for liberty in the country.

- **1960:** On November 25, Patria, Minerva, and Marí Teresa Mirabal are killed under Trujillo's orders.

  1999: November 25 has been designated the International Day against Violence against Women in the Mirabals' honor.

1960. Combined with the growing dissatisfaction of wealthier citizens in the Dominican Republic, these elements helped set the stage for Trujillo's downfall. On May 30, 1961, his car was ambushed by some of his former supporters and he was shot to death. Alvarez reveals in "Genetics of Justice" that Dominicans call his death not an assassination but an "*ajusticiamiento,* a bringing to justice." Indeed, the anniversary of his death is now a national holiday in the country.

The Post-Trujillo Era

Dominican politics continued to be marked by corruption after Trujillo's demise. In 1962, Juan Bosch defeated Joaquín Balaguer, who had been president under Trujillo, in the presidential elections. Bosch's liberal reforms were opposed by the United States and the Dominican military, however. Bosch was ousted by the military after only months in office. The years that followed contained further discord, including rigged elections and civil war. In 1965, the United States sent in Marines to occupy the country; in 1966, Balaguer again became president in a corrupt election. Balaguer was president until 1978, then was re-elected in 1986 and served until 1996, despite being almost ninety years old and nearly blind and deaf. From 1960 to

1994, when the novel ends, political and economic reform remained elusive for the country.

Dominican Culture and Economy

The culture in which the Mirabals live also contains restrictions and expectations not directly linked to Trujillo. The Dominican Republic is a predominantly Catholic country. Catholic beliefs and rituals inform the lives of everyone in the novel, even those who are not overtly religious. The people also hold widespread views about the roles of men and women in society. Alvarez's characters often speak of the male "macho" ethic, wherein a man must prove his strength, courage, and ability to run his own life and family. Contrasted to this ethic are the roles of women, which the Mirabal sisters often challenge. Women are expected to maintain primarily domestic lives as wives and mothers, although those limitations are not insurmountable. In the 1950s and 1960s, women were attending universities in the country, and many were assuming professional careers. The pressures to marry and bear children still impacted their lives, however.

Economically, the country has often struggled because of its reliance on agricultural exports that are subject to fluctuations in commodity prices. Farmers produce primarily sugar, but they also export coffee, cocoa beans, and tobacco. The economy also depends on mining exports, especially gold and silver. In the 1980s and 1990s, tourism has taken an increasingly central role in the country, becoming second in revenues only to agriculture. In fact, in the novel Dedé contends that the country has become "the playground of the Caribbean."

Critical Overview

Since its release in 1994, *In the Time of the Butterflies* has received largely positive reviews. Most critics praise Alvarez for bringing the Mirabal sisters' story to an American audience unfamiliar with their lives, struggles, and deaths. In their reviews of the novel, critics such as Janet Jones Hampton, Brad Hooper, Rebecca S. Kelm, and Kay Pritchett also comment on Alvarez's ability to effectively portray her characters' personal and domestic lives. Hampton, Hooper, and Pritchett commend Alvarez's focus on the political elements of her story. Pritchett, for example, contends in *World Literature Today* that Alvarez adeptly balances "the political and the human, the tragic and the lyrical." She also lauds Alvarez's style, which she says "seems to emerge from the core of woman's experience, passion, and grief."

Not all critics view the novel so favorably, however. Barbara Mujica and Roberto González Echevarría, for instance, find many areas of weakness in the work. Mujica asserts in *Americas* that Alvarez actually goes too far in humanizing her characters, making them "Smaller-than-life." She also believes that the characters "are rather too formulaic and unidimensional to hold our attention," which may hinder readers from reaching the more compelling passages in the latter stages of the book, areas in which "Alvarez has much to tell us about the strength of the human will."

In his important review in *The New York Times Book Review*, González Echevarría views Alvarez's characterizations differently. He believes that Alvarez "did not escape the temptation to monumentalize" the Mirabal sisters, which hurts the novel. In addition, he characterizes the Mirabal sisters as "reactive and passive," saying that Alvarez portrays them "as earnestly innocent and vulnerable, but that diminishes their political stature and fictional complexity." The world that Alvarez creates, according to González Echevarría, also includes "far too many misdeeds and misfortunes"

while still failing to make the reader aware "of a broader, more encompassing political world."

Other significant reviews disagree with González Echevarría's evaluation of the novel. Ilan Stavans commends the book in *Nation* and, unlike González Echevarría, he does not see the Mirabal sisters as passive. Instead, they offer a potent challenge to their society. Stavans asserts that Alvarez takes a unique approach to the Trujillo era by examining "the martyrdom of these three Dominican women as a gender battlefield." The sisters are raised in a chauvinistic society, confront the limitations this society places on women, and are killed by a dictator who must constantly demonstrate masculine power. For Stavans, though, the prominence of the Mirabals is balanced by the overarching presence of Trujillo, who is such a pervasive figure that Stavans says, "it seems to me he becomes the central character."

In *The Women's Review of Books,* Ruth Behar also comments on Alvarez's feminist approach to her topic. Behar believes that Alvarez joins other Latina writers "in the feminist quest to bring Latin American women into the nation and into history as agents," not merely as passive figures under male dominance. Behar also examines Alvarez's portrayal of the power of dictators to assert themselves in everyone's lives. She also considers Alvarez's treatments of history and revolution in the book. Behar holds that "This is a historical novel in which forgetting wins out over remembering. Alvarez offers a paradox: her novel bears witness to the urgency of her quest for memory, but for her characters healing comes only through forgetting." She criticizes Alvarez for not fully considering the corruption of revolutionaries turned dictators, but ultimately she compliments her for "showing that although revolutions turn sour, they matter."

Two critical articles have been printed on the novel. The first is "Recovering a Space for a History between Imperialism and Patriarchy: Julia Alvarez's *In the Time of the Butterflies*" by Elizabeth Coonrod Martínez, and the second is "Historiographic Metafiction in *In the Time of the Butterflies* " by Isabel Zakrzewski Brown. As do Stavans and Behar, Martínez compares Alvarez to other contemporary Latina and Chicana writers who focus on gender conflicts and represent Latin American history through women's lives. Martínez contends that like other Latin American women writers, Alvarez portrays the two sexes joined together in a common struggle, not separated by individual agendas. She also praises Alvarez for humanizing the Mirabal sisters while still constructing a political message that criticizes other nations, including America, for complicity with the Trujillo regime.

Brown also examines the feminist issues in the novel. Her approach, however, is historical. She treats the novel within the context of "historiographic metafiction," a term coined by critic Linda Hutcheon to describe the self-aware uses of history in contemporary novels. A significant portion of her article is dedicated to comparing Alvarez's fictional representations with the existing biographies of the Mirabals, detailing Alvarez's transformations of fact. She ultimately criticizes Alvarez for fashioning the Mirabal sisters into stereotypes and being "unable to avoid the mythification process she had professed to elude."

Criticism

Darren Felty

Felty teaches English at Trident Technical College in Charleston, South Carolina. In the following essay, he explores Alvarez's stated objectives in In the Time of the Butterflies *and the ways in which her characters fulfill these objectives.*

In her postscript to *In the Time of the Butterflies,* Julia Alvarez discusses her intentions in the novel. She says that she wanted to bring the story of Patria, Minerva, María Teresa, and Dedé Mirabal to the English-speaking public. All of the Mirabal sisters except Dedé rebelled against the dictator of the Dominican Republic, Rafael Trujillo, and were murdered by Trujillo's men in 1960.

Alvarez seems to recognize that many people might take exception to her book, which fictionalizes the lives of the real Mirabal sisters. Alvarez is careful to point out that the work is not a biography. She says that the reader is not to perceive these characters and events as factual. Instead, she asserts that "what you will find here are the Mirabals of my creation, made up but, I hope, true to the spirit of the real Mirabals." She also contends that the reader will not find the "legendary" Mirabals who have become more myths than actual people. In fact, she intends for her novel to counteract such myths, which make people believe that the Mirabals' courage is inaccessible to ordinary people.

To accomplish her goals, Alvarez must maintain a difficult balance. She must convey her sense of the Mirabal sisters and their importance while not posing her account as anything but an imaginary reconstruction. Because this strategy has become more common with contemporary American novels, many readers are willing to accept the fictionalizing of factual events. Still, Alvarez must work to persuade readers that her version of events provides genuine insight. Therefore, she needs to "humanize" her characters without trivializing them, show their significance without glorifying them, and maintain consistent characters without relying solely on stereotypes.

Some critics believe that Alvarez has fallen short in these areas. Others, however, find her portraits compelling and inspiring. This debate revolves around Alvarez's narrative strategies and her ability to create characters. While the reader does not know if Alvarez conveys the spirit of the *actual* Mirabal sisters, her use of alternating first person narratives allows her to generate a sense of her characters' courage and the magnitude of their sacrifices, which, ultimately, seems her central aim.

Prominent reservations about Alvarez's novel involve her inability to create believable or engaging characters. For example, Barbara Mujica observes in her review for *Americas* that Alvarez's Mirabal sisters are "Smaller-than-life" and "are rather too formulaic and unidimensional to hold our attention." Isabel Zakrzewski Brown also comments in her article "Historiographic Metafiction in *In the Time of the Butterflies*" in the *South Atlantic Review* that Alvarez resorts to stereotypes in the novel. She reaches a somewhat different conclusion than Mujica, however, though her appraisal is still negative. Brown believes that Alvarez's stereotyped sisters "come together to form a perfect whole: the now legendary Mirabal sisters. Alvarez thus is unable to avoid the mythification process she had professed to elude." In his review "Sisters in Death," Roberto González Echevarría offers a criticism similar to Brown's in *The New York Times Book Review,* saying that Alvarez "did not escape the temptation to monumentalize" the Mirabals.

The degrees to which Alvarez stereotypes or glorifies her characters are valid concerns. One could contend, like Brown, that Alvarez reduces her characters to "the pious one, Patria; the pragmatic one Dedé; the rebellious one, Minerva; and the innocent one, Mate [María Teresa]." However, one must also take into consideration both Alvarez's own implicit commentary on such stereotypes and her efforts to show the characters' divergences from these patterns.

What Do I Read Next?

- Like *In the Time of the Butterflies,* Alvarez's first novel, *How the García Girls Lost Their Accents* (1991), revolves around the lives of four sisters. In this semi-autobiographical work, she depicts their struggles both as Dominican immigrants to the United States and as women.

- *Something to Declare,* published in 1998, is a collection of personal essays by Alvarez. She discusses several aspects of her life, including her search for information about the Mirabal sisters in "Chasing the Butterflies" and the impact of Trujillo on her family in "Genetics of Justice".

- *The Woman Warrior* (1976) by Maxine Hong Kingston inspired Alvarez. This acclaimed work is based on Kingston's experiences. It foregrounds Chinese cultural expectations, such as the imposition of gender restrictions and the perceived dangers of storytelling, with which contemporary Chinese-American women must contend.

- Edwidge Danticat's 1998 novel *The Farming of Bones* employs fiction to portray the impact of Trujillo's 1937 massacre of Haitian immigrants in the Dominican Republic.

- In her poem "Parsley," Rita Dove evokes the horror of Trujillo's 1937 massacre and constructs a psychological portrait of the dictator. She focuses on the test Trujillo's men used to determine who would be killed: a person's ability to properly pronounce the Spanish word for parsley.

- *The Inhabited Woman* by Nicaraguan writer Gioconda Belli tells the story of a successful woman, Lavinia, who is influenced by the spirit of a female Indian warrior to rebel against both gender restrictions and her country's military dictatorship. This title was translated by Kathleen March in 1994.

- Gabriel García Márquez's novel *The Autumn of the Patriarch* is a psychological study of a cruel, lonely, and paranoid Latin American dictator. Employing a complex structure and a "stream-of-consciousness" style, the book is challenging to read. The first U.S. edition appeared in 1976 and was translated by Gregory Rabassa.

- In his famous work *The Prince,* which appeared in English in 1907, Niccolo Machiavelli details the means of sustaining political power. The work is known for its disregard for abstract rights and morality in favor of practical, brutal solutions to political problems.

- Adolf Hitler wrote *Mein Kampf* (translated as *My Battle*) before he rose to power in Germany. The book provides a frightening insight into racial hatred and Hitler's prescription for maintaining an authoritarian society.

Alvarez uses Dedé's narrative, in particular, to show how the Mirabals have already been reduced to formulaic portrayals. While briefly describing her sisters to the American interviewer who visits her, Dedé employs a "fixed, monolithic language" that she always uses with "interviewers and mythologizers of her sisters." She realizes that her listeners want definitive characterizations that support their own simplistic notions of the Mirabals. To be heroic, it seems, the Mirabal sisters must not be complex. Still, even in her stereotyping Dedé provides germs of truth. Her summaries are necessarily shorthand versions meant to create an overall sense of her sisters.

Alvarez employs much the same strategies because even a long work of fiction cannot capture the sisters' full complexity. In fact, Alvarez ascribes to Dedé her own methods: working to inspire while also lending an air of normalcy to the Mirabals. Like Dedé, she grounds her depictions in her characters' daily lives and loves in order to foreground their humanity. In doing so, she reveals how these sometimes mundane details are a means of understanding the sisters' rebellions. Alvarez also employs the sisters' weaknesses, fears, and even their selfishness to emphasize their strength in overcoming these hindrances.

Minerva would appear to be the most challenging character to create because she is the most "mythologized" of the sisters. She is the one most identified with the resistance against Trujillo because of her beauty, her public rebellions, her conspicuous intelligence, and her leadership in the underground movement. Alvarez exhibits these same attributes in her Minerva, especially her vehement, outspoken hatred of injustice in any form.

Yet Alvarez also complicates Minerva's character by having her struggle to maintain her outward strength. After her prison sentence, Minerva lives in her mother's house. For a time, she feels overwhelmed and cannot uphold others' expectations of her. As she says, "My months in prison had elevated me to superhuman status." She then finds herself merely performing a role she cannot actually fulfill: "I hid my anxieties and gave everyone a bright smile. If they had only known how frail was their iron-willed heroine. How much it took to put on that hardest of all performances, being my old self again."

Though Minerva eventually regains her fortitude and fiery will, these moments allow the reader to see beneath her "heroine" status to a woman who longs for peace, comfort, and her children. They also allow Alvarez to demonstrate the process of creating and maintaining simplistic public personas. Minerva becomes a symbol even before her death, and the living woman must cope with this status and even perpetuate it for the benefit of others. Alvarez thereby uses Minerva in this instance to reveal the dehumanizing consequences of such processes, which can cut people off from sympathy and understanding.

Initially, the least appealing of Alvarez's characters is María Teresa, or Mate. The reader does not acquire a sense of intimacy with her, perhaps because her narrative is told through diary entries that are most often addressed to the diary book itself, which creates a distancing effect. In addition, the younger Mate lacks the more engrossing conflicts that her sisters possess in their narratives. Even when she joins the underground movement, her commitments seem more shallow than Minerva or Patria's. She joins largely because of her feelings for her eventual husband, Leandro Guzmán. Thus, she seems to romanticize her involvement rather than comprehend the true repercussions of her actions.

By making Mate more childish and less of an ardent revolutionary, Alvarez shows her as someone guided by impulse and heedless emotion. These features may reflect a stereotypical youthful impetuousness, but they also limit the reader's admiration for her, which, if intentional, is a risky strategy for Alvarez to adopt. Not until Mate enters prison does she begin to grow in stature. By having Mate record her fear, doubts, and suffering in her journal, Alvarez drives home the reality of the prisoners' harrowing situation and the strength it takes to endure in this environment. Thus, after Alvarez deflates Mate's "heroine" status, she allows her to mature, creating a far more compelling character.

On the surface, Patria might seem the most mundane of the sisters, since she married young and lived a common, domestic life. However, Alvarez uses these characteristics to shape Patria's motivations for joining the revolution. If one were to stereotype her, she would be "the maternal one," even more so than Brown's description of her as "the pious one." She is a passionate mother, and even her religion contains a profound element of maternal concern for others. She becomes an active member in the underground after witnessing a boy's death during a military attack and thinking, "Oh my God, he's one of mine!" She then takes on a tone of defiance as she contemplates the destruction of the people, her "human family." She prays, "I'm not going to sit back and watch my babies die, Lord, even if that's what You in Your great wisdom decide."

Unlike Minerva and Mate, most of Patria's rebellions are internal. She has sexual longings that contradict her outward piety, and, after her child is born dead, she loses her religious faith for a time but tells no one. In addition, though she joins the rebellion, she is not as vocal as her sisters. Through her portrayal of Patria's strong emotions and deep commitments to others, Alvarez poses her as resolved and motivated by powerful feeling. In these respects, Alvarez creates a consistent, engaging character who exhibits some elements of stereotyping but is not defined by them.

Of all the sisters, Dedé proves the most complicated and engaging. These features perhaps result from the fact that she is the surviving sister, the one who did not give her life for a cause. They also result from her role as the book's central narrator and Alvarez's depiction of the growth of her character since 1960. Even while her sisters are alive, though, Dedé exhibits personal doubts and makes mistakes that have more resonance because of her lack of heroic actions. Most overtly, she marries Jaimito though she is secretly attracted to another man, and, of the four sisters, hers is the only seriously unhappy marriage. In addition, she readily admits to putting up a cheerful front and, in 1994, closely examines her own motivations for her previous actions, which her sisters, of course, cannot do.

Through Dedé, Alvarez explores the failures of courage that kept so many people from opposing Trujillo. She also explores the capacity for courage that lies hidden in people until times of crisis. After her sisters' deaths, Dedé had to remain strong for her nieces and nephews, as well as for those who admired her sisters. She did so and became "the grand dame of the terrible, beautiful past." This role might limit her to being a formulaic "oracle" figure, but Alvarez effectively portrays Dedé's honest appraisals of her failures, her unwillingness to hide from her guilt, and her resolve to keep living and finding happiness. Thus, while she retains consistent features throughout the book, they do not undermine the vibrancy of her character.

From beginning to end, Alvarez presents herself as an advocate for the Mirabal sisters. As a result, she cannot completely escape the charge that she glorifies their lives, nor can one deny the stereotypical elements of her characters. These deficiencies do not compromise the strengths of her book, however. She creates enough believable moments to evoke genuine emotional responses, particularly in her treatments of Patria and Dedé, and to emphasize the humanity of these women and their families.

She also implicitly raises the question of who has the right to speak for the Mirabals. Dedé is the keeper of the family flame, but she does not presume to become her sisters' mouthpiece. The Mirabal family servant Fela, however, believes that the dead sisters speak through her, and Alvarez herself gives the sisters distinctive fictional voices. Thus, Alvarez highlights how people, including herself, use the Mirabal sisters for their own purposes. Through Dedé's comments on speaking to interviewers, Fela's activities, and her own postscript, Alvarez highlights the constructed nature of her characters. Yet, she also stresses the *need* to construct them in order to inform others and enrich people's lives, whether it be those in the novel or Alvarez's own readership. And her constructions are compelling enough to inspire many to share her

assertion "Vivan las Mariposas!" or "Long live the Butterflies!" Therefore, by her own yardstick, Alvarez's novel is a success.

Source: Darren Felty, in an essay for *Novels for Students*, Gale, 2000.

Elizabeth Martinez

In the following essay, Martinez describes Alvarez's book as a "fictionalized biography that moves its characters forward in the shadow of impending doom" as they "become involved in the underground movement against dictator Rafael Leonidas Trujillo."

November 25th is observed as International Day Against Violence Toward Women in many Latin American countries. That was the day in 1960 when three young sisters who had been fighting to overthrow a brutal dictatorship in the Dominican Republic were assassinated. Known as the butterflies (originally their underground code name), the Mirabal sisters became beloved national heroines. They and their era are the subject of Julia Alvarez's devastating, inspiring book.

Good novels with political themes are a rare treat. Here we have not one but two: along with *Butterflies* comes *Mother-Tongue* by Chicana poet Demetria Martinez, winner of the 1994 Western States Book Award for Fiction. Her story of a young Chicana who falls in love with a Salvadoran refugee tortured as a counter-insurgent in his own country, now exiled to the U.S., is haunting and simply beautiful.

Both authors have interwoven political and personal themes with powerful effect. Both books center on young women maturing, and celebrate women. Both reveal powerful links between the spiritual and the political. Both follow a journal structure, with different voices speaking at different times. Both are treasures.

Also, both books are written by Latina women and thus form part of the flowering of fiction, poetry, essays, and plays by Chicanas and other Latinas here over the past decade. Opposing this creative explosion has been a Euroamerican tendency to find our history, mores, language, most artistic expression, and all but the fair-skinned just too alien. The problem lies not only in institutional racism; it's also the cultural and spiritual borders imposed by the dominant society. To cross, you need much more than a green card.

In the worlds of film and television, cultural gringoism is almost pathetic. During the last few years alone, one Hollywood movie after another—from *House of the Spirits* to *The Perez Family* —has found it necessary to have stars of European background play Latina/o characters. The sound of Meryl Streep repeatedly mispronouncing her husband's name, Esteban, may rasp in my ears forever. Television doesn't even bother to whiten; it just makes us invisible. As for the print media, they may publish reviews of art, theater, dance, films, and books with Latino themes—but how many Spanish surnames can you find among the reviewers? And of these, how many are even vaguely progressive?

In the world of literature, Latin American writers (for example, Isabel Allende and Carlos Fuentes) have been the ones to slip over the border most easily. In general, Chicano or other homegrown Latino writers have been quietly labeled a bunch of lightweights.

Mainstream recognition did not begin at all until the discovery that the Chicano world could be colorful, amusing, exotic, quaint, magical. Rarely was that world projected as full of anger at racism, struggles for justice, or revolutions of the body and spirit. It's better to be cute than political, individual than collective-minded, and you should pray to be compared with *Like Water for Chocolate*.

Now come the new books by Julia Alvarez and Demetria Martinez, both with radical themes that include criticism of U.S. policy and Anglo values. They have had flattering reviews, but profound political or social questions raised in each book go ignored: most critics seem happier with the romancing.

Julia Alvarez's book is a fictionalized biography that moves its characters forward in the shadow of impending doom, yet never victimizes, never negates human complexity. *Las mariposas*—the butterflies—were born to semi-rural comfort, servants, and a convent education. Their background did not suggest that one by one they would become involved in the underground movement against dictator Rafael Leonidas Trujillo. But they do, each in accordance with her own character and within her world of parents, lovers, husbands, and children. The transformation of the sisters—Minerva, Patria, and Maria Teresa—shows how a person can become a traitor to her class. How concessions that seem trivial may lead down one road and a refusal to make such compromises can lead down its opposite. How rebels are not always born but can be made.

You suspect Minerva will be the first when, in front of a crowd, she slaps Trujillo for sexual harassment (and then leaves the party with her family before Trujillo has left, which is literally against the law). It's not such a big step from there to running guns.

The highly religious Patria seems least likely to join the movement but she does, after witnessing a hideous government massacre of peasants. Her long journey from traditional Catholicism to revolution—a journey made by many priests also—is a major theme in this book, as in Latin American liberation theology.

Maria Teresa, the youngest and least political or even spiritual, first declares that love of a man goes deeper for her than some higher ideal, but she, too, joins. Only Dede, the fourth sister, following her conservative husband's wishes, does not join the others in their new life, in prison, and in death.

As a result, Dede lives to tell the sisters' story and how they were ambushed driving back from a visit to their husbands in prison. On a winding mountain road along the north coast of the Dominican Republic, their jeep is stopped and they are shot to death. The press reports how the bodies of the famous beautiful sisters have been found with their jeep and driver at the bottom of a 150-foot cliff—clearly the victims of an "accident". But the Dominican people know better; they know.

Within a year Trujillo was overthrown, but this didn't lead to a society of the sisters' dreams. Instead it was more killings, hapless new rulers, and the rise of "the prosperous young", living in luxury where guerrillas had once fought. "Was it for this, the sacrifice of the butterflies?" asks the survivor Dede, who takes center stage in the last pages of the book, grappling with guilt and grief. Her question can resound with U.S. movement activists from twenty-five years ago as precious victories of that era undergo reactionary assault today.

In the same mood, Dede describes how, at an event honoring the sisters, she thinks of the younger people: "to them we are characters in a sad story about a past that is over". But not quite, Dede tells an old friend: "I'm not stuck in the past, I've just brought it with me into the present. And the problem is not enough of us have done that".

Julia Alvarez, now a professor at Middlebury College, was brought to the U.S. at age ten by her family to escape Trujillo's repression. After her first successful book, *How the Garcia Girls Lost Their Accents,* Alvarez faced a huge challenge in telling the story of the butterflies. The Mirabal sisters are revered in the Dominican Republic; their family home is a shrine, where Patria's wedding dress lies on the bed ready to wear, and the braid of young Maria Teresa's hair rests under glass. To write a book about such icons could mean trouble, controversy.

Sure enough, some Dominicans have berated Alvarez for daring to humanize the sisters, and for other supposed crimes. Most of this seems to come down to petty jealousy, perhaps with a dash of wounded *macho,* toward someone who left the country and "made it" in the U.S. Reviewers in this country have displayed similar emotions, as in the major *New York Times* review, which bristled with hostility and leveled totally absurd criticism like, "There is indeed much too much crying in this novel".

Not that the book is perfect. It tells us almost nothing about the issue of color and the particularities of Afro-Dominican experience. And it somewhat veils the issue of class. But nothing makes me less than joyous that Julia Alvarez wrote this book, telling a story unknown to most people in this country.

Activists and progressives can also contemplate the author's own, last message about the butterflies: "by making them myth, we lost the Mirabals once more, dismissing the challenge of their courage as impossible for us, ordinary men and women".

Source: Elizabeth Martinez, in a review of *In the Time of the Butterflies,* in *The Progressive,* July 1995, p. 39.

Robert Gonzalez Echevarria

In the following essay, Echevarria criticizes Alvarez's book for monumentalizing the Mirabals' story, for not making their characters complex enough, and for not connecting the period of the Mirabals to broader Latin American history.

Hispanic writers in the United States have published several novels of unquestionable merit, the most recent success being Cristina Garcia's "Dreaming in Cuban". Most deal with the pains and pleasures of growing up in a culture and a language outside the mainstream. If becoming an adult is a trying process under ordinary circumstances, doing so within varying and often conflicting expectations can be even more bewildering and alienating. It makes growing up, which is by its very nature self-absorbing, doubly so. A person can emerge not a harmonious blend, but simultaneously two (or more) selves in conflict. This predicament is much more dramatic when people speak two or more languages, for the inner life can be like a United Nations debate, complete with simultaneous translations and awkward compromises.

All this is, of course, the stuff of literature, which is why it has become the central concern of Hispanic writers in this country. It was the explicit theme of Julia Alvarez's delightful first novel, *How the Garcia Girls Lost Their Accents,* and it is the subtext of her second, *In the Time of the Butterflies.* But by dealing with real historical figures in this novel, Ms. Alvarez has been much more ambitious than she was in her first, as if she needed to have her American self learn what it was really like in her native land, the Dominican Republic.

On the night of Nov. 25, 1960, Patria, Minerva and Maria Teresa Mirabal—three sisters returning from a visit to their husbands, political prisoners of the dictator Rafael Leonidas Trujillo—were murdered by Trujillo's henchmen. This was one of those appalling atrocities that galvanize opposition to a murderous regime and signal the beginning of its demise. Indeed, Trujillo was slain six months later, and the Dominican Republic began a tortuous and tortured attempt at democracy. The Mirabal sisters, already admired for their resistance to the Trujillo regime before they were murdered, became part of the mythology of the Dominicans struggle for social and political justice, and the day of their death is observed in many parts of Latin America today.

In an epilogue, Ms. Alvarez, who was 10 years old when her family came to the United States in the year the Mirabal sisters were assassinated, runs through the usual commonplaces about the freedom of the historical novelist in the handling of facts, and expresses her desire to do more than merely add to the deification of the Mirabals. In fictionalizing their story she has availed herself of the liberties of the creative writer, to be sure, but alas, I am afraid she did not escape the temptation to monumentalize.

Ms. Alvarez's plan is flawless. As she proved in her first novel, she is skilled at narrative construction, though she lacks a compelling style and her English is sometimes marred by Hispanisms. (Once we accept the idea of English-speaking Mirabals, there is no reason for them to have accents.)

In the Time of the Butterflies opens with a thinly disguised version of Ms. Alvarez, an Americanized Dominican woman who wants to write something about the Mirabals and is looking for information. She visits the family home, now a kind of shrine, run by Dede, the surviving fourth sister, who had remained at home that night, and who expectedly, is tortured by guilt and haunted by the burden of memory. Dede's recollections and musings open and close the novel, nicely framing the action.

The core of the book is made up of chronological reminiscences by the murdered sisters from childhood to the time of their brutal demise. Because we know their fate in advance, everything is colored by sadness and anger. The Mirabals are a traditional provincial Dominican family, portrayed in cliched fashion—a middle-class rural clan anchored by the inevitably philandering but supportive patriarch and the warm, caring and wise mother. Happy, bourgeois families like the Mirabals were, for many years, the heart of the Trujillo dictatorship's support.

As Ms. Alvarez tells their story, the Mirabal sisters are drawn into politics by Trujillo's intolerable wickedness rather than by any deeply felt or intellectually justified commitment. The sisters appear on the whole to be reactive and passive. Their education in religious schools, and their chaste and rather naïve development into womanhood take up too many tedious pages. Probably to heighten the evil import of Trujillo's deeds, the Mirabals are portrayed as earnestly innocent and vulnerable, but that diminishes their political stature and fictional complexity.

Ms Alvarez clutters her novel with far too many misdeeds and misfortunes: rape, harassment, miscarriage, separation, abuse, breast cancer. Are the sisters victims of fate, Latin American machismo, American imperialism or only the particularly diabolical nature of Trujillo's dictatorship? Eulogy turns into melodrama and history becomes hagiography. There is a touch of the maudlin even in the title—the Mirabals were affectionately known in their lifetime as the mariposas, the butterflies. There is indeed much too much crying in this novel.

Hispanic Americans today have "old countries" that are neither old nor remote. Even those born here often travel to their parents' homeland, and constantly face a flow of friends and relatives from "home" who keep the culture current. This constant cross-fertilization makes assimilation a more complicated process for them than for other minority groups. This "living origin" is a determining factor for Hispanic writers in the United States, as William Luis, a professor of Latin American literature at Vanderbilt University and the leading authority on this phenomenon, has pointed out. This is why the most convincing parts of *In the Time of the Butterflies* have to do with Dede, the survivor, and her anguished role as memorialist, which in turn becomes Ms. Alvarez's role. It is here that we best understand the depths of Ms. Alvarez's despair and the authenticity of her effort to represent the inner drama of her conversion to an American self.

There is for Hispanic writers in the United States the added burden of a very active popular literary tradition in Spanish, including some of the most distinguished names in contemporary world literature: Carlos Fuentes, Mario Vargas Llosa, Gabriel Garcia Marquez, and Octavio Paz. In its concern with history and dictatorship, *In the Time of the Butterflies* seems to be echoing Garcia Marquez, and the emphasis on a clannish rural family is reminiscent not only of that modern master but also of his disciple Isabel Allende.

But the actual history in *In the Time of the Butterflies* is very blurry. I find no connection between the specific dates Ms. Alvarez gives to mark periods in the Mirabals' lives and either Dominican or broader Latin American history. Serious historical fiction establishes links between individual destiny and pivotal political events. It shows either the disconnection between the individual and the larger flow of sociopolitical movements or on the contrary the individuals as a pawn of history. In either case there is irony, but in this novel the reader is not made aware of a broader, more encompassing political world.

In the Time of the Butterflies reads like the project the Americanized Dominican woman at the beginning of the novel ("a *gringa dominicana* in a rented car with a road map asking for street names") would have come up with after pondering the fate of the Mirabal sisters from her perspective as a teacher on a United States college campus today. Had Julia Alvarez concentrated more on her dialogue with Dede she would have produced a better book. It would have had the touch of irony provided by the realization that the *gringa dominicana* would never really be able to understand the other woman much less translate her.

Source: Robert Gonzalez Echevarria, "Sisters in Death", in *New York Times Book Review*, December 18, 1994, p. 28.

Sources

Julia Alvarez, "A Brief Account of My Writing Life," *Appalachian State University Summer Reading Program,* http://www.geocities.com/CollegePark/Library/4061/alvarez.html, 1997.

Julia Alvarez, "Genetics of Justice," in her *Something to Declare,* Algonquin Books of Chapel Hill, 1998, pp. 103-11.

Ruth Behar, "Revolutions of the Heart," *The Women's Review of Books,* May, 1995, pp. 6-7.

Jonathan Bing, "Julia Alvarez: Books that Cross Borders," *Publishers Weekly,* Vol. 243, No. 51, pp. 38-39.

Isabel Zakrzewski Brown, "Historiographic Metafiction in *In the Time of the Butterflies,*" *South Atlantic Review,* Spring, 1999, pp. 98-112.

Roberto González Echevarría, "Sisters in Death," *The New York Times Book Review,* December 18, 1994, p. 28.

Elizabeth Coonrod Martínez, "Recovering a Space for a History between Imperialism and Patriarchy: Julia Alvarez's *In the Time of the Butterflies,*" *Thamyris,* Autumn, 1998, pp. 263-79.

Barbara Mujica, a review in *Americas,* March-April, 1995, p. 60.

Kay Pritchett, a review in *World Literature Today,* Autumn, 1995, p. 789.

Ilan Stavans, "Las Mariposas," *Nation,* November 7, 1994, pp. 552-56.

For Further Study

Julia Alvarez, "Chasing the Butterflies," in her *Something to Declare,* Algonquin Books of Chapel Hill, 1998, pp. 197-209.

In this essay, Alvarez describes her attempts to find information on the Mirabal sisters and her progress toward writing a novel about them.

Aurora Arias, "The Mirabal Sisters," *Connexions,* Vol. 39, 1992, pp. 4-5.

This article gives a brief account of the Mirabal family, focusing most prominently on Minerva.

Janet Jones Hampton, a review in *Belles Lettres: A Review of Books by Women,* Spring, 1995, pp. 6-7.

Hampton praises the novel and identifies is overriding theme as "every person's accommodation of injustice."

Brad Hooper, a review in *Booklist,* July, 1994, p. 1892.

Hooper's one paragraph review is positive and says that the novel effectively balances domestic and political drama.

Rebecca S. Kelm, a review in *Library Journal,* August, 1994, p. 123.

In this very brief review, Kelm highly recommends the book and praises Alvarez for focusing on the characters' personal lives.

Susan Miller, "Family Spats, Urgent Prayers," *Newsweek,* October 17, 1994, p. 77.

Miller commends Alvarez for her character depictions and compares her to Denise Chavez.

Review in *Publishers Weekly,* July 11, 1994, p. 62.

This anonymous review asserts that while the novel begins slowly, it eventually reaches "a gripping intensity." It also claims that Marí Teresa's story begins as the least engaging then grows into the most moving of the four sisters' tales.

Heather Rosario-Sievert, "Conversation with Julia Alvarez," *Review: Latin American Literature and Arts,* Spring, 1997, pp. 31-37.

In this interview, Alvarez discusses her writing background, her challenges as a Latina writer, her sources of inspiration, and her view of the Dominican Republic.

Ava Roth, "Sisters in Revolution," *Ms. Magazine,* September-October, 1994, pp. 79-80.

Roth describes how Alvarez details the Mirabal sisters' many rebellions. She believes that Alvarez provides a story that is as much inspiration as tragedy.z

The Last of the Mohicans

James Fenimore Cooper

1826

When *The Last of the Mohicans* was published in 1826, James Fenimore Cooper was riding a growing wave of fame and critical acceptance. Following on the success of his last two books, *The Last of the Mohicans* was praised at the time for its non-stop adventure, realism, and intricate plotting. Using historical sources ranging from actual characters, such as Colonel Munro and Major Heyward, to John Heckewelder's *An Account of the History, Manners, and Customs, of the Indian Nations, Who Once Inhabited Pennsylvania and the Neighbouring States,* and adding to them his own knowledge of the history of the area in which the novel was set, Cooper laid the foundation of his novel with fact and real events.

The Last of the Mohicans introduces Cooper's most well-known character, Natty Bumppo. It is an abduction narrative, and follows the adventures of Bumppo and his two Mohican Indian companions—father and son, Chingachgook and Uncas. They set out to free Munro's two daughters, Cora and Alice, from repeated kidnapping by a group of Huron Indians, led by their chief, Magua.

While well received and praised in its day, *The Last of the Mohicans* has since gone through a cycle of neglect and insult, and back into critical favor. Later critics found it very unrealistic, and considered its characters stereotyped. Cooper was taken to task for his portrayal of the Indians in the book. Uncas and Chingachgook were thought to be too idealized, and Magua far too villainous. The women in *The Last of the Mohicans* and Cooper's

other books were considered to be mere damsels in distress, and completely undeveloped as characters. By the 1950s, Cooper had regained supporters, and was placed once again in the position as the father of the American novel. His lapses in style, sometimes poorly developed characterizations, and other literary offenses have been largely forgiven due to his role as pioneer of the American novel.

Author Biography

By the time *The Last of the Mohicans* was published in 1826, Cooper was the leading literary figure in America—a financial, critical, and public success. Cooper, born in New Jersey in 1789, had been a novelist for just six years, finding his calling at age thirty after a five-year stint in the navy.

His early years were largely marked by the influence of his father. He was sent to Yale, from which he was expelled after allegedly blowing up another student's door with gunpowder. His father then enlisted him in the navy. After his father's death in 1810, Cooper resigned his post and married. For the next ten years he settled into the life of a Federalist gentleman, serving in the state militia and as secretary to both the Bible and Agricultural Societies. It was not until 1820, his fortunes flagging and his inheritance running out, that Cooper began his literary career. While reading a popular English novel of the day to his wife, Cooper remarked that he could do better. His wife took him up on the challenge.

Published anonymously, his first work, *Precaution,* a drawing-room-style English comedy, was received poorly. He followed it with *The Spy,* a historical romance set in the Revolutionary War, which sold well and established the American novel as a genre. It was to set the tone of his literary output. For the next seventeen years Cooper worked only within the genre of historical fiction.

In 1823, Cooper published *The Pioneers,* the first of the five books of the Leatherstocking tales, which introduced Natty Bumppo, the archetypal frontiersman. The book sold 3,500 copies on its first day. Next came *The Pilot* (1823), a work of historical nautical fiction, another genre that Cooper was to develop, laying the groundwork for Herman Melville's *Moby Dick.*

The Last of the Mohicans was published in 1826. Still the most widely read of Cooper's works,

James Fenimore Cooper

it finds Natty Bumppo in the prime of his life. In the same year, Cooper and his family moved abroad, spending the next seven years in Europe. During that time, he published *The Prairie* (1827), a Leatherstocking tale about Bumppo at the end of his life, and *The Red Rover,* a work of nautical fiction. While abroad, Cooper became increasingly involved in politics, and began writing nonfiction as well as his novels, his first being *Notions of the Americans* (1828).

Upon returning home in 1833, he produced seven books (none fiction) in four years, four of them about European travel. In 1834, he and his family moved back to the family home in Cooperstown, New York, where he would spend the rest of his life. Cooper continued to produce both nonfiction and novels until his death in 1851, including the last two books of the five Leatherstocking tales, *The Path-Finder* (1840) and the *Deer-Slayer* (1841).

Plot Summary

The Journey Begins

Set in 1757 during the third year of the French and Indian War, the novel opens as Cora and Alice Munro are being escorted to Fort William Henry where they will meet up with the commander of the fort—their father, Colonel Munro. The two women are accompanied by Major Duncan Heyward, a gallant young officer who soon falls in love with Alice, and David Gamut, a ridiculous travelling psalm singer and music teacher. The small group is led by Magua, a mysterious and terrifying Huron, who suggests a "short-cut" that will lead them into an ambush he has prepared. The group are rescued from this fate when they run into Hawkeye, a skilled woodsman also known as Natty Bumppo (his birth name) and Le Longue Carabine (which means "Long Rifle"). With him are his two Mohican friends, Chingachgook and his son, Uncas. Major Heyward tells Hawkeye and his friends about his growing distrust of Magua, and the newcomers agree. Hawkeye and his companions then attempt to seize the "treacherous savage," but the guide escapes into the forest.

Hawkeye predicts that Magua will be back, and—fearing an attack by unfriendly Indians—leads the group to Glenn's Falls. The group takes shelter in a warren of caves behind the waterfall and spends an uneasy night. The sound of horses screaming early in the morning alerts them to danger, and they find themselves under attack by a band of Iroquois. Gamut is injured, and he, Cora, and Alice hide in the caves while the others plan a defense. Out in the forest Hawkeye, Heyward, Chingachgook, and Uncas engage in a bloody struggle with the Iroquois. They begin to run out of ammunition and prepare to die honorably. Cora begs them to go for help instead, so Hawkeye and the two Indians slip out down the river. Heyward stays to defend the girls, and they are all captured when a group of Hurons led by Magua enter the caves and uncover their hiding place.

Captured

Major Heyward attempts to trick Magua into releasing them, suggesting that Colonel Munro will pay good money to have his daughters returned. It seems to be working, until Magua asks to speak to Cora alone and reveals his true motives. Driven by a mix of lust for her and hatred of her father, Magua wants to take Cora as his wife. This will be his revenge upon Colonel Munro, who has whipped him in public for being drunk. He promises Cora that if she consents he will free her beloved sister, but she refuses to comply. Enraged, Magua stirs up the Hurons into a fury of vengeful feelings, and the whole group attacks the prisoners and lashes them to trees. As they stand waiting to be burnt alive,

Heyward breaks free and struggles with one of their captors. Just as he is about to be killed, Hawkeye and the two Mohicans arrive at the scene. The Hurons, terrified of Le Longue Carabine, flee, and Alice, Cora, Gamut, and Heyward are freed. Again, Magua manages to elude them.

The group continues toward Fort William Henry only to find it besieged by 10,000 French troops led by the Marquis de Montcalm. In thick fog, they make a mad dash for the fort and are rescued at the last minute. The girls are joyously reunited with their father, Colonel Munro. Heyward asks the Colonel for Alice's hand in marriage. In response, Munro reveals some of his past in order to ensure Heyward's commitment to his daughter.

The Fort William Henry Massacre

The British await reinforcements from General Webb. De Montcalm intercepts a letter from Webb, and reveals to Munro and Heyward that no reinforcements are coming—Munro is to surrender the fort. The Marquis allows them to retain their military honor, and promises that they can leave the fort "unmolested." However, he neglects to arrange a troop escort for the defeated British, and as they leave the fort they are suddenly attacked by a group of 2,000 Indians. The British are massacred in the bloody attack, during which Magua recaptures Alice and Cora and takes them into the forest. Gamut follows.

Munro, Heyward, Hawkeye, Chingachgook, and Uncas, who is now in love with Cora, follow their trail north through the forest. They find Gamut who tells them that Alice is still held captive by the Hurons and Cora is with the more peaceful Delaware. Uncas is captured, but using a cunning plan of swapped identities, Heyward and Hawkeye rescue both Uncas and Alice. They flee to safety with the Delaware, who free Cora when Uncas reveals that he is a chief and a Delaware descendant. The next day, Magua and his men come to the Delaware camp to demand the return of their captives. Tamenund, the Delaware chief, judges that Magua's desire to marry Cora makes his claim on her legitimate. Uncas vows that he and his friends will pursue them.

Tragedy

Followed by Hawkeye, the Mohicans, and a group of warriors, Magua and Cora set off for the Huron village. The two groups come into bloody conflict, and Uncas, Hawkeye, Heyward, and Gamut chase Magua and two warriors into a cave. Cora is as brave and strong-willed now as she has shown herself to be in earlier situations, and she refuses to move when her captors demand that she must. Attempting to force her, Magua threatens to kill her. His companions take him all too seriously, and another Huron advances to stab her to death. Desperately attempting to avert the tragedy, Uncas leaps into the fray from an overhanging ledge. He is too late to save Cora, and in the battle that follows he is killed by Magua, who is then shot by Hawkeye. The final chapter is one of sorrow for both the whites and the Indians. The bereft Munro returns to his territory with Heyward and Alice, who are now engaged. Hawkeye returns to the forest with Chingachgook. As the English leave, Hawkeye pledges eternal friendship with Chingachgook, the "Last of the Mohicans."

Characters

Big Serpent
See Chingachgook

Bounding Elk
See Uncas

Nathaniel Bumppo

Natty Bumppo is the hero of *The Last of the Mohicans*. Also known as Leatherstocking, the Deerslayer, and the Pathfinder in the other four books of the Leatherstocking tales, Natty Bumppo is known throughout this novel as Hawkeye. Hawkeye acts as guide and protector, rescuing half-sisters Cora and Alice Munro from Magua and his band of Huron Indians twice, and leading Major Heyward and Colonel Munro on several occasions. In the end, he shoots and kills Magua, who had killed Uncas, son of Chingachgook. This cements the bond of Hawkeye and Chingachgook's friendship, and at the end they wander off together.

Hawkeye is the archetype of the American frontier hero. Scout, tracker, marksman, he embodies the spirit of the West—the capable man. Hawkeye is in his thirties, at the peak of his physical powers. Civilized, mannered, and garrulous, he can at times be humorous and long-winded, or give over to boasts and superstition. He is a man of dual natures, however, and can be as stoic and silent as his Indian companion, Chingachgook. Although a somewhat idealized character, Hawkeye is not without his flaws. He is always quick to point out his "blood without a cross," making sure that none mistake him for an Indian or even someone of

mixed heritage. He is also prejudiced—quick to pass judgment on the Indians of the tribes other than the one with which he is allied.

Natty Bumppo
See Nathaniel Bumppo

Le Cerf Agile
See Uncas

Chingachgook

A middle-aged Mohican Indian and father of Uncas, Chingachgook is the longtime companion of Hawkeye. Last chief of his near vanished tribe, he is by the end of the book the title character, after Uncas perishes at the hand of Magua. Chingachgook speaks only when necessary, and then mostly to Uncas or Hawkeye, and almost always in his native tongue. He has not adapted at all to white ways, despite his long association with Hawkeye. In fact, he kills and scalps a French sentry after the party has been allowed to pass, merely because he is a representative of the enemy. Chingachgook is, however, always forthright and consistent in his dealings with the whites with whom Hawkeye throws in his lot.

David Gamut

David Gamut is a religious singing teacher, or psalmist, of New England. Odd-looking and rather clumsy, he serves no purpose in the world of Hawkeye, since as he cannot shoot, or make maps, or travel great distances. His singing does, however, make Hawkeye cry. It later serves to save his own life when in the midst of an Indian massacre he begins singing, and the marauding Hurons think him insane.

A thoroughly ineffective man, Gamut takes no part in battles, and when the Munro sisters are abducted by Magua, he merely follows them, doing nothing to hinder the kidnapping. He acts as a reinforcement of the idea that the world of civilization is powerless in the wilderness. Like the cowardice of General Webb, Gamut cannot or will not do anything to stop the actions of his own enemies. He also serves to symbolize the civilized side of spirituality in contrast to Hawkeye's more pagan view. The conflict between Gamut and Hawkeye represents the Lord, the church, and holy books versus the raw fact of nature.

Le Gros Serpent
See Chingachgook

Daniel Day-Lewis starred as Hawkeye (Natty Bumpo) in the 1992 film adaptation of Cooper's novel.

Hawkeye

See Nathaniel Bumppo

Duncan Heyward

An English soldier, Major Heyward is initially the protector of the Munro sisters. Courageous, handsome, and gallant, he appears at first to be the hero, but rapidly loses the role to Hawkeye, the only white man competent in the ways of the uncivilized world in which he finds himself. A symbol of the overly confident outsider, Heyward trusts Magua to lead him and the two women to safety, thus causing the abduction and subsequent problems. Although armed and nominally a soldier, Heyward finds himself largely useless. He falls in love with Alice, the younger, more civilized and, importantly, most pure-blooded and white of the two Munro sisters. Eventually, he breaks from his role of conventionality, disguising himself as Hawkeye to get into the Huron camp and attempt to effect the release of the captive women. In the end, he returns to the civilized world in which he has a place.

Major Heyward

See Duncan Heyward

Le Longue Carabine

See Nathaniel Bumppo

Magua

Magua, the antagonist of the novel, first appears as a simple guide, but is soon revealed to be the chief of the Huron Indians. A former soldier in Munro's army, his taste for whisky causes him to be punished by a brutal horsewhipping. This loss of dignity sets him on the path of vengeance, and he tries several times to kill the daughters of Colonel Munro.

Magua has been tainted by his service to the whites, and he has lost some of his Indian character. Besides the scars he bears on his back, like a common soldier or slave, his consumption of alcohol has caused him to walk spread-legged, unlike other Indians, and this makes him easy to track. This fact is pointed out by both the "true" Indians, Uncas and Chingachgook, and even Hawkeye.

Although initially making clear his desire to kill the Munro sisters, at several points he makes an offer of marriage to Cora. For whatever reason, Magua cannot go through with the murders of the two, and eventually tries to use his abduction of Alice to convince Cora to enter into a willing union with him. Later, he even looks to Tamenund to grant him express permission to take her away. This betrays his deeper feelings for the girl, as he could simply have spirited her away again. Rather than killing her, Magua wants Cora to desire him, and seeks either her approval, however coerced, or the approval of an authority figure.

Magua is the most complex of the Indian characters in the book. Not motivated by greed, military duty, or simply doing what is right, he seeks vengeance for himself. Allying himself first with the English, and later with the French, Magua has no true loyalty to either. Instead, he serves his own need for vengeance. He regains his place in the Huron tribe, which had previously shunned him, by leading them into battle to collect scalps and booty. This is incidental to him, and like all of his actions, is simply the means to an end. Magua appears to be the savage reflection of the noble Indian portrayed by Uncas. Similarly graceful, strong, and handsome, he is treacherous rather than noble, and driven by vengeance rather than love or fellowship.

The Marquis of Montcalm

Montcalm is the leader of the French army that besieges Fort Henry. He is a cunning, selfish man. He insists on speaking French with Major Heyward during their surrender negotiations, yet understands every word of their English conversation. Montcalm is devious; he grants generous terms of surrender to Munro and his men, only to allow the Huron Indians to sweep down and slaughter them once they are out of the safety of the fort. Montcalm illustrates the less noble side of white behavior, acting as an opposite to the actions of Colonel Munro.

Alice Munro

Alice is the archetypal damsel-in-distress of adventure fiction. The younger half-sister of Cora, she is by far the more conventionally feminine of the two. She faints under stress, speaks only when spoken to, and only follows the actions of others, especially her sister. Major Heyward, the civilized suitor to Uncas's primitive, falls in love with her. Despite her inability to act for herself or offer any attempt at self-preservation, she is the one who lives in the end, while her more forthright sister is killed.

Colonel Munro

Colonel Munro is the father of Cora and Alice Munro, and the commander of Fort Henry. A Scotsman, Munro is no stranger to serving his military posts in strange lands, having met and married Cora's mother in the West Indies. Betrayed by his

Media Adaptations

- *The Last of the Mohicans* was most recently adapted to film in 1992. This version, directed by Michael Mann, starred Daniel Day Lewis, Madeleine Stowe, and Russell Means. A Morgan Creek production, this film is available on home video and DVD.

- In 1977, the book was adapted for a made-for-TV movie, directed by James Conway, and featuring Steve Forrest, Michele Marsh, and Ned Romero.

- In 1957, there was a TV series based on the characters from the book, and bearing its title. It starred Lon Chaney Jr. as Chingachgook.

- Two film adaptations of the book were made in the 1930s. Ford Beebe's 1932 version, starring Harry Carey, Edwina Booth, and Hobart Bosworth; and George B. Seitz's 1936 version, starring Randolph Scott, the aptly named Alice Munro, and Robert Barrat.

- There were also two silent films based on the novel. In 1911, director Theodore Marston's production starred Frank Hall Crane, and, in 1920, Clarence Brown directed Harry Lorraine, Barbara Bedford, and Theodore Lurch in the film.

- Several foreign film versions of the book have been made. The BBC produced a TV version in 1971. Directed by David Maloney, it starred Kenneth Ives, Patricia Maynard, and John Albineri. There were two European attempts at adapting the book to film in 1965. From Spain, there was Mateo Cano's version, starring Jose Marco David, Luis Induni, and Sara Lezana. A joint Italian, German, and Spanish production of *The Last of the Mohicans* was directed by Harold Reinl, starring Oberst Munroe, Karin Dor, and Ricardo Rodriguez.

superior, General Webb, and bereft of his murdered daughter Cora, Colonel Munro finds himself defeated by the forces of both Old World and New in the end.

Cora Munro

Cora is the older of the two daughters of Munro. Dark-haired and bolder than her sister, Cora is of mixed racial heritage. Her mother is descended from slaves of the West Indies, her father is Scottish. With her mixed blood, Cooper allows her a more forthright, less feminine nature and greater freedom of action. When her sister, Alice, is abducted by Magua after fainting, she goes along, pursued by the hapless and useless David Gamut, to see that she does not meet her fate alone. Later, Uncas falls in love with her. After he dies at the hand of Magua, Cora is herself killed.

Nimble Deer

See Uncas

Nimble Stag

See Uncas

Le Renard Subtil

See Magua

Tamenund

Tamenund, chief of the Delaware, grants Magua the right to have Cora Munro as a wife. Based on a real man, Tamenund is the only Indian introduced within the context of his own people. He speaks prophetically of the eventual downfall of his people and the other Indians at the hand of the white men in their inevitable push West.

Uncas

At the outset of the book, Uncas, the son of Chingachgook, is the title character, the last of the Mohicans. He falls in love with Cora, the older and far less "civilized" of the Munro girls. In attempting her rescue from Magua, chief of the Hurons, who intends to marry her, Uncas is killed, thus leaving his father as the last of the Mohicans. At his death, the tribe dies with him; he is the only son of the last chief.

Uncas is an idealized portrait of the Indian: strong, graceful, beautiful. Although initially he seems to be merely along with the party because of his father, his actions eventually become his own, rather than simply following the lead of both his father and Hawkeye. Uncas is also set up as the foil for two of the other characters in the book. He provides the wild, untamed suitor to the Munro sisters in contrast to Major Heyward's civilized being. He is also the noble, handsome, and perfect Indian to Magua's treacherous, scarred, and evil savage.

General Webb

General Webb is the cowardly commanding officer of Colonel Munro, and makes the decision of surrender that sends the inhabitants of Fort George to their deaths. He is characterized by his absence. He does not appear in the text, but rather is spoken of and makes decisions outside of the narrative. Unsure of how to use his command, or what the dangers and strengths of it are, he prefers instead to not act. His inaction causes the fatal events of the last part of the book. He gives up Fort Henry to the French without a skirmish, causing the deaths of the people who had lived within it. This in turn results in the recapture of the Munro sisters, and ultimately in the deaths of both Cora Munro and Uncas.

Themes

Heredity

A recurring theme of *The Last of the Mohicans* is that of personal lineage and its inescapable effects. The idea of lineage is illustrated in several ways, most obviously in the hereditary title of chief that is passed from father to son. This is most direct in the case of Chingachgook, a chief and a Mohican, who passes that lineage to Uncas, the titular last Mohican who will become the last chief, or sagamore, upon his father's death. "When Uncas follows in my footsteps, there will no longer be any of the blood of the sagamores, for my boy is the last of the Mohicans." It is also clear in Hawkeye's repeated insistence that he is "a man without a cross." He obsessively points out that his "white" blood makes him purebred and civilized, despite his time among the Indians. Magua, too, is inheritor of the title of chief from his own people. Cora's forthright and passionate nature is due to her "uncivilized" lineage, as her mother was descended from native peoples of the West Indies. Her sister, of white stock, is retiring and calm.

Cutural Destruction

Though *The Last of the Mohicans* is clearly an abduction narrative or historical novel, it can also be read as a long essay about the destruction of cultures. Most obviously, the death of the Mohican tribe, embodied by the murder of Uncas, last son of the last chief, acts as a microcosm of the programmatic destruction of Native American culture. It is also shown through the degradation of Magua's character. He too is a chief, and his heritage has been tainted not by murder but by his interaction with whites—both English and French—and the evils of their culture, especially whisky. It is this sin, drinking the "firewater" of the white man, that leads to his savagery, treachery, and ultimate death. Subtler still is the symbolism of Cora's mother, a woman of West Indian slave origin. In her story, and in the genetic legacy she passes to her daughter, the novel recalls the earlier destruction of native culture in the first conquests of the whites. At the same time, the destruction of culture is effected through "miscegenation"—both metaphorically and literally. Just as West Indian culture has been destroyed, so intermarriage has destroyed the individuality of Cora's racial heritage.

The metaphoric role of interracial relationships is reinforced in Uncas's story. His love for a woman of white extraction leads to his death, just as his involvement with white politics leads to his moral decay. In much the same way, each character in *The Last of the Mohicans* experiences the dangers of mixing and losing one's place in one's culture. The Hurons have destroyed themselves by allying with the French, and becoming actively involved in the white man's destruction of both their way of life and their culture. Even Chingachgook has partnered himself with a white, both because there are no others of his tribe and because no other tribes are trustworthy. The "purity" of Indian Nation loyalties are no longer clear because they have begun to choose sides and align themselves with one white nation or the other, precipitating their own destruction. Chingachgook's fate is sealed as soon as he chooses Hawkeye as a companion. Though Hawkeye is a solitary white man, not "white culture," and although he appears more or less uninterested in the conflicts and conquests of the invaders, Chingachgook has nonetheless left his own world and culture. In the end, Tamenund is the only chief who still remains with his own tribe, and he foresees the death of Native American ways of life. As he says, "The pale faces are masters of the earth, and the time of the redmen has not come again. My day has been too long.... I have lived to see the last warrior of the wise race of the Mohicans."

Opposing Forces

Cooper makes wide and varied uses of opposites as a major theme. These range from the obvious—French versus English armies, and Indians against whites—to subtler, character-based oppositions. Of the characters, Hawkeye is a man of the woods, a native in his own environment, and he is revealed through his juxtaposition with a variety of

Topics for Further Study

- One of Hawkeye's most insistent assertions is that he is "a man without a cross." Why is being "pure-blooded" so important to him? Research the history of racial anxiety in early America: why was "miscegenation" considered such a threat?

- Uncas and Major Heyward are both solitary men who fall in love with the Munro daughters. What do they have in common? How are they different? Consider the characters of both men as they are revealed by the different sisters with whom they fall in love.

- Consider the character of the itinerant singing master, David Gamut. What archetype of early American culture does he symbolize? Look at his character in light of Washington Irving's hero, Ichabod Crane. How is Cooper's Gamut a reworking of Crane? What does this reworking achieve?

- *The Last of the Mohicans* is often seen as a tribute to the doomed cultures of Native Americans. Research the history of Indian clearances in the eighteenth century. How historically accurate is Cooper's depiction?

- Cooper is considered the first American author, and *The Last of the Mohicans* is often read as the first truly American novel. What is American about it?

"civilized" and "rude" men. Major Heyward is a soldier who cannot fight in the ways in which he needs in order to survive in Hawkeye's world. Uniformed and educated in the arts of war, Heyward can do nothing except follow Hawkeye's lead in all things once he is outside the confines of the fort. Removed from the world he knows, Heyward is useless. David Gamut, the psalmist, represents an ordered and civilized spirituality in contrast to Hawkeye's natural, pagan world. Chingachgook is the other side of Hawkeye's wilderness existence. Where Hawkeye is careful and reserved, his Mohican companion is rash, killing nominal enemies who offer no threat, and wishing to rush into conflict without consideration. Hawkeye is always quick to point out that though he has spent thirty years in the woods and living among the Indians, he has no Indian blood in his veins. For Chingachgook, it is just the opposite. He is to be perceived for what he is, an Indian.

Uncas, too, is used as a foil for multiple characters. Most obviously, he stands in contrast with Magua. Where Uncas is handsome, strong, and unmarked, Magua is savage-looking, devious, and bears the scars and marks of battles and his own foolishness. Uncas lives in the wilderness, with his father and Hawkeye. Magua has been cast out from his people, and serves first the English and then the French army, and later returns to his tribe. Though both are to be chiefs of their respective nations, Uncas does not have a nation to rule, and Magua's has cast him out. In the simplest terms, Cooper has set Uncas up as the ideal, noble Indian, and made Magua the crafty, vicious savage. Uncas and Major Heyward are used as opposites, both filling roles as potential suitors for the Munro sisters. Uncas is silent, classically beautiful, as the girls remark, and makes his love for Cora known through his actions, including his eventual death. He also acts as a contrast with Major Heyward, who loves Alice. Heyward, handsome as well but not classically so, is a talkative man of words and little action, who neither fights for nor gives his life for Alice. He becomes a part of her rescue by following the party, following the instructions of Hawkeye, and by simply being in the right place at the right time.

Style

Point of View

The Last of the Mohicans is told from a third person limited point of view. The narration of the story explains the events and actions of the novel, but does not give insight into the characters' thoughts or motivations. The only way to gain this information is by interpreting what the *dramatis personae* do and say. This perspective is further limited by the centrality of Hawkeye to the narrative. With very few exceptions, Cooper limits the scope of the narration to events that directly involve Hawkeye.

At the beginning of the story, the narration and point of view follow first David Gamut, then the Munro sisters and Major Heyward. Cooper shifts the story to introduce Hawkeye, Chingachgook, and Uncas, only to lead them to the party consisting of Heyward, the Munro sisters, Gamut, and Magua. From that point, there is a minimum of interruptions of the point of view directly involving Hawkeye.

The point of view shifts to the Munro sisters and Heyward when they are captured by the Huron Indians, and follows them until they are to be killed by their captors. Once Hawkeye and the Mohicans effect their rescue, the narrative once again follows them, until the capitulation of Fort Henry to the French. At that point, during the ensuing battle between the Hurons and the English, Cooper once again focuses on the Munro sisters and Gamut as they are led away by Magua. The story then moves to Hawkeye, Colonel Munro, and Heyward as they follow the sisters and their abductor. There are only a few shifts of scene to keep the reader informed as to their fate, while Cooper mostly gives the story over to the events and actions of Hawkeye and his party.

The Historical Romance

Set in the third year of the French and Indian War, *The Last of the Mohicans* is a historical novel, but does not attempt to provide a straight telling of any recorded events of the time. Cooper, like one of the other popular authors of his day, Sir Walter Scott, lends more importance to the narrative than to the historical context in which it is set. The book is not entirely fictional, however. He makes reference to the massacre of Fort William Henry, and some of the characters of the novel are based at least in part on actual figures: Colonel Munro, of the English army, and the Marquis de Montcalm, of the French. The names of the Indian tribes, the Delaware, Huron, and Mohawk, are of course factual, and "Mohican" is a corruption of "Mohegan."

There are some deviations from the facts. Despite the title and events of the book, there were members of the Mohican tribe still extant in the area when Cooper wrote his novel. In fact, the Mohicans, or Mohegans, as they are now more commonly known, were not wiped out by the French and Indian War. Members of the tribe still exist today, and are still living in the upper New York State area. The novel is set within the area in which Cooper himself lived. By the time it was written, the rural areas of New York State were no longer the wild forests of Cooper's novel, and the frontier had long ago moved West. Basing his story in the area around him, Cooper was able to draw on the memories and histories local to himself.

The historical romance was one of the two largest selling and most popular genres of fiction of the day. After taking the English drawing-room comedy for the model of his first novel, Cooper turned to the other form, where he found success. Duplicating the work of Scott down to estimated word length, he adapted an already accepted form of writing to the American narrative, and set down for posterity the tales and legendary characters of his own nation. This allowed him use of archaic language, a major component of the historical romance, as well as a certain suspension of disbelief. Only in the world of historical romance could two maidens be abducted multiple times, affording the author many chances to describe the heroism of Hawkeye and his companions, and to describe, over and over again, the dangers and savagery of those they faced.

Historical Context

The 1760s: The French and Indian War

The French and Indian War, which is the setting of *The Last of the Mohicans,* lasted seven years. Originally, the conflict was between England and France, with various tribes supporting both sides. The failure of the English to use their allies in an effective manner, and their poor treatment of those who did assist them, led most to leave, either not taking part or going over to the side of the French. While the Cherokee originally sided with the English, they soon joined the Delaware, Miami, Potawatomi, Chippewa, Micmac, Abenaki, Ottawa, Shawnee, and Wyandots on the side of the French. The forces of France had much more in the way of Indian support from the outset, as the French were much less numerous than the English, and were perceived as less of a threat to themselves and their territories.

The Indians viewed the French in this way because the French had, for the most part, inserted themselves into existing standards of intertribal diplomacy. The English were rude by comparison. The French were also much more content to let their allies act as autonomous forces, arming them and letting them go and choose their own targets and battles. The English merely tried to conscript them into their armies. Many, like Magua in *The Last of the Mohicans,* did not adapt well, either to the strange and strict ways of their military leaders, or to the problems inherent in liquor.

The Last of the Mohicans, *set in 1757, uses the French and Indian War as a backdrop. A few Native American tribes, most notably the Iroquois, chose to fight on the side of the British during the fierce battles between England and France for dominance in North America.*

At the outset of the war, the importance of the Native Americans as allies was minimal. That changed in 1759, when the Iroquois Confederacy joined the forces of England in the attack on Fort Niagara, an important French base. Their numbers swelled by the Iroquois, the English army eventually waited out the French, who had no means of getting supplies, reinforcements, or food. The Iroquois were widely believed to have been the decisive factor, and the battle was an important one in the fight to drive the French away.

By allying themselves with the English and driving the French away, the Iroquois Nation hoped to gain more in the way of considerations for their autonomy and lands. Also, by forming the Iroquois Nation of many differing tribes, they were attempting to marshal a force great enough to eventually drive all foreigners from their lands. Neither goal was achieved, since the English gave them nothing in the way of treaties or equality and the Iroquois Nation itself fell to infighting and separation of its constituent tribes.

Compare & Contrast

- **1760s:** During the French and Indian War, the Indian presence in land that colonists desire is a secondary concern of the British. They are more interested in defeating France.

  1820s: Public outcry for the removal of Indians from the path of westward expansion reaches critical mass. The solution is a series of broken treaties, military actions, and forced migrations that aim to remove the Indians to the West.

  Today: Legal challenges to the Bureau of Indian Affairs reach record numbers. There is more public sympathy for the plight of the Native Americans than ever before. Amnesty International joins the fight to free Leonard Peltier, an Oglala Sioux many believe to be wrongly convicted of two murders. Native rights movements demand that old treaties be honored.

- **1760s:** Both America and Canada are ruled by European powers and are neither autonomous entities, nor heavily colonized past their eastern edges. The major cities lie along the East Coast, and Native Americans still hold most of the rest of the country, living in their traditional cultures and groups. The Indians are regarded as a nuisance and a menace.

  1820s: Now a sovereign nation, the United States begins its westward expansion. Pioneers have pushed as far west as Minnesota. Native cultures in the Mississippi Valley are being decimated, and public opinion, exacerbated by newspaper accounts of the day, perceives the Indian as a constant danger. Having no legal protections, their treaties are ignored and the Indians are forced west and slaughtered in vast numbers at any sign of resistance.

  Today: Native Americans are a legally protected minority, falling under the set of laws known as Affirmative Action. Confined mostly to westward reservations, Native Americans have the highest rate of suicide, unemployment, and drug and alcohol addiction of any ethnic group in the United States. On a more positive note, financial gains are being made by the use of casinos on sovereign native lands, and Canada has granted a new and sovereign province to its natives.

The 1820s: National Indian Policy and the Birth of American Literature

The 1820s were an age of great transition for the United States. Just eight years before, the United States had defeated the British in the War of 1812. At the beginning of the decade, the American South became the world's largest producer of cotton. This in turn spurred the growth of the industrial economy in the northern states, as more and larger textile mills were built to use the raw material. In 1821, the United States wrested Florida from the Spanish and defeated the Native tribes of the state at the same time.

The success of the U.S. military in its territorial conquests and war victories was matched by the high rate of economic growth in the country as a whole. However, America had no reputation whatsoever for its artistic or cultural output among the older, more established nations of Europe. The folk-ways and people of America were unique, a greater mix than any before in the world. But there was nothing that was looked on as a lasting, permanent monument to the nation for the rest of the world to take part in—until *The Last of the Mohicans.*

Cooper produced *The Last of the Mohicans* as an apparent tribute to the vanishing cultures of the Native Americans. At the time of the publication of Cooper's book in 1826, the U.S. government had been pushing the Indians further West with greater speed and force than at any time before. In 1824, the Indian problem had come to a head in President James Monroe's State of the Union address. He declared that the only solution to the "Indian problem" was their removal to lands further west, far from the white settlers.

Immediately after the publication of the address in national newspapers, Cooper began work on *The Last of the Mohicans.* This work, conceived both in tribute to and as apology to the American Indian, was the first American fiction to be accepted in Europe as a significant and serious novel. While the policy of the U.S. government and the actions of its army worked to move the Indians west, destroying their way of life and cultural identities, the readers of the world came to know them "as they were." Cooper produced a novel that set the public's perception of the American Indian for years to come, but the irony was that he wrote it even as their way of life was being destroyed forever. The greater irony is that rather than approach the culture and problems of the Indians of his day, Cooper chose instead to concentrate on a past that was already gone.

Critical Overview

Initial Responses

The critical response to Cooper's *The Last of the Mohicans* was overwhelmingly positive. An American work of fiction was at last praised on both sides of the Atlantic for its realism, adventure, and characters. The editor of *Escritor* called Cooper "a genuine talent who has successfully bound realism in the guise of romance." The *Literary Gazette* praised his "ability to maintain interest and paint vivid characters and scenery," while *Literary World* referred to his "real life scenery created with faithfully presented narrative." *New York Review and Atheneum Magazine* described Cooper as "an imaginative writer," exhibiting "extraordinary power." The *Liverpool Repository* stated that Cooper was superior to Sir Walter Scott as an imparter of information.

Cooper's characters excited reviewers, but there was no consensus as to which were the best. His portraits of Indian life were praised by the *Literary Chronicle and Weekly Review* and *Monthly Review*. *Panaromic Miscellany* went so far as to call it "the most vivid and truthful portrait of Indians that has yet been written." *New York Review and Atheneum Magazine* claimed that Cora and Alice Munro were "delightful creations." Some critics and reviewers tempered their praise with criticism. *The Monthly Review* stated that while "Cooper has woven a tale of incredible suspense," it "need not have culminated in the tragedy that it did." The *United States Literary Gazette* said, "while *The Last of the Mohicans* is superior of those of a similar type that have preceded it" the book is "capable of improvement." The writer went

on to criticize the plot as "simple" with "little variety." *The New York Review and Atheneum Magazine* said that "if the author fails at all, it is in his ability to keep his characters' motive consistent with their actions."

Some condemned the novel entirely. W. H. Gardiner, writing in *The North American Review*, said that "Cooper goes out of way to put his characters into impossible situations that do nothing for the plot except clutter it with far too much action." One reviewer, in *United States Review and Literary Gazette*, attacked the author's research. Instead of faulting Cooper's acknowledged sources, however, he blamed Cooper for using the "absurdities and improbabilities" of Heckewelder's *An Account of the History, Manners, and Customs, of the Indian Nations, Who Once Inhabited Pennsylvania and the Neighbouring States.* John Neal, writing for the *London Magazine,* referred to *The Last of the Mohicans* as "the Last American Novel," condemning it as "the worst of Cooper's novels—tedious, improbable, unimaginative and redundant." In fact, Cooper's novel was so well known that two of his contemporaries published parodies of him: William Makepeace Thackeray's "The Stars and Stripes" in *Punch* (October 9, 1847), and Bret Hart's *Muck-a-Muck: A Modern Indian Novel after Cooper.*

A Reputation in Decline

Cooper's literary reputation seemed untouchable, but had declined even before his death in 1851. Thomas Lounsbury savaged both the man and his work, and Cooper's critical demise was assured and hastened by Mark Twain's "Fenimore Cooper's Literary Offenses," published in the July 1895 *American Review.* By the turn of the century, *The Last of the Mohicans* had become nothing more than a boy's adventure story. The criticism continued in the twentieth century. James Holden chronicled a list of Cooper's historical inaccuracies in his 1917 book, *'The Last of the Mohicans': Cooper's Historical Inventions, and His Cave.* John A. Inglis, of the *Society of Antiquaries of Scotland,* took Cooper to task for his use of Colonel Munro, noting that with the exception of his nationality, Cooper got nothing about the historical figure correct, even misspelling his name as "Munro" instead of the correct "Monro."

Detractors were going to extraordinary lengths to attack Cooper, and he had few defenders—most notably William Brownell, Brander Matthews, and William Phelps. However, their work was far more biographical in nature than scholarly, and did little to repair the damage of their colleagues. There were also a few tongue-in-cheek critiques of the novel, most notably John V. A. Weaver's "Fenimore Cooper—Comic," published in *Bookman.* Weaver argued that "Cooper could not have written such an incredibly bad book and been serious about it." He suggested that Cooper was in fact trying to create the "great comic novel of the nineteenth century."

A New Appreciation

After World War I, there was a sudden rebirth in the popularity and critical estimation of Cooper's work. In *Fenimore Cooper: Critic of His Times,* Robert E. Spiller sought to prove that Cooper was a profound social critic and serious author, refuting the perception of Cooper as an author of adventure stories. Suddenly, a vast cross section of authors and critics were reexamining *The Last of the Mohicans.* No longer taken at face value, it was reinterpreted in a variety of ways and used to illustrate the social ideals inherent in the work. In *Studies in American Fiction,* Dennis W. Allen pointed out the semiotic differences in the viewpoints of the white and Indian characters. Frank Bergmann explored the racial tolerance of the book, but also touched on Cooper's apparent reluctance to make solid statements about race. In *New Left Review,* George Dekker claimed that "miscegenation … provided the vehicle by which Cooper was able to investigate the more general problem of race relations." Terence Martin suggested in *The Frontier in History and Literature: Essays and Interpretations* that Cooper had trouble fitting a civilized man into the wilderness, or a wild man into civilization, and turned to the racial themes to inquire into the nature of the frontier.

There were also those who sought to defend Cooper's facts, style, and characters. Explaining away Cooper's tendency to play fast and loose with facts, Daniel J. Sundahl said in *Rackham Journal of the Arts and Humanities* that the book "is flawed in historical detail, for Cooper sacrificed fact for literary effect." He went on to suggest that the development of Hawkeye as a well-rounded character actually harms the book. "To assume that Cooper indulged in prolonged study is fallacious," stated *American Literature* contributor Thomas Philbrick, in an attempt to diffuse the belief that Cooper mixed up facts and chronology. Philbrick claimed that while the author did use reference works for his writing, he was by no means devoted to them.

T. A. Birrell's 1980 preface to Cooper's *Last of the Mohicans* claimed that the author had created a new literary form: "dramatic poetry as fiction." James Fenimore Cooper has once again been raised to his place as first man of American letters. His lapses in style, broad and underdeveloped characters, and convoluted, unrealistic plots are forgiven in the new view of Cooper as the father of the American novel.

Criticism

Tabitha McIntosh-Byrd

McIntosh-Byrd is a doctoral candidate and English literature instructor at the University of Pennsylvania. In the following essay, she critiques the role of mediation in the construction of romance, race, and national identity in The Last of the Mohicans.

The Last of the Mohicans is centered on Hawkeye, the figure of the pioneer and pathfinder who provides the link through which wilderness and civilization can be mediated. Throughout Cooper's novel, both Hawkeye and the reader are presented with a series of oppositions based on culture, race, and geography that create seemingly irreconcilable tensions and paradoxes. Indeed, the text itself is driven by an overarching narrative and generic paradox—the uneasy reconciliation of fact with fiction, history with romance.

Cooper's blend of fact and fiction has been extensively analyzed. Set in the third year of the French and Indian War, *The Last of the Mohicans* elides the boundaries that separate history and literature in order to create a quasi-mythic narrative of American history within which the New Man can be understood. Hawkeye, the archetypal American, straddles the fiction/fact divide, linking the actual events and persons of the period to the demands of Cooper's genre. Colonel Munro, the Marquis de Montcalm, the Indian nations, and the Fort William Henry massacre all find their basis in fact, though all are significantly altered by their incarnations in a romance.

The traditional narrative model of the romance is a quest, and its traditional textual movement tracks the protagonist as she or he enters unknown territories and worlds that transcend normal existence. This model also serves as the basis of the historical romance, Cooper's chosen genre, which

What Do I Read Next?

- *Bury My Heart at Wounded Knee* is Dee Brown's 1971 history of Indian massacres in nineteenth-century America. Brown's book forced America to reassess the cowboys-and-Indians myths of the Old West and its historical treatment of native people.

- *The Prairie* is Cooper's 1827 novel about an old Natty Bumppo in the newly independent United States. Iowa is called "The Hawkeye State" in honor of Cooper's hero.

- *Persuasion* is Jane Austen's 1818 novel about a young woman's search for happiness. This is the novel that Cooper is alleged to have been reading when he announced that he could write a better book.

- *Waverley,* Sir Walter Scott's 1814 novel about the Jacobite Rebellion, was a publishing phenomenon, and sold in massive numbers both in Britain and the United States. In it, Scott established the historical novel as a popular literary genre.

- Nathaniel Hawthorne's 1850 novel, *The Scarlet Letter,* is a historical novel that reassesses myths about early American life. The story of Hester Prynne and her punishment questions the morality of Puritanism and investigates the interaction of colonial America with the wilderness and its inhabitants.

- *A Narrative of the Captivity and Restoration* is Mary White Rowlandson's 1682 account of being captured by a band of rebelling Indians. One of the earliest "abduction narratives," Rowlandson's story reveals the religious, cultural, and political tensions between the colonizers and the indigenous people.

- *Letters from an American Farmer* is J. Hector St. John de Crevecoeur's 1782 "novel" about American life before and during the Revolution. Structured as a series of fictional letters from a self-made farmer, Crevecoeur's book was immensely popular in Europe, where it was largely responsible for creating the standard perception of U.S. character—self-reliance, hard-work, honesty, and sympathy with nature.

---

is normally structured by the movement between hostile civilizations, worlds, or stages of cultural development. In so doing, the form allows narrative articulation of cultural self-analysis and awareness. By allowing the "Self" culture to come into conflict with its "Other," the central features of the former are thrown into relief. In the American versions of the genre, this definitional clash of cultures gains intense significance. By endlessly enacting and reenacting the distinctions between New American and Native American cultures, historical romances act as a primary tool of self-definition for a young country that finds itself in need of a stable self-identity. In *The Last of the Mohicans* this series of clashes takes place between multiple "Selves" and "Others," and serves several purposes. Hawkeye, as the hero of the romance quest, travels between the Old and New Worlds and is in permanent contrast with both. Moving uneasily be-

tween his affiliations with the "natural" Delaware and the "pure-blooded" Europeans, Hawkeye creates a version of American identity that challenges the old order while retaining many of its key myths of lineage and purity.

Cooper's novel is most easily understood through an analysis of these kinds of oppositions. The narrative gains its momentum from the juxtaposition of such opposed elements as French and English, Indian and white, and from more particularized juxtapositions of characters and types. The complexity of the novel's structure is suggested by the density of such contrasts, which not only provide comparisons between the Old and New Worlds, but also refract those worlds in upon themselves, removing the possibility of simplistic assessments. Uncas and Magua, both chiefs without a tribe, stand in contrast to each other and with the contrasted Europeans, provoking a more complex negotiation of cultures than is at first apparent. Where Uncas is handsome, strong, and unmarked, Magua is "a savage" in appearance, painted and scarred by custom, war, and punishment. The level of scarification serves a clear symbolic function. Just as Uncas is a "pure" Indian, untainted by corrupt contact with Europeans, so he is "untouched" in appearance, while Magua's increasing corruption is literally inscribed into his flesh. Uncas in turn mirrors Major Heyward, both of them in love with one of the Munro sisters, but only the former capable of adequately defending them. Moving outwards in the ripple of textual associations, the relationships of Webb/Munro, Munro/de Montcalm, and Heyward/Gamut provide interior commentary-through-comparison on the European worldview.

Following the generic conventions of the romance, Hawkeye's character is created through an assembled chiaroscuro of contrasts with all of these representatives of various cultures. A "woodsman" and "beaver expert," Hawkeye's dangerous wildness is made valorous and valid by what he is *not:* neither a "civilized" nor a "rude" man. Major Heyward, uniformed, chivalrous, and educated in all the arts of war, is literally and figuratively "lost" as soon as he leaves the fort. Where his environment is circumscribed and dangerously finite, Hawkeye's natural medium *is* the environment in its most general sense—the wilderness. David Gamut, the psalmist, epitomizes an ordered and civilized spirituality inflated to a ridiculously hyperbolic level. Physically jarring and unable to assimilate into any of the situations in which the characters find themselves, Gamut becomes representative of the Old World religion against which American culture is defining itself. When he is juxtaposed with Hawkeye, the latter thus takes on a quasi-Jeffersonian naturalism by contrast, one in which harmony with nature and the self is elevated above formal protestation of faith as a signifier of moral virtue.

However, the near paganism of Hawkeye's "natural religion" is carefully distanced from the spirituality of the "Natural men"—the Mohicans. Chingachgook and Uncas, the new American counterparts of Hawkeye's dual cultural alignments, are separated from the hero both by the narrative and the character himself. While Hawkeye's "natural" instincts are in contrast to the formalized uselessness of both Heyward and Gamut, they are also configured as "rational" or "civilized," when juxtaposed with the behavior of his comrades. Where Hawkeye is careful, reserved, and feared as the dead-shot "Longue Carabine," Uncas is rash,

killing nominal enemies who offer no threat and rushing headlong into conflict. Significantly, it is neither a European nor a native, but only Hawkeye—the man who is of both and neither cultures at the same time—who is compassionate enough to waste his ammunition in putting a dangling enemy out of his misery. As a "man without a cross" who lives with natives but remains insistently white, Hawkeye is allowed to negotiate all possible worlds by remaining either genetically or geographically detached.

What happens if these series of opposed elements blend instead of finding or creating a removed mediation point, as Hawkeye does? Cooper's "romance" gains much of its thematic momentum from answering this question through the use of "romance"—the metaphoric role of sexual relationships between members of opposed cultures. Significantly, the protagonist is resolutely excluded from this literal "mediation" of cultures, providing a model of "untainted" communication instead. Thus while Hawkeye is, as he insists to a hyperbolic degree, a "man without a cross," many of the other characters are either symbolically or actually "crossbred," and the results are never shown to be positive. Cora's mother is a woman of West Indian slave origins, and though Colonel Munro takes great pride in his daughter's heritage, it is clear that he expects it to retard her progress through life. Cora's "bursting blood" recalls both the destruction of an earlier culture, as well as the cultural erasure signified by assimilation: just as West African culture has been destroyed, so intermarriage has destroyed the individuality of Cora's racial heritages. The result is not decay but vitality, the excessive life that is uneasily demarcated as both positive and negative within the text. Unlike her blonde and feeble sister, Cora is determined and heroic, but the only textual resolution available to her character is death or further "crossbreeding." Only "savages" fall in love with Cora.

The metaphor of interracial blending is reinforced in the story of Cora's lover. Uncas's love for a European woman leads to his death in the same way that his involvement with white affairs leads to his moral decay. On a broader symbolic level, this pattern can be applied to much of the novel's treatment of culture. Chingachgook identifies the "blending" of European and native cultures through the trade of "firewater" as the primary and devastating force of European colonialism. The Hurons are shown in the process of self-destruction through alliance with de Montcalm's forces, which threaten to destroy both their ways of life and their culture. By Magua's own analysis his character is destroyed by his interaction with whites—both English and French—and the evils of their culture, especially whisky. His sexual obsession with Cora, who symbolizes both colonizer and colonized, compounded with his drinking—Chingachgook's Original Sin of colonialism—leads to his punishment, revenge, and the cycle of treachery that ends in his death. Even Chingachgook, despite his integrity, embraces the dispersal of his culture when he accepts Hawkeye as his "brother." Though Hawkeye is a solitary white man, and a new kind of white man at that, Chingachgook has nonetheless been forced by genocide and cultural self-destruction to leave his own world when he accepts Hawkeye as family. In this new, American idea of family, only Hawkeye has the ability to re-transmit his culture to another generation, and their interracial relationship thus signifies death even as it appears to provide narrative hope. As Tamenund says, "I have lived to see the last warrior of the wise race of the Mohicans."

The core paradox of Cooper's historical romance lies in the uneasy ambiguity of its hero's mediation of these opposed cultures. Both Cooper and his protagonists work from the assumption that the modern stages of historical development are inherently better than the "savagery" of prior stages. At the same time, they also view the present as a dangerous challenge to the communal values and hierarchical relationships of the recent past. Both European and native cultures are shown to be violently disrupted throughout *The Last of the Mohicans,* with established systems of leadership and conduct broken down by alcohol, war, corruption and cultural contamination. Hawkeye, the only man to successfully negotiate these disruptions, is also significantly removed from the social hierarchy that has reformed itself by the novel's closing pages. The "man without a cross" may be the new American archetype, but he is also its Other—a man who dwells in the borderlands that separate Europe and the natives, with no familial or emotional ties to the people who comprise the power elite of either side.

The end of Cooper's historical romance thus intimates both stability and disruption—an uneasy celebration of both the return of hierarchical order and the heroism of the man who remains outside of that hierarchy. It allows identification with a socially mobile outsider and simultaneously promises that real social mobility will be denied him. In exactly the same way, it validates the possibility of a superior native culture even while it is careful to

A map of North America depicting some of the white settlements, native villages, and forts involved in the French and Indian War, 1689-1763.

make that culture an irretrievably dying one. If, as many literary theorists have claimed, the historical romance genre acts as a stabilizing force for the demands of social hierarchy, then the main impulse of *The Last of the Mohicans* is not the articulation and celebration of "natural," or "wild," self-identity, but instead the exact opposite. Hawkeye is both hero and antihero of his own story in a culture that seeks to distance itself from the Old World, even as it tries to retain the social structure that makes that world possible. As a stalemate of conflicting Anglophobic and Anglophiliac impulses, it provides an extremely ambiguous fictional pathway to later American history.

Source: Tabitha McIntosh-Byrd, in an essay for *Novels for Students,* Gale, 2000.

James A. Levernier

In the following essay, Levernier examines the changing critical status of The Last of the Mohicans.

For more than a century after its publication in 1826, *The Last of the Mohicans* was by far the most widely read of any of the novels of James Fenimore Cooper. Nonetheless, while praised for its strong narrative interest, *The Last of the Mohicans* was generally disparaged as the least substantive of the Leatherstocking Tales, with *The Prairie, The Pioneers, The Pathfinder,* and *The Deerslayer* receiving far greater critical acclaim. According to its 19th-century critics, *The Last of the Mohicans* satisfied the popular demands of audiences that craved adventure, but it did so at the expense of both content and realism. Particularly objectionable was Cooper's depiction of Indians, whom reviewers found hopelessly romanticized and not at all historical. As one commentator explained, Cooper's Indians "have no living prototype in our forests. They may wear leggins and moccasins, and be wrapped in a blanket or a buffalo skin, but they are civilized men, not Indians." Even Francis Parkman, who found worth in Cooper's mythic dimensions, felt that the Indians of the Leatherstocking Tales were "either superficially or falsely drawn." As a result, *The Last of the Mohicans* was for the most part dismissed as "almost pure adventure with slight social import."

Ironically, only in the 20th century, when the novel began to decline in popularity, did critical distinctions between novels of realism and novels of romance pave the way for scholars to discern in *The Last of the Mohicans* depths that had gone unnoticed for decades. To begin with, scholars attacked the notion that the novel lacked historical veracity. Research into Cooper's sources indicated that although he wrote the book in approximately four months he had researched his materials quite carefully. Among the many historical and anthropological sources attributed to the novel are Alexander Henry's *Travels and Adventures* (1809), Jonathan Carver's *Travels Through the Interior Parts of North-America* (1778), David Humphrey's *Life of Israel Putnam* (1788), Alexander Mackenzie's *Voyages from Montreal* (1802), and *The History ... of Captains Lewis and Clark* (1814).

Additional research further determined that the Indian materials in the novel were derived from a careful reading of such works as John Heckewelder's *History, Manners, and Customs of the Indian Nations* (1818) and Cadwallader Colden's *History of the Five Indian Nations* (1727). Literary sources include *The Iliad, The Odyssey,* and *The Aeneid,* as well as *Paradise Lost* and the novels of Scott and Austen. Leatherstocking himself is thought to be based on John Filson's "Adventures of Col. Daniel Boone" (1784), and mistakes in historical accuracy, including the eloquent language of Cooper's Indians, are in general attributable to

Cooper's sources, who at the time when they wrote were considered the foremost experts on the subjects they addressed. Even Cooper's landscape portraits, once thought to be hopelessly romantic backdrops to his fiction, came to be seen as complex symbolic structures that provide insight into the metaphysical foundations for a pre-Conradian analysis of the relationship between the wilderness and civilization.

Cooper himself said, however, that in writing *The Last of the Mohicans* he created a novel "essentially Indian in character," and it is in exploring what one analyst described as "the question of the relations between men of different races in the New World" that critics have found in the book a theme of "national, even hemispheric significance." Within this context, Cooper's vision of historical progress is seen as profoundly pessimistic and astutely prophetic. Extended into the wilderness setting of the novel, the rivalries between the French and English for control of the North American continent continue to propagate racial and nationalistic prejudices that the events of the narrative violently display. At the same time, the brutality of the Indians undercuts the romantic myth that in the wilderness of the New World the civilizations of the past will undergo a pastoral revitalization. Of the three characters in the novel capable of offering the possibility for moral renewal through a blending of the virtues of the Old and New Worlds, Cora and Uncas die, and Leatherstocking, described as a "man without a cross"—in other words, someone without preconceived prejudices who is open to the possibility of a new kind of moral order—remains childless and eventually vanishes into the wilderness. According to one critic, "In the bloodshed of William Henry the determining power of history is affirmed." People are seen as "incapable of change," and history becomes nothing more than "an endlessly repeating decimal" in which America's future will "necessarily recapitulate the European and the tribal past."

Source: James A. Levernier, "*The Last of the Mohicans:* Overview," in *Reference Guide to American Literature, 3rd ed.,* edited by Jim Kamp, St. James Press, 1994.

John Miller

In the following excerpt from a review of The Last of the Mohicans, *Miller praises Cooper's depiction of native American life and discusses the plot and characterizations of the novel, finding the characters Uncas, Chingachgook, and Bumppo (here called Hawk-eye) especially well presented.*

[In *The Last of the Mohicans* Cooper has] attempted to offer a picture of Indian character and life; and we may be justified, by a personal acquaintance with the aboriginal tribes of the North-American wilderness which falls to the lot of few Europeans, in pronouncing with confidence that it is a representation of admirable fidelity. That the author has availed himself of the narrative of John Hunter and of the notices of the missionary Heckewelder, is extremely probable; but we are convinced that the tale could never have been written, with the peculiar graphic truth which marks every page of his delineations of Indian manners, unless he had himself mingled with the red children of his country's forests. Elaborate relations of their general usages, and even imitations of their nervous and figurative language, might be copied from books: but here we have a thousand little peculiarities of habit, gesture, tone, and attitude, thrown as it were incidentally and unconsciously into the narrative, but which could not possibly have been noted except by familiar and watchful observance from the life. We are particular in remarking the easy and perpetual recurrence of these little characteristic touches, because they serve to determine the pretensions of the work to the highest praise which can be bestowed upon it. They certify that it is all that it claims to be, an authentic exhibition of the wildest and most fearfully romantic state of society, which the world has ever known.

The structure of the tale itself is sufficiently simple, but the narrative is frequently worked up to an intensity of horror and an agony of suspense which are really much more than interesting: the anxiety of the reader becomes engrossed, and his imagination excited, in many of the situations of the story, to a degree which is absolutely painful. Indeed it is a positive fault in the romance that the personages, for whom our sympathies are keenly awakened, encounter one unrelieved and perpetual crisis of terrific danger through three whole volumes of adventure. They are never for an instant secured from the appalling contingencies of a conflict with the Indian. Throughout the entire tale, the lair and ambush are around them and the war-whoop in their ears: the death-shot from the unerring rifle is the least of their dangers; and the tomahawk, the scalping knife, and the demoniac refinements of savage torture, appear as their hourly and impending lot. The first volume is filled with the thrilling details of an encounter with the Indians, which should seem to terminate, after a quick succession of imminent perils and as many sudden escapes, in the temporary safety of the res-

cued victims. These adventures are conceived with vivid invention, and the circumstances are told with amazing animation and force of description. Through this first volume we are led by the author in breathless rapid interest: our attention is never off the stretch; and yet we seek no relief, until we have seen the objects of our sympathy beyond their first series of dangers. But then it is that we encounter the prominent defect of the work. The second volume resembles the first, and the third is a repetition of the second. Without respite, without variety of interest, and almost without any change of scene, machinery, or action, we are led in an uniformity of horror through two volumes more of Indian ambushes, pursuits, battles, massacres, and scalpings. [The characters of Chingachgook, Uncas, and the white hunter] prove conspicuous actors … and are, beyond all comparison, the most remarkable and best drawn characters in the book. One of them, the white hunter, who is introduced to us only by his *noms de guerre* of Hawk-eye and La Longue Carabine, is a specimen (of the better sort, indeed,) of a class of men still to be found in the American forests. His qualities are adroitly elicited by a hundred little characteristic niceties of opinion and action, which, though perhaps they might not be quite understood by our home-bred readers, are all struck off from the original with most admirable tact. In the strange mixture of the habits of civilised and Indian life, the corresponding confusion of moral opinions and principles, an enthusiastic respect for the finer qualities of the red people, coupled always with the superior pride of pure European blood, and the perpetual boast of being 'a man without a cross;' in all these points, he who is familiar with the population of the American forests will at once recognise Hawk-eye for the true exemplar of a whole class. He is the genuine representative of the white hunter, who has naturalised himself among the red people, preserving some of the lingering traits and humaner features of civilised man, but acquiring the stern insensibility to danger and suffering, the patient endurance of privation, the suppleness and activity of limb, and even in part the wonderful sagacity of the senses, by which the native warrior supports and guards his life, and tracks out his path in the darkness, and solitude, and bewildering mazes of his gigantic forests.

The two Indian companions of Hawk-eye are father and son, 'the Last of the Mohicans,' a once celebrated tribe of the Delaware nations. Mr. Cooper will not be accused, by those at least who know any thing of the Indian character, of having, with any undue and foolish partiality for the virtues of savage life, depicted it too favourably for truth. But as in Magua he has displayed all the worst and most revolting features of the Indian mind, so may his portraits of the two Mohicans, Chingachgook and Uncas, be received as accurately representing in their persons all that is dignified and estimable, and the amount of this is far from small, in the simple children of the lake and forest.

Source: John Miller, in a review of *The Last of the Mohicans,* in *The Monthly Review,* London, Vol. II, No. VII, June, 1826, pp. 122-31.

Sources

Dennis W. Allen, "By All the Truth of Signs: James Fenimore Cooper's 'The Last of the Mohicans,'" *Studies in American Fiction,* Autumn, 1981, pp. 159-79.

T. A. Birrell, Preface to James Fenimore Cooper's *Last of the Mohicans,* 1980.

George Dekker, "Lillies That Fester: 'The Last of the Mohicans' and 'The Woman Who Rode Away,'" *New Left Review,* November-December, 1964, pp. 75-84.

Escritor, February, 1826, pp. 21-22.

W. H. Gardiner, "Cooper's Novels," *North American Review,* July, 1826, pp. 150-201.

John A. Inglis, "Colonel George Monro and the Defence of Fort William Henry, 1757," *Society of Antiquaries of Scotland Proceedings,* January, 1970, pp.72-73.

Literary Chronicle and Weekly Review, July 29, 1826, pp. 469-73.

Literary Gazette, April 1, 1826, pp. 198-200.

Literary World, October 19, 1826, p. 312.

Liverpool Repository, July-August, 1826, pp. 384, 448.

Terence Martin, "Leatherstocking and the Frontier: Cooper's 'The Last of the Mohicans,'" *The Frontier in History and Literature: Essays and Interpretations,* Verlag Moritz Diesterwag, 1962, pp. 49-64.

Monthly Review, June, 1826, pp. 122-31.

John Neal, "The Last American Novel," *London Magazine,* May, 1826, pp. 27-31.

New York Review and Atheneum Magazine, March, 1826, pp. 285-92.

"North American Indians," *United States Review and Literary Gazette,* April, 1827, pp. 40-53.

Panaromic Miscellany, April 30, 1826, pp. 533-34.

Thomas Philbrick, "The Sources of Cooper's Knowledge of Fort William Henry," *American Literature,* May, 1964, pp. 209-14.

Robert E. Spiller, *Fenimore Cooper: Critic of his Times,* Minton Balch, 1955.

Daniel J. Sundahl, "Details and Defects: Historical Peculiarities in 'The Last of the Mohicans,'" *Rackham Journal of the Arts and Humanities,* 1986, pp. 33-46.

Mark Twain, "Fenimore Cooper's Literary Offenses," *North American Review,* July, 1895, pp. 1-12.

United States Review Literary Gazette, March 15, 1826, pp. 87-94.

John V. A. Weaver, "Fenimore Cooper—Comic," *Bookman,* March, 1924, pp. 13-15.

For Further Study

John Gottlieb Ernestus Heckewelder, *An Account of the History, Manners, and Customs, of the Indian Nations, Who Once Inhabited Pennsylvania and the Neighbouring States: Communicated to the Historical and Literary Committee of the American Philosophical Society, Held at Philadelphia, for Promoting Useful Knowledge,* printed and published by Abraham Small, 1818.
> Heckewelder's book has been identified as Cooper's main source of information in drawing his Indian characters.

Donald A. Ringe, *James Fenimore Cooper,* Twayne, 1988.
> Biography and critical overview of Cooper's literary career.

Marilyn Gaddis Rose, "Time Discrepancy in 'The Last of the Mohicans,'" *American Notes and Queries,* January, 1970, pp. 72-3.
> Rose considers Cooper's skills as a historian, and suggests that while he kept his facts straight, he had a tendency to deviate from chronology.

Seymour I. Schwartz, *The French and Indian War, 1754–1763: The Imperial Struggle for North America,* Simon & Schuster, 1994.
> A history of the French and Indian War that forms the backdrop to *The Last of the Mohicans.*

William Thorp, "Cooper Beyond America," *North York History,* October, 1954, pp. 522-29.
> Illustrates the literary influence that Cooper had on European literature of the nineteenth century.

W. M. Verhoeven, editor, *James Fenimore Cooper: New Historical and Literary Contexts,* Rodopi, 1993.
> A collection of new essays that assess Cooper's novels from a historically materialist perspective.

Lolita

Vladimir Nabokov
1955

When Vladimir Nabokov's *Lolita* was first published in 1955 in Paris, it was soon banned for its controversial content. Yet as an underground readership grew, the novel gained international attention, and, as a result, the bans were lifted. Immediate responses to the work were understandably mixed. Many critics condemned it as pornographic trash, citing its "obscene" descriptions of a pedophile's sexual activities. Others applauded the work's originality and sparkling wit. The novel has now, however, gained almost universal approval as a brilliant *tour de force*. Readers find middle-aged narrator and protagonist Humbert Humbert to be both perpetrator and victim of his disastrous obsession with the young Lolita. In his record of his relationship with her, Humbert becomes a complex mixture of mad lecher who "breaks" the life of a young girl and wild romantic who suffers in his pursuit of his unattainable ideal. Donald E. Morton in his book *Vladimir Nabokov* argues that "what makes *Lolita* something more than either a case study of sexual perversion or pornographic titillation is the truly shocking fact that Humbert Humbert is a genius who, through the power of his artistry, actually persuades the reader that his memoir is a love story." Nabokov's technical brilliance and beautiful, evocative language help bring this tragic character to life.

Vladimir Nabokov

Author Biography

Vladimir Nabokov was born on April 23, 1899, in St. Petersburg, Russia. Twenty years later, during the Bolshevik Revolution, he and his aristocratic family fled to Berlin. After graduating with honors from Cambridge in 1922, Nabokov lived in Berlin and Paris where he wrote and taught English and tennis. In 1925, he married Vera Slonim, who became his lifelong helpmate and mother of his only child, Dmitri.

In 1940, Nabokov immigrated to the United States where he soon became a citizen and embarked on an illustrious teaching career at Stanford, Wellesley, Cornell, and Harvard. After he moved to America, he began writing in English, a change that he notes with despair in his Afterword to *Lolita:*

> My private tragedy, which cannot, and indeed should not, be anybody's concern, is that I had to abandon my natural idiom, my untrammeled, rich, and infinitely docile Russian tongue for a second-rate brand of English, devoid of any of those apparatuses—the baffling mirror, the black velvet backdrop, the implied associations and traditions—which the native illusionist, frac-tails flying, can magically use to transcend the heritage in his own way.

Critics, however, insist that Nabokov's American period was his most successful. During his years in the United States, he completed his highly acclaimed *Bend Sinister* (1947), *Lolita* (1955), *Pale Fire* (1962), *Lectures on Literature* (1980), and *Speak Memory* (1951), as well as other noteworthy works. Nabokov died on July 2, 1977, in Montreux, Switzerland. During his lifetime, he was awarded the Guggenheim fellowship for creative writing in 1943 and 1952, the National Institute of Arts and Letters grant in literature in 1951, a literary achievement prize from Brandeis University in 1964, the Medal of Merit from the American Academy of Arts and Letters in 1969, the National Medal for Literature in 1973, and a nomination for a National Book Critics Circle Award in 1980 for his *Lectures on Literature.*

Plot Summary

Lolita chronicles the life of its narrator and protagonist, Humbert Humbert, focusing on his disastrous love affair with a young girl. In this dark, comic novel, Nabokov paints a complex portrait of obsession that reveals Humbert to be both a middle-aged monster and a wild romantic who fails to attain his ideal.

Part I

In the Foreword, fictitious Freudian psychiatrist John Ray, Ph.D., who claims to be editing Humbert's manuscript titled "Lolita or The Confession of a White Widowed Male," notes that Humbert died in prison in November 1952 of heart disease a few days before the beginning of his trial. He also reveals that Mrs. Richard F. Schiller, who the reader will discover at the end of the book is Lolita, died in childbirth on Christmas Day, 1952. Ray, whom Nabokov later admitted he "impersonated," warns readers that they will be "entranced with the book while abhorring its author."

Humbert begins his memoir with "Lolita, light of my life, fire of my loins. My sin, my soul." He admits that Lolita had a precursor, and that "there might have been no Lolita at all had I not loved, one summer, a certain initial girl-child." During the summer of 1923, Humbert and Annabel, both thirteen, fell "madly, clumsily, shamelessly, agonizingly in love with each other," but were unable to find an opportunity to express it. When Humbert notes that Annabel died four months later of typhus, he wonders, "was it then ... that the rift in my life began; or was my excessive desire for that child only the first evidence of an inherent singularity?" He asserts his conviction, though, that "in a certain magic and fateful way Lolita began with Annabel." He defines Lolita as a nymphet, a category of young girls between the age of nine and fourteen who exhibit "fey grace, the elusive, shifty, soul-shattering insidious charm," and a certain "demonic" nature.

After Annabel's death, Humbert became obsessed with "nymphets," a condition that eventually prompted him to marry in order to keep his "degrading and dangerous desires" under control. After a few unhappy years, his wife Valeria left him for another man, and he departed for America, where he worked in his late uncle's perfume company. He was hospitalized several times for mental breakdowns before he moved to a small New England town where he could write.

Part II

Humbert rents a room from middle-aged widow Charlotte Haze, who has a twelve-year-old daughter named Dolores, or, as Humbert would come to call her, Lolita. He immediately begins a "pathetic" obsession with Lolita that prompts him after several weeks to marry Charlotte in order to be closer to her daughter. One day after reading his diary, which contains vivid descriptions of his true feelings for her and Lolita, a furious Charlotte confronts him and demands that he leave. Refusing to hear his excuses, she runs out of the house, but before she can mail some letters that will expose him, a car runs her over. "McFate," as Humbert calls it, has just given him the opportunity to have Lolita to himself.

After the funeral, Humbert picks Lolita up from camp and tells her that her mother is about to undergo a serious operation. That night, he takes her to the Enchanted Hunters Hotel, where he plans to drug her and then spare "her purity by operating only in the stealth of night, only upon a completely anesthetized little nude." The sleeping pill he gives her, however, does not have the effect he had hoped for, and so he cannot fulfill his desires. After a restless night, Lolita wakes up, looks at Humbert lying next to her, and promptly seduces him. Later, she tells him she had sexual experiences with a boy at camp. The fact of her previous sexual encounters helps ease his guilty feelings until he notices that "a queer dullness had replaced her usual cheerfulness." Later, when she wants to call her mother, he admits she is dead. That night she comes crying to his bed, for "she had nowhere else to go."

Part III

During the next year, as the two travel across America posing as a typical father and daughter on a cross-country trip, Humbert admits that he constantly has to bribe Lolita for sexual favors. He threatens to send her to a reformatory school if she tells anyone about their relationship. At the end of the year, they settle in Beardsley, a northeastern college town where he works on his book and she enrolls in a private girls' school. He keeps "a sharp eye on her" there, restricting her privileges. After an argument, Lolita announces her desire to leave the town and to travel again, and so the two begin another cross-country odyssey. This time Humbert suspects that someone, probably a detective, is following them. During their trip, Lolita comes down with the flu and has to be hospitalized, while Humbert fights his symptoms in a hotel room. When he recovers and calls the hospital to arrange for her discharge, an administrator informs him that her "uncle" had picked her up the day before. Enraged, he begins a desperate search for her and her "abductor" as he heads back east.

Humbert spends the next "three empty years" on the East Coast where he meets and has a brief relationship with a young, rather dim-witted, woman. After receiving a letter from Lolita, who is pregnant, married, and in need of money, he travels to her home where she fills in the missing parts of their story. She explains that she ran off with Clare Quilty, the director of her school play, because he was "the only man she had ever been crazy about." When Quilty pressured her to engage in group sex and in pornographic movies, she left, and eventually married Dick, her "sad-eyed" husband. Even though she now has "ruined looks" and is "hopelessly worn at seventeen," Humbert confesses, "I knew as clearly as I know I am to die, that I loved her more than anything I had ever seen or imagined on earth, or hoped for anywhere else." When she refuses to come back to him, Humbert gives her some money and leaves, acknowledging that he has broken her life. Eventually, bent on revenge, he tracks down Quilty, and after a prolonged struggle, kills him. His final request is that the manuscript he has written about himself and Lolita be published only after he and Lolita have died, so that "in the minds of later generations" the two can share "immortality."

Characters

Mona Dahl

Lolita's "elegant, cold, lascivious, experienced" girlfriend. Humbert decides she "had obvi-

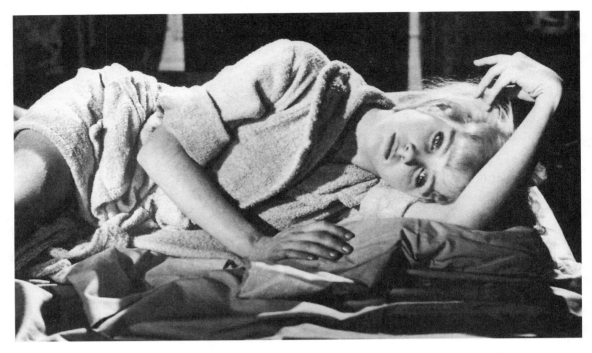

Sue Lyon played Lolita Haze in Stanley Kubrick's 1962 film. Although Nabokov created the screenplay, Kubrick rewrote much of the text for the final version of the movie.

ously long ceased to be a nymphet, if she ever had been one."

Jean Farlow

Jean and her husband John are Charlotte's friends. In an effort to prevent the pair from paying too much attention to his plans, Humbert suggests that Lolita is the product of an affair he had years ago with Charlotte. Humbert considers Jean "absolutely neurotic" and notes that she "apparently developed a strong liking for me." Jean dies of cancer two years later.

John Farlow

Farlow looks after Charlotte's estate after she dies.

Gaston Godin

Gaston, who teaches French at Beardsley College, finds Humbert and Lolita a house to rent. Humbert trusts him because he is "too self-centered and abstract to notice or suspect anything." While revealing a "colorless mind and dim memory … nonetheless, everybody considered him to be supremely lovable." Humbert suggests a sinister motive behind Gaston's enjoyment of the company of the small boys of the neighborhood: "There he was

devoid of any talent whatsoever, a mediocre teacher, a worthless scholar, a glum repulsive fat old invert, highly contemptuous of the American way of life, triumphantly ignorant of the English language— there he was in priggish New England, crooned over by the old and caressed by the young—oh, having a grand time and fooling everybody."

Charlotte Haze

Lolita's mother appears as both victimizer and victim. Humbert rents a room from her and eventually marries her so that he can be close to Lolita. Charlotte is a type of middle-aged woman "whose polished words may reflect a book club or bridge club, or any other deadly conventionality, but never her soul; women who are completely devoid of humor … utterly indifferent at heart to the dozen or so possible subjects of a parlor conversation, but very particular about the rules of such conversations, through the sunny cellophane of which not very appetizing frustrations can be readily distinguished." She "combined a cool forwardness … with a shyness and sadness that caused her detached way of selecting her words to seem as unnatural as the intonation of a professor of speech." Charlotte resents Lolita's affection for Humbert and so packs her off to camp. Humbert writes, "she was more afraid of Lolita's deriving some pleasure from me than of my enjoying Lolita." Yet she turns into a "touching, helpless creature" with Humbert, at least until she discovers his true feelings about her and Lolita. "McFate" conveniently removes her from Humbert's life when she is hit by a car.

Dolores Haze

See Lolita

Humbert Humbert

A name invented by the author/narrator of "Lolita, or the Confession of a White Widowed Male." Humbert is a witty, cultured European with a destructive obsession for young girls. For several years he lives with Lolita, his young stepdaughter, whom he coerces into granting him sexual favors. In his recreation of his life with Lolita, he calls himself "an artist and a madman." He tries to convince the "ladies and gentlemen of the jury," of the following partly true description:

> the majority of sex offenders that hanker for some throbbing, sweet-moaning, physical but not necessarily coital, relation with a girl child, are innocuous, inadequate, passive, timid strangers who merely ask the community to allow them to pursue their practically harmless, so-called aberrant behavior, their little hot wet private acts of sexual deviation without the police and society cracking down upon them. We are not sex fiends! ... We are unhappy, mild, dog-eyed gentlemen, sufficiently well integrated to control our urge in the presence of adults, but ready to give years and years of life for one chance to touch a nymphet. Emphatically, no killers are we. Poets never kill.

Yet at other points, Humbert admits that his "pathetic" obsession with Lolita "broke" her life. In the Foreword, the narrator suggests that Humbert writes of himself and Lolita with "a desperate honesty," and comments on "how magically his singing violin can conjure up a tendress, a compassion for Lolita that makes us entranced with the book while abhorring its author." Humbert dies of heart disease in prison, while awaiting his trial for the murder of Lolita's lover, Clare Quilty.

Valeria Humbert

Valerie is Humbert's first wife. He marries her in an effort to control his desire for young girls. Humbert admits he fell for "the imitation she gave of a little girl," but soon discovers she is at least in her late twenties. Initially his naivete prevents him from seeing that he "had on his hands a large, puffy, short-legged, big-breasted and practically brainless *baba*.... Her only asset was a muted nature which

Media Adaptations

- *Lolita* was twice adapted for the screen. The first version was directed in 1962 by Stanley Kubrick from Nabokov's screenplay and starred James Mason, Shelley Winters, and Sue Lyon as Lolita. This initial film was released by Warner and is available from Warner Home Video.

- The second film version, featuring a screenplay by Stephen Schiff, was directed by Adrian Lyne and stars Jeremy Irons, Melanie Griffith, and Dominique Swain. The film was released in 1997 by Trimark and is available from Vidmark/Trimark Home Video.

- The novel was also recorded in an audio version read by Jeremy Irons and released by Random House Audio in 1997.

did help to produce an odd sense of comfort in [their] small squalid flat." When she falls in love with another man, Humbert leaves for America. Later, he finds out that she died in childbirth.

Lolita

In the first lines of the novel, Humbert characterizes Lolita as "light of my life, fire of my loins. My sin, my soul." Readers see her from Humbert's point of view, which presents an often idealized but sometimes realistic image of this young girl, with whom he had an incestuous relationship for several years. Initially he defines Lolita as a nymphet, a category of young girls between the age of nine and fourteen who exhibit "fey grace, the elusive, shifty, soul-shattering insidious charm," and a certain "demonic" nature. He admits, "what drives me insane is the two fold nature of this nymphet—of every nymphet, perhaps; this mixture in my Lolita of tender dreamy childishness and a kind of eerie vulgarity, stemming from the snub-nosed cuteness of ads and magazine pictures, from the blurry pinkness of adolescent maidservants in the Old Country ... ; and from very young harlots disguised as children in provincial brothels." Sometimes he sees her as a combination of naivete and deception, of charm and vulgarity, of blue sulks and rosy mirth…. When she chose, [she] could be a most exasperating brat … [with her] fits of disorganized boredom, intense and vehement griping, her sprawling, droopy, dopey-eyed style—a kind of diffused clowning which she thought was tough in a boyish hoodlum way. Mentally, I found her to be a disgustingly conventional little girl.

Most often, Humbert projects Lolita as a vision of innocent beauty, as when he watches her play tennis:

[E]verything was right: the white little-boy shorts, the slender waist, the apricot midriff, the white breast-kerchief whose ribbons went up and encircled her neck to end behind in a dangling knot leaving bare her gaspingly young and adorable apricot shoulder blades with that pubescence and those lovely gentle bones, and the smooth, downward-tapering back.

Yet, almost against his will, Humbert recognizes that "Dolores Haze had been deprived of her childhood by a maniac." After she leaves Humbert, Lolita lives for a time with Clare Quilty. He throws her out after she refuses to allow him to put her in a pornographic film. A few years later she dies during childbirth.

Miss Pratt

Miss Pratt is headmistress at Beardsley School for girls. She tells Humbert that Lolita's grades are slipping and that she appears "morbidly uninterested in sexual matters." In an effort to help Lolita, she convinces Humbert to let her be in the school play.

Clare Quilty

Lolita runs off with him during her second cross-country trip with Humbert, who drops clues throughout the text that Quilty is a projection of an extreme version of himself. Nevertheless, he constructs a history for him. Quilty had known Lolita's mother, since his brother had been her dentist. He was the mysterious man who sat in the shadows at the Enchanted Hunter and quizzed Humbert about Lolita. Intrigued by their relationship, he followed the pair to Beardsley, where he wrote and produced a play for Lolita, who considered him "a genius," a "great guy," and "full of fun." This "great guy," however, encourages Lolita to engage in group sex and to participate in pornographic films. When she does not agree, he kicks her out. Humbert finds him "gray-faced" and "baggy-eyed" before he shoots him.

Themes

Art and Experience

When Humbert calls himself an artist, he reveals his attempt to impose some kind of meaningful order on his baser instincts. In his record of his life with Lolita, he tries to create a work of art that will grant immortality for the two of them by foregrounding his aesthetic sense of Lolita's beauty, and at the same time, by obscuring his morally corrupt crimes against her. Yet, he is often unable to accomplish this, as evidenced when he imagines himself as a painter, expressing the poignancy and heartbreak that defines his relationship with Lolita. He suggests his murals would recreate

a lake. There would have been an arbor in flame-flower…. There would have been a sultan, his face expressing great agony (belied, as it were, by his molding caress), helping a callypygean slave child to climb a column of onyx. There would have been those luminous globules of gonadal glow that travel up the opalescent sides of jukeboxes. There would have been all kinds of camp activities on the part of the intermediate group, Canoeing, Coranting, Combing Curls in the lakeside sun. There would have been poplars, apples, a suburban Sunday. There would have been a fire opal dissolving within a ripple-ringed pool, a last throb, a last dab of color, stinging red, smarting pink, a sigh, a wincing child.

At other times, he turns to art to help ease his burden of guilt: "Unless it can be proven to me … that in the infinite run it does not matter a jot that a north American girl-child named Dolores Haze had been deprived of her childhood by a maniac, unless this can be proven (and if it can, then life is a joke), I see nothing for the treatment of my misery but the melancholy and very local palliative of articulate art."

Appearances and Reality

Humbert's struggle to create art relates to another important theme—appearance versus reality—when he tries to present an idealistic portrait of Lolita and his relationship with her. He continually insists on the innocence of Lolita, which is crucial to his vision of and therefore his desire for her. He insists that "under no circumstances would [he] have interfered with the innocence of a child." She, however, was never quite the innocent he envisions. While at camp, she engaged in sexual activities and thus felt confident enough to seduce Humbert during their first night together. Later, in response to his control of her, she turns into a "cruel manipulator" who demands cash for sexual favors.

At the same time, she was more vulnerable than Humbert is willing to admit, and he took advantage of that vulnerability, as when he comforted her after she learned her mother was dead. He offers a symbolic assessment of his destruction of her innocence when he admits that "our long journey had only defiled with a sinuous trail of slime the lovely, trustful, dreamy, enormous country that by then, in retrospect, was no more to us than a collection of dog-eared maps, ruined tour books, old tires, and her sobs in the night—every night, every night—the moment I feigned sleep."

Victim and Victimization

Humbert becomes both victim and victimizer in his relationship with Lolita. He admits that he forced a "singular and bestial cohabitation" on her and "that even the most miserable of family lives was better than the parody of incest, which, in the long run, was the best I could offer the waif." Yet he was also victimized by his uncontrollable obsession with her, which he eloquently chronicles.

Anger and Hatred

Humbert's self-loathing prompts him to create a double who can absolve him of guilt. Clare Quilty becomes the manifestation of his illicit desire for Lolita. When he kills Quilty in a fit of revenge, he tries to erase the pain and suffering he caused her. Previously, his remorse over his obsession with young girls caused several breakdowns and subsequent hospitalizations. Yet, the absurd encounter with Quilty at the end of the novel suggests that Humbert recognizes his responsibility for his and Lolita's tragic relationship.

Style

Point of View

Humbert serves as the first person, unreliable narrator in *Lolita*. His "impassioned confession" unfolds from his very subjective point of view. In the Foreword, a fictitious Freudian psychiatrist, who is supposedly preparing Humbert's manuscript, informs us, "No doubt, [Humbert] is horrible, he is abject, he is a shining example of moral leprosy, a mixture of ferocity and jocularity.... [B]ut how magically his singing violin can conjure up a tendresse, a compassion for Lolita that makes us entranced with the book while abhorring its author." At certain points, however, Humbert also gains our compassion in response to his often witty,

Topics for Further Study

- At one point in the novel, Humbert admits that he never found out the laws governing his relationship with Lolita. Investigate what rights Humbert had as a stepfather in 1955 and what the penalties for incest were.

- Research the psychological term "obsession" and apply it to Humbert.

- Read Thomas Mann's *Death in Venice* and compare and contrast each novel's treatment of obsession and its effects.

- Investigate the effects of incest on children and compare your findings to the effects Lolita's relationship with Humbert had on her.

sometimes agonizing recount of his obsession with Lolita.

Setting

Humbert and Lolita twice travel across the United States, stopping frequently along the way at roadside motels, attractions, and restaurants, "where the holy spirit of Huncan Dines had descended upon the cute paper napkins and cottage-cheese-crested salads." The trip serves as a metaphor of the juxtaposition between Old World culture and Middle America's unsophisticated, brash materialism. Middle-aged European Humbert appreciates the natural beauty of the landscape while modern American Lolita prefers movie magazines, candy, and gift shop trinkets. The Enchanted Hunters Hotel is a witty allusion to Humbert's "enchanted" state as he "hunts" Lolita.

Structure

Humbert calls his manuscript a "confession," which it partly is. He frequently addresses "the ladies and gentlemen of the jury" during breaks in his account of his relationship with Lolita in an obvious attempt to gain their sympathy. The novel contains elements of parody, especially at the beginning and at the end. In the Foreword, Nabokov

A scene from the 1997 film adaptation of Nabokov's novel with Jeremy Irons as Humbert Humbert and Dominique Swain as his juvenile love interest, Lolita.

creates a fictitious Freudian psychologist who warns readers to look out for life's "potent evils"—a very pedantic reading of the book. This characterization relates to Humbert's encounter with Quilty at the end of the book. In the comical wrestling scene that culminates in Humbert being all "covered with Quilty," Nabokov pokes fun at the Freudian concept of dual personalities, as Humbert tries to find a way to absolve himself.

Symbolism

The text abounds with symbolism in its verbal puns, settings, and characterizations. The most important symbol occurs in the characterization of Clare Quilty, who appears as a manifestation of Humbert's evil self. Humbert gives us several clues to Quilty's real identity: He calls himself "Mr. Hyde" (referring to *Dr. Jekyll and Mr. Hyde*, Stevenson's famous novel on dual personalities); Quilty reminds him of his uncle; and, in the hilarious parody at the end of the novel, when the two wrestle over control of the gun, Humbert writes, "I rolled over him. We rolled over me. They rolled over him. We rolled over us." When Humbert kills Quilty, he tries to absolve himself of his guilt, as suggested in the judgment he handed down: "because you took advantage of a sin ... because you

took advantage of my inner essential innocence because you cheated me ... of my redemption.... because you stole her ... because of all you did because of all I did not you have to die." Humbert, of course, has proven himself to be guilty of all these crimes.

Historical Context

Sexuality in the 1950s

Traditional attitudes about sex began to change during the 1950s—the time in which *Lolita* appeared and just after the period in which Humbert and Lolita were sexually intimate. Dr. Alfred Kinsey's reports on the sexual behavior of men and women (1948, 1953) helped bring discussions of this subject out in the open. Although many Americans clung to puritanical ideas about sexuality, they could not suppress questions that began to be raised about what constituted normal or abnormal sexual behavior. Movie stars like Marilyn Monroe and Brigitte Bardot, who openly flaunted their sexuality, intrigued the public; and *Playboy* magazine, begun in 1953, gained a wide audience. Hugh Hefner, publisher of the magazine, claimed that the magazine's pictures of naked women were symbols of "disobedience, a triumph of sexuality, an end of Puritanism." *Playboy* itself promoted a new attitude toward sexuality with its "playboy philosophy" articles and its centerfolds of naked "girls next door." In the 1960s relaxed moral standards would result in an age of sexual freedom. Yet, most Americans in the 1950s retained conservative attitudes toward sexuality: they did not openly discuss sexual behavior, and promiscuity—especially for women—was not tolerated.

The Affluent Society

In *The Affluent Society,* published in 1958, John Kenneth Galbraith examined American consumerism in the 1950s, a time when more than ever before Americans had the money not only to acquire necessities but also to spend on "conveniences" and "improvements" to their lives. The higher standard of living enjoyed by Americans during this period resulted from the United States's participation in World War II, which enabled the country to become the strongest and most prosperous economic power in the world. Money poured into defense spending helped to create a successful military-industrial complex that bolstered the economy: companies produced goods that caused them to become prosperous and hire more workers, who would in turn buy more goods.

In this "age of plenty," customers could choose from a wide variety of innovations; the two most popular were new automobiles and suburban homes, both of which became important status symbols. Car manufacturers sold 21 million new cars during this period, most with powerful V-8 engines, tail fins, and lots of chrome. Developer William J. Levitt dotted the American suburban landscape with developments that crammed together hundreds of inexpensive, assembly-line houses with wall-to-wall carpeting and fully mechanized kitchens. The number of new homeowners in the 1950s increased by an unprecedented 9 million.

Americans' new materialism resulted from their eagerness to forget the hardships of the economic depression of the 1930s and the war that dominated the 1940s. Now the focus was on obtaining a good white-collar job, marrying, and raising a family in a suburban home with a lawn and a backyard barbecue. As the work week decreased to forty hours, Americans enjoyed more leisure time for personal comfort and entertainment.

Attitudes toward class distinctions also changed during the 1950s. Many Americans echoed Ernest Hemingway's assertion that the only factor that set the rich apart from the rest of the classes was that "they have more money." As more members of the middle class acquired the goods that had previously been reserved for the wealthy—the large shiny cars, the backyard swimming pools, the memberships to golf clubs—some class lines began to blur. Having and spending money lost the stigma it had had in the previous two decades when the wealthy had been criticized for lavish lifestyles in the face of depression and war. With the economy booming, the rich spent as they had in the twenties, and the burgeoning middle class emulated their habits. The introduction of department stores and restaurant charge cards also helped ordinary Americans spend much like the rich did.

Critical Overview

Lolita's interesting publishing history begins after Nabokov finished the novel in 1954 and submitted it to four American publishers, all of whom rejected it due to its shocking themes. Refusing to make any revisions to the manuscript, Nabokov sent it to Olympia Press in France, a company known for publishing pornography. After publication, however, France banned the "obscene" book, which cemented its popularity with underground readers. When tourists brought the book into America and Britain, U.S. Customs agents grudgingly allowed it in, but British officials convinced France to confiscate any remaining copies. In response to these censorship efforts, novelist Graham Greene, in a *London Times* article, declared it to be one of the ten best books of 1955. The controversy surrounding *Lolita* brought it international attention. As a result, the bans were rescinded and in 1958 this now notorious novel was published in the United States by G. P. Putnam & Sons. It immediately soared to the top of the *New York Times* bestseller list where it remained for over a year.

The controversial novel earned mixed reviews after its publication in America. Many critics found it to be immoral, including a writer for *Kirkus Reviews,* who called for the book to be banned, insisting, "That a book like this could be written—published here—sold, presumably over the counters, leaves one questioning the ethical and moral standards.... Any librarian surely will question this for anything but the closed shelves." A

Catholic World reviewer argues that its subject matter "makes it a book to which grave objection must he raised." A writer for *Library Journal* echoes these criticisms, stating "thousands of library patrons conditioned to near-incest by *Peyton Place* may take this in stride. However better read before buying. Although the writer prides himself on using no obscene words, he succeeds only too well in conveying his meaning without them." Orville Prescott in his review in *The New York Times* finds two reasons to attack the novel: *Lolita,* he writes, "is undeniably news in the world of books. Unfortunately it is bad news. There are two equally serious reasons why it isn't worthy of any adult reader's attention. The first is that it is dull, dull, dull in a pretentious, florid and archly fatuous fashion. The second is that it is repulsive."

Several other critics, however, offer their strong support of the novel, dismissing the charges of pornography and praising its artistic presentation of humor and tragedy. *New Yorker* reviewer Donald Malcolm considers *Lolita* "an artful modulation of lyricism and jocularity that quickly seduces the reader into something very like willing complicity." In *The Annotated Lolita,* editor Alfred Appel Jr. declares the book to be "one of the few supremely original novels of the century," while *San Francisco Chronicle* reviewer Lewis Vogler calls it "an authentic work of art which compels our immediate response." Those who praise the novel, however, sometimes have difficulty with its complexity, a typical characteristic of Nabokov's works. Andrew Field in *Nabokov: His Life in Art* writes, "Virtually all of the foremost literary critics in the United States and England have written about Nabokov, with enthusiasm often bordering on awe ... but their eloquence, where one wants and would expect explication, betrays the fact that they are at least as ill at ease with Nabokov as they are fascinated by him."

Nabokov's literary success continued after the publication of *Lolita,* which is now widely considered to be one of the outstanding novels of the twentieth century. During the next twenty years he produced works, including *Pale Fire,* his autobiographical *Speak Memory,* and *Lectures on Literature,* that solidified his literary reputation. Most critics would agree with writer Anthony Burgess's conclusion in *The Novel Now: A Guide to Contemporary Fiction* that Nabokov is "a major force in the contemporary novel."

Criticism

Wendy Perkins

Perkins is an Associate Professor of English at Prince George's Community College in Maryland. In the following essay, she examines how the narrative form of Lolita *reveals the main character's attempt to artistically recreate his relationship with a young girl.*

Some critics read Vladimir Nabokov's *Lolita* as a story of Humbert's unrequited love for the title character; others consider it a record of the rantings of a mad pedophile, with, as Humbert himself admits, "a fancy prose style." Nabokov's innovative construction, in fact, highlights both of these aspects as it reinforces and helps develop the novel's main theme: the relationship between art and experience. By allowing Humbert to narrate the details of his life with Lolita, Nabokov illustrates the difficulties inherent in an attempt to order experience through art. As he tries to project an ideal vision of his relationship with Lolita, Humbert manipulates readers' responses to him in order to gain sympathy and to effect a suspension of judgment. Ultimately, though, tragic reality emerges within his art.

In *'Lolita' and the Dangers of Fiction* Mathew Winston comments on Humbert's motive: "The artist wants to fix once for all the perilous magic of nymphets. The lover wants to write a history that will glorify his beloved for future generations.... In his final words, 'this is the only immortality you and I may share, my Lolita,' Humbert appears as Renaissance sonneteer, boasting that he will make his love immortal in his writing." Humbert does accomplish his goal in part: his manuscript contains beautiful and heartfelt descriptions of "the perilous magic of nymphets"; it also records, however, the devastating results of his illicit obsession for a young girl.

Humbert tries to manipulate his readers' response throughout his memoir by presenting a poetic portrait of Lolita and his life with her. He admits, "I hope I am addressing myself to unbiased readers." In an effort to provide himself with an excuse for his obsession with Lolita, he details his relationship with Annabel, Lolita's "precursor" at the beginning of the novel. Of his adolescent relationship with Annabel, he writes, "the spiritual and the physical had been blended in us with a perfection that must remain incomprehensible to the matter-of-fact, crude, standard-brained youngsters of today." He suggests that educated readers will thus comprehend the beauty of that relationship, as well as his with Lolita.

Before he begins the details of his life with Lolita, Humbert introduces the following idea: "Between the age limits of nine and fourteen there occur maidens who, to certain bewitched travelers, twice or many times older than they, reveal their true nature which is not human, but nymphic (that is demoniac); and these chosen creatures I propose to designate as 'nymphets.'" This description suggests he was a "hunter," "enchanted" by the "nymphet" Lolita almost against his will. He asserts that "under no circumstances would [he] have interfered with the innocence of a child."

In another effort to suspend readers' judgment, Humbert frequently interrupts his memoir with descriptions of sexual customs in other countries and other time periods. He notes that society dictates sexual taboos and that they change from culture to culture and in different time periods. "Let me remind my reader" he begins, that in the past girls Lolita's age frequently married and that artists like Dante and Petrarch "fell madly in love" with young girls. Thus, he intimates, readers should not impose judgment on him based on twentieth-century moral standards.

Humbert provides eloquent descriptions of Lolita that reveal the "incomparable" and "poignant bliss he feels in her presence." In the following passage, he mythologizes her as he reveals his exquisite pleasure over watching her play tennis:

> I remember at the very first game I watched being drenched with an almost painful convulsion of beauty assimilation. My Lolita had a way of raising her bent left knee at the ample and springy start of the service cycle when there would develop and hang in the sun for a second a vital web of balance between toed foot, pristine armpit, burnished arm and far back-flung racket, as she smiled up with gleaming teeth at the small globe suspended so high in the zenith of the powerful and graceful cosmos she had created for the express purpose of falling upon it with a clan resounding crack of her golden whip.

Humbert illustrates the depths of his feeling for her when he admits that in his assessment of their life together, everything "gets mixed up with the exquisite stainless tenderness seeping through the musk and the mud, through the dirt and the death, Oh God, oh God. And what is most singular is that she, *this* Lolita, *my* Lolita, has individualized the writer's ancient lust, so that above and over everything there is Lolita."

What Do I Read Next?

- *Death in Venice* (1913), by Thomas Mann, is a tragic tale of an acclaimed author's obsession for a young boy and an exploration of the nature of beauty.

- Nabokov's 1962 *Pale Fire,* a hilarious look at a different kind of obsession, presents a brilliant parody of literary scholarship.

- *Speak Memory* (1951), by Nabokov, is a moving account of his life and family.

- Nabokov wrote *Lolita: A Screenplay* for the 1962 film version of his novel. Stanley Kubrick rewrote much of it when he transferred it to the screen.

The wit and humor Humbert invests in his artistic reconstruction of his past further gain readers' sympathy and restrict their efforts to judge him. *New Yorker* contributor Donald Malcolm observes, "an artful modulation of lyricism and jocularity ... quickly seduces the reader into something very like willing complicity." The memoir contains several examples of Humbert's verbal brilliance and quick wit, but the most inventive occurs at the end during his comic scene with Clare Quilty, presented as Humbert's evil twin. In their death struggle, which recalls another lesser artform, Humbert notes,

> I rolled over him. We rolled over me. They rolled over him. We rolled over us.... [E]lderly readers, will surely recall at this point the obligatory scene in the Westerns of their childhood. Our tussle, however, lacked the ox-stunning fisticuffs, the flying furniture. He and I were two large dummies, stuffed with dirty cotton and rags.... When at last I had possessed myself of my precious weapon, and the scenario writer had been reinstalled in his low chair, both of us were panting as the cowman and the sheepman never do after their battle.

Humbert, however, cannot hide the reality of Lolita's suffering in his idealized portrait of her. He often, almost uncontrollably, undercuts his romantic vision with disturbing details of his responsibility for her "broken" life. At one point he admits, "I simply did not know a thing about my darling's mind and that quite possibly, behind the awful juvenile cliches, there was in her a garden and a twilight, and a palace gate—dim and adorable regions which happened to be lucidly and absolutely forbidden to me … living as we did, she and I, in a world of total evil…. [O]h my poor, bruised child. I loved you…. I was despicable and brutal, and turpid, and everything … and there were times when I knew how you felt, and it was hell to know it." Another time he writes, "I recall certain moments … when after having had my fill of her … the tenderness would deepen to shame and despair." Ironically, though, Humbert's brutal honesty gains him a measure of respect from his readers.

Humbert reveals his complex nature when he insists, that to love a nymphet, "you have to be an artist and a madman." In the Foreword, the fictitious Freudian psychiatrist John Ray Jr. insists, "No doubt, he is horrible, he is abject, he is a shining example of moral leprosy, a mixture of ferocity and jocularity…. [B]ut how magically his singing violin can conjure up a tendresse, a compassion for Lolita that makes us entranced with the book while abhorring its author." Donald E. Morton, in his *Vladimir Nabokov,* argues, "What makes *Lolita* something more than either a case study of sexual perversion or pornographic titillation is the truly shocking fact that Humbert Humbert is a genius who, through the power of his artistry, actually persuades the reader that his memoir is a love story. It is this accomplishment that makes the novel a surprising success from the perspective of Humbert Humbert's desires and intentions." Yet while readers recognize the poignant love story in *Lolita,* they also identify it as a tale of cruel victimization, and in its entirety as an illustration of the artist's difficult task in successfully ordering experience through art.

Source: Wendy Perkins, in an essay for *Novels for Students,* Gale, 2000.

Chester E. Eisinger

In this overview, Eisinger argues that Lolita *is not so much about its plot as it is about art; he asserts that the novel's "primary if not its sole reality is language."*

The apparent subject of Vladimir Nabokov's *Lolita* is the titillating perversion of a madman who virtually kills his wife in order to make captive and lasciviously possess her 12-year-old daughter; and

when the child, who has in fact seduced him, escapes him, running off with another man, he apparently kills that man. This lurid tale would seem to invite either a sensational or a moral response. The problem Nabokov deliberately sets for himself, however, is to persuade the reader to transcend the erotic content and eschew moral judgment in order to perceive his novel as an artistic creation and not as a reflection or interpretation of reality. *Lolita* is not immoral or didactic, he has said; it has no moral. It is a work of art. The apparent subject of the novel is Humbert Humbert's perverted passion for a nymphet. But we come closer to the real subject if we perceive that his passion is his prison and his pain, his ecstasy and his madness. His release from the prison of his passion and the justification of his perversion is in art, and that is the real subject of the novel: the pain of remembering, organizing, and telling his story is a surrogate for the pain of his life and a means of transcending and triumphing over it; art, as it transmutes the erotic experience, becomes the ultimate experience in passion and madness.

Late in the book Humbert says that unless it can be proved to him that it does not matter that Lolita had been deprived of her childhood by a maniac, then he sees nothing for the treatment of his misery but the palliative of articulate art. At the end of the novel, addressing Lolita, he says, I am thinking of angels, the secret of durable pigments, prophetic sonnets, the refuge of art. Here is the only immortality he and Lolita may share. Here is the only balm that will soothe. Here, in art, are the forms that will control the passionate furies while the music of the words cloaks it all in saving beauty.

Not that "reality" doesn't intrude. Nabokov sought and captured the way schoolgirls talk; he conveys the feel and the smell of American motel rooms in all their philistine vulgarity. But a major thrust of the novel is toward undermining and mocking the concepts of fact, reality, and truth in fiction, toward destroying, in short, the very bases of literary realism. Nabokov undercuts a firm conception of reality by involving Nabokov the "author," Humbert the "narrator," and John Ray the supposititious editor in the making of the book, creating an ambiguity and uncertainty about authorship, reliability, and authority which attack the validity of fact, reality, and truth: can we trust the criminally insane Humbert as the primary source of our knowledge of events and people, especially since "Humbert Humbert" is Humbert's own invention? And more especially since his diary, presumably the original source of the narrative, has been destroyed? Or the pompous Ray, who speaks of newspapers which carry the story of Humbert "For the benefit of old-fashioned readers who wish to follow the destinies of the 'real' people beyond the 'true' story ...," a man who asserts that the tale tends toward a moral apotheosis? The factitious factual character of the story that Ray emphasizes is only a device for encouraging our conventional expectations as readers of traditionally realistic fictions which make traditional moral judgments. Nabokov will disappoint these expectations just as he has deliberately confused the point of view and the identity and relationship of the characters. The techniques of the novel are forms of play for him, as art itself is play.

Writing his memoirs in prison, Humbert says, Oh, my Lolita, I have only words to play with. It is the case that word play and pure sound are one source of the wit and joy of the novel, as Humbert imagines the nymphet he would coach in French and fondle in Humbertish. Nabokov uses language so that it draws attention to itself. It is frequently more important than the action of the novel. It is thus possible to argue that if Humbert had only words to play with, he never had a flesh and blood 12-year-old girl at all. She is a fantasy, imagined by a madman imprisoned as much in his cell as he is in his lust. Indeed the entire book may be a fantasy. When Humbert kills Clare Quilty, the playwright who abducted Lolita, the characters move as though they were underwater or with that heavily retarded motion common to nightmare. Quilty may be as unreal as Lolita, Humbert's alter ego haunting him for his guilt in relation to the child. Lolita is thus an occasion for Humbert's fantasy of sex and Quilty for his fantasy of violence and revenge. It is as necessary to transmute the pain of one's fantasy life into art as it is the pain of one's conscious and quotidian life. Whether Lolita and Quilty are "real" or not, language will serve as a means of dealing with them.

It is not only through language that Lolita is removed from the "real" world. As a nymphet, she is nymphic, that is, daemonic. A nympholept like Humbert instantly recognizes and always burns for such a creature. When he gets her into bed, in an inn called appropriately enough for a magical, mythical experience The Enchanted Hunters, he thinks of her as an immortal daemon disguised as a female child. Thus it is possible to read Lolita as a daemonic spirit residing in the human id, that is, as an irrational, self-destructive force related to the primitive in man that will overwhelm his rationality with the frenzy of its appetite. The price of this

ecstasy is its inevitable pain. And so we return to language, because only it, only art, will bring these demonic energies under control. And that is the essence of the entire novel: its primary if not its sole reality is language.

Source: Chester E. Eisinger, "*Lolita:* Overview," in *Reference Guide to American Literature, 3rd ed.,* edited by Jim Kamp, St. James Press, 1994.

Phillip F. O'Connor

In the following essay, O'Connor discusses Lolita *as a parody of several popular genres, as a work rich in characterization, and as the catalyst for Nabokov's success as a writer.*

Lolita stays like a deep tattoo. Critics tumble over one another racing to publish articles on its twists, myths and artifices. Paperback houses have reprinted it again and again. It is the second most often cited title in *Book Week*'s Poll of Distinguished Fiction, 1945-65. It has been made into a movie, a successful one at that. Sales and critical attention have opened the way for the appearance of many of Nabokov's other novels, particularly his early or Russian novels. Without *Lolita,* Nabokov's rise to literary sainthood might have been delayed beyond his natural years. Indeed, it might never have occurred.

Nabokov's twelfth novel was brought out in 1955 by Maurice Girodias' Olympia Press in Paris when the author was fifty-six years old. It had been rejected by four American publishers on a variety of grounds, all, according to Andrew Field, stemming from "a compound of fright and incomprehension" (*Nabokov, His Life in Art*). Though Girodias had now and then published the works of distinguished writers such as [Lawrence] Durrell, [Samuel] Beckett and [Jean] Genet, he was known mainly for an output of "dirty books." He saw in *Lolita,* some of whose literary values he recognized, mainly a weapon in the fight against moral censorship. Nabokov was soon forced to insist that he would be hurt if his work became a *succes de scandale.* The author needn't have worried; during the year following its publication, *Lolita* was given not a single review and soon became just another book on the Olympia list, not even sufficiently pornographic to compete with some of Girodias' other titles, such as *White Thighs* and *The Sex Life of Robinson Crusoe.*

An early sign of the lastingness of *Lolita* seems to be the unanimity of contempt it aroused in snobs and slobs alike after it did find a public of sorts.

Orville Prescott in the daily *New York Times* (August 18, 1958) declared:

> *Lolita,* then, is undeniably news in the world of books. Unfortunately it is bad news. There are two equally serious reasons why it isn't worthy of any adult reader's attention. The first is that it is dull, dull, dull in a pretentious, florid and archly fatuous fashion. The second is that it is repulsive.

Prescott shared contempt with "Stockade Clyde" Carr, a barracks-mate of Nabokov's former student and, later, editor, Alfred Appel, Jr. Appel found and purchased the Olympia edition in Paris in 1955 and brought it back to his Army post, where Clyde, recognizing the publisher said, "Hey, lemme read your dirty book, man!" Urged to read it aloud himself, Clyde stumbled through the opening paragraph: "Lo … lita, light … of my life. Fire of my … loins. My sin, my soul. Lo … lee … ta" then tossed down the book and complained, "It's goddam littachure!" … Nabokov seems to have anticipated some of the fads, fashions and contempts of both schools. In the foreword to the novel, Nabokov's alter-ego, or mask, the scholar John Ray, Jr., says " … those very scenes one might ineptly accuse of a sensuous existence of their own, are the most strictly functional ones in the development of a tragic tale, tending unswervingly to nothing less than moral apotheosis." Nabokov's works are full of such clues and warnings, but only sensitive readers pick them up. In fact, *Lolita* remained an underground novel until 1956 when Graham Greene in *The London Times* placed it on his list of the ten best novels published during the previous year. As Field points out:

> Greene's pronouncement aroused great controversy, but also stimulated the interest of many important and respected critics and writers, who, with few exceptions, were quick to recognize the enormous importance and non-pornographic nature of the novel.

By 1959 many literary people had taken and followed Greene's signal (I might say, "*Not until 1959 …*"). V. S. Pritchett in *The New Statesman* appreciated the novel and addressed the problem of the so-called pornographic content, no doubt aware that the U.S. Customs Bureau had for a time confiscated copies of *Lolita:*

> I can imagine no book less likely to incite the corruptible reader; the already corrupted would surely be devastated by the author's power of projecting himself into their fantasy-addled minds. As for minors, the nymphets and schoolboys, one hardly sees them toiling through a book written in a difficult style, filled on every page with literary allusions, linguistic experiment and fits of idiosyncrasy.

Such praise seems mild, given what we now know of the general richness of the novel. To one degree or another, for example, critics have demonstrated that *Lolita* is a full-blown psychological novel with roots deep in nineteenth century models; a detective novel with conventions that date back to Poe, perhaps beyond; a confessional novel; a Doppelganger Tale; an extended allegory for the artistic process; a sexual myth more complicated and mysterious than comparable Freudian stereotypes; even a fable with correspondences to the Little Red Riding Hood story. And of course it to some degree parodies these types.

In his final confrontation with Quilty, "the kidnapper," Humbert, "the detective," comically plays his role to the extreme. Then, as if to remind us that popular genres often share both conventions and cliches, Nabokov mixes matters; that is, for moments at least, a scene from a detective novel becomes, as well, a scene from a Western, "detective" becoming "cowboy," etc. Quilty has just knocked Humbert's pistol ("Chum") under a chest of drawers:

> Fussily, busibodily, cunningly, he had risen again while he talked. I groped under the chest trying at the same time to keep an eye on him. All of a sudden I noticed that he had noticed that I did not seem to have noticed Chum protruding from beneath the other corner of the chest. We fell to wrestling again. We rolled all over the floor, in each other's arms, like two huge helpless children. He was naked and goatish under his robe, and I felt suffocated as he rolled over me. I rolled over him. We rolled over me. They rolled over him. We rolled over us.

The final sentences signal exhaustion, not only in the narrator and his opponent but, as importantly, in the author who lurks behind them and the reader who waits ahead. Yet Nabokov still isn't satisfied; as parodist he has recognized and used the possibilities for exhaustion in the detective/Western, pushing the scene to its sterile limits; now he provides the rewarding twist, presented in Humbert's comment:

> In its published form, this book is being read, I assume in the first years of 2000 A.D. (1935 plus eighty or ninety, live long, my love); and elderly readers will surely recall at this point the obligatory scene in the Westerns of their childhood. Our tussle, however, lacked the ox-stunning fisticuffs, the flying furniture…. It was a silent, soft, formless tussle on the part of two literati, one of whom was utterly disorganized by a drug while the other was handicapped by a heart condition with too much gin. When at last I had possessed myself of my precious weapon,— both of us were panting as the cowman and the sheepman never do after their battles.

Heretofore in the scene we've been presented with a mocking of roles and literary genres; but now we find connections between poor detective writing and poor Western film making, specifically in the fight-scene cliche. Not only do genres share cliches; so do modes (fiction and film).

Here, as in many of Nabokov's novels, parody is close to essence. Literature is not the only object of Nabokov's playful pen. Material as unrelated as the author himself (anagramatically called Vivian Darkbloom) and artifacts of the American culture, such as motels, come under the writer's amused eye. That Nabokov's work and its parts are at the same time themselves and imitations of themselves is no surprise to readers of *The Real Life of Sebastian Knight, Laughter in the Dark,* and other of the author's subversive fictions.

Characters imitate literary or historical figures outside the work (Humbert Humbert as Edgar Allan Poe), they imitate characters within the work (Humbert as Clare Quilty) and they imitate themselves (Humbert, the lecherous father and Humbert, the dutiful father). They constantly confront mirrors, adopt disguises or masks, and become, at least in terms of *motif* butterflies, hunters and chess pieces. Word-games abound, particularly those that involve repetitions (Humbert Humbert or John Ray, Jr. JR JR) and connotative resonances (like the surname Haze). Punning and similar games which allow a kind of verbal playback appear frequently. Clues, false clues, symbols and allusions are bounced against each other like the white dot in an electronic tennis game, though the author's hand remains steadily, constantly on the controls. And beneath all the trickery and games, as if in concession to realists like [Gustave] Flaubert and Saul Bellow there lies a more or less traditional, a tragic, love story.

Humbert's comment on the fight, quoted above, also reveals a quality that readers attending Nabokov's parodic vision may easily overlook: a depth of characterization. There are dimensions to Lolita, Quilty, Charlotte and others in the novel. Humbert is extraordinarily complicated: a lover, criminal, detective, cowboy, mocker, serious in each endeavor, even the most foolish. After noting "this mixture in my Lolita of tender dreamy childishness and a kind of eerie vulgarity," Humbert shares the depths of his feelings for her, saying:

... all this gets mixed up with the exquisite stainless tenderness seeping through the musk and the mud, through the dirt and the death, Oh God, oh God. And what is most singular is that she, this Lolita, my

Lolita, has individualized the writer's ancient lust, so that above and over everything there is—Lolita.

The subject here, however, is the novel and its readers: what happened and what might have happened. Consider. Because *Lolita* survived, as literature, as a popular novel, it prepared the way for subsequent Nabokov works, especially *Pale Fire* and *Ada,* which might otherwise have found no audience of notable size, might not even have been published by a commercial press. In sustaining a reasonably healthy life for itself, *Lolita* also made possible the translation and publication of Nabokov's important early novels, including *Mary, King, Queen, Knave, The Defense* and *The Eye.* Further, it brought invitations for Nabokov's short stories from editors of good-paying magazines who previously had ignored his work.... Finally, it provided for the author that glowing credential of a writer's popular success, a movie, which came about largely because of solid paperback sales. A work, then, which at the beginning was completely ignored, then existed as a controversial under-the-counter pornographic novel was finally published by a respectable house (The first Putnam edition appeared in August, 1958, and there were seventeen printings in the following thirteen months.) seemed to catapult its author into daylight. Yet this was decades after he had begun writing. How strange, especially when one recalls that *Lolita* was not discovered by an informed critic making a studied response *or* by an enterprising editor at a commercial publishing house but as the result of the bare mention of it made by another practitioner of Nabokov's lonely craft, a mention that itself might have gone unnoticed had the novel lacked the power to stir and sustain controversy. The oddness of it all might appeal to no one more than to Nabokov himself.

And so it did.

In "An Afterword to Lolita" he recalls his experiences with the four American publishers who'd rejected his novel before he sent it to Girodias: He found some of the reactions "very amusing." One reader thought the book would be all right if Lolita were turned into a twelve-year-boy and he was seduced by Humbert, "a farmer, in a barn, amidst gaunt and arid surroundings, all this set forth in short, strong, 'realistic' sentences." Nabokov insists that everybody knows that he detests symbols and allegories,

... an otherwise intelligent reader who flipped through the first part described *Lolita* as "Old Europe debauching young America," while another flipper saw in it "Young American debauching old Europe."

Publisher X, whose advisers got so bored with Humbert that they never got beyond page 188, had the naivete to write me that Part Two was too long. Publisher Y, on the other hand, regretted that there were no good people in the book. Publisher Z said if he printed *Lolita,* he and I would go to jail.

The author, after years of absurd neglect, had developed a shell of protection; any response now would amuse him. In jail or an asylum he would surely have laughed, perhaps scribbled out the folly of his fate on the walls of his cell.

I've intended my remarks to be informative and stimulating, not conclusive, and therefore I must warn myself away from the temptation to make something definite of all of this. The best closing is to be found in some of the words Nabokov himself wrote about *Lolita.* They seem to be a gentle phosphorescent light by which trailing fish—critics, teachers, writers, students, publishers and the like—might be guided. When he thinks of the novel, he says:

> … I seem always to pick out for special delectation such images as Mr. Taxovich, or that class list of Ramsdale School, or Charlotte saying "waterproof," or Lolita in slow motion advancing toward Humbert's gifts, or the pictures decorating the stylized garret of Gaston Godin, or the Kasbeam barber (who cost me a lot of work), or Lolita playing tennis, or the hospital at Elphinstone, or pale, pregnant, beloved, irretrievable Dolly Schiller dying in the Gray Star (the capital town of the book), or the tinkling sounds of the valley town coming up the mountain trail (on which I caught the first known female of *Lycaeides sublivens* Nabokov).

These parts he calls "the nerves of the novel." They are the "secret points, the subliminal co-ordinates by means of which the book is plotted."

And surely, I dare add, some of the reasons the novel has survived even its own audiences.

Source: Phillip F. O'Connor, "*Lolita:* A Modern Classic in Spite of Its Readers," in *A Question of Quality: Seasoned "Authors" for a New Season, Vol. 2,* edited by Louis Filler, Bowling Green University Popular Press, 1980, pp. 139-43.

Sources

Alfred Appel Jr., *The Annotated Lolita,* McGraw, 1970.

Anthony Burgess, *The Novel Now: A Guide to Contemporary Fiction,* Norton, 1967.

Catholic World, October, 1958.

Kirkus Reviews, June 5, 1958.

Andrew Field, *Nabokov: His Life in Art,* Little, Brown, 1967.

Library Journal, August, 1958.

Donald Malcolm, review in *The New Yorker,* November 8, 1958.

Donald E. Morton, *Vladimir Nabokov,* Unger, 1974.

Orville Prescott, review in *The New York Times,* August 18, 1958.

Lewis Vogler, review in *San Francisco Chronicle,* August 24, 1958.

Mathew Winston, "'Lolita' and the Dangers of Fiction," *Twentieth Century Literature,* December, 1975, pp. 421-27.

For Further Study

Martin Amis, review in *The Atlantic,* September, 1992.
Analyzes Humbert's psyche and the effect he has on others in his life, including Lolita, as well as acts of cruelty and moral issues in *Lolita.*

Roger Angell, "Lo Love, High Romance," *The New Yorker,* August 25 & September 1, 1997, pp. 156-59.
Revisits the novel as a new movie version is released in 1997.

Frank S. Meyer, review in *National Review,* December 11, 1995.
Examines Nabokov's intentions behind writing *Lolita.*

Rex Weiner, "'Lolita' Gets Old Waiting for a Date," *Variety,* June 2, 1997.
Discusses the controversy surrounding the distribution of the 1997 film version of *Lolita.*

On the Beach

Nevil Shute
1957

The antiwar novel has a grand literary tradition. Erich Maria Remarque's *All Quiet on the Western Front* (1929), Dalton Trumbo's *Johnny Got His Gun* (1939), and Norman Mailer's *The Naked and the Dead* (1948) are prime examples of novels that realistically portray the madness and brutality of war. While Nevil Shute's *On the Beach* is not as well-known as these other novels, it carries a powerful message about the dangers of nuclear warfare.

In his novel, Shute focuses on a group of ordinary people who wait for the inevitable radioactive fall-out of a devastating nuclear war to arrive in Melbourne, Australia. Many critics hailed the book as an insightful and humane cautionary fable. *On the Beach* continues to sell well for a forty-year-old novel, which suggests that the moral of the story remains relevant today.

Author Biography

Born Nevil Shute Norway, Shute was born on January 17, 1899, in a suburb of London, England. His father, Arthur Hamilton Norway, was the assistant secretary of the General Post Office in London. In 1912 his father was appointed head of the post office in Ireland. After moving to Dublin, Shute was sent to the Shrewsbury School in Oxford; in the summer, he stayed with his family in the countryside near Dublin.

In 1915, Shute's only brother, nineteen-year-old Fred, died in France during World War I. A

Nevil Shute and Scottish ballerina Moira Shearer autograph books at Harrod's, London.

short time later, Shute served as a stretcher-bearer during the 1916 Easter Rebellion in Ireland. During the fighting, Irish rebels occupied and burned his father's post office. He entered the Royal Military Academy and trained for several months to become a gunnery officer for the Royal Flying Corps, but a childhood stammer prevented him from getting a commission. Desperate to fight for England, he enlisted in the infantry, but the war ended before he saw any combat.

After graduating from Oxford in 1923, he worked at the de Havilland Aircraft Company. At this time he wrote his first novel, *Stephen Morris,*

which wasn't published until after his death. His first published novel was *Marazan,* which appeared in 1926.

He eventually left de Havilland's to work on the R-100 airship project. The R-100 was one-half of a two-airship project commissioned by the government. Although the R-100 flew a successful round-trip to Canada, the government version of the aircraft—known as the R-101—was poorly designed and crashed in an accident over France during its first flight. The project was canceled, and Shute went on to form his own company, Airspeed Ltd., in 1930.

Shute married Frances Heaton in 1931. After publishing his third novel, *Lonely Road* (1932), he stopped writing to focus his attention on his new company.

In 1938 Shute resigned from Airspeed Ltd. and began writing again. With the advent of World War II, he joined the British Navy and was appointed head of the engineering section at the Admiralty Department of Miscellaneous Weapon Development. He went with the invasion fleet to Normandy on D-Day as a correspondent for the Ministry of Information.

After the war, Shute spent the next several years traveling. In 1945 he was a correspondent in Burma, and a few years later, he toured America by automobile in 1947. A few years later he flew his own airplane to Australia, which provided him with the subject matter for *A Town Like Alice* and *Round the Bend* (1951). In 1950 he moved to Australia.

Shute's later books were influenced by his growing interest in Eastern mysticism. He wrote and traveled extensively in the last decade of his life. In 1958 he had a major stroke. Only a year later he suffered a second one, but he was still able to complete his last novel, *Trustee from the Toolroom* (1960). On January 12, 1960, Shute fell ill while writing in his study. He died later that evening.

Plot Summary

Chapter 1

On the Beach opens with Lieutenant Commander Peter Holmes of the Royal Australian Navy preparing for a new naval assignment. One year earlier, there had been a devastating nuclear conflict in North America, Europe, and Asia. As a result, billions of people have died from nuclear radiation, which will eventually reach Australia.

However, Peter is happy to be getting a new assignment. After he fetches milk for his wife, Mary, and his infant daughter, Jennifer, he travels to Melbourne to learn the nature of his new appointment.

In Melbourne, Peter is appointed as the liaison officer to the U.S. submarine, the *U.S.S. Scorpion.* He has met the captain, Commander Dwight Towers, and remembers him as a "… quiet, soft-spoken man of thirty-five or so with a slight New England accent."

When the war had erupted a year earlier, the *Scorpion* was cruising near Australia. When Towers was unable to raise a radio signal from the United States, he set course for Yap Island, a small cable post under U.S. control:

> Here he learned for the first time of the Russian-Chinese war which had flared up out of the Russian-NATO war, that had in turn been born of the Israeli-Arab war, initiated by Albania.

Consequently, Towers placed his submarine under Australian command.

Peter decides to tour the submarine before his official posting begins. He informs Towers of their orders: to cruise north to Cairns, Port Moresby (New Guinea), and Darwin to search for signs of life. The Australian Royal Navy also has plans for a much longer voyage, but Peter doesn't know where.

He invites Towers to spend some time as a guest at his home in Falmouth near the beach. Towers agrees to spend a night so he can go for a swim. Later, Peter and Mary introduce him to Moira Davidson, a young family friend. Towers and Moira have a drink in town before going to the Holmes household.

Moira continually flirts with Towers, and he is surprised to find he still has his sense of humor. Later, after the party, a drunk Moira begins to cry because she will never be able to have a family like Mary. Towers sympathizes, but he is unable to bring himself to comfort her. He asks Mary to put her to bed.

Chapter 2

The morning after the party, Towers goes to church and reflects upon his late family. He and Moira arrange to meet again before the *Scorpion* leaves for their first mission.

When Towers returns to his submarine, he discovers that a civilian scientific officer has been assigned to the mission. A reserved, somewhat morose, young man named John Osborne is in charge of observing and recording radiation levels during the cruise through the northern Coral Sea. Osborne is described as having a "lean, intelligent face" and a "loose, ungainly figure."

Moira arrives the following day for a tour of the submarine. While changing her clothes in Towers's cabin, she sees photographs of his late family. She vows to herself to make their evening date fun. During their date, Towers suggests to her that she should go to school instead of spending most of her time drinking.

At the end of their date, he promises to call when he returns from his mission. The next day, he learns from the First Naval Member that the radiation is now as far south as Townsville. He is forbidden to allow anyone on his submarine once he reaches that point.

Chapter Three

The mission is discouraging: there are no signs of life in Darwin or Port Moresby; they see only a dog in Cairns; they find a ghostly tanker floating between Cairns and Port Moresby, but the radiation is too high to board the ship.

The men discuss the origins of the war, which seem to be mysterious. For some reason, Albania bombed Naples. Tel Aviv was then bombed, spurring an Israeli-Arab war. Towers reveals that the Americans bombed the Soviets by mistake. Egyptians using Russian bombers attacked London and Washington D.C., and the Americans retaliated by attacking Russia. China also attacked Russia, and the Soviets retaliated.

Returning to Melbourne, the men learn that one of the crew has contracted measles. Towers also learns that the only other remaining submarine in the American fleet, the *U.S.S. Swordfish,* cruised along the eastern seaboard of the United States and found no signs of life.

Towers spends more time with Moira at Falmouth. He tells her that he suspects that his submarine will be sent on a mission to the United States. He also tells her about his family, and he reveals his belief that he will somehow be reunited with them in the afterlife. Moira begins to understand his need to be faithful to the memory of his family.

Chapter Four

Peter and Mary begin planning flower and vegetable gardens. Moira finds the idea ridiculous because the couple will not be alive to see the gardens grow, but Towers understands the need for some kind of hope in a time of crisis:

> "Maybe they don't believe [that the radiation will soon kill them]. Maybe they think they can take it all with them and have it where they're going to, someplace. I wouldn't know." He paused. "The thing is, they just kind of like to plan a garden. Don't you go and spoil it for them, telling them they're crazy."

Moira invites Towers to her parent's farm for a few days of rest and reflection. He accepts, and they spend several days helping Moira's father work on the farm.

Towers is ordered to take the *Scorpion* on a long and dangerous mission to Seattle to investigate a mysterious radio signal. Peter later discusses radiation sickness with the pharmacist, Mr. Goldie. Goldie instructs Peter on the use of the mercy-killing drugs. He tells him that they will be available for free when the radiation reaches Melbourne.

Chapter Five

Peter fears that he may not return from his next mission, so he reluctantly explains to Mary the symptoms of radiation sickness and the possibility that she may have to inject Jennifer with poison and take a suicide tablet herself in order to end their suffering. Mary is appalled and the couple has a terrible argument. Later, she realizes that Peter is only trying to protect them from prolonged agony and she apologizes for her reaction.

Osborne practices racing his Ferrari on the deserted highways and a race track. Driving the car excites him and fills him with confidence. Moira reveals to Towers that she has been taking classes. Having trouble accepting the deaths of his family members, Towers purchases an expensive bracelet for his wife and a fishing rod for his son, but he cannot locate a Pogo stick for his daughter. He is deeply moved when Moira promises to find one for him while he is on the cruise.

Chapter Six

The submarine safely makes it across the Pacific and into Puget Sound. They find no signs of life in Seattle. The submarine locates the source of the radio signal, a radio installation on Santa Maria Island.

Lieutenant Sunderstrom, an officer familiar with the installation, dons a protective suit to go ashore. He discovers that a broken window frame rattling on a transmitting key is the source of the radio signal. He sends a message to Australia to inform them that all is well, shuts the installation down, and returns to the submarine to be decontaminated.

Mary and Moira are informed that the men have completed the first half of their voyage safely. Moira tells Mary that she is in love with Towers, but that he would never be able to marry her. The *Scorpion* returns to Melbourne and Towers discovers that he has been appointed the Commanding Officer of the U.S. Naval Forces.

Chapter Seven

Towers comes down with a fever and spends several days in bed at the Davidson farm. Moira gives him a Pogo stick engraved with his daughter's name. Osborne visits the farm and shows them his Ferrari. He informs them that the radiation is showing no signs of slowing down. Towers gets well after several days of rest.

As the weeks pass, Osborne prepares for the time trials of the Australian Grand Prix, Peter and Mary work on their garden, and Towers works on the submarine while dating Moira. Osborne wins a position for the Grand Prix.

Chapter Eight

The only other surviving American naval vessel, the *U.S.S. Swordfish,* is at port in Montevideo, Uruguay, when the radiation reaches it. Towers reluctantly orders the commander to sink the submarine in deep water. The *Scorpion* is now the last submarine in the U.S. Navy.

On a shopping trip, Peter and Mary find Melbourne dirty and almost deserted. Towers is forced to discipline some of his crew when drunkenness becomes a problem.

Osborne wins the Australian Grand Prix. Later, Osborne calls Towers to inform him that the first cases of radiation sickness have appeared in Melbourne.

Chapter Nine

Towers informs Peter that he will soon be taking the *Scorpion* out to sea to sink it. He will go down with the ship, and bids Peter farewell. Osborne visits his mother for the last time. He puts her dog to sleep after his mother has committed suicide.

Peter and Mary both get radiation sickness, but Peter rebounds. He visits Osborne to ask him if recovery is possible; Osborne tells him it is temporary and Peter returns home to his wife. Osborne takes his tablet behind the wheel of his beloved Ferrari.

Peter injects the baby with poison. He and Mary take their tablets in bed together after expressing their love for each other. Moira visits Towers for the last time at the submarine; they are both very sick. She asks to go with him and he reluctantly refuses. Moira drives to a point where she can watch the submarine cruise away. There, she takes her tablet with a glass of brandy.

Characters

Bill Davidson

Bill is Moira's father. An old-fashioned sheep rancher, he is glad to welcome Dwight Towers to his home for a visit. The two men discuss the grim effects the nuclear holocaust will have on Australia. Bill plans to remain on his farm when the radiation reaches Melbourne. In the end, he and his wife express regret that Tower and Moira do not marry.

Moira Davidson

Moira Davidson is a friend of Peter and Mary Holmes. She copes with her impending death by constant drinking and promiscuity. However, her relationship with American naval officer Dwight Towers changes her.

At first she is flighty and flirtatious with him, but the officer's good nature and loyalty to his dead family touches her. Unfortunately, Moira gradually realizes that Towers will never be able to completely give himself to her because he is faithful to the memory of his wife.

Yet her relationship with Towers inspires her to quit drinking and find constructive ways to spend her last days. In addition, she strives to make his last months in Australia as pleasant as possible. She brings him home to her family, mends his clothes, and takes him on a fishing trip. Although Towers will not take her with him when he leaves to sink the submarine, she dies with dignity and peace.

Mrs. Davidson

Mrs. Davidson is Moira's mother. She helps Moira mend Towers's clothes.

Sir Douglas Froude

Sir Douglas is John Osborne's great-uncle and a former general in the Australian army. In his final months, he devotes himself to drinking the three thousand bottles of vintage port stored in the cellars of the exclusive Pastoral Club.

Mr. Goldie

Mr. Goldie is the plainspoken pharmacist who describes the symptoms of radiation sickness to Peter Holmes. He demonstrates the use of the suicide tablets and syringes and informs Holmes that there will be no charge for the poison when it is needed.

Jennifer Holmes

Jennifer Holmes is the infant child of Peter and Mary Holmes. At the end of the novel, Holmes

The film version of On the Beach, *directed by Stanley Kramer and released in 1959, starred Gregory Peck as Dwight Towers and Ava Gardner as Moira Davidson.*

must inject the child with poison when the family becomes fatally ill from radiation poisoning.

Mary Holmes

Mary Holmes is the English wife of Lieutenant Commander Peter Holmes. She is supportive of her husband's naval career, even though it calls for him to be away from his family as the final days of civilization approach.

Mary's life revolves around her infant daughter, Jennifer. She has difficulty coming to terms with reality of her family's inevitable deaths and the devastation around her. To avoid it, she occupies her time by caring for her baby, housekeeping, and planning a garden that nobody will live to see.

Before leaving on an extended voyage to the United States, Peter explains to Mary that she may have to euthanize Jennifer and take a suicide tablet herself if the radiation reaches Melbourne before he returns from his mission. Mary is angry and horrified; she accuses him of trying to rid himself of his wife and child in order to run off with another woman.

It is at this point in the novel that Mary finally understands the reality of the situation. After her husband returns from his last mission, they spend their remaining time together working on the garden. They commit suicide together at the end of the novel.

Peter Holmes

Lieutenant Commander Peter Holmes of the Australian Royal Navy is appointed as the liaison officer to U.S. Commander Dwight Towers at the beginning of the novel. Peter is a good and generous man, loyal to the navy and a dutiful, loving husband to his wife, Mary. He becomes friends with Towers and introduces him to Moira Davidson. In his duties as liaison officer, Holmes goes on two missions aboard the American nuclear submarine, the *U.S.S. Scorpion.*

Before the second and final voyage, Peter reluctantly demonstrates the use of the suicide drugs to Mary in case he should not return. They have a terrible argument, but Mary ultimately recognizes the necessity of her husband's actions.

Fortunately, he does return from the mission in time to spend his final days with his family. When the first cases of radiation sickness appear in Melbourne, he bids farewell to Towers. Although Holmes and Mary get radiation sickness at approximately the same time, a couple of days later he feels as if his health is coming back. He tells John Osborne, only to be told that his recovery is only temporary. Peter decides the time has come, and he injects his baby daughter with the poison. Then he takes his tablet with Mary, committing suicide.

John Osborne

John Osborne is the pragmatic scientist assigned to the *U.S.S. Scorpion.* He studies the spread of radiation in the area. He is somewhat pessimistic and dour, as demonstrated by his comments when the submarine reaches Port Darwin:

> They learned nothing, save for the inference that when the end had come the people had died tidily. "It's what animals do," John Osborne said. "Creep away into holes to die. They're probably all in bed."
>
> "That's enough about that," the captain said.
>
> "It's true," the scientist remarked.

However, Osborne's personality changes whenever he is near his treasured racing car, a red Ferrari he obtains from a widow. Osborne, knowing the end is near, plans to fulfill his lifetime dream of racing in a Grand Prix (even though he has never raced before).

In one of the more exciting passages in the book, Osborne competes in the time trials for the Grand Prix. Several racers are killed in the trials, but Osborne perseveres and gains a place in the race. Later, Towers and Moira learn of Osborne's victory in the Grand Prix while they are on a fishing trip. In the end, Osborne takes his tablet as he sits behind the wheel of his beloved Ferrari.

Mrs. Osborne

Mrs. Osborne is John Osborne's mother. John shares a few moments with her before going to the office for the last time. She worries about her pet dog, a Pekinese named Ming. When John returns from the office, he finds his mother has taken her pill and left him a note saying goodbye. He euthanizes the dog and puts it in its basket next to his mother's bed.

Mr. Paul

At the beginning of *On the Beach,* Peter Holmes acquires milk from a farmer named Mr. Paul. His conversation with the farmer reveals the grim conditions of postwar Australia in the novel. They discuss the difficulty of obtaining fuel and other items, and the decreasing value of money is demonstrated by the farmer's casual attitude when Peter promises that he will pay for any milk that Mary needs when he returns.

Lieutenant Sunderstrom

Lieutenant Sunderstrom volunteers to go ashore to investigate the communications installation on Santa Maria Island in order to determine the origin of the mysterious radio signal. At one time stationed on the island, he is familiar with the layout of the area. Protected by a radiation suit, he determines that the signal was caused by a broken window frame resting on a transmitting key. He yearns to take a carton of Lucky Strikes that he finds at the installation, but he knows they are hot with radioactivity. He does, however, sneak back three issues of *The Saturday Evening Post.*

Ralph Swain

Radar operator Yeoman First Class Ralph Swain jumps ship when the submarine surfaces near the shore of his hometown in United States. They are unable to convince him to return as he swims to shore. The submarine returns after Sunderstrom's mission on Santa Maria Island only to find Swain fishing. The young man reports that

Media Adaptations

- *On the Beach* was adapted as a film by John Paxton in 1959. This critically acclaimed film version was directed by Stanley Kramer and features an all-star cast, including Gregory Peck as Dwight Towers, Ava Gardner as Moira Davidson, Anthony Perkins as Peter Holmes, and Fred Astaire as Julian (John in the novel) Osborne. It is available on videotape and DVD.

- There is also a 1989 audiotape version of the novel, read by James Smillie, available from Chivers Audio Books.

- A television movie version is currently in production, scheduled for broadcast in 2000. Australians Bryan Brown (Osborne) and Rachel Ward (Moira Davidson) are featured.

everyone in the city is dead. He apologizes for jumping ship, but tells the captain that he wants to die in his hometown. The captain wishes him luck and the submarine returns to Australia.

Dwight Towers

Dwight Towers is the captain of the U.S. submarine, the *U.S.S. Scorpion.* The *Scorpion* was cruising near Midway when the nuclear holocaust devastated most of the civilized world. The Australian Royal Navy ultimately sends the submarine on two missions: one to the northern coast of Australia, and one to the western coast of the United States.

Towers becomes friends with the Australian liaison officer, Lieutenant Commander Peter Holmes. Peter and his wife, Mary, introduce him to Moira Davidson, a family friend. Moira, a vivacious young woman, falls in love with him.

Towers comes to care deeply for Moira, but he cannot completely reciprocate her feelings because he is faithful to the memory of his dead wife. In fact, he behaves as if his family isn't dead. He tries to buy a special gift for each family member, such as an expensive bracelet for his wife and a fishing

Topics for Further Study

- Study the anti-nuclear movements of the past several decades. Who were the leaders of these movements? Were they successful in their efforts? What effects have nuclear accidents at power plants, such as Three Mile Island and Chernobyl, had on these movements?

- In one passage of *On the Beach,* Towers and Moira go to a museum to view paintings influenced by the devastation of the nuclear holocaust. Using whatever media you wish (pencils, paint, collage, video, etc.), make your own "statement" about nuclear warfare.

- Several of the characters in *On the Beach* spend their last days fulfilling lifelong dreams. Osborne races his car in the Grand Prix, Mary works on her garden, and Sir Douglas Froude attempts to drink thousands of bottles of port. Write an essay describing what you would do if you had only six months left to live.

- Create a timeline for the novel. How fast does radiation spread? Does the novel accurately portray what would happen in a nuclear war? How would the world's weather patterns impact the spread of radiation? Illustrate your timeline by using maps.

- Watch the film version of *On the Beach* and compare it to the novel. You might also watch other films dealing with nuclear warfare, such as *Testament* and *The Day After,* and compare them to *On the Beach.*

pole for his son. However, he cannot locate a Pogo stick for his daughter. He is moved when Moira has one specially made for him.

Towers spends a considerable amount of time with Moira. Yet he is still unable to completely relinquish the memory of his wife. His loyalty to his job prevents him from allowing her to join him on the submarine at the end of the novel. Moira drives as close as she can to the point where Towers will sink the submarine. She vows to meet him in the afterlife as she takes her suicide tablet.

Themes

Death

The inevitability of death is the major theme of *On the Beach.* With the radiation cloud approaching Melbourne, the characters in the novel are very aware of their impending deaths. The main characters are all relatively young and they struggle with the intrinsic *unfairness* of this tragedy, as Peter does when he tries to explain the situation to his wife:

> "It's the end of everything for all of us," [Peter] said. "We're going to lose most of the years of life we've looked forward to, and Jennifer's going to lose all of them."

Shute explores the way various people react to the sobering reality of death. Several of the characters in *On the Beach* are in denial, which means they ignore their impending death. For example, Mary plans a garden that she will never live to see. Towers buys thoughtful presents for his late family and remains faithful to his dead wife.

Other characters resort to self-indulgence in the face of death. Sir Douglas Froude plans to drink the entire wine inventory of the Pastoral Club. At the beginning of the novel, Moira is a somewhat promiscuous drunk. Through her growing feelings for Towers, she transforms into a selfless heroine; she tempers her drinking and self-pity in order to care for him although she knows he will never reciprocate. This selflessness is also a viable and recognized reaction to death.

Another reaction to death is to take outrageous challenges. In the novel, John Osborne's obsession with racing illustrates this reaction. Osborne is a dreary and meek man until he gets behind the wheel of his Ferarri. When Towers asks Osborne what the car is like in a race, Osborne's reply is reminiscent of someone who has been on a great roller-coaster ride:

> "You get scared stiff. Then directly it's over you want to go on and do it again."

War

On the Beach can be viewed as a cautionary fable that is meant to warn readers about the dangers of nuclear war. Written during the height of the arms race between the United States and the Soviet Union, many people believed that World War III was inevitable.

Shute is more concerned with exploring the reactions of the characters to the war's aftermath than he is with the war itself, but it is obvious that he believes that the idea of a "winnable" nuclear war is ridiculous and irresponsible. This attitude is reflected during the final conversation between Peter and Mary:

"Couldn't anyone have stopped it?" [asked Mary.]

"I don't know ... Some kinds of silliness you just can't stop." [Peter] said. "I mean, if a couple of hundred million people all decide that their national honour requires them to drop cobalt bombs upon their neighbour, well, there's not much that you or I can do about it. The only possible hope would have been to educate them out of their silliness."

Hope

In the novel, Shute recognizes the human capacity for hope under even the worst of circumstances. The Royal Australian Navy sends the *U.S.S. Scorpion* on two missions in the hope that they will find some signs of life. Peter and Mary plan a garden. However, the most stirring example of hope in the novel is Towers's fervent belief that he will be joining his wife and children in the afterlife. His hope also inspires Moira at the very end of the novel:

She took the cork out of the bottle. It was ten past ten. She said earnestly, "Dwight, if you're on your way already, wait for me."

Then she put the tablets in her mouth and swallowed them down with a mouthful of brandy, sitting behind the wheel of her big car.

Euthanasia

Euthanasia, or mercy-killing, is one of the most controversial themes of *On the Beach*. In the novel, euthanasia is used in order to save people from the horrible affects of radiation poisoning.

Radiation sickness has horribly debilitating effects on the human body. The Australian government doles out a free drug to the general public so that people may end their lives painlessly. Syringes are also provided so that people may be injected by another person. The pharmacist, Mr. Goldie, recognizes the implications of this development:

"There must be terrible complications over the religious side," he said. "I suppose then that it's a matter for the individual."

There are indeed "terrible complications." One of the most traumatic episodes in the book takes place when Peter tries to explain to Mary that it may be necessary for her to kill her own infant daughter to spare the child from suffering. Mary is understandably horrified, and she accuses Peter of trying to rid himself of her and the baby so he can

run off with another woman. Peter angrily describes an appalling scenario to shock some sense into her:

"There's another thing you'd better think about," he said. "Jennifer may live longer than you will ... You can battle on as long as you can stand, until you die. But Jennifer may not be dead. She may live on for days, crying and vomiting all over herself in her cot and laying in her muck, with you dead on the floor beside her and nobody to help her. Finally, of course, she'll die. Do you want her to die like that? If you do, I don't." He turned away. "Just think about it, and don't be such a bloody fool."

In the end, Peter is responsible for injecting his daughter with the drug. Shute examines this disturbing theme in a very straightforward manner. The novelist seems less troubled by the moral issues of euthanasia than by the circumstances that might force a man to kill his own daughter.

Style

Science Fiction

Science fiction is a type of narrative that utilizes real or imagined scientific theories and technology. Although Shute is not typically recognized as a science fiction writer, *On the Beach* can be considered a science fiction novel because it contemplates the consequences of a global nuclear war.

Some critics do not take science fiction literature seriously as a genre. However, since the late 1950s, many science fiction authors have tackled themes of enormous importance with spectacular results. Many of the writers associated with the genre, such as Harlan Ellison, Kurt Vonnegut, and J. G. Ballard, have earned the respect of critics for their insightful and stylish work.

The devastating potential of a nuclear war is the subject of many science fiction novels and short stories. Pat Frank's *Alas, Babylon* (1959), Harlan Ellison's "A Boy and His Dog" (1969), and Russell Hoban's *Riddley Walker* (1980) are just a few diverse examples. Shute is more concerned with the psychology of his characters and their reactions to their grim circumstances than he is with the war itself, but the speculative nature of the work identifies it as science fiction.

Setting

The setting of *On the Beach* is an important plot element. Australia's location spares the country from the awful destruction that takes place in other parts of the world during the war. Unfortunately, there is no escaping the radioactive fall-out that accompanies the widespread use of nuclear weapons. The earth's winds gradually move the radiation cloud southward.

Most of the novel's action takes place in and around Melbourne. As the city is in Australia's southern region, it would be of the last cities in the world to be affected by the radiation. The inhabitants of Melbourne are therefore forced to watch as the entire populations of the cities to the north die of radiation sickness.

Shute evokes a nightmarish atmosphere. For example, most of Australia's large cities are located on the coasts. This allows the *Scorpion* to directly observe the ghostly, deserted streets of Cairns and Darwin. The crew realizes that in just a few months Melbourne will look the same. Thus, the setting of the novel allows Shute to examine the behavior of characters who are aware of their terrifying predicament.

Point of View

On the Beach is written in the third-person point of view. In other words, the reader is provided with an omniscient narrative perspective in order to get the thoughts of many characters.

The majority of the book concerns the thoughts and feelings of the five major characters: Peter Holmes, Mary Holmes, Dwight Towers, Moira Davidson, and John Osborne. However, the reader is also privy to the thoughts of secondary characters, such as Lieutenant Sunderstrom.

Stereotype

There are several familiar stereotypes in *On the Beach*. Both Peter Holmes and Dwight Towers are presented as loyal, brave military men. Mary is portrayed as the devoted mother.

Perhaps most recognizable is the mousy, pragmatic scientist, John Osborne, who is characterized by his serious, sullen demeanor. Of course, he is a completely different man when he is behind the wheel of his Ferrari. He then becomes a daredevil. All of these are common stereotypes in modern fiction.

Historical Context

Australia

On the Beach is set on the island continent of Australia. As mentioned above, the setting of the

story is important as its location spares it from the destruction that takes place in the rest of the world.

Australia is the only continent occupied by a single nation. As two-thirds of the continent is desert or semi-desert, over 86% of the population lives in cities. It is the most urbanized country in the world.

When Dwight Towers visits the Davidson family's farm, he comments on the beauty of the surrounding countryside. Mrs. Davidson's reply reveals Australia's historical origins:

> "Yes, it's nice up here," said Mrs. Davidson. "But it can't compare with England. England's beautiful."

The American asked, "Were you born in England?"

"Me? No. I was born in Australia. My grandfather came out to Sydney in the early days, but he wasn't a convict. Then he took up land in the Riverina. Some of the family are there still."

The history of Australia is an interesting one. After the great navigator James Cook (1728–1779) charted the waters off the eastern coast of the continent in 1770, the English began to use New South Wales (as Australia was known at the time) as a penal colony.

The first governor-designate of New South Wales, Arthur Philip, established a settlement in Sydney Harbour on January, 26, 1788 (now celebrated as Australia Day). He had with him eleven ships, 443 seamen, 586 male and 192 female convicts, and 211 marines, as well as officials, wives, and children. Over the next several decades, there were 825 passages by convict ships transporting more than 150,000 criminals to Australia.

However, Edward Gibbon Wakefield (1796–1862), a British official who led the efforts to colonize the continent, realized that a stable, civil society could not depend entirely on the transportation of convicts. The proceeds of land sales were used to subsidize the migration of free settlers. By 1839 there were twice as many free settlers as there were convicts. Abolitionist sentiment in England, along with the resentment of the free settlers, ultimately led to the end of the use of exile as punishment for crimes.

Australia was granted independence from England on January 1, 1901. The nation maintained a close relationship with England through most of the twentieth century. Australia was a firm ally of the United States during the Cold War.

However, Australia increasingly began to view itself as an Asian nation with people of European

United States President John F. Kennedy and Soviet Premier Nikita Khrushchev met in Vienna in June, 1961, to soften the hostility between their countries, leading adversaries during the Cold War. The meetings, however, were largely unsuccessful and the threat of nuclear war remained.

descent. Although Australia's contact with America and Europe remains close, the country now has vital trading partners in the economic powerhouses of East Asia.

On February 13, 1998, Australia's legislators proposed a referendum to turn the country into a fully independent republic by severing its ties to the British Crown. The proposed Republic of Australia would replace the monarchy with an Australian citizen as president. However, in 1999, the nation voted against the referendum. Today, Aus-

tralia enjoys one of the world's highest standards of living, ranking sixteenth among the industrialized nations.

Aborigines

It might seem surprising that there is no mention of aboriginal culture in *On the Beach*. However, Shute's characters probably wouldn't have had much contact with the aborigines.

The aborigines are Australia's indigenous people. Scientists believe that the aborigines canoed to

Compare
&
Contrast

- **1954:** The United States launches the first nuclear-powered submarine, the *U.S.S. Nautilus.* In 1958 the *Nautilus* becomes the first ship to cross the North Pole.

  Today: The U.S. Navy operates approximately eighty nuclear submarines. However, reductions in defense budgeting target the latest class of nuclear attack sub, the Seawolf. Originally, the government planned to build thirty of the two-billion-dollar subs; this number was reduced to three.

- **1957:** On October 4, the Soviets launch Sputnik, the first man-made satellite, into orbit. This signals the beginning of the space race between the Soviet Union and the United States.

  Today: The U. S. space program continues to dominate space exploration. Plans are implemented to explore the surface of Mars and groundbreaking information is gathered from the Hubble telescope.

- **1957:** Australia remains close to its Western allies. Prime Minister Robert Menzies strives to attract U.S. and European investment in the country. However, the nation's growing independence from Great Britain is symbolized by the change in its monetary unit from the British pound to the dollar in 1966. Australia begins to consider itself as an Asian nation.

  Today: Despite its increasingly Asian identity, the people of Australia vote against a parliamentary referendum to become a republic.

- **1961:** American forces secretly invade Cuba on April 17 to quash Fidel Castro's communist government. The Bay of Pigs invasion, as it was known, is a disaster. The 1500 troops led by the CIA are forced to retreat. One year later, President John F. Kennedy forces the Soviets to remove nuclear missiles from Cuba during the Cuban Missile Crisis. The United States agrees to remove its missiles from Greece and Turkey in return.

  Today: Fidel Castro remains in power in Cuba. However, Castro attempts to improve his country's image by allowing Pope John Paul II to visit in 1998 and by hosting the Ibero-American summit in November, 1999.

Australia from Southeast Asia approximately 30,000 to 50,000 years ago. The aborigines were hunter-gatherers living in tribes located for the most part in the northern part of the continent.

Unfortunately, like their Native American counterparts, contact with European settlers was detrimental to their culture and their existence. When the first settlers arrived in 1788, there were approximately 750,000 aborigines. Early settlers viewed the aborigines as uncivilized savages and attacked them remorselessly over the next century. By 1930, only 67,000 aborigines remained in Australia.

Colonial leaders recognized the problem as early as 1860 when the first protection act was passed. Many reserves were also established for aboriginal use and the aboriginal people presently own 11% of Australia's land. Aborigines were granted Australian citizenship by the government in 1967, although they were not granted the right to vote until 1984.

The Cold War

On the Beach is influenced by the historical events of the Cold War between the United States (along with its Western European allies) and the Soviet Union. According to the second edition of *Webster's New Twentieth Century Dictionary,* a *cold war* can be defined as a sharp conflict in diplomacy, economics, etc. between states, regarded as potentially leading to war. During a 1947 congressional debate, American financier Bernard Baruch was one of the first people on record to use the term.

In an infamous 1946 speech, Winston Churchill warned that the United States and its allies had to be on guard against Soviet expansionism. His remarks seemed prescient when, in June 1948, the Soviet Union began the Berlin blockade, cutting off Berlin from the West. The United States began a vast airlift to keep Berlin supplied with food and fuel. In August of 1949, tensions increased even further when the Soviet Union detonated its first atomic device. For the first time, war had the potential to wipe out the human race.

America and its allies sought to impose a "policy of containment" on the Soviet Union and the spread of communism. They created the North Atlantic Treaty Organization (NATO) to prevent the Soviet Union from expanding in Western Europe. The Soviets responded by signing the Warsaw Pact with its Eastern European satellites.

Like many other people at the time, Shute believed that one of these conflicts would eventually lead to a full-scale nuclear war. The Cold War was considered over when the Berlin Wall collapsed on November 9, 1989. However, there is still a great concern over the use of nuclear weapons—as demonstrated by the nuclear testing done by India and Pakistan in 1998.

Critical Overview

On the Beach received mixed reviews when it was published in 1957. Most critical reaction focused on the antiwar theme. In a review published in a 1957 edition of the *Atlantic,* critic Edward Weeks wrote:

> Only a very humane writer could have told a story as desolate as this and made it seem at once so close and implacable. The book held a kind of cobra fascination for me. I didn't want to keep looking, but I did to the end.

The eminent critic Edmund Fuller deemed *On the Beach* "[a]n austere, grim, moving, important book that could become real." Fuller asserted that Shute had skillfully written a suspenseful novel in spite of the fact that the reader knows how the book will end:

> His success in this is manifest in the concern we feel for his characters; for concern, identification, and anguish—not surprise—are the essence of suspense.

However, it is those same characters that create problems for other critics. Several maintained that the characters are boring or unrealistic. For example, in a review published in the October 1957 edition of the *Canadian Forum,* critic Edith Fowke wrote:

> Despite its powerful theme, Nevil Shute's book is a very bad novel. The people in it are dull and unimaginative, and the ending is anticlimactic rather than apocalyptic. In fact, his characters are so flat and unappealing that you may well feel their final death from the inevitable radioactive sickness is no great loss.

Several other critics suggested that the death of the characters in the novel is a relief. Of course, to be fair, more than one critic pointed out that the lives of the characters are deliberately portrayed as being average in an effort to make readers empathize. As for an anticlimactic ending, Shute foreshadows this on the title page of his novel with a quote from T. S. Eliot's "The Hollow Men":

> In this last of meeting places / We grope together / And avoid speech / Gathered on this beach of the tumid river.... / This is the way the world ends / This is the way the world ends / This is the way the world ends / Not with a bang but a whimper.

There has been very little critical attention for Shute's novel. As it is a dated work of popular fiction, there is little for scholars to study. However, it still attracts some interest as a cautionary fable. Perhaps the fairest assessment of the novel was written by Robert H. Estabrook in the August 12, 1957, issue of *The New Republic: "On the Beach* is not great literature, but it is not, either, a mere science fiction thriller.... It falls, actually, into the category of an evangelical effort, in the form of a novel, to save the world from its own folly. Hence, its significance lies in the possibility that it might stimulate action through capturing the popular imagination...."

Criticism

Don Akers

Don Akers is a freelance writer with an interest in literature. In the following essay, he compares Shute's fictional war scenario in On the Beach *with historical events in the past several decades.*

While the literary merits of Nevil Shute's *On the Beach* may be debated, there is no doubt that

What Do I Read Next?

- For those interested in other novels by Nevil Shute, his most popular work is probably *A Town Like Alice* (1950). It chronicles Jean Paget's experiences during World War II in Malaya and her subsequent life in the Australian outback.

- Pat Frank's *Alas, Babylon* (1959) is an American novel about the survivors of a nuclear war living in Florida. A loafer named Randy Bragg turns into a leader after a bomb is dropped on Miami.

- Russell Hoban's 1980 novel, *Riddley Walker,* is set in England thousands of years in the future after a nuclear war wipes out most of the life on the planet. It relates the story of a young man's life in a neo-barbarian society. The novel is notable because of Hoban's clever use of language.

- *The Making of the Atom Bomb* (1986), written by Richard Rhodes, is an in-depth history of the development of the atom bomb. The book won several awards, including the Pulitzer Prize and National Book Critics Circle Award.

- *Australia: A Traveler's Literary Companion* (1998) is a collection of stories by some of Australia's most celebrated writers, including Peter Carey, Robert Drewe, and aboriginal writers Oodgeroo and Kabul Ooodgeroo Noonuccal. The stories present vivid portraits of Australian culture and society.

---

he struck a nerve with the readers of popular fiction in 1957.

World War II concluded with the nuclear obliteration of Hiroshima and Nagasaki. However, the end of the most destructive war of the twentieth century signaled the beginning of a new conflict: the Cold War. After defeating Germany and Japan, the Soviet Union separated from its western allies. Winston Churchill coined the term "iron curtain" in a 1946 speech describing this separation. Tensions escalated between these former allies when the Soviets detonated their own nuclear bomb in 1949.

During the next decade, a variety of events intensified worry over world peace: the Korean War; the communist witch-hunts in the United States; and the launching of the Soviet satellite Sputnik the same year *On the Beach* was published. Shute was one of many observers who believed another regional conflict like the one in Korea could very well lead to a devastating nuclear confrontation between the superpowers.

The war scenario Shute created would have been impossible during the time frame in which he set his novel (the early sixties). Of course, today's readers have the benefit of hindsight, and some elements of Shute's scenario are still worth examining. Shute based his novel on the various political conflicts of his day. Some of these animosities still exist, but today's world is much different than it was in the 1950s. Fortunately, the threat of a nuclear war between the superpowers has abated. There are still, however, great concerns over nuclear proliferation.

At this point, a brief review of Shute's fictional war is necessary. The novel begins just after Christmas, 1962. The story of the thirty-seven-day war that takes place almost a year before the opening of the novel are revealed in the thoughts and conversations of the characters. There are many gaps in their understanding of the war; in fact, even military men Dwight Towers and Peter Holmes are bewildered by many of the events and why they happened.

Early in 1962, Albania dropped a nuclear bomb on Naples, Italy. Albania's behavior is never explained. In an apparently related event, an unidentified Arab country bombed Tel Aviv, igniting an Arab-Israeli conflict. Shortly after the bombing of Tel Aviv, American and British airplanes flew over Egypt in a show of force. The Egyptians then sent a force of thirteen bombers, all of them manufactured by Russia and identified as Russian aircraft, to bomb Washington, D.C. and London. One reached the United States and two made it to London.

NATO, believing that the Russians had bombed the United States and England, dropped bombs on several Russian cities before learning that the Egyptians were to blame. China, in an attempt to take advantage of Russia's war with NATO, dropped bombs on several Russian industrial cities. However, the Soviets had been planning an attack on China even before the war with NATO. They retaliated against China swiftly. Over 4700 nuclear bombs were used during the course of the war. Much of the world is destroyed and it is only a matter of time before the radioactive fall-out wipes out the remaining life on the planet.

One of the inaccuracies in Shute's scenario is in his overestimation of the rate of nuclear proliferation among the nations of the world. When Shute wrote the book in 1957, only the United States, Soviet Union, and Great Britain had detonated nuclear weapons. By 1962, when the war in the novel takes place, France was the only nation to join the nuclear powers. Thus, it would have been impossible for the rest of the countries in Shute's book to use a nuclear bomb.

As of 1999, the United States, Russia, Britain, France, China, and Israel are recognized as major nuclear powers. India and Pakistan recently joined the "nuclear club," although their delivery systems are not as advanced as the aforementioned nations. There are approximately thirty-six additional countries with some form of nuclear capability (Albania is not one of them).

While a nuclear clash between the superpowers may not be as likely as it was in Shute's era, there is as much concern about proliferation now than there ever was. The United States and its allies fear that various "rogue states," such as Iraq, Iran, Libya, and North Korea, may develop nuclear weapons and endanger the rest of the world with their instability.

Here, Shute may yet prove to be prescient. His characters do not blame the major powers for the start of the war. They blame the "Irresponsibles," meaning the smaller, unstable countries (such as Albania and Egypt in the novel), for beginning a war that quickly grew out of control. Today's readers can see a power-hungry dictator like Saddam Hussein in Iraq playing the role of an "Irresponsible."

As mentioned above, there is no explanation given for Albania's bombing of Italy in the novel. In 1957 Albania was a Warsaw Pact country. Albania strengthened its ties with the Soviet Union when Yugoslavia broke with Stalin in the late 1940s. One can only speculate on the Albanian bombing in the novel; perhaps it was in retaliation for Italy's invasion of the country in World War II.

Shute also connects the bombing of Naples with the bombing of Tel Aviv for some reason. Perhaps this was a show of support by an Arab country for the large Muslim population of Albania. Of course, there is no mystery as to why an Arab nation such as Egypt might have bombed Israel during the early sixties. Israel was not even a decade old when Shute published his novel. The new country was surrounded by enemies and, in 1956, Israel went to war with Egypt and captured the Gaza Strip on the Sinai Peninsula. Israel fought several wars with its Arab neighbors over the next three decades.

However, Israel and Egypt signed a historic peace treaty mediated by President Jimmy Carter on March 26, 1979. In the last decade, the world has watched with hope as the Israelis and Palestinians bargain for a lasting peace.

One of the most frightening elements of Shute's fictional war is the "accidental" bombing of Russia. NATO bombs the Soviet Union in retaliation for the bombing of Washington, D.C. and London, when in fact the Egyptians are responsible. The mistakenly launched nuclear missile has been a plot element in several novels, including Eugene Burdick and Harvey Wheeler's *Fail-Safe* (1962), and films, such as Stanley Kubrick's *Dr. Strangelove or: How I Learned to Stop Worrying and Love the Bomb* (1964).

The idea is disturbing precisely because it is within the realm of possibility. After all, fallible human beings design and operate complex nuclear weapons systems. The men and women who make decisions regarding the use of these systems are not perfect. In fact, a web edition of *Scientific American* (November 1997) posted a chilling article detailing a very close call.

On January 25, 1995, Russian radar technicians picked up a troubling blip on their screens. A rocket had been launched somewhere off the coast of Norway. An American submarine could conceivably launch a rocket from that range capable of dropping eight nuclear bombs on Moscow within fifteen minutes. Boris Yeltsin was contacted immediately as the technicians tracked the trajectory of the rocket. Yeltsin was holding the electronic case that could fire Russian nuclear missiles in response. For the first time ever, that case was activated for emergency use:

> For a few tense moments, the trajectory of the mysterious rocket remained unknown to the worried Russian officials. Anxiety mounted when the separation of multiple rocket stages created an impression of a possible attack by several missiles. But the radar crews continued to track their targets, and after about eight minutes (just a few minutes short of the procedural deadline to respond to an impending nuclear attack), senior military officials determined that the rocket was headed far out to sea and posed

On August 9, 1945, the United States dropped an atomic bomb on Nagasaki, an industrial port city in Japan. The explosion destroyed nearly half of the city and killed about forty thousand people.

no threat to Russia. The unidentified rocket in this case turned out to be a U.S. scientific probe, sent up to investigate the northern lights. Weeks earlier the Norwegians had duly informed Russian officials of the launch from the offshore island of Andoya, but somehow word of the high-altitude experiment had not reached the right ears.

Although the circumstances of the "accident" in Shute's novel are quite different, the above account demonstrates the terrifying possibility of an accidental launching of nuclear missiles.

On the Beach also details an abominable concept in its description of the war between the Rus-

sians and the Chinese: radiological warfare. Rather than use their nuclear arsenals as defensive weapons, the two nations simultaneously plan to drop hydrogen bombs on each other in a strategic use of radiation.

First of all, as noted above, this would have been impossible in 1962 because the Chinese had not yet developed a bomb. Second, even though Sino-Soviet relations deteriorated after the death of Joseph Stalin, both countries were too involved in their own affairs to meddle with each other. Finally, it is hard to believe that either government would choose to follow such an insane path. Sino-Soviet relations were normalized once again when Mikhail Gorbachev met Deng Xiaoping during a 1989 summit in Beijing.

In conclusion, the Cold War tensions that influenced the creation of a work like *On the Beach* are today virtually nonexistent. The world rejoiced when the symbol of communist oppression, the Berlin Wall, was brought down in November of 1989. Of course, even though a major conflict doesn't appear imminent, there are some potentially dangerous situations in various hot spots around the globe. The recent ethnic and religious hostilities in the Balkans serve as an example.

Shute's intent was to educate people on the madness of nuclear war. One would like to think that he accomplished his objective, but a recent vote in the U.S. Senate might indicate otherwise. Partisan conflict prevented the ratification of a worldwide nuclear test ban treaty. Certain U.S. senators might serve their constituents better if they were to read *On the Beach*.

Source: Don Akers, in an essay for *Novels for Students,* Gale, 2000.

Gene LaFaille

In the following review LaFaille contrasts the book to Pat Frank's Alas, Babylon.

Nevil Shute's *On the Beach,* although certainly intended for a mainstream audience when it was first published in 1957, immediately attracted the attention of the science fiction community because of its brilliant and horrifying depiction of the end of human life after an atomic war. *On the Beach* begins in Melbourne, Australia, in 1963, one year after a limited exchange of atomic weapons between China and Russia resulted in a wider conflict between the superpowers, as well as a series of regional conflicts with further atomic warfare. The result of this cataclysm is that there are no outward signs of human life after an atomic war. *On the Beach* begins in Melbourne, Australia in 1963, one year after a limited exchange of atomic weapons between China and Russia resulted in a wider conflict between the superpowers, as well as a series of regional conflicts with further atomic warfare. The result of this cataclysm is that there are no outward signs of human life in the Northern Hemisphere, and all life appears to be dying as the radioactive fallout is swept further and further south toward Australia by the wind. The impact of this approaching death on the increasingly restricted lives of the people of Australia over the

course of the next year is admirably chronicled in *On the Beach,* but the focus of the novel is on the interaction of American naval officer Dwight Towers and Australian naval officer Peter Holmes, as well as on their friends and families. Towers, commander of the nuclear submarine *U.S.S. Scorpion,* which had been forced to travel to Australia in order to survive the holocaust, has left his family in America, where by now everyone is certainly dead. Holmes is the father of a new baby; his wife cannot fathom the finality of the approaching doom. Thrown together by the demands of this emergency and the need to work together in order to have a purpose in life, each struggles to maintain his sanity and values in a society that is slowly losing its grip on what is normal....

Despite the possibility of becoming a hysterical work, as did Pat Frank's *Alas, Babylon, On the Beach* never succumbs to that level, maintaining the narrative thread of an unrelenting fate even in the most tearful of situations. Women of the 1990s may be offended by the limited and stereotypical roles for women in this work, but *On the Beach* accurately reflects 1950s society. Moreover, it is the message that is important, and that message is as powerful after thirty-five years as when it was written. *On the Beach* is mesmerizing in its intensity, and almost impossible to put down once begun. This is very highly recommended for grade nine to adult collections in school and public libraries.

Source: Gene LaFaille, review of *On the Beach,* in *Wilson Library Bulletin,* Vol. 66, No. 10, 1992, p. 131.

Julian Smith

In the essay below, Smith discusses how Shute came to write On the Beach, *noting the author's progress from optimism to pessimism and back again before, during, and after the novel's writing.*

Saturday, November 6th. The blast at Amchitka had gone off six hours before, generating lord only knows what shockwaves in the Pacific, not to mention concerned comments on the eleven o'clock news. The news ended, and the first of the late movies began: Stanley Kramer's *On the Beach,* based upon Nevil Shute's novel.

An epiphany! That movie of all movies on that night of all nights. The first important film treatment of nuclear holocaust, it premiered all around the world just thirteen years ago last November. I sat through it to the bitter end—everyone dead and a banner flying across the screen: THERE'S STILL TIME, BROTHER.

Thirteen years. And we're still playing with our devil toys. Is there really still time, brother, before the world ends, not with a bang but a whimper? The newscaster made a cute allusion to Eliot's lines, but I'm not being cute here, for Shute's novel took its title and epigraph from "The Hollow Men":

In this last meeting place
We grope together
And avoid speech
Gathered on this beach of the tumid river....
This is the way the world ends ...

Feeling on the beach myself, I sit down to tell you the story of how Nevil Shute, a most unlikely pacifist, came to write what is probably the most famous and best-selling antibomb novel of, as the expression goes, all time.

Oddly enough, I discovered the genesis of *On the Beach* with the help of a federal agency (no, not the CIA). It all started right in the middle of the campus unrest following the first of our annual territorial extensions of the Vietnam war, and during a period when I was having most grave doubts about the wisdom of ever having anything further to do with our government. It was then that I was co-opted most sinisterly via a travel and research grant from the National Endowment for the Humanities. Why had my soul, I wondered, suddenly become so valuable? So it came to pass that I found myself bestilled in the National Liberty of Australia, there charged with somehow making a "wider application of humanistic knowledge and insights to the general public interest". Luckily, I discovered letters and notes, some on the back of the proverbial envelope, tracing the growth of *On the Beach*. And therein lies the story of an engineer and novelist who suddenly came to the realization that the technology he had espoused all his life might not after all be capable of creating an earthly paradise.

An earthly paradise—Shute took pride in the fact that he used the money from the only prize he won at Oxford to buy a slide rule and a copy of William Morris' *The Earthly Paradise*. But he quickly forgot his Morris. From the end of the First War to the outbreak of the Second, he was an aeronautical engineer. After a very responsible position in England's disastrous rigid-airship program in the twenties, he became a founder and managing director of an aviation firm that helped develop a number of technologies (in-flight refueling, for one) that would make air warfare the tremendous success it is. In 1939, angered by the shortsightedness of air-raid planning for the coming war, he wrote a very accurate description of the impact of

bombing on the civilian population of England. The book was a great popular hit but somehow missed pointing out that dropping bombs on people was, well, immoral. And during the war he headed the engineering staff for a secret Admiralty department charged with developing clever ways of dispatching the Boche. Chief among his toys was a gigantic flame-thrower for knocking down low-flying planes. Ultimately impractical, the flamethrower scheme gave him the idea for a novel in which the heroes have lots of fun squirting *dirty* burning oil on Germans in order to kill and maim them in a particularly nasty way meant to impress the dispirited French. Oh, noble aspirations of man. Oh, William Morris.

How did this man of the machine, this author of twenty-odd romantic potboilers, decide to write *the* classic story of the end of the world? The answer, very simply, is that he didn't decide any such thing, that he set out quite cheerfully to write a kind of Australian Swiss Family Robinson about civilization carrying on Down Under after the big war Up Above.

It was exactly the same thing that happened to Mark Twain when he started *A Connecticut Yankee in King Arthur's Court:* let's think of all the funny and wonderful things that could happen to a clever Yankee thrown back to the sixth century. Poor Twain, he set his Yankees in motion, and before he could stop him, Hank Morgan had machine-gunned, dynamited, and electrocuted thirty thousand knights—and found himself surrounded, trapped, and doomed by a pile of rotting corpses. What a paradigm of total war was there! So with Shute, as we will see.

The idea for *On the Beach* "started as a joke", Shute wrote a friend. "Now that I was living in Australia I kidded my friends in the northern hemisphere, telling them that if they weren't careful with atomic explosions they'd destroy themselves and we Australians would inherit the world". "The idea stayed in my mind in that form for about a year, in a slightly cynical or humorous form", he wrote an interviewer; but when research on the subject showed him that Australia would not escape a general doom but would only have a one-year reprieve, "it became an attractive speculation—what would ordinary people in my part of the world do with that year"? An *attractive* speculation. How Mark Twain must have smiled when his friends who roam through the world seeking the ruin of souls told him about that one. Behold, he who builds attractive speculations upon the misery of others shall be cast down.

The casting down of Nevil Shute began even before he started writing *On the Beach*. In mid-1954, while the idea for the book was still in its cynical form, he spent six weeks visiting West Australian oil-exploration sites. If civilization was to flourish in oil-poor Australia in the absence of the northern nations, a large part of the drama would be found in the discovery of native oil resources. It would be an exciting story, the kind he had been telling since his first Australian novel, *A Town Like Alice* (1950). At about the time he started research for the after-the-war book, he gushed to an interviewer that Australia "is a country with everything before it. It's what's called an expanding economy. Every time you drive along the road to town you see a new factory going up. It gives you a kind of kick to see that".

But within a year of the trip to the would-be oil fields, he had written his dreariest, most static novel, *Beyond the Black Stump,* in which an American oil-survey team finds no oil, in which the Australian heroine forsakes her family's remote sheep ranch for the bright America she discovers in the *Saturday Evening Post*—and returns disillusioned to her starting point. Never had he written such a book; the sense of movement and change and expansion that had marked his earlier books was suddenly aborted and would soon be followed by that almost motionless story of waiting for the end of mankind.

"When I was a student I was taught that engineering was 'the art of directing the great sources of Power in Nature to the use and convenience of man.'" Shute had operated throughout his professional life on that principle, but something had made him change: perhaps it was the result of thinking about the abuse of those great sources of Power in Nature that had made nuclear catastrophe a constant threat. But there is no way of knowing how the change came about—among the piles of notes and letters, no external clue to the internal process that darkened him, convinced him of a universal fate.

On the Beach envisions a world done in by gadgets, but a world that still loves the gadgets which have destroyed and will outlast their markers and quondam masters. The best example is the cataclysmic auto race that comes late in the novel. Round and round the track goes mankind, concerned only with proving that one machine is faster than another, concerned more with the efficiency of the machine than the safety of the men who use them or worship them. Shute was not mocking man, only explaining how things are. In fact, he bought a brand new Jaguar XK 140 when he started writing *On the Beach* and raced it himself in order to write about racing in the novel—or that was his excuse. From beginning to end, the novel is suffused with man's love for his creations: the scientist who carefully prepares his Ferrari for eternal storage before taking a suicide pill in the driver's seat; the captain who takes his submarine out to sea and sinks it, crew and all, rather than leave it behind "unprotected". Best of all, the book's last sentence: back on the beach a young woman watches the submarine disappear, then takes her pills, "swallowing them down with a mouthful of brandy, sitting behind the wheel of the big car". Drug, drink, car: the best the world has to offer. No criticism intended.

Ah, Amchitka. We don't intend to *use* our bombs, you understand. We just want to see if they will work.

On the Beach's message, if any, is that the human race was a nice try. Unfortunately, it worked too well, trundling down the path until it found a way to destroy itself. This is not the novel of an angry man or even an anxious man, but of a man who has seen the possibilities and accepted them. Mankind endures in obedience only, making its appointed rounds, going about its business as usual, indulging in that hobgoblin of little minds (for the average human mind *is* little): consistency. Once a thousand rockets have been launched by mistake, why not launch the rest?

The novel's obvious sincerity has kept it alive, and so has its versatility. It has been praised by pacifists, theologians, philosophers, political scientists—and now crops up on environmental reading lists. Indeed, it was probably the first important fictional study of ecological disaster. The Australian heroine rejects her fate as unfair, for "No one in the Southern Hemisphere ever dropped a bomb.... We had nothing to do with it. Why should we have to die because other countries nine or ten thousand miles away from us wanted to have a war"? Having discovered Spaceship Earth for himself, Shute probably did more than any other writer of the fifties to make a large audience understand that men must suffer equally the results of what they do at home or allow to happen far away. Moreover, the novel's stoicism and objectivity left the burden for feeling on the reader, made it clear that the author didn't care one way or another how his audience reacted. After all, "It's not the end of the world", says Shute's alter ego, the auto-racing scientist. "It's only the end of us. The world will go on just the same, only we shan't be in it. I daresay it will get along all right without us".

Another writer talented at looking at the future, Philip Wylie, suggested that *On the Beach* "ought to be compulsory reading at the Pentagon, West Point, Annapolis. Ike should set aside his western and puzzle his way through it". When I came across a letter from John Kennedy, then a senator, thanking Shute's American publishers for sending him a copy of the novel, I wondered for a minute whether he would have dared the Cuban Missile Crisis had he read *On the Beach*. Then I came back to reality: presidents don't need novelists to tell them what can happen—they already know, or are supposed to. No, Shute was talking to the ordinary reader, the man charged with the extraordinary responsibility of telling his politicians what to do. And when I read John Kennedy's letter, I suddenly remembered that 1962, the year Shute chose for Armageddon, was also the year of the Cuban Missile Crisis. And if the reader in 1973 quivers a bit when he remembers that Shute's Russian-Chinese war grew out of Arab-Israeli conflict, then Shute's little time bomb is still lethal.

Exactly a hundred years before Shute's doomsday, Henry Adams made his own prediction in a letter to his brother: "Man has mounted science, and is now run away with. Some day science may have the existence of mankind in its power, and the human race commit suicide by blowing up the world".

Is there really still time, brother?

EPILOGUE

Shute finished his novel in late 1956. In November, 1959, the month he saw Kramer's film, he began the story of a miraculous birth in the Australian wilderness, an epiphany witnessed by "three wise men" bearing a series of gifts that sound like a return to the wishful thinking that preceded the writing of *On the Beach:* the gifts of oil to Australia through known coal deposits, of water by magnetic distillation, of defense against radioactivity. In other words, self-sufficiency in industry and agriculture combined with protection from the follies of the rest of the world—all sanctified

through an implied or explicit Second Coming. He had recovered the optimism that the creation of *On the Beach* had robbed him of. He never lived to finish the novel, but died two months later while Kramer's film was premiering all around the world. It was almost as though he had been struck down before he had a chance to undercut his own last testament to the world.

Source: Julian Smith, "On the Beach at Amchitka: The Conversion of Nevil Shute," *South Atlantic Quarterly,* Vol. 72, 1973, pp. 22-28.

Sources

Bruce G. and Harold A. Blair and Frank N. VonHippel, "Taking Nuclear Weapons Off Hair-Trigger Alert," *Scientific American,* http://www.sciam.com/1197issue/1197von-hippel.html.

Robert H. Estabrook, "After Armageddon," in *The New Republic,* Vol. 137, No. 20, August 12, 1957, p. 20.

Edith Fowke, in a review in *Canadian Forum,* Vol. 37, No. 166, October, 1957.

Edmund Fuller, in a review in the *Chicago Sunday Tribune,* August 4, 1957, p. 1.

Bruce Ryan, "Australia," in Compton's Encyclopedia Online v 3.0, http://comptonsv3.web.aol.com.

Edward Weeks, in a review in the *Atlantic,* Vol. 200, No. 80, August 1957.

For Further Study

Richard Rhodes, *Dark Sun: The Making of the Hydrogen Bomb,* Simon & Schuster, 1995, 731 p.
    The sequel to his Pulitzer Prize-winning history *The Making of the Atom Bomb* (1986).

Nevil Shute, *Slide Rule: The Autobiography of an Engineer,* Morrow, 1954, 254 p.
    Shute's autobiography chronicles his experiences as an engineer and a writer.

Julian Smith, *Nevil Shute,* Twayne, 1976, 166 p.
    Smith provides the only critical biography of Nevil Shute. Although this book is no longer in print, it is available in its entirety on the web at *http://www.cha-neover.com/shutebio/.*

H. A. Taylor, *Airspeed Aircraft since 1931,* Putnam, 1970, 206 p.
    Recounts the history of Shute's aircraft company.

Out of Africa

**Isak Dinesen
1937**

Isak Dinesen's autobiographical novel, *Out of Africa,* recounts the years she spent on a coffee plantation in East Africa. Published in 1937, the book garnered critical and popular acclaim, especially in Britain and America. The award-winning 1985 film version, which won an Oscar for best picture, prompted a resurgence of interest in the book and helped place it on the best-seller list several years after her death.

Out of Africa is comprised of a series of Dinesen's observations of the African landscape and character sketches of the East Africans and transplanted Europeans she met there. In her article in *The New York Times Book Review,* Katherine Woods maintains, "Africa lives through all this beautiful and heart-stirring book because of that simple and unsought-for fusion of the spirit, lying behind the skill which can put the sense of Africa's being into clear, right, simple words, through the things and people of the farm."

Yet *Out of Africa* is not just an account of what the author found in Africa; it is also the story of how an independent and courageous woman came to understand and define herself. Woods concludes that Dinesen "tells the story with quiet and noble beauty. And one knows that her wish for life as a whole has been fulfilled by Africa: she did not let it go until it blessed her."

Isak Dinesen

Author Biography

On April 17, 1885, Dinesen was born Christence Dinesen in Rungsted, Denmark. Her love of painting prompted her to study art at the Royal Academy of Fine Arts in Copenhagen, where she developed an eye for landscape details—a talent that would be reflected later in her writing.

She continued her studies in Oxford, Paris, and Rome and began to write short fiction and novels. In 1907 a literary magazine in Denmark published her short story, "The Hermits," under the pseudonym Osceola.

After a failed love affair with her cousin, Hans Blixen-Finecke, Christentze (she preferred to be called Karen), announced to her family that she planned to marry Hans's twin brother Bror, a big-game hunter and writer.

The couple married and moved to Kenya, where, with financial aid from her family, they purchased six thousand acres of land. Her marriage to Bror did not survive (they were divorced in 1921), but her love of the land and the people of Africa endured through the hardships she faced as a woman managing a coffee plantation on her own.

While in Africa, Dinesen wrote letters and composed stories that she would share with visiting friends. She left Africa in 1931 after financial problems forced her to sell the farm and returned to Denmark where she completed her first book, *Seven Gothic Tales* (1934).

In 1937 the memoirs of her time in Africa, *Out of Africa,* was published; she used the pseudonym Isak, which is Hebrew for the word "laughter." From 1931 until her death in Rungsted on September 7, 1962, this prolific author produced short story collections, essays, novels, poetry, plays, and memoirs written in both Danish and English.

Plot Summary

Part I: Kamante and Lulu

Out of Africa opens with a description of East Africa—of its views "immensely wide" and its "heroic and romantic air." From 1913–1931 Isak Dinesen (the pseudonym of Karen Christentze Dinesen Blixen) owned and operated a coffee plantation on the outskirts of what is now Nairobi, Kenya, until financial problems forced her to sell it and return to her home in Denmark. Her six thousand acres of land is used for different purposes: six hundred for the coffee beans and one thousand for the East African "squatters" who work the farm a set number of days for the right to live there. The remaining acres include a wide expanse of forest.

Dinesen finds it difficult to get to know the East Africans who work on her farm but eventually becomes friendly with them. Moreover, she is impressed with their courage, sincerity, and closeness to the land. She admits, "The discovery of the dark races was to me a magnificent enlargement of all my world."

One day on the farm, she meets Kamante, the nine-year-old son of one of her squatters. She tries to treat the sores covering his thin legs but is unsuccessful and so sends him to the Scotch Mission hospital where he stays for three months while his legs heal. Kamante is "a wild creature" when she first meets him, "so utterly isolated from the world, and, by a sort of firm deadly resignation, completely closed to all surrounding life."

After he returns from the Mission, he becomes one of Dinesen's trusted servants and friends. He helps her care for Lulu, a young antelope, who causes the house to become "one with the African landscape." In this section, Dinesen also introduces two other servants, Farah Aden and Ismail, and an old, eccentric Dane named Knudson.

Part II: The Shooting Incident

One night Kabero, the seven-year-old son of an old squatter named Kaninu, accidentally shoots two boys. One soon dies while the other, whose lower jaw has been shot off, slowly recovers in the hospital. The old men on the farm decide to set a Kyama on the case, made up of an assembly of elders authorized by the government to settle disputes among the squatters. The men, however, have trouble resolving the case and after a long period of disruption among the families, which includes accusations of sorcery, Chief Kinanjui is called to pass judgment. The matter is finally settled.

Part III: Big Dances

Native dances called Ngomas are held and soon become "the greatest social functions of the farm." One night, warriors from the neighboring Masai tribe attend the Ngoma and fighting erupts. In order to keep the authorities out of the incident, Dinesen nurses the injured men back to health.

Foreign visitors to the farm include some of Farah's Indian friends, members of his wife's family, and Emmanuelson, a Swede who is befriended by the Masai. Dinesen enjoys the company of these guests as she learns of their culture and experiences.

Two visitors who become great friends are British expatriates Barkeley Cole and Denys Finch-Hatton. They bring her fine wine, gramophone records, books, and good conversation about their African adventures. She in return offers them the comforts of home and recites the stories she has written for their entertainment. Both men help her get to know the people and the landscape of her new home.

Part IV: The Wild Came to the Aid of the Wild

This section includes fragments of Dinesen's comments on her surroundings. In these brief tales and verbal snapshots, she reveals her appreciation of the independence, resilience, and beauty of the people and animals she observes. She also notes the harsh existence suffered by many.

When World War I comes to East Africa, she travels the rough terrain bringing provisions and ammunition to the British troops on the border and forges a special bond with the Africans who ac-

company her. When Denys flies her in his plane over the landscape, she marvels at its beauty.

Part V: Farewell to the Farm

Seasons of drought and falling coffee prices force Dinesen to sell the farm. During the long departure process, she gradually disengages herself from the land and its people. She sells most of the contents of the house and refuses to allow Chief Kinanjui to end his life at her farm, fearing the wrath of government officials. At this point Dinesen admits, "I had not got it in me any longer to stand up against the authorities of the world."

Her two closest friends have died—Barkeley of heart failure and Denys in a plane crash. Yet she does fulfill two promises before she leaves: she buries Denys on a hill overlooking the farm and within view of Kilimanjaro and Mount Kenya. Later, when she hears reports of lions standing or lying on his grave for long periods of time, she finds it "fit and decorous" that the lions should "make him an African monument."

When her squatters come to her with fears about their forced relocation after the farm is sold, she helps them find a place to live. She explains, "it is more than their land that you take away from the people, whose native land you take. It is their past as well, their roots and their identity." As she prepares to depart, her friend Ingrid Lindstrom and the women on the farm give her comfort. She watches the landscape disappear from the window of her train out of Nairobi.

Characters

Farah Aden

Farah is Isak Dinesen's Somali servant. He remains with her the entire time she is in Africa and serves as her interpreter with the squatters.

Belknap

Belknap is Dinesen's American mill manager, an "exceptionally capable, inspired mechanic, but of an uneven mind." His mood swings are "a kind of emotional daily gymnastics to a lively temperament, much in need of exercise, and to which too little was happening."

Karen Blixen

See Isak Dinesen

A still from the 1985 film version of Out of Africa *captures the beauty of Kenya's sweeping landscape.*

Mr. Bulpett

Old Mr. Bulpett, also known as Uncle Charles, often comes to the farm for dinner. Dinesen regards him as an ideal English Victorian gentleman, noting he had swum the Hellespont, climbed the Matterhorn, and been romantically involved with a famous woman.

Barkeley Cole

Like Denys Finch-Hatton, Barkeley is a British expatriate who becomes good friends with Dinesen. From his neighboring farm on Mount Kenya, he brings her fine wine, books, and conversation while she offers him "a chosen, comfortable corner of the world." Like Denys, he is an outcast.

A good judge of people, he harbors no illusions about life. Although he suffers from heart problems, he is also "a source of heat and fun." He dreams of running off with Dinesen to have adventures in foreign countries, but their lack of money keeps them in Africa. During his time in Africa, he became intimate with the Masai and so could speak with them "of the old days in their own tongue." Before Dinesen leaves the farm, he dies of heart disease.

Isak Dinesen

Out of Africa is Dinesen's autobiography of her time in Kenya where she owns and operates a coffee plantation. She also acts as doctor, teacher, judge and friend to those who work for her and live on her land.

During her eighteen years on the farm, she develops a great love of the land and its people and forges strong friendships with them that last a lifetime. This love is evident in the stories, character sketches, and observations that she begins to record during lonely nights at the farm. After a series of financial setbacks, she is forced to sell the farm and leave her beloved Africa.

Emmanuelson

Emmanuelson is a gregarious Swede who works at a hotel in Nairobi. He asks Dinesen for a loan to help him journey to Tanganyika after losing his job. He explains he is an actor and hopes to find work there. She worries he will perish in the hot sun or be attacked by lions and/or Masai warriors. Six months later a letter arrives with her money and the news that he reached Tanganyika, ironically, with the aid of the Masai.

Esa

Esa is a servant on the farm. When his brother dies and leaves him a black cow, the once gentle and unassuming Esa determines "that from now fortune was going to smile on him" and so begins to develop "a terrible confidence in things." He decides to take a second wife, but she is young and headstrong and keeps running away from him. Eventually she poisons him and he dies.

Fathers

The fathers are a group of priests who live in the nearby French Roman Catholic Mission. When Dinesen attends Sunday mass, they provide news of the colony, "like a small lively group of brown, furry bees,—for they all grew long, thick beards." While showing keen interest in the life of the colony, they are "in their own French way exiles, patient and cheerful obeisants to some higher orders of a mysterious nature."

Denys Finch-Hatton

Finch-Hatton is an athlete, musician, art lover, and fine sportsman. When he decides to stay in East Africa, he moves in with Dinesen. He teaches her Latin, encourages her to read the Bible and the Greek poets, and brings her a gramophone that becomes "the voice of the farm." They enjoy the land together, whether on safari or from his plane. The East Africans admire his "absolute lack of self-consciousness, or self-interest," and his "unconditional truthfulness."

After he dies in a plane crash, Dinesen notes that "he had watched and followed all the ways of the African Highlands, and better than any other white man, he had known their soil and seasons, the vegetation and the wild animals, the winds and smells ... their people. He had taken in the country, and in his eyes and his mind it had been changed, marked by his own individuality, and made part of him."

Ismail

Ismail is a strict Mohammedan Somali gun-bearer who works for Dinesen during her first years in Africa.

Kabero

Kabero is the seven-year-old son of the old squatter Kaninu. While playing one day, Kabero accidentally shoots two boys and runs off to live with the Masai. When he returns, he is a young man, "a Masai from head to foot," with a "rigid, passive, and insolent bearing."

Media Adaptations

- *Out of Africa* was adapted as a film by Kurt Luedtke and based on Dinesen's autobiography and her *Letters from Africa.* Sydney Pollack directed and Meryl Streep and Robert Redford (as Denys Finch-Hatton) starred. It is available from MCA/Universal Home Video.

- The book was recorded in an audio version read by Julie Harris, West Audio, May 1988.

Kamante

Kamante is the nine-year-old son of one of her squatters. She tries to treat the scores covering his thin legs but is unsuccessful; subsequently, she sends him to the Scotch Mission hospital where he stays for three months. Kamante is "a wild creature" when she first meets him, "so utterly isolated from the world, and, by a sort of firm deadly resignation, completely closed to all surrounding life.... He had no wish for any sort of contact with the world round him, the contacts that he had known of had been too cruel for that."

When he returns from the hospital, he works as her servant for the next twelve years until she leaves the country. He takes care of her dogs, assists her doctoring, and becomes her cook.

Kaninu

Kaninu is Kabero's father.

Chief Kinanjui

Chief Kinanjui rules over more than one hundred thousand Kikuyus, the tribe that lives on the farm. He helps Dinesen settle disputes among the squatters.

Kitosch

Dinesen tells the story of this native man who dies after being flogged by his white master. After being tied up all night, Kitosch had decided that he wanted to die, and shortly thereafter, did.

Old Knudson

An old blind Danish man, Knudson is allowed to remain on Dinesen's farm for six months until his death.

Ingrid Lindstrom

Ingrid is Dinesen's neighbor and friend. She comforts Dinesen during her final days in Africa, understanding "to the bottom of her heart, with great strength, with something of the strength of the elements themselves, what it is really like, when a woman farmer has to give up her farm, and leave it."

Themes

Search for Self

The predominant theme of *Out of Africa* is the search for self. Soon after Dinesen relocates to East Africa, she finds herself alone in a foreign land with the enormous responsibility of trying to operate a successful coffee plantation. In order to accomplish this, she must get to know the land and the East Africans who work for and with her. In the process, she learns more about herself.

During her time in Africa, Dinesen transforms from a Danish aristocrat to a woman who forges a spiritual union with her new home. At one point she asks: "If I know a song of Africa ... of the Giraffe, and the African new moon lying on her back, of the ploughs in the fields, and the sweaty faces of the coffee-pickers, does Africa know a song of me?"

Later, she answers that question when she acknowledges, "The grass was me, and the air, the distant invisible mountains were me, the tired oxen were me. I breathed with the slight wind in the thorntrees."

Individual vs. Nature

One way Dinesen explores her self-identity is through her relationship with the land, which she finds challenging yet beautiful. She learns to stand her ground with lions and to cross a desert. When she decides to take provisions to British troops on the border at the outbreak of World War I, she travels for three months through rough terrain with a caravan of East Africans. She remembers, "The air of the African highlands went to my head like wine, I was all the time slightly drunk with it, and the joy of these months was indescribable."

Topics for Further Study

- Research the colonization of Kenya. Discuss how East Africans were treated during the first part of the twentieth century. How has the situation changed?

- Read Dinesen's *Letters from Africa,* and compare it to *Out of Africa.* What details did Dinesen omit from the latter work? Why do you think she omitted them?

- Investigate the culture of the Masai and of the Kikuyu. How does your research compare to Dinesen's characterizations of these tribes in *Out of Africa?*

- Some critics find examples of racism in Dinesen's autobiographical novel. Summarize their arguments and defend or refute them.

She also found incredible grace in the landscape. When a young antelope she names Lulu decides to take up residence at her farmhouse, she determines that "Lulu came in from the wild world to show that we were on good terms with it, and she made my house one with the African landscape, so that nobody could tell where the one stopped and the other began."

She later maintains that "the years in which Lulu and her people came round to my house were the happiest of my life in Africa. For that reason, I came to look upon my acquaintance with the forest antelopes as ... a token of friendship from Africa."

Freedom

Dinesen finds "infinite freedom" in Africa, explaining that "it is there that things are going on, destinies are made round you, there is activity to all sides, and it is none of your concern." While on the farm, she experiences a kind of freedom not usually allowed a woman at that time. Through her interactions with the land and the people of Africa, Dinesen acts a farmer, a doctor, a teacher, a judge, a storyteller, and a friend.

Courage

To live and flourish in Africa, Dinesen exhibited much courage. She deals with lonely nights on the farm by composing stories that she later relates to friends who visit. She learns how to survive the harsh environment and shoots game when necessary. She also shows courage when she accepts her failure to keep the farm and her departure from the land that she has grown to love.

Culture Clash

In *Out of Africa,* Dinesen records the clash between the European settlers and the East Africans, which involve issues of class conflict and prejudice. In fact, she compares the treatment of the Africans to the treatment of oxen: "the oxen in Africa have carried the heavy load of the advance of European civilization ... all of that we have taken away from the oxen, and in reward we have claimed their existence for ourselves."

Unlike most of her fellow Europeans, Dinesen embraces the differences she finds between herself and the East Africans and often adopts their customs and attitudes. Her relationship with them evolves into friendship.

Style

Point of View

Dinesen—or Karen Blixen as she identifies herself in the work—serves as narrator/storyteller throughout *Out of Africa.* This narrative method brings not only the African people and landscape to life; it also provides a chronicle of the narrator's journey of self-discovery.

Setting

One of the work's focal points is the harmonious relationship the African people have with the land. Dinesen also comes to enjoy this type of connection, as evident in the following passage from the book:

> The plains with the thorntrees on them were already quite dark, but the air was filled with clarity to grow big and radiant in the course of the night was now just visible, like a silver point in the sky of citrine topaz. The air was cold to the lungs, the long grass dripping wet, and the herbs on it gave out their spiced astringent scent. In a little while on the sides the cicada would begin to sing. The grass was me, and the air, the distant invisible mountains were me, the tired oxen were me. I breathed with the slight wind in the thorntrees.

Dinesen's details about Africa create a mythic vision of the land. By the end of the book, the setting becomes a reflection of her mood. As she prepares to leave, she insists "the attitude of the landscape towards me changed. Till then I had been part of it.... Now the country disengaged itself from me, and stood back a little, in order that I should see it clearly and as a whole." This final vision is symbolic of all she feels she is leaving behind.

Structure

Out of Africa's unique structure contains fragmented yet interrelated stories, character sketches, and observations of Africa and its people.

Symbolism

Dinesen's story fragments and character sketches, as well as her setting details, are often symbolic. In one story she writes of a time when her manager, while trying to break an ox for the farm, tied it up for the night. The next morning they discovered that a leopard had attacked it and so the ox had to be destroyed. When Dinesen concludes, "he would not be yoked now," she alludes to the strong desire for freedom that she found everywhere in Africa.

In another episode, she explains that she once shot an iguana, thinking that its multicolored skin would make "pretty things" for her. She discovered, however, that once dead, all the color had drained from it. Later she bought an embroidered bracelet from a native that looked lifeless when she put it on her own arm. These incidents show her the importance of the individual spark of life and of preserving that uniqueness.

Historical Context

British East Africa

In the latter part of the nineteenth century, European countries, especially Britain and Germany, began to colonize an area of British East Africa that is now called Kenya. The Europeans realized that the sparsely populated land promised political and economic opportunities.

In 1887 the Imperial British East Africa Company, a trading organization under government control, rented the land from the sultan of Zanzibar, who ruled over the area. By 1895 the influence of the British government in the East Africa increased when it established a "Protectorate," a

Kenyan warriors of the Kikuyu tribe assemble, dressed in ceremonial costume.

system often established in colonized countries. A protectorate established an official relationship between the colonizers, usually powerful Europeans, and then colonized in an area that had not yet established a political system of its own.

In an effort to secure political and economic control of the land, the British planned the construction of an extensive rail system. When the costs of the project began to mount, the government encouraged settlers from other countries to buy large parcels of East African land. The British had a difficult time, though, convincing Europeans to travel such a long distance and settle in a foreign land under harsh conditions.

Some settlers did come, especially middle- and upper-class Europeans who could afford to set up a comfortable lifestyle and to take financial losses as they learned new farming techniques. These settlers maintained a distance from the East Africans and relegated them to an inferior, servant status. The number of settlers increased dramatically in the early part of the twentieth century from approximately six hundred in 1905 to more than five thousand in 1914. Farmers made up the largest part of this population, followed by government officials and missionaries.

Kikuyu

The Kikuyu people lived in the area of East Africa where Karen Blixen had her farm. Marshall S. Clough in *Fighting Two Sides: Kenyan Chiefs and Politicians, 1918-1940* observed that the Kikuyu's customs were influenced by the mountainous African landscape. He maintains that "the first pioneers settled the land ridge by ridge—Kikuyu families staking their claims and others moving on to stake theirs—and the ridges, easily defended and dangerous to assault, developed into self-sufficient little communities."

This lack of central government helped the European colonizers set up their own system. Settlers were able to take over East African land from the Kikuyu with the aid of the British Protectorate. After suffering a wave of smallpox, drought, and insects that destroyed their crops, the Kikuyu put up little resistance, holding onto the false assumption that the presence of the Europeans would be temporary.

Nairobi

In the nineteenth century, the Uganda Railroad made Nairobi an important trade center and the center of British East Africa. The city offered relatively comfortable accommodations for European set-

Compare & Contrast

- **1895:** The British government establishes the East Africa Protectorate, which controls the political and economic life of the people of what is now called Kenya.

  1963: Kenya gains independence.

  Today: Kenya remains an independent republic with a parliamentary form of government.

- **Late 1890s:** The Uganda Railroad makes Nairobi an important trade center and the center of British East Africa. The city offers relatively comfortable accommodations for Euro-

  pean settlers, who bring many of their customs with them.

  Today: Nairobi is the capital of Kenya with a population of approximately 1.5 people.

- **1910s:** In the patriarchal cultures of Europe and America, women's roles are strictly limited; they have few legal rights. In Dinesen's case, as a settler in British East Africa, women are afforded more freedom and opportunity.

  Today: As a result of the women's liberation movement of the 1960s and 1970s, women in the Western world have more freedom, legal options, and opportunities.

tlers, who had brought many of their customs with them. While they enjoyed betting at the racetrack and relaxing at the Muthaiga Club, where they could play polo, golf, and tennis, impoverished East Africans and Indian immigrants lived in shacks on the edge of the town.

Dinesen recounts in *Out of Africa:* "During all my time, Nairobi was a medley place, with some fine new stone buildings, and whole quarters of old corrugated iron shops, offices, and bungalows, laid out with long rows of eucalyptus trees along the bare dusty streets…. And it was a live place, in movement like running water, and in growth like a young thing, it changed from year to year, and while you were away on a shooting safari."

Critical Overview

Isak Dinesen gained worldwide acclaim for her literary achievements. The autobiographical *Out of Africa* enjoyed popular and critical success, especially in the United States and Britain. Most reviewers applauded her lyrical style.

Katherine Woods, in her 1938 article for *The New York Times Book Review,* finds Dinesen's

prose in *Out of Africa* "without redundancies, bared to its lines of strength and beauty. There was no fat on it, and no luxuriance anywhere, she says of her African landscape; so in the book there is no sentimentality, no elaboration."

As a result, Woods concludes that Dinesen presents a clear vision of Africa, which "lives through all this beautiful and heart-stirring book because of that simple and unsought-for fusion of the spirit, lying behind the skill which can put the sense of Africa's being into clear, right, simple words, through the things and people of the farm."

Furthermore, Woods asserts:

> In this personal record out of Africa, so sincere and natural, so direct and clear, there is that penetration, restraint, simplicity and precision which, together, mark the highly civilized mind, and that compassion, courage and dignity which mark civilization, in the best sense, in the human heart. This writing is poignant and exquisite, it has an echoing reticence, it is swift in profundity or insight or tenderness or irony. And no description of this book, highly as it may praise its solid substance, can in itself do justice to its effortless, expressive, wholly individual beauty of form, or even list the evocations and suggestions that lie within, or are touched by, its very simplicity.

In his article in the *Saturday Review of Literature,* Hassoldt Davis describes her style "as cadenced, constrained, and graceful as we have today." In the same review, however, Davis finds fault with the book's structure, insisting that "the tale of increasing tragedy which fills the latter half of the book seems not quite so successful as her earlier chapters."

Another criticism of the book is that it presents a romantic colonialist portrait of Africa and its people. However, some critics disagree. Anthony Burgess contends that the novel "never fails in grace, sharpness, and humanity." In fact, most commentators find the book expresses a genuine *joie de vivre* and contend Woods' claim that it is "something rare and lovely, to read again and again."

Dinesen's literary success continued after the publication of *Out of Africa,* but none of her works became as popular. Her highly regarded body of work and standing as a masterful storyteller earned her two Nobel Prize nominations.

When Ernest Hemingway received his Nobel Prize for Literature in 1954, he stated that it should have been awarded to her. Dinesen recognized her gift, as quoted by Donald Hannah, when she wrote:

> I belong to an ancient, idle, wild and useless tribe, perhaps I am even one of the last members of it, who, for many thousands of years, in all countries and parts of the world, has, now and again, stayed for a time among hard-working honest people in real life, and sometimes has thus been fortunate enough to create another sort of reality for them, which in some way or another, has satisfied them. I am a storyteller.

Criticism

Wendy Perkins

Wendy Perkins, an Associate Professor of English at Prince George's Community College in Maryland, has published articles on several twentieth-century authors. In this essay she focuses on Dinesen's portrait of herself as an independent, nontraditional woman in Out of Africa.

The film version of *Out of Africa* presents Karen Blixen as a courageous woman who can shoot lions alongside her lover Denys Finch-Hatton and withstand the long separations from her husband Baron Bror Blixen. The film portrays Blixen/Dinesen to be an independent woman, but one who has had that independence thrust on her after first her husband's then her lover's desertion, leaving her to fend for herself on her African coffee plantation. Several scenes show her pleading

with one or the other to stay and help her adapt to her new home.

In her autobiographical novel, however, Dinesen refuses to define herself through her relationships with the men in her life. In Africa she takes on a very nontraditional female role during the early part of the twentieth century, finding her identity not through romantic relationships, but through her relationship with the land and its people.

The screenplay was adapted from several of Dinesen's works including *Letters from Africa,* which provides details about her relationship with her husband and Finch-Hatton. The film portrays her difficult relationship with her husband including a bout with syphilis, which she contracted from him. During the Baron's frequent absences, Dinesen began an affair with Finch-Hatton.

Yet the Hollywood version of the romance between the two overshadows the romance Dinesen records in her autobiography—with the people and land of Africa. In the book, she mentions her husband only in passing and provides no details of their relationship. She writes of a strong friendship between herself and Finch-Hatton. The depth of her feeling for him becomes evident only at the end of the book when her sorrow over his death intermingles with her sorrow over leaving Africa.

Unlike the film version, Dinesen's autobiography is a selected, perhaps idealized, memory of her life in Africa, constructed as a portrait of a woman who strips off her traditional feminine identity so she can more fully become part of her experience there.

Dinesen's love affair with the land becomes evident from the first pages of the book. She describes the landscape as having "no fat on it and no luxuriance anywhere." Its "tall solitary trees" and "views immensely wide" gave "a heroic and romantic air." She writes, "everything that you saw made for greatness and freedom." She found "infinite freedom" in the African night, claiming "it is there that things are going on, destinies are made round you, there is activity to all sides, and it is none of your concern."

As she interacts with the land, she discovers her own sense of freedom. Her independent spirit, denied European woman during that period, emerges as she adopts traditionally male roles. Dinesen hunts big game along side Finch-Hatton, manages a coffee plantation, and transports arms and supplies across harsh terrain to border troops. Of this last experience she writes, "The air of the African highlands went to my head like wine, I was all the time slightly drunk with it, and the joy of these months was indescribable. I had been out on a shooting Safari before, but I had not till now been out alone with Africans."

At one point, she struggles with her own identity in her new world, asking, "If I know a song of Africa, of the Giraffe, and the African new moon lying on her back, of the ploughs in the fields, and the sweaty faces of the coffee-pickers, does Africa know a song of me?" After living and working on the land, however, she was able to define herself in relation to it:

> The plains with the thorntrees on them were already quite dark, but the air was filled with clarity and over our heads, to the west, a single star which was to grow big and radiant in the course of the night was now just visible, like a silver point in the sky of citrine topaz. The air was cold to the lungs, the long grass dripping wet, and the herbs on it gave out their spiced astringent scent. In a little while on the sides the cicada would begin to sing. The grass was me, and the air, the distant invisible mountains were me, the tired oxen were me. I breathed with the slight wind in the thorntrees.

More evidence of her growing relationship with the land emerges in her story of Lulu, a young antelope that became "a member of the household." Dinesen notes:

> The free union between my house and the antelope was a rare, honourable thing. Lulu came in from the wild world to show that we were on good terms with it, and she made my house one with the African landscape, so that nobody could tell where the one stopped and the other began.... The years in which Lulu and her people came round to my house were the happiest of my life in Africa. For that reason, I came to look upon my acquaintance with the forest antelopes as ... a token of friendship from Africa.

Dinesen's relations with the East Africans also helped define her nontraditional identity. As she interacts with them, she becomes a teacher, a doctor, an employer, a judge, and a friend. Sidonie Smith, in "The Other Woman and the Racial Politics of Gender: Isak Dinesen and Beryl Markham in Kenya," argues that "figuring herself as honorable, resourceful, courageous, dependable, hardworking, and socially responsible, [Dinesen] identifies herself as a hybrid of 'manliness' and 'womanliness.'"

In "Isak Dinesen: An Appreciation," Janet Lewis concludes that in *Out of Africa* Dinesen views the "world through the eyes of the other" and thus is able to define herself in relation to it. Lewis writes, "I don't know whether her deep understanding and empathy—if we hesitate to call it sympathy—with the Kikuyu was a natural thing to her,

What Do I Read Next?

- *Anecdotes of Destiny,* a 1985 collection of short stories by Dinesen, includes "Babette's Feast," a tale of a woman's struggle to define herself in a new and harsh landscape.

- Ernest Hemingway's *Green Hills of Africa* (1935) is a stirring account of a safari he and his wife joined in 1933. In the work, Hemingway reveals what the experience taught him about Africa and about himself.

- In *Letters from Africa* (1981) Dinesen provides more details about her life on her farm in Africa. Both works were used as source material for the successful film version of *Out of Africa.*

- Beryl Markham's *West with the Night,* published in 1942, chronicles her exciting life as an African bush pilot in the 1930s.

and a part of her own disposition and training, but I have a feeling that she learned some of this fortitude and gallantry from the Natives of Africa."

Smith adds, "Learning from the Africans how to live in accordance with [the landscape], this white woman represents herself as being as one with Africa in a powerful commingling of subjectivity and place." Thus as she opened herself to the experience of learning from them, she embarked on a journey of self-discovery.

Only at the end of the book does Dinesen identify her feminine qualities. Of her last weeks on the farm when her friend Ingrid Lindstrom came to spend time with her, Dinesen writes:

> Ingrid understood and realized to the bottom of her heart, with great strength, with something of the strength of the elements themselves, what it is really like, when a woman farmer has to give up her farm, and leave it.... We closed our two minds round the disaster of the hour. We walked together from the one thing on the farm to the other, naming them as we passed them, one by one, as if we were taking mental stock of my loss, or as if Ingrid were, on my behalf, collecting material for a book of complaints to be laid before destiny. Ingrid knew well enough

from her own experience that there is no such book, but all the same the idea of it forms part of the livelihood of women.

At this point, Dinesen expresses a strong connection with the women who worked the land with her and who were the most sorry to see her go. Unlike with her friend Ingrid, however, she identifies with them in nontraditional ways. She describes them as having "a hard life" and becoming "flinthard under it … wilder than the men…. They were afraid of nothing." Her portrait suggests these women found similar qualities in her, for they had "always been friends."

As Dinesen prepares to leave Africa, she seems to lose a sense of herself as she started to break her connections with the land and the people. She admits: "When I first began to make terms with fate, and the negotiations about the sale of the farm were taken up, the attitude of the landscape towards me changed. Till then I had been part of it…. Now the country disengaged itself from me, and stood back a little, in order that I should see it clearly and as a whole."

She also "disengaged" from the people. When she fears legal repercussions over allowing Chief Kinanjui to die in her home, she refuses his request. Yet she could not disengage herself completely from Africa. During the Ngoma held in her honor during her last days on the farm, she realizes that "the people were with me, and I with the people, well content."

In her record of her observations of the people and landscape of Africa, Dinesen defines herself in relation to what she sees. Ironically she gains a sense of individuality as she became part of the landscape.

Out of Africa omits the details of her life during her years on the farm that identify her in traditional ways and instead foregrounds her independent spirit. The resulting work creates a poetic portrait of her relationship with Africa and its people and an idealized, but perhaps truer, vision of self.

Source: Wendy Perkins, in an essay for *Novels for Students,* Gale, 2000.

John Burt Foster Jr.

In the following excerpt from an essay in which he discusses both Out of Africa *and Saul Friedländer's memoir of the Holocaust,* When Memory Comes *(1978), Foster examines the ways in which Dinesen's autobiographical persona represents an amalgamation of the cultures she experienced: her native Danish culture, the British colonial culture in East Africa, and the native African cultures.*

The phrase "cultural multiplicity" in my title is a deliberate variation on "multiculturalism," whose core meaning raises issues of curricular choice, educational philosophy, and public policy. "Cultural multiplicity," by contrast and for the purpose of this essay, refers to a more intimately personal cultural site: to the conflicts, the feelings of tension, the revelations of affinity, or the sense of triumph that can come from living among several cultural traditions and to some degree internalizing their diversity. Though this condition of multiplicity is not limited to border regions, states of exile, or diasporas, it is obviously one that has flourished at such points of cross-cultural contact. But multiplicity, I should stress, can only arise when more than two cultures meet at once, so that binary strategies of either polarization or synthesis must yield to more complex processes of negotiation, shifting alliances, and interplay.

Autobiography, and especially modern autobiography, provides fertile ground for exploring the varying ways people experience cultural multiplicity. As we all know, the twentieth century has witnessed a vast number of cultural migrations and displacements. The life story of someone who has undergone such large-scale change, even if seen as just the retrospective account of a personality formed by several cultures, can already reveal a great deal about multiplicity. But such an autobiography should not be read merely for the author's explicit thesis or conclusions. In particular, the writer's delight in transcribing certain memories can lead to a saturation effect, to an excess of detail about the past that can ultimately convey more than the author is willing to state outright.

At the same time, moreover, no autobiography concerns itself solely with the past events that are its ostensible subject matter. Unlike other forms of life-writing, such as letters or a diary, an autobiography has been composed at a certain temporal remove from the events it records, so that the author's present self can deeply influence such elements of the narrative as point of view, choice of events, and style. Some theorists of autobiography even hold that in the last analysis the genre deals with the authorial present more than the remembered past. As a result the texture of the writing can act as a gauge of the author's *current* state of multiplicity, at least to the extent that one's cultural identity is registered in words, as opposed to gestures, clothing, eating habits, and the like. Readers of autobiography thus gain access to a realm suspended between the written past and the writing present, a realm that ambiguously interweaves the story of an experience that the author views as formative with a provisional settling of accounts at the time of writing.

For an example of how saturation and temporal ambiguity can combine to reveal cultural multiplicity, let me turn to Vladimir Nabokov, whose work first alerted me to these issues and thus helped guide my approach to the two books I shall be discussing in this essay, Saul Friedländer's *When Memory Comes* and Isak Dinesen's *Out of Africa*. At one point in his autobiography, *Speak, Memory,* Nabokov recalls the bedtime ritual of his pre-World War I Russian boyhood, which in his multilingual family culminated with prayers recited not in Russian but in English. Then, as the remembered scene sharpens in the telling, and thus becomes "saturated," some pictures come to mind. Nabokov recalls an icon above his bed, then the nearby watercolor of an "eerily dense European beechwood." This memory, in turn, reminds him of the English fairy tale of a boy who actually entered such a picture, and Nabokov rounds off the scene by stating that in time he too visited that enchanted beechwood.

In cultural terms, what is most striking about this passage is the infusion of English elements into a Russian childhood. Beyond this documentary element, Nabokov has located a retrospective basis for his switch in the late thirties from writing in Russian to writing in English, as shown by the very fact that a decade later he composed most of *Speak, Memory* in English. Yet the detail of the European beechwood lingers as a mysterious third term. As the book develops, aspects of this motif will reappear to complicate the Anglo-Russian dualism in several ways. As a beechwood in Vermont, it calls attention to Nabokov's glide from a British to an American sense of English, while as an explicitly European setting it foreshadows his exile in Germany and France in the twenties and thirties. As a visual artifact, finally (and here we should note that in Russian the words for icon and image are the same), it implies that European as well as Russian models have guided Nabokov's interest in image-making throughout his literary career.

The dense textuality of this passage thus conveys both the cultural multiplicity of a certain childhood moment and the even more complex outcome known to the author as he writes. Nabokov's basic attitude in reviewing his life story deserves atten-

tion as well. It is emphatically triumphant, with the mature writer now realizing that he has indeed earned the fairy-tale privilege of entering an enchanted picture—one that permits unexpected new developments and rich juxtapositions in the cultural realm. As we turn to Friedländer's and Dinesen's autobiographies, we shall encounter similar experiences of cultural multiplicity, which nonetheless contrast with Nabokov's in two key respects. First, Friedländer's dramatic religious odyssey and Dinesen's two decades among the peoples of East Africa involve more drastic cultural challenges than even Nabokov's passage from Russia through western Europe into the English-speaking world. And second, although Nabokov's cultural multiplicity depends upon his being a refugee from Lenin and then Hitler, *When Memory Comes* and *Out of Africa* both grow out of and bear more immediate witness to even harsher historical conflicts—to the Jewish Holocaust and to African colonialism. Still, both books address the reader in ways that recall a major border-crossing built into the very words on the page of *Speak, Memory*. Neither the original French of Friedländer's autobiography nor the English that Dinesen used to compose one version of hers is the language spoken at the time of writing by those authors in their intimate, everyday lives....

Cross-cultural interaction [leads to] complex negotiations in Dinesen, but let me begin by acknowledging a certain falsity to her position in East Africa, where the British colonial regime was then seeking to create an area of exclusive European settlement in the Kenyan highlands. Thus the unintended irony of an ad recently cited in *Public Culture,* under the heading "Out of Africa 1906": "Between the years 1906 and 1939, a trickle, then a light rainfall, then a downpour of Englishmen, Germans, Scots, and some remarkable women began to fall upon the immense gorgeous plateau of East Africa" [*Public Culture,* Vol. 6, No. 1, Fall, 1993]. Such prose raises troubling questions about the popular reception of Dinesen's book, or at least about the movie that borrowed its title. But if the ad undercuts the justification of Dinesen's very presence in Africa as well as some of her romantic attitudes about the landscape, her life story also includes situations whose rich cultural multiplicity points in a very different direction.

In fact, if we bracket the overarching colonial dichotomy which (as her autobiography makes clear) Dinesen herself learned to question, the multiplicity in *Out of Africa* surpasses even the triadic patterns in *Speak, Memory* and *When Memory Comes*. Thus in one key passage Dinesen reviews the great variety of cultures that mingled in East Africa in the 1920s, then concludes that "[a]s far as receptivity of ideas goes, the Native is more a man of the world than the suburban or provincial settler or missionary, who has grown up in a uniform community and with a set of stable ideas". The third of her book's five units, called "Visitors to the Farm," clearly identifies with this East African responsiveness to diversity, for she arranges her experiences in a broad panorama that includes the Kikuyu, the Masai, Asian Indians, Somalis, Scandinavians, and British, to name only the leading groups. And if the progression among these peoples seems to replicate the colonial hierarchy, it should be noted that when this unit closes by evoking the thrill of flying in the early days of aircraft, it circles back to an old Kikuyu, whose skepticism about the enterprise gets the last word.

Perhaps because Dinesen wrote this autobiography some years after the failure of her coffee farm in 1931 forced her back to Denmark, she can imagine herself as "out of Africa" in a sense quite different from that title's main implication of a direct, documentary account. Thus she knows that alongside the colonial order, and never totally displaced by it, there exist the cultural orders of the East African tribes, who have other interpretations for her presence in Kenya. In the unit called "A Shooting Accident on the Farm," in which the Kikuyu request her help in an inquiry into damages, she realizes that she also functions as part of *their* cultural system, in a process she calls "brass-serpenting." "They can turn you into a symbol," she remarks, then concludes, "in spite of all our activities in the land, of the scientific and mechanical progress there, and of Pax Britannica itself, this is the only practical use that the Natives have ever had of us." As this episode continues, however, Dinesen discovers that beyond accepting this passive role in the Kikuyu system of justice, she cannot help taking a more active part as well. Thus a key insight about the dispute flashes on her in Swaheli, and she takes steps which help settle the case. In a book the very existence of which depends upon the author's bilingualism in Danish and English, this further crossing of linguistic boundaries must be seen as a key token of cultural multiplicity.

One might be tempted to simplify Dinesen's East Africa by speaking of three main groups—the Europeans, the Muslims, and the local Africans. Certainly the community which forms on her coffee farm suggests as much, since it consists of Dinesen's British and Scandinavian friends, of her major-domo Farah and his Somali relatives, and of

the so-called Kikuyu "squatters," led by their chief Kinanjui. But such a scheme overlooks both some gaps in Dinesen's coverage and the strong tensions *within* two of these groups. Regarding the gaps, though she clearly knew Arab, Indian, and local African Muslims, she gives far more attention to the Somalis, an interest which might repay closer study than is possible here. Such a discussion would have to consider the chapter on Farah in *Shadows on the Grass* (1960), a second African memoir written more than twenty years later.

My purpose, however, is to consider tensions within the European and African groups. The bearing of these tensions on cultural multiplicity can be hard to see, given Dinesen's reticence about herself in *Out of Africa,* which is emphatically *not* an autobiography in the confessional mode. Thus, though she does show conflicts among different groups, she does not explain their personal relevance, except through saturated details whose connection with her personal life remains deeply encoded. This relative silence follows the narrative logic suggested by her portrait of old Knudsen, a fellow Dane who normally told grand stories about himself in the third person, but who only admitted "I am very sick" on the single occasion that he spoke in the first person. As a result, though *Out of Africa* describes the multicultural variety of East Africa with much zest, it obscures how Dinesen identifies with or negotiates among these traditions while coping with personal experiences of isolation, illness, and distress. The route to interpreting her cultural multiplicity, though finally rewarding, is thus a tortuous one.

Dinesen alludes to her problems as a Scandinavian in a British colony at the very end of her narrative. The occasion is the day when everyone in Nairobi avoided her because her lover Denys Finch-Hatton had just died in a plane crash, and she was the only person who did not know. Dinesen gets a nightmarish feeling that "I myself was somehow on the wrong side, and therefore was regarded with distrust and fear by everyone." She explains that this mood recalled her experiences some twenty years before, at the start of World War I, when she was mistakenly considered pro-German.

What she does not say is that her later feeling of separation probably included separation from Denys himself. Her book has already indicated that when visiting her farm he liked to hear her retell the stories she was then writing, thus he acquired a certain responsibility for Dinesen's crucial transition from writing in Danish to writing in English.

But subsequently, when her money problems had decisively worsened, he recited a poem that shows his unwillingness to get too closely involved: "You must turn your mournful ditty / To a merry measure, / I will never come for pity, / I will come for pleasure." This is the most explicit trace in the book of what Dinesen's biographer Judith Thurman says probably happened, that Dinesen and Finch-Hatton had ended their affair just before his death [see Thurman, *Isak Dinesen: The Life of a Storyteller,* 1982]. But rather than giving a direct account of their relationship, *Out of Africa* acts this story out on a literary plane: Denys' gift of English in the storytelling sessions ironically turns into the medium for a warning to "come no closer." This revelation of aloofness is then mirrored in the British who avoid Dinesen in Nairobi after her lover's death just as they shunned her in World War I.

A pointed answer to Denys' poem of disengagement appears in a final scene from *Out of Africa,* where Dinesen "cites back" at the British. Her farm has gone bankrupt and she must sell; but then she discovers that the Kikuyu squatters have no legal rights to the land. Not only will they lose their homes, but they will be resettled piecemeal, with no regard for their standing as a community. When she pleads for some compromise (which comes at the last minute, but only as an unprecedented exception to colonial policy), she thinks of Shakespeare. "You can class people according to how they may be imagined behaving to King Lear," she reflects, and, to the officials who cannot understand why the community should be preserved, she inwardly protests, "Oh reason not the need." Yet unlike Lear with his daughters, she suddenly realizes, "the African Native has not handed over his country to the white man in a magnificent gesture." Only when she has lost her own land, and with the added irony that it is the very land she is now disputing on behalf of the Africans, does Dinesen reconsider a vaunted achievement of the English, so that instead of offering an alibi for the civilizing mission of colonialism, she attacks the whole enterprise.

A Scandinavian counterweight to Dinesen's disillusionment with the British appears in the chapter describing the Swede Emmanuelson in "Visitors to the Farm." Dinesen overcomes her dislike for this former waiter at a Nairobi hotel when she learns that he was once a tragic actor and that he plans to walk to Tanganyika, a week-long journey through the harsh lands of the Masai. His passionate love of tragic drama implicitly sets him apart from the emotionally neutral British, and she also admires his affinity with the Masai, with whom he can communicate only by pantomime but who, it turns out, still show him "great kindness and hospitality." In fact, Emmanuelson clearly functions as an alter ego for Dinesen, not just because his isolation amidst a group of Africans echoes her isolation in World War I, but also because one of his favorite tragic texts is Ibsen's *Ghosts*. This saturated detail looks ahead to Dinesen's situation while writing *Out of Africa,* when she learned that the syphilis she had contracted from her womanizing husband had not, as she had once thought, been cured, but had become her fate, thus mirroring Ibsen's Osvald Alving, who similarly returned to Scandinavia after a long period abroad.

Dinesen does not write of her illness or of her husband in *Out of Africa,* but traces of this painful experience do mark her treatment of the two African tribes she knew best. In general she draws distinct contrasts—the proud Masai warriors versus the humbler Kikuyu agriculturalists, the slave takers versus the victims in the Arab slave trade. But despite strong tensions between the tribes in the past, the Masai have begun to intermarry with the Kikuyu, since, as Dinesen puts it, "the Masai women have no children and the prolific young Kikuyu girls are in demand." It is here that Dinesen's personal situation comes closest to the surface. For, as Thurman tells us, the Masai were infertile due to widespread syphilis, and it was from a Masai woman that Dinesen's husband probably got the disease that he then passed on to her. This history, I think, underlies and helps explain the evolution of Dinesen's sympathies for the local Africans, from a rather facile admiration for Masai warriors to a deeper identification with old Kikuyu women.

On the one hand, the young Dinesen was greatly taken with her Swedish husband's noble title. Though he is banished from her book, she nonetheless calls herself "Baroness Blixen" in a key passage, and once even indicated in a letter to her brother that the title was worth a case of syphilis. In her identification with the Africans, she sees this aristocratic mystique embodied in the Masai men. Their "rigid, passive, and insolent bearing" gives them the look of "creatures trained through hard discipline to the height of rapaciousness, greed, and gluttony," and, in a less lurid passage, their sense of freedom is said to be so strong that they cannot survive three months in prison.

However, the older Dinesen, who has lost her land and writes with the knowledge that she suffers from an incurable case of spinal syphilis, prefers to identify with the old Kikuyu women. Early in *Out of Africa* she pays tribute to these women, "who have mixed blood with Fate, and recognize her irony, wherever they meet it, with sympathy, as if it were that of a sister." Read hastily in the context of Dinesen's status as mistress of a coffee plantation, these words may seem condescending; what gives them a deeper resonance is the temporal ambiguity implied by the image of "mixing blood with Fate," which surely reflects the author's awareness of her illness as she wrote the autobiography in Denmark.

Somewhat later in the book, in a naming scene that contrasts "Baroness Blixen" with another, quite different Dinesen persona, the old women call her "Jambo Jerie." But this phrase, once spoken, will remain an enigma until much later: writing of her departure from Africa, Dinesen explains that "whenever a girl is born to a Kikuyu family a long time after her brothers and sisters, she is named Jerie." Dinesen clearly prizes this acknowledgment of honorary kinship from her elders. Not only did it give her the strength to face the distress of involuntary displacement—one of her last African memories is of an old Kikuyu woman carrying part of her dismantled house on her back—but even now, as she writes, it steels her against the arrival of old age. Her tribute is too long to quote in full, but here are some key phrases: "The old Kikuyu women have had a hard life, and have themselves become flint-hard … they were afraid of nothing. They carried loads … of three hundred pounds …, they worked in the hard ground … from the early morning til late in the evening…. And they had a stock of energy in them still; they radiated vitality…. This strength … to me seemed … glorious and bewitching." In a set of cross-cultural exchanges that began when her husband consorted with a Masai woman, Dinesen's narrative suppresses this all-too-painful personal event only to highlight another symptom of the same situation, the syphilis-enforced intermarriages between the Masai and the Kikuyu. Identifying with both tribes, she thrills at first to the aristocratic warrior ethic of the Masai but settles in the end for the toughness of her self-described sisters, the old Kikuyu women.

Thus in *Out of Africa*, for all its studied reticence, as well as in the more directly confessional When Memory Comes, the upheavals of twentieth-century history thrust the autobiographer into situations where it becomes possible to take part in three or more cultures. Saul Friedländer as boy and youth experienced central-European secular, French Catholic, and Israeli Jewish cultures; Isak Dinesen as an adult woman experienced Scandinavian, British, and East African cultures, with East Africa opening up to reveal both the Kikuyu and the Masai. In each case, as the autobiography develops, the author comes to occupy a complex multicultural site where the binary logic of simple biculturalism no longer applies, where even the two-dimensional concept of boundary lines may appear inadequate.

Instead, as the autobiographical persona passes through these worlds, the multicultural vision of external diversity turns inward, leading to what I call cultural multiplicity. In the intimacy of such questions as "Who do I admire?" or "What do I believe?" or "Where do I belong?"—questions which, amid the flux of experience, challenge and sometimes alter or widen one's deepest cultural affiliations—the autobiographer identifies with and assimilates certain specific traits of the multicultural world that he or she portrays. The result is an autobiographical text which projects a polycentric field of cultural forces, forces which interrelate across a spectrum of options from tension to negotiation, from conflict to triumphant resolution. Such an autobiography, moreover, communicates these possibilities to its readers, who as they read learn to share to some extent in the author's multiplicity. At our present moment, with its heightened and often polarized sense of cultural identity, this kind of cultural literacy seems well worth cultivating; for rather than associating identity with certain monolithic, unchanging traits, it acknowledges both the many-sidedness of experience and the capacity of that experience to stir complex sympathies.

Source: John Burt Foster Jr. , "Cultural Multiplicity in Two Modern Autobiographies: Friedländer's *When Memory Comes* and Dinesen's *Out of Africa,"* in *Southern Humanities Review,* Vol. XXIX, No. 3, Summer, 1995, pp. 205-18.

Katherine Woods

In the following review, Woods enthusiastically praises Out of Africa.

The book [*Out of Africa*] which Isak Dinesen has made from her life on an African farm is a surprising piece of writing to come from the author of *Seven Gothic Tales.* After dazzling the public with what Dorothy Canfield called "the strange slanting beauty and controlled fantasy" of the first book, this amazing Danish master of English prose has stepped now into the clearest reality, the utmost classic simplicity, the most direct—yet the most exquisitely restrained—truth. But it is an incandescent simplicity; the reality is of the spirit as well as of object and event; the truth is a cry from the heart. And after all the books that we have had out of Africa, I think this is the one we have been waiting for.

Like the Ngong hills—which are amongst the most beautiful in the world—this writing is without redundancies, bared to its lines of strength and beauty. "There was no fat on it, and no luxuriance anywhere," she says of her African landscape; so in the book there is no sentimentality no elaboration. It is an autobiographical book: in one sense, only partly an autobiography; in another sense doubly autobiographical. This is not a chronological record; and until close to the end it touches almost casually the course of the author's life. It is peopled with other characters, every one of them alive. And the author knows how the hills look just before the rains come; and how the bleak wind runs over the land and the scents and colors die when the rains fail; and how often the bright air will bring illusion, as if one were walking on the bottom of the sea. She can make a sudden parable of the resignation of the oxen, and understand the tragedy of the captured giraffes, so proud and innocent; and the ancient African forest, she says, is like an old tapestry. She knows the practical details, the hard work, of this farm life, too.

But before one has read many pages in her book one realizes how, in a deeper sense than that of mere chronicle, these clear objective details from a farm in Kenya are themselves wholly personal. Once, looking back on an evening errand in wartime in the Masai Reserve, she shows the reason:

> The plains with the thorntrees on them were already quite dark, but the air was filled with clarity—and over our heads, to the west, a single star which was to grow big and radiant in the course of the night was now just visible, like a silver point in the sky of citrine topaz. The air was cold to the lungs, the long grass dripping wet, and the herbs on it gave out their spiced astringent scent. In a little while on the sides the cicada would begin to sing. The grass was me, and the air, the distant invisible mountains were me, the tired oxen were me. I breathed with the slight wind in the thorntrees.

This is more than mere understanding. And Africa lives through all this beautiful and heart-stirring book because of that simple and unsought-for fusion of the spirit, lying behind the skill which can

put the sense of Africa's being into clear, right, simple words, through the things and people of the farm.

The farm was a coffee plantation, but much of it was grass land and part was primeval forest, and native squatters lived, by law and custom, on 1,000 of its 6,000 acres and had their own gardens and herds there. Across the river was the country of the Masai, a proud people who had been great fighters but were now a dying race. Hunting country was roundabout, and two missions were a few miles away (in opposite directions), and it was not a long drive to Nairobi, even in the early days by cart. Other Europeans came and went, and some lived in these same hills. That complex scene, that unpredictable cast of characters, of the European colony in Africa, can be found in this book. But Baroness Blixen (not yet known under her pen-name of Isak Dinesen) was very close to the native peoples and to all the immemorial life of the African wild. It was not easy to get to know the natives, she says: they understood her better than she understood them; but she felt a great affection for them, from the first.

She used to doctor them, from her simple knowledge. She had an evening school for them, with a native schoolmaster. She studied their language, and told them stories to which they loved to listen. They came to her—even the Masai across the river—to complain when a lion was taking their cows, and she would go out and shoot it; one night she and Denys Finch-Hatton shot two of these marauding lions, and the children came out from their school near by and sang a little song of triumph, which ended "in an intoxicated refrain, 'A-B-C-D,' because they came straight from the school and had their heads filled with wisdom." And the little herd-boys brought their sheep to graze on her lawns. She was the friend of the Kikuyu chief, and he sent for her to come to him when he was dying. And once when a serious dispute among the Kikuyu on the farm had gone beyond the power of her peace-making, she asked the chief to render judgment for her on the important matter of cows and witchcraft; for she was a sort of judge among them, too; the Elders held their council meetings before her house, and used to ask her for final decisions.

So, as the years went by, she came to know them: their justice which is so different from the white man's justice; their untroubled acceptance of life's uncertainties which is so different from the white man's shrinking from risk; their courage, which is "unadulterated liking for danger"; their strange dancing imagination, and their stillness and their hardness and their mocking mirth; the way, too, in which they could be "unreliable and yet in the grand manner sincere." And she came to know how the African natives will make of some certain European, for some certain reason, a symbol—a brass serpent lifted up in the wilderness—and even to see that she had become such a symbol, herself. In these and other ways she knew the African peoples among whom she lived, and whose friend she was. And unforgettably, through her book, she draws the portraits, and tells or suggests the stories of individuals—natives, Europeans, animals.

In this personal record out of Africa, so sincere and natural, so direct and clear, there is that penetration, restraint, simplicity and precision which, together, mark the highly civilized mind, and that compassion, courage and dignity which mark civilization, in the best sense, in the human heart. This writing is poignant and exquisite, it has an echoing reticence, it is swift in profundity or insight or tenderness or irony. And no description of this book, highly as it may praise its solid substance, can in itself do justice to its effortless, expressive, wholly individual beauty of form, or even list the evocations and suggestions that lie within, or are touched by, its very simplicity. *Out of Africa* is something rare and lovely, to read again and again.

At the last, it tears the heart with its disaster and its simple gallantry. Isak Dinesen had planted her own deep roots in this soil, long years before. And the roots were broken at last. She had to sell the farm, and leave Africa. After tedious effort she was able to assure her villages being kept together, when she had gone. But the farm was lost and divided. She tells the story with quiet and noble beauty. And one knows that her wish for life as a whole has been fulfilled by Africa: she did not let it go until it blessed her.

Source: Katherine Woods, "Isak Dinesen's Fine Record of Life on an African Farm," in *The New York Times Book Review,* May 6, 1938, p. 3.

Sources

Anthony Burgess, in a review in *The Observer Review,* September 6, 1981, p. 29.

Marshall S. Clough, *Fighting Two Sides Kenyan Chiefs and Politicians, 1918-1940,* University Press of Colorado, 1990.

Hassoldt Davis, in a review in *Saturday Review of Literature,* March 5, 1938.

Donald Hannah, *"Isak Dinesen" and Karen Blixen: The Mask and the Reality,* Putnam, 1971.

Janet Lewis, "Isak Dinesen: An Appreciation," in *The Southern Review,* Vol. 2, No. 2, March, 1966, pp. 297-314.

Sidonie Smith, "The Other Woman and the Racial Politics of Gender: Isak Dinesen and Beryl Markham in Kenya," in *De/Colonizing the Subject: The Politics of Gender in Women's Autobiography,* edited by Sidonie Smith and Julia Watson, University of Minnesota Press, 1992, pp. 410-35.

Katherine Woods, "Isak Dinesen's Fine Record of Life on an Africa Farm," in *The New York Times Book Review*, May 6, 1938, p. 3.

For Further Study

Thorkild Bjornvig, "Who Am I? The Story of Isak Dinesen's Identity," in *Scandinavian Studies,* Vol. 57, No. 4, Autumn, 1985, pp. 363-78.
    Bjornvig examines the relationship between identity and animals in Dinesen's work.

Louise Bogan, "Isak Dinesen," in *A Poet's Alphabet,* McGraw-Hill, 1970, pp. 104-06.
    Explores the autobiography's main themes and compares them to her other works.

John Davenport, "A Noble Pride: The Art of Karen Blixen," in *The Twentieth Century,* Vol. CLIX, No. 949, March 1956, pp. 264-74.
    This essay explores the autobiographical aspects of her works.

Henry Louis Gates Jr. and Lynn Davis, in *Wonders of the African World,* Knopf, 1999, 275 p.
    Traces Gates's journey through contemporary Africa, from Ethiopia to the lost city of Timbuktu and the fabled University of Sankore.

The Prince

Niccoló Machiavelli
1513

Niccoló Machiavelli's *The Prince* is arguably the most popular book about politics ever written. Its observations about human behavior are as true today as they were five hundred years ago. In this book, Machiavelli offers advice to politicians regarding how to gain power and how to keep it.

Although modern readers think that a "prince" is someone who is destined to inherit control of his country, the princes of Machiavelli's time were by no means that secure: the prince had to be careful to keep the support of his citizens if he wanted to remain in power. The methods that Machiavelli suggests for leaders to keep public support are just as relevant for today's elected officials as they were for leaders of the sixteenth century.

Although *The Prince* is taught in many schools, there are few reputable teachers who would recommend actually following the advice that Machiavelli offers; it is meant to serve the prince's selfish interests, not to serve society in general. The ideas in the book are stated so harshly and bluntly that the term *Machiavellian* has now commonly used to describe the process of being cunning and ruthless in the pursuit of power.

Previous political writers, from Plato and Aristotle in ancient times to the sixteenth-century humanists, treated politics as a branch of the area of philosophy that dealt with morals. Machiavelli's chief innovation was to break with this long tradition and present the study of politics as political science.

Niccolo Machiavelli

Author Biography

Niccoló Machiavelli was born in Florence on May 3, 1469. He is notable for his essays on politics, particularly his infamous treatise on power entitled *The Prince*.

Not much is known about Machiavelli's early life except that he came from a political family. His father was a lawyer and represented Florentine nobles of high social standing. However, even with this privileged position, he had to struggle to make enough money to support his wife and sixteen children.

In 1494 Machiavelli became a clerk at the chancery at Adrian. In 1498 the ruling family of Florence was forced out of power and a republican government assumed control. Machiavelli became a secretary to the Council of Ten, which was the governing body in charge of diplomacy and military organization for the new Florentine republican government.

In his work for the executive council he had the opportunity to observe the workings of foreign affairs firsthand. In addition, he got to meet with other political leaders to see how their countries were ruled. He carried out several diplomatic mis-

sions to Germany, Spain, and other Italian city-states.

One of the political rulers he came to know was Cesare Borgia, of the powerful Borgia family; in fact, *The Prince* often refers to the Cesare Borgia as the model for an ideal ruler.

In 1512 the Medici family regained power in Florence, putting an end to republican rule. As a result, Machiavelli was forced out of his job and temporarily imprisoned. He returned to his country estate near San Casciano after his release and wrote several books on politics, including: *On the Art of War, History of Florence, Discourses on Livy,* and *The Prince,* which was dedicated to Lorenzo de Medici in an attempt to gain favor with the ruling family.

In 1527 the republic was restored, but Machiavelli was not appointed to his old position because many in the new government felt that he was too closely associated with the Medici family. Machiavelli died later that same year. His most famous work, *The Prince,* was published in 1532—five years after his death.

Plot Summary

Dedicatory Letter

The cover letter that opens *The Prince* is addressed to Lorenzo de Medici, a member of the ruling family in Florence. The letter introduces the book as an attempt to gain Lorenzo's favor, referring to the work as "a gift" and promising to show him—through examples of how powerful men have behaved throughout history—the most proven way to govern his people.

Much of language of the "Dedicatory Letter" is meant to assure the prince that Machiavelli is indeed humble; he wants the prince to benefit from his experience while at the same time avoiding the appearance that he knows more than him. These two ideas are contradictory, and so Machiavelli makes a point of downplaying his own qualifications. Historically, this has been read as an attempt to secure a job within Medici's government, although the letter itself emphasizes the point that he was trying to be helpful with no personal gain.

Chapters 1-11

Although there are no formal divisions between the twenty-six chapters that comprise *The Prince,* it is easy to see that Machiavelli's work has

The villa of the ruling Florentine family, the Medici, figures predominantly in this seventeenth-century painting by Claude Lorrain. Machiavelli dedicated The Prince *to Lorenzo de Medici, offering it as a guide to successful government.*

been arranged in four distinct sections. The first eleven chapters discuss the various kinds of principalities that are possible, introducing readers to the strengths and weaknesses of each type.

The beginning of this section of the book starts with discussions of contemporary Italian politics, a subject that will be dropped by the end of this section. Machiavelli looks at examples from antiquity, which is meant to underscore the scholarly aspect of *The Prince.*

One of the central themes of the book is that a ruler should never leave anything to chance; rulers cannot rely on fate or on the support of oth-

ers, for it will usually end up proving unreliable. Machiavelli then explores possible ways for a prince to come to power.

Chapters 12-14

In this section, Machiavelli discusses ways for a political leader to organize his military—the most important function of a ruler. First, he examines the use of mercenary soldiers—men who are hired to fight, usually from a different country—and explores the problems with this method. For instance, he contends that history shows that mercenaries are motivated only by money; therefore, if there is a disruption in payment, the mercenaries will not fight. Also, soldiers from other countries might lack the nationalistic fervor to fight hard for a certain cause or ruler.

Moreover, he offers direct, specific advice for how political leaders should handle their armies. They should, for instance, always have an enemy. He recommends that steps be taken so that the soldiers do not get bored, for then they will get themselves into trouble.

Chapters 15-23

Like the first section of the book, the third spans the length of several chapters. The focus in this section is the prince's subordinates and associates.

It is in this section that the book's famous rejection of conventional morality can be found. Machiavelli proposes the idea that one who is a leader does not need to return loyalty with loyalty; the only thing the prince owes his subjects is military success.

If the rest of the book functions as a textbook, teaching old stories and traditional wisdom to young rulers who are curious about rulers from the past, this third section functions as a political tract, suggesting changes that need to come about if the prince is to rule effectively.

The first half of this section examines examples from history, while the second half emphasizes the present and the future.

Chapters 24-26

This final section has been viewed as a patriotic call to arms, as Machiavelli encourages the prince to take good care of Italy, act prudently, and leave nothing about his country or his subjects to chance.

As with the second section, the rhetoric rises throughout the course of these few chapters. The book ends as it began: examining contemporary Italy, leaving examples from history in the past.

Characters

Agathocles the Sicilian

Machiavelli cites Agathocles as an example of someone who attained his political control through crime. Agathocles lived from 361 to 289 BC and came from humble origins—his father was a pot-

Media Adaptations

- *The Prince* is available in a four-audiocassette version from Penguin Audiobooks, read by Fritz Weaver.

- An examination of Machiavelli's life and writings entitled *The Prince: Niccoló Machiavelli,* is available on an audiocassette from Knowledge Products of Nashville, Tennessee.

ter. He rose up through the military ranks in Syracuse to become the praetor.

One morning, he assembled the members of the Senate of Syracuse and with one signal had all of the Senators and the town's richest people killed, leaving no one to oppose his political control. Machiavelli credits him for taking control of his own destiny.

Alexander the Great

Alexander the Great was a Macedonian ruler in the fourth century BC. He is used as an example by Machiavelli on how to divide and rule conquered territory.

Alexander VI

The father of Cesare Borgia, Rodrigo became Pope Alexander VI in 1492. Machiavelli notes that it was Alexander who helped propel his son into power. While Machiavelli acknowledges Alexander's role in Cesare's career, he credits Cesare with making the political decisions that accounted for his rise to power.

Cesare Borgia

Many of Machiavelli's examples of the effective ways for a prince to gain and retain power refer to practices he observed in his acquaintance with Cesare Borgia. He recounts that after being given the opportunity to rule Romagna, Borgia secured his position by following a set of standards that should be followed by any new ruler.

In particular, Machiavelli attributes four key ruling strategies to Cesare Borgia: eliminating all challengers to the throne; gaining the favor of the powers in Rome, especially the Pope; winning the support of the College of Cardinals; and defeating his enemies quickly and efficiently.

Rodrigo Borgia

See Alexander VI

Charles VIII

Charles VIII was the French king who led the successful invasion against Italy in 1494. This invasion forced the Medici family to relinquish their control of Florence (which they later regained in 1512).

Liverotto da Fermo

Machiavelli uses Liverotto as an example of a prince who gained political power due to criminal means. An orphan, Liverotto was raised by his maternal uncle. After serving in the army, he returned to his uncle's home, asking if he could bring his entire army with him to impress his uncle's associates. After dinner, Liverotto took the powerful men aside, pretending that he had some secret to tell them. On his command they all were slaughtered. In the end, Liverotto's reign was stopped by one who could match him in deception and cruelty—Cesare Borgia.

Antonio da Venafro

Da Venafro was a professor of law in Sienna and minister of Pandolfo Petrucci, prince of Sienna. Machiavelli deems him a respected, intelligent advisor. His discussion about Antonio's good qualities and how they reflect on his prince represent a thinly-veiled attempt to stress how much Machiavelli's own good reputation and wise counsel would help the reputation of the prince who would hire him.

Remirro de Orco

De Orca is Cesare Borgia's minister in Romagna. He ruled with ruthless power and was much hated. When he had outlived his purpose—that is, when the people threatened to rise up and kill him—Borgia had him killed. His body was left in the public square one morning, cut in half. In this way, Borgia was able to claim that the cruelty perpetrated against the people had come from Remirro, and not from him.

Ferdinand of Aragon

Ferdinand of Aragon was the king of Spain at the time that Machiavelli was writing *The Prince*.

He was considered to be a new prince because he abruptly changed his style of ruling, becoming more aggressive later in his reign. His reputation grew by attacking Granada and by waging religious war against the Muslims that lived in Spain.

Louis XII

Louis was the French ruler from 1498 to 1515. Louis was an ally of the Venetians, and he is used as an example of how such alliances hurt city-states.

Girolamo Savonarola

Savonarola was a Dominican monk who preached to the people of Florence about self-government. He was instrumental in ousting the Medici family from power in 1498.

Valentino

See Cesare Borgia

Themes

Politics

The Prince is considered one of the more important and influential books about politics ever written. It is esteemed by generations of readers because it is thought to show how politics really works. The book presents itself as a handbook: it offers practical advice to a new prince or leader how to gain, consolidate, and keep political power.

Prior to Machiavelli, political theorists judged a prince's reign on how moral the prince was: did he go to church? Did he sin? Was he a good man? Yet with *The Prince*, Machiavelli contended that it wasn't how moral the prince actually was, but how he was perceived by his subjects. In other words, appearance was all that mattered; it didn't matter what a prince did in private, as long as he was upstanding, honest, and fair in public.

Fate and Chance

The concepts of fortune and virtue are recurring ones in *The Prince*. Although these words can mean a variety of things, in this book fortune refers to those events that are beyond human control, and virtue means the things people can do to control fate.

It would be counterproductive for a how-to manual of this type to use fortune to explain most of life's events. The point of Machiavelli's book is to recommend the most effective tactics to stay in

Topics for Further Study

- Choose a candidate from a recent United States presidential election. Analyze this candidate from a Machiavellian perspective. Does this person adhere to the Machiavellian philosophy? Or do they break his rules? Provide specific examples.

- Machiavelli makes no mention of the fact that during his lifetime some of history's greatest art was being produced in his hometown, Florence. Read about Florentine art during the Renaissance, and explain how the political situation contributed to the artistic situation at the time.

- The adjective "Machiavellian" is often used to describe rulers who are ruthless and deceptive. Research Adolph Hitler's rise and fall as leader of Germany in the 1930s and 1940s. Write a letter from Machiavelli to Adolph Hitler explaining why he lost World War II.

- Machiavelli almost never mentions women. Pick a novel that has female characters, and analyze the female characters in Machiavellian terms. They may not be leaders of countries, but do they act according to Machiavellian principles? Use specific examples from the novel.

power, not to put a damper on his activities. He estimates that half of our actions may be caused by fortune while free will controls the other half; but fortune has the greater significance because when it asserts itself it is like a raging flood, washing away all that is in its path.

Continuing with the flood metaphor, he notes that virtue can control the flow of fortune in the same way that dikes and dams control a flood. Rather than using the idea of fate or luck as an excuse—as a great many theorists do when things do not work out as expected—Machiavelli warns princes that they must prepare themselves against fortune and be ready to change their methods in order to accept what fortune brings. Yet because of this, he has more admiration for rulers who are reckless than those who are cautious—the cautious

ones are fooling themselves about how much they really control their fate.

Deception

According to Machiavelli, political leaders should be allowed to deceive their subjects. The test of a politician is not how well he keeps his word, but whether he is *perceived* to be honest.

It is not Machiavelli's goal to uphold morality, but to advise political leaders on the best way to strengthen their power. For him, the best way to remain in power is to tell the people what they want to hear—whether it is true or not.

According to this theory, it would actually be detrimental for a prince to tell the truth all of the time. In fact, he explains that a "prudent" ruler "cannot observe faith, nor should he, when such observance turns against him, and the causes that make him promise have been eliminated." Later in the same paragraph, he adds, "Nor does a prince ever lack legitimate cause to color his failure to observe faith."

"Observing faith," like "keeping faith," means to remain true and honest. With these lines Machiavelli is telling readers that the prince should break his promises when circumstances change and then lie about why he broke his promise. This sort of moral relativism—changing one's ethical code from one situation to the next—is effective for retaining the prince's hold on power, even though it violates most systems of ethics.

War and Peace

In Machiavelli's time, countries were constantly at war with one another. Therefore, the ability to effectively lead during wartime was a much more important measurement of a politician than it is in contemporary times. Much of the political theory in *The Prince* is centered on a principality's ability to defend itself against attacks.

Machiavelli approves of a strong army, but he cautions a prince to create such a force from his own subjects and to not rely on mercenaries or on soldiers borrowed from other lands. He does approve of taking control of other countries through military aggression.

His central message to princes is to keep their subjects happy; therefore, his subjects will stay loyal and fight off an invasion by a new ruler. As with most subjects, Machiavelli views war and peace as means to popularity, noting that the failure to stir up conflict in a relatively peaceful time will make rulers look weak.

Style

Point of View

Most of *The Prince* is written from the first-person point of view. In other words, the speaker of the work refers to himself directly, using the word "I." In this case, the speaker is the same person as the book's author, Niccoló Machiavelli.

In the "Dedicatory Letter" that opens the book, Machiavelli openly addresses Lorenzo de Medici, a member of the Florence ruling family. In the letter, Machiavelli states that what is written there will illustrate "my extreme desire that you arrive at the greatness that your future and your other qualities promise you." He addresses Lorenzo again near the end of the book, speaking directly of the current situation in Italy.

Throughout the book, though, he wrote with the formal "you," referring to a plural, a general readership, as modern readers might use the word in a statement like, "you need to take vitamins if you are going to stay healthy." As the English language uses one word, "you," for both the direct (singular) and general (plural) forms of address, it can be difficult to follow the subtle changes of point of view used by Machiavelli.

Structure

In presenting *The Prince* as a guidebook for new princes, Machiavelli rejected a conventional narrative structure and instead divided his book by issues of leadership. The textbook structure is based on logic: it starts with general types of political situations and examines them each for a few chapters before going on to a few chapters about how princes come to acquire new principalities, following that with a few chapters about war, then princes' styles and reputations, finishing with advice about the people who they keep close to them.

Overall, the structure of the book moves from general issues to specific issues. This structure also disguises the fact that Machiavelli is using the book as a resume; he is obviously auditioning for a job with Lorenzo de Medici.

Modernism

Critics often explore Machiavelli's pragmatic views by asserting that the Florentine author was a modernist born hundreds of years ahead of his time. In the late 1800s a movement within the Roman Catholic Church began to challenge the Church's teachings. Scholars who followed this movement—known as the modernist movement—sought to pub-lish their own philosophical works without having to seek the approval of the church.

While Machiavelli did not directly question the authority of the church, the very fact that he talked about the church only as a political institution and did not claim that the Pope had absolute divine knowledge is enough to categorize him with the modern philosophers of the eighteenth century. In 1907 Pope Pius X issued a papal encyclical that deemed the movement a synthesis of all heresies, a charge reminiscent of those levied against Machiavelli, who was referred to as an agent of the devil when *The Prince* was published.

Although Machiavelli's style was familiar to readers of his day, the fact that he used a textbook on political education to cover broader ideas about morality might be considered a modernist technique, especially by those critics who assert that he was trying to be ironic in *The Prince*. Irony occurs when there is a distance between what a work says and what the author means, and it is common for modernist works to use old, familiar forms ironically.

Historical Context

The Medici Family

Lorenzo di Medici was a member of a family who ruled Florence for almost three centuries (1434–1737). They lost control of Florence for only a brief time (1494 to 1512) when a reform government was established to run Florence. Machiavelli was a member of the reform government, and he lost his government post when the Medici family regained power in 1512. *The Prince* was written as Machiavelli's way of gaining the Medici family's favor by offering advice based on his experience in government.

The first Medici came to Florence from the surrounding farmlands around the year 1200. At that time Italy was not a unified country, but a land scattered with separate, powerful, feudal cities. Florence was one of the most prominent of these city-states.

It is believed that the family prospered in Florence. The social class system was strict: the wealthy merchant class, known as the *popolo grasso* ("the fat people"), suppressed the lower class, known as the *popolo minuto* ("the lean people").

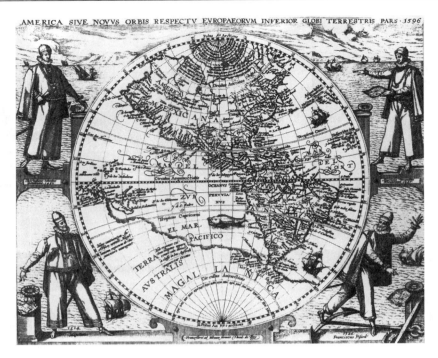

Among the accomplishments of Machiavelli's era were the explorations of Columbus, Magellan, and Vespucci, portrayed in this map of the Americas dated 1590.

The Ordinances of Justice (1293) established the city as a republic to be ruled under democratic principles. Although true democracy was never achieved—political rights were reserved for members of higher political standing—it did much to change the political landscape. Florence was looked on by other Italian city-states as a model of progressive thinking.

Giovanni di Bicci de Medici (1360–1429) was the first real politician of the family. He was a banker and a powerful member of the popular political party. Though he considered himself a businessman only dabbling in politics, Giovanni was elected *prior* of Florence three times.

It was his son Cosimo (1389–1464) who first established the family's control of the city, ruling Florence for thirty years. He was a brutal, aggressive leader. Yet he is also remembered as a financial supporter of some of the Renaissance's leading artists, including Donatello and Brunelleschi.

Cosimo's son, Piero (1414–1469), was a quiet, contemplative man. Yet Cosimo's grandson was one of the most powerful in Italian history: Lorenzo the Magnificent (1449-1492), who took control in 1469, the year of Machiavelli's birth.

Lorenzo was a strong-willed ruler and an outstanding patron of the arts. Among the great thinkers who stayed at his house were Leonardo di Vinci, Michelangelo, and Botticelli. Yet he was tyrannical and ruthless in his reign.

When he brought a Dominican friar named Girolamo Savonarola (1452–1498) to Florence in 1485, Savonarola quickly became a popular spiritual leader who raised public sentiment against the Medici family.

After Lorenzo's death, his son Piero (1471–1503) assumed leadership. Considered weak and foolish, Piero was very unpopular with his subjects. Savonarola and his supporters drove Piero from power in 1494. The Florentine Republic proved unstable, though, and the Medici family returned to power in 1512. They ruled the city until 1737.

Renaissance

The Renaissance began in Italy in the fourteenth century and spread to the rest of Europe in the sixteenth and seventeenth centuries. During the Renaissance, the agricultural-based economy and religious domination of the Middle Ages virtually disappeared and was replaced by a society gov-

Compare & Contrast

- **1500s:** Renaissance thinkers, like Machiavelli, emphasize logic and rational pragmatism over religious ethics in political analysis.

  Today: Political campaigns are driven more and more by advertising and market research. This allows candidates to support only popular positions, often to the chagrin of voters who doubt the morality and ethics of political candidates.

- **1534:** Giulio de Medici becomes the first in a long succession of Italian popes.

  Today: Elected in 1978, Pope John Paul II remains the preeminent Roman Catholic leader. He was the first Polish priest to be chosen for the position, ending an uninterrupted line of Italian popes.

- **1513:** Polish astronomer Nicolaus Copernicus begins writing his major work, *De Revolutionibus Orbium Coelestium.* Published after his death in 1543, it proposes that planets revolve around the sun.

  1633: Italian astronomer Galileo Galilei supports Copernicus' theories. As a result, he is jailed because the Roman Catholic Church teaches that Earth is the center of the universe.

  Today: It is accepted as fact the planets revolve around the sun.

erned by centralized political institutions and urban-centered, commercial economies.

The Renaissance is also characterized by great strides in the fields of mathematics, philosophy, medicine, and astronomy. Yet the greatest legacy of the Renaissance period is found in the field of art—and the greatest Renaissance artists lived in Florence.

Artistic advances were numerous and significant during this period. Linear perspective—the mathematical ordering of the scene portrayed on a painter's canvas so that things are proportional to their distance from the viewer—was developed by Filippo Brunelleschi. Leonardo Da Vinci painted the *Mona Lisa,* which remains the most recognized painting in the world. The sculptor Donatello as well as the painter Botticelli lived and worked in Florence. Even those artists who did not live there at least passed through Florence, eager to gain inspiration from the terrific artistic revolution that occurred during the period.

Critical Overview

Almost as soon as it was published in 1532, *The Prince* was derided as a controversial, heretical work. Sidney Angelo collected a handful of these early reviews that he found during his research:

> Throughout the sixteenth and seventeenth centuries we find Machiavelli depicted as the very hand of the devil; ad an "imp" of Satan; as "hell-bourne"; as a "damnable fiend" of the underworld; as the "gret monster-master of hell." John Donne once went so far as to describe a vision of the netherworld in which Machiavelli, attempting to gain a place in Lucifer's innermost sanctum, was out-argued by Ignatius Loyola, founder of the Jesuits. And it was even possible for Samuel Butler to suggest, facetiously, that "Old Nick" himself took his name from "Nick Machiavel."

The Prince was placed on the Papal Index of Prohibited Books in 1559, but historians disagree to whether this was for religious or political reasons.

More telling is the scathing reaction to Machiavelli by English minister Richard Harvey in his treatise *A Theological Discourse of the Lamb of God and His Enemies* (1590). After discussing how much Machiavelli's anti-Christian philosophy sickened him, comparing him to a spider who has gathered his venom from "old philosophers and heathen authors," Harvey warns to his readers:

> Be not deceived, God is not mocked, for whatever a man soweth that he shall also reap: for he that soweth

to the flesh, shall of the flesh reap corruption, but he that soweth to the spirit, shall of the spirit reap life everlasting.

Given that the purpose of *The Prince* was to raise revolutionary ideas— rejecting the old morality in favor of a new one—it is hardly surprising that early critics might find Machiavelli disturbing and heretical.

However, by the nineteenth century, critics became interested in Machiavelli's purposes for writing *The Prince*. His theories of moral relativism were no longer shocking. The ideas that Machiavelli had been condemned for were known all over the world. Critics began to praise him for his honesty and insight into the political arena.

For instance, Lord Macaulay Thomas Babington asserted in 1827 that ordinary readers could be expected to view Machiavelli as the most depraved and shameless of human beings, but that, in fact, "[h]is works prove, beyond all contradiction, that his understanding was strong, and his sense of the ridiculous exquisitely keen."

By the end of the 1800s, Machiavelli's ideas had become so commonly accepted that critics seldom felt the need to soften their praise of him. The introduction to the 1891 edition of *The Prince* contained glowing praise from the eminent sociologist Lord Acton John Emerich Edward Dalberg-Acton.

Dalberg-Acton rejected the moral objections to Machiavelli's work, maintaining that they may be legitimate but that his great contribution to the world of political discourse made them necessary. He praised Machiavelli as "the earliest conscious and articulate exponent of certain living forces in the present world," contending that the events that had occurred since the publication of the book had only served to make his ideas more relevant.

Twentieth-century students of Machiavelli have addressed his personal motives for writing *The Prince*. Critic Garrett Mattingly ridiculed the idea of the book as a serious guide. In fact, Mattingly made the case that the book's apparent attempt to aid and justify dictators contradicts everything else that Machiavelli wrote.

The book must be a satire of totalitarian rulers, Mattingly concluded, written at a time when its author would have been most hesitant to openly criticize political leaders—when he had just been freed from jail.

Many other recent critics have examined the specific question of what is meant by *Virtu*. Entire books have been written debating Machiavelli's

meaning, while other critics have concluded that he had no set meaning for the word at all.

Interestingly, the word "Machiavellian" is still used as an insult—implying dishonesty and greed—but there is seldom a question of Machiavelli's historical importance.

Criticism

David Kelly

Kelly is an instructor of literature and creative writing at College of Lake County, Illinois. In the following essay, he questions whether The Prince *can be considered useful for the modern student.*

Is it prudish of me to focus on the obvious antisocial element that most people notice first when they read *The Prince?* Is it naive to reject the version of reality that he was selling? Each time I read this book, I think of what a good movie it would make, filled as it is with tough, cynical lines giving those who hold high office advice that would be more appropriate in jail: that only suckers play by the rules. I wonder about our motives as a society, about what we hope to gain when we read this.

Like most good novels, its attraction to us is mixed—it can teach us something about the world, but it is also (and this is a facet too frequently ignored) a fine piece of entertainment. We shouldn't confuse the two and value it for what it is not. *The Prince* calls itself a primer for novice politicians, and it is full of iron-clad truths, but it does not really offer much advice that can be applied to life in any practical way.

We should have no problem admitting that we enjoy reading Machiavelli: we like the serious, efficient tone of his cutthroat attitude, even while pretending that we don't. It has been nearly five hundred years *The Prince* was written, and still we read it, analyze it, discuss it and assign it in schools. Ninety percent of books written are not in print five years after their initial publication, let alone fifty years or a hundred. There must be some reason for his popularity.

I think that there is an aspect of entertainment to be drawn from an idea like "cruelties badly or well used," that our culture is constantly trying to think up ways to fill that mysterious category of "cruelties well used" at the same time that it wants

T h e   P r i n c e

to tell us that cruelty has no place in the civilized world.

This ideal prince belongs to a long history of imaginary characters who make their own laws. Increasingly, as the world has gotten more crowded and laws more restrictive, we dream up do-gooders who transgress the conventional morality in their search for some higher good. There have always been, and always will be, the Zorros and Billy Jacks and Dirty Harrys and Buffy the Vampire Slayers, using bad means for good ends, and Machiavelli's ideal ruler falls right in with them.

The book explains that the prince must use cruelty sometimes, or else his subjects will quit their support of him and leave the government defenseless against anarchy and eventual overthrow by persons who would not use their cruelty so well. Our culture is brimming with antiheroes who are forced to step over to the dark side and engage in immoral behavior in order to preserve morality.

Their appeal may stem from a sense that the prevailing social order is absurd. It may come from an inherent sadism that, in a desire to watch somebody take advantage of somebody else, twists the rules of what is acceptable to make such bullying just. The important thing is that this rogue element is and always has been entertaining, a crowd-pleaser, and this is the category where I think *The Prince* belongs.

It is more problematic to consider *The Prince* an educational experience. It was written as a handbook—its only stated goal is to advise anyone who might come into control of a Renaissance city-state on how to maintain order. Compassion has no place except as a tool for keeping the people's support. Yet most of us are not princes, and we do not live in principalities. We have a right to wonder what this book has to offer beyond its entertainment value.

The book would be well worth serious attention if only because it has the educational value that any five-hundred-year-old artifact has. Curious Americans go to Colonial Williamsburg and wonder what the seventeenth century must have been like; they visit Civil War battlefields that saw action less than a hundred and fifty years ago. The works of Shakespeare (almost a century after Machiavelli) are important to us today because of the writer's artistry, but a common person's diary from the same time is also important for telling us who we are and where we come from.

Simply, the value of *The Prince* becomes one of those unsolvable chicken-and-egg questions

What Do I Read Next?

- A seminal philosophical work on the nature of politics, *Politics* was written by the Greek philosopher Aristotle after 335 B.C.

- Machiavelli's view of the world is applied to the modern political scene in Michael A. Ledeen's *Machiavelli On Modern Leadership: Why Machiavelli's Iron Rules are as Timely and Important Today As Five Centuries Ago* (1999).

- Giorgio Vasari was a painter during the Renaissance. First published in 1550, his book *Lives of the Painters, Sculptors and Artists* reminisces about his acquaintances with many of the key artists who lived in Florence during Machiavelli's time, including Michelangelo, Leonardo da Vinci, and Brunnelleschi.

- Jacob Burckhardt, a Swiss historian whose writings changed the way historians looked at the past, ushered in a new perspective on the Renaissance period. His 1860 book *A History of Italy in the Renaissance* is a groundbreaking work that introduces readers to Machiavelli, the Medici family, and many other key figures of the time.

about which came first: is the book valuable because it is so old, or have we kept it around to reach this old age because it is so valuable? Either way, we all have to agree that there's something useful there.

Unlike the common person's diary, which might or might not provide a few interesting bits of information here and there, *The Prince* appeared at a transitional point in world history—when the past meets the future. The book can serve as a portal between our world and medieval society. We can generalize by saying that the world Machiavelli was rebelling against was one ruled by religious assumptions that supported political systems that had been handed down intact for centuries.

Just as Renaissance artists made their marks by cutting through tradition and organizing their works according to their own innate sense of rationality, so too Machiavelli and Renaissance political scientists evaluated ideas based on their effectiveness. Unlike most progressives who have no patience for quaint, old-fashioned ideas, he treated such ideas as threats to the security of the principality.

When studying history, it is always enlightening to look at the examples that connect two different eras, and shows one way of life at the moment it evolves into the next. *The Prince* represents a moment of political transition, and for that, it is worth the modern reader's attention.

The advice the book offers, though, is hardly any more useful to us today than a medieval broadsword would be. No one can deny that his rules work, but why should we be impressed with that? There has never been any mystery about winning a fight by being the first one to throw the rules aside and resort to eye gouging and punching below the belt: it is the problem of playing within the rules that makes winning difficult. Manners go stale right out of the box. When the rules are ridiculous (which happens much less than they seem), then it is easy to agree with the suggestion that we crumple them up and start again.

Yet *The Prince* doesn't simply suggest that we give up obscure niceties like helping old women across streets: it tells political leaders they should lie to their subjects, and then lie about why they lied when they are caught; it tells them they should lure others into positions of trust, and then kill them; it tells them to hide behind others when their crimes are found; and to start wars even when there is no reason to, just for the sake of keeping the troops sharp.

Scholars since the Renaissance have been scandalized by *The Prince*—and for good reason. Machiavelli's rules do not make sense, and would only lead to disastrous policy. They rip out any hope that social order could be based on cooperation and replace it with sham cooperation. Do politicians need to be trained to act in their own self-interest? A power-mad, would-be dictator would look to Machiavelli to justify his or her actions, but ruthlessness flourishes enough without teaching it in schools.

If life is a jammed freeway, Machiavelli is the one who tells certain self-important people that they deserve to pull of onto the shoulder of the road and drive past everyone else. That sort of advice wasn't even good for society when there actually were royal personages around.

Yet we still endure generations of historians who praise Machiavelli for telling it like it is, for having the guts to stand up against a society that tries to suppress his frankness, as if from fear. They treat him like the lone honest voice in the wilderness.

By necessity, this stance requires one to look at the advocates of honesty and peace as dreamers, as pie-in-the-sky idealists. There really is no reason to think that believing a "hit them before they hit you" attitude is any more "realistic" than cooperation, although the less aggressive approach would, with no other evidence, be the sort of thing people would like to imagine.

There's no reason to equate backstabbing with reality. Idealizing treachery does not do anyone good except the treacherous, and the point of having a society is to minimize—if not eliminate—treachery. Lying and killing are not good for the general public, no matter how much Machiavelli dresses them up as the lesser evils when stood beside anarchy and social unrest.

If lying and killing are not for the public good, then it seems strange we would treat these guidelines as pearls of wisdom dropped at our feet. We wouldn't accept bank robbery or drug running as "effective" methods of raising money, although they can be—Machiavelli's recommendations to the prince are irrelevant when they are applied within a moral system, and they are blandly obvious in a place where morality is left out of the equation.

We have enough trouble getting politicians to do the things they say they will—who needs them reading books that tell them that honesty is irrelevant? If Machiavelli is "telling a truth that nobody else dared to tell" (a courageous line that graces the posters advertising movies about those antiheroes mentioned before), we might want to think about why no one has told it before.

A recent news article about the leader of a nationwide crime gang that made billions of dollars in drugs and extortion each year describes him as "smart and manipulative, a reader of Machiavelli who tried to project a positive image through food giveaways to the poor." This is the sort of "prince" who might use Machiavelli's advice, although it seems more likely that he already knew which opponents to kill, which underlings to threaten, before he had the time in prison to catch up on his reading.

It's more likely that he bought a copy of *The Prince* once and left it around unread, and the magazine writer picked up on it as a neat way to contrast the thuggishness of gang members with a methodical political education. It is no contrast.

The Prince can feed our imaginations about people claiming rights over and above those granted to ordinary people, and it can teach us history, but its advice has always been more ornamental than useful.

Source: David Kelly, in an essay for *Novels for Students,* Gale, 2000.

Harvey C. Mansfield Jr.

In the following essay, Mansfield provides an overview of The Prince, *describing the work as "the most famous book on politics when politics is thought to be carried on for its own sake, unlimited by anything above it."*

Anyone who picks up Machiavelli's *The Prince* holds in his hands the most famous book on politics ever written. Its closest rival might be Plato's *Republic,* but that book discusses politics in the context of things above politics, and politics turns out to have a limited and subordinate place. In *The Prince* Machiavelli also discusses politics in relation to things outside politics, as we shall see, but his conclusion is very different. Politics according to him is not limited by things above it, and things normally taken to be outside politics—the "givers" in any political situation—turn out to be much more under the control of politics than politicians, peoples, and philosophers have hitherto assumed. Machiavelli's *The Prince,* then, is the most famous book on politics when politics is thought to be carried on for its own sake, unlimited by anything above it. The renown of *The Prince* is precisely to have been the first and the best book to argue that politics has and should have its own rules and should not accept rules of any kind or from any source where the object is not to win or prevail over others. *The Prince* is briefer and pithier than Machiavelli's other major work, *Discourses on Livy,* for *The Prince* is addressed to Lorenzo de' Medici, a prince like the busy executive of our day who has little time for reading. So *The Prince* with its political advice to an active politician that politics should not be limited by anything not political, is by far more famous than the *Discourses on Livy.*

We cannot, however, agree that *The Prince* is the most famous book on politics without immediately correcting this to say that it is the most infamous. It is famous for its infamy, for recommending the kind of politics that ever since has been called Machiavellian. The essence of this politics is that "you can get away with murder": that no divine sanction, or degradation of soul, or twinge of conscience will come to punish you. If you succeed, you will not even have to face the infamy of murder, because when "men acquire who can acquire, they will be praised or not blamed" (Chapter 3). Those criminals who are infamous have merely been on the losing side. Machiavelli and Machiavellian politics are famous or infamous for their willingness to brave infamy.

Yet it must be reported that the prevailing view among scholars of Machiavelli is that he was not an evil man who taught evil doctrines, and that he does not deserve his infamy. With a view to his preference for republics over principalities (more evident in the *Discourses on Livy* than in *The Prince,* but not absent in the latter), they cannot believe he was an apologist for tyranny; or, impressed by the sudden burst of Italian patriotism in the last chapter of *The Prince,* they forgive him for the sardonic observations which are not fully consistent with this generous feeling but are thought to give it a certain piquancy (this is the opinion of an earlier generation of scholars); or, on the basis of Machiavelli's saying in Chapter 15 that we should take our bearings from "what is done" rather than from "what should be done," they conclude that he was a forerunner of modern political science, which is not an evil thing because it merely tells us what happens without passing judgment. In sum, the prevailing view of the scholars offers excuses for Machiavelli: he was a republican, a patriot, or a scientist, and therefore, in explicit contradiction to the reaction of most people to Machiavelli as soon as they hear of his doctrines, Machiavelli was not "Machiavellian."

The reader can form his own judgment of these excuses for Machiavelli. I do not recommend them, chiefly because they make Machiavelli less interesting. They transform him into a herald of the future who had the luck to sound the tunes we hear so often today—democracy, nationalism or self-determination, and science. Instead of challenging our favorite beliefs and forcing us to think, Machiavelli is enlisted into a chorus of self-congratulation. There is, of course, evidence for the excuses supplied on behalf of Machiavelli, and that evidence consists of the excuses offered by Machiavelli himself. If someone were to accuse him of being an apologist for tyranny, he can indeed point to a passage in the *Discourses on Livy* (II 2) where he says (rather carefully) that the common good is not observed unless in republics; but if someone else were to accuse him of supporting republicanism, he could point to the same chapter, where he says that the hardest slavery of all is to be conquered by a republic. And, while he shows his Italian patriotism in Chapter 26 of *The Prince* by exhorting someone to seize Italy in order to free it from the barbarians, he also shows his fairmindedness by advising a French king in Chapter 3 how he might better invade Italy the next time. Lastly, it is true that he sometimes merely reports the evil that he sees, while (unnecessarily) deploring it; but at other times he urges us to share in that evil and he virtuously condemns halfhearted immoralists. Although he was an exceedingly bold writer who seems to have deliberately courted an evil reputation, he was nonetheless not so bold as to fail to provide excuses, or prudent reservations, for his boldest statements. Since I have spoken at length on this point in another place, and will not hesitate to mention the work of Leo Strauss, it is not necessary to explain it further here.

What is at issue in the question of whether Machiavelli was "Machiavellian"? To see that a matter of the highest importance is involved we must not rest satisfied with either scholarly excuses or moral frowns. For the matter at issue is the character of the rules by which we reward human beings with fame or condemn them with infamy, the very status of morality. Machiavelli does not make it clear at first that this grave question is his subject. In the Dedicatory Letter he approaches Lorenzo de' Medici with hat in one hand and *The Prince* in the other. Since, he says, one must be a prince to know the nature of peoples and a man of the people to know the nature of princes, he seems to offer Lorenzo the knowledge of princes he does not have but needs. In accordance with this half-serious promise, Machiavelli speaks about the kinds of principalities in the first part of *The Prince* (Chapters 1-2) and, as we learn of the necessity of conquest, about the kinds of armies in the second part (Chapters 12-14). But at the same time (to make a long story short), we learn that the prince must or may lay his foundations on the people (Chapter 9) and that while his only object should be the art of war, he must in time of peace pay attention to moral qualities in such manner as to be able to use them in time of war (Chapter 14, end).

Thus are we prepared for Machiavelli's clarion call in Chapter 15, where he proclaims that he "departs from the orders of others" and says why. For moral qualities are qualities "held good" by the people; so, if the prince must conquer, and wants, like the Medici, to lay his foundation on the peo-

ple, who are the keepers of morality, then a new morality consistent with the necessity of conquest must be found, and the prince has to be taught anew about the nature of peoples by Machiavelli. In departing from the orders of others, it appears more fitting to Machiavelli "to go directly to the effectual truth of the thing than to the imagination of it." Many have imagined republics and principalities, but one cannot "let go of what is done for what should be done," because a man who "makes a profession of good in all regards" comes to ruin among so many who are not good. The prince must learn to be able not to be good, and use this ability or not according to necessity.

This concise statement is most efficacious. It contains a fundamental assault on all morality and political science, both Christian and classical, as understood in Machiavelli's time. Morality had meant not only doing the right action, but also doing it for the right reason or for the love of God. Thus, to be good was thought to require "a profession of good" in which the motive for doing good was explained; otherwise, morality would go no deeper than outward conformity to law, or even to superior force, and could not be distinguished from it. But professions of good could not accompany moral actions in isolation from each other; they would have to be elaborated so that moral actions would be consistent with each other and the life of a moral person would form a whole. Such elaboration requires an effort of imagination, since the consistency we see tells us only of the presence of outward conformity, and the elaboration extends over a society, because it is difficult to live a moral life by oneself; hence morality requires the construction of an imagined republic or principality, such as Plato's *Republic* or St. Augustine's *City of God*.

When Machiavelli denies that imagined republics and principalities "exist in truth," and declares that the truth in these or all matters is the effectual truth, he says that no moral rules exist, not made by men, which men must abide by. The rules or laws that exist are those made by governments or other powers acting under necessity, and they must be obeyed out of the same necessity. Whatever is necessary may be called just and reasonable, but justice is no more reasonable than what a person's prudence tells him he must acquire for himself, or must submit to, because men cannot afford justice in any sense that transcends their own preservation. Machiavelli did not attempt (as did Hobbes) to formulate a new definition of justice based on self-preservation. Instead, he showed what he meant by not including justice among the eleven pairs of moral qualities that he lists in Chapter 15. He does mention justice in Chapter 21 as a calculation of what a weaker party might expect from a prince whom it has supported in war, but even this little is contradicted by what Machiavelli says about keeping faith in Chapter 18 and about betraying one's old supporters in Chapter 20. He also brings up justice as something identical with necessity in Chapter 26. But, what is most striking, he never mentions—not in *The Prince,* or in any of his works—natural justice or natural law, the two conceptions of justice in the classical and medieval tradition that had been handed down to his time and that could be found in the writings on this subject of all his contemporaries. The grave issue raised by the dispute whether Machiavelli was truly "Machiavellian" is this: does justice exist by nature or by God, or is it the convenience of the prince (government)? "So let a prince win and maintain a state: the means will always be judged honorable, and will be praised by everyone" (Chapter 18). Reputation, then, is outward conformity to successful human force and has no reference to moral rules that the government might find inconvenient.

If there is no natural justice, perhaps Machiavelli can teach the prince how to rule in its absence—but with a view to the fact that men "profess" it. It does not follow of necessity that because no natural justice exists, princes can rule successfully without it. Governments might be as unsuccessful in making and keeping conquests as in living up to natural justice; indeed, the traditional proponents of natural justice, when less confident of their own cause, had pointed to the uncertainty of gain, to the happy inconstancy of fortune, as an argument against determined wickedness. But Machiavelli thinks it possible to "learn" to be able not to be good. For each of the difficulties of gaining and keeping, even and especially for the fickleness of fortune, he has a "remedy," to use his frequent expression. Since nature or God does not support human justice, men are in need of a remedy; and the remedy is the prince, especially the new prince. Why must the new prince be preferred?

In the heading to the first chapter of *The Prince* we see that the kinds of principalities are to be discussed together with the ways in which they are acquired, and then in the chapter itself we find more than this, that principalities are classified into kinds by the ways in which they are acquired. "Acquisition," an economic term, is Machiavelli's word for "conquest"; and acquisition determines the classifications of governments, not their ends or structures, as Plato and Aristotle had thought. How is acquisition related to the problem of justice?

Justice requires a modest complement of external goods, the equipment of virtue in Aristotle's phrase, to keep the wolf from the door and to provide for moral persons a certain decent distance from necessities in the face of which morality might falter or even fail. For how can one distribute justly without something to distribute? But, then, where is one to get this modest complement? The easy way is by inheritance. In Chapter 2, Machiavelli considers hereditary principalities, in which a person falls heir to everything he needs, especially the political power to protect what he has. The hereditary prince, the man who has everything, is called the "natural prince," as if to suggest that our grandest and most comprehensive inheritance is what we get from nature. But when the hereditary prince looks upon his inheritance—and when we, generalizing from his case, add up everything we inherit—is it adequate?

The difficulty with hereditary principalities is indicated at the end of Chapter 2, where Machiavelli admits that hereditary princes will have to change but claims that change will not be disruptive because it can be gradual and continuous. He compares each prince's own construction to building a house that is added on to a row of houses: you may not inherit all you need, but you inherit a firm support and an easy start in what you must acquire. But clearly a row of houses so built over generations presupposes that the first house was built without existing support and without an easy start. Inheritance presupposes an original acquisition made without a previous inheritance. And in the original acquisition, full attention to the niceties of justice may unfortunately not be possible. One may congratulate an American citizen for all the advantages to which he is born; but what of the nasty necessities that prepared this inheritance—the British expelled, Indians defrauded, blacks enslaved?

Machiavelli informs us in the third chapter, accordingly, that "truly it is a very natural and ordinary thing to desire to acquire." In the space of a few pages, "natural" has shifted in meaning from hereditary to acquisitive. Or can we be consoled by reference to Machiavelli's republicanism, not so prominent in *The Prince* with the thought that acquisitiveness may be natural to princes but is not natural to republics? But in Chapter 3 Machiavelli praises the successful acquisitiveness of the "Romans," that is, the Roman republic, by comparison to the imprudence of the king of France. At the time Machiavelli is referring to, the Romans were not weak and vulnerable as they were at their inception, they had grown powerful and were still expanding. Even when they had enough empire to provide an inheritance for their citizens, they went on acquiring. Was this reasonable? It was, because the haves of this world cannot quietly inherit what is coming to them; lest they be treated now as they once treated others, they must keep an eye on the have-nots. To keep a step ahead of the have-nots the haves must think and behave like have-nots. They certainly cannot afford justice to the have-nots, nor can they waste time or money on sympathy.

In the Dedicatory Letter Machiavelli presents himself to Lorenzo as a have-not, "from a low and mean state"; and one thing he lacks besides honorable employment, we learn, is a unified fatherland. Italy is weak and divided. Then should we say that acquisitiveness is justified for Italians of Machiavelli's time, including him? As we have noted, Machiavelli does not seem to accept this justification because, still in Chapter 3, he advises a French king how to correct the errors he had made in his invasion of Italy. Besides, was Machiavelli's fatherland Italy or was it Florence? In Chapter 15 he refers to "our language," meaning Tuscan, and in Chapter 20 to "our ancients," meaning Florentines. But does it matter whether Machiavelli was essentially an Italian or a Florentine patriot? Anyone's fatherland is defined by an original acquisition, a conquest, and hence is always subject to redefinition of the same kind. To be devoted to one's native country at the expense of foreigners is no more justified than to be devoted to one's city at the expense of fellow countrymen, or to one's family at the expense of fellow city-dwellers, or, to adapt a Machiavellian remark in Chapter 17, to one's patrimony at the expense of one's father. So to "unify" one's fatherland means to treat it as a conquered territory—conquered by a king or republic from within; and Machiavelli's advice to the French king on how to hold his conquests in Italy was also advice to Lorenzo on how to unify Italy. It appears that, in acquiring, the new prince acquires for himself.

What are the qualities of the new prince? What must he do? First, as we have seen, he should rise from private or unprivileged status; he should not have an inheritance, or if he has, he should not rely on it. He should owe nothing to anyone or anything, for having debts of gratitude would make him dependent on others, in the widest sense dependent on fortune. It might seem that the new prince depends at least on the character of the country he conquers, and Machiavelli says at the end of Chapter 4 that Alexander had no trouble in holding Asia because it had been accustomed to the government of one lord. But then in Chapter 5 he shows how this limitation can be overcome. A prince who conquers a city used to living in freedom need not respect its inherited liberties; he can and should destroy such cities or else rule them personally. Fortune supplies the prince with nothing more than opportunity, as when Moses found the people of Israel enslaved by the Egyptians, Romulus found himself exposed at birth, Cyrus found the Persians discontented with the empire of the Medes, and Theseus found the Athenians dispersed (Chapter 6). These famous founders had the virtue to recognize the opportunity that fortune offered to them—opportunity for them, harsh necessity to their peoples. Instead of dispersing the inhabitants of a free city (Chapter 5), the prince is lucky enough to find them dispersed (Chapter 6). This suggests that the prince could go so far as to make his own opportunity by creating a situation of necessity in which no one's inherited goods remain to him and everything is owed to you, the new prince. When a new prince comes to power, should he be grateful to those who helped him get power and rely on them? Indeed not. A new prince has "lukewarm defenders" in his friends and allies, because they expect benefits from him; as we have seen, it is much better to conciliate his former enemies who feared losing everything (compare Chapters 6 and 20).

Thus, the new prince has virtue that enables him to overcome his dependence on inheritance in the widest sense, including custom, nature, and fortune, and that shows him how to arrange it that others depend on him and his virtue (Chapters 9, 24). But if virtue is to do all this, it must have a new meaning. Instead of cooperating with nature or God, as in the various classical and Christian conceptions, virtue must be taught to be acquisitive on its own. Machiavelli teaches the new meaning of virtue by showing us both the new and the old meanings. In a famous passage on the successful criminal Agathocles in Chapter 8, he says "one cannot call it virtue to kill one's fellow citizens, betray one's friends, to be without faith, without mercy, without religion." Yet in the very next sentence Machiavelli proceeds to speak of "the virtue of Agathocles."

The prince, we have seen in Chapter 15, must "learn to be able not to be good, and to use this and not use it according to necessity." Machiavelli supplies this knowledge in Chapters 16 to 18. First, with superb calm, he delivers home-truths concerning the moral virtue of liberality. It is no use being liberal (or generous) unless it is noticed, so that you are "held liberal" or get a name for liberality. But a prince cannot be held liberal by being liberal, because he would have to be liberal to a few by burdening the many with taxes; the many would be offended, the prince would have to retrench, and he would soon get a name for stinginess. The right way to get a reputation for liberality is to begin by not caring about having a reputation for stinginess. When the people see that the prince gets the job done without burdening them, they will in time consider him liberal to them and stingy only to the few to whom he gives nothing. In the event, "liberality" comes to mean taking little rather than giving much.

As regards cruelty and mercy, in Chapter 8 Machiavelli made a distinction between cruelties well used and badly used; well-used cruelties are done once, for self-defense, and not continued but turned to the benefit of one's subjects, and badly used ones continue and increase. In Chapter 17, however, he does not mention this distinction but rather speaks only of using mercy badly. Mercy is badly used when, like the Florentine people in a certain instance, one seeks to avoid a reputation for cruelty and thus allows disorders to continue which might be stopped with a very few examples of cruelty. Disorders harm everybody; executions harm only the few or the one who is executed. As the prince may gain a name for liberality by taking little, so he may be held merciful by not being cruel too often.

Machiavelli's new prince arranges the obligation of his subjects to himself in a manner rather like that of the Christian God, in the eye of whom all are guilty by original sin; hence God's mercy appears less as the granting of benefits than as the remission of punishment. With this thought in mind, the reader will not be surprised that Machiavelli goes on to discuss whether it is better for the prince to be loved or feared. It would be best to be both loved and feared, but, when necessity forces a choice, it is better to be feared, because men love at their convenience but they fear at the convenience of the prince. Friends may fail you, but the dread of punishment will never forsake you. If the prince avoids making himself hated, which he can do by abstaining from the property of others, "because men forget the death of a father more quickly than the loss of a patrimony," he will again have

subjects obligated to him for what he does not do to them rather than for benefits he provides.

It is laudable for a prince to keep faith, Machiavelli says in Chapter 18, but princes who have done great things have done them by deceit and betrayal. The prince must learn how to use the beast in man, or rather the beasts: for man is an animal who can be many animals, and he must know how to be a fox as well as a lion. Men will not keep faith with you; how can you keep it with them? Politics, Machiavelli seems to say, as much as consists in breaking promises, for circumstances change and new necessities arise that make it impossible to hold to one's word. The only question is, can one get away with breaking one's promises? Machiavelli's answer is a confident yes. He broadens the discussion, speaking of five moral qualities, especially religion; he says that men judge by appearances and that when one judges by appearances, "one looks to the end." The end is the outcome or the effect, and if a prince wins and maintains a state, the means will always be judged honorable. Since Machiavelli has just emphasized the prince's need to appear religious, we may compare the people's attitude toward a successful prince with their belief in divine providence. As people assume that the outcome of events in the world is determined by God's providence, so they conclude that the means chosen by God cannot have been unworthy. Machiavelli's thought here is both a subtle attack on the notion of divine providence and a subtle appreciation of it, insofar as the prince can appropriate it to his own use.

It is not easy to state exactly what virtue is, according to Machiavelli. Clearly he does not leave virtue as it was in the classical or Christian tradition, nor does he imitate any other writer of his time. Virtue in his new meaning seems to be a prudent or well-taught combination of vice and virtue in the old meaning. Virtue for him is not a mean between two extremes of vice, as is moral virtue for Aristotle. As we have seen, in Chapter 15 eleven virtues (the same number as Aristotle's, though not all of them the same virtues) are paired with eleven vices. From this we might conclude that virtue does not shine of itself, as when it is done for its own sake. Rather, virtue is as it takes effect, its truth is its effectual truth; and it is effectual only when it is seen in contrast to its opposite. Liberality, mercy, and love are impressive only when one expects stinginess (or rapacity), cruelty, and fear. This contrast makes virtue apparent and enables the prince to gain a reputation for virtue. If this is so, then the new meaning Machiavelli gives to virtue, a meaning which makes use of vice, must not entirely replace but somehow continue to coexist with the old meaning, according to which virtue is shocked by vice.

A third quality of the new prince is that he must make his own foundations. Although to be acquisitive means to be acquisitive for oneself, the prince cannot do everything with his own hands: he needs help from others. But in seeking help he must take account of the "two diverse humors" to be found in every city—the people, who desire not to be commanded or oppressed by the great, and the great, who desire to command and oppress the people (Chapter 9). Of these two humors, the prince should choose the people. The people are easier to satisfy, too inert to move against him, and too numerous to kill, whereas the great regard themselves as his equals, are ready and able to conspire against him, and are replaceable.

The prince, then, should ally with the people against the aristocracy; but how should he get their support? Machiavelli gives an example in the conduct of Cesare Borgia, whom he praises for the foundations he laid (Chapter 73). When Cesare had conquered the province of Romagna, he installed "Remirro de Orco" (actually a Spaniard, Don Remiro de Lorqua) to carry out a purge of the unruly lords there. Then, because Cesare thought Remirro's authority might be excessive, and his exercise of it might become hateful—in short, because Remirro had served his purpose—he purged the purger and one day had Remirro displayed in the piazza at Cesena in two pieces. This spectacle left the people "at the same time satisfied and stupefied"; and Cesare set up a more constitutional government in Romagna. The lesson: constitutional government is possible but only after an unconstitutional beginning. In Chapter 9 Machiavelli discusses the "civil principality," which is gained through the favor of the people, and gives as example Nabis, "prince" of the Spartans, whom he calls a tyrant in the *Discourses on Livy* because of the crimes Nabis committed against his rivals. In Chapter 8 Machiavelli considers the principality that is attained through crimes, and cites Agathocles and Oliverotto, both of whom were very popular despite their crimes. As one ponders these two chapters, it becomes more and more difficult to find a difference between gaining a principality through crimes and through the favor of the people. Surely Cesare Borgia, Agathocles, and Nabis seemed to have followed the same policy of pleasing the people by cutting up the great. Finally, in Chapter 19, Machiavelli reveals that the prince need not have

the support of the people after all. Even if he is hated by the people (since in fact he cannot fail to be hated by someone), he can, like the Roman emperor Severus, make his foundation with his soldiers (see also Chapter 20). Severus had such virtue, Machiavelli says, with an unobstrusive comparison to Cesare Borgia in Chapter 7, that he "stupefied" the people and "satisfied" the soldiers.

Fourth, the new prince has his own arms, and does not rely on mercenary or auxiliary armies. Machiavelli omits a discussion of the laws a prince should establish, in contrast to the tradition of political science, because, he says, "there cannot be good laws where there are not good arms, and where there are good arms there must be good laws" (Chapter 12). He speaks of the prince's arms in Chapters 12 to 14, and in Chapter 14 he proclaims that the prince should have no other object or thought but the art of war. He must be armed, since it is quite unreasonable for one who is armed to obey one who is disarmed. With this short remark Machiavelli seems to dismiss the fundamental principle of classical political science, the rule of the wise, not to mention the Christian promise that the meek shall inherit the earth.

Machiavelli does not mean that those with the most bodily force always win, for he broadens the art of war to include the acquisition as well as the use of arms. A prince who has no army but has the art of war will prevail over one with an army but without the art. Thus, to be armed means to know the art of war, to exercise it in time of peace, and to have read histories about great captains of the past. In this regard Machiavelli mentions Xenophon's "Life of Cyrus," as he calls it (actually "The Education of Cyrus"), the first and best work in the literature of "mirrors of princes" to which *The Prince* belongs. But he calls it a history, not a mirror of princes, and says that it inspired the Roman general Scipio, whom he criticizes in Chapter 17 for excessive mercy. Not books of imaginary republics and principalities, or treatises on law, but histories of war, are recommended reading for the prince.

Last, the new prince with his own arms is his own master. The deeper meaning of Machiavelli's slogan, "one's own arms," is religious, or rather, antireligious. If man is obligated to God as his creature, then man's own necessities are subordinate or even irrelevant to his most pressing duties. It would not matter if he could not afford justice: God commands it! Thus Machiavelli must look at the new prince who is also a prophet, above all at Moses.

Moses was a "mere executor of things that had been ordered by God" (Chapter 6); hence he should be admired for the grace that made him worthy of speaking with God. Or should it be said, as Machiavelli says in Chapter 26, that Moses had "virtue," the virtue that makes a prince dependent on no one but himself? In Chapter 13 Machiavelli retells the biblical story of David and Goliath to illustrate the necessity of one's own arms. When Saul offered his arms to David, David refused them, saying, according to Machiavelli, that with them he could not give a good account of himself, and according to the Bible, that the Lord "will deliver me out of the hand of this Philistine." Machiavelli also gives David a knife to go with his sling, the knife which according to the Bible he took from the fallen Goliath and used to cut off his head.

Must the new prince—the truly new prince—then be his own prophet and make a new religion so as to be his own master? The great power of religion can be seen in what Moses and David founded, and in what Savonarola nearly accomplished in Machiavelli's own time and city. The unarmed prince whom he disparages in Chapter 6 actually disposes of formidable weapons necessary to the art of war. The unarmed prophet becomes armed if he uses religion for his own purposes rather than God's; and because the prince cannot acquire glory for himself without bringing order to his principality, using religion for himself is using it to answer human necessities generally.

The last three chapters of *The Prince* take up the question of how far man can make his own world. What are the limits set on Machiavelli's political science (or the "art of war") by fortune? At the end of Chapter 24 he blames "these princes of ours" who accuse fortune for their troubles and not their own indolence. In quiet times they do not take account of the storm to come. But they should—they can. They believe that the people will be disgusted by the arrogance of the foreign conquerors and will call them back. But "one should never fall in the belief you can find someone to pick you up." Whether successful or not, such a defense is base, because it does not depend on you and your virtue.

With this high promise of human capability, Machiavelli introduces his famous Chapter 25 on fortune. He begins it by asking how much of the world is governed by fortune and God, and how much by man. He then supposes that half is governed by fortune (forgetting God) and half by man, and he compares fortune to a violent river that can be contained with dikes and dams. Turning to par-

ticular men, he shows that the difficulty in containing fortunes lies in the inability of one who is impetuous to succeed in quiet times or of one who is cautious to succeed in stormy times. Men, with their fixed natures and habits, do not vary as the times vary, and so they fall under the control of the times, of fortune. Men's fixed natures are the special problem Machiavelli indicates; so the problem of overcoming the influence of fortune reduces to the problem of overcoming the fixity of different human natures. Having a fixed nature is what makes one liable to changes of fortune. Pope Julius II succeeded because the times were in accord with his impetuous nature; if he had lived longer, he would have come to grief. Machiavelli blames him for his inflexibility, and so implies that neither he nor the rest of us need respect the natures or natural inclinations we have been given.

What is the new meaning of virtue that Machiavelli has developed but flexibility according to the times or situation? Yet, though one should learn to be both impetuous and cautious (these stand for all the other contrary qualities), on the whole one should be impetuous. Fortune is a woman who "lets herself be won more by the impetuous than by those who proceed coldly"; hence she is a friend of the young. He makes the politics of the new prince appear in the image of rape; impetuous himself, Machiavelli forces us to see the question he has raised about the status of morality. Whether he says what he appears to say about the status of women may be doubted, however. The young men who master Lady Fortune come with audacity and leave exhausted, but she remains ageless, waiting for the next ones. One might go so far as to wonder who is raping whom, cautiously as it were, and whether Machiavelli, who has personified fortune, can impersonate her in the world of modern politics he attempted to create.

Source: Harvey C. Mansfield Jr. , in an introduction to *The Prince,* by Niccolo Machiavelli, translated by Harvey C. Mansfield, Jr., The University of Chicago Press, 1985, pp. vii–xxiv.

Garrett Mattingly

In the following excerpt, Mattingly proposes that The Prince *be interpreted as a satire.*

The notion that this little book [*The Prince*] was meant as a serious, scientific treatise on government contradicts everything we know about Machiavelli's life, about his writings, and about the history of his time.

In the first place, this proposition asks us to believe that Niccolo Machiavelli deliberately wrote a handbook meant to help a tyrant rule the once free people of Florence....

He has left proof of his devotion in the record of his activities and in the state papers in which he spun endless schemes for the defense and aggrandizement of the republic, and constantly preached the same to his superiors. One characteristic quotation is irresistible. The subject is an increase in the defense budget that Machiavelli's masters were reluctant to vote. He reminds them with mounting impatience that only strong states are respected by their neighbors and that their neglect of military strength in the recent past has cost them dear, and he ends with anything but detached calm:

> Other people learn from the perils of their neighbors, you will not even learn from your own, nor trust yourselves, nor recognize the time you are losing and have lost. I tell you fortune will not alter the sentence it has pronounced unless you alter your behavior. Heaven will not and cannot preserve those bent on their own ruin. But I cannot believe it will come to this, seeing that you are free Florentines and have your liberty in your own hands. In the end I believe you will have the same regard for your freedom that men always have who are born free and desire to live free.

Only a man who cared deeply for the independence of his city would use language like this to his employers. But Machiavelli gave an even more impressive proof of his disinterested patriotism. After fourteen years in high office, in a place where the opportunities for dipping into the public purse and into the pockets of his compatriots and of those foreigners he did business with were practically unlimited (among other duties he acted as paymaster-general of the army), Machiavelli retired from public life as poor as when he had entered it. Later he was to refer to this record with pride, but also with a kind of rueful astonishment; and, indeed, if this was not a unique feat in his day, it was a very rare one....

Machiavelli emerged from prison in mid-March, 1513. Most people believe that *The Prince* was finished by December. I suppose it is possible to imagine that a man who has seen his country enslaved, his life's work wrecked and his own career with it, and has, for good measure, been tortured within an inch of his life should thereupon go home and write a book intended to teach his enemies the proper way to maintain themselves, writing all the time, remember, with the passionless objectivity of a scientist in a laboratory. It must be possible to imagine such behavior, because Machiavelli schol-

ars do imagine it and accept it without a visible tremor. But it is a little difficult for the ordinary mind to compass.

The difficulty is increased by the fact that this acceptance of tyranny seems to have been a passing phase. Throughout the rest of his life Machiavelli wrote as a republican and moved mainly in republican circles....

The notion that *The Prince* is what it pretends to be, a scientific manual for tyrants, has to contend not only against Machiavelli's life but against his writings, as, of course, everyone who wants to use *The Prince* as a centerpiece in an exposition of Machiavelli's political thought has recognized. Ever since Herder, the standard explanation has been that in the corrupt conditions of sixteenth-century Italy only a prince could create a strong state capable of expansion. The trouble with this is that it was chiefly because they widened their boundaries that Machiavelli preferred republics. In the *Discorsi* he wrote,

> We know by experience that states have never signally increased either in territory or in riches except under a free government. The cause is not far to seek, since it is the well-being not of individuals but of the community which makes the state great, and without question this universal well-being is nowhere secured save in a republic.... Popular rule is always better than the rule of princes.

This is not just a casual remark. It is the main theme of the *Discorsi* and the basic assumption of all but one of Machiavelli's writings, as it was the basic assumption of his political career.

There is another way in which *The Prince* is a puzzling anomaly. In practically everything else Machiavelli wrote, he displayed the sensitivity and tact of the developed literary temperament. He was delicately aware of the tastes and probable reactions of his public. No one could have written that magnificent satiric soliloquy of Fra Timotheo in *Mandragola,* for instance, who had not an instinctive feeling for the response of an audience. But the effect of the publication of *The Prince* on the first several generations of its readers in Italy (outside of Florence) and in the rest of Europe was shock. It horrified, repelled and fascinated like a Medusa's head. A large part of the shock was caused, of course, by the cynical immorality of some of the proposals, but instead of appeasing revulsion and insinuating his new proposals as delicately as possible, Machiavelli seems to delight in intensifying the shock and deliberately employing devices to heighten it. Of these not the least effective is the way *The Prince* imitates, almost parodies, one of the best known and most respected literary forms of the three preceding centuries, the handbook of advice to princes. This literary type was enormously popular. Its exemplars ran into the hundreds of titles of which a few, like St. Thomas' *De Regno* and Erasmus' *Institutio principis christiani* are not quite unknown today. In some ways, Machiavelli's little treatise was just like all the other "Mirrors of Princes"; in other ways it was a diabolical burlesque of all of them, like a political Black Mass.

The shock was intensified again because Machiavelli deliberately addressed himself primarily to princes who have newly acquired their principalities and do not owe them either to inheritance or to the free choice of their countrymen. The short and ugly word for this kind of prince is "tyrant." Machiavelli never quite uses the word except in illustrations from classical antiquity, but he seems to delight in dancing all around it until even the dullest of his readers could not mistake his meaning. Opinions about the relative merits of republics and monarchies varied during the Renaissance, depending mainly upon where one lived, but about tyrants there was only one opinion. Cristoforo Landino, Lorenzo the Magnificent's teacher and client, stated the usual view in his commentary on Dante, written when Niccolo Machiavelli was a child. When he came to comment on Brutus and Cassius in the lowest circle of hell, Landino wrote:

> Surely it was extraordinary cruelty to inflict such severe punishment on those who faced death to deliver their country from slavery, a deed for which, if they had been Christians, they would have merited the most honored seats in the highest heaven. If we consult the laws of any well-constituted republic, we shall find them to decree no greater reward to anyone than to the man who kills the tyrant.

So said the Italian Renaissance with almost unanimous voice. If Machiavelli's friends were meant to read the manuscript of *The Prince* and if they took it at face value—an objective study of how to be a successful tyrant offered as advice to a member of the species—they can hardly have failed to be deeply shocked. And if the manuscript was meant for the eye of young Giuliano de Medici alone, he can hardly have been pleased to find it blandly assumed that he was one of a class of whom his father's tutor had written that the highest duty of a good citizen was to kill them.

The literary fame of *The Prince* is due, precisely, to its shocking quality, so if the book was seriously meant as a scientific manual, it owes its literary reputation to an artistic blunder....

Perhaps nobody should be rash enough today to call *The Prince* a satire, not in the teeth of all the learned opinion to the contrary. But when one comes to think of it, what excellent sense the idea makes! However you define "satire"—and I understand that critics are still without a thoroughly satisfactory definition—it must include the intention to denounce, expose or deride someone or something, and it is to be distinguished from mere didactic condemnation and invective (when it can be distinguished at all) by the employment of such devices as irony, sarcasm and ridicule. It need not be provocative of laughter; I doubt whether many people ever laughed or even smiled at the adventures of Gulliver among the Yahoos. And though satire admits of, and in fact always employs, exaggeration and overemphasis, the author, to be effective, must not appear to be, and in fact need not be, conscious that this is so. When Dryden wrote, "The rest to some faint meaning make pretense / But Shadwell never deviates into sense," he may have been conscious of some overstatement, but he was conveying his considered criticism of Shadwell's poetry. And when Pope called "Lord Fanny" "this painted child of dirt that stinks and strings," the language may be violent, but who can doubt that this is how Pope felt? Indeed the satirist seems to put forth his greatest powers chiefly when goaded by anger, hatred and savage indignation. If Machiavelli wrote *The Prince* out of the fullness of these emotions rather than out of the dispassionate curiosity of the scientist or out of a base willingness to toady to the destroyers of his country's liberty, then one can understand why the sentences crack like a whip, why the words bite and bum like acid, and why the whole style has a density and impact unique among his writings.

To read *The Prince* as satire not only clears up puzzles and resolves contradictions; it gives a new dimension and meaning to passages unremarkable before. Take the place in the dedication that runs "just as those who paint landscapes must seat themselves below in the plains to see the mountains, and high in the mountains to see the plains, so to understand the nature of the people one must be a prince, and to understand the nature a prince, one must be one of the people." In the usual view, this is a mere rhetorical flourish, but the irony, once sought, is easy to discover, for Machiavelli, in fact, takes both positions. The people can only see the prince as, by nature and necessity, false, cruel, mean and hypocritical. The prince, from his lofty but precarious perch, dare not see the people as other than they are described in Chapter Seventeen: "ungrateful, fickle, treacherous, cowardly and greedy. As long as you succeed they are yours entirely. They will offer you their blood, property, lives and children when you do not need them. When you do need them, they will turn against you." Probably Machiavelli really believed that this, or something like it, happened to the human nature of a tyrant and his subjects. But the view, like its expression, is something less than objective and dispassionate, and the only lesson it has for princes would seem to be: "Run for your life!"

Considering the brevity of the book, the number of times its princely reader is reminded, as in the passage just quoted, that his people will overthrow him at last is quite remarkable. Cities ruled in the past by princes easily accustom themselves to a change of masters, Machiavelli says in Chapter Five, but "in republics there is more vitality, greater hatred and more desire for vengeance. They cannot forget their lost liberty, so that the safest way is to destroy them—or to live there." He does not say what makes that safe. And most notably, with savage irony, "the duke [Borgia] was so able and laid such firm foundations … that the Romagna [after Alexander VI's death] waited for him more than a month." This is as much as to put Leo X's brother on notice that without papal support he can expect short shrift. If the Romagna, accustomed to tyranny, waited only a month before it rose in revolt, how long will Florence wait? Tactlessness like this is unintelligible unless it is deliberate, unless these are not pedantic blunders but sarcastic ironies, taunts flung at the Medici, incitements to the Florentines.

Only in a satire can one understand the choice of Cesare Borgia as the model prince. The common people of Tuscany could not have had what they could expect of a prince's rule made clearer than by the example of this bloodstained buffoon whose vices, crimes and follies had been the scandal of Italy, and the conduct of whose brutal, undisciplined troops had so infuriated the Tuscans that when another band of them crossed their frontier, the peasants fell upon them and tore them to pieces. The Florentine aristocrats on whom Giovanni and cousin Giulio were relying to bridge the transition to despotism would have shared the people's revulsion to Cesare, and they may have been rendered somewhat more thoughtful by the logic of the assumption that nobles were more dangerous to a tyrant than commoners and should be dealt with as Cesare had dealt with the petty lords of the Romagna. Moreover, they could scarcely have avoided noticing the advice to use some faithful servant to terrorize the rest, and then to sacrifice him to escape the obloquy of his conduct, as Cesare had sacrificed Captain Ramiro. As for the gentle, mild-mannered, indolent Giuliano de Medici himself, he was the last man to be attracted by the notion of imitating the Borgia. He wanted no more than to occupy the same social position in Florence that his magnificent father had held, and not even that if it was too much trouble.

Besides, in the days of the family's misfortunes, Giuliano had found shelter and hospitality at the court of Guidobaldo de Montrefeltre. Guiliano lived at Urbino for many years (there is a rather charming picture of him there in Castiglione's *Il Cortegiano*), and all his life he cherished deep gratitude and a strong affection for Duke Guidobaldo. He must have felt, then, a special loathing for the foreign ruffian who had betrayed and plundered his patron, and Machiavelli must have known that he did. Only a wish to draw the most odious comparison possible, only a compulsion to wound and insult, could have led Machiavelli to select the Borgia as the prime exemplar in his "Mirror of Princes."

There is one last famous passage that reads differently if we accept *The Prince* as satire. On any other hypothesis, the final exhortation to free Italy from the barbarians sounds at best like empty rhetoric, at worst like calculating but stupid flattery. Who could really believe that the lazy, insipid Giuliano or his petty, vicious successor were the liberators Italy awaited? But if we have heard the mordant irony and sarcasm of the preceding chapters and detected the overtones of hatred and despair, then this last chapter will be charged with an irony turned inward, the bitter mockery of misdirected optimism. For before the Florentine republic had been gored to death by Spanish pikes, Machiavelli had believed, as he was to believe again, that a free Florentine republic could play the liberator's role. Perhaps, since he was all his life a passionate idealist, blind to reality when his desires were strong, Machiavelli may not have given up that wild hope even when he wrote *The Prince*.

Source: Garrett Mattingly, "Machiavelli's *Prince*: Political Science or Political Satire?," in *The American Scholar*, Vol. 27, No. 4, Autumn, 1958, pp. 482-91.

Sources

Sidney Anglo, *Machiavelli: A Dissertation,* Harcourt, Brace and World, 1969.

Lord Macaulay Thomas Babington, *Critical, Historical and Miscellaneous Essays,* Sheldon and Company, 1862, pp. 267-320.

Lord Acton John Emerich Dalberg-Acton, "Introduction," in *Il Principo* by Niccolo Machiavelli, edited by L. Arthur Burd, Clarenon Press, 1891, pp. xix-xi.

Richard Harvey, *A Theological Discourse of the Lamb of God and His Enemies,* n.p., 1590, pp. 93-9.

Garrett Mattingly, "Machiavelli's *Prince*: Political Science or Political Satire?" in *The American Scholar,* Vol. 27, No. 4, Autumn, 1958, pp. 482-91.

John McCormick, "Winning a Gang War," in *Newsweek,* November 1, 1999, 46-9.

Leo B. Strauss, *Thoughts on Machiavelli,* University of Chicago Press, 1958, pp. 54-84.

For Further Study

Stanley Bing, *What Would Machiavelli Do?,* Harperbusiness, 2000, 160 p.

> Bing satirically applies Machiavellian principles to contemporary corporate culture.

Sebastian de Grazia, *Machiavelli in Hell,* Princeton University Press, 1989, 497 p.

> Biographical study that examines Machiavelli's life in terms of the ideas presented in *The Prince.*

Harvey C. Mansfield, *Machiavelli's Virtue,* The University of Chicago Press, 1996, 371 p.

> Mansfield provides an insightful analysis of Machiavelli's concept of virtue.

Vespasiano, *Renaissance Princes, Popes, and Prelates: The Vespasiano Memoirs,* Harper and Row Torchbooks, 1963, 475 p.

> These memoirs, which were kept in the Vatican library and studied only by scholars until the nineteenth century, provide readers with the background of Machiavelli's political career.

Robinson Crusoe

Daniel Defoe
1719

Daniel Defoe's *The Life and Strange Surprising Adventures of Robinson Crusoe* was published as a fictional memoir in 1719. It was so commercially successful that he quickly wrote a sequel. Realizing that fake autobiographies made a good profit, Defoe wrote four more first-person narratives before 1724. The best known are *Moll Flanders* (1722), *A Journal of the Plague Year* (1722), and *The Fortunate Mistress, or Roxana* (1724).

Today *Robinson Crusoe* remains a popular adventure narrative. In fact, the book gave rise to the "Robinsonade," adventure tales that rework the structural elements of Crusoe's island tale. Moreover, the character of Robinson Crusoe is recognized as a literary and cultural icon, like Don Quixote, Don Juan, and Faust; the story of a man stuck on a deserted island has become familiar to nearly everyone in the Western world.

Author Biography

Daniel Defoe was born in 1660 in Cripplegate, just outside the walls of the City of London. His parents, James and Alice Foe, were Dissenters—Protestants who refused to accept the authority of the Anglican Church (also known as the Church of England).

In 1670 Defoe's mother died and he was sent to boarding school. He attended Charles Morton's academy at Newington Green, where he received

an excellent education and developed a taste for political radicalism.

Defoe finished his studies at Morton in 1679 and entered the hosiery business. In 1684 he married Mary Tuffley, a wealthy young woman. He prospered in business and became a member of the Butcher's Company—one of several companies that controlled business in London. He also gained several influential friends in the government.

Unfortunately, Defoe overextended his investments—at one point he owed seventeen thousand pounds—and was sued eight times between 1688 and 1694, ending up in debtor's prison in 1692. However, King William III proved to be a true patron and by the late 1690s Defoe's fortunes were on the mend.

His first important work, *An Essay upon Projects* (1697), proposed social improvement schemes; his first profitable work was a political poem satirizing xenophobia, *The True-Born Englishman* (1701).

After the death of William III, Queen Anne succeeded him on the English throne. There was no one to protect Defoe when he was revealed as the author of *The Shortest Way with the Dissenters,* (1702), a pamphlet which satirically advocated extermination of religious nonconformists. For his work, Defoe suffered three days in the pillory—but he was somewhat vindicated when the crowd threw flowers instead of rotten vegetables. Meanwhile, he went bankrupt.

Robert Harley, the Tory who headed Queen Anne's government, made Defoe a spy and forced him to gather information on his political opponents. Defoe's opinion journal, *The Review,* became a mouthpiece for Harley's views. While a Tory spy, Defoe toured Britain and invested in Scotland. In 1707, the year that England and Scotland were united in the Act of Union, Defoe owned every newspaper in Edinburgh.

Queen Anne's death in 1714 precipitated the decline of the Tory Party and put Defoe—a Tory spy but a Whig at heart—in an awkward position. When Defoe was imprisoned for slanderous remarks, Lord Chief Justice Parker decided to release Defoe and make him a spy for George I. Defoe became saboteur of the anti-government Tory paper, *Weekly Journal.*

Meanwhile, Defoe experimented with prose and began to write innovative fiction. His first novel was his 1717 "memoir" chronicling the story of peace negotiations with France.

Daniel Defoe

In 1719 *Robinson Crusoe* was published to commercial success. It was followed by four more very popular "biographies," as well as essays on crime, the family, and economics. He died in 1731.

Plot Summary

Born in York

A retired German merchant named Kreutznaer settles in the York country where, due to the "usual corruption of words in England," the German name becomes Crusoe. In York, Mr. Crusoe marries a woman whose surname is Robinson.

Robinson Crusoe, born in 1632, is their third child. Early on, Crusoe's father determines that his son will become a lawyer. Unfortunately, Crusoe "would be satisfied with nothing but going to sea." His mother and father do not allow it.

To London and Trade

A year later Crusoe sneaks away and accepts passage to London. He leaves on September 1, 1651. During a terrible storm, he promises to return home to his parents. Yet after the ship sinks, he forgets his promise. Instead, he goes to London and befriends the captain of a vessel bound for Guinea. He joins the voyage.

After a successful voyage, Crusoe resolves to make another journey with his friend. Yet after his friend suddenly dies, he gives most of his money to the captain's widow, invests some money, buys trade goods with the remainder, and takes the same ship for another voyage. On the way to Guinea, Moorish pirates seize the ship and he is forced to become a slave.

Two years later, Crusoe escapes in a fishing boat with the slave boy Xury. They sail down the "Barbarian Coast" of West Africa. Finally, just off the Cape Verde Islands, a Portuguese ship bound for Brazil rescues them. With Xury's consent, he sells him along with the boat's inventory to the ship's master.

Deciding to make his fortune in the area, Crusoe purchases a slave and a Brazilian sugar plantation. He enjoys moderate success with the new venture. A bit restless, he becomes interested in leading a slave expedition to Africa. So, at the "evil hour, the 1st of September, 1659," he embarks for Guinea; tragically, a hurricane wrecks the vessel on a sand bar and only Crusoe survives.

"The Island of Despair"

Crusoe is shocked to find himself on the deserted island. His shock gives way to jubilation and thanksgiving for his survival. However, when he realizes the serious nature of his dilemma, he runs around in shock, paranoia, and fear. He finally falls asleep in a tree gripping a stick.

Crusoe spends several days cannibalizing the shipwreck for materials and provisions. With these salvaged goods, he begins to establish a fort— which he calls his "castle"—where he rules over a dog, some cats, and a parrot. He keeps a record of time, but after his ink runs out, he cannot maintain his journal.

Reviewing his life, he realizes that he has been selfish and cruel. He repents and resolves to lead a virtuous life. His days are filled with exploring the island, improving his castle, domesticating goats, experimenting with pottery, and developing other skills necessary for self-sufficiency.

Having secured shelter and food, Crusoe makes a boat. He constructs a small one, but he is nearly swept out to sea by dangerous currents. He uses the boat only for transportation to other parts of the island.

After twelve years, Crusoe nearly dies of fright over "the print of a man's naked foot on the shore." In a flurry of self-preservation, he expands his fortifications. He also discovers human bones and signs of cannibalism. Eleven years later, he witnesses a cannibal feast. A Spanish ship wrecks off the coast and Crusoe is able to salvage some provisions from the wreck.

The End of Solitude

One night, in his twenty-fourth year on the island, he dreams of saving one of the cannibals and civilizing him. Eighteen months later, on a Friday, his dream comes true. The savage falls at Crusoe's feet out of gratitude. Crusoe calls him Friday, and teaches him important English words like "Master," "Yes," and "No."

Gradually, Friday becomes civilized, converts to Christianity, and adopts English habits. Friday tells Crusoe about the Spanish castaways living with his tribe on the mainland. Crusoe begins work on a bigger boat to bring the Spaniards to his island.

In the twenty-seventh year, cannibals hostile to Friday's tribe (along with a few of their captives) visit the island. One of the captives is a European, so Crusoe and Friday attack the cannibals to free the captive: Crusoe shoots several of them and the rest of the cannibals flee. One of the captives turns out to be Friday's father. With people to help and good advice, Crusoe expands his agricultural production.

On the condition that they accept Crusoe's leadership, the Spaniard and Friday's father leave to fetch the rest of the Spaniards. Meanwhile, a group of English mutineers lands on the island to dispose of their captain and his loyal officers. Crusoe and Friday rescue them, capture the mutineers, and take back the ship.

The mutineers choose to stay on the island as Crusoe's subjects rather than return for punishment in England. Crusoe takes Friday to England as honored guests of the rescued English captain.

Back to Civilization

After an absence of twenty-eight years, Crusoe returns London in June, 1687. After the English captain gives him a reward, Crusoe learns that his parents are dead.

Crusoe discovers that he is rich because of some previous investments. After rewarding those who served him faithfully and selling his plantation, he returns to London.

Aidan Quinn played the title role in Crusoe, *the 1989 film version of Defoe's novel.*

Back in London, he marries and fathers three children. After his wife dies, he embarks on a final journey. On the way back, he visits his colony, which is thriving.

Characters

Captain of the Guinea Trading Ship

Arriving in London, Crusoe happens to meet the master of a ship bound for Guinea. The two men become friends, and Crusoe decides to make the journey too. Unfortunately, the man dies en route to Guinea.

Captain's Widow

The widow of Crusoe's friend the Captain of the Guinea Trading Ship is one of the two substantial female characters in the book. A trustworthy friend, she watches his money and becomes his London agent.

These responsibilities are appropriate to the gender roles governing the London financial district. Women as well as men were investors in the Bank of England—affectionately known as the lady of Threadneedle Street.

Comrade in Hull

Crusoe meets a friend in Hull who offers him a trip to London. This friend represents the youth of the English mercantile class as well as a life of adventure. He inspires Crusoe in his dreams of a life at sea.

The Comrade's Father

The Comrade's father is the master of the first vessel Crusoe travels on in Yarmouth, where he goes to recover. When his comrade tells his father that Crusoe was on the vessel as a sailor, he tells Crusoe that he ought to give up seafaring.

The Comrade's father resembles Crusoe's own father. They are both old-fashioned men and fearful of change. For them, a man's destiny is determined at birth.

Robinson Crusoe

The protagonist of Defoe's fictional autobiography, Crusoe is an adventurous man who rejects the expectations of his family and the constraints of the English middle class for a life on the high seas. After a devastating wreck at sea —of which he is the only survivor—he is forced to live confront his fear about being alone in order to survive

Media Adaptations

- Since the silent black-and-white film in 1916 with Robert Paton Gibbs, there have been some sixteen film adaptations of *Robinson Crusoe*. This count includes versions in French, Spanish, Russian, Swiss, and German.

- However, this count does not include all of the spin-offs, such as a female Crusoe—as early as a silent film made in 1917—or animations of Crusoe as a rodent in, *Rabbitson Crusoe* (1956). In 1965, *Robinson Crusoe* was made into a TV series. The book was made into a TV movie in the United Kingdom in 1974.

- The most recent movie adapted from Defoe's novel is *Robinson Crusoe* (1996), produced by USA pictures. Directed by Rod Hardy and George Miller, Pierce Brosnan stars as a lovestruck Robinson Crusoe separated from the object of his desire.

the harsh demands of his lonely and solitary existence.

Crusoe is not by nature a brave man. In time, his reason grows sharper and he conquers his fears. In fact, for a time he wanders the island without any weaponry. He learns how to do many diverse tasks, such as making an ax, baking bread, and building an elaborate shelter. When faced with marauding cannibals, he attacks them and rescues their captives. Finally, when he returns to London, he is able to readjust to English life and even gets married and has a family.

Friday

Friday is a native rescued by Crusoe; the young man eventually becomes his loyal servant. He is described by Crusoe as a Creole—a mix of African and Indian—and represents the wildness of nature. Through his relationship with Friday, Crusoe is able to confront his fear of the native people of the region.

When Friday offers to exchange ideas with Crusoe on religion or technology, Crusoe refuses to learn from his knowledge. For example, when they begin to build a boat together, Friday wants to show Crusoe how to burn out the inside. Crusoe, however, insists on the more laborious method of using a hatchet. Crusoe's reluctance to treat Friday as an equal symbolizes general European attitudes toward "the savage."

Eventually, Friday becomes Europeanized, accepting English customs and religious concepts. He symbolizes the process of colonialization.

Mr. Kreutznaer

Crusoe's father is an immigrant from the town of Bremen, Germany. A merchant by trade, Mr. Kreutznaer's name is changed in England to Crusoe. He is a "wise and grave man" who pleads with Crusoe to give up his notions of adventure and settle in England at a solid middle-class occupation like law.

Mrs. Kreutznaer

Although his mother refuses to intercede on Crusoe's behalf and win him his father's blessing, she does support her son in private. She represents the "proper woman" referred to at the end—a hard worker who is not afraid of risks.

Old Savage

The Old Savage is one of the captives rescued by Crusoe and Friday; surprisingly, he turns out to be Friday's father. He too pledges allegiance to Crusoe.

Portuguese Captain

The Portuguese Captain's ship rescues Crusoe from Africa, takes him to Brazil, and purchases Xury. He also helps invest Crusoe's money and acts as a father figure for him. He is an honest pilot of his crew and vessel and he serves Crusoe faithfully.

The Spaniard

The Spaniard is one of the captives rescued by Crusoe and Friday. After they release and give him a weapon, the group is able to kill many of the cannibals. The Spaniard turns out to be an honest fellow who advises Crusoe to expand the plantation. The Spaniard's belief in Roman Catholicism is of no importance to Crusoe; what matters to him is that the Spaniard has a good work ethic and a true sense of honor.

Mr. Wells

Mr. Wells is Crusoe's Portuguese neighbor; his plantation is next to Crusoe's in Brazil. Crusoe and Mr. Wells exchange labor and help each other when needed—a common practice for colonizers at that time. Accordingly, they become good friends and look out for each other's affairs. It is Wells who takes over the management of Crusoe's estate while he lives on his island. Wells represents the settler and plantation operator.

Xury

Xury is a servant that is forced into slavery with Crusoe. Fortunately, they are able to escape their masters. Xury, like Friday, naturally assumes the role of obedient and affectionate slave. Xury represents a European's notion of the non-European. He has better natural instincts—he is a natural hunter, a hide processor, he can see better at night (or day, for it is Xury who spots the Portuguese ship), and his sense of self-preservation is keener. Xury agrees to being sold into slavery on the condition that if he converts to Christianity he will be free in ten years.

Themes

Fear

Robinson Crusoe must overcome his fear in order to survive his long ordeal on the deserted island. The trial by fear begins when he runs about like a madman, scared of every shadow, and sleeps in a tree with a weapon: "fear banished all my religious hope, all that former confidence in God." He quickly realizes that he must recover his wits and reason if he is to survive.

At several points in the narrative, Crusoe is almost overwhelmed by his fear of the unknown. It propels him to colonize the island, securing his shelter and becoming self-sufficient. His ability to funnel his fear into productivity and creativity allows him to survive under extreme conditions.

Crusoe masters his fear when he faces the ultimate challenge—the devil. Investigating a cave, he is met by a pair of eyes. At first scared, he realizes that he can confront this enemy just like he has met every other challenge on the island. "He that was afraid to see the devil, was not fit to live twenty years in an island all alone."

With that, he rushes in to confront the devil and discovers a dying goat. He has passed his trial.

Topics for Further Study

- Research the ecological impact of colonialism. Use your research to explain the problematic overpopulation of cats on the island in the novel. What kinds of problems do we have today with exotic specie invasions? Investigate such a problem in your area.

- How is the character of Friday presented in the novel? How is he different from other representations of native people in Defoe's time? Read Aphra Behn's *Oroonoko*. Contrast the character of Prince in that novel with Defoe's Friday.

- *Robinson Crusoe* was very popular as a children's book. What do you think children were supposed to learn from Crusoe? What moral lessons, if any, can be drawn from his story?

- Many economists use *Robinson Crusoe* when explaining basic economic theory. What principles of economics does Crusoe demonstrate?

- Crusoe is an ex-slave trader, but is horrified by the Spanish treatment of native South Americans. Research the role of England in the slave trade. Is Crusoe's treatment of the native population any better than that of the Spanish Conquistadors?

- Based on the novel, what was the eighteenth-century family like? How does it differ from your family?

Had he not faced his fears, he would have run away in full belief that the devil lived in that cave. Instead, he investigates and confronts his fear.

Human Condition

Robinson Crusoe is a meditation on the human condition, and an argument for challenging traditional notions about that condition. Finding himself alone in a deserted island, Crusoe struggles to maintain reason, order, and civilization. His "original sin" is his rejection of a conventional life. When he leaves England for a life on the high seas, he refuses to be "satisfied with the station wherein God and Nature hath placed" him.

Crusoe struggles with—and eventually triumphs over—nature. The book suggests that this struggle is at the heart of human nature: man is on earth to triumph and gain profit from nature. Any profit makes sense in this view of the world, whether that means getting just one plank out of a huge tree or building a boat too heavy to bring to the water. Once Crusoe is able to overcome his fear and subdue nature is rewarded handsomely.

Money

Consistent with Defoe's writings on economics, money is an important theme in *Robinson Crusoe.* At the beginning of the narrative, Crusoe details how much money he has, what he does with it, and what he gains by his actions.

On the island, money loses all value. Crusoe has to find another way to measure his worth. While rummaging through a ship for salvage he laments aloud at the sight of some money, "O Drug! ... what are thou good for." At that point he realizes that just one knife is worth more than money. Usefulness is the key to evaluation of worth.

Crusoe's hope of returning to England is symbolized by these tokens of civilization—on the island, the money is only a reminder of his old life and he treasures it as a memento. In all of his other endeavors he freely admits his success or failure. But as a merchant, he knows that though separated from the world now, he can only reconnect with it if he has money. Once he returns to London, his old reliance on money returns.

Industrialization

Industrialization is defined here as a process whereby humans channel the forces of nature into the production and manufacture of goods for their economic consumption. This industrialization is Crusoe's occupation, according to his cultural background and his religion. He immediately sets out to be productive and self-sufficient on the island.

By the time of *Robinson Crusoe,* most villages were experiencing labor specialization. People began to buy bread instead of baking it. Thus Crusoe has to relearn many of these arts to survive. With practice, Crusoe is able to increase the level of industrialization on his island.

Crusoe has a few implements with which he is able to reconstruct a semblance of civilization as well as create more advanced technology. While building his house, he notes that every task is exhausting. In brief, he praises the idea of "division of labor" as he describes cutting timber out of trees, bringing the wood from the trees to the construction site, and then constructing his shelter. He soon devises labor-saving devices, thus increasing his efficiency and productivity.

The necessity of a sharp ax leads Crusoe to invent his own foot-powered sharpener. He has "no notion of a kiln," but he manages to fire pottery. He needs a mill for grinding his grain, but not finding a proper stone, he settles for a block of hard wood. The entire process of baking his own bread spurs a realization of how wonderful the state of human technology is.

People take the labor behind the necessities of life for granted when such items can be easily purchased in the market. Crusoe is not suggesting that people return to a world of self-sufficient households. Instead, as he goes about his Herculean tasks, like creating a simple shelf in his house, he comments that a carpenter could have finished the two-day job in an hour. Thus he appreciates the process of specialization that helps make industrialization so successful.

Style

Narrative

Robinson Crusoe is a fictional autobiography written from a first-person point of view, apparently written by an old man looking back on his life. The story also includes material from an incomplete diary, which is integrated into the novel.

Spiritual Fable

Robinson Crusoe can be viewed as a spiritual or religious fable. Defoe was very concerned with religious issues, and nearly became a Dissenter minister. In the preface of the book, Crusoe asserts that he aims to "justify and honour the wisdom of Providence in all the variety of our circumstance."

In so doing, Crusoe clearly sees himself as part of the tradition of religious instruction manuals. The book does show similarities to the four different types of spiritual fable. Firstly, Crusoe, like many Puritans, keeps a diary in which he records his progress toward salvation. Of this first form of spiritual biography, the best known is John Bunyan's 1666 *Grace Abounding.*

The second form of spiritual fable evident in Crusoe is the guide or advice tradition. This type of fable is aimed at particular audiences—seamen, farmers, young people, women—to point out the dangers of human existence, especially their own. The goal of such works is to show not just the dangers but the solution, usually a prayer.

The tale of Providence is the third tradition evident in Crusoe's story. In such tales, God is believed to be a being who intervenes in the affairs of people. Crusoe is constantly speculating on whether an event is due to God's intervention in providential terms.

The last form is the pilgrim allegory, like Bunyan's *Pilgrim's Progress (1678)*. This form was very popular but often amounted to no more than a modernization of the parable about the Prodigal Son, or the story of Jonah.

In this form, a young man leaves his home and consequently isolates himself from God. This act results from pride, discontent, or the rejection of a "calling." God intervenes, usually with violence, to bring about a change in the prodigal's direction back toward Himself. By this intervention, the man realizes he should have stayed home or accepted his calling and thus willingly confronts evils and hardships to return to God. Crusoe's adventure follows this pattern.

Verisimilitude

Although heavily influenced by religious concerns and technique, Defoe's use of realism, or verisimilitude, is perhaps the most singular aspect of the work. What Defoe did was apply and thereby popularize modern realism.

Modern realism—as formulated by Descartes and Locke but not fully outlined until Thomas Reid—holds that truth should be discovered at the individual level by verification of the senses. The realistic elements of *Robinson Crusoe* include the lists, time scale, repetition, diary, and Crusoe's ordinary nature. The reader could almost use *Robinson Crusoe* as a handbook if ever stuck on a deserted island.

Time

The concept of time is central to the structure of *Robinson Crusoe*. Defoe presents Crusoe's life chronologically. The details of Crusoe's life and activities mark the passage of time; and while exhausting to the modern reader, these small details reflect the concern with time during that period.

Allegory

Many critics view *Robinson Crusoe* as an allegory for Defoe's life. The first such attempt, by Charles Gildon, was spurred by a comment in the preface of Defoe's *Serious Reflections During the Life and Surprising Adventures of Robinson Crusoe*. Many scholars have since tried to match the known details about Defoe with the events in Crusoe. No one has been successful.

Earlier works by Defoe add credence to this view. His notebook of meditations, written when he was twenty-one, show that Robinson Crusoe's story was on his mind a long time, well before the sensational tales about Alexander Selkirk.

More clues can be found in Defoe's most autobiographical piece, *An Appeal to Honour and Justice* (1715). Defoe claims that he endured great solitude but had remained "silent under the infinite Clamours and Reproaches, causeless Curses, unusual Threatnings, and the most unjust and injurious Treatment in the World." Although it is impossible to be certain whether *Robinson Crusoe* is an allegory for Defoe, it is certain that Crusoe represents Defoe's thoughts on solitude and industriousness.

Historical Context

Dissenters

Dissenters (also Nonconformists) is a term that refers to Protestant ministers and congregations (among them: Quakers, Congregationalists, Presbyterians, and Baptists) who rejected the authority of the Anglican Church. Dissenters refused to participate in Anglican services, take communion, or conform to the tenants of the Church of England under the 1662 Act of Uniformity and the later Five Mile Act.

The Act of Uniformity decreed that all ministers adhere to the Book of Common Prayer. Those who refused were penalized by the Five Mile Act, which ordered that lawbreakers could not come within five miles of their home parish or town.

When William and Mary assumed the throne in 1688, their need for money and their belief in tolerance prompted them to pass the Toleration Act of 1689. This law allowed Dissenters to license their meeting houses with their own ministers, provided they took oaths of allegiance to England according to the Test Act.

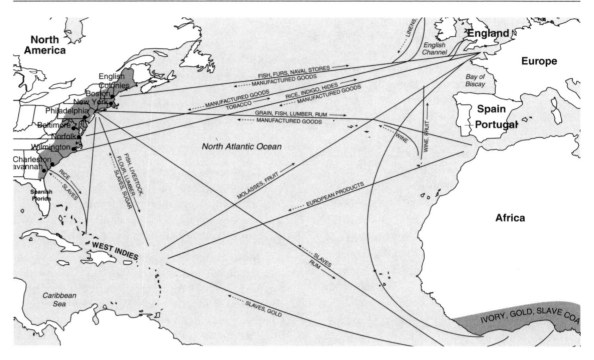

In the second half of the seventeenth century, trade between England, Europe, and overseas colonies boosted the British economy. This map depicts the triangular exchange of goods and slave labor that both Defoe and his protagonist practiced.

The Restoration

When Oliver Cromwell (1599–1658) came to power in England in 1653 he instituted a strict government based on Puritan principles. Although this benefited the middle class and the merchants, his excessive taxes, his rule by force, and the absence of trial by jury or parliamentary representation gradually led the English people to hate him more than they had Charles I.

When Cromwell died in 1658, his son Richard (1628–1712) assumed the reigns of power. His weakness soon led to his resignation, and the army and parliament verged on a civil war. However, the monarchy was restored to power when General George Monck invited Charles II to return.

Charles II (1630–1685) restored the British monarchy in May of 1660. An enthusiastic parliament convened in the following year, and became known as the "Cavalier Parliament." Its session lasted until 1679. The Church of England was restored by the Clarendon Code, which also demanded oaths of allegiance to the king. It also made it unlawful to raise arms against the king.

Colonialism

Two dominant European powers lost much of their power during the seventeenth century. Firstly, Spain's decline began after a series of naval losses. Secondly, Portugal was not able to withstand Dutch aggression. Although both nations would retain control over several colonies, by the end of the seventeenth century France and England became the dominant world powers.

England's colonies in North America— Jamestown, Virginia (founded 1607) and Plymouth, Massachusetts (founded 1620)—were becoming prosperous by the 1700s. The original English colonies in the New World were joined by new ones: the Carolinas (1663), Pennsylvania (1682), and islands in the West Indies.

Glorious Revolution

When Charles II died, James II (1633–1701) assumed the throne of England. A fervent Roman Catholic, James freed many Catholics, Quakers, and Dissenters from prison. Alarmed by his policies, the Earl of Argyll and the Duke of Monmouth joined to overthrow the King in 1685. They were defeated, due in large part to a lack of support from

Compare & Contrast

- **1600s:** Religion is a central focus of life. Many European countries—such as England, Spain, the Netherlands, and Portugal—persecute religious reformists and dissenters. As a result, many religious radicals emigrate to the New World in order to practice their religious beliefs.

  Early 1700s: Religious fervor cools. The *philosophes* in France are trying to eradicate religion from their country with little success.

  Today: Religious tolerance, while not universal, is accepted. The percentage of people that believe in some kind of organized religion remains high in most countries.

- **1600s:** Countries such as England, France, and Spain strive to remain formidable imperialistic powers. Maintaining colonial power and building a formidable military force is very expensive.

  Early 1700s: Between the banking developments in Amsterdam and the Bank of England, the foundations of modern national finance are laid and the concept of the national debt is created.

  Today: For poor nations, a national debt prevents them from challenging rich nations. In the wealthy nations, national debts cause much worry, but their existence is vital to the global financial market.

- **1600s:** Trade is mostly in raw goods, luxury items, or expensive manufactured items. Occupational specialization is accelerating in European economies. For example, a farmer might begin to focus on dairy production.

  Early 1700s: Manufactured goods are growing more plentiful while becoming less expensive. The average person can now buy bread, candles, and cloth from specialized merchants.

  Today: The economy of most Western countries has shifted away from manufacturing to technology.

---

the noble classes and the London merchants. Some suggest that Defoe himself was among those captured.

In 1688, James II had an heir and he proceeded to impose his Catholic agenda, including Catholicizing the army. The nobles and merchants decided to bet their lives on an "invasion," by extending an invitation to the Protestant rulers William and Mary of the United Provinces (Netherlands).

William III (1650–1702), having promised to defend English liberties and Protestantism, landed with an army in 1688 and marched unopposed on London. James II fled to Ireland where his supporters, the Jacobites, were strong. He had French backing as well as the support of some of the Scottish clans. The Scottish Jacobites were defeated by William III at Killiecrankie in 1689.

In the following year, William III defeated James II at the Battle of the Boyne in Ireland.

William then turned his attention to Europe. With English money and troops, he fought against the French in the War of the League of Augsberg until 1697. William's need for money led to the creation of the Bank of England (1694), and a commercial revolution which would enable Britain to eventually dominate global commerce.

England in 1719

In 1719 England was a more tolerant and stable country; as a result, emigration to America decreased. As Defoe reported while in London, the wages of workers in England were high and unemployment low. Competition in the textile trade resulted in an threatened market, but the English re-tooled and remained competitive.

After the instability of Cromwell and the Restoration, the Hanovers assumed the throne. By the Treaty of Utrecht, English vessels had access to Spanish trade. This latter development made economists like Defoe enthusiastic about the market.

When the stock market crashed as a result of the South Sea Bubble in 1721, a great number of previously wealthy people lost their fortunes. Unlike a similar bubble known as France's Mississippi Scheme, the incident did not cool English enthusiasm for capital speculation and stock trading. Consequently, England recovered from the South Sea Bubble to develop the financial resources necessary to launch the Industrial Revolution.

Critical Overview

Robinson Crusoe did not revolutionize the book industry in London, but it was a great commercial success; in fact, a second edition was released within only two weeks after the first had been published. Pirated editions came out within hours of the book's release. One of these pirated editions, known as the 'O' edition, is extremely valuable today.

Critical reaction to *Robinson Crusoe* is generally negative or patronizing. Many early commentators derided the novel as commercial and unrefined. Yet many commentators celebrated the adventurous hero, Robinson Crusoe.

Charles Gildon launched the first sustained attack on Defoe's novel with *The Life and Strange Surprizing Adventures of Mr. D-De F-*, in 1719. In his critique, Gildon focuses on the novel's inaccuracies, as well as a "Looseness and Incorrectness of Stile."

His most interesting criticism, however, charges Defoe with slander in regards to English shipping practices. He contends that there is "no Man so ignorant as not to know that our Navigation produces both Safety and our Riches and that whoever therefore shall endeavor to discourage this, is so far a profest Enemy of his Country's Prosperity and Safety." Little did Gildon, or anyone else at the time, realize that *Robinson Crusoe* was to inspire many colonial and pioneering dreams.

Decades later, Theophilus Cibber, a playwright and Shakespeare reviser, signaled a change in critical attitudes toward *Robinson Crusoe*. In his 1753 essay, he praises Defoe for his "moral conduct" and "invincible integrity." *Robinson Crusoe*, he says, "was written in so natural a manner, and with so many probable incidents, that, for some time after

its publication, it was judged by most people to be a true story."

Jean-Jacques Rousseau concurred with Cibber in 1762, when he recommended *Robinson Crusoe*. Furthermore, asserted Rousseau, since books are necessary, then *Robinson Crusoe* should be given to children for it teaches them self-sufficiency.

Scottish critics were just as enthusiastic about Defoe's novel. James Beattie included a review of *Robinson Crusoe* in his *Dissertations Moral and Critical* (1783). He maintained that the story is "one of those books, which one may read, not only with pleasure, but also with profit."

Sir Walter Scott, the leading advocate of verisimilitude in the early nineteenth century, praised the work for its realism. Scott also noted the tremendous impact it had on boys who go to sea for the first time "in the corner of the nursery." Robinson Crusoe's "situation is such as every man may make his own, and, being possible in itself, is, by the exquisite art of the narrator, rendered as probable as it is interesting."

In the second half of the nineteenth century, scholars began a debate to the real identity of Robinson Crusoe. Thomas Wright proposed that the character of Robinson Crusoe is based on Alexander Selkirk. So prevalent was this belief that maps even to this day mark Selkirk's island off the coast of Chile as Crusoe's island, despite the clear description in the novel of the island's location.

In his *Das Kapital*, (1867), Karl Marx deemed *Robinson Crusoe* as capitalist propaganda. Ian Watt, in his *The Rise of the Novel*, concurred with Marx's analysis. Moreover, Watt asserted that Puritanism was merely a precursor to capitalism.

With this perspective, Watt echoed the theory of his contemporary, Max Weber, while setting the terms for much of the debate surrounding the novel. In fact, with the exception of Diana Spearman and George A. Starr, the economic reading of the novel dominated critical perspectives of *Robinson Crusoe* until the 1980s.

Although James Joyce explored the colonialist theme of *Robinson Crusoe* as early as 1911, his comments were not published until 1964. Since then, writers such as Toni Morrison, Derek Walcott, and Edward Said have viewed the novel as an allegory of colonialism.

Peter Hulme argues for the importance of placing the novel within its historical context. Hulme's article does not bash Defoe but praises him for his "scrupulous attention to financial details" as well as his honesty.

Hulme suggests that the hero has two personalities: one is in isolation on an island working on his individualism while his "ghostly 'partner'" is enslaving people and managing a plantation. The most dangerous point of the book is when the two are reunited.

Criticism

Jeremy W. Hubbell

Jeremy W. Hubbell is a graduate student in History at SUNY Stony Brook and has written for a wide variety of business, academic, and educational publishers. In the following essay, he views Robinson Crusoe *as a guidebook for English colonialism.*

Today, the typical reading of Daniel Defoe's *Robinson Crusoe* assumes that the novel is central to the bourgeois myth. However, as Diana Spearman and others have pointed out, the story of a man in isolation for twenty-four years is a strange myth for a class of people dependent on an economic system that requires people to interact with one another through an economic medium.

Instead, Defoe's novel meditates on the redeeming qualities offered by the labor of colonialism for the Englishman. Work was the way to civilize the wilderness of the New World and achieve peace with God. The project of colonialism, as the Puritans were proving at the start of the eighteenth century, provided a profitable way of realizing God's directive in Genesis: "be fruitful, multiply, fill the earth and conquer it."

Although too old to follow God's directive, Defoe hoped to persuade the English people to engage in the good work. He even shows them how—the Englishman must be ruthless yet reasonable in order to conquer nature and receive God's reward. Defoe's novel encourages England to emulate the Puritans in their success.

He believed that Englishmen were destined to succeed at colonialism if they overcame their fear through the use of their psychological tools: their reason, their work ethic, and their Protestant faith. In *Robinson Crusoe*, Defoe imagines a *true-born Englishman* fulfilling his fantasy. Throughout the novel, Defoe makes clear that a man's power over

himself and nature depends upon ceaseless labor—this is the secret to the colonial project.

Before the colonialist can begin to work, security precautions must be taken. This is Crusoe's first concern. The next phase of conquest is the act of possession.

Both concerns are demonstrated during his escape from slavery and his dealings with Xury, who embodies the barbarities of both slavery and Africa. Crusoe has two advantages over the boy, in that he is bigger and he has a gun. In other words, Crusoe's first providential trial is a small contest. He passes and is and is amply rewarded.

In this first trial, his planning and stealth (both are forms of work) have already provided him with possessions, but Xury's subordination secures his claim to the ownership of the commandeered vessel, the stolen goods, and even Xury himself. This pattern of getting and securing by force is repeated throughout the novel. The power of the patriarch, however, comes only by the grace of God, and only after vast expenditures of labor.

On the island, Crusoe cannot immediately carry out this model as well as he wishes. He must first master himself. The process of mastering himself and his environment takes twenty years, finally culminating when he faces what he believes to be a devil, which turns out to be a dying goat.

During those twenty years, Crusoe illustrates the small steps towards self-sufficiency and self-mastery. His entire scheme of labor and conquest serializes the lesson of patience. Part of this lesson involves a day-to-day manufacture of an organized civilization.

He wants to construct a castle, but he must first "make me some tools." Thus, he recovers as many items of civilization as possible from the wrecked ship. Next, he sets about remaking civilization with those salvaged objects. He constructs a shovel, a table, and a chair. These things prevent him from existing "like a mere savage."

As a civilized man, he makes peace with God and institutes daily readings from the New Testament. From this point on, there are few skills he cannot master with the use of logic and reason, although issues of security and ownership remain unsettled.

The island contains no singular embodiment of nature to be conquered, so instead every element of the island presents a threat. Crusoe vacillates on how to deal with these threats. The first method involves visualization of mastery:

What Do I Read Next?

- Another of Defoe's fictional biographies, *The Fortunes and Misfortunes of the Famous Moll Flanders,* was published in 1722. It is the story of an orphan, Moll Flanders, who is brought up in the house of the Mayor of Colchester. Moll leads an interesting life as she is involved with a succession of men, journeys to Virginia, returns to England, becomes destitute and, consequently, a prosperous thief.

- *A Journal of the Plague Year* (1722) exhibits Defoe's talents as a journalist. The book details the devastating effects of a crippling plague.

- Defoe's *Roxana, or the Fortunate Mistress,* (1724) chronicles the story of Roxana. The daughter of French Huguenots, Roxana and her children are abandoned by her husband. Along with her trustworthy maid, Amy, Roxana leads a life of adventure and dissipation.

- One of the more famous Robinsonades grew out of the bedtime stories which Johann David Wyss (1743–1818) told to his family. Along with overseeing the education of his sons, Wyss loved to read tales of exploration such as those of Captain Cook and George Forster. His bed-

time stories were written down by the family and published in 1812 as *The Swiss Family Robinson.*

- Jules Verne was one of the most enthusiastic writers of the Robinsonade. Verne modernized Defoe's story. In his version, Robinson is a scientist who by accident finds himself in an unexplored world. His most explicit Robinsonade is the 1874 novel, *The Mysterious Island.* In this story a group of men in a hot-air balloon crash on an island, where they proceed to build mines, kilns, and factories.

- Robert Louis Stevenson's *Treasure Island* (1883) remains a popular adventure tale. The story takes place in the eighteenth century, and begins when Jim Hawkins secures an old treasure map. He recruits some friends to go look for the treasure.

- William Golding's 1954 novel, *Lord of the Flies,* is considered a contemporary Robinsonade. When a plane of schoolboys crashes on an island, the boys' attempt to create a semblance of civilization fails. The boys separate into civilized and primitive camps.

I came to an opening ... the country appeared so fresh ... it looked like a planted garden ... surveying it with a secret kind of pleasure ... to think that this was all my own; that I was king and lord of all this country indefeasibly, and had a right and possession; and, if I could convey it, I might have it in inheritance as completely as any lord of a manor in England.

Here, Crusoe is expressing a Lockean sentiment: the perception that "I own it" is half of ownership. Yet this is insufficient, because anyone or anything could perceive and state likewise.

So Crusoe uses fear to complete his conquest. A metaphor for his use of terror is found in his conflicts with his winged enemies, the crows. He employs terror in the same way the English crown does; he hangs three dead crows as if they were

"notorious thieves" and, consequently, he never sees another bird in that part of the island.

He also employs terror with the goats. He learns the value of entrapment and starvation as coercive devices, and soon has a tame herd serving his nutritional needs. The most radical element of terror Crusoe employs in his campaign against the armies of nature and barbarity is the fortification of his shelter. For this, he uses trees, cables, and the earth to make impenetrable shelter.

However, his construction never serves a defensive purpose. Rather, it signifies the completion of his ownership; with his ten-foot walls, there is no doubt that he rules the land he has surveyed.

Crusoe's power depends upon a constant supply of labor. Once he has conquered the island with his hedges, fences, granaries and boats, he begins to fear that the cannibals will take it all away from him. Clearly, God's work is never finished, but Crusoe soon finds help.

As in his earlier ceremony of possession, he visualizes having a servant before he even rescues Friday. Colonialism, according to Crusoe, demands a steady state of mind developed in the course of laborious exercises. Even when Friday shows him an easier way of constructing a boat, Crusoe sticks to his own method.

Crusoe's success results from a cruelty to self. By doing things the hard way, he learned hard lessons, and he wants Friday to imitate him. His relationship with Friday reflects his relationship with himself.

Away from the hectic world of 1719, Crusoe is on his island in perfect isolation. Not only is Crusoe geographically located where Defoe had pinned his hopes (a colony at the mouth of the Orinoco where Sir Walter Raleigh attempted a settlement), but he lives in the time of greatest hope.

Defoe admired many of Oliver Cromwell's projects, especially the Navigation Acts, so it is not surprising that Crusoe is lost to civilization in 1659, the year Cromwell's son, Richard, lost political power. Once on the island, Crusoe reinvents society for himself. The island becomes his benevolent garden and he laboriously constructs the infrastructure of civilization by subjugating nature.

This is precisely the process the Puritans went through. As Joyce Appleby describes them in his *Capitalism and a New Social Order,* "Far from turning into modern entrepreneurs, Puritan men became rural patriarchs…. who commanded their wives, controlled their [children] and kept out any deviants who might spoil the sweet harmony of their peaceable kingdom." Crusoe behaves in the same way, keeping out crows, cannibals, or anyone refusing his authority. Power, for Crusoe, comes down to control:

> It would have made a stoic smile to have seen me and my little family sit down to dinner; there was my majesty, the prince and lord of the whole island; I had the lives of all my subjects [two cats, a parrot who is the only one permitted to talk, and a dog] at my absolute command; I could hang, draw, give liberty, and take it away; and no rebels among all my subjects.

This, and like passages, express Crusoe's belief in his "undoubted right of dominion" over the whole island. Such a belief in patriarchal forms of government led Philip Morgan to comment in his opus, *Slave Counterpoint,* that "Defoe had shrewdly caught the tenor of idealized plantation life." Granted, Defoe remains anxious about his ownership until he can register his claim in a European court.

The story of Crusoe is a counterpoint to the attitude that prevailed in London at the time: work, not speculation, will offer people full employment and contentment. Defoe was prophesying doom for the stock market, but he was echoing the warnings and calls for moderation issued by Horace Walpole.

The only thing of value in Crusoe's story is his *right* to rule his work and accomplishments. All of his speculations lead only to his distraction and endangerment. With a cool head and reason, as well as the backing of God, Crusoe will be safe, fed, and happy—not to mention rich. Defoe hoped the same for England and its people.

If Defoe wanted to write a novel of capitalism, he would not isolate his hero on an island for twenty-four years. In fact, Defoe never tired of pointing out that a proper economy depends upon an individual's free access to the market, other people, currency, and an unimpeded right to invest and profit with that capital. Defoe did not write a novel about the trials and tribulations of those attempting to involve themselves in commerce. His novel does not resemble a Horatio Alger story.

Robinson Crusoe is a religious instruction manual, cautioning the people of England against capital speculation or abandonment of their Puritan work ethic. Furthermore, the novel suggests that the English are destined to reap the rewards of colonialism due to their work ethic and their religious convictions.

Unlike every other castaway story popular in Defoe's time, in which the "hero" essentially goes crazy as a result of solitude, Crusoe thrives utilizing the Puritan principles—reason, work, and God. That is the lesson he wanted to provide to the English people.

Source: Jeremy W. Hubbell, in an essay for *Novels for Students,* Gale, 2000.

Robert H. MacDonald

In the following essay, MacDonald argues that the novel is about order, both physical and psychic, and that the establishment of order is its main myth.

A favourite scene of the illustrators of *Robinson Crusoe* is Crusoe's discovery of the footprint on the sand. Crusoe can be seen peering downwards in surprise and shock at an oversize and remark-

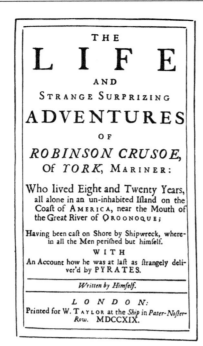

THE
LIFE
AND
STRANGE SURPRIZING
ADVENTURES
OF
ROBINSON CRUSOE,
Of *YORK*, MARINER:

Who lived Eight and Twenty Years,
all alone in an un-inhabited Iſland on the
Coaſt of AMERICA, near the Mouth of
the Great River of OROONOQUE;

Having been caſt on Shore by Shipwreck, wherein all the Men periſhed but himſelf.
WITH
An Account how he was at laſt as ſtrangely deliver'd by PYRATES.

Written by Himſelf.

LONDON:
Printed for W. TAYLOR at the *Ship* in *Pater-Noſter-
Row.* MDCCXIX.

The first edition of Defoe's novel, from which this title page is taken, was published as a fictional memoir in 1719.

ably distinct single footprint, which, when we check the story, oddly enough is still visible several days later. The image remains in the mind, a crystallization of what the book has come to mean to us, the hero in his shaggy goatskins, his isolation, his ever-present danger from unknown cannibals. The footprint scene comes well on in the novel, and its effect belongs as much to what popularity, posterity and Disneyland have done to Crusoe, as to the text itself. For the reader, an image as strong appears earlier: that of Crusoe driven by the earthquake from his refuge in the rock, sitting alone in the storm, outside his palisade. He is, he tells us, "greatly cast down and disconsolate," "very much terrify'd and dejected," and remains in his solitary, defenceless position for upwards of two hours. His wits quite leave him at first, he has no notion of what to do, and it is not until he all of a sudden decides that the wind and the rain which follow the earthquake are the consequence of the earthquake, and it would be safe for him to retreat once more into his cave, that he can make any motion at all. Defoe does not tell us so, but we imagine Crusoe as sitting and shivering, clasping his knees, his head bowed in despair.

Between them the two scenes might serve to epitomize two views of the novel: if the first is our dominant image, we see Robinson Crusoe as the resilient hero of adventure, the man who survived, the man alone, triumphant over not only nature but all outside danger. Giving the second image precedence in our imagination leaves us with a different Crusoe, a solitary, pathetic figure, an outcast, rejected by man and deserted by God. Chronologically, of course, these images need not be contradictory, and we can read the novel as the history of the outcast's triumph, his finding of God, and with God, strength. With this in mind, our memory of Crusoe as an orphan of the storm fades, and the scene of his isolation becomes but a prelude to his inevitable victory. Yet such a reconciliation seems unsatisfactory; the image of isolation is too strong to be forgotten.

The criticism of recent years has forced us to look at *Robinson Crusoe* with more respect, and has gone a long way to explain the novel's extraordinary force and strength. We know that the book is full of faults, that it is repetitious and often boring, that it is sloppily written by a forgetful author. We are aware that the time scheme is improbable and the end of the novel is tacked on. We are told that Crusoe's life is unrealistic, that he does not seem to suffer from the lack of company, or women, or an adequate diet. We know too that all these things matter very little, since the book has a mythic simplicity, an appeal that owes little to realism and nothing to chronology.

Yet what is the central myth of *Robinson Crusoe,* what is the one theme that gives the novel its organizing structure and its rationale? Ian Watt, in his familiar thesis of Crusoe as *Homo economicus,* argued for the novel as a myth of man alone, independent and free, while E.M.W. Tillyard placed the book in the tradition of epic. More recently, J. Paul Hunter has substantially reminded us of the background or religious allegory in the story, with Crusoe as a type of Adam, his sufferings and trials patterned upon the wanderings of the children of Israel. These views are well known, and each is necessary to an understanding of the novel: Crusoe *is* economic man, the hero of epic, *and* a reluctant pilgrim; he is all of these and more. Yet in thinking of him as a type we neglect his humanity, we forget how close he stands to ourselves. An article by Eric Berne on the psychology of the novel suggests a way of adjusting our perspective, in drawing attention to the man himself. Berne argues that Crusoe's behaviour on the island is motivated by his need to explore and secure the space around him, and in this Crusoe is at least partially successful. What is important about Berne's argument is not its conclusion—as a Freudian he sees Crusoe as something of a neurotic, the victim of an oral fixation—but his realization that the hero's conquest of the outer space of the island parallels the exploration of the inner space of the self.

I propose to look at this dual exploration from an archetypal viewpoint. Crusoe's quest is to find himself: a quest, both extraordinary and commonplace, heroic and human. He is the exceptional man, yet one of us; no neurotic, but a man undergoing the archetypal crises of life. Our response to him is one of sympathy, understanding and immediate recognition of his situation. *Robinson Crusoe*, I will argue, is a novel about order, both physical and psychic, and the establishment of this order is its dominant myth.

The island is Crusoe's microcosm; it contains the extreme conditions he must learn to cope with, the dangers and the delights, both around him and within his own self. On the island he learns to progress from spiritual ignorance to psychic integration. In the middle of the storm after the earthquake, we see him at perhaps his lowest point. He has survived his shipwreck, he has overcome his first fears of savages and wild animals, and he has laboriously salvaged innumerable articles from the hulk on the rocks. He has begun his system of fortification, erecting a semi-circular palisade of stakes around the face of a wall of rock, and he has tunnelled out his cave from this rock. Just before this point in the story, he seems to be well on his way to establishing himself in safety and some measure of repose, since he has seen his first miracle, the first sign of God's hand, in the discovery of the stalks of barley. Then comes the earthquake, which finds him inside his cave. His first action is to escape into the open, and he does this instinctively, being afterwards "like one dead or stupify'd." His first fear is of being buried himself, his next, that his tent and all his goods will be buried even if he is not. When the storm is over and he has had time to consider, he finds himself subject to two equal fears: one, of being swallowed up alive, the other, of being in the open, of "lying abroad without any fence."

Seeing the novel as a record of the hero's establishment of some kind of psychic order within his personality, this scene takes on a powerful meaning. We remember that Crusoe has been buried before: when he is shipwrecked we are told that the wave swallowed him up, and "buried me

at once 20 or 30 Foot deep in its own Body." Now, he again lives in fear of "being swallow'd up alive." His battle with Nature is cosmic; she seems a most terrifying and powerful force, ready to devour her unfortunate child. We remember that Crusoe is a Jonah, and that Leviathan lurks in the waves, even that he is a type of Christ, and must needs descend into the dark jaws of Hell before he can be reborn. With these mythic and allegorical parallels in our minds, we can see this earthquake scene as a second beginning, a thrusting out from the womb-like cave into the open world. Until Crusoe has become aware of his defencelessness he cannot (like Jonah) begin the ordering of his life.

One of the peculiarities of the beginning of the novel is the nature of Crusoe's sin. He tells us repeatedly that he is a sinner, and that his sin is filial disobedience. He is guilty not only for his refusal to obey his father, but also because he has resisted the will of God, who gives him clear signs that he should never go to sea. Yet in spite of these explanations, we sense that Crusoe's actual sin is only important as a rationalization, and that he is a victim of an unrelenting fate. His father's constant advice is that he should seek the "middle state," for the golden mean brings man's only chance of earthly happiness. This is "the just Standard of true Felicity," and it can only be Crusoe's "meer Fate or Fault" that stirs him to wander, for he is by no means content with this middle state, either in England or later on his plantation in Brazil, but must explore the extreme. This indeed is the eternal fate of the hero. Crusoe has been singled out, chosen for testing by Providence, and we can have no reluctance to accepting his claim to be the Wanderer; being someone very special, he becomes a surrogate for ourselves. As a story of crime and punishment, *Robinson Crusoe* is incomprehensible; as a record of an individual's struggle to accept the responsibilities of the heroic role, to go to limit of self and return sane, the novel is in the mythic tradition. Crusoe cannot reach an equilibrium until he has both discovered and come to an accommodation with the world of extremes. This world is both around him and within him, both in his conscious and his unconscious self.

What emerges from the first part of the story is the inevitability of Crusoe's role as wanderer, a man driven by Providence towards some critical moment. That this moment is not just retribution, nor yet another adventure, but a meeting with God and Self, is central to any thematic reading of the novel. Crusoe's God is of course an external power, controlling the elemental forces, showing Himself to Crusoe through the sea, the storm, the earthquake and nature, but He is at the same time within Crusoe, manifesting Himself in his thoughts and his dreams, directing his soul through secret stirrings. It does no historical injustice to the novel to see in this communication with God Crusoe's exploration of his psyche, and in particular, to recognize, in the gradual freeing of Crusoe's soul, his acceptance of his unconscious.

It is when he becomes sick with an ague that Crusoe has his first real experience of God and makes his first prayer. In the middle of his sickness he has a dream, in which "I thought, that I was sitting on the Ground on the Outside of my Wall, where I sat when the Storm blew after the Earthquake" when he sees a man descend from "a great black Cloud, in a bright Flame of Fire." This apparition seems unspeakable to Crusoe as it moves forward towards him with a "long Spear or Weapon" in its hand to kill him, and he is terrified when the figure speaks:

> I heard a Voice so terrible, that it is impossible to express the Terror of it; all that I can say, I understood, was this, Seeing all these Things have not brought thee to Repent, now thou shalt die: At which Words, I thought he lifted up the Spear that was in his Hand, to kill me.

Crusoe wakes filled with the horrors of this terrible vision.

This is clearly intended to be a symbolic conversation, the moment when Crusoe's Saul becomes Paul. The image of Crusoe's absolute isolation after the earthquake is repeated at the beginning of the dream: the two events in a sense are but one episode, when Crusoe is forced to reach down into his inner depths and find accommodation with his worst fears. In his half-conscious reflections upon his moral depravity immediately after his dream he casts his eye over his whole sinful life and comes to a true realization of his utter helplessness:

> now I have Difficulties to struggle with, too great even for Nature itself to support, and no Assistance, no Help, no Comfort, no Advice; then I cry'd out, Lord be my Help, for I am in great Distress.

From this point on his spiritual cure is hardly in doubt. Looking for tobacco as medicine for his sickness, he finds a Bible; looking in the Bible he finds guidance from the word of God. He is led to reconsider his past life, and given hope for the future. He comes to understand that from being confined upon a barren island, he has been delivered from a sinful career, from being imprisoned, he is now free.

On recovering from his sickness—which is of course spiritual as well as physical—he is able for the first time to set out upon a journey of exploration. He has a "great Desire to make a more perfect Discovery of the Island, and to see what other Productions I might find, which I yet knew nothing of." He crosses over into the other half of the island, finding that it is fruitful—his own part is barren—having meadows, a great deal of tobacco (the herb that had cured his illness), sugar canes, melons, and grapes. Going further, Crusoe finds a spring, and everything in "a constant Verdure…. that is looked like a planted Garden." He immediately imagines himself as the lord of this fair country.

It is clear that the effect of this scene is symbolic. Crusoe could not have found the fruitful part of the island until he had made peace with God; once he has realized he is no longer a prisoner the bars are open, and he is ready to be led into green pastures. On the psychological level, with his visionary dream Crusoe reaches into his unconscious, and is afterwards guided through his sickness by intuition and instinct. Until this point he has been resisting the forces within himself; after this dream he becomes resigned to his condition. On his recovery from his ague he is able to proceed further and explore the wonders of a new and delightful country, which in a sense may be said to stand for the unconscious itself. He builds a "bower" in this lotus land, and eventually sets up a little farm there, but significantly enough he never abandons his first home on the barren side of the island, telling himself that his rescue must come from that direction. The fruitful side has an almost seductive charm; there is something dangerous about it: it is from this side that the savages come when they do. Crusoe never thoroughly makes it his own, never quite surrenders himself, tempted though he is, to the "Pleasantness of the Place."

He is now able, however, to set up a reasonable and almost complete order in his new world after this first exploration of the island. He finds no want of food, and delights in all its variety. He tames first a parrot, then a young goat; added to his dog and cats they form his society. He professes himself increasingly comfortable, and his own house becomes a "perfect Settlement" to him. He still has his wanderings and doubts, but essentially he is at peace with himself:

> I began to conclude in my Mind, That it was possible for me to be more happy in this forsaken Solitary Condition, than it was probable I should ever have been in any other Particular State in the World; and

with this Thought I was going to give Thanks to God for bringing me to this Place.

It is at this point that we can see how completely Crusoe's inner order is reflected by his outer order. His actions at this stage of the novel are methodical and precise; working with hope in his breast he becomes increasingly constructive. He is an experimenter, hindered only by the inadequacies of his tools; he is a creator, limited only by his diminishing ignorance. We notice that Defoe's treatment of work is symbolic when we compare what Crusoe did before his dream and after. His first attempt to organize his solitary life was energetic rather than directed; with beaver-like industry he worked to create a world about him, making himself a home, fixing himself furniture, exploring a part of his neighbourhood. Immediately before his sickness he had worked frantically on a second salvage of the wreck, but all to very little purpose: he was frustrated by the tide and the sand; he could only hack pieces off the roll of lead, and the figurehead itself, freed by the wind, proved too heavy for him to move. He did manage to bring a mass of timber, planks and iron-work ashore, enough to build a boat "if I had known how." What characterizes this labour is its pointlessness. This is made quite plain by the contrast of the work done after his recovery from his sickness: now his labour is as tedious, but it is purposeful. He makes himself a board, and though it takes him five days before he can even begin to flatten the sides, he does succeed in his design, for he is patient. What does he need with boards, we might ask, remembering that he had salvaged enough planks from the ship to build a boat? The answer—unless we are willing to accept the explanation of the forgetful author—is that the labour is symbolic of his spiritual and physical cure; now Crusoe is a creator, who is building his own order. He does not want nor need the abundance of the wreck, which in a sense is tainted by his previous sin, but he must make do with natural material. He must make his own things, and he must make things work. So he proceeds by trial and error, often laboriously, but with a new sense of design. He discovers how to grow his corn, and in his many difficulties he is "content to work it out with Patience, and bear with the badness of the Performance."

In settling the small world about him, he adjusts to the cosmos itself, observing and taking note of the seasons. He organizes his agriculture according to these observations, sowing and harvesting at the proper times. He sets his daily routine in strict and sensible parts; no time is unaccounted for, no time is wasted:

> I was very seldom idle; but having regularly divided my Time, according to the several daily Employments that were before me, such as *First*, My Duty to God, and the Reading the Scriptures, which I constantly set a part some Time for thrice every Day. *Secondly*, The going Abroad with my Gun for Food, which generally took me three Hours in every Morning, when it did not Rain. *Thirdly*, The ordering, curing, preserving, and cooking what I had kill'd or catch'd for my Supply; these took up great Part of the Day....

He becomes an inventor, and after a fashion, a craftsman, discovering rough and ready ways to make his tools and pots. He sets himself up as the judge and executioner of his society, first over the animals (as with the birds that rob his field) and later over the savages and the mutineers. He still on occasion "wastes" his labour, spending long and fruitless hours on such a hopeless project as the first dug-out canoe, but this is a lapse, a backsliding from his real knowledge of God. In the main he is at peace with his inner self. He has long dialogues with his soul, questioning his fate and the workings of Providence, reassuring himself:

> Thus I liv'd mighty comfortably, my Mind being entirely composed by resigning to the Will of God, and throwing my self wholly upon the Disposal of his Providence. This made my life better sociable ...

He still has occasional meetings with the world of the unconscious which unnerve him, and show him the limits of his psychic order. On launching his second canoe, he is carried away by the current; on reaching firm land with much difficulty he regains his bower, and drops into a sleep of exhaustion. He is awakened by a voice calling his name, "where are you Robin Crusoe? Where are you? Where have you been?" This excursion into unknown waters is a frightening experience, and it is only after an extended self-explanation that he really accepts his questioner as "honest Poll," the "sociable Creature."

It is in the middle of a long and circumstantial account of Crusoe's ordered world—his plantations, his fortifications, his stores, his goats—that we are suddenly surprised, as he is himself, by the appearance of "the Print of a Man's naked Foot on the Shore." Crusoe of course is more than surprised, he is "Thunder-struck," and all his carefully constructed tranquility seems at once overturned. He hurries home to his fort, imagining intruders behind every bush, and immediately shuts himself up in great "Terror of Mind." His fears are far from rational: he finds it impossible "to describe how many various Shapes affrighted Imagination represented Things to me in, how many wild Ideas were found every Moment in my Fancy, and what strange unaccountable Whimsies came into my Thoughts by the Way." He supposes at times that the footprint belongs to the devil, for there is something supernatural about its appearance, something terrifying in it being a *single* mark. His musings at length take a more balanced note, and he turns once again to God, finding in His revealed work comfort and direction.

The footprint is a disruption of Crusoe's little kingdom; it is a sign that there have been trespassers about on the island. Its dramatic effect is all the more powerful for the detailed description we have just had of an island apparently tamed; now civilization is shown to be a facade, the inviolate society broken into almost by malevolent magic. Crusoe's immediate action is to re-organize his world, to set up more and yet more lines of defence about his fortifications, to crawl once more back into his island womb, to regret even the door on his cave. It is two years before he sees any further sign of the savages, and his mind, at first obsessed by thoughts of his own defence, then significantly enough turns to thoughts of revenge. "It would take up a larger Volume than this whole Work is intended to be, to set down all the Contrivances I hatch'd, or rather brooded upon in my Thought, for the destroying these Creatures." The savages are the intruders from another world; they must be met and destroyed before order can be restored.

It is as much Crusoe's inner peace that has been threatened as his outer order. Musing upon his now unsettled condition, he resolves to take direction from his unconscious:

How when we are in (a *Quandary,* as we call it) a Doubt or Hesitation, whether to go this Way, or that Way, a Secret Hint shall direct us this Way, when we intended to go that Way …

He makes it a rule of conduct from this time forth to obey these "secret Hints, or pressings of my Mind." To the Puritan this was a familiar way of receiving God's own instruction; Crusoe's speculations go a little further than usual, since he goes on to suppose that these "Intimations of Providence … are Proof of the Converse of Spirits, and the secret Communication between those embody'd, and those unembody'd…." It is just after these thoughts that he has another nasty fright in a second encounter with the devil, when, exploring a cave, he sees "two broad shining Eyes of some Creature,"

which terrifies him with a pair of loud, deep sighs. The devil turns out to be a goat. Crusoe once again in crawling into this enclosed and dark world—which reveals itself to be in its innermost depths the most "glorious Sight seen in the Island"—learns that the fear is of the unknown within and that indeed there is nothing so fearful as fear itself. Taking possession of this inner and most splendid cave, Crusoe fancies himself "like one of the ancient Giants," and for the first time feels quite safe from even "five hundred Savages."

Up to this point we have been shown a series of archetypal images in the life-voyage of this Wanderer: his disengorgement from the sea, more helpless and no wiser than Jonah himself; his isolation; his peril, first from (imaginary) wild animals, and later, from wild men; his burrowing back into the elemental earth: his expulsion from this womb to face the divine. As we have seen, this crisis, this meeting with the unconscious, is followed by the meticulous re-ordering of both the inner and the outer realities. The island, though still surrounded by the dangerous currents of the elemental waters, turns from prison into a kingdom, while the images of the wilderness give way to those of the enclosed garden. Now Crusoe, faced with the threat from the outside world, significantly seeks the solution within himself, enters the mouth of hell, confronts the devil, and finds in that cave of the unconscious a secure and hidden retreat.

He is by no means settled and easy after this experience in the cave, but still finds himself prey to innumerable doubts and fears. It is not until he meets his danger in the form of Friday that he becomes his old self once more: by taming, teaching and forming Friday after his own image he sets his world back to rights. Once the unknown becomes familiar, once he is able to make it his own and impose his own order upon it, it no longer offers a real threat to him. With Friday at his side, Crusoe spends "the pleasantest Year of all the Life I led in this Place."

Crusoe has now regained his confidence, and during the rest of the novel he is in command of his growing society. With the addition of Friday's father and the Spaniard "my Island was now peopled," and he is no longer just king in fancy. His resoluteness in guiding the attack on the savages, and later, in directing the defeat of the mutineers, makes us accept his title of "Governour" as real rather than ironic just as later, safe in Spain, his companions call him their "Captain." The order that he has imposed so carefully upon his own life is extended to those who come near him: he plans the rescue of the fourteen shipwrecked Spaniards, and he restores to his ship the captain and his companions, imposing resolute yet merciful justice upon the mutinous crew. The final imposition of order upon his by now expanded world is the settlement of his commercial affairs, whose notable success— and it is none of Crusoe's doing—is a reward for his finding of God and self.

He is now quite in touch with God and is content to be guided by the promptings of his inner self. His unconscious speaks to him in moments of crisis, and he listens: "I had some secret Doubts hung about me, I cannot tell from whence they came...." And they bid him to be on his guard, and so he is cautious. He speculates on the nature of such warnings, speaking of "certain Discoveries of an invisible World, and a Converse of Spirits." "Let no Man despise the secret Hints and Notices of Danger" he says, and later, on his way home to England, when he finds he has a "strange Aversion" to going to sea, he repeats the lesson: "let no Man slight the strong Impulses of his own Thoughts in Cases of such Moment."

Seen in this light, Crusoe's life becomes the experiencing and the ordering of the unknown. The peculiar scene of the wolves in the pass of the Pyrenees is felt as one last attack upon his psyche; by now he is so strong that even when "above three hundred Devils come roaring and open mouth'd" to devour him, and he tells us that he gives himself over for lost, we have little sense of crisis, and no fear for his safety.

This scene may be unrealistic, but realism, for all the detail of *homo economicus,* is not always Defoe's point. Crusoe's island is a world of creation and experience, and his twenty-eight years on the island should be read in somewhat of the same light as Jehovah's six days of creation. All is drawn into the myth of order: Crusoe becomes more than *homo economicus* and more than the Wanderer: he becomes, finally, every man who has ever tried to cope with a chaotic and hostile world.

Source: Robert H. MacDonald, "The Creation of an Ordered World in Robinson Crusoe," in *Dalhousie Review,* Vol. LVI, 1976, pp. 23-34.

Edwin B. Benjamin

In the following essay Benjamin discusses Defoe's contention that Robinson Crusoe *was autobiographical in nature, concluding that the book symbolized the author's spiritual development rather than an account of the historical facts of his life.*

Although Defoe claimed in the *Serious Reflections* that *Robinson Crusoe* was in part an allegory of his own life, attempts to connect details in the book with specific experiences in the life of Defoe have not been found convincing. Complicated as the connection is between Defoe's life and his works, I believe that the claim may yet be found valid if we look at the book as a symbolic account of a spiritual experience rather than a kind of cipher of its author's life. It is quite possible that the symbolism is by no means a part of Defoe's intention; as his imagination warmed to its task, the story began to take on its symbolic overtones, and his later comment is merely an attempt to defend himself against the charges of trying to pass off fiction as fact.

Allegory seems to have been always congenial to the Puritan mind as a legitimate province in which the imagination might exercise itself; and although at times in the eighteenth century it came to be looked down upon as a rather crude vehicle of literary expression, it continued longer as a vital tradition in the dissenting milieu in which Defoe's mind was molded than in more advanced intellectual and literary circles. Defoe can hardly have been unaffected by the forces that shaped Bunyan and that accounted for the continued popularity of his allegories. It is perhaps surprising that in view of his background we do not find more evidences of allegory in the work of Defoe.

Robinson Crusoe is far more than the account of a practical man's adjustment to life on a deserted island. Side by side with Crusoe's physical conquest of nature is his struggle to conquer himself and to find God. It is really a conversion story; like that of Augustine or Baxter, with the classic symptoms of supernatural guidance (in this case in a dream), penitential tears, and Biblical text. Despite repeated signs and warnings, Crusoe only gradually awakens to the necessity for salvation; and it is not until in his illness he stumbles to the tobacco box and comes upon the Bible that he crosses the hump. The final stage is his realization that his deliverance from the island is unimportant in comparison with his deliverance from sin through the mercy of God.

Now I began to construe the words mentioned above, *Call on me, and I will deliver you,* in a different sense from what I had ever done before; for then I had no notion of any thing being call'd deliverance, but my being deliver'd from the captivity I was in; ... but not I learn'd to take it in another sense. Now I look'd back upon my past life with such horrour, and my sins appear'd so dreadful, that my soul sought nothing of God but deliverance from the load of guilt that bore down all my comfort: as for my solitary life, it was nothing; I did not so much pray to be deliver'd from it, or think of it; it was all of no consideration in comparison to this.

From this point on, his mind is essentially at peace, and the remainder of his autobiography is in the nature of an account of the due rewards and powers of the man who has been saved.

Although Defoe's Christianity is at times fairly materialistic, especially in comparison with that of Augustine, Bunyan or Baxter, the account of Crusoe's conversion has a peculiar force and intensity to it that tempts one into believing it of some greater than ordinary personal significance to Defoe. It is indicative, I think, that as soon as Crusoe gets back to Europe, he sheds his Christianity like an old cloak and pursues his complacent way with only the most perfunctory expressions of gratitude to his Creator and Preserver (e.g., the scene in the Pyrenees when he is attacked by wolves). But whatever the personal associations of the story to Defoe, at least a part of the effectiveness of the novel is due to the way in which the parallel struggles set off and suggest one another. Some of the details of Crusoe's struggle with nature seem to symbolize his spiritual quest, though perhaps not intentionally on the part of Defoe. One notices that many of these are among the most emphatic and memorable incidents of the novel.

The main outline of Crusoe's story lends itself readily to allegorization. Given the notion of life as a voyage, which is at least as old as patristic commentaries on the *Aeneid,* both storm and desert island, punishment and proving ground, are logical corollaries. Contemporary use of some of these ideas can be found, for instance, in Matthew Greene's witty urbane *The Spleen.*

> Thus, thus I steer my bark, and sail.
> On even keel with gentle gale;
> At helm I make my reason sit,
> My crew of passions all submit.
> If dark and blustering prove some nights,
> Philosophy puts forth her lights;
> Experience holds the cautious glass,
> To shun the breakers, as I pass, …
> And once in seven years I'm seen
> At Bath or Tunbridge to careen.
> Though pleased to see the dolphins play,
> I mind my compass and my way….
> I make (may heaven propitious send
> Such wind and weather to the end)
> Neither becalmed nor over-blown,
> Life's voyage to the world unknown

However, it should be emphasized that the distinctive feature of *Crusoe* is that which is appar-

ently original with Defoe, the detailed account of Crusoe's adjustment to the island.

By no means all the details of the novel are allegorical. Some of these I have chosen may be found unconvincing, the well-disposed reader may wish to add others; but at least this will be a start toward isolating one of the elements that make the book such an appealing one.

The geography of the island is conceived in moral terms. The side of the island on which Crusoe lands and where he establishes his "home," as he calls it, although it affords a better prospect of the ocean, is less favored naturally than the other side that he explores later and where he builds his "bower." The latter yields not only a greater variety of fruits—aloes, limes, wild sugar cane, grapes—but a more numerous fauna. Goats abound in the rich meadow, also hares and fox-like creatures, and on the shore a great profusion of turtles, which are something of a rarity on the other side of the island. Crusoe is tempted to move, but decides against it—wisely, as it turns out; for the shore where the turtles can be found is the one where the cannibals are accustomed to land for their inhuman feasts. Also, the richness proves to be largely illusory. Crusoe doesn't dare eat the grapes until dried, for fear of flux; a batch he gathers and leaves overnight are "trod to pieces" and spread about by some "wild creatures"; the goats, though more numerous, are harder to catch because of lack of cover. In a curious passage in his second trip he describes descending into a large wooded valley where he becomes lost for several days in the forests and in a haze that springs up.

It is difficult not to sense allegory at work behind all this. Turtle, as in Pope and Fielding, is a symbol of luxurious living; the grapes are harder to fix, though there may be Biblical overtones here; and the hot misty forest has suggestions of sloth and lassitude: " … and then by easy journies I turn'd homeward, the weather being exceeding hot, and my gun, ammunition, hatchet, and other things very heavy." Since these experiences happen to Crusoe on his two exploratory trips shortly after his conversion, the thither side of the island becomes to him, like Egypt to the Israelites on the march to Canaan, a temptation to be resisted.

Fundamentally, the temptation to move is an appeal to a species of pride, not to remain where he had been cast up by divine Providence, but to go whoring after false gods. When it comes to attempting to escape from the island entirely, however, which presumably he must not do until a sign has been given, Crusoe shows that he is not proof against this sin. In his first effort, pride acts to blind his reason; he selects for his *periagua* a cedar so large (there is a significant reference to the temple of Solomon at this point) that when fashioned into a vessel, it cannot be launched by one man. Yet despite this warning he persists, builds a second boat, and, in maneuvering about the island, is almost swept away by currents to certain death. It is only then that Crusoe realizes where his unwillingness to accept his lot has led him; falling on his knees, he thanks God for his preservation and resolves "to lay aside all thoughts of my deliverance by my boat."

This incident acts as a turning point in Crusoe's career; from here on he makes no major mistakes, though he is capable of certain indiscreet plans in reference to the cannibals in the long course of his preoccupation with them.

Generally, the symbolism is clustered around the conversion. The peculiar effectiveness of the descriptions of the shoots of barley and the making of the earthen pot is probably due to their symbolic value in the religious context. Crusoe sheds tears at the realization that the stalks are "perfect green barley," and for the first time begins to reflect seriously on God's providence. Clearly, they are the seeds of grace stirring in his heart and sending forth their first tender sprouts. Similarly, Crusoe's ultimate success in fashioning an earthen pot after certain false starts is analogous to his ultimate success in attaining a spiritual goal. In a sense Crusoe is the pot himself. Several times he has been brought to the fire, but nothing had come of it. Finally, however, his trials redouble (fresh fuel is brought to the fire), he glows clear red, and emerges a serviceable, if not handsome pipkin of the Lord. The analogy may seem far-fetched at first; but one should remember, in addition to the fact that the very intensity of these descriptions suggests a special meaning for them, that dissenting circles were accustomed to think and to express themselves in terms of "chosen vessels" and seeds of grace or doctrine.

Other incidents may be susceptible of such an interpretation: the goatskin clothes he makes after his old ones wear out may be the new armor of faith, and the elaborate system of defense that Crusoe establishes on the island may suggest the invulnerability of the true believer; but the four examples I have chosen are the most obvious in respect to both their nature and their position in the narrative.

Source: Edwin B. Benjamin, "Symbolic Elements in Robinson Crusoe," in *Philological Quarterly,* Vol. XXX, No. 2, April 1951, pp. 206-11.

Sources

Joyce Appleby, *Capitalism and a New Social Order: The Republican Vision of the 1790s,* New York University Press, 1984.

James Beattie, "On Fable and Romance," in his *Dissertations Moral and Critical,* W. Strahan, 1783.

Theophilus Cibber, "De Foe," in *The Lives of the Poets of Great Britain and Ireland,* Vol. IV by Mr. Cibber and Other Hands, R. Griffiths, 1753, pp. 313-25.

Charles Gildon, *The Life and Strange Surprizing Adventures of Mr. D-De F-,* J. Roberts, 1719.

Peter Hulme, "Robinson Crusoe and Friday," in his *Colonial Encounters: Europe and the Native Caribbean, 1492–1797,* Methuen, 1986.

Philip D. Morgan, *Slave Counterpoint: Black Culture in the Eighteenth-Century Chesapeake and Lowcountry,* North Carolina Press, 1998.

Jean-Jacques Rousseau, "Rousseau on 'Robinson Crusoe'," in *Defoe: The Critical Heritage,* edited and translated by Pat Rogers, Routledge and Kegan Paul, 1972, pp. 52-4.

Sir Walter Scott, "Daniel Defoe," in *On Novelists and Fiction,* edited by Ian Williams, Routledge and Kegan Paul, 1968, pp. 164-83.

For Further Study

Alfred W. Crosby, in *Ecological Imperialism: The Biological Expansion of Europe, 900—1900,* Cambridge University Press, 1986.
    Crosby documents the ecological history of colonialist expansion. He details how epidemics destroyed incredible numbers of people who hitherto had no exposure to certain diseases. He also describes how animals and fauna of the Old World establish themselves in the New World, such as the practice of leaving goats on islands while exploring in order to have a source of European-style food.

Peter Earle, *The World of Defoe,* Atheneum, 1977.
    Earle examines Defoe's view of the world as well as social relations in the England of the eighteenth century.

Maximillan E. Novak, *Defoe and the Nature of Man,* Oxford University Press, 1963.
    Drawing on the authors contemporary with Defoe as well as Defoe's other writings, Novak provides a thematic analysis of Defoe's fiction.

John J. Richetti, *Popular Fiction Before Richardson* Clarendon Press, 1969.

Richetti traces the development of the novel by examining early works. This work is an essential resource for anyone interested in the origins of the novel genre.

Pat Rogers, *Robinson Crusoe,* George Allen and Unwin, 1979.
Rogers praises Defoe's novel for its mastery of narrative form as well as its exploration of psychological and spiritual experiences.

Arthur Secord, *Studies in the Narrative Method of Defoe,* University of Illinois Press, 1968.
Secord investigates Defoe's narrative methods.

Diana Spearman, *The Novel and Society,* London, 1966.
Spearman is one of the few twentieth-century critics to examine *Robinson Crusoe* as a book of religious instruction. Her motivation stems from the idea that a man alone on an island is a poor device for exploring economic theory—but a great one to explore an individual's relation with God in an increasingly secular world.

Ian Watt, *The Rise of the Novel: Studies in Defoe, Richardson and Fielding,* Chatto and Windus, 1957.
This seminal study analyzed the novel as a historical document reflecting human thought.

Roots: The Story of an American Family

Alex Haley
1976

Roots: The Saga of an American Family became a sensation immediately after its publication in 1976. It was adapted into a popular miniseries, and became one of the most-watched television programs in American history. Two sequels, *The Next Generation* and *The Gift,* quickly followed.

Roots appealed to readers of every background: for African American readers, the story inspired pride and a greater understanding of the past; and for readers of other ethnicities, it was a powerful look at an American family's immigrant past. Moreover, Haley's work is widely credited with starting the American genealogy craze.

The continuing controversy over Haley's writing and research methods and the facts of his narrative has not dimmed his achievement. *Roots* is viewed as a mythic saga of African American history, portraying the ways in which enslaved Africans endured suffering and fought for their place in American society. It has earned a place among the popular classics of American literature and remains a profoundly influential and well-loved book.

Author Biography

In 1921 Haley was born in Ithaca, New York. He grew up in Henning, Tennessee, and even after his family moved, he spent his summers there. Haley's mother, Bertha, died when he was only twelve

Alex Haley

years old. Haley's father, Simon, was a respected professor of agriculture who died just before *Roots* was completed.

Haley was an indifferent student and eventually joined the Coast Guard. He found he had a talent for writing, and began to submit pieces to magazines. When he left the service at age thirty-seven, he had become the chief journalist for the Coast Guard, a position that had been created for him.

After struggling to make ends meet in his new civilian life, Haley received an assignment from *Playboy* to interview Miles Davis, the first of what were to become infamous as "the *Playboy* interviews." Soon afterwards, he began to collaborate with Malcolm X on his autobiography, which after Malcolm X's death in 1965 became a bestseller.

After finishing his book on Malcolm X, Haley began researching his own family history. He traced the names of Tom and Irene Murray, his great-grandparents, and found a *griot* in Africa with knowledge of the Kinte family.

After twelve years of research, he wrote *Roots: The Saga of an American Family,* which became an immediate best-seller. It was adapted into the wildly popular television miniseries of the same name. The miniseries was followed by another, *Roots: The Next Generation,* and the television

movies *Roots: The Gift, Queen,* a drama about Haley's paternal grandmother, and *Mama Flora's Family,* centering on the life of his maternal great-grandmother.

After the publication of *Roots,* Haley spent much time lecturing around the country. On a lecture trip to Seattle in 1992, Haley suffered a heart attack and died at age seventy-one.

Plot Summary

Kunta Kinte

Roots begins in a small African village named Juffure with the birth of a son to Omoro and Binta Kinte. The boy is named Kunta Kinte in honor of his famous grandfather, Kairaba Kunta Kinte, who saved the people of Juffure from a terrible drought.

At the age of five, Kunta graduates to the second *kafo.* He begins to herd goats and go to school. When he is eight, Kunta goes with his father on a journey to visit the new village his uncles, Janneh and Saloum, have founded. By this time, he has formed a close relationship with his younger brother, Lamin.

At the age of ten, Kunta completes his schooling and goes through his manhood training with his mates. He moves into his own hut and gets his own land to farm. By fifteen, he has built a thriving farm. One day, while hunting for wood with which to make a drum, Kunta is captured by white slavers, known as the *toubob.*

On the long journey to the United States, the slavers place Kunta in the hold of a ship with dozens of other men. After a harrowing journey across the ocean, Kunta and the surviving men and women arrive in Virginia. Kunta begins plotting his escape.

Almost as soon as he has the strength, he tries to escape; he is quickly recaptured. He tries again three more times. On the fourth attempt, the two white patrollers who catch him cut off half of his foot. He quickly loses consciousness, and wakes to find himself on a new farm.

While he recovers, he is tended by Bell, a young African American slave who will later become his wife. Kunta soon meets Fiddler, a talkative man who teaches him English and tells him about events beyond the plantation. He is given the name "Toby" but he insists to Fiddler that Kunta Kinte is his real name.

Kunta begins to work in the plantation garden. He realizes that he prefers life on the plantation to the certainty of death if he tries to escape, though he knows that this acceptance will come at a terrible price to his soul. After Luther, the driver, is sold for helping a young girl escape, Kunta becomes the new driver for the master of the plantation, a doctor named Master Waller.

His new position makes him a source for information about current events. Fiddler resents Kunta's new position, although it does not destroy their friendship. One Thanksgiving, after he has driven Master Waller to a ball, he meets another African, one of the most joyous experiences of his life. Soon afterward, influenced by Boteng Bediako's words to him, "[s]eeds you's got a-plenty, you jes' needs de wife to plant 'em in," he marries Bell and they have a daughter, Kizzy.

Although Kunta loves his daughter, he does not approve of the friendship she forms with Miss Anne, Master Waller's niece. When he drives Kizzy to Miss Anne's house, he tells her about Africa and teaches her many Mandinka words, something Kizzy will pass on to her descendants. When Miss Anne and Kizzy are teenagers, they begin to drift apart, as Anne starts courting and their difference in status becomes too much to ignore.

Kizzy begins an affair with Noah, another slave, which ends in tragedy when she is caught trying to help Noah escape. Bell and Kunta plead with Master Waller not to sell Kizzy, but she is sold to a man named Tom Lea. She never sees her parents again.

Kizzy

Almost immediately, Tom Lea rapes Kizzy and impregnates her with her only child, a son Lea names George. Although Kizzy initially rejects George, she comes to love him—as do the other blacks in the quarters, Sister Sarah, Malizy, and Uncle Pompey. As soon as George is old enough, Kizzy teaches him about her father, Kunta Kinte.

By the time George is nine, he has begun to "preach," amusing the blacks and whites alike. Tom Lea decides to apprentice George to Uncle Mingo, who cares for Lea's fighting cocks. When he orders George to move in with Mingo, nearer to the birds, Kizzy, in her anger, blurts out that Lea is George's father.

Chicken George

George quickly becomes expert at handling the cocks, and begins to make money from "hack fight-ing" with other African Americans, using the master's rejected birds to stage side fights. After liaisons with women on neighboring plantations, George marries Matilda.

The religious and responsible Matilda—known as Tilda—quickly becomes part of the slave community on Lea's plantation. As George and Tilda's children grow up, George teaches them about their heritage. George's fourth son is named after Tom Lea, and grows up to become a blacksmith and the leader of the family.

George, Tom, and Tilda try to earn enough money to buy the family's freedom. Unfortunately their entire savings is lost when Tom Lea bets his own and George's money at a cockfight against Lord John Russell. George is sent to England with Lord Russell as part of Lea's payoff on the bet, though Lea promises George his freedom on his return to the United States.

In George's absence, Lea's fortunes continue to decline. He sells Tilda and her children, leaving Kizzy, Malizy, Sarah, and Pompey on the plantation. Lea agrees to Tom's request that he sell the older folks too, but Tom knows it might take years to do so. Uncle Pompey is found dead on the day they are due to leave.

Tom

Tom diligently works to save money to buy freedom for his family members. He marries a half-Native American woman, Irene, who brightens the family's lives. They quickly start a family of their own; the youngest is Cynthia, who will grow up to be Alex Haley's grandmother.

When George arrives from England, he gets his freedom from a drunken Tom Lea. He arrives on the Murray plantation for a reunion with his family, but is soon forced to leave because free blacks are not allowed to live in the state.

Soon after, the Civil War begins. Tom works for the Confederate Army, is accused of stealing, and nearly killed. The white boy who actually did the stealing, George Johnson, ends up begging for food from the slave cabins, and is made the overseer by Master Murray. Eventually Johnson endears himself to the slave community by working as hard as they do, and never exhibiting any prejudice. "Ol' George" remains a part of the community even after they are emancipated, which they are in 1865, at the war's end.

The family soon moves to Henning, Tennessee after George meets some whites who need their help building a new town. Tom earns the respect

In 1977, Roots *was adapted as a television miniseries, one of the most successful and critically acclaimed series ever aired. Levar Burton played Haley's ancestor, Kunta Kinte, kidnapped and brought from West Africa to America to be sold into slavery.*

of the whites after he builds a traveling blacksmith shop. The African Americans in Henning build a strong community of their own, and they construct a church that becomes the center of the community.

Tom forbids his daughter Elizabeth from marrying a "high yaller" light-skinned black man. Tilda dies, followed by a heartbroken George. Tom's youngest daughter Cynthia marries Will Palmer, who becomes the owner of Henning's only lumber business.

The Haleys

Cynthia and Will Palmer have a daughter, Bertha, who marries Simon Alexander Haley at a wedding that everyone in town—black and white—attends. Bertha and Simon quickly surprise Cynthia and Will with a son, Alex, who will grow up to write *Roots.*

Alex spends a lot of time in Henning as a child, developing a close relationship with his grandfather, Will Palmer, and his grandmother and great

aunts, particularly after his mother dies. After growing up and becoming a writer, Haley decides to research the family stories he so often heard as a child.

Alex meets a linguist who pinpoints the origins of the remembered African words, and he journeys to Africa. He arrives in Juffure to meet a *griot* who knows of the Kinte family, and learns of a man named Kunta Kinte who went to chop wood for a drum and is never seen again. Haley excitedly tells the *griot* that in *his* family story, an African named Kunta is captured after going to chop wood for a drum.

The men of Juffure give thanks to Allah for the return of one who has been long lost. The villagers call Haley "Mr. Kinte," which touches him deeply. Haley decides to write a book that will be a symbolic saga of all people of African descent. After twelve years of research, he writes *Roots.*

Characters

Bell

Bell is the cook on Master Waller's plantation. Eventually, she becomes Kunta's wife. When she is in labor, she tells Kunta about the two baby girls who were sold away from her when she was younger. In response, he gives their daughter the name Kizzy (the name means "you stay put").

Bell is sometimes exasperated by her husband's African ways and by his refusal to accept Christianity, but they have a deeply loving relationship based on mutual respect. Like Kunta, Bell is devastated by the sale of Kizzy.

Nyo Boto

Nyo is Kunta's grandmother, a woman who cares for the children of the village and fears no one. When he leaves on his first trip away from the village, she gives him a saphie charm to ward off evil spirits.

The Fiddler

One of the most colorful characters in *Roots,* Fiddler is "half-free," as he explains to Kunta, because his former master was drowned and he must stay near another master for protection. He plays his fiddle at parties and learns much about current events. He is the one, for example, who tells the other slaves about the Boston Massacre.

Fiddler is garrulous, likes to drink, and is a staunch friend to Kunta. He saves $700 hoping to buy his freedom, but is devastated to learn that Master Waller wants twice that amount to free him. In his anger and pain, he smashes his fiddle, and his playing is never the same after that.

Chicken George

Kizzy's flamboyant son, George is doted on by the adults on the Lea plantation. As he grows up, he becomes the apprentice to Uncle Mingo, and quickly becomes an expert trainer of gamecocks.

Often absent from his family's lives, George is not faithful to his wife, but is in his own way a loving father and husband. He plans to buy his family's freedom with money he's saved from cockfighting, but loses it all when Tom Lea—at George's urging—bets too much in a cockfight. George is forced to travel to England and work for Lord John Russell for several years, returning to find his family has been sold. Lea gives him his freedom, and he finds his family at the Murray plantation, only to be forced to leave the state.

When the family is emancipated in 1865, George rejoins them. The family journeys to Henning, Tennessee. After his wife Matilda's death, George dies from a bad burn.

Alex Haley

The author of *Roots,* Haley is the son of Simon and Bertha Haley. He grows up in Henning hearing stories of his African ancestors and his other relatives. After a long career in the Coast Guard, Haley becomes a writer; he is eventually driven to research his family's past. The high point of his life comes when he hears of his African ancestor, Kunta Kinte, while on a journey to Africa. After twelve years of research, Haley publishes *Roots.*

Simon Haley

A railroad employee who becomes a professor, Simon is Alex Haley's father. He is devastated by his wife's early death. *Roots* ends with an account of his funeral.

Ol' George Johnson

After begging on the Murray plantation, Ol' George is a white man that becomes the overseer. He earns the respect of the slaves by working hard and never exhibiting any prejudice. When the Murrays leave their plantation, he and his wife journey with them to Henning. Ol' George becomes a part

Media Adaptations

- *Roots* was adapted as a television miniseries in 1977, starring LeVar Burton, Ben Vereen, John Amos, Leslie Uggams, Maya Angelou, Cicely Tyson, Edward Asner, Harry Rhodes, and Robert Reed.

- A sequel, *Roots: The Next Generation,* was shown in 1979 as a miniseries. It covered the lives of Haley's ancestors after the Civil War. A Christmas movie, *Roots: The Gift,* heralded the return of Kunta Kinte, played by Burton, as well as the Fiddler, played by Louis Gossett, Jr., to network television.

of the black community and is subject to the same treatment the blacks suffer.

Binta Kinte

Binta is the mother of Kunta Kinte and his brothers Lamin, Suwadu, and Madi.

Janneh Kinte

Janneh is Kunta's uncle and the son of Kairaba Kunta Kinte and his first wife. Janneh and his brother Saloum have traveled over much of Africa before founding their own village.

Kunta Kinte

The protagonist of *Roots,* Kunta Kinte is born in Juffure, Africa, to Binta and Omoro Kinte. Soon followed by three brothers, Kunta grows up according to the traditional ways of his village. By fifteen, he already owns a thriving farm, has traveled within the Gambia, and has made plans for a trip to Mali with his brother Lamin.

When Kunta goes one morning to chop wood for a drum, he is captured and enslaved by the *toubob* (white slavers). After a harrowing journey to the African coast, Kunta is placed in the hold of a ship, which arrives in Virginia several weeks later. He attempts to escape from his captors four times, and on the last attempt his foot is cut off by two white patrollers.

While he recovers, he is sold to Master John Waller. Kunta becomes the gardener on the plantation, and later is assigned to be Waller's driver. Gradually Kunta learns English, aided by his friend the Fiddler, who teaches him many English words. Kunta becomes a part of the slave community, though he does not forget his African identity.

Unlike the other blacks on the plantation, Kunta refuses to become a Christian, and continues to pray to Allah. Likewise, he tells the other slaves his name is Kunta Kinte, not Toby, the name given him by his original master. Kunta marries Bell, the plantation cook, and they have a daughter, Kizzy. Kunta teaches Kizzy about his heritage, including his life in Juffure and many Mandinka words. Kunta and Bell are devastated when Kizzy is sold away from them at sixteen, after she has helped her lover Noah escape.

Lamin Kinte

Lamin is Kunta's younger brother. Lamin accompanies Kunta on his trip to find gold.

Omoro Kinte

The father of Kunta Kinte, Omoro is stern but loving. When Kunta loses a goat to a wild animal, he expects his father to punish him. Instead, Omoro tells Kunta that he still bears the scars from trying to save one of his own goats when he was a boy, and, out of his concern for Kunta, he tells him never to run toward a wild animal. Omoro also takes Kunta on his first trip, which gives Kunta a love of traveling.

Saloum Kinte

Saloum is Janneh's brother and Kunta's uncle.

Yaisa Kinte

Yaisa is Kunta's grandmother. When he is a child, she cares for him and tells him stories. Her death is Kunta's first experience of loss.

Themes

Assimilation and Separatism

Kunta Kinte's story illustrates an enduring theme of African-American life: the conflict between assimilation and separatism. In Africa, Kunta would never have been confronted with this issue,

Topics for Further Study

- Create a your own account of Kunta and Bell's time on the Waller plantation after their daughter Kizzy is sold. What do you think happened to these characters?

- Research your family tree. How far back can you go? What do you know about your family's history and heritage?

- Research the Haitian slave revolt and Kunta's hero, Toussaint Louverture. How did slave life in Haiti differ from slave life in the American colonies? How did conditions in Haiti make a successful slave revolt possible?

- Examine the central beliefs of the Quakers, who were the first American abolitionists. Did their religious faith and practice influence their commitment to abolitionism? How did other religions in the antebellum period treat the question of slavery?

but in the American colonies he is subject to the powerful pressures of assimilation.

Kunta tries to hold onto his African identity, which has always defined him. Yet he is forced to accept a new name. As a slave, his entire social context has been redefined. Kunta cannot fully express himself because he is not free; he has lost his autonomy, which had so defined him as a young man in Africa.

Moreover, Kunta is very lonely away from his home, family, and culture. In order to assuage his loneliness, he reaches out to the other blacks. Eventually Kunta realizes that he prefers life on the plantation to certain death, which he risks if he attempts to escape again.

Yet the knowledge that he has to surrender part of himself to survive is soul crushing, and he realizes that he has lost an essential part of himself. However, Kunta does pass on as much of his African knowledge as he can to his daughter, Kizzy, who in turn passes stories of her father on to succeeding generations, who cherish their

African heritage while seeking the American dream of freedom and success.

Coming of Age

The first part of *Roots* is a coming-of-age story: the young hero, Kunta Kinte, learns how to be an adult. This is not an emotional or intellectual journey so much as it is a process of learning the steps to adulthood. As a young child, Kunta hears stories that teach him his place in the world. When he is older, he has a job taking care of his father's goats and he attends school. At ten, he embarks on his manhood training, formally becoming an adult in his culture, which means he has his own farm and his own hut.

Kunta's continued growth into adulthood is halted by his descent into slavery. He must come of age all over again, learning a new language and culture. However, Kunta can never fully become an adult in a slave society. Like a child, he is forever subject to the whims of others. He has no freedom of movement, and most heartbreakingly, he cannot save his daughter Kizzy from being sold. Although Kunta behaves with an adult sense of responsibility, he is always subject to the humiliating realization that he is treated as less than a man, human being, and adult.

Human Rights

Roots is a story that illustrates the incompatibility of slavery with basic human dignity. The crux of incompatibility is the manner in which individual family members are sold without regard for family ties.

For instance, Kunta and Bell have their daughter sold away from them, and Kizzy suffers the same fate when Tom Lea sells her daughter-in-law and grandchildren from her. It is in these heart-rending scenes that the cruelty of treating humans like property is most evident.

Slaves who are sold away from their families never see them again, cannot attend a loved one's funeral, hold a grandchild, or celebrate a son's marriage. Master Waller can order Kunta to drive him to see his family whenever he wants, but when he sells Kizzy, Kunta knows he will never see her again. Although both Master Waller and Master Murray are portrayed as relatively fair owners, the constant threat of separation shows how inhumane slavery is and how their participation in slavery makes them inhumane.

Style

Narration

Roots is narrated by a third-person narrator. The device of a third-person narrator enables the text to change settings when the characters do. For example, when Kizzy is sold away from the Waller plantation, the narrative moves with her, recording her actions and thoughts on the Lea plantation. In this way the narrative moves from generation to generation, from Kunta Kinte to Bertha Palmer Haley.

At the very end of the book, the narration switches from the third person to the first person with the arrival of Alex Haley, the book's author. Haley records his own thoughts and actions in his own voice.

Setting

The setting of *Roots* changes as the characters are sold or move. It begins in Juffure, Kunta's village, and then moves to the ship in which Kunta is placed for his journey across the Atlantic.

The narrative then moves to Virginia, on the Waller plantations where Kunta lives. When Kizzy is sold away from the Waller plantation, the setting switches to Tom Lea's plantation in North Carolina. Kizzy's daughter-in-law and grandchildren are later sold to Master Murray in Alamance County, also in North Carolina. After emancipation, the family moves to Henning, Tennessee. At the end of the novel, Alex Haley journeys to Juffure and the narrative comes full circle.

Realism

Haley called his book "faction," a mix of fact and fiction. Although Haley creates the thoughts and dialogue of his characters, *Roots* is meant to be a realistic account of Mandinka culture and slave life in the American colonies and the United States. Haley frequently has his characters refer to historical events, and he relies on oral and written accounts in order to realistically imagine what the lives and thoughts of his characters may have been like.

Plot

The plot of *Roots* becomes more episodic as the story goes on. Haley presents the extraordinary events in the lives of his characters such as birth, marriage, death or sale, or important events like George's biggest gamecock matches or the Fiddler's inability to gain freedom. At times, the narrative skips years in the lives of the characters because not much of consequence occurs.

Several generations of this slave family, pictured in 1862, were born on the same plantation in South Carolina. Roots, *however, documents how many families were broken up and members sold to various masters, a practice that underscores the dehumanizing practice of treating slaves as property.*

Historical Context

American Slavery

Haley began writing his novels during the Civil Rights movement, and he researched and wrote *Roots* at a time when African Americans and European Americans were reevaluating slavery and its legacy. Many Americans believed in what has often been called the "*Gone With the Wind* version" of slavery, in which enslaved Africans were happy-go-lucky, childlike people who were cared for by benevolent, paternalistic masters. One consequence of the Civil Rights movement was the reevaluation of this myth.

The reality of slavery was much more complex. White masters were certainly invested in the myth of paternalism, which allowed them to justify the enslavement of human beings on the grounds that the relationship of slaves and masters was a reciprocal one—the master took care of his slaves and claimed the fruits of their labor.

Although African Americans opposed this myth, they were often able to use paternalism to demand rights. The slaves came to accept certain things as their due: the right to practice their religion; no work on Sundays; and the right to be adequately fed and sheltered. As Haley's characters do, the slaves also made distinctions between good and bad masters. They may have keenly felt the horrors of slavery in general but recognized that it was easier when they had a humane master.

Family was a very important concept for slaves who were under constant threat of being sold away from their families. A master who sold individual family members was a bad master. After they were emancipated in 1865, many slaves went to great lengths to find lost family members.

Frequently, slaves formed strong communities; they often considered all blacks on the plantation as members of their family, much like those on the Lea plantation do. Children grew up with an extended group of people who would care for them, and, in particular, allowed for children without fathers to experience the care and example of a male role model. Chicken George has this kind of relationship with Uncle Mingo, his mentor in cockfighting.

The romantic myth of slavery held that blacks and whites on plantations formed a kind of family unit. To some degree, this was true, and it can be seen in Matilda's concern for the Murrays after the black Murrays are freed. Yet, like many slaves, Matilda's concern only goes so far—she does not hesitate to move to Henning when she gets the chance.

Eugene Genovese notes that many slaves pretended devotion in order to make their own lives easier, but often the most "devoted" slaves on a plantation were the first to leave after the Civil War. Whites believed that blacks cared for them as if they were family, but even if some did, they chose to assert their own freedom rather than remain with their former masters. Most slaves valued their own kin far more than they did their masters and mistresses. Although proximity can lead to close bonds, most slaves found that it was difficult to love someone with the power to punish, sexually abuse, or sell them, even if that power was not exercised.

Sometimes, the blacks and whites on a plantation were relatives; the coercion or rape by whites of African American women was a common practice. As in Kizzy's situation, even when the man didn't use violence, it was impossible to obtain a

Compare & Contrast

- **1760s:** Thousands of enslaved Africans arrive at every port in the American colonies.

  1970s: African Americans explore their African heritage.

  Today: The term "African American" becomes the most popular term for Americans of African descent. Henry Louis Gates Jr. makes a series of public television programs about African cultures.

- **1760s:** Most white people cannot read. Slaves are legally prohibited from learning to read and write.

  1970s: In the first full decade of mandated school integration, many black students are bused to white schools in order to integrate these institutions. Busing becomes a controversial issue.

  Today: Many African Americans question the merits of integration. A sobering statistic: more black men are in jail than in college.

- **1760s:** African Americans are brought over to America as slaves to work on plantations in the South, as well as other areas of the colonies.

  1970s: The legacy of slavery and the realities of racism make race relations a controversial subject in America. A dialogue about racial issues is initiated as many artists, writers, cultural figures, and politicians bring race into the foreground of the American consciousness. Many African Americans become interested in their heritage and begin to appreciate the accomplishments of African Americans.

  Today: The wounds of slavery have still not healed. Racism still exists, but many laws have been enacted to battle institutionalized racism.

---

slave woman's consent for sexual relations because her owner had the power to make her submit.

It was not uncommon for the children and siblings of a master to also be his slaves, as in Chicken George's case. Although some slaveholders treated their own kin better than the other slaves they owned, often they treated them no differently.

In spite of the hardships of being owned, slaves created a strong culture that enabled them to survive. Chief among their comforts was religion, which enabled them to look forward to freedom in the next world. Their religious practices bound slaves together in a community created by God. Slaves took care of each other, calling each other "brother" and "sister" as at the Lea plantation, and helped each other to survive.

Contrary to the myth, all slaves felt the hardships of their slavery; as Tom says, it was sometimes impossible for whites to understand that "being owned by anyone could never be enjoyable." Some slaves did run away successfully, sometimes

with the help of whites and free blacks, though Kunta Kinte was never able to.

Most slaves, much like Kunta, decided to stay with their families and plantation communities. Although slaves longed for the rights whites took for granted, they made accommodations to slavery. The slaves' ability to accommodate slavery did not mean that they preferred it to freedom, as many whites insisted. Haley's book, which documents the slaves' yearning for freedom, was an eye-opener for many, blacks and whites alike, who believed the old myths about slavery.

Critical Overview

For the most part, *Roots* was a critical success, although no amount of critical acclaim could have overshadowed its overwhelming popular reception. Critics of *Roots* have tended to focus on the historical accuracy of the novel, Haley's use of dialect, and the book's emotional power.

Russell Warren Howe asserted that *Roots* "is crammed with raw violence and makes valid demands on the tearducts of the dourest reader."

Arnold Rampersad contended that Haley's "recreation of Kunta's middle passage journey in the hold of a slave ship is harrowing, the major place in the book where facts are incontrovertibly alchemized into vivid narrative."

Likewise, critics praised Haley's renderings of heart-wrenching scenes like the one where Kizzy is sold away from her parents, about which Paul Zimmerman wrote, "this soapy passage is heartbreaking."

Even critics who have found themselves moved by *Roots* have taken issue with the historical accuracy of the book. Some have argued that *Roots* is a mythic account, not a strictly factual one—more of an "unchallengeable testament of symbolic truth."

Nevertheless, other critics have continued to find fault with Haley's historical accuracy. Howe maintained that Kunta would never have identified himself as "African" while still in Africa, nor would he have seen African slavers as traitors. He wrote, "the people of his village, Juffure, did not see all 'Africans' as brothers. Indeed, they had no concept of Africa."

Other critics have maintained that Haley's portrayal of slave life unrealistic. David Herbert Donald contended that "he simply has not done enough reading about the South, about slavery, about American agriculture."

Some critics of Haley have also seen his portrayals of whites as monolithic. Howard Stein saw in *Roots* "a reversal of white stereotypes, popular and sociological, [which] obscures much of the interpersonal complexity and internal anguish in those both Black and White."

Almost all reviewers and critics of Haley noted his use of black dialect. Rampersad asserted that "Haley's ability to write dialogue and dialect is competent at best, and stilted and artificial far too often." Zimmerman deemed the dialect "authentic," but argued that it "grows wearing and turns ridiculous when forced to convey historical bulletins."

Several critics found fault with Haley's introduction of American historical events into the action of the book. Rampersad called the inclusion "uninteresting" and Donald wrote, "it is awkward that the only way Haley can devise to introduce chronology is to have house slaves rush down to the quarters announcing the latest big-house gossip."

Most critics have noted that Haley's portrayal of Kunta Kinte is by far his strongest characterization. Rampersad called Haley's "presentation of Kunta's unfolding consciousness of the strange new white world of America" "brilliant." Although some critics praised Haley's rendering of life in Juffure, Howe argued that "only when Juffure has become a distant childhood memory, and Kunta is acculturated into slave America, does the character become arrestingly true."

There have been periodic challenges to Haley's research methods and veracity. One critic, Philip Nobile, has argued that because "the uniqueness of *Roots* lay in the fact that it claimed to be painstakingly researched, and true," inconsistencies between Haley's account and historical records meant that Haley was basically a fraud.

In a rebuttal to this claim, Clarence Page argued that "the difference between fiction and journalism is that journalism deals with 'facts' while fiction deals with 'truths.' If so, it will always be easier for somebody to chip away at Haley's 'facts' than for anybody to deny his 'truths.'"

On the whole, most critics of *Roots* have tended to agree with Rampersad, who wrote that the book is "a work of extremely uneven texture but unquestionable final success."

Criticism

Jane Elizabeth Dougherty

Dougherty is a Ph.D. candidate at Tufts University. In the following essay, she explores Haley's use of the past in Roots.

When discussing *Roots,* Haley contended that he was "just trying to give his people a myth to live by." If one definition of myth is "a useable version of the past," Haley's saga certainly succeeds in overturning other myths about the Black American experience and giving African Americans a proud history.

Haley's book must be seen, at least in part, as a corrective to prevailing American myths about slavery and about Africa. Some critics have called *Roots* a counter-narrative to Margaret Mitchell's *Gone With the Wind,* which depicted happy-go-lucky, childlike slaves with no connection to their African heritage.

Instead, Haley presents a harrowing account of the devastating toll slavery took on American blacks and the cultural strategies they used to endure it, an account which is intended to give African American readers a useable version of their shared past.

Haley concludes *Roots* by asserting that he set out to write a book not only about his own family's history, but one that would serve as a "symbolic saga of all African-descent people—who are without exception the seeds of someone like Kunta who was born and grew up in some black African village, someone who was captured and chained down in one of those slave ships that sailed them across the same ocean, into some succession of plantations, and since then a struggle for freedom."

Haley assumes this task in part because he recognizes how fortunate his family is compared with many other African American families. Most African Americans cannot trace their ancestry back to a specific African ancestor because of the dislocations of slavery.

For example, in Haley's book, Bell has had two girls before Kizzy, both of whom were sold away from her. Neither girl would have grown up knowing who her parents were, nor where she had come from. Fortunately, Haley's family is able to stay together and they can pass their story on to their descendants. In addition, the Haley family takes pride in their African past, and they want to pass their story on because it says something about who they are: in their stories of their ancestor "Kintay," their hope for freedom stays alive.

It was long held by apologists for slavery that the Middle Passage made by enslaved Africans across the Atlantic effectively erased their identities. This *tabula rasa,* or blank slate theory, excused the social control slaveholders sought to exercise over their slaves by making slavery "paternalistic" in nature. In other words, it was believed that because their former identity was erased that Africans had to be treated like children.

In the myth of paternalism, as Eugene Genovese notes, the master became the slaves' father, caring for them because they could not care for themselves. For the myth of paternalism to operate effectively, the African past of the slaves had both to be destroyed and denigrated. The family of master, mistress, children, and slaves had to replace the African families left behind; for paternalism to

What Do I Read Next?

- *Song of Solomon* (1977), Toni Morrison's lyrical novel, recounts the story of a black man searching for his roots.

- Russell Banks's *Cloudsplitter* (1998) is a fictionalized account of the saga of John Brown narrated by his son, Owen Brown.

- *Praisesong for the Widow* (1983), written by Paule Marshall, presents a middle-aged black woman's journey into her own past.

- Chinua Achebe's classic novel, entitled *Things Fall Apart* (1958), chronicles life in an African village.

work effectively, slaves had to identify with their masters, not their African forebears.

Africa represented a powerful independent source of identity that had to be eliminated. Moreover, because African cultural practices were often adapted as survival strategies, and were used to undermine the all-encompassing power of slavery, it was felt that they had to be resisted, denigrated, and destroyed.

Through the character of Kunta Kinte, Haley offers a powerful counter-story to the myth of the *tabula rasa.* Kunta carries all his African experiences and expectations across the ocean with him in spite of the agony he endures on the passage. Indeed, he has a greater experience of his Africanness on the ship than he would have on the land, where, as Russell Warren Howe notes, he would have identified with clan, village, region, and religion before identifying as African.

Kunta's experience of his African identity is forged by the suffering he shares with the other men—all Africans—in the hold of the ship and by their common desire to resist the men who hold them there—all Europeans. The men comfort each other, pass on information, and plan their resistance. Through these communications, they become a community. Haley writes:

The relaying of any information from whatever source seemed about the only function that would justify their staying alive. When there was no news, the men would talk of their families, their villages, their professions, their farms, their hunts. And more and more frequently there arose disagreements on how to kill the toubob, and when it should be tried. Some of the men felt that, whatever the consequences, the toubob should be attacked the next time they were taken up on deck. Others felt that it would be wiser to watch and wait for the best moment. Bitter disagreements began to flare up. One debate was suddenly interrupted when the voice of an elder rang out, "Hear me! Though we are of different tribes and tongues, we must remember that we are the same people! We must be as one village, together in this place!"

Although the men forge a kind of pan-African community born of their suffering in the hold, Kunta retains his tribal identification. He stops speaking to his Wolof neighbor when he realizes that he is a pagan, and even in the American colonies, he instinctively identifies other blacks according to their tribes.

The American blacks have little time for what they call Kunta's "heathen Africanisms"; when Kunta tells his wife Bell that she is like a Mandinka woman, the highest compliment he can think of to pay her, Bell takes it as an insult. The American blacks have been taught to denigrate their own African heritage and to identify with the European culture of their masters; in fact, Kunta is astonished to see black slaves obediently following orders instead of rising in revolt.

Clearly, being forced to give up their African identities is one step toward identifying with the slave system; Kunta is named "Toby" as a symbolic attempt to rid him of his old identity and replace it with a slave identity. To the end of his life, Kunta will resist the master's attempts to separate him from his own identity, and insist that his name is Kunta, not Toby.

Although they denigrate their own African heritage, the American blacks have familiar practices. Kunta often notices how black American cultural practices are like African ones. Haley writes:

> And Kunta had been reminded of Africa in the way that black women wore their hair tied up with strings into very tight plaits—although African women often decorated their plaits with colorful beads. And the women of this place knotted cloth pieces over their heads, although they didn't tie them correctly. Kunta saw that even some of these black men wore their hair in short plaits, too, as some men did in Africa.

Kunta also viewed Africa in the way that black children here were trained to treat their elders with politeness and respect. He saw it in the way that mothers carried their babies with their plump little legs straddling the mothers' bodies. He noticed even such small customs as how the older ones among these blacks would sit in the evenings rubbing their gums and teeth with the finely crushed end of a twig, which would have been lemongrass root in Juffure. Although he found it difficult to understand how they could do it here in *toubob* land, Kunta had to admit that these blacks' great love of singing and dancing was unmistakably African.

Clearly, even the American blacks who denigrate their African heritage are engaging in cultural practices that are unmistakably African. These cultural practices bind the community together in a shared African American culture, which is separate from that of the master. These enduring Africanisms give the lie to the theory of *tabula rasa,* and thus loosen the grip of paternalism: the slaves maintain separate identities from their masters, building a powerful communal culture.

By far the most important element in the culture of the slaves is their religion. When Kunta goes to his first black Christian religious service, he is "astonished at how much it reminded him of the way the people of Juffure sat at the Council of Elders' meetings once each moon." In spite of this realization, Kunta remains true to his Muslim faith.

Yet for his descendants, Christianity represents a way to hold onto the idea of freedom. As Genovese notes, slaves identified with the sufferings of Jesus, and expected that one day a new Moses would lead them to the Promised Land of freedom. Likewise, Kunta's descendants expect to see their lost relatives in the next world, which helps them bear terrible separations in this one.

Genovese notes that many masters tried to control their slaves' religious expressions, but didn't succeed. They were more successful in their attempts to destroy and denigrate African culture. In particular, they sought to destroy those aspects of African culture that could be used against them. It was routine for tribesmen to be sold to different farms, lest they be able to plot insurrection or escape in their own languages.

Likewise, Kunta noted that the drumtalk that was a constant feature of life in African villages had been stilled in black communities in the American colonies. Drumming was made often made illegal in Southern communities because slaveholders thought it "agitated" their slaves, often not realizing that drumming was actually a way of communicating.

Kunta also noticed that American blacks had secret ways of communicating, much like the "sireng kato" language of his village. These secret methods of communication included special handshakes and ways of talking and, most famously, the secret messages in slave spirituals. For these reasons alone, the masters encouraged the destruction and denigration of African culture.

This denigration of African culture is a common feature of American life even today; most Americans, both black and white, are ignorant of the history, diversity, and magnificence of African life. Moreover, many blacks do not have direct access to their African heritage because of the dislocations of slavery. For many readers, *Roots* was their first chance to see an African past which they could admire.

As Chester Fontenot maintains, "this book stands as the first thorough attempt by an Afro-American to come to terms with his African heritage." Haley offers a powerful myth of a beautiful African culture and its enduring influence in black American life, and thus gives black American readers a profound source of pride. As Haley asserts, *Roots* is a myth his people can use.

Source: Jane Elizabeth Dougherty, in an essay for *Novels for Students*, Gale, 2000.

Helen Taylor

Taylor discusses the enormous success and popularity of Roots *in the following essay, paying particular attention to the feeling of connection to the past that it offered so many rootless people.*

> I acknowledge immense debt to the griots of Africa—where today it is rightly said that when a griot dies, it is as if a library has burned to the ground. The griots symbolize how all human ancestry goes back to some place, and some time, where there was no writing. Then, the memories and the mouths of ancient elders was [sic] the only way that early histories of mankind got passed along ... for all of us today to know who we are.

With these words, Alex Haley concludes the Acknowledgments page of his ambitious work, *Roots*. The tribute to the African griots he paid here, and in the final chapters of the book—not to mention at countless lectures and interviews after publication—was paid back to him by African-American critics. For instance, his biographer Mary Siebert McCauley entitled her study *Alex Haley, A Southern Griot*. In *The Black Scholar*, published

only months after the first transmission of the television mini-series, black columnist Chuck Stone praised Haley for producing, as he had intended, "the symbol [sic] saga of all of us of African ancestry." Calling him "the griot from Tennessee," he praised Haley for "painstakingly unraveling the umbilical cord that had stretched tortured distance from Africa to America." For many critics, and millions of readers and TV viewers, Haley unraveled that umbilical cord by using his own family's story, and his griot-like powers, to link the pre-literate African past to his own literary, professional present via the terrible saga of slavery. The griots passed stories on orally, "for all of us today to know who we are." Haley—as befitted a contemporary figure who was the culmination of centuries of oppression and resistance, slavery and freedom—gave his story massive pre-publicity circulation on campus lecture tours and in popular journals, then wrote it down for publication and subsequent TV serialization. Whatever his original intention, Haley (already a race hero for his authorship of *The Autobiography of Malcolm X,* 1965) slipped comfortably into the role of mythic national figure, welcoming claims made for the vast symbolic importance of *Roots* for his race and nation.

The impact of Haley and *Roots* has been profound. For African-Americans, deprived for centuries of their ancestral homes and families, enslaved and exploited, denied basic human and civil rights, including the crucial right to literacy, this book—published in Bicentennial Year, 1976—offered a fresh perspective on their history, community and genealogy. Although usually regarded as a novel, it was published originally as nonfiction, supporting Haley's apparently thoroughly researched claims that the book told the true story of his ancestors, traced back to the Mandinka tribe of Juffure, the Gambia. This was no tale found in books; it was a culmination of an epic quest. Haley had heard fragments of it first at his grandmother's knee in Henning, Tennessee, and had subsequently traveled the world, interviewing people, seeking sources, and eventually being led to an old African griot who revealed the name of his original ancestor Kunta Kinte.

The problem with this romantic account is that it has been disputed by several distinguished historians and journalists, who have challenged Haley's version of events, research methods, and source material. The most recent, and most damning, attack on the authenticity of Haley's claims comes from journalist Philip Nobile, arguing in the *Village Voice* that *Roots* is "a hoax, a literary painted mouse, a Piltdown of genealogy, a pyramid of bogus research." Far from being a griot and literary giant, in Nobile's account Haley is a liar, plagiarist and fantasist. Ever since *Roots* first appeared, many voices—most stridently, Haley's own—have been heard to defend and attack both book and TV series. It seems appropriate, in a journal issue devoted to "Voice," to examine the weight and validity of the various voices and silences which have surrounded this controversial text, one which claimed above all else that it derived from verbal accounts within a predominantly oral culture.

Roots begins in the year 1750 and records the story of the original ancestor of ex-Coast Guard journalist Alex Haley. Kunta Kinte, a Mandinka warrior, is captured into slavery, and taken to the South, where he becomes the first of a long line culminating in Alex, his brothers and sister. The book records the horrors of the Middle Passage, the cruelties and deprivations of slavery, the separation of families, economic and sexual exploitation, the rise of abolitionist fervor, Secession, the Civil War, Emancipation, and gradually a new prosperity for what became the Haley family. The main story ends with Alex's grandfather hanging up his sign, in 1893, "W.E. palmer Lumber Company" and his wife giving birth two years later to Bertha; the final page records the professional careers of Haley and his siblings. Pervading the book is the theme of loss of an idealized African culture, the ordered, patriarchal and hierarchical Muslim society in which Kunta Kinte would have played a major social and familial role.

Roots was an instant success. Its advance print-run of 200,000 sold out at once; 1.5 million hardback copies were sold in the first eighteen months, and millions have sold since. The novel was translated into at least thirty-three languages and distributed in twenty-eight countries. Among many major awards, it won the prestigious Pulitzer Prize. By the mid 1980s, 276 colleges and universities had adopted the book for black history curricula; it was popularly recognized as a sort of black family Bible.

In January 1977 (ironically because the programming director feared low ratings) the twelve-hour television mini-series was broadcast over eight consecutive evenings on ABC-TV to record American audiences. ABC research estimated that 130 million viewers saw some part of the series; virtually three-quarters of the TV audience watched the eighth, final part. (The previous record was set by the first broadcast of *Gone With the Wind* in November 1976, which attracted 65 per cent of the audience.) The huge success of the TV series (in Britain as well as the USA) was both astonishing to all concerned and seen by some as a major cultural event. "Haley's Comet," *Time Magazine* called it; black readers claimed it as the most important civil rights event since the 1965 Selma, Alabama, march. In Britain, reporting on the impact of the first U.S. broadcasts, the *Daily Express* (3 February 1977) referred to the way "30 million Americans fought blizzards, ice and fellow commuters to be home in time for *Roots*", while the *Daily Mail* reported the cancellation of night school courses, a huge drop in restaurant business, and the emptying of bars and hospital wards. In the *Sunday Telegraph* (30 January 1977) the series was described as "the most traumatic event in the nation's broadcasting since Orson Welles's 'War of the Worlds' produced panic in the 1930s." Audience figures were all the more amazing because 90 percent of the TV audience was white, and *Roots*—in an unprecedented eight sequential nights of broadcasting—became the film trade's dream "crossover": a feature which appealed to the urban black mass market as well as the majority white audiences. The TV series won 145 different awards, including nine Emmys.

Roots has enjoyed multiple intertextual circulations. Fifty cities declared "Roots Weeks"; the Governor of Tennessee (Haley's home state) proclaimed May 19-21, 1977 "Alex Haley Days"; while the Gambian Government pronounced Kunta Kinte's home in Juffure to be a national shrine and began to market "Roots trips." T-shirts, plaques, "Roots music" recordings appeared; "Roots-tracing kits" with imitation parchment genealogical charts became the rage (among whites as well as blacks). Schools were sent supplementary materials to use with the book and show, and colleges gave students credit for simply watching the mini-series. New black babies were named Kunta Kinte and Kizzy, after the show's main protagonists. As recently as 1988, in Eddie Murphy's successful comedy *Coming to America,* H[is] R[oyal] H[ighness] Akeem (Murphy) enters a barber's shop and is proclaimed by the barber "a Kunta Kinte"—an authentic African.

Haley himself became a folk hero. Letters arrived from all over the world addressed to "Alex Haley, 'Roots', America." De Burg notes he was the third most admired black man among black American youth (after Muhammed Ali and Stevie Wonder). In the prestigious "Black One Hundred," a list of the most influential blacks, Haley is still listed above major writers James Baldwin and Toni Morrison. He was invited to meet presidents and crowned heads, to front TV commercials, speak on talk shows, at prestigious lecture venues, and at autograph parties. He was given the key to many U.S. cities; special citations from the U.S. Senate and House of Representatives; profiles in magazines and newspapers galore. Two black colleges, Fisk and Lane, placed him on their boards, and dozens of publishers and hundreds of individuals sent him manuscripts for endorsement and patronage.

The (mainly Caucasian) critics who have waxed most fulsomely about *Roots* have made large, often extravagant claims for it. Despite a damning indictment of its literary style, writing in 1979 Leslie Fiedler recognized the cultural significance of the book and TV series. Noting that Kunta Kinte had become a household name, he said, "with *Roots,* a Black American succeeded for the first time in modifying the mythology of Black-White relations *for the majority audience*" (a majority which was of course white), and he goes on to argue how unlikely it might have seemed that this book, like Mrs. Stowe's, [would] be "read equally in the parlor, the kitchen and the nursery, but be condensed in the *Reader's Digest* and assigned in every classroom in the land." Almost a decade later, Harold Courlander (who had by then won a plagiarism suit against Haley) noted:

> *Roots* continues to be read and quoted, is found everywhere on library shelves, is a cornerstone of various black studies programs.... In short, the book has an established place in contemporary American literature and will be spoken of, no doubt, for some time to come.

Willie Lee Rose describes *Roots* simply as "the most astounding cultural event of the American Bicentennial."

Celebration of Haley's focus on roots recurs in the critical acclaim. David A. Gerber, by no means uncritical of the work's historicity and style, argues that "the lives of both Kunta Kinte and Malcolm X have filled a powerful emotional need for inspiring models of strength, dignity, and self-creation in a hostile or, at best, indifferent White world," and that Haley has reminded us "we know no way to think of the present or conceive of the future except with reference to our pasts ... to our roots." Judith Mudd, giving two Indian views of *Roots,* quotes justice V. R. Krishna Iyer, judge of the Supreme Court of India:

> The dignity of a race is restored when its roots are known ... and that explains how Gandhi in India

could resist the imperial rulers with knowledge of our strength and sustenance from our roots. *The Discovery of India* by Nehru was prompted by the same urge to trace one's roots which induced Alex Haley to research the black Americans' roots.

In 1992, after Haley's death, his editor and co-writer Murray Fisher quoted black leader Jesse Jackson: "[Haley] made history talk ... He lit up the long night of slavery. He gave our grandparents personhood. He gave *Roots* to the rootless."

This refrain, of roots to the rootless, is one reason I have dwelt on the enormous commercial, critical and indeed world-wide success of this text. *Roots* must be the only non-religious text to have achieved such universal success and endorsement; *Gone With the Wind* has probably out-sold it but certainly rarely found itself on a school or college syllabus, praised by statesmen and judges, and its writer was never compared with a figure of the stature of Nehru. This smash hit, which made its author a multi-millionaire, national black hero, and international roving ambassador, is of considerable cultural importance. If Haley is not the griot he is cracked up to be, the furore over the devaluation of *Roots* should be explosive.

Source: Helen Taylor, "'The Griot from Tennessee': The Saga of Alex Haley's Roots," in *Critical Quarterly,* Vol.37, No.2, Summer 1995, pp. 46-62.

Michael Steward Blayney

In this essay, Blayney argues that prior to Roots *white America did not perceive African Americans as having the same "noble" stature that had been accorded Native Americans.*

Time Magazine called it "Haley's Comet." Black readers hailed it as the most important event in civil rights history since the 1965 march on Selma, Alabama. In January 1977 *Roots* was proclaimed the most popular television program in the medium's history, with the last of eight consecutive episodes reaching an unprecedented 90,000,000 viewers. *Roots* attracted a larger audience than such all-time favorites as *Gone with the Wind* and the 1977 Superbowl. Spurred by the television success, Alex Haley's novel went into fourteen printings after its initial publication in October 1976. During and after the nights it was telecast long lines formed outside bookstores displaying *Roots.* Those too impatient to wait broke into bookstores to obtain copies of the bestseller. Haley was instantly transformed from writer into celebrity. The author's appearance at book parties frequently produced mile-long lines. Haley was deluged with fan mail, and he reportedly received about one thousand letters per week. Meanwhile, the American Broadcasting Company announced plans to air *Roots Two,* a production for 1979 which concentrated on the adventures of Haley's ancestors since the Civil War. Juffure, the village of Haley's famous African ancestor, Kunta Kinte, rapidly became a shrine for boatloads of tourists, and Gambian President Dawda Jwara declared the village a national monument. In South Africa, *Roots* threatened to spark an international incident when the white government there openly voiced its fears that the showing of *Roots* by the United States Information Service might provoke race riots. Meanwhile, the novel has been translated into twelve languages and made available to twenty-eight countries. The mini-series has been broadcast in thirty-two countries.

Despite the frequent criticism of *Roots* as a shallow melodrama, it has been granted academic respectability in 276 colleges and universities which adopted the novel as a standard part of the curriculum in black history. At least one Afro-American history text boasts Alex Haley as its consultant. Clearly, *Roots* is a significant phenomenon in American popular culture.

The almost universal acclaim the broadcast of *Roots* received startled its creators. In producing a period piece of slavery from the slave's perspective, ABC executives took a high-risk gamble. They feared that white audiences might refuse to watch a twelve-hour drama in which whites were consistently portrayed as villains against a group of heroic blacks. One reason well-known television personalities like Loren Greene and Edward Asner were given parts was to counter a possible negative white reaction. Despite its heavily charged racial theme, *Roots* enjoyed a popularity rare for any television presentation. While one can easily understand why blacks hailed Haley as a "savior," *Roots'* popularity among its larger white audience requires further explanation. It seems likely that *Roots* failed to appreciably affect white attitudes, and perhaps no novel or television program could hope to accomplish such an enormous undertaking.

Why then did the *Roots* phenomenon succeed in capturing the white imagination? To better understand the appeals of *Roots* for white Americans, we should consider the noble savage, that long-held romantic image of the American Indian. From the time of the earliest American settlements, whites, when not viewing Indians as agents of Satan, have frequently perceived the red man as living in har-

mony with nature, possessing deep spiritual wisdom and extraordinary courage. By contrast, blacks have been pictured as either comic Sambos or fiendish devils in literature and popular culture. Even the recent departure from some of the more vicious stereotypes since the end of the Second World War has failed to produce a black hero the stature of Hiawatha or Chief Joseph. It was not until the publication of *Roots* that Africans and the descendants of Africans for the first time became heroes in the tradition of the noble savage. The concept of the noble African is central to an understanding of *Roots'* appeal to whites, because unintentionally, both novel and broadcast provided whites with a safe Negro. Just as popular treatment of the legendary noble red man fails to address the contemporary situation of native Americans, so Kunta Kinte was palatable to white audiences precisely because of his failure to remind whites of the plight of contemporary blacks.

From the first white contacts with the New World, the American Indian has been romanticized. Christopher Columbus viewed Indians as innocent, kind, intelligent, and generous. Rationalistic philosophers of the eighteenth century invented the term noble savage as part of a larger attack upon the Christian doctrine of the fall of man. For these European philosophers, the Indian became an idealized "child of nature," not the savage fiend and child of the devil depicted by American frontiersmen. The noble savage experienced a primitive, unburdened existence in the wilderness free from tyrannical government and class distinctions. His simplicity enabled him to live in harmony with nature and his fellows. He was articulate, intelligent, and handsome. Being freer than civilized man, the noble savage was also happier. He was a stranger to the greed, materialism, and pretense of white civilization.

In his *Notes on the State of Virginia,* Thomas Jefferson praised the political system of American Indians as having very little external coercive power. Since laws of nature were part of their normal condition, man-made laws did not need to be imposed from without. Jefferson also admired Indians because their society possessed no artificial class distinctions, and he speculated on the possible racial amalgamation between Indians and whites. On the other hand, Jefferson opposed any future racial union between whites and blacks. For Jefferson, noble savages were found only in America. For white Americans like Jefferson, much of the Indian's nobility grew out of his integration with nature. Throughout the early years of discovery and settlement, many Americans perceived America in Edenic terms. In a similar way, Europeans portrayed the new world as a Garden of Eden, a paradise on earth. Those who held the garden image also intended to view the Indian as a noble savage.

The noble Indian spoke with an eloquence and a wisdom few white men possessed. Chief Logan's famous speech to Lord Dunmore, for example, was used in McGuffey's fourth-and fifth-grade readers in the 1850s and 1860s. The speech taught white children Christian ethics and further served to idealize the American Indian.

No early American writer popularized the myth of the noble savage more than James Fenimore Cooper. Cooper's Leatherstocking tales offered nineteenth century readers two types of Indians: the savage fiend and the noble savage. While in no way minimizing the importance of the Indian as the devil in Cooper's works, characters like Satanstoe, Uncas, Chingachgook, Hard-Heart, and Rivenoak all perpetuated the noble savage myth in the popular mind. Cooper gave his noble Indians physical beauty and a keen intelligence. Like the slaves in *Roots,* Cooper's Indians looked backward to an earlier age of glory. As a species already vanishing, at least some Indians could be sentimentally regarded. The hero Chingachgook, for example, emerges as a "brave and just minded Delaware," respected by his "fallen people." White civilization's depravity ultimately corrupts Cooper's Indian. The white man brings firewater which disrupts the Indian's harmonious integration with nature.

Unlike their image of the American Indian, the image of Africans held by whites was conceived in almost wholly negative terms. Sixteenth century Europeans likened Africans to the apes that inhabited the Dark Continent. For Elizabethan Englishmen, a fine line existed between black people and anthropoid apes like the chimpanzee ("orangoutangs"). Like apes, Africans were though of as lewd, wanton savages devoid of humanity. Similarly, Europeans imagined Africa a hostile, forbidding place inhabited by dangerous animals and an appropriate home for uncivilized men. Unlike America, the black man's home was never seen in idyllic paradisic terms. The black man was a savage, without nobility and a Garden of Eden. Perhaps for these reasons, Negroes were therefore fit only for the ignominious burden of slavery.

Despite his eighteenth century rationalist convictions, Thomas Jefferson found it impossible to place blacks on the same level, either intellectually or physically, with whites. Jefferson rejected environmental arguments for the intellectual equality of the races. Jefferson reluctantly concluded that Africans were therefore incapable of future intellectual growth. He favored African colonization, not integration, as the most desirable alternative to slavery, and opposed any future racial union between blacks and whites. Jefferson attributed the peculiar body odor of blacks to their skin glands, which secreted more, and to their kidneys, which secreted less than whites. Even on a purely aesthetic level, Jefferson chose red and white rather than black as nature's most beautiful colors.

James Fenimore Cooper's novels juxtaposed blacks to Indians. In *The Redskins,* the Littlepages' English servant observes that "the nigger grows uglier and uglier every year, ... while I do think sir, that the Indian grows 'andsomer and 'andsomer." Cooper believed that the black's intellect was also inferior to the Indian's, and because Indians possessed an integrity and independence surpassing blacks, the two were never natural allies. The common enemy, the white man, in no way made for common interest between the two races. For Cooper, the lack of nobility in the black man's character meant he could never rise to the level of the noble savage. The Indian's death provided another source of nobility over the African, for even though the red man was destroyed physically, he endured spiritually while the black man merely survived on a physical level.

White Americans during the nineteenth century often viewed the Negro as entertaining, but never as noble. Negroes figured largely in the popular culture of the early republic. The nineteenth century minstrel show, which accurately mirrored the common man's thinking, portrayed blacks as comic Sambo figures. The minstrel show served important cultural and psychological needs for their white audiences. Minstrels created "a ludicrous Northern Negro character that assured audience members that however confused, bewildered, and helpless they felt, someone was much worse off than they were." Minstrel shows provided a nonthreatening view of race at a time when race threatened the Union, while at the same time helping to justify racism.

In the twentieth century, a new form of popular culture, the motion picture, continued to deny black nobility. David Wark Griffith's *The Birth of a Nation* (1915) was in many respects the first modern motion picture. This hundred-thousand dollar spectacle achieved unparalleled heights of screen realism. Grifith boasted "magnificent settings, gorgeous costumes, thousands of actors and smiles, tears and thrills." In *The Birth of a Nation* the Negro was portrayed as a brute whose demonic instincts were unleashed with emancipation. Freedom for blacks during Reconstruction ended in tragedy as freedmen attempted to soil the purity of white womanhood. Only the dramatic intervention of the Ku Klux Klan at the film's climax saved the white South and reconciled the two sections.

With the advent of the talkies, negative black stereotypes were heard as well as seen. Two popular types in the 1930s were "coons" and "Toms." "Coons" were lazy, good for nothing and shiftless, and were constantly getting into trouble. The best known "coon" of the 1930s was Stepin Fetchit, who became the most successful Negro in Hollywood. Stepin Fetchit was laziness and ignorance personified. His performances followed in the tradition of the nineteenth century minstrel characters, for the characters he played lacked humanity, much less nobility.

Bill "Bojangles" Robinson, the most famous "Tom" of the era, frequently co-starred with Shirley Temple. Unlike Stepin Fetchit, "Uncle Billy" was well-mannered and always knew his place. Robinson delighted Shirley by dancing for her. He was both intelligent and reliable. For white audiences, he represented a safe, if hardly noble, Negro.

By the end of the thirties the black Hollywood image underwent considerable improvement. Negro characters in *Gone with the Wind* (1939) were a far cry from those in *Birth of a Nation.* In *Gone with the Wind* Hattie McDaniel turned in an exceptionally strong performance as the mammy of the O'Hara household. As both counselor and manager, she was much more than a fawning servant. McDaniel became the first black to receive an Oscar, an honor that divided liberals, some of whom objected to her demeaning servant role. Yet even those who found her role demeaning found it difficult to criticize her Oscar. *Gone with the Wind* represented a turning point in which Negroes began to take more attractive roles in films. Like McDaniel, however, most continued in traditionally inferior roles.

Despite improvement during and following the Second World War, the black image in American film remained fundamentally dissimilar from white perceptions of Indians as noble savages. War against a racist power necessitated opposition to racism at home. Typical of the improved image was

Dooley Wilson as Sam, the piano player in *Casablanca* (1942). Following the war *Home of the Brave* (1949) became the first movie to attack white bigotry openly. In *Lost Boundaries* (1948) whites rejected a light-skinned negro family that passes as white in a small New England community. Their race is finally discovered, and white friends turn against them until the town's minister persuades the community to accept the family.

In the 1950s and the 1960s individual stars and movies with racial themes won white audience approval, but none captured the white imagination like *Roots.* Dorothy Dandridge, Harry Belafonte, Sidney Poitier, Richard Roundtree, and Pamela Greer enjoyed widespread popularity among whites, but none of these stars performed in any motion picture whose popularity matched *Roots.*

Source: Michael Steward Blayney, *"Roots and the Noble Savage,"* in *North Dakota Quarterly,* Vol. 54, No. 1, Winter 1986, pp. 1-17.

Sources

David Herbert Donald, in a review in *Commentary,* December, 1976.

Chester J. Fontenot, "Radical Upbringing," in *Prairie Schooner,* Spring, 1977, pp. 98-9.

Eugene D. Genovese, *Roll Jordan Roll: The World the Slaves Made,* Vintage, 1974.

Russell Warren Howe, "An Elusive Past," in *The New Leader,* January 3, 1977, pp. 23-4.

Philip Nobile, "Was *Roots* One of the Great Literary Hoaxes?" in *The Toronto Star,* March 8, 1993, p. A13.

Clarence Page, "Alex Haley's Enduring Truths," in *The Courier Journal,* March 11, 1993, p. 8A.

Arnold Rampersad, in a review in *The New Republic,* Vol. 175, No. 23, December 4, 1976, pp. 23-4, 26.

Pascoe Sawyers, "Black and White," in *The Guardian,* September 13, 1997, p. 6.

Howard F. Stein, "In Search of 'Roots': An Epic of Origins and Destiny," in *Journal of Popular Culture,* Vol. XI, No. 1, Summer, 1977, pp. 11-17.

Paul D. Zimmerman, "In Search of a Heritage: Roots," in *Newsweek,* Sept. 27, 1976, p. 94.

For Further Study

Russell Adams, "An Analysis of the *Roots* Phenomenon in the Context of American Racial Conservatism," in *Presence Africaine,* Vol. 116, No. 4, pp. 125-40.

This article explores the factors that contributed to the success of *Roots.*

Helen Davis Othow, "*Roots* and the Heroic Search for Identity," in *CLA Journal,* Vol. XXVI, No. 3, March, 1983, pp. 311-24.

Chavis describes Haley's book as the embodiment of the "feverish search for meaning in an alien universe."

Elizabeth Stone, *Black Sheep and Kissing Cousins: How Our Family Stories Shape Us,* Penguin, 1989, 254 p.

Stone interviews one hundred people and records their family histories.

Tommie Morton Young, in *Afro American Genealogy Sourcebook,* Afragenda, 1998, 199 p.

Young provides a multitude of genealogical resources for those interested in exploring their own genealogy.

Rubyfruit Jungle

Rita Mae Brown
1973

When a small feminist press published Rita Mae Brown's *Rubyfruit Jungle* in 1973, the novel sold 70,000 copies despite being almost completely ignored by reviewers at major magazines and periodicals. In 1977 the book was reissued by Bantam Books and went on to sell over one million copies.

Rubyfruit Jungle chronicles the life of a young woman named Molly Bolt. Starting with her childhood in Pennsylvania, the book follows her adolescence in Florida and her later adventures in New York. Her relationships with other women are also a major source of focus and conflict in the novel. Many of the events and characters in the book draw from Brown's own early years.

Rubyfruit Jungle fits into the tradition of the picaresque novel, which typically follows the adventures of a socially or financially marginalized protagonist, such as Huck Finn in Mark Twain's *The Adventures of Huckleberry Finn* (1884). The book is unique within the picaresque tradition in that both the protagonist and the author are female.

Author Biography

Rita Mae Brown was born in Pennsylvania in 1944 and moved to Florida during her adolescence. She attended the University of Florida, but was expelled for her participation in a civil rights rally.

She later moved to New York and attended New York University, where she received a degree

Rita Mae Brown

in Classics and English. Later she received another degree in Cinematography from the New York School of Visual Arts. She also holds a doctorate in Political Science from the Institute for Policy Studies in Washington, D.C.

In the late 1960s, Brown turned her attention to politics. She became interested in several feminist and lesbian rights groups. In 1971 she was instrumental in forming the Furies, a lesbian and feminist group. Also she founded and edited the feminist research journal *Quest*.

In 1971 she published a book of poetry, *The Hand That Cradles the Rock,* and a translation of works from the original Latin, *Hrotsvitra: Six Medieval Plays.*

Her first published novel was entitled *Rubyfruit Jungle.* Turned down by major presses and agents, the book was finally published by a small feminist press and later purchased by Bantam Books for a wider release. Selling well in its limited first edition, the book went on to sell more than one million copies.

A picaresque, autobiographical novel, *Rubyfruit Jungle* has been compared to Mark Twain's *The Adventures of Huckleberry Finn.* It is widely regarded as the first popular novel with a lesbian protagonist.

In the years following *Rubyfruit Jungle,* Brown has published eleven novels, two collections of poetry, a book of essays, and a writer's instruction manual. She had also written seven mysteries with feline protagonists, co-credited to her cat, Sneaky Pie Brown. Brown has also won the Literary Lion Award from the New York Public Library, and was named Charlottesville's Favorite Author.

Brown has worked in both film and television. She wrote the screenplay for the 1982 horror film *Slumber Party Massacre,* and provided the voice-over narration for *Before Stonewall* (1985), a documentary about the gay and lesbian rights movement. Brown also wrote the 1993 made-for-TV movie *The Woman Who Loved Elvis.*

Plot Summary

Early Years

As *Rubyfruit Jungle* opens, a young girl named Molly Bolt lives with her adoptive parents in Coffee Hollow, Pennsylvania. An industrious girl, she thinks up a moneymaking scheme with Brockhurst Detwiler, a school friend.

As the only uncircumcised child in the area, Molly charges nickels to look at Brockhurst's penis—and dimes to touch it. When another student tells a teacher, her mother finds out. Irate, her mother informs her that she is adopted and illegitimate.

Shortly after this incident, Molly's Aunt Jenna goes into the hospital to deliver a baby. It lives for only two days and a few weeks later, Jenna dies of cancer. Molly has her first sexual experience in sixth grade with another girl, Leota Bisland. The family moves to Florida.

Florida

In the second section, Molly details her school years in Florida. She struggles to fit in, yet realizes that she is different from her classmates.

She has her first heterosexual experience with her cousin Leroy, who tells her about his own passive homosexual experiences. She enters high school and begins to hang out with a more select, popular clique. After spotting her principal with a teacher in an adulterous meeting, Molly secures financial backing for her successful run at student body presidency.

She has a sexual affair with a female classmate, Carolyn, one of her two best friends. After

Carolyn becomes jealous of the time Molly spends with her other best friend, Connie, and accuses Molly of sleeping with her, Molly reveals the affair to Connie. Connie has a strongly homophobic reaction, and Carolyn reacts badly, denying that she is a lesbian. She points out her own feminine traits and Molly's masculine ones.

After high school, Molly attends the University of Florida. She begins a lesbian relationship with her roommate, Faye. After tiring of the cold and silent treatment of the other girls in the dorm, Molly confronts them and reveals her relationship with Faye.

This proves to be disastrous: she is placed under psychiatric care; her scholarship is revoked on moral grounds; and Faye is put into a mental institution. Molly returns home on a Greyhound bus.

New York

When Molly arrives home, her mother announces that she is no longer welcome. Molly hitchhikes to New York. Nearly broke, she spends her first night in New York City sleeping in a car, where she meets her first New Yorker, a young man named Calvin.

Calvin, like Molly, is from Pennsylvania; he too has run away to New York because his family would not accept his sexuality. After taking her to a lesbian bar, Calvin departs for San Francisco. Molly takes a job at The Fling, a clone of the Playboy Club. There she meets Holly, a tall, beautiful black lesbian.

The two women become lovers. Holly reveals that she is a kept woman and encourages Molly to do the same. Molly goes so far as to attend a party to meet a potential sponsor—and even to have lunch with her—but cannot go through with it.

After Holly gets them both fired for assaulting a customer, they have a fight. Holly cannot deal with Molly's moral objection to being a kept woman. Eventually, Holly professes her love for Molly, but to no avail. The third section ends with Holly leaving in a cab.

Coming Home

In the final section of the book, Molly gets a job at the Silver Publishing Company. She has an affair with Polina, a married woman, and nearly consummates a relationship with Polina's other lover, Paul.

Initially repulsed by Molly's sexuality, Polina wants to explore her bisexuality—but Molly cannot handle Polina's sexual fantasies of being a man.

She eventually begins a liaison with Polina's daughter Alice. One day, Alice informs her mother that she and Molly are lovers. Her mother banishes Molly from both their lives.

In the aftermath of that incident, Molly leaves New York for a pilgrimage to her hometown in Pennsylvania, where she looks up her first lover. Leota has married and has two children. She thinks that what they did was "perverted."

Returning to New York City for her last year of film school, Molly decides to do her senior project on her mother's life. She once again makes a pilgrimage, this time to her second hometown in Florida. She arrives to find that her mother is dying of an unnamed disease.

Her mother now denies all of the things she said while Molly was growing up. In fact, she wants to make peace with her daughter. Molly films her mother talking about her life, then returns to New York and shows the film.

Characters

Alice Bellantoni

Polina's sixteen-year-old daughter, Alice is described as "a Renaissance princess come back to life." She expresses an active desire to have sex with her mother. She and Molly become lovers, but when Alice informs her mother of their relationship, she is never allowed to see Molly again.

Aunt Jenna

See Jennifer Denman

Polina Belantoni

Polina is a married woman who teaches medieval studies at Columbia University in New York City. When Molly reveals her sexuality to her, Polina reacts in a stereotypically homophobic way: she informs Molly that she is straight and already has a lover, Paul Digita. After seeing her psychiatrist for a while, Polina decides that it is okay for Molly to be a lesbian.

Eventually the two women become lovers. Polina can only achieve sexual climax by acting out fantasies of being a man. Their affair becomes more and more bizarre and ends after Polina's daughter reveals that Molly is her lover as well.

Leota B. Bisland

Leota is Molly's first lover. While the two girls were in the sixth grade, Molly believed that Leota was "the most beautiful girl I had ever seen." When Molly returns to her hometown many years later, she learns that Leota is married and has two children. When Molly asks her if she ever thinks about what happened between them, Leota says no, and goes on to say "anyway, that was perverted, sick."

When Molly professes her happiness as a lesbian, Leota says that she should be institutionalized. Leota represents the unfulfilled lives of women who deny their true selves in order to conform to society's expectations.

Carl Bolt

Carl is Molly's father and always defends her against her mother. After giving Molly his blessing and acceptance, Carl dies of a heart attack. His tolerant and loving attitude toward his daughter is a conscious reworking of expected gender behavior in which the mother is generally shown to be the more sympathetic figure.

Carrie Bolt

Carrie is Molly's adoptive mother. Unfortunately, she is quick to remind Molly that she is illegitimate and not her "real" daughter. At the outset, Carrie is a sharp-tongued woman, and constantly criticizes her daughter for her masculine ways.

Carrie is scandalized by her daughter's election to student body president. She believes that Molly wants to go to college so that she can forget her roots and family. Eventually, they have a serious fight when Carrie learns that Molly is a lesbian. She throws Molly out of the house.

Carrie does not reappear in her daughter's life for many years. When Molly returns to Florida to film Carrie for her senior film project, she is dying of an unnamed disease. Older and wiser, she regrets the way she has treated Molly over the years and yearns for the chance to improve their relationship.

Molly Bolt

The protagonist and narrator of the book, Molly lives with her adoptive parents at the beginning of the story. Yet she never feels completely loved and accepted, because her mother frequently reminds her that she was born an illegitimate orphan.

In the 1970s, when Rubyfruit Jungle *was published, the taboos against homosexuality were rebuked at gay pride demonstrations such as this Gay Freedom Day Parade in San Francisco in June, 1977.*

A lesbian, Molly faces much discrimination as a result of her sexual identity. For example, she is kicked out of college, accused of being mentally ill, and banished from her mother's home when her homosexuality is revealed. She decides to move to New York City to find the more tolerant and creative atmosphere she craves.

Molly symbolizes the liberated woman of the late 1960s and early 1970s. She has more options than women of past generations. Yet while she is able to experiment sexually, she still has trouble finding true love. She is able to pursue higher education at the university level, but faces the same sexist obstacles. Molly still has to search for love and fulfillment like any other character.

Broccoli

See Brockhurst Detwiler

Calvin

A gay, African American street hustler, Calvin is the first person Molly meets in New York. He introduces her to Ronnie Rappaport so she can make money. Raised in Philadelphia, Calvin has run away from a girl he got pregnant in order to convince his father that he wasn't gay.

Calvin serves as a strange mirror image for Molly. Whereas her high school girlfriend was the captain of the cheerleaders, Calvin was having sex with the football team. They both grew up poor, and are both from Pennsylvania. He moves to San Francisco.

Craig

A masculine, young biker, Craig introduces Leroy to gay sex.

Ep Denman

Ep is Leroy's father.

Jennifer Denman

The mother of Leroy and Ted, Jennifer looks like a grandmother at the age of thirty-three. She has a baby named Carl, but it dies two days later. She dies of cancer within two weeks. Jenna is symbolic of the many women trapped in exhausting domestic roles. Her death functions as a metaphor for the psychic "death" that awaits Molly if she decides to conform to society's ideas of femininity.

Leroy Denman

Leroy is Molly's cousin and best friend as a child. He is also her first male lover. After his family moves to Florida, Leroy rebels against society: he gets a wild hairstyle and dresses like the other poor hoodlums in his school.

Leroy is confused about his identity as a male and allows a gay man, Craig, to perform oral sex on him. He becomes less tolerant of Molly's sexuality as he ages.

When Molly sees him when she returns to Florida several years later, Leroy is married with children. He had joined the Marines as a young man, and they "straightened him right out." He still feels close to Molly.

Leroy symbolizes the fears and confusion of men in the new era of greater freedom for women. He is unsure about his role in this changing environment. Like Molly, he too explores his sexuality. While seemingly fine with incest, he is afraid of being perceived as "queer."

Brockhurst Detwiler

Broccoli is a childhood friend of Molly's in Pennsylvania. Broccoli has the distinction of being the only uncircumcised boy in the area, and Molly convinces him to go into business: charge people money to see his penis.

Paul Digita

Paul is Polina's lover. When Molly makes a date with him, he lures her home for sex. He can only achieve orgasm by pretending that he is a woman.

Ruby Drollinger

Ruby is the heroine's biological mother who never appears in the book. Molly's adoptive mother makes reference to her several times. According to Carrie, Ruby was a "bull-headed woman" like her daughter.

Florence

Florence is Molly's aunt and Jennifer's mother. She is noted for staying calm during crisis situations. She dies while Molly is in New York.

Holly

Molly's first lover in New York City, Holly is a tall, beautiful African American lesbian. A "kept woman," she introduces Molly to her benefactor, a well-known actress named Kim Wilson. Holly attempts to get Molly to find a patron of her own.

Molly judges Holly unfavorably because she is a "kept" woman. As a result, the two women fight and they never see each other again. Molly and Holly have almost the same name—similar characters whose moral and personal progression represents the results of very different individual choices.

Miss Marne

Miss Marne is the dean of women at the University of Florida. She places Molly under psychiatric care when Molly's sexuality is revealed. To Molly, Marne appears to be a lesbian herself. It is a well-known fact that Marne lived with the same woman for fifteen years. Forced to hide her identity, Marne is so fearful of being exposed as a lesbian that she punishes the other lesbians on campus.

Mighty Mo

A butch lesbian who tries to pick Molly up in a bar, Mo introduces Molly to the concept of role division within the lesbian community.

The Mouth

See Florence

Connie Pen

Connie is one of Molly's best friends in high school. Connie cannot handle the fact that Molly is a lesbian, but seems find Carolyn acceptable because she denies being gay—even though she admits to having sex with Molly. Her homophobia ends her friendship with Molly.

Leota B. Phantom

See Leota B. Bisland

Faye Raider

Faye is Molly's college roommate. She takes Molly under her wing, buying her clothing and generally taking care of her. She drinks a lot, and takes Molly to her first lesbian bar. Though not professing to be a lesbian, Faye ends up in a relationship with Molly. When the affair is exposed, she leaves school and her parents place her in a psychiatric institution.

Ronnie Rappaport

The son of a rich department store owner, Ronnie can only achieve sexual gratification from being pelted with fruit.

Rhea Rhadin

One of Molly's coworkers at Silver Publishing, Rhea and Molly have a contentious and competitive relationship.

Carolyn Simpson

One of Molly's two best friends in high school, Carolyn "was the school goody two shoes." When first introduced, she is a virgin. Later, she gets drunk in the park and has sex with Molly. Their affair ends when Molly tells Connie that she and Carolyn are lovers. Carolyn responds with defensive homophobia, claiming that she is not a lesbian. Molly finds this unforgivable, and they part company.

Cheryl Spiegelglass

Cheryl is a childhood friend of Molly's in Pennsylvania. After informing Molly that girls can't be doctors, Molly punches her in the mouth.

Earl Stambach

A classmate of Molly's in Pennsylvania, Earl gets her in trouble by telling their teacher about Molly's business with Detwiler.

Themes

Gender

Rubyfruit Jungle explores the impact of gender conditioning. From the very beginning of Molly's childhood, she is under constant pressure to be feminine. Her mother expects Molly to become skilled in cooking, cleaning, and other domestic skills in order to marry, while her adoptive father wants her to go to college. Even her best friend, Leroy Denman, can't understand what Molly wants to be when she gets older.

In an early scene, Molly, Leroy, and another friend named Cheryl decide to play nurses. When Molly announces that she will be a doctor Cheryl disagrees, saying: "You can't be a doctor. Only boys can be doctors. Leroy's got to be the doctor." Molly disagrees and insists that she will be the doctor because she is "the smart one." Cheryl counters with, "It doesn't matter about brains, brains don't count. What counts is whether you are a boy or a girl." Molly promptly punches her in the mouth.

As this vignette makes clear, Molly must fight against the gender expectations from women as well as men.

In the aftermath of Molly's fight with Cheryl, Molly's mother announces that "she's gonna make a lady" out of her, teaching her to "act right, cook, clean, and sew." For her, femininity is constructed from a series of tasks and chores that must be repeated daily. Being female becomes a ritual—a set of proscribed actions that must be invoked day after day. Crucially, these rituals take place in the home. Molly argues that she "can learn them things at night," and should be allowed to explore all day.

Attempting to conciliate, Leroy announces that he, too, will stay in. Molly's mother immediately assaults his masculinity, "telling him what would happen to him if he picked up women's ways ... soon they'd take him to the hospital and cut his thing off." For all of these characters, actual confinement within the home symbolizes female experience and identity.

Gender and Sexuality

As a lesbian, Molly is subject to much discrimination. Her mother rejects her, eventually kicking her out of the house. Her former lovers deny their sexuality for fear of being identified as a lesbian. Even as a young girl, Molly knows that society expects her to be heterosexual; therefore, she tries to have boyfriends and subscribe to gender roles as a teenager.

Topics for Further Study

- Research the defining characteristic and history of the picaresque novel. How much does Molly conform to or diverge from the traditional picaresque hero?

- Investigate the equal rights movements of the sixties and seventies. Is Molly Bolt a radical feminist? Provide reasons for your answer.

- *Rubyfruit Jungle* was rejected by all the major publishing houses in the United States. Finally published by a small firm, it sold more than seventy thousand copies. Look at the *New York Times* bestseller lists for 1973 and 1977, the years Brown's novel was published and re-issued. What kind of books consistently made the lists? How were the top sellers of each year different? Why do you think *Rubyfruit Jungle* became a bestseller?

- Molly Bolt comes of age in a pre-AIDS culture. Research the history of sexual liberation movements in the 1970s and how the AIDs crisis of the 1980s changed perceptions and behavior. How much is *Rubyfruit Jungle* a product of its time? How might Brown's story be different if it were written in 1993, instead of 1973?

After Leroy and Molly have sex for the first time, Molly becomes the more sexually aggressive partner. For Leroy, this is fundamentally wrong; society has taught him that the man should be the one in control, and Molly should play the passive role in sexual relations.

In fact, Molly's aggressiveness symbolically castrates Leroy—he actually becomes impotent. His sense of self is inextricably linked with society's concepts of correct male and female behavior. When faced with deviation from this norm, he loses power over the totemic symbol of his male identity—the phallus.

Here, as in his brief experimentation with homosexuality, Leroy finds himself the victim of his social conditioning.

Molly's complex negotiations of sex, sexuality and gender act as a sustained critique of the more simplistic versions of sexual liberation in the novel. Although she is celebrated as a lesbian heroine, Molly's sexual experiences are far more complicated and varied than her exalted status in popular culture would imply.

Realizing the limits of her own freedom, Molly has boyfriends to prove her heterosexuality to the worlds of her high school and college. Her first lover is male, and she retains a deeply eroticized relationship with her closest male friends.

For too many of the supporting characters of *Rubyfruit Jungle,* the sexual liberation of the 1960s and 1970s is seen only as a brief inversion of the status quo. These inversions last only for a short time—usually to vent frustrations—and then order can be restored.

This is seen very clearly in the episode concerning Molly's sexual liaisons with Polina and Polina's lover, Paul. The only way Polina can achieve sexual satisfaction is through her fantasy of being a man. Paul's fantasies involve being treated as a female with large breasts.

The symbolism of their names underscores this inversion of gender roles—Polina is a feminine version of Paul, and Paul the masculine version of Polina.

Style

The Picaresque Novel

Rubyfruit Jungle is considered a prime example of a picaresque novel. This form of literature dates back at least as early as 1554, with the publication of *Lazarillo de Tormes.* Perhaps the best-known example is *Don Quixote,* by Miguel Cervantes. More recent examples include Henry Fielding's *Tom Jones* (1749) and Mark Twain's *The Adventures of Huckleberry Finn* (1884).

The picaresque genre is structured as a loosely organized series of episodes that detail the journey and adventures of a hero or heroine. Lessons are learned through bitter and humorous experiences. Often, the hero of the picaresque is a marginalized character, either socially or economically.

Rubyfruit Jungle follows the conventions of the picaresque in many ways. Molly's journey is as bawdy and sexual as that in *Tom Jones.* Stylistically, *Rubyfruit Jungle* has been compared with Twain's picaresque hero; specifically, both protagonists are orphans, poor, from rural backgrounds, and don't seem to understand the reality of racism.

However, Brown's novel is significantly different from the traditional model. Unlike the characters in most picaresque stories, Molly rarely uses her experiences to learn about herself, but rather to learn about other people. She remains developmentally static, and while the lessons are learned, they don't significantly alter her.

Rubyfruit Jungle is also innovative in its choice of a heroine. While Defoe's *Moll Flanders* was a female picaresque, *Rubyfruit Jungle* is the first to have both a female character and a female author. Like Defoe's book, *Rubyfruit Jungle* has a large sexual component—but rather than sexuality as the character's downfall, Brown takes the experiences of the character and uses them to empower and mature her.

While sometimes autobiographical, the picaresque form is often used to employ broad satire and social commentary. *Don Quixote* has been deemed a satirical political statement about both government and church. Twain utilizes Huckleberry Finn to satirize cultural issues such as racism and child abuse.

In the same way, Brown uses Molly and her adventures to reveal the prejudice inherent in most people's view of minorities. She employs farce, caricature, and absurdity to explore human foibles and failings.

Symbolism

The most obvious significance of the novel's title—*Rubyfruit Jungle*—is a metaphor for genitalia. As Molly defines it, "I think of [women's] genitals as a, as a ruby fruit jungle … thick and rich and full of hidden treasures."

In the creation of the description and the phrase, Molly is formulating a female-centered set of sexual language and imagery, just as her sexual liberation is mapping out a new terrain of experience. However, the phrase and image have more complex applications. Molly's mother is called Ruby, making Molly the metaphoric "fruit" of Ruby.

The narrative itself, which tracks Molly's journey through hostile rural and urban landscapes, could be considered her "jungle." The title can thus be read as a literal description of the narrative: the fruit of Ruby in her jungle, or, more gracefully phrased, *Rubyfruit Jungle.*

Molly's encounter with Ronnie reveals another significant meaning for the title. The son of a wealthy department store owner, Ronnie achieves sexual climax by being pelted with fruit; Molly is paid a hundred dollars to throw grapefruits at him. This is her only act of prostitution in the book, and would seem at first to be a celibate act.

If, as Leroy makes so clear, sex is defined as a man touching a woman in the dark, then this episode must be considered as entirely asexual. The direct sexual symbolism of the scenario is fully realized when two things are considered. First, the common grapefruit is also known as the ruby red grapefruit.

Second, when interpreting the scene through Molly's own definition of female genitalia, it is clear that in the purest symbolic sense, she is having sexual intercourse with Ronnie. For Molly Bolt, sexuality is created by a wide variety of acts and relationships.

Historical Context

1973

Rubyfruit Jungle was published in a very tumultuous year in American history. The U. S. military was integrated by gender as the women-only branches were eliminated. The last U.S. combat personnel were withdrawn from Vietnam, officially ending the Vietnam War.

In Roe v. Wade, the Supreme Court established a woman's right to abortion. Billie Jean King scored an enormous symbolic victory for female athletes when she beats Bobby Riggs in "The Battle of the Sexes," a televised tennis tournament watched by nearly forty-eight million people.

The 1950s: The Beginning of Civil Rights

The first part of *Rubyfruit Jungle* is set in the early 1950s. There are no overt signs of racism or segregation because Molly lives in a very segregated area. Yet when Molly's family moves to Florida, she experiences racism for the first time. She discovers that African Americans are considered "separate but equal" by law: they must use separate washrooms, drinking fountains, and even theaters and restaurants.

By the middle of the decade, the civil rights struggle was gaining momentum. In 1955 Rosa Parks symbolizes the movement when she refuses

Compare
&
Contrast

- **1973:** Gays and lesbians begin to form support groups and lobby to raise public awareness of the important roles of gays and lesbians in society. Discrimination and violence force many homosexuals to hide their sexual identities, and there is no legislation to protect gays and lesbians from discrimination on the job.

  Today: Although not widely accepted, gays and lesbians have made significant strides in teaching tolerance and fighting ignorance. Hate crimes against homosexuals still occur on a frequent basis, and a "don't ask, don't tell" policy is implemented in the U. S. military. Yet most companies prohibit sexual discrimination against gays and lesbians and steps are taken to legitimize gay marriage in some states, such as Hawaii.

- **1973:** A symbolic victory for female athletes is scored when Billie Jean King beats Bobby Riggs in "The Battle of the Sexes," a televised tennis tournament watched by nearly forty-eight million people.

  Today: On the heels of the victory of the U. S. women's soccer team and the success of the WNBA, women's athletics are gaining respect and popularity throughout the United States.

- **1972:** After languishing since 1923, the Equal Rights amendment (known as the ERA) is passed by Congress on March 22, and sent to individual states for ratification. Hawaii approves it within the hour. By the end of the week, so have Delaware, Nebraska, New Hampshire, Idaho and Iowa. Yet by the end of the decade, political pressures have killed the amendment.

  Today: Many feminist groups seek to reintroduce the ERA, hoping that with the more tolerant and enlightened atmosphere it will pass.

---

to give up her seat on a public bus. The same year, the Daughters of Bilitis, the first lesbian organization, was founded in San Francisco.

In 1956, the Supreme Court ruled that segregation on public transport is unconstitutional. That next year, the court passed the first civil rights legislation since right after the Civil War. Martin Luther King formed the Southern Christian Leadership Conference to fight segregation and achieve civil rights, and on May 17, he spoke to a crowd of 15,000 in Washington, D.C.

The Early to Middle 1960s: Turbulence and Change

In November of 1961, the Interstate Commerce Commission banned segregation in interstate travel. The Congress on Racial Equality (CORE) began the first Freedom rides through the South. The same year the birth control pill became accessible to adult women, which gives women control over reproduction and greater sexual freedom.

On November 22, 1963, President John F. Kennedy was assassinated. The same year, the Equal Pay Act was passed, assuring women equal pay for equal work. Later that year, the report issued by the President's Commission on the Status of Women documents discrimination against women in virtually every area of American life.

Betty Friedan's best-seller, *The Feminine Mystique,* explores the "problem that has no name"— the condition of the American woman. Five million copies are sold by 1970, laying the groundwork for the modern feminist movement. The following year, the Civil Rights Act of 1964 was passed. In December, Dr. King became the youngest recipient of the Nobel Peace Prize.

Late 1960s and Early 1970s: The Early Feminist Movement

In 1967 the Chicago Women's Liberation Group organized—they are the first women's group to use the term "liberation." Shortly afterward, the

New York Radical Women was founded. In 1968 they begin a process of sharing life stories to generate political awareness, a process that becomes known as "consciousness raising." Similar groups are formed all over the country.

On April 4, 1968, Dr. Martin Luther King was assassinated. There were riots and disturbances in 130 cities, with some twenty thousand arrests. New York Radical Women garnered much media attention when they protest the Miss America Pageant in Atlantic City.

The first national women's liberation conference was held in Chicago. The National Abortion Rights Action League (NARAL) was founded.

By the end of the 1960s, the crusade for women's rights had made great strides. In 1969, Betty Friedan organized the first Women's Equality Day, August 26, to mark the fiftieth anniversary of women's right to vote. By 1971 more than one hundred newsletters and newspapers focusing on the women's movement were being published across the country. The non-partisan National Women's Political Caucus was founded to encourage women to run for public office.

In 1972, Title IX of the Education Amendments decreed that "no person in the United States shall, on the basis of sex, be excluded from participation in, be denied the benefits of, or be subjected to discrimination under any education program or activity receiving federal financial assistance." In Eisenstadt v. Baird, the Supreme Court ruled that the right to privacy encompasses an unmarried person's right to use contraceptives.

After languishing since 1923, the Equal Rights amendment (known as the ERA) was passed by Congress on March 22, 1973, and sent to individual states for ratification. Hawaii approved it within the hour. By the end of the week, so had Delaware, Nebraska, New Hampshire, Idaho and Iowa.

Critical Overview

Rubyfruit Jungle was initially rejected by several major publishers because its subject matter was considered too controversial for mass market public appeal. First published by a small, independent feminist press, Daughters, Inc., it sold a surprising seventy thousand copies.

During its initial publication run, *Rubyfruit Jungle* was widely ignored by the major newspapers and magazines. One of the few reviews it re-

ceived was in *Ms.*, where Marylin Webb called the book "an inspiring, bravado adventure story of a female Huck Finn named Molly Bolt." It was not until Bantam Publishing republished the novel in 1977 that more mainstream reviews began to appear.

New Boston Review's Shelly Temchin Henze traced the parallels between *Rubyfruit Jungle* and the work of Mark Twain: "Imagine, if you will, Tom Sawyer, only smarter; Huckleberry Finn, only foul-mouthed, female, and lesbian, and you have an idea of Molly Bolt." She asserted that Brown's novel was "a symbol of a movement, a sisterly struggle" and a "classic American success story."

Dismissing those who deem the book revolutionary, she maintained that "*Rubyfruit Jungle* is not about revolution, nor even particularly about feminism. It is about standing on your own two feet, creaming the competition, looking out for Number One."

In *The Village Voice*, Bertha Harris underscored the unique character of Molly Bolt. She contended:

> While American heroes may occasionally be women, they may not be lesbian. Or if they are, they had better be discreet or at least miserable. Not Molly. She is lusty and lewd and pursues sex with relentless gusto.

Harris also maintained that "much of Molly's world seems a cardboard stage set lighted to reveal only Molly's virtues and those characteristics which mark her as the 'exceptional' lesbian."

However, she turned the faults of the book into good points, contending:

> it is exactly this quality of *Rubyfruit Jungle* which makes it exemplary (for women) of its kind: an American primitive, whose predecessors have dealt only with male heroes. Although Molly Bolt is not a real woman, she is at least the first real image of a heroine in the noble savage, leather-stocking, true-blue bullfighting tradition in this country's literature.

A second *Village Voice* critic, Terry Curtis Fox, described the novel as a typical coming-of-age story. Fox summarized it as a tale of "sensitive member of outside group heads toward American society and lives to tell the tale."

Fox noted that the protagonist was not strictly aimed at a lesbian audience, noting that "you don't have to be gay or female to identify with Molly Bolt—she is one of the outsiders many of us believe ourselves to be. 'Molly Bolt' can laugh at herself as well as others, and make us laugh too."

Since the publication of *Rubyfruit Jungle,* it has come to be regarded as both a milestone and a classic. Constantly turning up on top ten lists for gay and lesbian readers, and annually listed on the *Index of Censorship*'s Banned Books List, *Rubyfruit Jungle* has made a lasting impact on American readers.

Brown's later works have been nowhere near as successful, nor have they garnered as much critical notice or acclaim. In fact, there has been more focus on Brown as a genre writer: a Southern writer, a lesbian writer, or a writer of mysteries. As Annie Gottlieb maintained in *The New York Times Book Review,* "Ever since *Rubyfruit Jungle,* Rita Mae Brown's subject has been the misfit between human passions and societal conventions. In her view, sexuality is a first cousin of imagination, involving an irrepressible urge to honor and rival the crazy abundance of life."

She viewed "the comic futility and wasteful pain that Miss Brown sees in the effort to confine desire within the one standard form: respectable heterosexual marriage." While *Rubyfruit Jungle* is not regarded as a classic of American literature, it remains a popular and influential novel.

Criticism

Tabitha McIntosh-Byrd

Tabitha McIntosh-Byrd is a doctoral candidate at the University of Pennsylvania. In the following essay, she maintains that Rubyfruit Jungle *resists easy classification.*

Rubyfruit Jungle is a difficult novel to classify in regard to its subject and its genre—as well as its wider cultural reception. Although commentators often label the book as a lesbian, feminist, or Southern novel, Brown's text does not fit in these three simple classifications and is as resistant to stable categorization as feminism, gender difference, or sexuality are to final definitions.

Most often called a "lesbian picaresque," the novel is perhaps best read as a reaction to the gender politics and theories of the 1970s—an exploration of both the benefits and intellectual constraints offered by its feminist and lesbian contemporaries. By sketching the history of lesbian feminist criticism and contextualizing *Rubyfruit Jungle* within that history, it can be read as a precursor to later theoretical movements—especially

the deconstructivist and analytic movements that culminated in Queer theory.

The slippage of categories within Brown's novel, as well as its general refusal to conform to genre labeling, act as a sustained challenge to the biases and assumptions of a liberation politics that was predominantly white and middle class. By tracking the elisions, departures, and slippages of sex, gender, and geography throughout the novel, *Rubyfruit Jungle* can be seen to be not just a "freak" bestseller, but also a radical renegotiation of the cultural meaning of "freakishness."

Lesbian criticism grew from the political theory and movements of lesbian feminism, as well as the women's and gay liberation movements. Reacting to the homophobia of heterosexual feminists on one hand, and the sexism of gay men on the other, lesbians created new groups and theories for the goal of "lesbian liberation," and lesbian feminism.

Within this new movement, lesbianism was intensely politicized; it was viewed as the way to achieve the ultimate goal of feminism—defeat of the patriarchal power structure. Lesbianism became not so much a form of sexuality as a metaphor for anger—what the radical lesbians collective called "the rage of all women" in their 1970 manifesto, "The Woman-Identified Woman." Lesbian critics began to formulate a perspective on cultural creativity that grew out of the "particularity" of lesbian experience.

In this theory, the lesbian perspective was understood as a unique and singular perspective. Lesbian perspective viewed patriarchal culture as a marginalized outsider, and could be found in literary work as a silenced "Other" who needed to be deciphered.

With this formulation of lesbian experience came the idea that the role of the author was to express her unique lesbian perspective in her texts, while the role of the reader was to find and therefore "decode" them. From this interchange of ideas came the idea that lesbianism frees women from the constraints and oppressions of patriarchy, making lesbians the *de facto* role models for all women.

In the 1970s lesbian theory started with a set of extremely rigid assumptions: that a category called "lesbian" existed; lesbians share key experiences and ideas; and that literary texts, as well as politics, are generated by lived experience. All of these assumptions were called into question by later theorists.

Critics such as Diana Fuss questioned the "essentializing" aspect of this view of lesbian existence, claiming that it constructed only one possible lesbian identity that promoted certain forms of lesbians and lesbianism over others. Instead, they offered an anti-essentialist construction of lesbianism that took into account gender, sexuality, race, and class.

In this way, the lesbian becomes one manifestation of what Teresa de Lauretis calls the "eccentric" subject—a self that is multiple and shifting, continually constructed and reconstructed at the margins, instead of a singular and particularized special category.

Within this cultural history, labeling Rita Mae Brown's book a lesbian or feminist novel has immediate political and theoretical ramifications. In the first instance, it implies the existence of a particular perspective on the construction of sex and gender—an expectation that the text will be an encoded document from the margins which critiques patriarchal culture.

At the same time, "lesbian" is understood to be a unifying, monolithic term that acts as the culmination of *all* women's rage, regardless of race and class—it excludes all men, regardless of race, class, and sexuality. Feminism is an equally loaded term, implying—again—a presentation of women's shared experience of oppression that writes out class, race, and geography. Nowhere is this more paradigmatically revealed than in a cursory investigation of the label "Southern."

The first and most basic misidentification of *Rubyfruit Jungle* is that of Southern novel. Molly is one of Teresa de Lauretis "ec-centric" subjects whose life is always in movement. She spends her early childhood in Pennsylvania, before moving to Florida and finally to New York.

Pennsylvania is usually considered either an Appalachian or Eastern seaboard state—neither southern nor northern but somewhere mid-Atlantic. Florida, while geographically southern, is not traditionally considered one of the southern states. Its population is and always has been made up of newcomers—retired people, job seekers, seasonal workers, and immigrants. Lacking the accents and cultural background of the other southern states, Florida is southerly rather than a quintessential part of the American South.

New York figures in *Rubyfruit Jungle* as the quasi-real, symbolic melting pot of American imagination. When Molly attempts to go home, she is forced to understand that she does not have one:

What Do I Read Next?

- *Six of One* (1983) is Rita Mae Brown's novel about love, war, and sibling rivalry.

- Brown's novel, *Sudden Death* (1984), tells the story of sex, betrayal, ambition, and greed amongst professional women tennis players.

- *The History of Tom Jones: A Foundling* (1749), written by Henry Fielding, explores every facet of eighteenth-century English society from brothels to drawing rooms. The protagonist of the book, Tom Jones, is a picaresque hero—an adventurer with a conscience who has many sexual adventures before getting married.

- Saul Bellow's *The Adventures of Augie March* (1954) is a picaresque novel that recounts the life of a Jewish man.

- Lisa Alther's 1976 bestseller, *Kinflicks* chronicles the story of a young woman who discovers the joys of liberation and sexual experimentation in the 1960s.

- *The Well of Loneliness* (1928) is Radclyffe Hall's groundbreaking and controversial novel about a lesbian's search for happiness.

the people who constitute her environment are transient too, and her home is nothing but a shifting landscape. Her first lover is now a married woman with children—she has "crossed the border," giving up her ambiguous sexuality and going to the clearly defined areas of wife, mother, and heterosexual.

Molly's development therefore takes place in border states and spaces for explicit symbolic purposes. In an extended conceit, the text plays with the double meaning of the word "state." Molly travels between states—Pennsylvania, Florida, New York—as she moves between "states" of life and identity—childhood, adolescence, and adulthood. The geographical doubling and redoubling parallels her precarious travels towards maturity in a topography that she must constitute herself.

Unable to fit into the metaphoric landscape of the heterosexual state/states, Molly territorializes her own. Tellingly, the actual states in which she lives are archetypally transitional, just like her uneasy transition between archetypes of femininity.

Taken from a border state and going first to a southern and then a northern context, Molly adapts herself, her speech, behavior, and even her wardrobe, to fit into her new environments. Even her name changes—from Brown to Bolt—reflecting her constant self-inscription, as well as signifying her perpetual motion: "bolt-ing."

Rubyfruit Jungle is densely layered with investigations into the role of gender conditioning, but it resists categorization as simply a feminist text, especially within the expectations of the period in which it was written. Molly's rebelliousness is neither radical nor reformist feminism. Instead, it is based on her own socioeconomic background, and the complex role that race, class, and gender play in the creation of her options and opportunities.

This perspective reaches its culmination in her film school senior project. While the other students—all male—are making projects based around violence that self-consciously attempt to reject social and cinematic conventions, Molly's project is a traditional narrative—a documentary that tracks her mother as she goes about her life. In creating a "realistic" document of this kind, Molly rejects the cultural politics that demand a unique outsider perspective in the creation of "radical" art.

The alignment of narrative experimentation with the privileged middle class forces the reader to accept Molly's realistic style—as well as the novel's—as a class-based response to the elitism of the cultural avant-garde.

Just as Molly rejects the option of experimenting in the service of feminist particularization, so *Rubyfruit Jungle* resists a narrative of gender creation in which women are constructed and men constructing. Throughout the text, it is the adult *women* who inculcate gender in both boys and girls, and both sexes experience being "gendered" as one of delimitation and destruction. Molly and Leroy have their genders forced onto them by their parents, their contemporaries, and finally themselves.

In a critical early scene, they play "nurse" with a friend. When Molly announces that she will be a doctor, she is told that she can't: "Only boys can be doctors. Leroy's got to be the doctor._ What counts is whether you are a boy or a girl." In the aftermath of the violence that ensues, both Molly

and Leroy experience an intensification of "gendering."

For Molly this means being literally locked into her proscribed female space—the home. For Leroy it means threatened castration if he stays inside: "soon they'd take him to the hospital and cut his thing off." Later, when Molly acts as the sexual aggressor, Leroy's childhood lessons show themselves: slippage from ideal gender behavior causes him to become impotent. Acting out the internalized fears from him childhood, Leroy "castrates" himself rather than perform in a female role.

Molly's complex negotiations of sex, sexuality, and gender function as a sustained critique of the more simplistic versions of sexual liberation in the novel, and undermine all of the key assumptions inherent in 1970s lesbian feminism. Her sexual experiences are far more complicated and varied than the unitary theories of a lesbian perspective allow.

Neither the novel nor Molly presents a stable definition of the category "lesbian," an essential prerequisite to constructing lesbian theory. Traveling through the underworld of gay and lesbian New York, Molly finds and rejects many people, none of whom conform to narrowly defined types, and all of whom are constructed as much by their gender, class, and race as they by their sexuality.

In experimenting with and ultimately rejecting various forms of self-defined lesbianism, Molly uncovers much diversity. Ranging from the "butch and femme" couples who enact male/female stereotypes, to the liberated women who are kept by mistresses, *Rubyfruit Jungle* explores the different ways lesbians interact and live in contemporary society.

Molly is self-conscious about her sexuality, adapting to societal norms in the same way that she changes her clothing and her accent. She has boyfriends in high school and college, and she retains a deeply eroticized relationship with her closest male friends. In doing so, she "bolts" away from the confining stereotypes of gender-appropriate sexuality or politically expedient labeling.

For too many of the supporting characters of *Rubyfruit Jungle,* the sexual liberation of the 1960s and 1970s is seen as a chance for inversion or destruction of the status quo. Both simple rejection and binary opposition are consistently presented as an insidious form of acceptance in Brown's text.

Instead of validating the patriarchal power structure by becoming its "Other"—the "rage of all women"—Molly refuses to ignore the class dynamics that tie her to Leroy, or the gender politics that separate her from her Mother. She is not Everywoman, but one woman in an "ec-centric" orbit through her culture, escaping from labels of the kind that are printed on the cover of every copy of *Rubyfruit Jungle*.

Source: Tabitha McIntosh-Byrd, in an essay for *Novels for Students*, Gale, 2000.

Sources

Terry Curtis Fox, in a review in *The Village Voice*, October 9, 1978.

Annie Gottlieb, "Passion and Punishment," in *New York Times Book Review*, March 21, 1982, p. 10.

Bertha Harris, in a review in *The Village Voice*, September 12, 1977.

Shelly Temchin Henze, in a review in *New Boston Review*, April-May, 1970.

Marylin Webb, in a review in *Ms.*, March, 1974.

For Further Study

Carol Marie Brown, *Rita Mae Brown*, Twayne, 1993, 191 p.

> A biographical and critical study. The author also discusses the parallels between the lives of Brown's characters and her own experiences.

Dudley Clendinen and Adam Nagourney, *Out for Good: The Struggle to Build a Gay Rights Movement in America*, Simon & Schuster, 1999, 716 p.

> An exhaustive account of the struggle for equal rights for homosexuals in the twentieth century.

Alice Echols, *Daring to Be Bad: Radical Feminism in America, 1967–1975*, University of Minnesota Press, 1989, 416 p.

> The first full-length study of radical feminism from the late 1960s to the early 1970s.

Leslie Fishbein, "Ruby Fruit Jungle: Lesbianism, Feminism, and Narcissism," in the *International Journal of Women's Studies*, Vol. 7. No. 2, March-April, 1984.

> An in-depth examination of Brown's major themes.

Diane Silver, *The New Civil War: The Lesbian and Gay Struggle for Civil Rights (The Lesbian and Gay Experience)*, Franklin Watts, 1997, 191 p.

> Aimed at a high school audience, this book includes a brief survey of historical perspectives on homosexuality and an examination of the diversity of contemporary gay and lesbian life in the United States.

Tex

S. E. Hinton
1979

Susan Eloise Hinton is considered the unquestioned master of young adult (YA) literature. Although not nearly as famous as *The Outsiders* or *Rumble Fish,* Hinton's fourth novel, *Tex,* is deemed by many critics to be her best artistic effort.

Tex explores the same themes of her earlier novels: youth, the loss of innocence, the coming of age, and violence. It also utilizes similar plot devices. Yet this novel differs from earlier efforts because of its inclusion of an articulate female character, Jamie.

The novel chronicles a year in the life of a young, easygoing lad named Tex McCormick. In the course of the book, Tex must face questions about his family's future—particularly his brother's yearning to leave Oklahoma and his father's abandonment. He must also address his burgeoning sexuality and questions about sex and women.

Author Biography

Born in 1950, S. E. Hinton has spent her entire life in Tulsa, Oklahoma. While growing up in Tulsa, Hinton was a keen observer of her friends and fellow classmates. Although not a member of any social clique, she got along well with her schoolmates. As she told William Walsh, "everyone looked at me sort of strangely, but I was accepted."

S. E. Hinton

Hinton began to write when her fifth-grade teacher gave the students a story writing assignment. The result was a fantastic, mystical story about the sun and moon. The exercise hooked her on writing, and several events over the next few years convinced her to write a story revealing the absurd but brutal world of teen cliques.

During her junior year of high school, while her father was ill with cancer, Hinton began writing *The Outsiders* (1967). The novel has sold more than four million copies in the United States.

The huge commercial success of *The Outsiders* enabled Hinton to go to college at the University of Tulsa. While attending university, she met her future husband, David E. Inhofe, a mail-order businessman. They have one son, Nicholas David.

Since then, she has written several more novels, including the critically well-received *Tex*. She also lectures and plays an active role in her son's school. In the early eighties, she worked on the film adaptations of her novels.

In 1988 she published her last novel to date, *Taming the Star Runner*. Since then, she has written two works for young children, *Big David, Little David* (1994) and *The Puppy Sister* (1995).

Plot Summary

Tex opens on what seems to a routine day at school for Tex, the teenage protagonist of the novel. After school, Tex returns home to find that his brother Mason has sold his horse, Negrito, as well as his own horse, Red, because they have run out of money. Tex reacts violently to this news, and he and Mason fight.

Tex goes to look for the horses and runs into his friends Jamie and Johnny Collins. They are shocked by the bruises on Tex's face. Soon after, Mason pulls up in the truck and orders Tex to come home with him.

Mason's friend, Bob Collins, visits and Mason tells him that his father—who has been touring with a rodeo—is the one he should have punched out. He is sick of being the man of the house and hopes he can leave soon on a basketball scholarship.

Bob drives Tex and Johnny to the county fair. They visit a fortuneteller, who tells Tex that some people go, and some people stay—he will stay. After leaving the fair, the boys visit Charlie Collins and Tex gets drunk for the first time.

When Mr. Collins finds them passed out the next morning, he blames Mason and Tex for being bad influences on his boys. That same night, Mason's friend Lem Peters shows up to announce that he's become a father. They sneak into the Collins' house to share the news. Jamie insults Lem by telling him that he and his wife don't know anything about taking care of kids. Mason later agrees with her.

After a fight with Johnny, Tex goes to look for him at the gravel pits. After Johnny fails to jump the creek with his motorcycle, Tex manages to make it. Mason is displeased to hear about Tex's stunt. He discovers he has an ulcer after he goes to the city hospital for tests.

On the way to visit Lem, Tex learns that Mason is a virgin because he doesn't want to endanger his future by getting some girl pregnant. Tex realizes what Mason means when they discover that Lem is dealing drugs.

Returning from the city, Mason and Tex pick up a hitchhiker. Suddenly, the man puts a gun to Mason's ribs and tells Tex to drive to the state line. When Tex sees a patrol car behind them, he spins out into a ditch and the hitchhiker dies in a shootout with police. Tex and Mason learn that the hitchhiker had killed one man and tried to kill another.

The news story about Mason and Tex's encounter with the hitchhiker is shown in Dallas. Their father finally calls, saying he'll be home the next day. Soon after his arrival, Mason and Pop have an argument about his long absence. When Tex goes to school that day, he is sent to the principal for talking so much about the incident with the hitchhiker.

Despite his promise, Pop does not take Tex to buy back Negrito. Mason takes Tex instead, but when the new owners refuse to sell Negrito, Tex tells Mason he'll hate him for the rest of his life.

Tex starts to date Jamie against her father's wishes. Jamie tells Tex that Cole is more impressed with Mason than his own kids, who are all disappointing to him.

At an important basketball game, Mason is injured. After the game, an opposing fan insults Jamie and Tex hits him. Later, while they are making out, Tex goes too far. Jamie tells him she's not ready for sex. When he tells her he loves her and wants to marry her, she replies that she doesn't think it will work out. Like Mason, she can't wait to leave town; Tex wants to stay. They break up.

A month later, Johnny and Tex are suspended for gluing caps on the school typewriters before midterms. When Cole and Mason confront the two young men, Mason stands up to Cole by telling him that neither Johnny nor Tex is a bad kid.

The principal informs Tex that Mr. Kencaide has offered him a summer job taking care of horses. Tex is overjoyed. When Pop finally arrives at the school, he and Mason get into a fight because Pop doesn't take Tex's pranks seriously. In the course of the argument, Mason blurts out that Pop is not Tex's biological father. Shocked, Tex runs out of the school.

Tex meets up with Lem and they go to the apartment of a drug connection, Kelly. Lem and Kelly argue. Tex tries to leave the scene, but Kelly pulls a gun on him. Tex grabs the gun.

It is only after they leave the apartment that Tex tells Lem he's been shot in the struggle. He wakes up in the hospital, where Mason tells him he beat up Lem Peters. Later, Pop explains that Tex's mother had had an affair while he was in prison years ago. Tex asks him if that was why Pop paid more attention to Mason when they were growing up, and Pop says, "I reckon it was."

When Jamie visits, she tells Tex what happened when he was brought to the hospital: Mason beat up Lem and wept when he found out Tex was going to be okay. Tex and Jamie kiss, and Tex realizes she's the only girl for him.

When Mason announces that he's not going to college, Tex tells him he should, that he'll hate Tex if he stays. The story ends with the final reconciliation of the two brothers.

Characters

Blackie Collins

Blackie refuses to live up to the expectations of his demanding father, Cole. Rather than enroll in college, Blackie runs off to San Francisco.

Charlie Collins

The oldest of the Collins children, Charlie is a medical student who lives in an apartment in the city. A popular guy, he represents the perfect son.

Cole Collins

Cole Collins represents the corporate, middle-class white man. He has high expectations for his children and blames their failures on the influence of the McCormick boys, whom he perceives as bad boys. Eventually he realizes his mistake through his interaction with Mason. He also recognizes Tex's bravery.

Jamie Collins

Jamie is Tex's love interest and the only girl among the five Collins children. Like Mason, she is destined to leave the country for the city. This is symbolized by her insistence that the window be kept open while she sleeps. Cole is disturbed by her refusal to adopt conventional ideas of womanhood. As Jamie tells Tex, "being a girl doesn't mean I'm going to be a devoted little mother just like Mona."

Jamie is a feminist. Mason respects her for speaking her mind, especially the way she sees through Lem. Jamie says what she thinks, particularly about sex. She has no intention of risking pregnancy, but she is curious about sex.

Johnny Collins

Johnny is Tex's best friend. He is "flame-haired as a matchstick," and is also described as flighty, which frustrates his brother Cole. He receives a motorcycle for his birthday; unfortunately, the privilege of riding the motorcycle is the way his father tries to maintain his control over the boy.

Matt Dillon (middle) played the beleaguered title character in the film version of Tex, with Emilio Estevez and Meg Tilly as Johnny and Jamie Collins. In this scene from the movie, Tex is troubled by a fight he has just had with his brother.

Johnny dotes on Tex, and they are such good friends that when they pass out on the ride home from the fair they are "flopped together like puppies."

Mona Collins

Mona is Cole's wife. She represent the traditional role of women in marriage: she basically goes along with everything Cole says and lets him make all of the important decisions in their lives.

Robert Collins

Bob Collins is Mason's best friend. As the oldest Collins boy at home, he tries to have the same influence over Jamie and Johnny as Mason has on Tex.

Roger Genet

Roger is a hoodlum and the school bully. It seems that he will eventually follow the path of Lem Peters and the Hitchhiker. Tex gets along with Roger; in fact it is Roger who drives Tex out to the gravel pits.

Hitchhiker

For Tex, the Hitchhiker symbolizes the criminal life. Tex realizes he has a choice to make and he decides, with Mason's influence, to reject that life.

Mrs. Johnson

The only positive adult role model in the story, Mrs. Johnson is the vice-principal and guidance counselor of the school. Tex respects her because she is consistent in her level of care and punishment. She takes a genuine interest in his future. When she reveals how close he came to being expelled, he realizes the seriousness of his situation. He accepts her offer to work for Mr. Kencaide.

Mace

See Mason McCormick.

Mason McCormick

Mason is Tex's older brother. He is one of the most popular guys in school and an excellent athlete. Yet Mason has many problems: he can't wait to leave his rural home and move to the city; he worries about Tex's future; and he is afraid of getting close to women because he does not want an

Media Adaptations

- Walt Disney released a film adaptation of *Tex* in 1982. Hinton assisted director Tim Hunter with the casting, scriptwriting, and directing. The movie was filmed in Tulsa, and Hinton's own horse starred as Negrito. Matt Dillon starred as Tex and Emilio Estevez played the role of Johnny Collins.

unwanted pregnancy. Mason is forced to step into the role of parent and head of household because of his father's absence.

Mason wants respect. For this reason, he does not ask his friends for money or to buy the horses: "You think I could take knowing you guys had our horses on top of everything else you've got?" To Mason's shame, he belongs to a poor family and it "hacks him off" whenever he thinks about it too much.

It is Mason that reveals that Pop is not Tex's father. In the end, the brothers are completely reconciled. Tex gives Mason the blessing he needs to leave town and pursue his dream. In turn, Mason is happy that Tex is growing up and choosing the right path in life.

Pop McCormick

Tex's father represents the absent parent— he spends six months a year on tour with the rodeo. He is not close with his sons. Pop fears that Tex will wind up in prison like he did (he went to prison for running moonshine).

Texas McCormick

Texas McCormick, the protagonist and narrator of the novel, is a good-natured young man growing up in Tulsa, Oklahoma. He looks up to his older brother Mason, and looks forward to a life in Tulsa, probably training horses. He enjoys hanging out with his best friend Johnny, doesn't have much interest in school, and likes to pull pranks. During the novel, he also falls in love with Johnny's sister, Jamie.

Tex is not close to his father. He feels that he has been treated differently his whole life. At the climax of the novel, when he realizes that Pop is not his biological father, he understands why. With this new information, he realizes that he wants to stay in Tulsa. He is able to reassure Mason that he will be okay, so that his brother can go to college.

Connie Peters

Connie is Lem's wife. A new mother, she is careful that either she or Lem stays "straight" to care for the baby. A drug user, Connie uses speed to keep her weight down. Although Connie managed to leave the rural life for the city, she represents the things that Jamie is terrified of—accidental pregnancy, forced marriage, and domestication. She also represents motherhood in the story.

Lem Peters

Lem was once Mason's best friend. He fell in love with Connie; unfortunately both families were opposed to the match. Yet that only encouraged them. When she became pregnant, they married and broke off contact with their families. With only a high school education and limited employment prospects, he turns to drug dealing in order to make ends meet.

Tex

See Texas McCormick

Themes

Change

Tex faces many life changes during the course of *Tex;* like many young adolescents, he wants to avoid dealing with them. To escape his problems, he attends the local fair—riding the rides and losing himself amongst the happy people.

Tex knows that Mason is determined to leave home; but he is annoyed that Mason will no longer go with him to the fair. This action represents Mason's embracing of adulthood and inevitable separation from Tex. Rejecting adulthood, Tex childishly says to Mason, "I ain't going to outgrow it, either. I'll think the Fair is fun no matter how old I get."

As is typical of storybook characters at the fair, Tex has an encounter with a fortuneteller. She informs him that change is inevitable, but it doesn't have to change him:

Topics For Further Study

- Due to the commercial success of Hinton's novels, young adult literature has become a popular genre. Educators are divided as to whether this is a good development. Some assert that it panders to a poor education system in which teachers are so desperate to foster literacy skills that they use such "easy" texts. Other commentators and librarians applaud that fact that young adults *want* to read these books. What do you think? What are your favorite young adult books?

- In an article for the *New York Times* in 1967, Hinton wrote:

  You've heard of people reading the symptoms of a disease, and then suddenly developing the disease? Well, you can't pick up a magazine or a newspaper that doesn't declare that teen-agers are rebellious, over-worked, over-pampered, under-privileged, smart, stupid and sex-crazed. No wonder some develop the symptoms.

  Reflecting on the book and on your own experience, explain how perceptions behave as a disease. Apply your thoughts to the general perception today of youth and postulate whether anything has changed since Hinton's 1967 article.

- To the charge that her fiction contains too much violence, Hinton maintains:

  Adults who let small children watch hours of violence, unfunny comedy, abnormal behavior and suggestive actions on TV, scream their heads off when a book written for children contains a fist fight. But violence too is a part of teen-agers' lives. If it's not on television or in the movies, it's a beating up at a local drive-in. . . .

  What do you think of censorship, such as the "v-chip" or banning books at the library? Write an essay outlining your opinion on the issue.

- In *Tex,* what is the attitude towards guns and drugs? Today, we worry about loners and troublemakers selling narcotics, pulling guns, and planting bombs. What has changed in our society since 1979? Has society become more violent?

Your next year: change. My advice: Don't change. Your future: There are people who go, people who stay. You will stay.

The fortuneteller's words bother him. Later, he learns that Jamie and Mason are leaving. Eventually, he accepts these events. He realizes that change will come and that people who are important to him will leave. Others will stay. He also recognizes that one day he will choose his own fate: whether to stay in Oklahoma or leave, like his brother.

Education

Tex's education does not take place only in school; it involves learning about what it takes to be a man from other men and the world around him. This happens through interaction.

Tex describes this process at the beginning of the story. While riding his horse, Tex relates his theory of horse handling: he never hits his horse but respects it, while nudging Negrito toward the behavior he would prefer. This is why he holds in the reigns before allowing the horse to run.

As a result of this respectful interaction, Negrito behaves like a person. The other horse, Red, is not so well behaved. "Mason had never treated him like a person, so Red had never acted like one." When you acknowledge a horse, the horse will acknowledge your command. In the same way, when a young man is allowed to be a young man, he will become one. This passage to manhood is not an easy one.

In school, Tex learns from observing the behavior of other people. He also realizes the effects of his pranks on students and teachers. From his own experience, he finds pranks and ditch-jumping far less rewarding than being respected by Mr.

Kencaide for his horse-riding skills and his ability to help other people.

Love and Relationships

"Love ought to be a real simple thing," according to Tex. Yet he realizes that "with humans it gets so mixed up." At first Tex believes that love leads to pain, both physical and emotional. Yet by the end of the novel, he feels differently—that expressing love is fulfilling and rewarding. His growing romantic feelings for Jamie also signal a new perspective on love and relationships opening up for the young protagonist.

Except for the thorny and unresolved question of sex, Tex's lessons about love are all very similar. He realizes he has to accept people for who they are. He comes to an understanding with Pop, reconciles with Johnny, is acknowledged by Cole, and settles things with Mr. Kencaide. Finally, he is able to reach out to Mason.

Style

Narration

Tex is characterized by simple first person narration; in other words, the story is told from Tex's perspective. There are no superfluous tricks or scenes. Everything in the narration relates to the plot, and the reader knows only what Tex knows.

Setting

The majority of the novel takes place in the country, which represents space and peacefulness. On the other hand, the city is full of cars, people, and danger. Each setting presents a challenge to the hero and his friends.

Climax

Within the conventions of fiction, the action—both emotional and actual—gradually rises until it reaches a crisis point. This is known as the climax.

The climax of *Tex* occurs in the school office, when Tex hears how close he came to being expelled and witnesses Mason fighting with Pop. Mason utters the very line of the climax, "he is my brother even if he isn't your son." The action of the novel reaches its greatest moment of tension when the truth of Tex's conception is revealed.

Bildungsroman

A *bildungsroman* is a kind of German novel, typically about a boy struggling through his for-mative years. Such tales involve survival of physical and mental anguish in high-pressure schools or military academies. There is a positive ending, as the main character survives his earlier foolishness and mistakes and grows as a person.

Hinton has redefined this class of literature into a distinctly American genre. In these stories, a troubled youth—typically a boy one mistake away from expulsion or prison—gains a moral center. Moreover, it is often a retrospective account that relates moral lessons; *Tex* exemplifies this new kind of *bildungsroman*.

Historical Context

The Late Seventies

During the late 1970s, the United States struggled to overcome the upsetting legacy of the Watergate scandal, the subsequent resignation of Richard Nixon, and the wounds of American participation in the Vietnam War. Adding to the frustration of many Americans was a volatile economic situation: high inflation, high unemployment, and a worldwide energy crisis.

In addition, farming communities and small towns begin to disappear across America. This trend was exacerbated in the 1980s, especially in farming communities like that in Hinton's Oklahoma. Record numbers of farming families went bankrupt as a result of this farming crisis.

The Carter Administration

Running as an outsider, Jimmy Carter (1924–) won the presidential election of 1976. Two issues challenged the Carter Administration: first, the energy crisis caused the cost of living to increase by thirteen percent; second, the Islamic revolution in Iran resulted in the taking of American hostages in Iran. In November 1979, Carter had allowed the hated Iranian leader—known as the shah of Iran—to enter the United States for medical treatment; and in retaliation, fifty-three Americans were taken hostage from the American embassy in Tehran.

When Carter refused to return the shah to Iran, the captors refused to release the hostages. In April an attempt to rescue the hostages failed. Secretary of State Cyrus Vance resigned over the mission and its failure. Carter came under relentless media and political attack for his unsuccessful efforts to free the hostages, who were finally released shortly af-

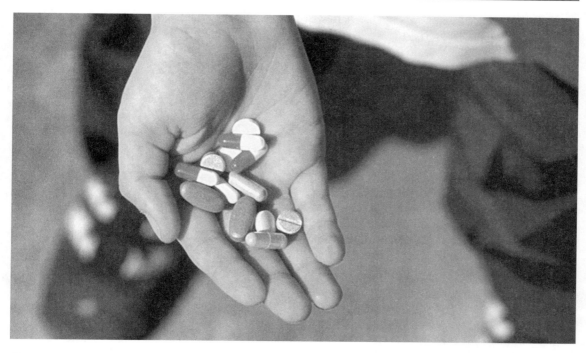

Often praised for the realism of her books, Hinton doesn't shy away from a portrayal of teenage pregnancy, drinking, violent fighting, and drug dealing.

ter Ronald Reagan was sworn in as president in January, 1981.

On the brighter side, the Carter Administration successfully negotiated the SALT II nuclear treaty with the Soviet Union, which allowed for the nuclear missiles on both sides to balance out. Carter also facilitated better relations between Egypt and Israel through landmark negotiations known as the Camp David Accords (1978), which led to a historic Egyptian-Israeli peace treaty.

Energy Crisis

Periods of industrialization depend on easy and cheap access to low-cost fuels, usually fossil fuels. Between 1952 and 1972, energy consumption doubled while generation of electrical energy more than tripled in the United States. With such an abundant supply of energy, the United States and many other nations continued to increase consumption.

In order to guarantee a constant supply of oil, industrialized nations essentially colonized countries rich in oil beginning in the late nineteenth and early twentieth centuries. After World War II, these countries regained their sovereignty; by the late 1960s, they began to assert their independence in

matters of the pricing and export of oil. Protesting United States aid to Israel, Arab members of the Organization of Petroleum Exporting Countries (OPEC) place an embargo on oil to the United States.

As a result of the embargo, the price of crude oil doubled in 1973. Further price increases followed—most of them in 1979. A barrel of oil, which cost $7.00 in 1972, increased to $33.50 in 1982. Industrialized nations implemented energy conservation programs, but not before recession set in and, in the United States, inflation indices reached nearly twenty percent.

The energy crisis affected every sector of the American economy. The lessons of oil dependency, however, are lost and consumption levels increased and even surpassed 1972 levels as prices fell throughout the 1980s.

Women's Liberation

In *Tex,* Jamie often refers to the concept of "women's lib." This movement was prominent in the 1970s, as women struggled to fight gender discrimination and bring attention to specific issues such as equal pay for equal work and abortion rights. Organizations such as the National Organization of Women (also known by the acronym NOW) also fought for the passage of the Equal Rights Amendment (ERA), as well as fought against sexual harassment and date rape.

Critical Overview

Hinton is considered the most successful writer for young adults in contemporary times. In fact, she is often credited with creating the genre of "young adult literature" as a viable and attractive genre for junior high and high school audiences. Critics have generally been impressed with her work since her first novel, *The Outsiders,* was published in 1967.

Critics compare her favorably with Ernest Hemingway in terms of sentence structure, minimal description, and the exploration of conventional male and female roles. She has often been faulted for these same qualities: in particular, that her work presents an unreal and violent male culture where viable female personalities, let alone mothers, scarcely exist. Despite the criticism, Hinton remains popular among young readers. She continues to win awards, especially from librarians.

The most contentious issue in Hinton's work is her use of violence. Some commentators view the violence as integral—not gratuitous—to her work. Another of Hinton's tendencies is to revisit the same themes with the same devices in each novel. In fact, most of her stories are about young male protagonists who survive several obstacles to gain self-knowledge.

Many readers and fans of Hinton's agree with Jay Daly's praise in his *Presenting S. E. Hinton.* There he wrote:

> *Tex* is clearly the most seamless of her books. The voice is consistent and appropriate throughout. It is Tex's voice, Tex's consciousness. The controlling, manipulating hand of the author is far in the background.

Yet critics view *Tex* as a breakthrough for Hinton, partly for her successful development of a strong, complex female character. Cynthia Rose, in "Rebels Redux," notes that Hinton is undoubtedly influenced by Jim Carroll's *The Basketball Diaries* because Hinton's heroes are also delinquents. Like Carroll, Hinton focuses solely on males, until the character Jamie in *Tex.*

Rose contends that Hinton's early female characters fulfill the "good girl/bad girl stereotype in a manner which recalls *West Side Story.*" This pattern is shattered by the articulate Jamie, who is not just a tomboy but a young woman obviously influenced by the women's liberation movement. Jamie reflects the fact that girls have more options of expression than they once did.

June Harris concurs with Rose's assessment that Hinton finally "uses an interesting female." Harris also asserts that *Tex* is Hinton's best novel, but the story might possibly have too much action in such a short span. For Harris, *Tex* not only reveals Hinton's maturity but also raises some questions. Harris asserts:

> Tex uses a line that is almost verbatim the same line used by Mark in *That Was Then, This Is Now:* "Nothing that bad ever happened to me." Tex also suffers from the same sort of unexplained nightmares as Ponyboy Curtis in *The Outsiders.* Is such repetition simply a dearth of imagination, or does Hinton cannibalize her own work for plot ideas?

It is true that many of the central themes of *Tex* can be found in earlier works.

One critic, Michael Malone, is not enthralled by the Hinton phenomenon. He derides the depiction of the "tough as nails" youth as a heroic cowboy. In fact, he illustrates how outrageous the depiction is. Even *Tex,* maintains Malone, "the most recent, the least riddled with gang romance and the best of the books" features an ex-convict who kidnaps the protagonist and then is shot in a drug deal gone wrong a few pages later.

In response to a comment by Tim Hunter, director of the Disney film adaptation of *Tex,* who said he liked Hinton because she weaves social problems into the fabric of her stories, Malone contends that "in fact, the fabric is mythic. There are no verisimilar settings."

According to Malone, Hinton continues to celebrate juvenile delinquency and broken families. Malone even has a comment on Hinton's abilities:

> Moreover, while praised for its "lean Hemingway style" and natural dialogue, Hinton's prose can be as fervid, mawkish and ornate as any nineteenth-century romance, although this is less true in the later books, especially *Tex.*

Yet many critics believe that Hinton's fiction is valuable and praiseworthy for its exploration of troubled youth. More immediately, she gives young adults something that they like to read. The story has a message that appeals to countless kids in reformatory schools and prisons; many have written to Hinton to say that they appreciate her novels and her characters.

Criticism

Jane Elizabeth Dougherty

Dougherty is a Ph.D. candidate at Tufts University. In the following essay, she examines the themes of change and stability in Tex.

As Jay Daly notes, throughout S. E. Hinton's novel *Tex,* the narrator, Tex McCormick, divides the people he meets into two groups: those who go and those who stay. In the beginning, this seems like a straightforward division, but by the end of the novel, it is clear that the question of whether to go or to stay is a complex one.

Not only is it difficult for the characters to choose whether to go or to stay, it is clear by the end of the novel that sometimes the only way to stay somewhere emotionally is physically to go. Through Tex's ruminations on the differences between those who stay and those who go, Hinton's themes of change and stability emerge.

Tex knows that he is a "stayer"—that he will probably always remain in his hometown. In part, this is because he enjoys rural life, particularly working with horses, which he calls the "best high" he knows. He has experienced true communion with his horse Negrito, whom he treats like a human. Tex prefers the joys of the country to the temptations of the city, saying that

> Me, I liked living in the country and some of the other kids liked it, too. Some of them pretended they did because they couldn't live anywhere else. Then you had the people like Mason, who were itching to stay out. I couldn't quite figure out why.

Throughout the novel, Tex identifies his brother Mason as a "goer." Mason expresses his dissatisfaction with their life in the country, hoping for a basketball scholarship in order to get out of town. Tex is worried about Mason's desire to leave; he is the only stable element of Tex's life, once Tex's horse Negrito is sold. Mason takes care of Tex, worries about him, and supports him.

By contrast, Tex loses his girlfriend Jamie because he wants to get closer, both physically and emotionally, than she wants. The other Collins kids are discouraged from seeing Tex and Mason by their father, Cole.

Tex's mother is dead, and his father isn't around much. When Pop is around, he indulges Tex, which Mason sees as evidence of Pop's lack of concern for the kid. When Tex gets in trouble at school, Mason punishes him. Pop is amused by Tex's behavior, especially since Tex was mimicking something Pop had done when he was a boy. Mason is disgusted by what he sees as Pop's lack of concern, as Tex notes:

> I couldn't see what else he could do, besides take it calmly, but Mason was absolutely enraged.
>
> "Okay," he stalked around the room like a frenzied panther. "Okay, so you can't take Tex serious. So you can't give a damn about what happens to him. All right, I'm trying to live with that. Then think about me! For God's sake, how do you think I feel, seeing you being 'nice' to him, like you'd be nice to a goddamn stray puppy! While I'm the one who has to look out for him and what's going to happen when I'm not here?"
>
> Pop and I were both staring at him. I was ready to call in the straight jacket people.
>
> "Geez, make it easier on me if nothing else! He is my brother even if he isn't your son!"

Tex is stunned by this news, but it makes sense to him emotionally. When he lies in the hospital after being shot, he asks Pop if the reason he clearly favored Mason was because he wasn't his son. Despite Tex's hopes that Pop will blame it on birth order or personality, Pop says simply that he reckons that was the reason.

It is clear that the only person Tex can rely is Mason—and it appears that Mason badly wants to leave. In spite of Tex often feeling angry with Mason, he is aware that Mason cares about him and is there for him.

Yet Mason wants to go to college. Indeed, Mason has seen what can happen to those trapped by circumstance. Throughout the novel, Lem Peters is an example to Mason of the costs of staying. Lem has impregnated and married his girlfriend at the age of seventeen and descends into drug use and dealing. When Tex asks Mason if he's "gone all the way," Mason replies:

> "I never could stand the thought of getting tied down," he went on. "I never wanted anybody to have any kind of a hold on me. Look what happened to Lem. Nobody is ever going to stop me from getting out of here."
>
> Well, I knew that. But, boy, that was desperate! It was almost scary.
>
> "It hasn't been easy. And don't think I haven't had plenty of chances."
>
> "Sure," I said. Lord, I knew he had chances. Being the school hero gave a guy chances.
>
> "When I get to college, and at least have that much ... if I can get over the feeling I won't be trapped...."

Mason longs for a sense of security and safety, but he believes that he can only acquire it by leav-

What Do I Read Next?

- Hinton wrote her first book while still attending Tulsa's Will Rogers High School. *The Outsiders* (1967) focuses on the interaction of familiar social groups: the lower-class "greasers" and the upper-class "socs." The book remains popular among teenagers, though parents often complain that it is too violent.

- *That Was Then This Is Now* (1971) is Hinton's second book. This novel chronicles the story of two foster brothers. One brother becomes popular with girls and does well in school, while the other gets involved with drugs and crime.

- Hinton's 1975 novel, *Rumble Fish,* revisits the themes of her first novel. The protagonist of the story, Rusty-James, struggles to earn a tough reputation through his relationship with Motorcycle Boy.

- First published in 1944, Esther Forbes' *Johnny Tremain* remains a popular novel for young adults. Johnny is a young apprentice silversmith with a maimed hand. He becomes involved in the Revolutionary War through his relationship with James Otis, John Hancock, and John and Samuel Adams.

- Paule Marshall's 1959 novel, *Brown Girl, Brownstones* is a good complement to *Tex*. Selina's family are Barbadian immigrants who move to Brooklyn. She faces the tough challenges of sexism and racism in her new home.

- James Joyce's *A Portrait of an Artist as a Young Man* (1916) is considered to be the greatest *bildungsroman* in the English language. In this story, Stephen Daedalus is completing his studies at Trinity College in Dublin, Ireland, but is distracted by aesthetic questions and the temptations of the flesh.

---

ing town. For his part, Tex attributes Lem's misfortune to leaving—Lem has left the country for the city, and Tex thinks to himself that Lem "should have stayed."

In the contrast between Mason and Lem, it becomes clear to Tex that although there are people who go and people who stay, sometimes people don't know which category they fall into. Lem's example makes Tex realize that sometimes people make the wrong choices for themselves. Daly notes that Tex is himself extremely self-aware, but Tex notices that other people do not always know themselves as well as he knows himself.

Tex's girlfriend Jamie is a person who doesn't know herself. She tells Tex that sometimes she loves everyone, and other times she hates everyone. She recognizes that her uncertainty is part of adolescence, and that she is not yet ready to establish a firm identity. Her conversation with Tex in the truck makes him realize that people can be ambivalent about whether to stay or go. Secure in the knowledge that he will stay, he tells Jamie he wants to marry her.

I wanted to know Jamie was going to be there the rest of my life.

"I can see me marrying you," Jamie said slowly.

"Yeah?"

"Yeah. When I'm eighteen or nineteen and scared of the way things are changing, the way people are going off in different directions, and the simple life looks romantic, a good way to keep everything the same . . . yeah, I can see me marrying you. It'd last about a year."

Jamie recognizes that because of her own fear of change and willingness to romanticize "the simple life," she may make the wrong choice. She does not yet know whether she is one who goes or one who stays, and she can't be with Tex until she figures that out.

Likewise, even Mason feels ambivalent about whether to stay or go. At the end of the novel, he tells Tex: "I don't know what to do. I can't go. I can't stay. Sometimes I feel like I really am going to go nuts." He is torn about leaving Tex alone.

Ultimately, Mason does decide to stay with Tex—at least while Tex is still in high school—

and to defer his college scholarships. Yet Tex tells him that he should go. He realizes that the best hope of Mason "staying" is actually for him to go—that their loving relationship will continue only if Mason does go.

In this way, the boundary between the people who stay and the people who go is shown to be an ambiguous one—even an artificial one. The only way Tex and Mason can really stay together is by Mason's departure. In this way, change becomes the best way to maintain stability. Hinton's novel shows that sometimes you have to stay to go, and go to stay—and that stability can mean change and change can be the best way to maintain stability.

Source: Jane Elizabeth Dougherty, in an essay for *Novels for Students,* Gale, 2000.

Jay Daly

In the following essay Daly discusses Hinton's growing maturity of style as reflected in Tex.

There was close to universal agreement among the reviewers on the new "mature" style of *Tex,* usually the result of comparison with the youthful exuberance of *The Outsiders* or with the more personal, more demanding *Rumble Fish.* There will always be strong individual arguments for readers who prefer the unalloyed intensity of *The Outsiders* or the spine-tingling mythmaking of *Rumble Fish,* but there is little doubt that, as an example of mature, polished storytelling, *Tex* is Hinton's most successful effort. All the discipline and control she had to force into *That Was Then, This Is Now* is here brought effortlessly to bear. *Tex* doesn't take the chances that *Rumble Fish* took, but it knows what chances it is willing to take and how to handle them.

In fact *Tex* is clearly the most seamless of her books. The voice is consistent and appropriate throughout. It is Tex's voice, Tex's consciousness. The controlling, manipulating hand of the author is far in the background. For us, the readers, it has disappeared.

This is a style of writing that puts the welfare of the book, and the integrity of the book's voice, above its own need to show off. The most successful fiction—that which will last beyond one day in the sun—always seems to work its magic upon the reader in concealment, lying in wait like an enemy agent, familiar and friendly and certainly unsuspected, until at some point it explodes into an awareness that is truly subversive, that shakes the foundations of the reader's version of comfortable reality. *Tex*'s subversion is a modest one, as befits a book of such "unexpected contentment" but in its own way, in the conclusions it draws, the world view that gradually comes into focus behind its exceptional main character, it is as meaningful, and as important, as the shattering monochrome vision of *Rumble Fish.*

The structure of the book resembles that of the conventional novel much more than anything we've seen before. There are no tricks, no frame chapters or flashbacks. Hinton shows the same restraint with regard to her structure as she has with her style. The approach is straightforward, without embellishment, without anything that might distract the reader from the important matter at hand: the story, as conveyed through the continuing, sure voice of the narrator.

The story rolls along in real time, event upon event, so as to achieve a kind of momentum, a not-to-be-averted quality that reminds us of the carnival gypsy: "There are people who go, people who stay. You will stay". There is no intervention by a more knowing narrator with access to the future, no one to tease us with hints of secrets he knows and we will only later find out. Tex knows no more than we do about his future. He knows only what he's been told by gypsies and what he's inferred from meetings with hitchhikers and drug dealers, which isn't much. Tex's is a future without the kind of guarantees an omniscient narrator provides. It's the kind of future that needs to be lived in order to see what will happen.

The structure of the novel emphasizes the flow of events. It is the opposite of the staccato structure of *Rumble Fish,* whose technique emphasizes the here-and-now (and the timeless), rather than the gradual flow of time. Chapters in the earlier books are shorter and tend to concentrate on one scene, with the result that—though there are some powerfully rendered scenes—the overall effect is episodic. The action in the earlier books tends to move in an almost cinematic fashion, from scene to scene, with the mood and flow of the story building up out of an accumulation of episodes. There is nothing wrong with this technique and when it works it works very well but the structure of *Tex* is the more traditional (let's say, literary, rather than the cinematic) way to do it.

The structure of the book is, finally, in keeping with the *ars est celare artem* (true art conceals art) approach of its style. Understated, conventional, it defers at all times to the story line, to character and plot.

The plot, outlined earlier, is certainly not lacking in action scenes. Why is it then that we don't emerge from the book with the sense of having read an action/adventure story, as we certainly might have with *The Outsiders,* and even with the other books? Part of it has to do with the more controlled, more confident writer Hinton has become. The action scenes, while still vividly written, are more integrated into the flow of the story line. The impulse of the younger writer might have been to make sure that her action scenes packed a wallop—something she knew she could achieve—to compensate for what she might have felt were inadequacies in other areas. By the time of *Tex* she seems to have become more comfortable with her talent, and those inadequacies, real or imagined, no longer hold much sway on her.

The result is, once again, a more organic, integrated novel. Nothing stands out; nothing detracts from the movement of the book as a whole. Even the central scene with the hitchhiker—major melodrama on the face of it: it could easily have been made as obvious a turning point as the church fire in *The Outsiders*—is quickly disarmed by the horseplay of the television/local hero scenes and by the new turning point (or so we think) of the return of Pop. It is rather surprising, in fact, to note that the hitchhiker, as we shall see, is a rather important figure in the book, so quickly does he come and go.

Another point to consider is that events and scenes don't make it into S.E. Hinton novels as a result of serendipity. Certainly not since *The Outsiders* anyway. All the novels since then have been very clearly worked over, shaped and controlled by the author. Hinton's method of plot construction is a painstaking process, based—as it has been from the beginning—on character, on the reactions of characters to incidents, and to the more subtle structural weave that surrounds them. This is not something that comes without effort.

Her comments in the interview published in the 1983-84 *University of Tulsa Annual* are instructive as to both her methods and her goals.

> I have a real hard time plotting things anyway. And I always have an end in mind. The beginning is kind of easy because you can put characters in any situation. Getting from point A to Z is just so hard for me, and I get off on tangents and write 50 pages on a minor character. So I think, this isn't going in the direction I thought, and I tear it up. What's going to happen next? I need to get "Tex" from there over here, but how do I do that? Sometimes I put it away for months at a time.

Behind her usual self-deprecating tone (the same voice that says the gas bill is an inspiration) there are clues to the close attention paid to the requirements of fitting plot with character: the false starts and wrong turns, the clear direction of the book from its inception, and the occasional frustration when the fit between character and event is wrong ("Sometimes … months at a time").

Hinton is, as she has said from the start, a "character writer." "I always start off with characters, and I have to know my characters real well…. It doesn't matter if they show up in the book or not, I have to know them." When you know your characters real well, when you know "what they eat for breakfast, what their sign is," then you will not sacrifice them to the poor fit of an overblown crisis scene. No, their actions and reactions must be true to themselves, or there is no reason to write the book at all.

"I like to think my books show character growth in some way, that the character is always different in the end than he was in the beginning." Action is Character, we will recall, was Fitzgerald's uppercase imperative to himself in the notebooks for *The Last Tycoon.* We have applied this prescription to *The Outsiders* and seen where the book met—and failed to meet—its requirements. With *Tex* it must be introduced once again because, while the character of the first-person narrator, and character in general, is important in all the books, in *Tex* it is truly sine qua non, that without which there is no book. And the character is, of course, Tex.

We are inside Tex's head and with his thoughts from the first line. Once inside his head we never leave; we're coaxed into believing in that voice from the start, and the voice never falters, so our belief remains strong. It's clear that just one "clanger," just one miscalculation of what the character might do or say in a given situation, can destroy the illusion of reality and the reader's complicity in making that illusion seem real. Many's the novel that one such foolish move has reduced from the miraculous to the merely good. *Tex,* whether it be miraculous or not, at least makes no foolish moves.

S.E. Hinton knows Tex, intimately. She knows how he thinks and, like a good actor drawing on the experience of her own emotion to animate a character, how he feels. Consequently, the voice does not seem contrived; it is a true voice.

Other than Ponyboy (whom Hinton admits is perhaps the closet to being an extension of herself, her own voice at the time), she has never taken the easy way out with her narrators. Bryon Douglas was an intellectual jigsaw puzzle, a snapshot of bitterness, or betrayal, or self-reliance, or ... but the pieces never could be made to fit. Rusty-James, whom Hinton has termed "my biggest challenge as a writer," emerged out of an inarticulate haze to steal the book away from his "perfect" brother. Now Tex, neither as bright and analytical as Bryon nor as emotion-driven and vulnerable as Rusty-James, comes to us with his "unexpected contentment."

There is a flip side to the requirement that successful characters be always true to themselves, always "in character," and that is that they not be boring, that they be, in some sense, unpredictable, unexpected. Dallas Winston was unpredictable in this sense, as was, because innocence is always unexpected, Rusty-James. Thus, when Margery Fisher uses the word unexpected to describe Tex in the phrase above, she renders him a distinct compliment.

What about the second part of her compliment, the "contentment" part? What is contentment, anyway? Fisher goes on to define it more expansively as "his cheerful approach to life as it is and not as he would like it to be," which is close, but doesn't quite explain it. Tex's approach to life-as-it-is when life-as-it-is happens to include the sale of his horse hardly qualifies as cheerful. No, Tex is too complicated and real a character to be reduced simply to "cheerful," nor is he always content, satisfied with things as they are, particularly in the early parts of the book. Contentment is an appropriate word, though; it describes something special about Tex, something that distinguishes him from the other Hinton narrators. What it describes, however, is not some quality he possesses in abundance, something he brings to all his human interactions like the wisdom of Solomon, but rather a state of being he achieves, by the end of the book, with the considerable help of other qualities that he does possess in abundance.

Included among Tex's better qualities is his honesty. We believe everything Tex tells us (as opposed to Bryon Douglas, for example, or even Ponyboy) because we believe that he would no sooner lie to us than he would to himself. What Tex knows about himself he will not conceal from us, or from himself. This sometimes means revealing things that are unpleasant. After he tells Mace that he will hate him for the rest of his life, he sees a muscle in his brother's face jump, "and I knew I'd

hurt him. It felt good. It was the first time I realized hurting somebody could feel really good."

Tex's honesty (or maybe his inability to be dishonest) makes for a tricky kind of relationship with "the truth." For Mason, truth is "a present I always wanted," but it is a gift for him because it is something he can use. Tex does not have that luxury. For Tex, who cannot compromise his honesty, truth is often better left unknown. Once known, it cannot be ignored or used as he sees fit. Tex won't turn away from unpleasant truths. This is what he tries to explain to Mason in a scene after the shootout in which the hitchhiker was killed.

> "Texas," [Mason] said, "why did you have to go look, after they'd killed him? It wasn't exactly a sideshow at the Fair." I was shocked that he could think such a thing. What kind of a creep did he think I was, anyway? "I had to," I said finally. " Mason, I killed that guy, as sure as if I'd pulled the trigger. I knew it when I ditched the truck. I couldn't just walk off like nothing had happened. I had to face what I did."

This is a rare kind of integrity in a character, a rare sense of responsibility.

Even more rare—in a character of any age but surely in one so young and presumably self-involved—is the kind of generosity Tex shows toward those around him. It is this generosity of spirit, which he exhibits throughout the book, that paves the way for his unexpected contentment at the end. Not that he's perfect, or ego-less, or free from any taint of spite. He wouldn't be human if he were. But that's what makes so continuously surprising his naturally generous character, his impulse to think the best of people, to give them their best possible lives and to let them diminish those lives if they must themselves.

He looks into oncoming cars on the highway and sees not featureless strange faces but people with stories, stories that are just as important to them as our stuff is to us. Miss Johnson—the vice principal—"might swat me once in a while, but she always asked me how we were getting along, if we'd heard from Pop," and made other such overtures that, for Tex, were enough to show that she cared whether he lived or died. "If you get the feeling somebody cares about what happens to you, then you don't mind if they swat you once in a while." Johnny Cade, who had to endure the latter without ever feeling the former, would have agreed.

Miss Johnson's asking about Pop brings up another good case, because Tex's generosity extends particularly to him, especially because Pop does practically nothing to earn it. He forgets Tex's birthday. He show his obvious preference for Mason, who doesn't even "much like being named after Pop," over and over again. He goes to a pool game in Broken Arrow rather than helping to get Negrito back as he had promised he would do (this last an insensitivity that even the movie version of *Tex* apparently could not stomach; Pop goes with Tex and Mace to try and get the horse back in the movie). Still at the end of it all, Tex forgives him, the way a patient, loving parent forgives a wayward child. It's not Pop's fault if he forgets. As Tex notes, "He doesn't have a very long attention span."

He is also generous toward the hitchhiker. He needs to explain, if not to justify, the fact of his existence. "Mace, something really bad must have happened to that guy." But his motivation for generosity toward the hitchhiker is a bit more complicated than that which prompts his generosity as a rule; we will look more closely at this later.

Tex is also a creature of hope. Hope is a conclusion that is perhaps impossible for the generous spirit to avoid. It is the conclusion of Smoky the Cowhorse that sometimes bad things happen—they can nearly take the heart out of you—but if you hang on you will see that, like Tex in his time of troubles, "in the morning I'd still be alive, and sometimes the pain seemed a fraction less." This is a definition of hope, to expect that day by day you will awaken and the pain will seem "a fraction less."

Tex also has more conventional hopes, like the poignant "Mason would be gone for college pretty soon and then Pop would have to notice me a little more. I mean, I'd be the only kid, then," but the hope that animates the book is Smoky's hope. "I've been bashed up pretty good, Mason, but I'm going to make it." And we have no doubt that he will.

All these qualities give Tex a kind of innocence, an attitude he shares with characters like Johnny and Ponyboy and Rusty-James, characters who are, at least on the surface, as far from innocent as a street kid can get. There are, of course, two ways of defining innocence: (1) freedom from sin, guilt, imperfection, etc. and (2) freedom from *knowledge* of sin, guilt, imperfection, etc. In this world, since the Fall, there is no innocence in the first sense. There is only innocence within terms of the second definition, and for Hinton characters this innocence is usually under attack, it by nothing else then always by the eroding effects of time in a world of unfriendly truths. Mason's "present; I always wanted," truth, is, like Eve's apple, a gift of uncertain value.

Tex's innocence is particularly vulnerable because of his unwillingness to compromise his honesty. He manages to hold onto his enduring innocence, despite all the assaults made upon it, because it is important to his generous view of life. Mason puts it this way, when Tex refuses to feel anything but happiness for Lem and his new baby: "Tex, you are not stupid, and you're not all that ignorant. But how anybody as simple-minded as you are has managed to survive for fourteen years is beyond me." Tex answers back quickly, revealing the temporary, fragile nature of the simple-mindedness (innocence) that Mason deplores: "'Well, I had a wonderful smart sweet brother lookin' out for me,' I said. I'm not sarcastic by nature, but I reckon you can learn anything if you're around it long enough." The fruit of the Tree of Knowledge includes sarcasm, and much worse.

The theme of innocence, of staying gold, arises in *Tex* nearly unchanged from its statement in *The Outsiders* (and its counter-statement in *That Was Then, This Is Now*). As long as Tex stays "simple-minded," as long as he stays a kid, he stays gold. "I ain't going to outgrow [the fair]," he says to Mace. "I'll think the Fair is fun no matter how old I get." It's Peter Pan again, but Peter's solution, as we saw in *The Outsiders,* is incompatible with life in the real world. One cannot stay gold and stay around. Tex, who is from the beginning one who will stay around and knows it, must make another, more realistic solution. This is where *Tex* takes over and expands upon *The Outsiders*. This is where *Tex* is, in many ways, the summation statement of the unresolved concerns of all three earlier books.

Tex is a character study, and it is an action novel, but at its core it is also a novel of ideas. Not surprisingly, the ideas the novel feels impelled to grapple with are those we have seen before, the troubling, unresolved problems of *The Outsiders, That Was Then, This Is Now,* and to some extent *Rumble Fish.* And *Tex* the novel is like Tex the character; it wants to find solutions to these problems; it wants to make a working arrangement that will let them all live in the real world. To do so it must deal directly with problems of the real world that have left earlier characters bitter, or puzzled, or just numb.

Source: Jay Daly, "Tex: Those Who Go and Those Who Stay," in *Presenting S. E. Hinton,* Twayne, 1987, pp. 94-103.

Jean Duncan with Carol Dye, Joan Lazarus, Diane Schwartzmann, Jill A. Hendin, and Rita Hendin

The following review is a synopsis of the novel, highlighting a teen's relationships and his path to young adulthood.

In *Tex,* S.E. Hinton has created another engaging character—a carefree, easygoing, fifteen-year-old who learns some hard lessons on the road to maturity. Hinton's skillful handling of the first person narrative easily involves the reader in Tex's changing feelings and relationships with his brother, his father, and his friends.

Tex is an appealing Huckleberry Finn sort of character—natural, mischievous, and instinctive. He and his seventeen-year-old brother, Mason, shift for themselves, with only a memory of a mother and an "absent minded" father who is away "rodeoing" most of the time. Mason (or Mace), as serious as Tex is carefree, is forced to be the father and manager of the family, and the responsibility gives him an ulcer and a burning desire to leave. Tex, in his immaturity, cannot understand Mason's dilemma. He resents Mace's authority and misinterprets his concern and worry. He is also jealous of his father's attention to Mace, and he yearns for affection from Pop, whom he tries to emulate.

Tex and his world begin to change when Mace sells his horse to pay bills. His resentment of Mace turns to real bitterness and Tex suffers some traumatic losses. Besides his horse, he loses forever the hope that he will be someone special to Pop, and he almost loses his life. However, he also gains a lot including a growing awareness of how much a girl's affection means to him, an acceptance of Pop as a person, and a better understanding of how much he and Mace really mean to each other.

Source: Jean Duncan with Carol Dye, Joan Lazarus, Diane Schwartzmann, Jill A. Hendin, and Rita Hendin, "Tex" in *English Journal,* Vol. 70, No. 4, April, 1981, pp. 76-77.

Sources

Jay Daly, "*Tex:* Those Who Go and Those Who Stay," in *Presenting S. E. Hinton,* Twayne Publishers, 1987, pp. 89-111.

June Harris, in review in *Contemporary Popular Writers,* edited by Dave Mote, St. James Press, 1997.

S. E. Hinton, "Teen-Agers are for Real," in *The New York Times Book Review,* August, 1967, pp. 26-9.

Michael Malone, in a review in *The Nation,* Vol. 242, No. 9, March 8, 1986, pp. 276-78, 290.

Cynthia Rose, "Rebels Redux: The Fiction of S. E. Hinton," in *Monthly Film Bulletin,* Vol. 50, No. 596, September, 1983, pp. 238-39.

William Walsh, in an interview in *From Writers to Students: The Pleasures and Pains of Writing,* edited by M. Jerry Weiss, International Reading Association, 1979, pp. 32-8.

For Further Study

Jay Daly, *Presenting S. E. Hinton,* Twayne, 1987, 127 p..
A guide to the first five of Hinton's novels, including major themes of each book.

Gene Lyons, "On Tulsa's Mean Streets," in *Newsweek,* October 11, 1982, pp. 105-6.
Examines Hinton's works that have been adapted as films.

Kevin Phillips, *Boiling Point: Republicans, Democrats and the Decline of Middle-Class Prosperity,* HarperCollins, 1994, 307 p.
A political analyst for the Republican Party during the 1968 election, Phillips has been praised for his work on economic issues. In *Boiling Point,* he gives a comprehensive picture of middle-class prosperity in decline.

Brett Singer, *The Petting Zoo,* Simon and Schuster, 1979, 254 p.
Like *Tex,* this young adult novel focuses on themes of maturity, independence, and burgeoning sexual relationships.

Glossary of Literary Terms

A

Abstract: As an adjective applied to writing or literary works, abstract refers to words or phrases that name things not knowable through the five senses.

Aestheticism: A literary and artistic movement of the nineteenth century. Followers of the movement believed that art should not be mixed with social, political, or moral teaching. The statement "art for art's sake" is a good summary of aestheticism. The movement had its roots in France, but it gained widespread importance in England in the last half of the nineteenth century, where it helped change the Victorian practice of including moral lessons in literature.

Allegory: A narrative technique in which characters representing things or abstract ideas are used to convey a message or teach a lesson. Allegory is typically used to teach moral, ethical, or religious lessons but is sometimes used for satiric or political purposes.

Allusion: A reference to a familiar literary or historical person or event, used to make an idea more easily understood.

Analogy: A comparison of two things made to explain something unfamiliar through its similarities to something familiar, or to prove one point based on the acceptedness of another. Similes and metaphors are types of analogies.

Antagonist: The major character in a narrative or drama who works against the hero or protagonist.

Anthropomorphism: The presentation of animals or objects in human shape or with human characteristics. The term is derived from the Greek word for "human form."

Antihero: A central character in a work of literature who lacks traditional heroic qualities such as courage, physical prowess, and fortitude. Antiheroes typically distrust conventional values and are unable to commit themselves to any ideals. They generally feel helpless in a world over which they have no control. Antiheroes usually accept, and often celebrate, their positions as social outcasts.

Apprenticeship Novel: See *Bildungsroman*

Archetype: The word archetype is commonly used to describe an original pattern or model from which all other things of the same kind are made. This term was introduced to literary criticism from the psychology of Carl Jung. It expresses Jung's theory that behind every person's "unconscious," or repressed memories of the past, lies the "collective unconscious" of the human race: memories of the countless typical experiences of our ancestors. These memories are said to prompt illogical associations that trigger powerful emotions in the reader. Often, the emotional process is primitive, even primordial. Archetypes are the literary images that grow out of the "collective unconscious." They appear in literature as incidents and plots that repeat basic patterns of life. They may also appear as stereotyped characters.

Avant-garde: French term meaning "vanguard." It is used in literary criticism to describe new writing that rejects traditional approaches to literature in favor of innovations in style or content.

B

Beat Movement: A period featuring a group of American poets and novelists of the 1950s and 1960s—including Jack Kerouac, Allen Ginsberg, Gregory Corso, William S. Burroughs, and Lawrence Ferlinghetti—who rejected established social and literary values. Using such techniques as stream of consciousness writing and jazz-influenced free verse and focusing on unusual or abnormal states of mind—generated by religious ecstasy or the use of drugs—the Beat writers aimed to create works that were unconventional in both form and subject matter.

Bildungsroman: A German word meaning "novel of development." The *bildungsroman* is a study of the maturation of a youthful character, typically brought about through a series of social or sexual encounters that lead to self-awareness. *Bildungsroman* is used interchangeably with *erziehungsroman,* a novel of initiation and education. When a *bildungsroman* is concerned with the development of an artist (as in James Joyce's *A Portrait of the Artist as a Young Man*), it is often termed a *kunstlerroman.* Also known as Apprenticeship Novel, Coming of Age Novel, *Erziehungsroman,* or *Kunstlerroman.*

Black Aesthetic Movement: A period of artistic and literary development among African Americans in the 1960s and early 1970s. This was the first major African-American artistic movement since the Harlem Renaissance and was closely paralleled by the civil rights and black power movements. The black aesthetic writers attempted to produce works of art that would be meaningful to the black masses. Key figures in black aesthetics included one of its founders, poet and playwright Amiri Baraka, formerly known as LeRoi Jones; poet and essayist Haki R. Madhubuti, formerly Don L. Lee; poet and playwright Sonia Sanchez; and dramatist Ed Bullins. Also known as Black Arts Movement.

Black Humor: Writing that places grotesque elements side by side with humorous ones in an attempt to shock the reader, forcing him or her to laugh at the horrifying reality of a disordered world. Also known as Black Comedy.

Burlesque: Any literary work that uses exaggeration to make its subject appear ridiculous, either by treating a trivial subject with profound seriousness or by treating a dignified subject frivolously. The word "burlesque" may also be used as an adjective, as in "burlesque show," to mean "striptease act."

C

Character: Broadly speaking, a person in a literary work. The actions of characters are what constitute the plot of a story, novel, or poem. There are numerous types of characters, ranging from simple, stereotypical figures to intricate, multifaceted ones. In the techniques of anthropomorphism and personification, animals—and even places or things—can assume aspects of character. "Characterization" is the process by which an author creates vivid, believable characters in a work of art. This may be done in a variety of ways, including (1) direct description of the character by the narrator; (2) the direct presentation of the speech, thoughts, or actions of the character; and (3) the responses of other characters to the character. The term "character" also refers to a form originated by the ancient Greek writer Theophrastus that later became popular in the seventeenth and eighteenth centuries. It is a short essay or sketch of a person who prominently displays a specific attribute or quality, such as miserliness or ambition.

Climax: The turning point in a narrative, the moment when the conflict is at its most intense. Typically, the structure of stories, novels, and plays is one of rising action, in which tension builds to the climax, followed by falling action, in which tension lessens as the story moves to its conclusion.

Colloquialism: A word, phrase, or form of pronunciation that is acceptable in casual conversation but not in formal, written communication. It is considered more acceptable than slang.

Coming of Age Novel: See *Bildungsroman*

Concrete: Concrete is the opposite of abstract, and refers to a thing that actually exists or a description that allows the reader to experience an object or concept with the senses.

Connotation: The impression that a word gives beyond its defined meaning. Connotations may be universally understood or may be significant only to a certain group.

Convention: Any widely accepted literary device, style, or form.

D

Denotation: The definition of a word, apart from the impressions or feelings it creates (connotations) in the reader.

Denouement: A French word meaning "the unknotting." In literary criticism, it denotes the resolution of conflict in fiction or drama. The *denouement* follows the climax and provides an outcome to the primary plot situation as well as an explanation of secondary plot complications. The *denouement* often involves a character's recognition of his or her state of mind or moral condition. Also known as Falling Action.

Description: Descriptive writing is intended to allow a reader to picture the scene or setting in which the action of a story takes place. The form this description takes often evokes an intended emotional response—a dark, spooky graveyard will evoke fear, and a peaceful, sunny meadow will evoke calmness.

Dialogue: In its widest sense, dialogue is simply conversation between people in a literary work; in its most restricted sense, it refers specifically to the speech of characters in a drama. As a specific literary genre, a "dialogue" is a composition in which characters debate an issue or idea.

Diction: The selection and arrangement of words in a literary work. Either or both may vary depending on the desired effect. There are four general types of diction: "formal," used in scholarly or lofty writing; "informal," used in relaxed but educated conversation; "colloquial," used in everyday speech; and "slang," containing newly coined words and other terms not accepted in formal usage.

Didactic: A term used to describe works of literature that aim to teach some moral, religious, political, or practical lesson. Although didactic elements are often found in artistically pleasing works, the term "didactic" usually refers to literature in which the message is more important than the form. The term may also be used to criticize a work that the critic finds "overly didactic," that is, heavy-handed in its delivery of a lesson.

Doppelganger: A literary technique by which a character is duplicated (usually in the form of an alter ego, though sometimes as a ghostly counterpart) or divided into two distinct, usually opposite personalities. The use of this character device is widespread in nineteenth- and twentieth-century literature, and indicates a growing awareness among authors that the "self" is really a composite of many "selves." Also known as The Double.

Double Entendre: A corruption of a French phrase meaning "double meaning." The term is used to indicate a word or phrase that is deliberately ambiguous, especially when one of the meanings is risqué or improper.

Dramatic Irony: Occurs when the audience of a play or the reader of a work of literature knows something that a character in the work itself does not know. The irony is in the contrast between the intended meaning of the statements or actions of a character and the additional information understood by the audience.

Dystopia: An imaginary place in a work of fiction where the characters lead dehumanized, fearful lives.

E

Edwardian: Describes cultural conventions identified with the period of the reign of Edward VII of England (1901-1910). Writers of the Edwardian Age typically displayed a strong reaction against the propriety and conservatism of the Victorian Age. Their work often exhibits distrust of authority in religion, politics, and art and expresses strong doubts about the soundness of conventional values.

Empathy: A sense of shared experience, including emotional and physical feelings, with someone or something other than oneself. Empathy is often used to describe the response of a reader to a literary character.

Enlightenment, The: An eighteenth-century philosophical movement. It began in France but had a wide impact throughout Europe and America. Thinkers of the Enlightenment valued reason and believed that both the individual and society could achieve a state of perfection. Corresponding to this essentially humanist vision was a resistance to religious authority.

Epigram: A saying that makes the speaker's point quickly and concisely. Often used to preface a novel.

Epilogue: A concluding statement or section of a literary work. In dramas, particularly those of the seventeenth and eighteenth centuries, the epilogue is a closing speech, often in verse, delivered by an actor at the end of a play and spoken directly to the audience.

Epiphany: A sudden revelation of truth inspired by a seemingly trivial incident.

Episode: An incident that forms part of a story and is significantly related to it. Episodes may be either self-contained narratives or events that depend on a larger context for their sense and importance.

Epistolary Novel: A novel in the form of letters. The form was particularly popular in the eighteenth century.

Epithet: A word or phrase, often disparaging or abusive, that expresses a character trait of someone or something.

Existentialism: A predominantly twentieth-century philosophy concerned with the nature and perception of human existence. There are two major strains of existentialist thought: atheistic and Christian. Followers of atheistic existentialism believe that the individual is alone in a godless universe and that the basic human condition is one of suffering and loneliness. Nevertheless, because there are no fixed values, individuals can create their own characters—indeed, they can shape themselves—through the exercise of free will. The atheistic strain culminates in and is popularly associated with the works of Jean-Paul Sartre. The Christian existentialists, on the other hand, believe that only in God may people find freedom from life's anguish. The two strains hold certain beliefs in common: that existence cannot be fully understood or described through empirical effort; that anguish is a universal element of life; that individuals must bear responsibility for their actions; and that there is no common standard of behavior or perception for religious and ethical matters.

Expatriates: See *Expatriatism*

Expatriatism: The practice of leaving one's country to live for an extended period in another country.

Exposition: Writing intended to explain the nature of an idea, thing, or theme. Expository writing is often combined with description, narration, or argument. In dramatic writing, the exposition is the introductory material which presents the characters, setting, and tone of the play.

Expressionism: An indistinct literary term, originally used to describe an early twentieth-century school of German painting. The term applies to almost any mode of unconventional, highly subjective writing that distorts reality in some way.

F

Fable: A prose or verse narrative intended to convey a moral. Animals or inanimate objects with human characteristics often serve as characters in fables.

Falling Action: See *Denouement*

Fantasy: A literary form related to mythology and folklore. Fantasy literature is typically set in non-existent realms and features supernatural beings.

Farce: A type of comedy characterized by broad humor, outlandish incidents, and often vulgar subject matter.

Femme fatale: A French phrase with the literal translation "fatal woman." A *femme fatale* is a sensuous, alluring woman who often leads men into danger or trouble.

Fiction: Any story that is the product of imagination rather than a documentation of fact. Characters and events in such narratives may be based in real life but their ultimate form and configuration is a creation of the author.

Figurative Language: A technique in writing in which the author temporarily interrupts the order, construction, or meaning of the writing for a particular effect. This interruption takes the form of one or more figures of speech such as hyperbole, irony, or simile. Figurative language is the opposite of literal language, in which every word is truthful, accurate, and free of exaggeration or embellishment.

Figures of Speech: Writing that differs from customary conventions for construction, meaning, order, or significance for the purpose of a special meaning or effect. There are two major types of figures of speech: rhetorical figures, which do not make changes in the meaning of the words, and tropes, which do.

Fin de siecle: A French term meaning "end of the century." The term is used to denote the last decade of the nineteenth century, a transition period when writers and other artists abandoned old conventions and looked for new techniques and objectives.

First Person: See *Point of View*

Flashback: A device used in literature to present action that occurred before the beginning of the story. Flashbacks are often introduced as the dreams or recollections of one or more characters.

Foil: A character in a work of literature whose physical or psychological qualities contrast strongly with, and therefore highlight, the corresponding qualities of another character.

Folklore: Traditions and myths preserved in a culture or group of people. Typically, these are passed on by word of mouth in various forms—such as legends, songs, and proverbs—or preserved in customs and ceremonies. This term was first used by W. J. Thoms in 1846.

Folktale: A story originating in oral tradition. Folktales fall into a variety of categories, including legends, ghost stories, fairy tales, fables, and anecdotes based on historical figures and events.

Foreshadowing: A device used in literature to create expectation or to set up an explanation of later developments.

Form: The pattern or construction of a work which identifies its genre and distinguishes it from other genres.

G

Genre: A category of literary work. In critical theory, genre may refer to both the content of a given work—tragedy, comedy, pastoral—and to its form, such as poetry, novel, or drama.

Gilded Age: A period in American history during the 1870s characterized by political corruption and materialism. A number of important novels of social and political criticism were written during this time.

Gothicism: In literary criticism, works characterized by a taste for the medieval or morbidly attractive. A gothic novel prominently features elements of horror, the supernatural, gloom, and violence: clanking chains, terror, charnel houses, ghosts, medieval castles, and mysteriously slamming doors. The term "gothic novel" is also applied to novels that lack elements of the traditional Gothic setting but that create a similar atmosphere of terror or dread.

Grotesque: In literary criticism, the subject matter of a work or a style of expression characterized by exaggeration, deformity, freakishness, and disorder. The grotesque often includes an element of comic absurdity.

H

Harlem Renaissance: The Harlem Renaissance of the 1920s is generally considered the first significant movement of black writers and artists in the United States. During this period, new and established black writers published more fiction and poetry than ever before, the first influential black literary journals were established, and black authors and artists received their first widespread recognition and serious critical appraisal. Among the major writers associated with this period are Claude McKay, Jean Toomer, Countee Cullen, Langston Hughes, Arna Bontemps, Nella Larsen, and Zora Neale Hurston. Also known as Negro Renaissance and New Negro Movement.

Hero/Heroine: The principal sympathetic character (male or female) in a literary work. Heroes and heroines typically exhibit admirable traits: idealism, courage, and integrity, for example.

Holocaust Literature: Literature influenced by or written about the Holocaust of World War II. Such literature includes true stories of survival in concentration camps, escape, and life after the war, as well as fictional works and poetry.

Humanism: A philosophy that places faith in the dignity of humankind and rejects the medieval perception of the individual as a weak, fallen creature. "Humanists" typically believe in the perfectibility of human nature and view reason and education as the means to that end.

Hyperbole: In literary criticism, deliberate exaggeration used to achieve an effect.

I

Idiom: A word construction or verbal expression closely associated with a given language.

Image: A concrete representation of an object or sensory experience. Typically, such a representation helps evoke the feelings associated with the object or experience itself. Images are either "literal" or "figurative." Literal images are especially concrete and involve little or no extension of the obvious meaning of the words used to express them. Figurative images do not follow the literal meaning of the words exactly. Images in literature are usually visual, but the term "image" can also refer to the representation of any sensory experience.

Imagery: The array of images in a literary work. Also, figurative language.

In medias res: A Latin term meaning "in the middle of things." It refers to the technique of beginning a story at its midpoint and then using various flashback devices to reveal previous action.

Interior Monologue: A narrative technique in which characters' thoughts are revealed in a way that appears to be uncontrolled by the author. The interior monologue typically aims to reveal the inner self of a character. It portrays emotional experiences as they occur at both a conscious and unconscious level. Images are often used to represent sensations or emotions.

Irony: In literary criticism, the effect of language in which the intended meaning is the opposite of what is stated.

J

Jargon: Language that is used or understood only by a select group of people. Jargon may refer to terminology used in a certain profession, such as computer jargon, or it may refer to any nonsensical language that is not understood by most people.

L

Leitmotiv: See *Motif*

Literal Language: An author uses literal language when he or she writes without exaggerating or embellishing the subject matter and without any tools of figurative language.

Lost Generation: A term first used by Gertrude Stein to describe the post-World War I generation of American writers: men and women haunted by a sense of betrayal and emptiness brought about by the destructiveness of the war.

M

Mannerism: Exaggerated, artificial adherence to a literary manner or style. Also, a popular style of the visual arts of late sixteenth-century Europe that was marked by elongation of the human form and by intentional spatial distortion. Literary works that are self-consciously high-toned and artistic are often said to be "mannered."

Metaphor: A figure of speech that expresses an idea through the image of another object. Metaphors suggest the essence of the first object by identifying it with certain qualities of the second object.

Modernism: Modern literary practices. Also, the principles of a literary school that lasted from roughly the beginning of the twentieth century until the end of World War II. Modernism is defined by its rejection of the literary conventions of the nineteenth century and by its opposition to conventional morality, taste, traditions, and economic values.

Mood: The prevailing emotions of a work or of the author in his or her creation of the work. The mood of a work is not always what might be expected based on its subject matter.

Motif: A theme, character type, image, metaphor, or other verbal element that recurs throughout a single work of literature or occurs in a number of different works over a period of time. Also known as *Motiv* or *Leitmotiv*.

Myth: An anonymous tale emerging from the traditional beliefs of a culture or social unit. Myths use supernatural explanations for natural phenomena. They may also explain cosmic issues like creation and death. Collections of myths, known as mythologies, are common to all cultures and nations, but the best-known myths belong to the Norse, Roman, and Greek mythologies.

N

Narration: The telling of a series of events, real or invented. A narration may be either a simple narrative, in which the events are recounted chronologically, or a narrative with a plot, in which the account is given in a style reflecting the author's artistic concept of the story. Narration is sometimes used as a synonym for "storyline."

Narrative: A verse or prose accounting of an event or sequence of events, real or invented. The term is also used as an adjective in the sense "method of narration." For example, in literary criticism, the expression "narrative technique" usually refers to the way the author structures and presents his or her story.

Narrator: The teller of a story. The narrator may be the author or a character in the story through whom the author speaks.

Naturalism: A literary movement of the late nineteenth and early twentieth centuries. The movement's major theorist, French novelist Emile Zola, envisioned a type of fiction that would examine human life with the objectivity of scientific inquiry. The Naturalists typically viewed human beings as either the products of "biological determinism," ruled by hereditary instincts and engaged in an endless struggle for survival, or as the products of "socioeconomic determinism," ruled by social and economic forces beyond their control. In their works, the Naturalists generally ignored the highest levels of society and focused on degradation: poverty, alcoholism, prostitution, insanity, and disease.

Noble Savage: The idea that primitive man is noble and good but becomes evil and corrupted as he becomes civilized. The concept of the noble savage originated in the Renaissance period but is more closely identified with such later writers as

Jean-Jacques Rousseau and Aphra Behn. See also Primitivism.

Novel of Ideas: A novel in which the examination of intellectual issues and concepts takes precedence over characterization or a traditional storyline.

Novel of Manners: A novel that examines the customs and mores of a cultural group.

Novel: A long fictional narrative written in prose, which developed from the novella and other early forms of narrative. A novel is usually organized under a plot or theme with a focus on character development and action.

Novella: An Italian term meaning "story." This term has been especially used to describe fourteenth-century Italian tales, but it also refers to modern short novels.

O

Objective Correlative: An outward set of objects, a situation, or a chain of events corresponding to an inward experience and evoking this experience in the reader. The term frequently appears in modern criticism in discussions of authors' intended effects on the emotional responses of readers.

Objectivity: A quality in writing characterized by the absence of the author's opinion or feeling about the subject matter. Objectivity is an important factor in criticism.

Oedipus Complex: A son's amorous obsession with his mother. The phrase is derived from the story of the ancient Theban hero Oedipus, who unknowingly killed his father and married his mother.

Omniscience: See *Point of View*

Onomatopoeia: The use of words whose sounds express or suggest their meaning. In its simplest sense, onomatopoeia may be represented by words that mimic the sounds they denote such as "hiss" or "meow." At a more subtle level, the pattern and rhythm of sounds and rhymes of a line or poem may be onomatopoeic.

Oxymoron: A phrase combining two contradictory terms. Oxymorons may be intentional or unintentional.

P

Parable: A story intended to teach a moral lesson or answer an ethical question.

Paradox: A statement that appears illogical or contradictory at first, but may actually point to an underlying truth.

Parallelism: A method of comparison of two ideas in which each is developed in the same grammatical structure.

Parody: In literary criticism, this term refers to an imitation of a serious literary work or the signature style of a particular author in a ridiculous manner. A typical parody adopts the style of the original and applies it to an inappropriate subject for humorous effect. Parody is a form of satire and could be considered the literary equivalent of a caricature or cartoon.

Pastoral: A term derived from the Latin word "pastor," meaning shepherd. A pastoral is a literary composition on a rural theme. The conventions of the pastoral were originated by the third-century Greek poet Theocritus, who wrote about the experiences, love affairs, and pastimes of Sicilian shepherds. In a pastoral, characters and language of a courtly nature are often placed in a simple setting. The term pastoral is also used to classify dramas, elegies, and lyrics that exhibit the use of country settings and shepherd characters.

Pen Name: See *Pseudonym*

Persona: A Latin term meaning "mask." *Personae* are the characters in a fictional work of literature. The *persona* generally functions as a mask through which the author tells a story in a voice other than his or her own. A *persona* is usually either a character in a story who acts as a narrator or an "implied author," a voice created by the author to act as the narrator for himself or herself.

Personification: A figure of speech that gives human qualities to abstract ideas, animals, and inanimate objects. Also known as *Prosopopoeia*.

Picaresque Novel: Episodic fiction depicting the adventures of a roguish central character ("picaro" is Spanish for "rogue"). The picaresque hero is commonly a low-born but clever individual who wanders into and out of various affairs of love, danger, and farcical intrigue. These involvements may take place at all social levels and typically present a humorous and wide-ranging satire of a given society.

Plagiarism: Claiming another person's written material as one's own. Plagiarism can take the form of direct, word-for-word copying or the theft of the substance or idea of the work.

Plot: In literary criticism, this term refers to the pattern of events in a narrative or drama. In its simplest sense, the plot guides the author in composing the work and helps the reader follow the work. Typically, plots exhibit causality and unity and have a beginning, a middle, and an end. Sometimes, however, a plot may consist of a series of disconnected events, in which case it is known as an "episodic plot."

Poetic Justice: An outcome in a literary work, not necessarily a poem, in which the good are rewarded and the evil are punished, especially in ways that particularly fit their virtues or crimes.

Poetic License: Distortions of fact and literary convention made by a writer—not always a poet—for the sake of the effect gained. Poetic license is closely related to the concept of "artistic freedom."

Poetics: This term has two closely related meanings. It denotes (1) an aesthetic theory in literary criticism about the essence of poetry or (2) rules prescribing the proper methods, content, style, or diction of poetry. The term poetics may also refer to theories about literature in general, not just poetry.

Point of View: The narrative perspective from which a literary work is presented to the reader. There are four traditional points of view. The "third person omniscient" gives the reader a "godlike" perspective, unrestricted by time or place, from which to see actions and look into the minds of characters. This allows the author to comment openly on characters and events in the work. The "third person" point of view presents the events of the story from outside of any single character's perception, much like the omniscient point of view, but the reader must understand the action as it takes place and without any special insight into characters' minds or motivations. The "first person" or "personal" point of view relates events as they are perceived by a single character. The main character "tells" the story and may offer opinions about the action and characters which differ from those of the author. Much less common than omniscient, third person, and first person is the "second person" point of view, wherein the author tells the story as if it is happening to the reader.

Polemic: A work in which the author takes a stand on a controversial subject, such as abortion or religion. Such works are often extremely argumentative or provocative.

Pornography: Writing intended to provoke feelings of lust in the reader. Such works are often condemned by critics and teachers, but those which can be shown to have literary value are viewed less harshly.

Post-Aesthetic Movement: An artistic response made by African Americans to the black aesthetic movement of the 1960s and early '70s. Writers since that time have adopted a somewhat different tone in their work, with less emphasis placed on the disparity between black and white in the United States. In the words of post-aesthetic authors such as Toni Morrison, John Edgar Wideman, and Kristin Hunter, African Americans are portrayed as looking inward for answers to their own questions, rather than always looking to the outside world.

Postmodernism: Writing from the 1960s forward characterized by experimentation and continuing to apply some of the fundamentals of modernism, which included existentialism and alienation. Postmodernists have gone a step further in the rejection of tradition begun with the modernists by also rejecting traditional forms, preferring the anti-novel over the novel and the antihero over the hero.

Primitivism: The belief that primitive peoples were nobler and less flawed than civilized peoples because they had not been subjected to the tainting influence of society. See also Noble Savage.

Prologue: An introductory section of a literary work. It often contains information establishing the situation of the characters or presents information about the setting, time period, or action. In drama, the prologue is spoken by a chorus or by one of the principal characters.

Prose: A literary medium that attempts to mirror the language of everyday speech. It is distinguished from poetry by its use of unmetered, unrhymed language consisting of logically related sentences. Prose is usually grouped into paragraphs that form a cohesive whole such as an essay or a novel.

***Prosopopoeia*:** See *Personification*

Protagonist: The central character of a story who serves as a focus for its themes and incidents and as the principal rationale for its development. The protagonist is sometimes referred to in discussions of modern literature as the hero or antihero.

Protest Fiction: Protest fiction has as its primary purpose the protesting of some social injustice, such as racism or discrimination.

Proverb: A brief, sage saying that expresses a truth about life in a striking manner.

Pseudonym: A name assumed by a writer, most often intended to prevent his or her identification as the author of a work. Two or more authors may work together under one pseudonym, or an author may use a different name for each genre he or she publishes in. Some publishing companies maintain "house pseudonyms," under which any number of authors may write installations in a series. Some authors also choose a pseudonym over their real names the way an actor may use a stage name.

Pun: A play on words that have similar sounds but different meanings.

R

Realism: A nineteenth-century European literary movement that sought to portray familiar characters, situations, and settings in a realistic manner. This was done primarily by using an objective narrative point of view and through the buildup of accurate detail. The standard for success of any realistic work depends on how faithfully it transfers common experience into fictional forms. The realistic method may be altered or extended, as in stream of consciousness writing, to record highly subjective experience.

Repartee: Conversation featuring snappy retorts and witticisms.

Resolution: The portion of a story following the climax, in which the conflict is resolved. See also *Denouement.*

Rhetoric: In literary criticism, this term denotes the art of ethical persuasion. In its strictest sense, rhetoric adheres to various principles developed since classical times for arranging facts and ideas in a clear, persuasive, appealing manner. The term is also used to refer to effective prose in general and theories of or methods for composing effective prose.

Rhetorical Question: A question intended to provoke thought, but not an expressed answer, in the reader. It is most commonly used in oratory and other persuasive genres.

Rising Action: The part of a drama where the plot becomes increasingly complicated. Rising action leads up to the climax, or turning point, of a drama.

Roman a clef: A French phrase meaning "novel with a key." It refers to a narrative in which real persons are portrayed under fictitious names.

Romance: A broad term, usually denoting a narrative with exotic, exaggerated, often idealized characters, scenes, and themes.

Romanticism: This term has two widely accepted meanings. In historical criticism, it refers to a European intellectual and artistic movement of the late eighteenth and early nineteenth centuries that sought greater freedom of personal expression than that allowed by the strict rules of literary form and logic of the eighteenth-century neoclassicists. The Romantics preferred emotional and imaginative expression to rational analysis. They considered the individual to be at the center of all experience and so placed him or her at the center of their art. The Romantics believed that the creative imagination reveals nobler truths—unique feelings and attitudes—than those that could be discovered by logic or by scientific examination. Both the natural world and the state of childhood were important sources for revelations of "eternal truths." "Romanticism" is also used as a general term to refer to a type of sensibility found in all periods of literary history and usually considered to be in opposition to the principles of classicism. In this sense, Romanticism signifies any work or philosophy in which the exotic or dreamlike figure strongly, or that is devoted to individualistic expression, self-analysis, or a pursuit of a higher realm of knowledge than can be discovered by human reason.

Romantics: See *Romanticism*

S

Satire: A work that uses ridicule, humor, and wit to criticize and provoke change in human nature and institutions. There are two major types of satire: "formal" or "direct" satire speaks directly to the reader or to a character in the work; "indirect" satire relies upon the ridiculous behavior of its characters to make its point. Formal satire is further divided into two manners: the "Horatian," which ridicules gently, and the "Juvenalian," which derides its subjects harshly and bitterly.

Science Fiction: A type of narrative about or based upon real or imagined scientific theories and technology. Science fiction is often peopled with alien creatures and set on other planets or in different dimensions.

Second Person: See *Point of View*

Setting: The time, place, and culture in which the action of a narrative takes place. The elements of setting may include geographic location, characters' physical and mental environments, prevailing cultural attitudes, or the historical time in which the action takes place.

Simile: A comparison, usually using "like" or "as", of two essentially dissimilar things, as in "coffee as cold as ice" or "He sounded like a broken record."

Slang: A type of informal verbal communication that is generally unacceptable for formal writing. Slang words and phrases are often colorful exaggerations used to emphasize the speaker's point; they may also be shortened versions of an often-used word or phrase.

Slave Narrative: Autobiographical accounts of American slave life as told by escaped slaves. These works first appeared during the abolition movement of the 1830s through the 1850s.

Socialist Realism: The Socialist Realism school of literary theory was proposed by Maxim Gorky and established as a dogma by the first Soviet Congress of Writers. It demanded adherence to a communist worldview in works of literature. Its doctrines required an objective viewpoint comprehensible to the working classes and themes of social struggle featuring strong proletarian heroes. Also known as Social Realism.

Stereotype: A stereotype was originally the name for a duplication made during the printing process; this led to its modern definition as a person or thing that is (or is assumed to be) the same as all others of its type.

Stream of Consciousness: A narrative technique for rendering the inward experience of a character. This technique is designed to give the impression of an ever-changing series of thoughts, emotions, images, and memories in the spontaneous and seemingly illogical order that they occur in life.

Structure: The form taken by a piece of literature. The structure may be made obvious for ease of understanding, as in nonfiction works, or may be obscured for artistic purposes, as in some poetry or seemingly "unstructured" prose.

***Sturm und Drang*:** A German term meaning "storm and stress." It refers to a German literary movement of the 1770s and 1780s that reacted against the order and rationalism of the enlightenment, focusing instead on the intense experience of extraordinary individuals.

Style: A writer's distinctive manner of arranging words to suit his or her ideas and purpose in writing. The unique imprint of the author's personality upon his or her writing, style is the product of an author's way of arranging ideas and his or her use of diction, different sentence structures, rhythm, figures of speech, rhetorical principles, and other elements of composition.

Subjectivity: Writing that expresses the author's personal feelings about his subject, and which may or may not include factual information about the subject.

Subplot: A secondary story in a narrative. A subplot may serve as a motivating or complicating force for the main plot of the work, or it may provide emphasis for, or relief from, the main plot.

Surrealism: A term introduced to criticism by Guillaume Apollinaire and later adopted by Andre Breton. It refers to a French literary and artistic movement founded in the 1920s. The Surrealists sought to express unconscious thoughts and feelings in their works. The best-known technique used for achieving this aim was automatic writing—transcriptions of spontaneous outpourings from the unconscious. The Surrealists proposed to unify the contrary levels of conscious and unconscious, dream and reality, objectivity and subjectivity into a new level of "super-realism."

Suspense: A literary device in which the author maintains the audience's attention through the buildup of events, the outcome of which will soon be revealed.

Symbol: Something that suggests or stands for something else without losing its original identity. In literature, symbols combine their literal meaning with the suggestion of an abstract concept. Literary symbols are of two types: those that carry complex associations of meaning no matter what their contexts, and those that derive their suggestive meaning from their functions in specific literary works.

Symbolism: This term has two widely accepted meanings. In historical criticism, it denotes an early modernist literary movement initiated in France during the nineteenth century that reacted against the prevailing standards of realism. Writers in this movement aimed to evoke, indirectly and symbolically, an order of being beyond the material world of the five senses. Poetic expression of personal emotion figured strongly in the movement, typically by means of a private set of symbols uniquely identifiable with the individual poet. The principal aim of the Symbolists was to express in words the highly complex feelings that grew out of everyday contact with the world. In a broader sense, the term "symbolism" refers to the use of one object to represent another.

T

Tall Tale: A humorous tale told in a straightforward, credible tone but relating absolutely impossible events or feats of the characters. Such tales were commonly told of frontier adventures during the settlement of the west in the United States.

Theme: The main point of a work of literature. The term is used interchangeably with thesis.

Thesis: A thesis is both an essay and the point argued in the essay. Thesis novels and thesis plays share the quality of containing a thesis which is supported through the action of the story.

Third Person: See *Point of View*

Tone: The author's attitude toward his or her audience may be deduced from the tone of the work. A formal tone may create distance or convey politeness, while an informal tone may encourage a friendly, intimate, or intrusive feeling in the reader. The author's attitude toward his or her subject matter may also be deduced from the tone of the words he or she uses in discussing it.

Transcendentalism: An American philosophical and religious movement, based in New England from around 1835 until the Civil War. Transcendentalism was a form of American romanticism that had its roots abroad in the works of Thomas Carlyle, Samuel Coleridge, and Johann Wolfgang von Goethe. The Transcendentalists stressed the importance of intuition and subjective experience in communication with God. They rejected religious dogma and texts in favor of mysticism and scientific naturalism. They pursued truths that lie beyond the "colorless" realms perceived by reason and the senses and were active social reformers in public education, women's rights, and the abolition of slavery.

U

Urban Realism: A branch of realist writing that attempts to accurately reflect the often harsh facts of modern urban existence.

Utopia: A fictional perfect place, such as "paradise" or "heaven."

V

Verisimilitude: Literally, the appearance of truth. In literary criticism, the term refers to aspects of a work of literature that seem true to the reader.

Victorian: Refers broadly to the reign of Queen Victoria of England (1837-1901) and to anything with qualities typical of that era. For example, the qualities of smug narrowmindedness, bourgeois materialism, faith in social progress, and priggish morality are often considered Victorian. This stereotype is contradicted by such dramatic intellectual developments as the theories of Charles Darwin, Karl Marx, and Sigmund Freud (which stirred strong debates in England) and the critical attitudes of serious Victorian writers like Charles Dickens and George Eliot. In literature, the Victorian Period was the great age of the English novel, and the latter part of the era saw the rise of movements such as decadence and symbolism. Also known as Victorian Age and Victorian Period.

W

Weltanschauung: A German term referring to a person's worldview or philosophy.

Weltschmerz: A German term meaning "world pain." It describes a sense of anguish about the nature of existence, usually associated with a melancholy, pessimistic attitude.

Z

Zeitgeist: A German term meaning "spirit of the time." It refers to the moral and intellectual trends

Cumulative Author/Title Index

Cumulative Nationality/Ethnicity Index

Hemingway, Ernest
  A Farewell to Arms: V1
  The Old Man and the Sea: V6
  The Sun Also Rises: V5
Hinton, S. E.
  Tex: V9
  The Outsiders: V5
Hurston, Zora Neale
  Their Eyes Were Watching God:
  V3
Kerouac, Jack
  On the Road: V8
Kesey, Ken
  One Flew Over the Cuckoo's
  Nest: V2
Keyes, Daniel
  Flowers for Algernon: V2
Kincaid, Jamaica
  Annie John: V3
Kingsolver, Barbara
  The Bean Trees: V5
Kingston, Maxine Hong
  The Woman Warrior: V6
Knowles, John
  A Separate Peace: V2
Le Guin, Ursula K.
  Always Coming Home: V9
  The Left Hand of Darkness: V6
Lee, Harper
  To Kill a Mockingbird: V2
London, Jack
  The Call of the Wild: V8
Lowry, Lois
  The Giver: V3
Mason, Bobbie Ann
  In Country: V4
McCullers, Carson
  The Heart Is a Lonely Hunter: V6
Melville, Herman
  Billy Budd: V9
  Moby-Dick: V7
Mitchell, Margaret
  Gone with the Wind: V9
Morrison, Toni
  Beloved: V6
  The Bluest Eye: V1
  Song of Solomon: V8
Oates, Joyce Carol
  them: V8
O'Connor, Flannery
  Wise Blood: V3
Plath, Sylvia
  The Bell Jar: V1
Potok, Chaim
  The Chosen: V4
Rölvaag, O. E.
  Giants in the Earth: V5
Salinger, J. D.
  The Catcher in the Rye: V1
Sinclair, Upton
  The Jungle: V6
Steinbeck, John

The Grapes of Wrath: V7
Of Mice and Men: V1
The Pearl: V5
Stowe, Harriet Beecher
  Uncle Tom's Cabin: V6
Tan, Amy
  The Joy Luck Club: V1
Twain, Mark
  The Adventures of Huckleberry
  Finn: V1
  The Adventures of Tom Sawyer: V6
Tyler, Anne
  The Accidental Tourist: V7
  Dinner at the Homesick
  Restaurant: V2
Vonnegut, Kurt, Jr.
  Slaughterhouse-Five: V3
Walker, Alice
  The Color Purple: V5
Wharton, Edith
  Ethan Frome: V5
Wouk, Herman
  The Caine Mutiny: V7
Wright, Richard
  Black Boy: V1
  Native Son: V7

Asian American
Kingston, Maxine Hong
  The Woman Warrior: V6
Tan, Amy
  The Joy Luck Club: V1

Asian Canadian
Kogawa, Joy
  Obasan: V3

British
Adams, Douglas
  The Hitchhiker's Guide to the
  Galaxy: V7
Austen, Jane
  Pride and Prejudice: V1
Ballard, J. G.
  Empire of the Sun: V8
Blair, Eric Arthur
  Animal Farm: V3
Brontë, Charlotte
  Jane Eyre: V4
Brontë, Emily
  Wuthering Heights: V2
Carroll, Lewis
  Alice's Adventurers in
  Wonderland: V7
Chrisite, Agatha
  Ten Little Indians: V8
Conrad, Joseph
  Heart of Darkness: V2
Defoe, Daniel
  Robinson Crusoe: V9

Dickens, Charles
  Great Expectations: V4
  A Tale of Two Cities: V5
Forster, E. M.
  A Passage to India: V3
Golding, William
  Lord of the Flies: V2
Hardy, Thomas
  Tess of the d'Urbervilles: V3
Huxley, Aldous
  Brave New World: V6
Marmon Silko, Leslie
  Ceremony: V4
Orwell, George
  1984: V7
  Animal Farm: V3
Shelley, Mary
  Frankenstein: V1
Shute, Nevil
  On the Beach: V9
Swift, Jonathan
  Gulliver's Travels: V6
Tolkien, J. R. R.
  The Hobbit: V8
Woolf, Virginia
  To the Lighthouse: V8

Canadian
Atwood, Margaret
  The Handmaid's Tale: V4
Kogawa, Joy
  Obasan: V3

Chilean
Allende, Isabel
  The House of the Spirits: V6

Colombian
García Márquez, Gabriel
  Love in the Time of Cholera: V1
  One Hundred Years of Solitude:
  V5

Danish
Dinesen, Isak
  Out of Africa: V9

Dominican
Alvarez, Julia
  How the García Girls Lost Their
  Accents: V5
  In the Time of Butterflies: V9

European
American
Hemingway, Ernest
  The Old Man and the Sea: V6

Cumulative Nationality/Ethnicity Index

Subject/Theme Index

Subject/Theme Index